American Government

A Complete Coursebook

Ethel Wood and Stephen C. Sansone

GReaT SøuRCe
EDUCATION GROUP
A Houghton Mifflin Company

AUTHORS | **Ethel Wood**

Princeton High School
Princeton, New Jersey

Ethel Wood has taught World History, U.S. Government, and Comparative
Government for more than 16 years at Princeton High School. Previously
she had taught in Texas at the high school, community college, and university levels. In addition, she is the author of "Teaching Guide: Comparative
Government and Politics."

Stephen C. Sansone

Waukesha South High School
Waukesha, Wisconsin

Stephen C. Sansone has taught U.S. History, Government, and Honors
Government for more than 20 years in the Waukesha School District and
is currently at Waukesha South High School. He is also the author of the
Teacher's Activity Book and numerous articles, including most recently
"Get Your Students Involved in Civics" for *Social Education* (1998–99).

DESIGN | **Oversat Paredes**

ILLUSTRATIONS | **Robert Neubecker**

ACKNOWLEDGMENTS | **Text acknowledgments are on page iv.**

Printed in the United States of America

International Standard Book Number: 0-669-46795-2

1 2 3 4 5 6 7 8 9 —RRDC— 05 04 03 02 01 00 99

CONSULTING AUTHOR | **Dr. Michael Hartoonian**
Professor of Education
University of Minnesota

Dr. Hartoonian has taught, lectured, and served as an education, business, and government consultant throughout the United States, Central America, Asia, and Europe. He has authored more than 50 articles and written and contributed to numerous books. He is also a past president of the National Council of Social Studies (1995-96).

READERS & REVIEWERS | *Academic Consultants*

Prof. Dennis Dresang
University of Wisconsin
Madison, Wisconsin

Prof. William McLaughlin
Purdue University
West Lafayette, Indiana

Government Teachers

Michael Barry
Loyola Academy
Wilmette, Illinois

Karen Moore
Williamson High School
Williamson, West Virginia

Tom Baumann
Adlai Stevenson High School
Lincolnshire, Illinois

Paul Rykken
Black River Falls Senior High
Black River Falls, Wisconsin

Ann Connor
Academy of Notre Dame
Villanova, Pennsylvania

Maria Schmidt
Westfield High School
Westfield, New Jersey

Karen Coston
Blacksburg High School
Blacksburg, Virginia

George Westergaard
South Eugene High School
Eugene, Oregon

Jana Eaton
Unionville High School
Kennett Square, Pennsylvania

Mark Wise
John F. Kennedy School
  of Government
Harvard University
Cambridge, Massachusetts

Ellen Harmon
T.C. Williams High School
Alexandria, Virginia

David LaShomb
Brainerd High School
Brainerd, Minnesota

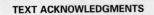

TEXT ACKNOWLEDGMENTS

54 Adapted from "Banned In the USA," *Time,* July 6, 1998, p. 32.

98 Adapted with permission from *The American Dream,* by Smith, Lew, 1983, Scott Foresman–Addison Wesley.

115 Copyright © 1993 by *The New York Times.* Reprinted by permission.

127 Copyright © from *Encyclopedia of Associations,* 1998 Edition. Reprinted by permission of The Gale Group.

180 Republished by permission of Dow Jones, Inc. via Copyright Clearance Center, Inc. © 1998 Dow Jones and Company, Inc. All Rights Reserved Worldwide.

208 From *Newsweek,* Oct 20, 1997, © 1997 Newsweek, Inc. All rights reserved. Reprinted by permission.

245 Sheldon Goldman, "The Bush Imprint on the Judiciary: Carrying on a Tradition." *Judicature* 74[April/May 1991], pp. 298-99; also Sheldon Goldman and Matthew D. Saronson, "Clinton's Nontraditional Judges: The Triumph of Affirmative Action," *Judicature* 78 [Sept/Oct 1994].

245 *Government by the People* by Burns *et al.,* ® 1995.

308, 309 Courtesy of American Civil Liberties Union.

Contents

Unit II: Political Behavior and Participation

Unit III: Institutions of National Government

Unit IV: Civil Liberties and Civil Rights

Unit VII: Skills Handbook

Contents

Unit VIII: Almanac

Introduction

This coursebook has been designed to be:

★ student-friendly

★ comprehensive

★ up-to-date

★ skills-intensive

We believe books should be easy to read and make it easy to find the information you want. Too often books include so much stuff that it's actually hard to find what you want. This coursebook provides short previews at the beginning of each chapter, highlighted vocabulary at the bottom of the page, and a convenient handbook to make using it easy. The coursebook was even designed to be a small, more manageable size.

We use the word *coursebook* because we've included here a "complete course"—that is, a thorough background on the subject of government without a lot of unnecessary details. We cover all the essentials—of the subject, the vocabulary, and the skills you'll need to understand government in the future.

This introduction walks through each of the main parts of the coursebook. Take a moment to read the next few pages. It will help you get the most from this coursebook.

In this introduction . . .

Book Organization

American Government: A Complete Coursebook has four main sections:

★ This **Introduction** provides a general introduction to the coursebook.

★ The **Units and Chapters** discuss American government and form the main part of the book.

★ A **Skills Handbook** teaches a broad range of skills needed to understand, speak, and write about government.

★ An **Almanac** offers such resources as key documents as well as recents facts and data.

UNIT ORGANIZATION

This *American Government* coursebook is divided into 6 main units:

I. Constitution and Foundations of Government

II. Political Behavior and Participation

III. Institutions of National Government

IV. Civil Liberties and Civil Rights

V. Public Policy and Comparative Government

VI. State and Local Government

Within each unit are two or more chapters that explore key concepts and topics within that unit. For example, Unit I, "Constitution and Foundations of Government," contains four chapters that describe the basic concepts underlying American government.

Constitution

Constitution and Foundations of Government

CHAPTER ORGANIZATION

Each chapter opens with a one-page introduction, or preview, to the material that tells why the topic is important to American government and lists the sections within the chapter. A three-stars icon signals a summary that concludes the chapter.

Preview

Summary

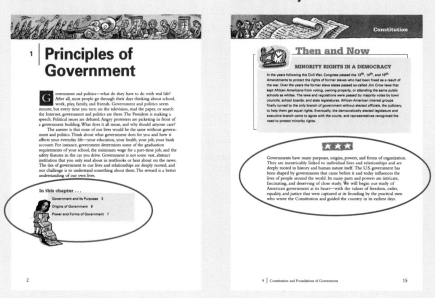

Chapter Features

Definitions for more than 300 key terms in government appear at the bottom of the page on which the term is first used. These terms also appear in the glossary that begins on page 562. In the text, the most essential terms are printed in red and in a tinted box in the footnote. Other vocabulary words are boldfaced in the text and are outside the box in the footnote.

def·i·ni·tions

amendment—a formal statement of change to a law or constitution.

Bill of Rights—the first ten amendments to the Constitution of the United States.

lame duck—an elected official during the period between failure to win re-election and the inauguration of a successor.

Other Features

Many features woven through the coursebook illuminate timely examples, highlight key ideas, or illustrate major points of comparison.

★ **HEADLINES** Current events reflect important ideas about government every day. These features highlight just a few examples from contemporary issues.

★ **VERSUS (VS.)** Contrasts between positions are highlighted through these features to make the essential distinctions clear.

★ **QUOTES** Great ideas inspired the Founders of America and lie at the heart of the Constitution. To focus on some of these great ideas, brief quotes are placed to emphasize their influence or highlight a particular point.

★ **E.G.** The abbreviation E.G. stands for "for example." This feature offers further detail or elaboration of an idea in the chapter.

★ **THEN AND NOW** To illustrate historical moments from the past, the *Then and Now* features recall important occurrences in America's history, showing how events of the past still influence the present.

★ **TIMELINE** To make the sequence of events clear, timelines appear in places to reinforce the order historical events or the key steps in a process.

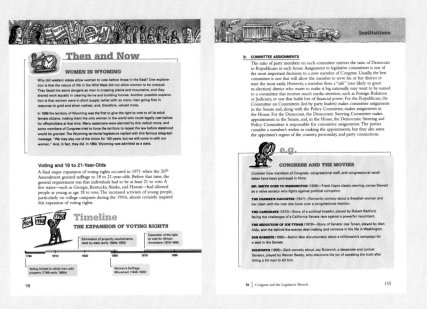

SKILLS HANDBOOK

Participating in government at any level requires that you understand and can express your opinions on all kinds of matters, from reading U.S. census tables to writing your senator. Yet even the seemingly simplest of tasks requires a great many skills. Critical reading, distinguishing facts from opinions, summarizing, organizing, writing, and revising might all be needed just to write a letter to your local paper. The Skills Handbook offers checklists, practical advice, and examples to help. Check it out.

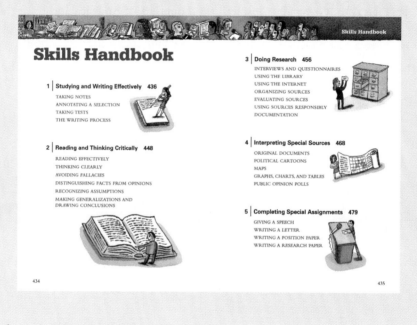

1. Help with *Determining Cause-and-Effect*

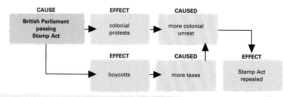

DETERMINING CAUSE-AND-EFFECT In a cause-and-effect relationship, a cause triggers an event that can then become the cause of another event. Ask why something (the effect) happened. The answer tells the cause, or the reason. Because effects are sometimes obvious, it's usually more important to spend time discussing the causes and how they really caused the events. Be clear about immediate or long-term causes and effects, too.

2. Helpful *Web Sites* to aid your research

USEFUL GOVERNMENT WEB SITES

The White House www.whitehouse.gov
The House of Representatives www.house.gov
The Senate www.senate.gov
The Bureau of the Census www.census.gov

3. Help in *Interpreting Original Sources*

Original Documents

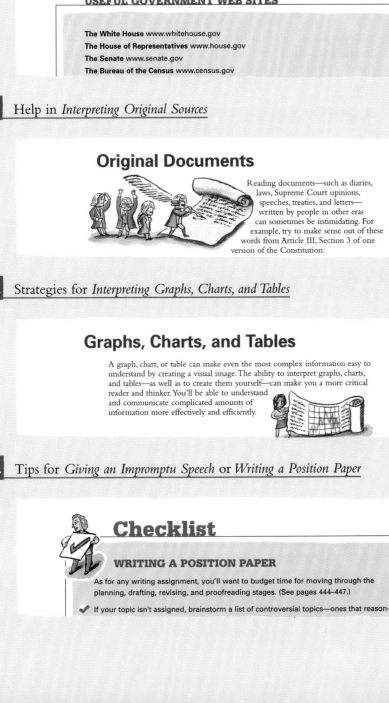

Reading documents—such as diaries, laws, Supreme Court opinions, speeches, treaties, and letters— written by people in other eras can sometimes be intimidating. For example, try to make sense out of these words from Article III, Section 3 of one version of the Constitution:

4. Strategies for *Interpreting Graphs, Charts, and Tables*

Graphs, Charts, and Tables

A graph, chart, or table can make even the most complex information easy to understand by creating a visual image. The ability to interpret graphs, charts, and tables—as well as to create them yourself—can make you a more critical reader and thinker. You'll be able to understand and communicate complicated amounts of information more effectively and efficiently.

5. Tips for *Giving an Impromptu Speech* or *Writing a Position Paper*

Checklist

WRITING A POSITION PAPER

As for any writing assignment, you'll want to budget time for moving through the planning, drafting, revising, and proofreading stages. (See pages 444–447.)

✔ If your topic isn't assigned, brainstorm a list of controversial topics—ones that reason-

ALMANAC

Keeping up-to-date with political events can be trying. Law on financing political campaigns, the position of the independent counsel, the latest restrictions on school prayer—all of these issues and others change. The Almanac attempts to pull together both timely data and lists as well as classic, time-tested documents such as the Bill of Rights and the Constitution. It also includes informative—and amusing—background on key events and figures in American government and politics. Cross-references to the Almanac are placed where appropriate in the coursebook.

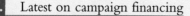

1. Latest on campaign financing

THE RUSH FOR MONEY

★ Political fund-raisers estimate that a viable presidential candidate in campaign 2000 must raise between $22 million and $25 million by the end of 1999. That amounts to more than $60,000 a day.

★ The candidate with the most cash at the end of the year before the election has become the party's nominee in the past five elections.

★ The cost of presidential campaigns has steadily increased. In 1992, presidential candidates spent about $296 million. According to Federal Election Commission (FEC) records, in 1996 presidential candidates spent more than $393 million.

★ The amount the government is contributing to presidential campaigns is

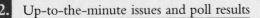
2. Up-to-the-minute issues and poll results

CONTROVERSIAL ISSUES—1998

★ California voters approved slot machines and unrestricted expansion of gambling on Native American land.

★ Voters in Hawaii approved a constitutional amendment giving their state legislature the power to ban same-sex marriage.

★ Michigan voters rejected a proposal that would have legalized physician-

3. Fascinating facts about Congress

CONGRESSIONAL TRIVIA

★ Carl T. Hayden of Arizona has the all-time record for length of service. Hayden served a total of 56 years, 10 months, and 28 days (in the House from 1912 to 1927 and then in the Senate between 1927 and 1969).

★ Strom Thurmond (SC) is the longest-serving member of the Senate. He began serving on November 7, 1956, in the second session of the 84th Congress.

★ John Dingell (MI) is the longest-serving member of the House. He began his service

4. Milestones of the presidency

1829—THE INAUGURATION OF ANDREW JACKSON

The election of Andrew Jackson is often seen as a turning point in ideas about the presidency. Jackson made an effort to establish a direct relationship between himself and the people. In fact, his presidency got off to a wild start. The first President born in a log cabin and born west of the Allegheny Mountains, he was also the first President not descended from an aristo-

5. Important Supreme Court cases

Important Supreme Court Cases

Marbury v. Madison (1803)
Established the power of the Supreme Court to declare an act of Congress or of the executive branch unconstitutional

McCulloch v. Maryland (1819)
Expanded Congress's ability to use its implied powers

Unit I

Constitution and Foundations of Government

1 | Principles of Government

Government and politics—what do they have to do with real life? After all, most people go through their days thinking about school, work, play, family, and friends. Government and politics seem remote, but every time you turn on the television, read the paper, or search the Internet, government and politics are there. The President is making a speech. Political issues are debated. Angry protesters are picketing in front of a government building. What does it all mean, and why should anyone care?

The answer is that none of our lives would be the same without government and politics. Think about what government does for you and how it affects your everyday life—your education, your health, your job, your bank account. For instance, government determines some of the graduation requirements of your school, the minimum wage for a part-time job, and the safety features in the car you drive. Government is not some vast, abstract institution that you only read about in textbooks or hear about on the news. The ties of government to our lives and relationships are deeply rooted, and our challenge is to understand something about them. The reward is a better understanding of our own lives.

In this chapter . . .

Government and Its Purposes

"Politics and government seem so complicated that a person can't really understand what's going on." Does that sound like you or someone you know? In fact, according to a poll from The National Election Studies, 63 percent of people do feel this way.

The key to understanding **government** is to think about its various parts—what they are, why they exist, and how they work. Let's start out by looking at some basic ways to talk about countries and their governments. Take a look at a globe or a political map of the world. Think about the nearly 200 countries whose outlines you see. The **nation–state,** or country, is the world's basic political unit. Nation–states commonly share several important characteristics.

FOUR CHARACTERISTICS OF NATION-STATES

★ **TERRITORY** Of course, a nation-state must have land for people to occupy. The amount and types of land vary dramatically. For example, Russia contains more than six million square miles, but large areas are frozen tundra. In contrast, Bahrain occupies only 240 square miles of desert and coastal land.

★ **POPULATION** Populations, like territories, vary greatly in size and types. The population of the United States, for instance, is much larger and more culturally mixed than that of Sweden, whose people share more similar cultural backgrounds.

★ **SOVEREIGNTY** A strong nation-state has the power to determine its form of government and its economic and social policies. Whether one country has the right to interfere in the sovereignty of another country has become an increasingly difficult and pressing issue in the world today.

★ **GOVERNMENT** Each nation-state has a national government. Although they take many forms, governments are generally made up of people who have the authority and power to rule. If the government is weak, however, the result is often chaos or even war. For example, in the late 1990s, the authority of the government of the Congo was challenged by large groups of its own citizens, and a bloody civil war followed. The result was a new, but not necessarily stronger, government.

def·i·ni·tions

government—the institutions, people, and processes by which a nation-state or political unit is ruled and its public policy created and administered.

nation–state—a political unit with a defined territory, organized under a government and having the authority to make and enforce the law.

Keeping a government strong is not an easy task, partly because individuals must be convinced to follow the rules. In **politics,** successful leaders, or politicians, often maintain or gain control by developing good relationships with the people, and frequently they must persuade one group to see the point of view of another. Leaders must always keep in mind the reasons governments exist and then use their skills to see that those purposes are fulfilled.

PURPOSES

Think for a moment about a band of prehistoric men and women. Our images of them are shaped by scientific research and discoveries and a generous use of imagination. We do know that they generally lived in groups and that survival was not easy. Dangers lurked everywhere. Another group of humans could attack to steal food and shelter, or huge meat-eating animals could devour the band. People could die from starvation, the cold, the heat, or accidents. To ensure survival, people huddled together and began to find ways to protect themselves. Unknowingly, they were blazing a path for generations to follow. Their efforts help us understand the existence and purposes of government.

From their earliest beginnings, governments almost certainly have had three basic purposes:

1. Protection

One characteristic of all government is **sovereignty,** or the right to be free from outside interference. Throughout history, leaders have organized warriors to defend the community, from prehistoric tribes to modern armies. The United States, for example, has a military force of more than 1.5 million troops, as well as powerful nuclear weapons.

2. Maintenance of public order

Almost always, governments have taken responsibility for protecting citizens from violence against one another. Modern governments pass hundreds of laws and maintain large police forces and court systems to protect the public, ensure an orderly daily existence, and promote a sense of justice.

def·i·ni·tions

politics—the methods or tactics involved in managing government and gaining power.

sovereignty—the authority of a state's right to rule itself.

3. Resolution of social conflicts

In human societies conflicts between groups are unavoidable. Central to many of these disagreements is the idea that some groups are unjustly treated. Left unresolved, these conflicts may lead to rioting or war. Traditionally, governments sometimes have suppressed conflicts by use of force, but if their authority is respected, people have tended to accept their decisions peaceably, whether by a king's decree or a democratic election.

In modern times governments are expected to serve several other purposes:

4. Responsibility for a stable economy

The role of government in creating and maintaining a healthy economy has varied widely throughout history. For example, in the late nineteenth-century United States, government was expected to leave the economy alone. In contrast, some modern governments actually own the major industries, and others regulate business practices of private citizens and monitor the currency or money.

5. Provision of public service

Many modern governments provide a transportation and communications network for public use, and most take some measures to protect public health and safety. More controversial is the extent of government responsibility for individual welfare, such as the needs of the poor, unemployed, aged, and disabled. Some countries have extensive welfare benefits; others do not.

Origins of Government

Governments almost certainly evolved gradually, and no one can give a definitive explanation of how they first came to exist. Four theories, however, help us consider their possible origins.

1. The *Evolution Theory* sees government as an extension of family relationships. Even in prehistoric times, families were organized under a system that gave parents authority over children. As more families banded together over time to form tribes, the system of parental rule evolved into tribal rule. Often the elder adults assumed the leadership role, forming a type of mini-government.

2. The *Force Theory* claims that governments were formed as a result of one group's conquest of another. The victorious group would then impose its rules on the conquered group, forcing it into submission. Supporters of this theory cite evidence from both prehistoric and modern times. For example, during World War II, Adolph Hitler forced other European countries to submit to Germany through his *blitzkrieg* ("lightning war") tactics.

3. The *Divine Right Theory* was widely accepted in most European nations from the fifteenth to eighteenth centuries. According to **divine right,** rulers inherit their power from God. Once blessed with this power, the royal family and its heirs become God's representation on Earth. Therefore, defiance of the ruler represents a sin against the church. Ancient civilizations—such as those in China, Egypt, and South America—also believed in divine right and gave godlike qualities to their leaders.

4. The *Social Contract Theory* was developed as a response to the Divine Right Theory by seventeenth- and eighteenth-century philosophers, such as John Locke, James Harrington, Thomas Hobbes, and Jean Jacques Rousseau. According to the theory of **social contract,** humans developed government and named rulers to establish order in the chaotic natural world in which they lived. By agreeing to cooperate with each other and follow a set of rules, people brought order and safety to their lives. The power to govern was a result of decisions made freely by people, not handed down by God. This theory was the inspiration for the American revolution against English rule.

divine right—the belief that rulers derive their authority directly from God and are accountable only to Him.

social contract—the concept that the governed and those governing have obligations to each other, that the people being governed will support the government, and that the government will protect the basic rights of the people.

e.g.

EARLY NATIVE-AMERICAN GOVERNMENTS

The governing systems of early Native Americans offer evidence for the Evolution Theory of the origins of government. At the time the United States was founded, more than 500 culturally different groups had occupied the land for centuries, and most of them had governments based on family life.

Peoples in areas poor in food resources, such as the Paiutes of the Nevada desert, lived in small groups of two or three couples and their children. Life consisted of hunting, fishing, gathering plant foods, and moving camp several times a year. They usually met with other small groups for only a few weeks of feasting, trading, and visiting in the summer. Under these circumstances government was simple, not much beyond the authority structure of the family.

Most Native American groups, however, lived in villages, since agriculture allowed them to stay in one place for longer periods of time. Government was more complex, but still family-based. In most cases, villages formed loose alliances with nearby villages and were governed by councils.

Power and Forms of Government

Notice that all four of these theories define government in terms of power—that is, a small group's ability to get other people to act according to its wishes. Those who govern have some degree of power over the governed. If their decisions are accepted by the people who give them the right to rule, they have the authority to exercise that power, and people recognize the right of the government to exist. Power is generally held by only a few. People who have legitimate power over others may be called **elites.**

---

elite—a small and privileged group who have a disproportionate share of money or political influence.

ELITES

Most Americans—who believe in equality for all, not special privileges for the few—do not like to think about the existence of political elites, at least in the United States. But as much as we might not want to admit it, elites may be identified in nearly every country, past and present, including the United States. Who are they? Political scientists have four main theories to describe and explain the actions of elites, whose political or economic power give them unusual influence in government.

1. Marxist Theory

In his famous theory, Karl Marx argued that those who hold control of the economy have the real power in a society, and government is merely a tool of the rich. In American society, the elites would be leaders of the biggest corporations and financial institutions.

2. The "Power Elite"

Other theorists believe that corporate leaders are important, but that some elites come from other areas as well. For example, C. Wright Mills, an American sociologist, argued in his book *The Power Elite* that important policies are made by three groups: corporate leaders, top military officers, and a few key political leaders.

3. The Bureaucrats

According to this theory, elites are not well-known, visible heads of state or business tycoons, but the people behind the scenes, the bureaucrats whose expertise and specialized talents are responsible for managing societies. Leaders may come and go, but the bureaucrats carry out the day-to-day workings of government and hold the real power. The scholar most often associated with this theory is Max Weber, a German historian and sociologist who believed that all institutions, not just government, have fallen under the control of large bureaucracies.

4. The Pluralists

According to the pluralists, elites are not easily identified as one specific group holding power, money, or prestige. In modern society, these resources are held by a variety of people, and no single elitist group has a monopoly on them. Pluralists do not argue that all resources are held equally. They believe that power is split among so many different types of elites (business people, political leaders, union bosses, journalists, bureaucrats, university leaders) that many people have the chance to influence decision-making.

FORMS OF GOVERNMENT

Each of the elite theories (Marxism, Mills's elites, Weber's bureaucracy, and pluralism) identifies which people in a society hold real power. Even though influential people may have much in common across cultures, political power may be spread among elites in three different ways: according to geographic locations, the separation of powers between executive and legislative branches, and the number of people who hold power.

1. Geographic Distribution

All countries have capital cities, but they differ in how much political power is held there. Governments may center their power in one location, they may scatter power among several places equally, or they may do something in between.

A. UNITARY SYSTEMS

The most common way that countries distribute power is to centralize it in one place, forming a **unitary government.** Local units of government have only those powers given to them by the central government, and they usually are limited and can be changed easily. In fact, the central government can redraw the boundaries and even eliminate local units of government. One advantage of unitary systems is that laws and policies are applied in the same way to each citizen. These systems also avoid costly duplication of government efforts. However, if a country becomes very large geographically, running the government from one location may be difficult.

Unitary governments may be organized in a variety of ways. Some are run by dictators, and others are modern democracies. Examples of countries with this kind of government are France, Japan, Denmark, Great Britain, and China.

B. FEDERAL SYSTEMS

In a **federal government,** central and state governments have different spheres of authority, although their powers may overlap considerably. Countries may divide powers differently between central government and its subdivisions, but some powers are always given exclusively to each level, while others are shared. For example, the central government may hold the sole power to coin money, while both the central and local governments may have the power to tax. Federal systems allow for more flexibility and freedom for the subdivisions, but their governments are often more difficult to coordinate.

def·i·ni·tions

unitary government—a form of government in which all of the powers of the government are held by a single unit or agency.

federal government—a form of government in which governmental powers are divided between a central authority and a number of regional political subdivisions.

Another common problem is the tendency to duplicate efforts, promoting the criticism of wastefulness and inefficiency.

Fewer than 30 modern countries have federal systems of government. Australia, Canada, Germany, India, Mexico, and the United States are among them.

C. CONFEDERATIONS

A **confederation** has a very weak central government and very strong, nearly independent state or local governments. A confederal structure is usually formed when several states or countries want to cooperate in matters of common concern, but also retain their own separate identities. By their nature, confederations tend to be very short-lived; their governments are too weak to keep the states together, and the states often see little need to stay together for a long period of time.

The United States experimented with the confederal system when the First Continental Congress drafted the Articles of Confederation shortly after the Declaration of Independence was written. During the mid-nineteenth century, the southern states seceded from the United States and declared the formation of the Confederate States of America (CSA), thus igniting the Civil War. Quite predictably, the new, weak central government of the CSA had a difficult time coordinating the South's war effort. After it collapsed at the end of the war, no U.S. states attempted to form any other confederations.

An example of a confederation in the modern world is the Commonwealth of Independent States (CIS), which was formed by former Soviet Union Republics when the USSR broke up in 1991. Like most confederations, its central government is so weak that it may break apart. A bold attempt to confederate is currently being conducted in phases, in an experiment called the European Union.

2. Legislative and Executive Branches

Almost all modern governments have a branch that is responsible for making laws—called a legislative branch—and a branch that is responsible for executing the laws—called an executive branch. Power is not always shared equally between these branches. For example, a country ruled by a dictator usually has a legislature, although it may function as a puppet with no real power. Today the practice of dividing power among branches of government takes two basic forms: parliamentary and presidential.

def·i·ni·tions

confederation—a political system in which a weak central government has limited authority, and the states have ultimate power.

Headlines

THE EUROPEAN UNION

Shortly after World War II ended, some European leaders—who sought to unite their nations to prevent another war—began talking about establishing an economic confederation that they first called the Common Market. The main idea of the European Union was to get countries to reduce trade barriers and form a common currency that would be accepted and used in every European country. After years of discussion, in January of 1999, 11 European nations began to share a single currency, the euro. The European Union (EU) was never intended to be political, so it cannot strictly be called a government, but it does represent an economic confederation. Despite the difficulty of convincing countries to give up their old currencies, the new euro market will be huge and powerful, with an economic strength that many economists believe will be equal to or exceed that of the United States. The euro will give the European Union clout.

A. PARLIAMENTARY GOVERNMENT

The English model was widely copied and is now more common than the presidential. Although the countries with **parliamentary governments** may vary in form, they all tend to fuse the two branches together. The chief executive is called a prime minister or premier, and he or she is a member of the legislature, as are the members of the cabinet, who are the chief executive's advisers. The prime minister is the leader of the majority party or a coalition of parties in parliament, and he or she chooses the cabinet members from among the members of the legislature. The prime minister is not popularly elected, except as a member of parliament, but is chosen by his or her political party. Because the prime minister is selected by the majority party, the chief executive does not serve a fixed term.

B. PRESIDENTIAL GOVERNMENT

The United States was an early experiment in the form of **presidential government.** The presidential system separates, rather than fuses, the powers of the legislative and executive branches. The two branches are relatively independent, though they each have the power to check and balance the other. The chief executive is a president who usually holds a fixed term and is chosen separately from the legislature, often by popular vote.

def·i·ni·tions

parliamentary government—a form of government in which the executive leaders are chosen by and responsible to the legislature.

presidential government—a form of government in which the legislative and executive branches are separate and function independently.

HYBRID GOVERNMENTS

Just as species of plants may be crossed to produce new variations, some countries have combined the parliamentary and presidential systems to create a hybrid form. France, for example, has both a prime minister and a president. The prime minister, or premier, generally works closely with the legislature, and the president has an independent power base. The French system, set up in 1958, has been adopted recently by the Russian Republic, although the two hybrids are not exactly alike. Since the Russian government was established only in 1993, its success or failure remains to be seen.

3. Number Who Participate

Throughout history, the number of people who participate in government has varied widely. In the fourth century B.C., the Greek philosopher Aristotle made a memorable early attempt to classify governments according to members who participate: rule by one, rule by few, and rule by many. Although he could not have anticipated it, Aristotle's simple classification organizes many types of governments that have existed since his time.

A. RULE BY ONE

Aristotle used the term *autocracy* to define rule by one. *Auto* means "self," so loosely interpreted, it describes "rule by oneself."

ABSOLUTE MONARCHY In Greek, *mono* means "single" or "alone," and in a **monarchy,** a ruler gains power through inheritance. Rule by monarchs evolved during the Middle Ages into absolutism, a form of government in which monarchs had no restraints on their power. As parliaments and advisers came to share power, absolutism gave way to democratic forms of government, but their old titles—such as king, czar, and sultan—are still recognizable today. Modern monarchs are ceremonial or constitutional, and they generally have little power.

DICTATORSHIP Modern versions of autocracy are often called **dictatorships.** Dictators or totalitarians usually seize and keep power by force. They allow no political opposition and impose many controls on the citizens.

---

monarchy—government in which the ruler's power is hereditary.

dictatorship—a form of government in which an absolute ruler controls the power, often through fear or force, and ignores the will of the people.

B. RULE BY A FEW

Aristotle used the term *oligarchy* to define government in which a small group holds the power to rule. *Oligos* in Greek means "few." Oligarchies have assumed many forms.

ARISTOCRACY In Greek, *aristos* means "most virtuous, noblest, or finest." Rule by the aristocracy, then, means rule by the finest. In some aristocracies the ruling group has been determined by social position or wealth. Another ancient Greek, named Plato, believed in "philosopher kings," or rule by highly educated scholars.

THEOCRACY In Greek, *theos* means "god." In a theocracy, the power to rule lies in the hands of a religious group, such as priests. Today, theocracies rarely exist in pure form, although in some countries religious groups still have a powerful influence on government.

POLITICAL PARTY A modern version of rule by a few is control by a political party. The most obvious examples are the USSR, which existed from 1917 to 1991 under control of the communists, and China, controlled by the Communist party since 1949. In both countries leaders were carefully selected and controlled from within the top ranks of the party.

C. RULE BY MANY

Aristotle used the term **democracy** to define rule by many. *Demos* in Greek means "people," so loosely translated, democracy is rule by the people. Many variations of rule by many have existed since his time.

DIRECT OR PARTICIPATORY DEMOCRACY Democracy began in the city-states of ancient Greece. Most citizens participated directly in either holding office or making policy (excluding nonproperty owners, slaves, and women, who were not citizens). Today, a **direct democracy** may exist in communities, but not very easily on a national level. For example, in some New England towns, the citizens of a community gather once or twice a year to vote directly on major issues and expenditures of the town.

def·i·ni·tions

democracy—a system of government by the people, exercised either directly or through elected representatives.

direct democracy—a democratic system of government in which all citizens participate in politics and decision-making, such as New England town meetings.

DEMOCRATIC CENTRALISM This form of government, which operates on the premise that a government is democratic if it serves the true interests of the people, is associated with communist regimes of the twentieth century. The leaders claim to discover the people's interest through discussions within the Communist party and then make decisions based on their beliefs about what the people want and need. This form of democracy is far from Aristotle's definition because very few, not many, actually rule.

REPRESENTATIVE DEMOCRACY A **representative democracy** is the most common democratic form in modern times, although it was developed centuries ago in ancient Rome. Instead of allowing all of the eligible citizens to participate in the government, a small number are elected to serve as representatives. Because the representatives are elected by the people, government is indirectly by the many.

One criticism of this system is that the representatives become elites who make decisions on their own and, in reality, lead a government by the few. On the other hand, supporters of representative democracies argue that people elect representatives because they respect the representatives' judgments. Those elected see the overall picture and understand the need to protect the rights of all.

representative democracy—a democratic system of government in which policies are made by officials accountable to the people who elected them.

Then and Now

MINORITY RIGHTS IN A DEMOCRACY

In the years following the Civil War, Congress passed the 13th, 14th, and 15th Amendments to protect the rights of former slaves who had been freed as a result of the war. Over the years the former slave states passed so-called Jim Crow laws that kept African Americans from voting, owning property, or attending the same public schools as whites. The laws and regulations were passed by majority votes by town councils, school boards, and state legislatures. African-American interest groups finally turned to the only branch of government without elected officials, the judiciary, to help them get equal rights. Eventually, the democratically elected legislature and executive branch came to agree with the courts, and representatives recognized the need to protect minority rights.

Governments have many purposes, origins, powers, and forms of organization. They are inextricably linked to individual lives and relationships and are deeply rooted in history and human nature itself. The U.S. government has been shaped by governments that came before it and today influences the lives of people around the world. Its many parts and powers are intricate, fascinating, and deserving of close study. We will begin our study of American government at its heart—with the values of freedom, order, equality, and justice that were captured at its founding by the practical men who wrote the Constitution and guided the country in its earliest days.

2 | Beginnings of American Government

I magine a society in which everyone has complete freedom and no laws restrict behavior. What would happen? Would there be complete chaos? If you think so, then you agree with most of the Founders of American government—men like John Adams, George Washington, Benjamin Franklin, and Thomas Jefferson. While they believed that people should have freedom, at the same time they knew that complete freedom would lead to disorder. A compromise had to be reached: a balance between liberty and order.

The Founders' goal was to create a government that would protect freedom without sacrificing order, one that would promote the values of equality and justice. They believed in democracy, but they doubted people's ability to handle it. Their product, the Constitution of the United States, was crafted in 1787 to provide a delicate balance among liberty, order, and justice. It came after years of national debate, first as colonists from Great Britain, and later as independent citizens struggling to hold the new nation together.

In this chapter . . .

English Influence

The English wrestled with the balance between liberty and order and the meaning of justice and democracy for many years before they established the colonies in America. Because the United States was first a part of colonial Britain, the English political system profoundly influenced the colonists.

EARLY TRADITIONS

By the seventeenth century, England had already established important political traditions:

★ **LIMITED GOVERNMENT** The power of the monarch was limited, not absolute. As early as the thirteenth century, the nobles demanded of the king the right to be consulted before taxes were levied. The king was eventually expected to consult with commoners as well, and the first traces of Parliament emerged. By the seventeenth century, **limited government** was well established, with Parliament as a check on the monarch.

★ **REPRESENTATIVE GOVERNMENT** The British Parliament was (and still is) a representative assembly divided into two bodies, the House of Lords and the House of Commons. The English set up similar **representative governments** in the American colonies, though the colonists were not allowed representatives to the British Parliament.

IMPORTANT DOCUMENTS

The colonists based their early governments on the English traditions reflected in three early documents.

1. The Magna Carta, written in 1215, was signed by King John on Runnymede field after he was chased and caught by nobles angry with him for his absolute rule. The document protected nobles from arbitrary acts by the king, guaranteed rights (such as trial by jury), and forbade the king from taking life, liberty, or property without good reason. The Magna Carta represents the first attempt to limit the absolute power of the monarchy.

def·i·ni·tions

limited government—a system in which government's powers are restricted and individuals' rights are protected.

representative government—a system in which policies are made by officials accountable to the people who elected them.

2. The Petition of Right, written in 1628, was intended to curb the actions of another monarch, Charles I, who ignored the rights of others to have a say in government. Unlike the Magna Carta, the Petition of Right extended these rights to commoners, or people not of the nobility. The king's powers were limited in a number of ways. He could not imprison political critics without trial by jury, he could not declare military rule during times of peace, and he could not levy taxes without Parliament's consent.

3. The English Bill of Rights, created in 1688 after years of tension between Parliament and the monarchy, was signed by William and Mary of Orange. Parliament offered to make them joint monarchs in exchange for their signature on the Bill of Rights, which guaranteed free parliamentary elections, freedom from cruel and unusual punishment, and the rights of citizens to a fair and speedy trial.

The Colonies and the Beginnings of Independence

The struggle to put together a government for the fledgling American nation in the late eighteenth century was in many ways an experiment—no one knew what its outcome would be. In many ways, however, the English system of government itself contained the seeds of the American Revolution. The English tradition emphasized limiting the power of the ruler, and the colonists learned that lesson well.

EARLY COLONIAL GOVERNMENTS

In the early years of the American colonies, governments took three forms, all based on English traditions. The colonies became a laboratory for developing governments, from which the Founders drew heavily when they drafted the United States Constitution. At the foundation of each colony was its **charter,** a written agreement between the colony and the king of England (or with Parliament in the case of Georgia), which authorized its existence and set up rules of operation. The three forms of colonial governments were:

---

charter—a legal document issued by a monarch or other authoritative power conferring certain rights and powers upon a person, people, or corporation.

1. Royal Colonies

Charters of royal colonies subjected the government to direct control of the monarchy. Governors and royal councils were appointed by the king. Governors were very strict, had nearly full authority, and closely obeyed the instructions of the king. Royal colonies did have **bicameral** legislatures, but only the lower houses were elected by property owners. The royal councils functioned as the upper houses. There were eight royal colonies: Georgia, Massachusetts, New Hampshire, New Jersey, New York, North Carolina, South Carolina, and Virginia.

2. Proprietary Colonies

Three colonies (Delaware, Maryland, and Pennsylvania) were directly controlled by a proprietor, not the king. The proprietors were granted land by the king and were given great powers to govern. The charters were not as strict as those of the royal colonies, and the colonists generally held less resentment toward the king. The proprietors appointed governors, royal councils, and judges, and the lower house of the legislature was elected by property owners. William Penn (1644–1718) was the most famous of the colonial proprietors. He organized the colonies of Pennsylvania and Delaware to protect basic religious freedom. Pennsylvania's single-house, or **unicameral,** legislature granted more liberties than any other colonial government.

3. Charter Colonies

Connecticut and Rhode Island convinced the king to grant the power to rule directly to the colonists. They had a great deal of independence and were nearly self-governing. Governors, councils, and upper and lower houses of the legislatures were elected by property-owning colonists, and judges were appointed by the legislature.

All colonists elected representatives to government, although only to the lower house of the legislature in all but the two charter colonies. The desire for self-government is thus apparent in all the colonial charters. In fact, a famous group of colonists asserted themselves even before they arrived in America. At Plymouth Rock in 1620, men aboard the *Mayflower* drew up an agreement to govern by majority rule, and their Mayflower Compact reinforced the idea that governments are formed by agreement among citizens for their own benefit.

def·i·ni·tions

bicameral—having or consisting of two legislative chambers or houses.

unicameral—having or consisting of one legislative chamber or house.

GROWING RESENTMENT AND COLONIAL UNITY

In a letter to a friend, John Adams wrote that the real revolution was the "radical change in the principles, opinions, and sentiments, and affections of the people." Adams understood that the American Revolution occurred as a result of a change in the colonists' interpretation of the balance of liberty and order and their definition of equality, democracy, and justice. They eventually decided that the English system erred on the side of order at the expense of liberty and did not grant the colonists equality or allow democratic self-government.

The early relationship between the colonies and the English monarch was good until about 1765, with little talk about revolution. The monarch provided a currency system and defense for the colonies. Both England and America benefited from trade. The colonies supplied raw materials and labor, and the mother country the means of production, much of the capital, and transportation. As long as the colonies fulfilled their economic promise, England was content to allow them control of their internal affairs.

The English victory over France in the French and Indian War in 1763 had some unexpected, dramatic results. The cost of protecting the vast amounts of territory gained from France in North America was overwhelming, especially since the war itself had been expensive. King George III and the British Parliament decided that the colonists should help pay for their own defense. They began enforcing old taxes more strictly and even passed some new ones. The colonists did not approve.

Colonial Boycotts

Resistance to the new tax policies began in 1765, when Parliament passed the Stamp Act. It required that all printed materials be stamped, indicating that a tax had been paid to the king. The colonists protested the new tax and called for a **boycott** on all trade with England. They organized the Sons of Liberty to put pressure on merchants to honor the boycott and were successful in convincing England to repeal the Stamp Act.

Despite the repeal, England still believed that the colonists should help shoulder the expense of their defense, and Parliament continued to pass new taxes. The angry colonists protested their loss of control over tax decisions, and discontent began to grow, especially in the trade-centered Northeast. Violence erupted in 1770 in what came to be known as the Boston Massacre. British soldiers fired on a group of angry colonists, killing five. Three years later, the resentment had increased to the point that the colonists protested a new tea monopoly. In December of 1773, the tea was dumped in the Boston Harbor, in the famous Boston Tea Party.

---

boycott—a method of expressing protest in which people are urged not to use or buy goods and services or deal with certain people or companies.

The Continental Congresses

The English government reacted to the Boston Tea Party with a series of additional laws in 1774 that colonists called the Intolerable Acts, a name that reflected their growing resentment toward British regulations. The result was the gathering of 55 delegates from 12 colonies (all except Georgia) in Philadelphia during September and October of 1774. This First Continental Congress resolved to send a Declaration of Rights to King George protesting Britain's actions. They also resolved to boycott British goods and to call for a Second Continental Congress to convene in May of 1775.

Then and Now

THE LETTERS OF JOHN AND ABIGAIL ADAMS

Some of the most valuable information about the inside workings of the Second Continental Congress, as well as the personal concerns of the delegates, comes from the correspondence between John Adams of Massachusetts and his wife, Abigail. The two reflect political concerns about equality between the sexes and a teasing regard for one another in the following exchange:

"In the new Code of Laws . . . I desire you would Remember the Ladies, and be more generous and favorable to them than your ancestors . . . Remember all Men would be tyrants if they could. If . . . care and attention is not paid to the Ladies we are determined to foment [begin] a Rebellion, and will not hold ourselves bound by any Laws in which we have no voice, or Representation. . . . Men of Sense of all Ages abhor those customs which treat us only as the vassals [servants] of your Sex. . . ."

Abigail Adams, March 31, 1776

Her husband responded:

"As to your extraordinary Code of Laws, I cannot but laugh . . . We have been told that our Struggle has loosened the bands of Government every where. That Children and Apprentices were disobedient—that schools and Colleges were grown turbulent . . . But your letter was the first Intimation that another [group] more numerous and powerful than all the rest were grown discontented . . . you are so saucy. . . . you know that [our Masculine systems] are little more than Theory . . . in Practice you know We are the subjects."

John Adams, April 14, 1776

The American Revolution actually began before the Second Continental Congress met. In April 1775 British troops were sent to the Massachusetts towns of Lexington and Concord to arrest rebellious political leaders and destroy the colonists' weapons. The colonists resisted, and the battle for independence intensified.

The list of delegates who gathered for the Second Continental Congress included George Washington, Benjamin Franklin, John Adams, Patrick Henry, John Hancock, and Thomas Jefferson. On July 4, 1776, the American Revolution officially began with the acceptance of the Declaration of Independence by the delegates from all 13 colonies.

THE DECLARATION OF INDEPENDENCE

The Declaration of Independence, written largely by Thomas Jefferson, is one of the most famous American documents ever written. (See Almanac page 492.) The first paragraphs give a stirring philosophical argument that justified the brazen act of declaring independence. The bulk of the document is an item-by-item list of complaints against the British government. However, the fame of the Declaration of Independence comes from its statement of philosophy, which became the basis for the establishment of the government. Those important first paragraphs express the most enduring beliefs of American society, the values that define the relationship between liberty and order and the meaning of equality, democracy, and justice. These paragraphs reflect the profound influence of the seventeenth-century philosopher John Locke on Thomas Jefferson.

Influence of John Locke

The Declaration of Independence was signed by American colonists during a time of political and philosophical change in Europe known as the Enlightenment. The colonists' conceptions of the balance between liberty and order and their interpretations of equality, democracy, and justice were shaped by such European philosophers as Hobbes, Montesquieu, Voltaire, and Locke. All were critics of absolute monarchy in Europe, and most of the delegates to the Second Continental Congress had read their works.

John Locke (1632–1704) was an early Enlightenment philosopher whose famous work, *The Second Treatise of Government*, powerfully influenced Thomas Jefferson as he wrote the Declaration of Independence. Locke's writings reflect the power struggle between the king and British parliament. His basic principles include:

★ **NATURAL RIGHTS** Locke imagined a "state of nature"—a time that existed before "civilization." Locke held that in this state people have equality, are governed only by the laws of nature, and hold natural rights, including life, liberty, and property.

★ **CONSENT OF THE GOVERNED** Locke argued that government must be based on the consent of the governed. In other words, the people must agree on who their rulers will be. If the government reasonably honors its responsibilities to the people, a social contract exists, and the people should allow the government to rule. If, however, the government betrays the people's trust and breaks the contract by abusing natural rights, the people may abolish it and form a new one.

With these revolutionary ideas in mind, Jefferson claimed in the Declaration of Independence that people should rule instead of being ruled. Moreover, each person was important as an individual, "created equal," and endowed with "unalienable rights."

 **Vs.**

LOCKE AND JEFFERSON

The parallels between the phrases from *The Second Treatise of Government* and the Declaration of Independence are striking.

TREATISE

"The state of nature has a law to govern it . . ."

"to preserve life, liberty, and property"

"men being by nature all free, equal and independent"

DECLARATION

"Laws of Nature and Nature's God"

"life, liberty, and the pursuit of happiness"

"all men are created equal"

The Confederation Period

The Second Continental Congress was only a voluntary association of the states. In May 1776, the delegates urged all the colonies to form new state governments to fill the void left as British officials fled to England. Then, after the Declaration of Independence, the Congress appointed a committee to draw up a plan for a permanent union of the states. The first governments of the newly declared states consisted of 13 different **constitutions,** one from each colony, as well as the first national constitution, the **Articles of Confederation.** The state constitutions included many features that were later incorporated into the national constitution, such as three separate branches, checks and balances, bicameral legislatures, and a bill of rights.

ARTICLES OF CONFEDERATION

After making the bold move to declare independence, the Second Continental Congress turned to the practical issue of establishing a new government based on liberty, not the heavy restrictions placed by the British Crown in the name of order. Since the delegates rejected the tyranny of a monarchy, they quite logically decided that the central government should not be strong. They believed that state legislatures were closest to the people and should be granted power to determine their own policies. When they finally established a government under the Articles of Confederation in 1781, the delegates saw the new government as little more than an agreement among the states. The balance between liberty and order tilted far to the side of liberty, and, as a result, the country sank into turmoil and chaos.

When peace came, many parts of the new country were devastated, and major cities—such as New York and Boston—in shambles. The United States was heavily in debt and surrounded by powerful European countries—England to the north in Canada, and Spain to the south and west. What was to prevent either country from striking and defeating the struggling country? The love of liberty appeared to bring the new country to the brink of disaster.

The Articles of Confederation had outlined a plan of government that had some success—the negotiation of peace and the passage of the Northwest Ordinance of 1787, which limited slavery in the Ohio Valley. But the Articles also had serious weaknesses. Because each state retained its sovereignty,

def·i·ni·tions

constitution—a plan, often written, that details the rules, functions, and principles of a government.

Articles of Confederation—the first constitution of the United States, adopted by the original 13 states in 1781 and lasting until 1788 when the present Constitution was ratified.

the central government could not regulate trade or control a national currency. It had no power to tax and could only request financial support from states. No national judicial system was created to settle disputes among states, and the legislature had no power to make states obey laws and policies that were passed.

e.g.

THE IROQUOIS CONFEDERATION

The Articles of Confederation were influenced not only by the delegates' desire to reject the British government, but by their admiration for the government systems of Native Americans, many of whom had created confederacies for protection. The Iroquois Confederation consisted of Five Nations (groups with common cultures and identities), including the Mohawk, Onondaga, Oneida, Cayuga, and Seneca. Their constitution consisted of verbal agreements that were eventually written down in 1850. According to legend, the confederation began about 1570 when two leaders, Dekanawida and Hiawatha, convinced people in their regions to stop fighting one another and join together to resist invasions from other nations. Clans from the various nations elected representatives to the Confederation Council, which discussed common concerns and coordinated collective actions and decisions.

THE STRUGGLE FOR BALANCE

By 1786, the leaders of the United States were forced to rethink the government they had created. Most of the Founders did not believe that ordinary people were capable of running their own government. They rejected direct democracy in favor of a **republic.** But some trusted the judgment of ordinary citizens more than others, just as some believed in more limits on liberty than others advocated.

Samuel Adams and Patrick Henry were vocal leaders of the independence movement who most resisted a strong central government. Their point of view was immortalized in words that Henry spoke to the Virginia House of Burgesses: "Give me liberty, or give me death!"

def·i·ni·tions

republic—a democracy in which the supreme power lies with the citizens who vote for officials and representatives responsible to them.

Liberty vs. Order

Thomas Jefferson and James Madison both valued liberty highly, but they realized the need to check the chaos that complete liberty brings. Jefferson and Madison believed that strong state governments should balance the central government because local leaders could best represent the citizens.

Although he spoke out strongly against British control, John Adams was more suspicious of liberty than were Jefferson and Madison. He convinced all the states except Pennsylvania to put in bicameral legislatures, with an upper house of men of property to watch over the more hot-headed representatives of the ordinary people.

George Washington, charged with leading the ragtag Continental Army during the Revolutionary War, understood the need for central control. Washington believed in freedom of religion, speech, and other liberties, but he was much more concerned with holding the struggling young nation together and maintaining order and stability by strengthening the unity of the states.

Alexander Hamilton, a lawyer from New York, tilted the delicate balance decidedly toward order. Concerned about the huge war debts, he wanted the new national government to take a strong lead over the states in economic matters.

Quote

"The spirit of resistance to government is so valuable on certain occasions that I wish it to be always kept alive. I like a little rebellion now and then. It is like a storm in the atmosphere."

Thomas Jefferson, letter to Abigail Adams
January 29, 1787

Toward Unity and Order

Economic problems and social unrest in the 1780s led to growing dissatisfaction with the Articles of Confederation and the conviction that the central government must be strengthened. The states fiercely quarreled over boundary lines and **tariffs,** and some even began to deal directly with foreign nations. The national government owed $40 million to foreign governments and to American soldiers for war service. An economic depression left states, as well as farmers and small merchants, deep in debt.

---

tariff—a duty or tax imposed on imported or exported goods.

In 1786, the economic troubles erupted in Shays's Rebellion in western Massachusetts. Led by Daniel Shays, angry farmers armed themselves with pitchforks, marched on the Springfield Arsenal to get weapons, and blocked the entrance to courthouses to prevent actions on farm foreclosures. Because the weak federal government could do nothing to help the state militia put the rebellion down, the farmers raged on, frightening people all across the country. Even though the Massachusetts militia eventually stopped the farmers, Shays's Rebellion set the stage for the delicate balance to tilt toward the side of order.

In the summer of 1786, Alexander Hamilton took the lead in calling together concerned leaders to consider revising the Articles of Confederation. Delegates from five states met in Annapolis, Maryland, and though they were too few to take definitive action, they did request that the state legislatures approve and send delegates to a convention in Philadelphia in May of 1787. The states complied, and the meeting that they called is known as the Constitutional Convention.

Creating and Ratifying the Constitution

On May 25, 1787, 55 delegates representing all the states except Rhode Island attended a meeting that would produce the United States Constitution. The meeting was held in the State House of Pennsylvania, the same Philadelphia building in which the Declaration of Independence had been written 11 years earlier. Today, the building is appropriately called Independence Hall.

THE CONSTITUTIONAL CONVENTION

The most famous delegates were George Washington (the president of the Convention), Benjamin Franklin, Alexander Hamilton, and James Madison. The delegates were all well-known men of their day—mostly wealthy planters, successful lawyers and merchants, and men of independent wealth who had served in their state legislatures. Eight had signed the Declaration of Independence, and many were college graduates, well acquainted with eighteenth-century philosophers. No women, Native Americans, or African Americans attended.

Almost as important were the political leaders who were not there. Patrick Henry refused to come because he suspected something was wrong (he said he "smelt a rat"), and Samuel Adams was not selected by Massachusetts to come. Thomas Jefferson was serving as minister to France and John Adams as envoy to Britain, so neither was able to attend. Quite understandably, without those important individuals, the balance was swayed to order, especially under the influence of Alexander Hamilton and George Washington.

Issues and Compromises

The delegates—the Framers of the Constitution—discussed alternatives, offered compromises, and reached decisions that became the basic principles of American government. James Madison, a young delegate from Virginia, put the decisions into words and gave the document its shape. Therefore, he is usually known as the "Father of the Constitution."

THE VIRGINIA PLAN vs. THE NEW JERSEY PLAN

The Virginia delegates acted boldly within days of the opening of the Constitutional Convention. Governor Edmund Randolph proposed a plan of government that would replace the Articles of Confederation. The Virginia Plan was challenged by the small states in the New Jersey Plan, proposed by Attorney General William Paterson of New Jersey.

THE VIRGINIA PLAN	THE NEW JERSEY PLAN
The legislature should be bicameral, with a lower house elected by the people and an upper house selected by the lower house from nominees submitted by state legislatures.	The legislative branch should be unicameral with representatives selected by state legislatures.
Representation in each house should be based on population and/or money contributed to the national government by the state.	All states should be represented equally in the legislature.
The executive would be chosen by the legislative branch and could serve only one term. Together with the judicial branch, the executive could veto acts of the legislature.	The executive branch would be made up of several persons and would have no veto power over the legislature.
The judicial branch should consist of judges chosen by the legislative branch.	Supreme Court members should be appointed by the executive branch for life.

One important issue involved equality of the states. Some thought that state governments should remain powerful and equal to one another because they ensured that a tyrannical central government would not emerge. Others believed that equality could best be achieved by considering the populations of each state. The earliest and most time-consuming argument at the Convention took place between the large states, who believed that representation in the national legislature should be based on population, and the small states, who supported equal representation of each state. These two positions were embodied in the Virginia Plan, supported by the large states, and the New Jersey Plan, supported by small states.

The conflict between the plans was finally settled after weeks of heated debate by a compromise suggested by the Connecticut delegates. Under the Connecticut or Great Compromise, Congress would be bicameral, with equal representation of the states in the upper house and representation by population in the lower house. The Compromise passed by a razor-thin majority, but it enabled the delegates to move on to other equality issues.

Three-Fifths Compromise

The Three-Fifths Compromise addressed whether or not slaves should be counted in the populations of the southern states. Most delegates from the southern states argued that slaves should be counted, and most from the North took the opposite view. The compromise they reached lasted until slavery was abolished in the late 1860s. It serves as a bizarre example of concessions given on both sides. For purposes of determining representation and taxation, each state was to count three-fifths of all its slaves.

In addition to the issues of equality, the Founders were also very concerned about the poor state of the American economy and the need to preserve individual liberties. Opinions varied as to how serious the economic problems were, but most believed that the economic powers of the new national government should be strengthened. Even though the delegates ultimately tilted the balance between liberty and order toward increasing order, they believed that the Constitution established a limited government that would not threaten individual freedoms. But when the delegates submitted the document to the states for ratification, the critics complained vigorously about how little the Constitution said about individual liberty.

Then and Now

RATIFICATION OF THE CONSTITUTION

The vote for ratification of the Constitution was close in several states, but the Federalists finally managed to win in all of them. Delaware was the first state to ratify, on December 7, 1787. In May of 1790, Rhode Island became the 13th state to vote for ratification. The vote was close, 34–32, and came more than a year after George Washington had become the first President.

RATIFICATION

Nonetheless, the Constitution was signed on September 17, 1787, by 39 of the remaining delegates (several had gone home early for a variety of reasons), and the document was submitted to the states for **ratification.** At least nine states had to give their approval, a requirement that took two years. A fierce debate took place in many of the state legislatures, and for a while it appeared that the new Constitution was doomed.

Federalists and Anti-Federalists

The debate polarized people into two camps: those who supported the Constitution, the **Federalists,** and those who did not, the **Anti-Federalists.** The Federalists supported the greatly increased powers of the central government and believed that individual liberties were sufficiently protected by the proposed Constitution. The Anti-Federalists believed that liberty was sacrificed to order and demanded the Constitution explicitly guarantee individual freedoms and rights. (See Almanac page 515.)

def·i·ni·tions

ratification—the formal approval, or act of validating, a constitution, a constitutional amendment, or a treaty.

Federalists—supporters of a strong federal government, as described in the Constitution.

Anti-Federalists—those who opposed the adoption of the Constitution.

The Federalist

The criticisms of the Anti-Federalists mobilized the men who had crafted the Constitution to action. As the issues were debated not only in the state legislatures but at dinner parties and in public squares, James Madison, Alexander Hamilton, and John Jay published articles under pseudonyms (James Madison called himself "Publius") that illustrated the Constitution's principles. Their 85 essays, known as *The Federalist,* clearly explain the intent of the Founders.

Consider, for example, Madison's explanation, in *The Federalist* No. 51, for why a strong government was necessary: "If men were angels, no government would be necessary. If angels were to govern men, neither external nor internal controls on government would be necessary." Since men are not angels, he reasoned, governments must control people, but they also must be controlled themselves. Such arguments eventually convinced all 13 states to approve the Constitution, especially after they agreed that a very important addition be made to preserve individual liberties—a Bill of Rights that explicitly listed liberties to be protected from encroachment by the central government.

The road to the creation of the Constitution was long, difficult, and filled with uncertainties. The Founders all valued freedom and order, but they disagreed on the balance between them. Through experimentation, rational discussion, and compromise, they reached a delicate consensus, a carefully constructed blueprint to guide the new nation. The document they created was destined to become the oldest written constitution in the world, a model for countless others, and the cornerstone to the United States government today.

3 | **The Constitution**

R ules . . . do we need them? Even though most people complain about them and sometimes even break them, without rules we would have chaos. Sometimes rules take the form of oral instructions, customs, and traditions, but throughout history, many societies have created a set of written rules.

A constitution is a set of principles and rules for governing a country, but it also represents an unwritten collection of traditions and customs that people want to preserve. The United States Constitution, together with the Bill of Rights, provides a blueprint for government, the rules that must be followed. More importantly, the Constitution and the amendments protect our basic values: democracy, justice, equality, and, of course, the delicate balance between liberty and order.

Consider some amazing facts: The Constitution is the supreme law of the land and consists of only 4,300 words. It is the oldest written document of its kind in the world today. While so much has completely changed during the last two centuries—the size and shape of the country and its economy, family life, and laws—the Constitution has remained much the same, with the exception of only 27 amendments. Why? First, the rules of the Constitution are based solidly in important beliefs, customs, and traditions that citizens have valued through the years. Second, the rules preserve enduring values but allow the necessary flexibility to apply the principles to a changing society.

In this chapter . . .

Basic Principles

The Constitution reflects the Founders' belief that controls had to be placed on both the governed and the governors. Democracy must be checked by rulers, and rulers must be checked by democracy. By spreading the power among many, the Constitution prevents any one person or group from taking control of the government, ensuring a degree of democracy. At the same time, it gives the government enough power to avoid mob rule and the tyranny of the majority. The Founders carefully crafted the Constitution to rest on basic principles that reflect a near-perfect balance: popular sovereignty, separation of powers, checks and balances, limited government, and federalism.

1. POPULAR SOVEREIGNTY

Remember that most of the Founders believed John Locke's argument that government must be based on the consent of the governed. In other words, the people must agree on who their rulers will be. **Popular sovereignty** means that people are the most important source of governmental power. But note that everyone's rights were not equal. The Constitution paid almost no attention to social equality and hardly mentioned slavery.

Over time, the principle of popular sovereignty has been expanded by amendments to the Constitution that grant more groups the right to vote: African Americans (the 15th Amendment), women (the 19th Amendment), and young people between the ages of 18–21 (the 26th Amendment). Abraham Lincoln immortalized the principle of popular sovereignty when he declared in his 1863 Gettysburg Address that the Civil War was fought so that "government of the people, by the people, and for the people should not perish from the earth."

As democratic as we might like to think the Founders were, it is important to notice that they allowed the people to vote directly only for members of the House of Representatives—not for the President, judges, or senators. Clearly, they believed that most of the power should be trusted to government leaders, who must be prevented from becoming tyrants.

def·i·ni·tions

popular sovereignty—the fundamental principle that the power to govern belongs to the people and that government must be based on the consent of the governed.

2. SEPARATION OF POWERS

One way that the Constitution prevents one person or group from controlling the government is to separate the powers among three branches of government—legislative, executive, and judicial—so that power is distinct but shared. **Separation of powers** was not a new idea in 1787, because most of the colonies practiced it for more than 100 years before the Constitution was written. Many people believed that the first national government under the Articles of Confederation failed partly because the legislature had no strong executive to check legislative abuses or question and challenge its power. As a result, the constitutional separation of powers became a basic principle of government. Congress was given the function of making laws; the President was given the power to execute and administer laws; and the courts were given the responsibility of interpreting and applying laws.

3. CHECKS AND BALANCES

The Framers of the Constitution did not believe that separation of powers was enough to prevent both oppression by rulers and tyranny of the majority. Because they feared that different officials with different powers might pool their authority and act together, they decided to allow each branch some authority over the actions of the others. In a system of **checks and balances,** no one person or group would be likely to take over the whole government. "Ambition must be made to counteract ambition," as Madison wrote in *The Federalist* No. 51.

def·i·ni·tions

separation of powers—the division of government's executive, legislative, and judicial powers into three separate branches.

checks and balances—a system in which political power is divided among the three branches of government, with each having some control over the others.

For example, even though Congress is responsible for passing laws, the President may veto those laws. Congress, in turn, may refuse to provide funds that the President requests for implementing his programs. Over the years, the courts have developed the power to interpret laws according to the Constitution, but federal judges must be appointed by the President and approved by the Senate. As a result of checks and balances such as these, no branch functions alone, but each is dependent on the others to fulfill its duties.

4. LIMITED GOVERNMENT

Madison's quote reflects the Founders' concern about oppression by rulers, which was as strong as their fear of tyranny of the majority. The principle of limited government guarantees that government does not hold all the power and that it does only those things that people allow it to do. Government officials are subject to law themselves and held to the principles established in the Constitution. Presidents may be impeached, representatives may be voted out of office, and potential judges may be denied confirmation by the Senate.

5. FEDERALISM

Federalism reflects the Founders' desire to balance liberty and order. They believed that the government under the Articles of Confederation lacked a strong central government and allowed states and their citizens too much liberty. Yet they didn't want the oppressive rule of a distant central government, such as that of the British government during colonial times. Federalism spreads—and splits—the powers between national and state governments. For example, only the federal legislature can declare war, only state governments can conduct elections, but both levels of government can levy and collect taxes.

def·i·ni·tions

federalism—the division of governmental power, as expressed in the United States Constitution, between the national government and the states.

SEPARATION OF POWERS AND CHECKS AND BALANCES IN THE CONSTITUTION

Executive Branch

★ Nominates federal judges
★ Grants pardons or reprieves for federal offenses

★ Implements laws
★ Vetoes laws passed by Congress
★ Calls special sessions of Congress
★ Suggests legislation
★ Sends messages to Congress

Judicial Branch

★ Declares executive actions unconstitutional

★ Interprets laws and treaties
★ Declares laws passed by Congress unconstitutional

Legislative Branch

★ Passes laws and sends them to the President
★ Impeaches and removes the President
★ Overrides presidential veto by $\frac{2}{3}$ vote
★ Controls appropriation of money
★ Confirms presidential appointments
★ Ratifies treaties

★ Impeaches and removes federal judges
★ Confirms judicial appointments
★ Establishes lower federal court

Headlines

GENDER, ETHNICITY, AND RACE IN THE CONSTITUTION

Critics of the Framers often say that the Constitution reflects the interests of white, well-to-do males and does not address the concerns of women or minority groups. It is true that no women or minorities attended the Philadelphia convention and that the Constitution did not extend voting rights beyond propertied white males. In addition, each time the Constitution has a pronoun, it is the masculine form—*he* or *him*.

However, as Robert Goldwin discussed in a 1987 article in *Commentary*, the Constitution does not specify men; instead it grants rights to *persons* or *citizens*. In fact, when African Americans were granted the right to vote in 1870 and women in 1920, it was not necessary to change any existing language in the Constitution because the document itself did not deny any groups the right to vote. Thus, the Constitution again proved itself to be a flexible document, based on broad principles, rather than on specific, easily outdated rules.

Structure of the Constitution

An important secret of the longevity of the Constitution is its brevity. The original document had only some 4,300 words and could be carried around in a coat pocket. Rather than going into specific details, the Constitution provided a general blueprint. Its structure may be divided into three parts: the Preamble, the articles, and the amendments, including the Bill of Rights. The full text of the Constitution, including the amendments, is included in the Almanac on page 497.

1. THE PREAMBLE

The Preamble lists six goals for American government: "to form a more perfect union, establish justice, insure domestic tranquillity [peace], provide for the common defense, promote the general welfare, and secure the blessings of liberty." The Preamble is a good example of the enduring nature of the Framers' work. Even though these words were written more than 200 years ago, these goals are just as important for government today as they ever were.

2. THE ARTICLES

Each of the seven articles of the Constitution covers a general topic and is divided into sections that cover more specific details. For example, Article I, by far the longest, contains ten sections. Each section in turn contains a number of clauses, which are often just one sentence long (although some of the sentences are complex). If the Constitution were a plan for a building, the articles could be thought of as the working blueprints for seven main floors.

The articles clearly reflect the basic principles of government. For example, Articles I, II, and III create the three branches of the national government and reflect separation of powers and checks and balances. Article I establishes the legislative branch, Article II addresses the executive branch, and Article III defines the nature of the judiciary. The remaining four articles clarify the relationship between the states and the federal government (Article IV), explain the process for amending the Constitution (Article V), establish the supremacy of national law (Article VI), and outline the ratification process (Article VII).

3. THE BILL OF RIGHTS AND ADDITIONAL AMENDMENTS

Only 27 **amendments,** or changes, have been made to the Constitution. The first ten, called collectively the **Bill of Rights,** were added in 1791 to convince the state legislatures to ratify the Constitution. Originally 12 amendments were proposed, but only ten were adopted; one, about congressional pay, was eventually adopted as the 27th Amendment. The Bill of Rights keeps the national government from limiting personal freedoms.

Amendments 11 through 27 were added between 1798 and 1992. None of them change the basic principles of the Constitution, but they do reflect significant changes in its interpretation through the years. For example, the 13th Amendment abolished slavery, and the 15th extended the right to vote to African Americans. The 17th Amendment established the direct election of senators, thus broadening popular sovereignty. The principle of limited government was affirmed by the 22nd Amendment, which limited a President to two terms in office. The 19th and 26th Amendments further extended popular sovereignty by giving the vote to women and to 18-year-olds respectively. Other amendments created a federal income tax, shortened the time **lame ducks** are in office, and provided for a succession to the presidency. All in all, the additions are remarkably few.

def·i·ni·tions

amendment—a formal statement of change to a law or constitution.

Bill of Rights—the first ten amendments to the Constitution of the United States.

lame duck—an elected official during the period between failure to win re-election and the inauguration of a successor.

38

e.g.

THE 27TH AMENDMENT: 202 YEARS, 7 MONTHS, AND 23 DAYS IN THE MAKING

Salaries for government officials are set by Congress. Representatives and senators determine their own pay. This privilege sounds wonderful, but if Congress abuses it, voters will certainly let them know. The 27th Amendment addresses this awkward power. Ratified in 1992, it says that no increase in the pay of members of Congress can take effect until after the next congressional elections, giving citizens the opportunity to react to the increase through their votes.

Oddly, the 27th had first been proposed as a part of the Bill of Rights by James Madison in 1789, when both representatives and senators made $6 a day. Because it was a part of the Bill of Rights, no deadline was set for its ratification. The Supreme Court had made it clear that amendments must be ratified within a "reasonable time," but the congressional pay amendment never entirely died.

In 1982, Gregory Watson, a student at the University of Texas writing a paper on the Equal Rights Amendment, discovered the languishing amendment and started a ratification movement. In 1992—only 202 years after Madison proposed it—the amendment became a part of the Constitution.

The Amendment Processes

The Founders anticipated the need to change the Constitution, so they set out a formal amendment process in Article V. Their decision was a carefully designed balance between the need for flexibility and the danger of frivolous additions. They believed that the amendment process should be difficult enough to prevent Congress or the states from endlessly slapping on amendments, making the original document meaningless.

THE FORMAL AMENDMENT PROCESS

According to Article V, amendments may be proposed in two ways, and they may be approved by the states in two ways, creating four possible paths that a proposed amendment may take. Congress selects the methods of ratification and sets time limits (now seven years) for ratification. The chart below illustrates these paths.

TWO WAYS TO PROPOSE AMENDMENTS

Proposed by $\frac{2}{3}$ vote of each house of Congress

Proposed by a national constitutional convention requested by at least $\frac{2}{3}$ of state legislatures.

TWO WAYS TO RATIFY AMENDMENTS

Ratified by at least $\frac{3}{4}$ of the state legislatures

Ratified by specially called conventions in at least $\frac{3}{4}$ of the states

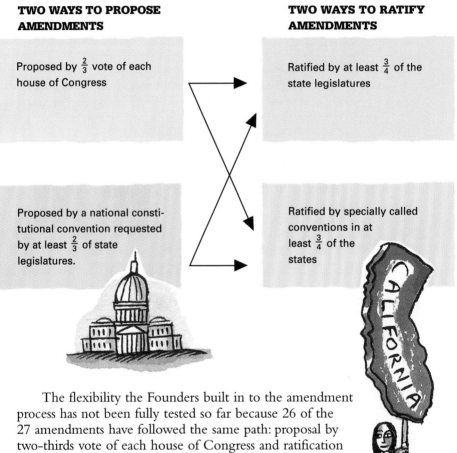

The flexibility the Founders built in to the amendment process has not been fully tested so far because 26 of the 27 amendments have followed the same path: proposal by two-thirds vote of each house of Congress and ratification by at least three-fourths of the state legislatures. Only the 21st Amendment was adopted by a different method. There has not been a constitutional convention held since 1787, perhaps because of the fear that delegates might possibly vote to throw out the whole Constitution.

Then and Now

REPEALING THE "NOBLE EXPERIMENT"

With support from reformers concerned about drinking excesses, Congress, and President Woodrow Wilson, the 18th Amendment was passed in 1919, putting Prohibition into effect. Although the worthiness of the reformers' goals is seldom questioned, the effects were disastrous. The country was split in its opinions of Prohibition, this so-called "noble experiment," with people in rural areas more likely to support it than those in cities.

By 1933 the members of Congress clearly wanted to repeal the 18th Amendment but were afraid that legislators from states with large rural populations would oppose it. They anticipated that a 21st Amendment, to repeal Prohibition, would have a much better chance of passing if special delegates to state conventions made the decision, since those delegates would not have the legislators' worries about getting re-elected. They were right. The 21st Amendment is the only one to be proposed by two-thirds of the members of both houses of Congress and ratified by conventions held in three-fourths of the states, and it is the only one that has ever repealed a previous amendment.

THE INFORMAL AMENDMENT PROCESS

The actual words of the Constitution have changed only by the formal amendment process, but the American system of government is dramatically different today from what it was in 1789. The United States Constitution is written broadly enough so that change may occur within the political system without going through the formal amendment process and altering the document's language. Informal changes in the Constitution occur in at least four ways, including legislative and executive actions, judicial interpretation, and the development of political custom.

1. Legislative Actions

Congress has passed many laws that spell out and add to the Constitution's provisions. For example, although Congress is granted the power to "lay and collect taxes" in Article I, Section 8 of the Constitution, the clause does not specify what may be taxed nor how much tax may be collected. Congress has made and changed those decisions through the years. Similarly, in Article III, Section 1, the Constitution creates "one Supreme Court, and . . . such inferior courts as the Congress may from time to time ordain and establish." Through legislative actions—such as setting up other federal courts—Congress has interpreted the Constitution's meaning.

2. Executive Actions

Just as laws have defined the meaning of the Constitution, the manner in which the President carries out his duties has shaped our interpretation of the great document's words. For example, according to Article I, Section 8, only Congress can declare war, and yet Article II, Section 2 states that the President is the commander in chief of the army. Presidents have acted under this authority to make war without a congressional declaration, although they often consult with congressional leaders. Prominent examples include the Korean conflict of the early 1950s and the Vietnam War in the 1960s and '70s. In the 1990s, President Bush sent American troops to the Gulf War, and President Clinton sent soldiers to Bosnia because they interpreted their roles as commanders in chief to allow them to commit American troops to the conflicts.

3. Judicial Interpretations

The courts, even more than the legislative and executive branches, generally have been most influential in interpreting the Constitution when disputes arise. The power of the courts was greatly enhanced in the 1803 case of *Marbury v. Madison,* in which the Supreme Court claimed for itself the power of judicial review. Implied but never explicitly stated in the Constitution, this power allows courts to decide whether executive and legislative actions of state and national governments are in accord with the Constitution. Their decisions, always made within a historical and social context, are an important source of informal amendments to the Constitution.

4. Changing Customs

In the two centuries since the government was founded, many unwritten customs have become accepted as constitutional, even though they are not part of the Constitution. For example, nowhere is the President's cabinet mentioned, but the customary, established cabinet positions—such as secretary of state and secretary of the treasury—were first created by George Washington, and they have remained as fixtures in the executive branch ever since. Article II, Section 2 does say that the President may consult "the principal officer in each of the executive departments," so the idea of cabinet positions is loosely based in the Constitution.

The original Constitution did not place any limit on the number of terms that a President may serve. Yet the two-term custom was set in place by George Washington when, in his Farewell Address, he recommended that no one should hold the office for a longer time. The custom was not broken for almost 150 years, until Franklin Roosevelt sought and won a third term in 1940 and a fourth in 1944. As popular as Roosevelt was, the unwritten custom was still judged to be best, and in 1951 it became a formal amendment that limited a President to two elected terms or a maximum of ten years in office.

The two-term controversy reflects the importance of beliefs, customs, and traditions in shaping the broad principles of the Constitution. The rules and guidelines that the seven articles put in place are important because they not only preserve enduring values, but allow the necessary flexibility to apply the principles to a changing society. Throughout this book, we will see how the major principles of separation of powers, checks and balances, limited government, popular sovereignty, and federalism continue to shape the American system as it enters the twenty-first century.

4 | **Federalism**

I n one sense, federalism is like a marble cake. One color batter is swirled into a different color and baked until done. When the cake is sliced, every piece is different, with designs going in every direction. No distinct layers exist, and the batters, even though they mix together, are clearly distinct. And so it goes with federalism.

Just as the Founders did not allow the legislative, executive, and judicial branches total independence, they did not explicitly layer state and national government. The Constitution separates the powers of states from those of the national government, but it also recognizes that powers may be shared. The patterns that result are not always neat; they provide, not surprisingly, for ambiguity and conflict, as in the swirling contrasts of the marble cake. In fact, although federalism reflects one of the most important founding principles of the United States, it has been the most important single source of political conflict in the history of the government.

In this chapter . . .

Federalism and the Constitution

The mere existence of national and state governments does not make for federalism. The key ingredient is power that is divided and shared between them, so that each has substantial functions.

e.g.

INTERPRETATIONS OF FEDERALISM

The "marble cake" analogy was proposed by Morton Grodzins. Although Grodzins's analogy for federalism is a useful way to look at it, other interpretations are possible:

★ **DUAL FEDERALISM,** prevalent for the first hundred years or so after the American Revolution, interprets the Constitution to give limited powers to the national government, leaving most power to states. Each level of government dominates its own sphere—like the layers of a cake—with the Supreme Court serving as umpire between the levels.

★ **COOPERATIVE FEDERALISM** defines federalism as a system to provide goods and services to the people, thus requiring cooperation among various levels of government. This point of view is a variation of the marble cake analogy.

★ **NEW FEDERALISM,** advocated by recent Presidents Richard Nixon, Ronald Reagan, and George Bush, emphasizes shrinking the size and responsibilities of the national government and returning more power to the states.

The Constitution recognizes only national and state governments, but in a practical sense, the United States has thousands of governments at other levels, such as counties, municipalities, towns, and school districts. However, it is up to the states to create these other governments and empower them, so the relationship between the states and local governments is usually thought of as one. Understandably, dividing powers and responsibilities among these governments is a complex task, but the formal constitutional framework of the U.S. federal system is relatively simple:

★ The national government has only those powers delegated to it by the Constitution (except for inherent powers explained below). Within the scope of its powers, the national government is supreme.

★ The state governments have the powers not delegated to the national government, except those denied to them by the Constitution or their state constitutions.

★ Some powers are prohibited to both state and national governments; others are denied only to the states, and still others only to the national government.

POWERS OF THE NATIONAL GOVERNMENT

The Constitution gives three types of powers to the national government: the delegated, the implied, and the inherent powers. **Delegated powers,** or expressed powers, are those specifically written in the Constitution (Article I, Section 8) giving Congress 27 powers. They include the power to collect taxes, to coin money, to regulate commerce, to raise and maintain armed forces, to declare war, and to grant patents and copyrights.

In addition to delegated powers, **implied powers** may be reasonably inferred from the Constitution by right of the **Elastic Clause,** (Article I, Section 8), which gives Congress the right "to make all laws which shall be necessary and proper for carrying into execution the foregoing powers, and all other powers vested . . . in the government of the United States." The Supreme Court uses the Elastic Clause, or the Necessary and Proper Clause, to give the national government some very broad powers.

In the field of foreign affairs, the national government has **inherent powers** that don't depend on specific clauses of the Constitution. The national government has the same authority in dealing with other nations as a sovereign state. Among the important inherent powers are those to acquire territory, to recognize foreign states, to set immigration policy, and to protect the United States from rebellion.

def·i·ni·tions

delegated powers—the powers, also called enumerated or expressed powers, that are specifically granted to the federal government by the Constitution.

implied powers—those delegated powers of the national government that are not specifically stated in the Constitution, but that are implied by the interpretation of the Elastic Clause.

Elastic Clause—the clause in the Constitution that allows Congress to pass laws as necessary to carry out its authorized powers; also called the Necessary and Proper Clause.

inherent powers—the powers, usually in foreign affairs, that grow out of the very existence of the national government.

POWERS OF THE STATES

Reserved powers are those held by the states that are not delegated to the national government nor denied to the states. They are not explicitly listed, but are guaranteed by the 10th Amendment as "reserved to the states respectively, or to the people." Traditionally, some of the more significant powers reserved for the states include establishing local government, conducting elections, regulating trade within a state, and ratifying amendments to the Constitution.

Although the division of powers can be confusing, it is logical. The assumption is that state governments should regulate their internal affairs—such as welfare, education, standards of behavior, and public convenience. Next time you question, for example, whether it is constitutional for your state to pass a law allowing public schools to require drug screening for athletes, remember the concept of reserved powers. It leaves states much leeway to pass laws, as long as they don't violate other provisions of the Constitution.

CONCURRENT POWERS

Concurrent powers are held by both national and state governments. They are those powers that the Constitution does not grant exclusively to the national government and that it does not deny the states. Concurrent powers include levying and collecting taxes, establishing and maintaining separate court systems, making and enforcing laws, providing for the health and welfare of citizens, and borrowing money.

PROHIBITED POWERS

Prohibited powers, or restricted powers, are denied either to the national government, the state governments, or both. The Constitution specifically denies some powers to the national government in Article I, Section 9. For example, it can't tax exports, nor can it interfere substantially with the ability of the states to perform their responsibilities. States are prohibited from a number of activities, including making treaties with foreign governments, printing or coining money, taxing imports or exports, and engaging in war.

def·i·ni·tions

reserved powers—the powers that the Constitution sets aside for the state governments.

concurrent powers—the powers that both national and state governments have.

prohibited powers—the powers that are denied to the federal government, the state government, or both; also called restricted powers.

Federal and State Responsibilities

The Constitution not only defines federal and state powers, but it outlines federal responsibilities to states. It also outlines state responsibilities to the national government and states' obligations to one another.

1. FEDERAL RESPONSIBILITIES

The Constitution requires that the national government guarantee "to every state in this union a republican form of government" (Article IV, Section 4). The Framers meant to distinguish a republic, or representative government, from a monarchy (too much order) and a direct democracy (too much liberty). That a state sends representatives and senators to the national Congress is recognition of this federal responsibility.

The Constitution also emphasizes the responsibility of the national government to keep order and to protect states against "domestic insurrection." To fulfill this responsibility, the President has the authority to dispatch troops to put down insurrections when so asked by state authorities, or when state authorities are not enforcing federal laws. For example, President Dwight Eisenhower dispatched federal troops in 1957 to enforce federal policy in Little Rock, Arkansas. The governor and the state militia forbade the integration of Central High School by blocking African-American students from the building.

Another obligation of the federal government to the states is the admission of new states. Also, by promising federal money, the government may also establish standards for states to follow. For example, the federal government provides money to build highways and to fund vocational programs in public high schools.

2. STATE RESPONSIBILITIES

States must meet their responsibilities to the federal government in several ways. For instance, a militia may be organized by a state and called for in time of need. Since 1903 the state militias have been organized under the National Guard. The President, acting in the role of commander in chief of the military, may activate them at any time. In many emergencies, such as floods or civil disturbances, the governor of the state activates the Guard.

The states are also responsible for the elections for all public officials, including national senators, representatives, and the President. The procedures may vary from state to state, or even from election to election. States also set up procedures for voter registration and determination of polling places. In addition, states determine congressional districts, and they play a key role in the amendment process. No amendment can be added to the Constitution unless three-fourths of the states approve.

3. STATES' OBLIGATIONS TO EACH OTHER

The Constitution outlines certain obligations that each state has to every other state. For example, each state must give "full faith and credit" to the public acts, records, and civil judicial proceedings of every other state. This provision recognizes marriages in all states, as well as business contracts. If the **Full Faith and Credit Clause** (Article IV, Section 1) did not exist, a person might be able to avoid obligations, such as automobile loans, by simply crossing a state border.

What about criminal penalties? Almost all criminal law is state law, and if someone robs a store or commits a murder, he or she cannot escape prosecution by crossing state lines. The Constitution requires a person charged with a crime in another state to be returned to that state for trial or imprisonment. This practice is called **extradition.**

A complex obligation among the states is the requirement that citizens of one state receive the privileges and immunities of any other state where they happen to be. In other words, if you are a citizen of New York traveling in Texas, you have the same right to police protection there as do Texas citizens. Many exceptions are allowed to this obligation, however. For example, a state university has the right to charge a lower tuition to citizens of its state than to citizens of other states. Likewise, only citizens of a state may vote in its state elections.

Full Faith and Credit Clause—the clause in the Constitution stating that acts or documents considered legal in one state must be accepted as valid by all other states.

extradition—the legal process in which an alleged criminal is returned to the state or country where the crime was committed.

The Changing Nature of Federalism

Differing views about the nature of the division of power between the states and the national government have existed since the Constitution was created, and those opinions reflect the political attitudes and issues of particular periods.

ESTABLISHING NATIONAL SUPREMACY

A debate in 1791 over the establishment of a national bank—Alexander Hamilton supported it and Thomas Jefferson argued against it—reveals two conflicting interpretations of the Elastic Clause. Hamilton argued that because Article I, Section 8 gave Congress the power to "make all laws which shall be necessary and proper for carrying into execution the foregoing [delegated] powers," Congress had the authority to create a national bank to help carry out the government's power to tax and borrow money.

Thomas Jefferson strongly challenged Hamilton's view. He didn't want to see the Elastic Clause stretched so broadly, arguing that the national government's powers ought to be more limited.

McCulloch v. Maryland

Agreeing with Hamilton's view, President Washington signed the bill establishing the First Bank of the United States. However, in 1819 the argument over national supremacy erupted again in the Supreme Court's decision in *McCulloch v. Maryland* (1819). In 1818 Maryland passed a law taxing the national bank's Baltimore branch. When the Baltimore branch refused to pay, the state sued the cashier, James McCulloch, for payment. Maryland challenged the constitutionality of the bank, arguing that the power to create a national bank was not among those granted by the Constitution. McCulloch was convicted, but he appealed the case to the Supreme Court.

The Court dismissed the charges against McCulloch, ruling that the First Bank of the United States was constitutional, based on the Elastic Clause. Chief Justice John Marshall reasoned that "the government of the United States, though limited in its power, is supreme within its sphere of action." According to Marshall, "all means which are appropriate . . . which are not prohibited, but consistent with the letter and spirit of the Constitution, are constitutional."

The Civil War

Conflicting views of federalism surfaced again in controversies around slavery. The Civil War (1861–1865) was not simply a conflict over slavery; it was also a struggle between states and the national government. John C. Calhoun, a prominent politician from South Carolina and advocate for states' rights, argued that if the government attempted to ban slavery, a state had the right to declare a federal law unconstitutional and null and void within the boundaries of the state. Southern states followed Calhoun's view when they seceded from the Union to form the Confederate States of America. They argued that since states had formed the Union in the first place, they had the right to leave. The national government under President Abraham Lincoln disagreed, claiming national supremacy. The North's victory guaranteed that the union of states could not be dissolved.

 **Vs.**

STATES' RIGHTS POSITION vs. NATIONALIST POSITION

Over the years four basic differences between the states' rights and the nationalist points of view have been the source of countless conflicts.

STATES' RIGHTS	NATIONALIST
The Constitution is a compact among the states.	The Constitution was created by the people, not the states.
Because it was created by the states, the federal government is subordinate to the states.	The national government should take the lead in making government decisions.
Any doubt about whether a power belongs to the national or state government should be settled in favor of the states.	The powers expressly delegated to the national government should be expanded as necessary and proper to carry out its expressed powers.
State governments are closer to the people and better serve their wishes than the national government.	The national government stands for all the people, while each state speaks for only part of the people.

The Commerce Clause

The Supreme Court also promoted the supremacy of national government by its interpretation of the so-called Commerce Clause (Article I, Section 8, Clause 3) through its decision in *Gibbons v. Ogden* (1824). The clause empowers Congress to regulate interstate commerce, and the Supreme Court has expanded this power by ruling that the meaning of commerce is very broad. This case questioned whether the national or state government should regulate boats carrying passengers across the Hudson River between New Jersey and New York. According to the states' rights advocates, commerce involved only products, not passengers. The Court rejected this argument and declared that commerce encompasses virtually every form of commercial activity and thus comes under federal authority.

Over the years, the Court has expanded its definition of commerce to give the national government power over almost any widespread activity— including radio signals, electricity, telephone messages, and insurance transactions. During the 1930s, President Franklin Roosevelt and Congress used the Commerce Clause to require all businesses engaged in interstate commerce to pay a national minimum wage for workers.

The Court even relied on the interstate commerce power to uphold the Civil Rights Act of 1964. This act prohibited racial discrimination in public places, such as restaurants, hotels, and movie theaters. The law was first challenged in 1964 by a Georgia motel owner (*Heart of Atlanta Motel v. United States*) and later that year by the owners of an Alabama restaurant (*Katzenbach v. McClung*). In both cases, the law against discrimination was upheld. The justices reasoned that since public hotels and motels serve interstate travelers and restaurants serve food that has crossed state lines, interstate commerce is involved.

Then and Now

THE COMMERCE CLAUSE AND NATIVE AMERICANS

The Commerce Clause of the Constitution authorized the national government to regulate commerce not only with states and nations but also "with the Indian Tribes." Especially during the nineteenth century, the national government came into constant conflict with Native Americans, and questions of sovereignty and inherent powers were similar to those defining national and state relationships. The result was basically the same: the supremacy of the national government. From 1770 to 1870, Congress increased its role in Indian affairs—regulating trade with Native Americans, ceding land rights to settlers moving west, and controlling almost all facets of Native Americans' government.

Incorporation of the Bill of Rights

The increasing tilt toward the supremacy of the national government has been clearly apparent in several examples. One is the expanded protection of civil liberties. The Bill of Rights originally did not protect against abuses by state governments. Over the years, through a process called incorporation, the Bill of Rights was gradually applied to the states.

THE 14TH AMENDMENT

After the Civil War, Congress was concerned that southern state governments might keep former slaves from exercising rights they did not have as slaves—voting, buying property, or holding public office. In an effort to stop such discrimination, Congress passed the 14th Amendment in 1868. It read, in part: "No state shall . . . deprive any person of life, liberty, or property, without due process of law."

Many felt that this amendment, which clearly contradicted the *Barron v. Baltimore* (1833) decision, would require the protections in the Bill of Rights to be applied to every state. However, judges have a great deal of discretion on how broadly to interpret the Constitution, and the Supreme Court took no significant action to apply the 14th Amendment until the case of *Gitlow v. New York* (1925). Benjamin Gitlow was convicted of a felony under New York state law for passing out leaflets that supported socialism and called for the overthrow of the government. Even though the Supreme Court upheld the state law (the justices ruled against Gitlow), the majority opinion contained a very important statement: Freedom of speech and of the press were among the "fundamental personal rights" protected from infringements by the state by the Due Process Clause of the 14th Amendment. Since then, civil liberties protection from abuse by the states has been applied to most of the guarantees in the Bill of Rights.

UNIQUE STATE AND LOCAL LAWS

Federalism means that state and local laws are often unique and sometimes baffling. Consider these from around the nation:

Weaverville, North Carolina—No unleashed miniature pigs in public

Howey-in-the-Hills, Florida—No run-down façades with chipped paint

South Padre Island, Texas—No wearing of socks or ties

State of Texas—No walking in the streets if there is a sidewalk

Mount Prospect, Illinois—No harboring pigeons or bees

Topeka, Kansas—No alcohol in a teacup

Manhattan, Kansas—No indoor furniture on outdoor porches

Salt Lake City, Utah—No spitting on sidewalks

Coos Bay, Oregon—No possession of paint, ink, or chalk with intent to apply graffiti

FEDERALISM TODAY

The Constitution's primary concern is the division of power between the national and state governments. But federalism today is much more complex, affecting many local governments: counties, municipalities, towns, school districts, and special districts. Each has special duties that often overlap with others, and each passes laws and regulations that apply to its populations. Their relationships are often complex, especially in recent times when the federal government provides funds and regulations that affect the lower levels.

Federal Grants

The federal government has always influenced the states through **grants-in-aid,** or money to finance their programs. Grants-in-aid have existed for more than 200 years. Government first granted land to states in order to finance education and contributed cash to help them pay for their militias. However, since the massive aid given by New Deal programs in the 1930s, grants have dominated relations with the states.

def·i·ni·tions

grants-in-aid—federal funds given to a state or local government for a particular project or program.

★ CATEGORICAL GRANTS are given for a specific purpose. Strict formulas govern which parts of the country get which **categorical grants,** and they are usually subject to detailed federal restrictions, or strings. There are hundreds of grant programs, but a few—including Medicaid and Aid to Families with Dependent Children (AFDC)—account for most of the total spending. Project grants are a type of categorical grant awarded on the basis of competitive applications.

★ BLOCK GRANTS increased in popularity as a result of complaints regarding the cumbersome paperwork and the many strings attached to categorical grants. **Block grants** are devoted to a general purpose, such as education or drug abuse treatment, and have fewer restrictions on their use than categorical grants. The states are allowed to decide the specifics on how to use them and are responsible for channeling the funds to the local governments. Block grants are sometimes criticized because specific programs are overlooked. For example, dropping aid to school libraries and putting it into block grant money has caused some school libraries to close.

def·i·ni·tions

categorical grants—a type of grant-in-aid given by the federal government to a state for specific purposes.

block grants—a type of grant-in-aid given by the federal government to a state for a general purpose, such as fighting crime or improving education.

★ REVENUE SHARING, first proposed by economists in the Lyndon Johnson administration (1963–1969), became a favorite of the Nixon administration (1969–1974.) In **revenue sharing,** a portion of federal income tax monies was automatically returned to state and local governments. The money could be used in almost any policy area at the discretion of the state and local governments. In 1987, the program ended, a victim of a budget cut at a time when deficits soared and there was no revenue to share.

Since state and local governments must apply for categorical grants, they spend a great deal of time investigating grant programs, making applications, and competing for a limited amount of money available. A problem with this competition is that some state and local governments get more than others; the discrepancy is not necessarily based on need but on persuasive power. To address this situation, recent Presidents have supported block grants, which minimize the political connections between Congress and lobbyists. Members of Congress, on the other hand, often resist consolidation of grants because it gives them less control over where the money goes. The situation continues to create considerable tension between Congress and the President.

def·i·ni·tions

revenue sharing—government financing in which money collected in federal income tax is distributed to state and local governments.

Federal Mandates

Conditions of aid are the traditional strings attached to federal aid. They define what state and local governments must do if they want to get some grant money. A newer type of control is a **mandate,** an order from the federal government that is not necessarily backed with money. In other words, the government can tell the states what to do without giving them the funds to carry out the orders.

Most mandates concern civil rights and the protection of the environment. The federal government wants to make it clear that state and local governments may not discriminate in the operations of their programs. Today the anti-discrimination mandates apply not only to race, sex, age, and ethnicity, but to the physically and mentally disabled as well. Environmental groups have convinced the federal government to set standards for clean air, beaches, and drinking water. Though few people disagree with the importance of these federal standards, state and local governments often complain that they shouldn't bear the burden of paying for them.

The Founders designed federalism as a balance between order and liberty, between a powerful and distant central government and a disorganized and dangerous popular government. As a result, they created a complex, controversial division of power. To some, the many levels of government provide opportunities for participation; to others, the division of powers proves confusing. To some, federalism checks the growth of tyranny; others feel it may block the will of the majority. To some, federalism allows for much needed diversity among states, while others believe such diversity results in inequality.

Federalism is a basic principle in the Constitution. Though its nature has changed vastly over the years, it is still an important characteristic of government today. As a source of constant conflict, federalism has been partially responsible for a great civil war, has sometimes blocked national legislation, and has produced bickering among states. On the other hand, it has prevented tyranny, has allowed for diversity, and has provided people more opportunities to participate in democracy. Without the fundamental principle of federalism, the United States would be a dramatically different country today.

def·i·ni·tions

mandate—a rule issued by the federal government to the states.

Unit II

Political Behavior and Participation

5 | Political Parties

Think for a moment about Democrats and Republicans. What good do political parties do? Each party often appears to focus on arguments with its opponent, and once Presidents, representatives, and senators are elected, they usually try to distance themselves from party politics. The general impression is that political parties are somehow a necessary evil. Some people are pleased that their influence has weakened in recent years, believing that if parties were abolished, the United States would be a better country.

A negative attitude toward parties is not new. The Constitution, not accidentally, does not mention political parties, largely because the Founders worried about their possible negative effects—divisiveness and pursuit of selfish interest. When James Madison spoke of the "evils of factions" in *The Federalist* No. 10, he almost certainly had political parties in mind. George Washington even stressed his opposition to political parties in his Farewell Address to the nation in 1796. Washington worried that "the baneful effects of the spirit of party" might distract American citizens "with ill-founded jealousies" and open "the door to foreign influence and corruption."

However, no matter how much the Founders spoke against a political party, most of them eventually joined or helped to form one. For example, Thomas Jefferson wrote in a 1789 letter that if he could only "go to heaven" with a party, he "would not go there at all." Yet he founded the Democratic-Republican party a few years later. This early ambivalence toward parties has profoundly affected their status in the country.

In this chapter . . .

Party Systems and Party Roles

Political parties exist in some form in almost every country in the world today, forming a key connection between people and their governments. The functions of parties vary widely, but in general they almost always form because competing groups want their points of view to influence the government.

PARTY SYSTEMS

Any person or group of people may start a political party. Members of a party share similar beliefs, but not necessarily all the same beliefs. People may band together in political parties for practical reasons. In some countries, one party may form chiefly to oppose another party. In other countries, two large groups may compete for power. In others, many smaller groups may form, making it difficult for any one party to gain a majority. The end results are one-party, two-party, and multiparty systems.

One-Party Systems

In a **one-party system,** the party captures control of the government and, through various means, doesn't allow other parties to form. The party is the government. The party leaders make policy, and often political differences occur only within the party itself. Most one-party systems allow elections, but they are not competitive because only that party's candidates appear on the ballot.

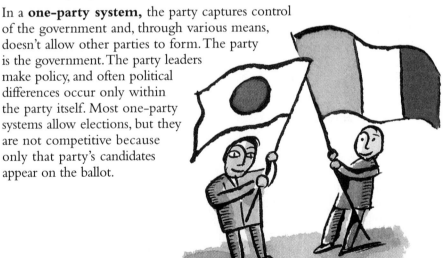

def·i·ni·tions

political party—a group of people organized to influence government through winning elections and setting public policy.

one-party system—a political system in which only one party exists or routinely controls the government.

Headlines

During the twentieth century, the Communist party took over the governments in a number of countries: first in Russia, and later in China, Cuba, North Korea, and Vietnam. During the communist regime in Russia (a member of the Union of Soviet Socialist Republics, or USSR), which was toppled in 1991, no opposition parties were allowed, and the head of the party was also the chief of state. Today, however, Russia has numerous political parties, and the country is attempting to establish competitive elections for both the presidency and the legislature.

Two-Party Systems

The **two-party system** is a rarity, occurring in only about 15 countries in the world today. But the United States has had two major political parties—the Republicans and the Democrats—throughout most of its history. Even though minor parties do exist, many believe those two parties have the only reasonable chance to win national elections. Even on the state and local levels, nearly all elected officials belong to one party or the other. A recent exception was the 1998 election of Reform party candidate Jesse Ventura as governor of Minnesota. On the national level, one party is sometimes more powerful than the other, and the rival may be declared "dead," but the balance of power between the parties always changes over time.

---

two-party system—a political system in which only two major parties compete for control of the government.

Multiparty Systems

Multiparty systems are far more common than two-party systems. Most European countries today (for example, Germany and Italy) have multiparty systems. They usually arise in countries with strong parliamentary systems. The legislature is the most important branch of government, and the head of government is the leader of one of the major parties in the legislature. Because the people only elect representatives to the legislature, and government leaders are party leaders, no separation of powers between legislative and executive branches exists.

Parliamentary systems that use a **proportional representation** method for elections tend to have multiple parties. Parties have a good chance of getting their representatives elected to parliament, because parties get the same percentage of representatives as they have votes in the population. For example, if a party receives 10 percent of the vote, and parliament has a total membership of 500, the party will get 50 members. This system encourages minor parties to form **coalitions,** or loose alliances, to create a majority vote so that legislation can be passed.

ROLES OF PARTIES

Political parties exist because they fill at least four important functions, especially in democratic countries with competitive elections.

1. Recruiting and Labeling

Imagine an election without political parties, an election with 75 candidates in which citizens could vote for anyone. How would voters choose wisely? People would have to study the beliefs and qualifications of them all before making an informed decision. Parties simplify the process by selecting candidates so that voters can make up their minds among just a few people. Candidates run for public office with a party label that serves as a seal of approval. Parties provide the labels in the minds of voters to help them identify a candidate's political views.

def·i·ni·tions

proportional representation—a system in which candidates are elected in proportion to the popular vote they received.

multiparty system—a political system in which many parties exist and compete for control of the government.

coalition—an alliance, often temporary, of people, parties, or nations to achieve a common goal.

2. Acting as Watchdogs

Parties that don't have control of the legislative or the executive bodies are the vocal critics of majority parties. Members of other parties usually hold a significant number of seats in government. They represent an opposing view and voice concerns over the policies and decisions of the party in power.

3. Getting Out Information

Parties go to considerable effort to publicize their points of view on various issues. Each party campaigns for its candidates, takes stands on issues, and criticizes the candidates and stands of the opposition parties. In the process, citizens learn and develop opinions about society's pressing problems.

4. Running the Government

Political parties play a key role in running the government. Congress and the state legislatures are organized according to party affiliations. Party leaders generally see that their members support the party's position when considering potential laws and policies. Most appointments to executive positions, both federal and state, are made along partisan, or party, lines.

INFLUENCE OF PARTIES IN THE UNITED STATES

How do the Republicans and Democrats really influence U.S. government and politics? What is the true nature of their power? We can begin to find the answers by looking at three areas of their influence: with voters, with party workers, and with leaders in government.

1. The Party and Voters

How do you join the Republican or Democratic party? How much does it cost, and how do you maintain your party membership? The answer to these questions is that you have to do almost nothing. In most European nations, people formally join a party, carry membership cards, pay dues, and vote regularly for party candidates. In the United States, all you have to do is choose to be a Republican or Democrat. You are free to identify yourself as such, or you can keep it a secret. No one will stop you from changing parties as frequently as you like.

Indeed, the ability to switch party loyalties is part of protecting individual liberties and rights. Today one of the clearest trends in politics is the tendency for people to see themselves as **independent.** They often vote for a President from one party and a senator or governor from another. Or, they may vote for one party's presidential candidate in one election, and four years later, vote for the other party's candidate. Each party does, however, have its share of loyal supporters and a core of party workers who work for candidates, contribute money, encourage others to vote, attend party meetings, and participate in local party organizations.

2. Party Organization

To understand party organization, we need to think about the concept of power. Many organizations, such as business corporations and even the government, give a great deal of power to the people at the top. For example, boards of directors run most corporations, communicating their wishes to their CEOs (Chief Executive Officers), who then give orders to vice presidents and managers. They, in turn, tell workers what to do.

In contrast to this top-down decision-making, political parties work from the bottom up. This is sometimes known as a **grassroots** organization. Even though each party has a national chairman and other leaders on top, those people have very little control over the people on lower levels. Instead, local and state party organizations do as they please. The national committee leaders must listen to those at the state and local levels in order to coordinate their efforts—such as getting their presidential candidate elected. The 50 state party organizations are each unique.

def·i·ni·tions

independent—a voter who does not belong to or consistently support one of the main political parties.

grassroots—people at the local level; average voters, not professional politicians.

A. LOCAL PARTIES

From the late nineteenth century until the 1930s, the local urban political party was the only influential party organization in America. Many cities were dominated by party machines, which were tightly knit local organizations with strong leaders who held firm control of party members in the city. Much of their power came from a **patronage** system, trading money, political jobs, or other favors from government for votes for the party's candidate.

The abuses of the party machine, which contributed greatly to the negative public image of the parties, were gradually lessened with stricter voter registration laws and civil service reforms. The reforms, however, cost the parties their source of strength. Without the machines or a developed national organization, parties in the twentieth century have struggled to keep their power in the political process.

B. NATIONAL PARTY ORGANIZATION

On the national level, parties historically have been fragmented and decentralized. Although both parties are much better financed and organized than they used to be, local and state party organizations are only loosely tied to the national party organizations. People generally feel the local parties represent their interests better.

On paper, the national Democratic and Republican parties look very much alike. Ultimate authority rests with the national convention and the representatives that meet every four years to nominate a presidential candidate. Between these conventions, the party is managed by a national committee. In Congress, each party has a committee that provides support and campaign funds to party candidates for congressional seats.

3. The Party and Government

Because many of the people who hold government offices—at any level—are party members, political parties play a key role in running and staffing the government. Congress and the state legislatures are organized and carry on their work on the basis of party membership. For example, in both the Senate and the House of Representatives, the majority party leads the legislative process. It wields more control over which legislation is considered and passed than does the opposition. Congress is carefully organized according to a two-party system, a fact that makes it more difficult for a minor third party to influence government. Even though Presidents sometimes like to distance themselves from their party, they must pay attention to party politics if they want their programs to succeed.

def·i·ni·tions

patronage—the practice of rewarding political allies and supporters with jobs.

66

America's Two-Party System

For more than two centuries the two-party system has endured in the
United States. It has had varying degrees of influence on American government. Why, when most other democratic countries have numerous political
parties whose candidates are elected to public office, does the United States
still have only two parties? Minor parties have formed, and they sometimes
have received a significant number of votes. However, none of them has
lasted. There must be some good reasons, and indeed there are at least three.

1. HISTORICAL INFLUENCE

The force of historical tradition is a major reason the United States continues to
have a two-party system. Since the nation began with two parties—the Federalists
and the Anti-Federalists—people have grown used to the system. The longer it
has persisted, the more unthinkable it has become to have it any other way.

2. AMERICAN POLITICAL BELIEFS AND VALUES

Another factor that has influenced America's two-party system is the shared
principles and ideals of the American people. In many other countries, the
range of beliefs is greater, and disagreements run deeper. For example, France
has a communist party that, though weaker than it once was, still gets a
significant amount of support. It also has a strong right-wing nationalist party
whose members have almost the opposite political views from the communists.
Likewise, Nigeria has for many years been locked in a serious dispute over
who should control policy: the military or the proponents of democracy.
The broad ideological **consensus** in the United States encourages just two
large parties—with overlapping points of view—whose main focus is to win
elections, not to represent vastly different sets of beliefs.

3. WINNER-TAKE-ALL SYSTEM

Probably the single most important reason that the United States has a two-
party system is the **winner-take-all** electoral system, instead of proportional
representation. In nearly all elections, from the race for the presidency to

def·i·ni·tions

winner-take-all—an electoral system in which the person with the most votes wins; no majority
is needed.

consensus—collective opinion, general agreement.

contests at the local level, the winner is the one who receives the largest number of votes. The winner does not need to have more than 50 percent of the vote, only one vote more than his or her opponents. Because a party does not gain anything by finishing second, minor parties can rarely overcome the assumption that a vote for them is "wasted."

Elections for national and most state representatives are based on **single-member districts.** One person represents the people within a small area, or district, of a state. No matter how many people run, the person with the largest number of votes wins. This encourages parties to become larger, spreading their "umbrellas" to embrace more voters. Parties without big groups of voters supporting them have little hope of winning, and often even have a hard time getting their candidates listed on the ballot.

Parties in American History

Although America's political parties started with a clouded reputation and George Washington's stern disapproval, they gradually gained strength over the years. By the late nineteenth century, political parties dominated elections and government decision-making. In the twentieth century, their influence has declined somewhat, and voters are not as loyal to their political parties as they once were.

Throughout American history, until the last 30 years or so, one party was dominant for long periods of time. This majority party won most elections, although it may have suffered from internal squabbles or run weak candidates and temporarily lost power. Each of five party eras ended with a critical election in which loyalties shifted, eroding support for the dominant party.

THE FIRST PARTY SYSTEM: 1796–1828

The origins of the two-party system lie in the conflicting views over the role of the national government. Opposing party views began over the battle on the ratification of the Constitution. Alexander Hamilton, co-author of *The Federalist* and first secretary of the treasury, was most concerned about the economic stability of the new country. He strongly believed that a national bank would solve many financial problems. His supporters formed the Federalist party, American's first political party. The Federalists were

def·i·ni·tions

single-member district—an electoral district in which only the one candidate with the most votes is elected to office.

short-lived, partly because of Hamilton's early and untimely death (he was killed in a duel with Aaron Burr), and otherwise because of the persistence of his opponent, Thomas Jefferson. The people who supported the Federalists generally believed in strong central government and the economic interests of northern businessmen, who generally benefited from a strong national bank.

The party that destroyed the Federalists was led by Virginians Thomas Jefferson, James Madison, and James Monroe. First called the Anti-Federalists and later the Democratic-Republicans, their dominance was so complete that the Federalists didn't even bother to run a presidential candidate in 1820. The Democratic-Republicans supported states' rights and state banks and were first popular in rural areas, particularly in the South. They gained support by broadening their policies, stealing support from the Federalists and practicing for the first time the "broadening the umbrella" technique.

THE FIRST DEMOCRATIC ERA: 1828–1860

The critical election of 1828 marked the founding of the modern American political party by Andrew Jackson and his new coalition of westerners, southerners, new immigrants, and long-time citizens. Jackson was at first a Democratic-Republican, but once he became President, the name of the party was shortened to Democratic. The Democrats' primary goals were to broaden voting rights and political and economic opportunity for ordinary citizens and to eliminate privileges for the elite. Another democratic reform of the era was the establishment of the convention, or an assembly of representatives from around the country, to nominate the party's presidential candidate. The convention replaced the old system in which the party leaders did the choosing.

Although the Democrats dominated the era, an opposition party, the Whigs, emerged. The Whig party, led by Henry Clay and Daniel Webster, never stated its purposes very well, except that its supporters were opposed to the Democrats. The Whigs won few elections on local, state, or national levels, although they understood the appeal of military heroes as presidential candidates. They managed to elect two war heroes to the presidency—William Henry Harrison in 1840 and Zachary Taylor in 1848. The Whigs' most serious internal problem—two distinct groups of supporters, one of northern industrialists and one of southern planters—eventually split the party.

THE REPUBLICAN ERA: 1860–1932

In the 1850s the issue of slavery dominated American politics. The Republicans arose in the 1850s as the anti-slavery party, and their candidate, Abraham Lincoln, became President in the critical election of 1860. His election sparked the secession of the southern states and the beginning of the Civil War. After the war, the Republicans controlled government and politics for more than 60 years. The South, however, remained Democratic and resentful of the Republicans who had opposed them during the war.

Once southern states returned to the Union by 1876, the Democratic party once again challenged the Republicans—Grover Cleveland was elected in 1884 and 1892. However, in the critical 1896 election, Democrat William Jennings Bryan lost to William McKinley, and the Republicans regained the presidency, exerting their control for another 36 years (except for Woodrow Wilson's victories in 1912 and 1916).

During this era the parties gained significant power, and many elected officials served as "puppets" for the party leaders. One of the most powerful party leaders was Mark Hanna, whose hand-picked candidates—among them President William McKinley—usually won the elections. Under party bosses like Hanna, political parties usually became associated with graft and corruption, stuffed ballot boxes, and bribery. In reaction to the corruption, a progressive movement began to try to take power away from the bosses. The reforms greatly influenced the succeeding eras.

THE SECOND DEMOCRATIC ERA: 1932–1968

The Great Depression caused the end of the Republican era and brought to power Democratic President Franklin Roosevelt. The critical election of 1932 formed the famous New Deal Coalition of eastern immigrants, southern and western farmers, African Americans, urban dwellers, labor union members, and intellectuals. These groups strongly supported the New Deal programs designed to help the country recover from the depression. Roosevelt was elected to office four straight times. Even though the depression ended, his policies extended through the presidency of Lyndon Johnson during the 1960s. The Democrats maintained their programs and policies designed to help labor, the working classes, and minorities. Even though Republican war hero Dwight Eisenhower won the presidency in 1952 and 1956, the Democrats generally controlled Congress and dominated state and local elections.

THE ERA OF DIVIDED GOVERNMENT: 1968–PRESENT

Beginning in the 1950s, the issue of civil rights for African Americans began to crack the New Deal coalition. Many southern whites, who had been loyal Democrats since the Civil War, did not approve of the Democratic party's pro-civil rights policies, and they began to defect to the Republican party in increasing numbers. A second issue—the Vietnam War—further split the coalition during the 1960s. The result has been a period without a single critical, realigning election, a period of divided government, in which one party controls the presidency and the other is the majority party in Congress. Between 1968 and 1992, the Democrats captured the presidency only once (Jimmy Carter in 1976), but they controlled both houses of Congress for most of the same period. Democrat Bill Clinton was elected in 1992, but the Republicans captured both houses of Congress two years later. Although Clinton was reelected in 1996, the Republicans retained control of Congress in both the 1996 and the 1998 elections, keeping the trend of divided government alive.

Since 1968, divided government has prevailed not only at the federal level, but at the state and local levels as well. Many state governors deal with legislatures dominated by the opposing party, and citizens tend to vote a **split ticket** on all levels of government.

def·i·ni·tions

split ticket—a vote for candidates of more than one party in the same election.

Minor Parties

Even though the two-party system is deeply entrenched in United States politics, minor third parties have popped up consistently through American history. They don't last, largely because the winner-take-all electoral system gives them almost no chance of winning elections. The names of most of them are forgotten: the Free Soil party, the Know Nothings, the Liberty party, the Poor Man's party, and the Greenback party. Others, like the Populists, Progressives, and States' Rights Democrats (Dixiecrats) have certainly influenced the course of political history.

TYPES OF MINOR PARTIES

The minor parties that have won electoral votes tend to be **economic protest parties,** often based in a particular region. Minor parties are sometimes **splinter parties,** which split from a major party. The Populists were an influential economic protest party that gathered support from midwestern and southern farmers who felt taken advantage of by big banks and companies. The Progressive party of 1912 and the Progressive party of 1924 splintered from the Republicans, gaining 88 electoral votes in 1912 and 13 votes in 1924. Often these parties form around charismatic figures—Theodore Roosevelt in 1912 (Bull Moose) or George Wallace in 1968 (American Independent). Like all third parties, they faded as issues changed, sometimes because the major parties eventually broadened their goals and addressed their concerns.

Other minor parties do not always take on the goal of winning elections and electoral votes. **Ideological parties** often profess broad political beliefs and values that are radically different from the mainstream. For example, the Communist party (1920s to the present) wants to replace capitalism with socialism, a point of view that has never won electoral votes. Although members know they will not win, they persist in running candidates for office, hoping that they can eventually bring about a revolutionary change. **Single-issue parties** have as their main goal to influence one major social, economic, or moral issue; too narrowly focused to win large groups of voters, they often have no real desire to continue after the issue is resolved. For example, the Free Soil party formed in 1848 to prevent the spread of slavery and faded away in 1852.

---

economic protest party—a political party dominated by feelings of economic discontent.

splinter party—a political party that has split off from a major party because of a serious disagreement.

ideological party—a political party based on a particular set of beliefs or ideology.

single-issue party—a political party focused on one issue.

SELECTED MINOR PARTIES IN AMERICAN POLITICS

ELECTION YEAR	PARTY	PERCENT OF VOTE	ELECTORAL VOTES	CLAIM TO FAME
1832	Anti-Masonic	7.8	7	The first party to use a national convention to nominate its presidential candidate.
1860	Secessionist Democrats	18.1	72	One of two splinter parties in the realigning election of 1860 that caused the Republicans to win.
1892	Populists	8.5	22	Sponsored reforms that favored "the people," particularly farmers.
1912	Progressive (Bull Moose)	27.4	88	Divided the Republicans and caused the election of a Democratic President for the first time in more than 50 years.
1948	States' Rights (Dixiecrats)	2.4	39	Splintered the Democrats and blocked civil rights legislation for years.
1968	American Independent	13.5	46	The party of segregationist George Wallace that tried to broaden its appeal to all "forgotten" Americans.
1996	Reform	8.4	—	The party, led by billionaire Ross Perot (that grew out of Perot's 1992 campaign as an independent), which drew support from those dissatisfied with the two major parties.

THE INFLUENCE OF MINOR PARTIES

Besides attracting new groups of voters, minor parties have shaped American politics in two major ways:

1. Influencing the Outcomes of Elections

Even though minor parties have never won the presidency, and few have elected candidates to Congress, they sometimes get enough votes to determine which candidate from the major parties wins. For example, Teddy Roosevelt's Bull Moose party siphoned votes from Republican William Howard Taft, so that Democrat Woodrow Wilson won the election of 1912. In 1968, George Wallace's American Independent party undermined Democratic support in the South, helping Republican Richard Nixon to win. Some observers believe that in 1992 and 1996 Ross Perot's campaigns hurt the Republicans more than the Democrats, ensuring victory for Democrat Bill Clinton.

2. Encouraging the Major Parties to Face Important Issues

The "umbrella" nature of the two major parties causes them to look for ways to attract more voters. They pay attention to votes lost to a minor party that addresses a significant or appealing issue. Often the Democrats or Republicans will adopt the policies of the minor parties in order to attract voters back. In fact, the actions of minor parties have helped bring many significant issues to the public's attention—from women's voting rights and the income tax to the Social Security program and voter referendums.

For example, the Progressive party championed eight-hour workdays and better working and living conditions for the urban poor, and both major parties eventually adopted this point of view.

Political parties have played an important, though varying, role in American government and politics for the past 200 years. Sometimes, as in the late nineteenth and early twentieth centuries (through the domination of party bosses and political machines), parties have been extremely powerful. At other times, such as in the 1990s, political parties seem to be not only less well organized but less influential with both voters and candidates. Yet party candidates have persistently won elections, with very few nonparty candidates winning public office on any level of government. Furthermore, as controversial as it is, many believe the two-party system has worked well for the United States. Are political parties a necessary evil, or has the tarnish given them by George Washington and other Founders unfairly maligned them? Whatever your opinion, political parties are almost certainly here to stay.

6 | Elections and Campaigns

ompetitive elections are an essential component of a democratic society. In this country, elections take place on all levels and for many different positions and purposes, from school clubs and neighborhood groups to the presidency of the United States. Almost all Americans have some experience with elections. Probably you or a friend have been nominated for or elected to a leadership position in a club, team, or organization. In reality, the United States has more elected officials than any other country today, a fact that creates many opportunities for ordinary citizens to participate in government and politics.

Campaigns and elections on state and local levels, as well as for the presidency, form the foundation of the democratic process. The goal of campaigns is still to win on election day, but developments in the twentieth century have radically changed the nature of campaigns. The weakening of the parties' control over the electoral process and the growing initiative of the candidates themselves, the increased significance of electronic media, and controversies surrounding campaign financing—all have altered the country's electoral process. Does the new process produce better candidates for public office and thus better government? Keep that question in mind as you read this chapter.

In this chapter . . .

The Electoral Process and Elections

Almost every weekday throughout the year brings some type of election somewhere in the United States. Each voter is eligible to elect people to many different offices, and collectively Americans fill more than 500,000 different public offices. Preceding most elections is a campaign, or an effort to convince voters to elect a particular individual—most often either a Democrat or Republican—to a position.

LAWS AND THE ELECTORAL PROCESS

The Constitution sets certain conditions and requirements for elections, and Congress has passed a number of laws and regulations. However, the rules vary a great deal because states and communities still have the primary responsibility for the process that individuals follow in order to be elected to public office. Most election laws are set by states. Despite the variations, some common rules apply to all American campaigns and elections.

★ Scheduling Elections

In many parliamentary systems, such as Great Britain and Canada, elections may be called by the prime minister at any time, as long as they fall within a specified period (five years in Great Britain). In the United States, elections are scheduled far in advance, according to rules set by national or state legislatures and according to specifications within the Constitution. The Constitution also gives Congress the power to regulate dates and other aspects of the presidential election process, such as those involving the electoral college. Elections are held at scheduled times no matter what, even in times of war or national crisis. Because elections are regularly scheduled, most elected officials—members of Congress, the President and Vice President, state legislators, and local officials such as mayors or school board members—have fixed terms of office and may not serve indefinitely.

★ Polling Places and Ballots

State laws restrict the size of **precincts,** the basic geographical units in which elections are conducted. In turn, precinct election boards regulate the specific polling places and the voting process used in each precinct. They often also count the votes cast.

---

precinct—an election district of a city or town, often the smallest voting district.

Congress has required the use of secret ballots, and the most widely used form is the **Australian ballot.** Printed at government expense, it lists all the candidates and is given out only at the polls to qualified voters. More than half of all votes in national elections are registered on voting machines. Voters make their choices by pulling levers or through electronic vote-counting methods, such as punch-card ballots tallied by computers.

TYPES OF ELECTIONS

Elections may be categorized many different ways. Most people make clear distinctions between local, state, and national elections and think of the presidential selection as different from all the rest. Many candidates—those running for a city council, a state legislature, or the presidency—participate in the two basic types of elections in the United States: the primary or caucus and the general election.

Primaries

Primaries play a key role in the **nomination** process. First used in the late nineteenth and early twentieth centuries, **direct primaries** are held in the spring before the **general election** in the fall and are regulated by state law. As usual in America's federalist system, each state's rules for primaries differ. However, two basic forms of direct primaries are used.

★ In a **closed primary,** voting is limited to registered party members. Currently, most states and the District of Columbia use some variation of the closed primary. Qualified voters are required to declare their political affiliation before they vote. In most states, names must be checked against a party roster before individuals may vote. In other states, an individual may register as a member of a party at the polling place, but sometimes party officials may be stationed at the polling places to challenge a person's right to vote. If challenged, the voter often is required to swear allegiance to the party. In this way, political parties can eliminate a **cross-over vote,** in which members of rival parties vote for weaker candidates.

def·i·ni·tions

nomination—the process of selecting and naming candidates for office.

direct primary—a nominating election in which all party members may vote to choose the party's candidate for the general election.

general election—a regularly scheduled election in which all voters select the winners for each office.

closed primary—a type of direct primary in which only registered party members may vote.

Australian ballot—a uniform ballot printed by the government distributed at the polls and able to be marked in secret.

cross-over vote—a vote in which a member of one party votes in the other party's primary.

★ An **open primary,** currently used in only a few states, is a party nominating election in which any qualified voter may participate. No one has to declare a party choice at registration or at the polls. When voters come to the polling place, they pick the party primary in which they wish to vote. Because the idea of the open primary is to allow voters to switch freely from one party to another, the variations can be confusing. For example, a **blanket primary** is one in which all voters receive the same ballot that lists every candidate for nomination from all parties. Parties still run candidates, but the voter may select a Republican for one office and a Democrat for another. Alaska, California, and Washington have blanket primaries.

In some states, a **runoff primary** is required if no candidate wins a majority of votes. The two highest vote-getters in the direct primary run again, with the winner earning the right to run in the general election. Runoffs may be held in either partisan (party-based) or nonpartisan primaries.

Caucuses

To add to the various types of party nominating processes, some states don't hold primary elections. They choose candidates through a party **caucus,** or a meeting for party members only. While caucus nominations were common in the eighteenth and early nineteenth centuries, by the 1840s, conventions had replaced caucuses as the most common means of nominating candidates. Used only infrequently today for state and local nominations, caucus selections remain important in presidential politics. Local caucuses select members of the state party caucuses, who meet separately to select which presidential candidate each party will support. Of particular importance as early indicators of the popularity of presidential candidates are the Iowa caucuses, traditionally held in February.

def·i·ni·tions

open primary—a type of direct primary in which voters may choose on election day the party primary they want to vote in.

caucus—a meeting of leaders of a political party to select candidates. In a congressional caucus, party leaders and members meet to decide party strategies and conduct party business.

blanket primary—a type of open primary in which voters may vote for candidates of more than one party on an office-to-office basis.

runoff primary—a second primary between the two candidates who received the most votes in the first primary.

The General Election

Once parties determine their candidates for office, the nominees face one another in a general election. By law, candidates for Congress must be selected on the Tuesday after the first Monday in November in even-numbered years. Since the President and Vice President have four-year terms, they are selected in every other general congressional election, but always in an even-numbered year as well. State and local general elections may occur in odd-numbered years and not necessarily in November. But since they must follow primaries, most general elections occur in late spring, summer, or fall. The most important thing to remember is that in a general election the winner fills the public office.

Then and Now

THE PRE-TWENTIETH-CENTURY ELECTORAL PROCESS

Primaries were not common before the early twentieth century. In the earliest years, party leaders met together in a caucus to select candidates for the general elections. Even then, on the national level, they voted directly only for representatives to the House. Senators were chosen by state legislators, and the President by the electoral college. A national convention, with delegates selected from all states, was begun in the 1830s during Andrew Jackson's presidency to make the process more democratic. However, the party bosses soon took over the conventions and maintained control until the early twentieth century, despite charges of unfair and often corrupt practices.

Among later reforms were the institution of state primaries and direct election of senators. The purpose was to give more political power to the people and limit the control of party bosses. Gradually, as more states adopted the practice, political parties lost more and more power.

Campaigns

Campaigns for election to public office in the United States range from very simple to quite complex. If an individual is running for local office, the campaign may consist of talking to voters at meetings, passing out campaign flyers, putting up yard signs, getting attention in the local newspaper, and perhaps calling people on the phone. On the national level, and also often the state level, campaigns have two distinct phases:

★ the campaign before the party nomination, and

★ the effort between the time of the nomination and the general election.

Different techniques and financing rules apply to each phase. In addition, on the national level, congressional campaigns may be distinguished from presidential ones. To investigate the nature of campaigns, consider first a presidential campaign and then a congressional one.

PRESIDENTIAL CAMPAIGNS

How does an individual win the presidency of the United States, probably the world's most powerful office? It definitely doesn't just happen. Even though every President ever elected has done it his own way, each has followed some generally accepted rules of selection. For instance, no person since George Washington has ever won the presidency without first being nominated by a major political party. Tactics have changed dramatically during the twentieth century—from the "whistle-stop" train tour around the country and casual personal appearances of the early days to today's high-technology campaign of media events and publicity.

Quote

"For four years, that's all I did. I mean, all I did. That's all you think about. That's all you talk about. . . . That's your leisure. That's your luxury. . . . I told someone, 'The question is not whether I can get elected. The question is whether I can be elected and not be nuts when I get there.'"

Walter Mondale, Vice President of the United States (1977–1981) and 1984 presidential candidate

1. The Decision to Run

The first step in running for the presidency is to assess the price—the monetary, psychological, and personal toll. Potential candidates also consider the odds, usually doing extensive polling and hiring media experts to judge their chances of success. Candidates must seriously evaluate their money and support. If they don't have a family fortune or high name recognition, then how will they raise money from supporters? Since many campaigns unofficially begin shortly after the previous presidential election, and all successful attempts require media attention, they can be very expensive.

Once a decision is made to run and the public announcement made, candidates must decide on the best strategy for getting support in the primaries. Should the campaign concentrate on a few large states, or should candidates make efforts in all 50 states? The initial phases of the run for the presidency are characterized by hopeful candidates announcing their intentions and then as the primaries get under way, dropping out one by one.

2. Winning Delegates

Although the practice of holding presidential primaries and caucuses has taken a great deal of party control away, to be successful it seems a candidate must still win enough delegates to win the nomination of the Democratic or Republican parties. By tradition, the primaries and caucuses begin in February before the November general election in a presidential election year. They continue, state by state, until June. All states must complete their primaries and caucuses before the national convention delegates meet.

For years the first primary has been held in New Hampshire, a state with only four electoral votes. The campaigning in New Hampshire is usually intense because those that do better than expected receive a great deal of publicity. The Iowa caucus, also held in February, captures a great deal of media attention. A victory, or even a good showing, generates publicity, support, and money. On the other hand, poor results can doom a campaign.

Over the years, primaries have become a series of media events. For example, the Democrats created "Super Tuesday," a day in early March when several southern states hold their primaries. A few weeks before the big day, the candidates flock to the South to campaign rigorously because their very survival may depend on it. What the primaries boil down to for both parties is a process of elimination.

3. The Convention

Before primary elections began in the early twentieth century, the real choice of the presidential candidate was made at the party's convention, which is held traditionally in July or August before the November general election. The delegates, selected by state party organizations, usually came to the conventions with instructions from party leaders about who to vote for. Races were often close, and voting sometimes went through several rounds before one candidate could win enough delegates. Occasionally a **dark horse candidate** might emerge. In 1996, a candidate needed the votes of 996 of 1,990 Democratic party delegates to capture the nomination. To win the Republican nomination, a candidate needed to have the support of 2,146 of 4,290 delegates.

Then and Now

103 BALLOTS

In the Democratic national convention of 1924, it took 103 ballots and 9 days for New Yorker John W. Davis to win the nomination of a sharply divided Democratic party. Davis, a conservative Wall Street lawyer, lost to Republican Calvin Coolidge, winning just under 29 percent of the popular vote.

In the last 20 years, however, each party has known who its candidate would be before the convention even began. With no suspense about the presidential nomination, the convention is more like a pep rally, an opportunity to show the public that the party is organized, enthusiastic, and 100 percent behind its candidate and its party **platform.** Again, media attention is crucial. Both parties put forth their best stars. In 1996, for example, the Republicans scored exceptionally well when Elizabeth Dole, the wife of candidate Bob Dole, gave a speech for her husband that captured the media's attention.

dark horse candidate—one who receives unexpected support as a candidate for the nomination of a political convention.

platform—the formal written statement of the principles and beliefs of a political party.

e.g.

PARTY CONVENTIONS: DAY BY DAY

Both Republican and Democratic conventions represent the most important assembly of party members on the national level. They last for four days, and their major business is the formal nomination of the party's presidential and vice-presidential candidates.

★ **DAY ONE**—The party selects a number of people to give welcoming speeches, with the evening **keynote address** as the highlight of the day. The keynote speaker is chosen carefully, usually an up-and-coming star, or someone popular with a group that the party wants to influence. For example, in 1996, the Republicans chose Christine Todd Whitman, the articulate, popular governor of New Jersey, whom they thought would attract moderate voters, particularly women.

★ **DAY TWO**—Various party committees—such as Rules, Credentials, and Permanent Organization—meet to attend to party business. Of particular importance is the agreement on the party platform and the writing of the individual statements, or planks. Also discussed are particular issues, such as national defense, welfare spending, taxes, AIDS, and the death penalty.

★ **DAY THREE**—The highlight of the day is the nomination of the candidate. The roll is called alphabetically, state by state. The emphasis is on show, and each state pats itself on the back with self-congratulatory comments as it reveals its choice. Sometimes delegates dress in ways designed to attract the cameras—such as Republicans wearing large elephant hats or Democrats with flashy donkey pins. A pep rally atmosphere prevails.

★ **DAY FOUR**—The convention turns its attention to the selection of the Vice President. The nominee tries to choose a running mate who will "balance the ticket," or provide added appeal to voters. This may mean a Vice President who differs in philosophy, age, or gender, or is from a different region of the country. The final events of the convention are the candidates' acceptance speeches, typically covered on television during prime time.

---

keynote address—an opening speech of a national nominating convention that sets the tone of the upcoming campaign.

4. The General Election Stage

Until the last few presidential elections, the campaign for the general election traditionally kicked off the day after Labor Day. After the conventions, the party nominees would often relax before going into the second and final phase of the election campaign: the Democratic nominee against the Republican nominee. That's not so in today's media-driven campaign. In effect, the nominees campaign continuously until the general election day in early November.

Once candidates have their party's nomination, the campaign generally refocuses to appeal to all American voters, not just members of one political party. For Democrats and Republicans alike, the tone usually moderates to capture the voter in the middle, the independent who has little party loyalty.

Over the years, more and more staff members have been hired by both parties to formulate campaign strategies and to contend with what has been called a "media circus." Both parties have long employed campaign managers to coordinate all elements of the campaign. Today many other paid consultants handle advertising, interpret polls, coordinate travel and schedules, write speeches, secure endorsements, and manage the candidate's public image. An effective campaign requires a competent organization of political advisers, public relations experts, creative media producers, and, of course, fund-raisers.

Because television plays such a significant part in modern campaigns, it's not surprising that televised debates—between not only presidential but also congressional, state, or local candidates—have grown more common. With the exception of 1964 and 1972, presidential debates have been held in every election between 1960 and 1996.

Timeline

RUNNING FOR THE PRESIDENCY

The presidential campaign may start at any time, sometimes almost as soon as the previous election is over, but usually not until about a year and a half before the election.

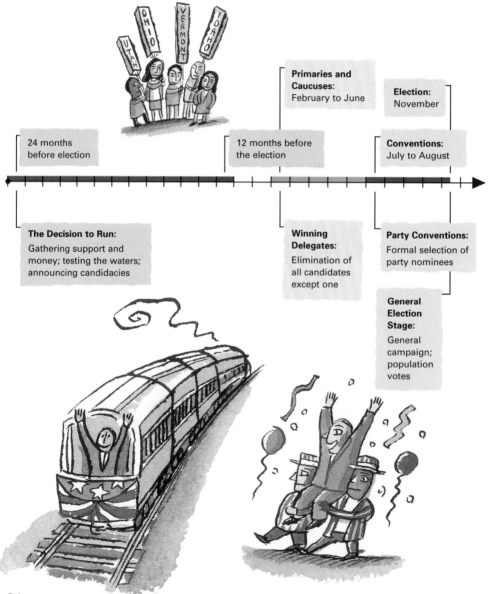

Primaries and Caucuses: February to June

Election: November

24 months before election

12 months before the election

Conventions: July to August

The Decision to Run: Gathering support and money; testing the waters; announcing candidacies

Winning Delegates: Elimination of all candidates except one

Party Conventions: Formal selection of party nominees

General Election Stage: General campaign; population votes

CONGRESSIONAL CAMPAIGNS

Races for seats in the House of Representatives and the Senate follow a schedule similar to that for the presidency, although announcements generally are not made as far ahead. Because congressional races are much smaller than presidential races, they are less expensive, although costs are rising. Also, congressional races are generally less competitive than are presidential ones.

Presidential popularity may affect both House and Senate races. The effect of presidential popularity on other offices is known as the **coattail effect.** For example, in 1980 and 1984, Ronald Reagan's popularity helped many lesser known Republican candidates "ride the coattails" to victory. The strength of the coattail effect is often debated because a popular **incumbent** does not always provide the party's candidates a boost. In 1988, the Republicans suffered a loss of six congressional seats when George Bush won the presidency, and the Democrats lost ten when Bill Clinton was elected in 1992. A reverse coattail effect can happen too, as it did in 1964 with Republican candidate Barry Goldwater and in 1972 with Democratic candidate George McGovern.

Campaign Financing

The high cost of campaigning and the sources of campaign funds have always been controversial topics. (See Almanac page 525.) The amount of money needed to win a federal election these days, particularly the presidency, is enormous. Not surprisingly, the Federal Election Commission (FEC) requires candidates and parties to make records of contributions public. The Clinton and Dole campaigns spent about $232 million in the 1996 campaign, not including about $69 million in "issue ads" paid for by the Republican and Democratic National Committees. For federal, state, and local elections combined in 1996, campaign spending was estimated at $4.1 billion.

The largest chunk of money goes to buy television and radio ads. For example, the Democratic National Committee launched a massive television advertising campaign in October 1995 designed to bolster President Bill Clinton's image. The ads, which almost certainly contributed to the Clinton re-election victory, cost about $44 million. Although candidates for congressional seats spend less, incumbents with large campaign funds can scare away challengers, and advertising can win elections. One of the most expensive Senate

def·i·ni·tions
_____

incumbent—a person currently holding a political office or position.

coattail effect—the favorable influence that a popular candidate has on the voters' selection of other candidates in his or her party.

campaign was the 1994 California race between Democrat Dianne Feinstein and Republican Michael Huffington. The cost was $44 million; Feinstein won.

The FEC oversees disclosure requirements, sets limits on contributions and expenditures, and administers all federal law about campaign finances. Two major issues arise concerning campaign funds: control of overall costs and limits on individual contributions.

SOURCES OF FUNDS

Parties and their candidates draw their funds from two sources: private contributors and the public treasury. Presidential candidates receive part of their money from the federal government; candidates for all other offices are funded primarily from private sources.

Private Sources

The candidates themselves provide some of the funds needed for campaigns. Some candidates are able to finance a large part of their own political campaigns, especially on the local level. At the state and national level, few candidates are able to afford the costs. An exception was billionaire Ross Perot, who contributed some $65 million of his own money to his campaign as an independent in 1992.

Private individuals contribute to the campaigns they support. Until the 1970s, no limits on individual contributions were in place. Many people believed that this arrangement gave an unfair advantage to the wealthy who could buy political influence through their contributions. Today, both the federal and state governments regulate the amount of money a private individual may donate to a political campaign. Contrary to popular belief, most campaign funds come from individual donors, often from people of modest means who contribute $100 or $200 each.

Another private source of campaign funds is **political action committees** (PACs). These political arms of special interest groups have greatly increased since the 1970s. In 1974, only 600 PACs existed; today more than 4,000 contribute to political campaigns. PACs are created by any group that wants to influence government, such as corporations, labor unions, and professional organizations. They pool voluntary contributions of their members into a single fund and give their funds to favored candidates. According to Federal Election Commission (FEC) statistics, in 1995–96, PAC campaign contributions totaled almost $218 million.

def·i·ni·tions

political action committee—a political arm of an interest group set up to contribute to political campaigns; often simply called PACs.

Public Sources

In an effort to offset the influence of wealthy private donors, the federal government offers to help fund presidential campaigns. If candidates accept these funds (both Bob Dole and Bill Clinton did in 1996, each receiving $61.8 million), they must limit their spending to just that amount. The government provides matching funds for all money raised from individual donors who contribute no more than $250 each. So, if Joe Smith from Indiana gives $200 to the Democratic party presidential candidate, the government will match the contribution with another $200. Minor party candidates may also qualify for money if they have received at least 5 percent of the popular vote in the previous election, or if they can raise $5,000 from small contributors in each of 20 states. Congressional candidates receive no government funds and, as a result, have increasingly relied on PAC money.

REFORM LAWS

Congress passed various reform laws in the 1970s because of disclosures that President Richard Nixon's campaign committee had engaged in questionable or illegal money-raising schemes during the 1972 election. In 1974, the Federal Election Commission was established to enforce tougher restrictions on campaign financing. Amendments to the 1971 Federal Election Campaign Act (FECA) included limits on individual and PAC contributions but did not limit overall spending by candidates.

MAJOR FEDERAL CAMPAIGN FINANCE RULES

GENERAL REGULATIONS

The Federal Election Commission (FEC) polices campaigns and has the power to investigate and prosecute violators. All contributions over $100 must be disclosed, giving the name, address, and occupation of the contributors. No cash contributions may exceed $100, and no foreign contributions may be accepted.

CONTRIBUTION LIMITS

	To a candidate or candidate committee per primary or general election	To a national party committee per year	To any other political committee per year	Total per calendar year
Individuals	$1,000	$20,000	$5,000	$25,000
PACs	$5,000	$15,000	$5,000	No limit

LOOPHOLES AND CONCERNS

Although the campaign finance rules have ended many abuses, making it harder for candidates to rely on the influence of a small group of wealthy private donors, accusations that candidates have found loopholes, or ways to get around the laws, continue. The debate over campaign finance flared up after the election of 1996, with many citizens and legislators demanding new rules to address three major concerns.

1. Soft Money

Political parties are allowed to spend as much as they want as long as the money goes to party-building activities, such as voter registration campaigns, get-out-the-vote drives, or issue ads—that is, ads supporting party positions on issues. This spending of **soft money,** unlike hard money spent promoting specific candidates, is largely unregulated. No limit at all exists on the amount donors can give to a party as long as it goes into soft money accounts. Independent expenditures by PACs and interest groups on independent advertising, not coordinated with the campaign, are also unlimited. During the 1996 campaign, the amount of soft money raised by the two major political parties skyrocketed to an unprecedented $262 million, three times more than in 1992. Although the parties may not have done anything illegal, both appeared to have stretched the definition of party-building activities.

Headlines

PARTY-BUILDING ACTIVITIES?

Many critics accused both parties of allowing soft money to make its way into the presidential campaign coffers in 1995–1996. For example, the Democratic National Committee used soft money to pay for a series of television commercials basically the same as campaign ads. President Clinton's approval ratings subsequently improved. Likewise, the Republican National Committee was criticized for paying for a 60-second commercial—largely about Bob Dole's life—crafted by Dole's advertising team with footage originally shot for the Dole campaign. In late 1998, both campaigns were fined heavily by the FEC. Clinton's campaign was told to return $7 million to government coffers, and Dole was fined $17 million.

def·i·ni·tions

soft money—money not regulated by federal law, used by political parties for general expenses.

2. Fund-Raising Tactics

After the re-election in 1996 of Bill Clinton and Al Gore, critics claimed that their fund-raising tactics were unethical, if not illegal. For example, Clinton was accused of inviting donors to spend a night in the Lincoln bedroom of the White House or to have coffee with the President. Others cited inadequate security and background checks of contributors visiting the White House. An investigation was launched into telephone calls to potential donors made from Vice President Gore's office. Although the calls were not challenged by the Justice Department, Republicans in Congress and media critics accused Gore of misusing the power of his office to ask for donations.

3. The High Cost of Campaigns

Campaign expenditures rapidly increased between the time of the reform laws in the 1970s and the 1990s. When the total cost of the election of 1996 across the country weighed in at $2.7 billion, many critics called for new regulations that would create ceilings for overall campaign spending. Others argued that the amount was not excessive, especially compared to advertising costs that many big corporations incur. For example, the Phillip Morris tobacco company spent about $2.8 billion on advertising in 1995.

A fair, competitive election process is a fundamental principle of a democratic society. But critics of America's electoral process argue that the media plays too large a role in primaries and campaigns. They think that laws unfairly discourage independent or minor party candidates, that campaign costs are excessive, and that, despite reform legislation, corrupt and unethical campaign financing practices still exist. Those who defend America's electoral process counter that media coverage—no matter the cost—is critical to educating voters, that the two-party system works well, that primaries keep party bosses from exerting unhealthy control, and that stiff federal regulations eliminate most of the campaign financing problems. So, how fair and efficient is the electoral process in the United States? The answer to that question is not simple, and the debate continues.

7 | Political Participation and Voter Behavior

A mericans often think that they have little to do with politics and that they aren't involved in government decisions or policies. Some people even claim that government never does anything for them or that no one in politics pays attention to what ordinary citizens think and want. For example, in a 1996 survey by The National Election Studies at the University of Michigan, 53 percent of adults questioned said that people don't have a say in what the government does. What may be overlooked, however, are the numerous ways that people can and do participate in government.

Political participation is a vital part of a strong democracy. But, does more participation necessarily mean a better country? The United States is a representative, not a direct, democracy. How much should citizens leave up to government officials? Do low voter turnout rates in the United States mean that Americans don't care about their government? How much thought do people give to the candidates and policies that they support? Consider these questions as we look at the various ways that citizens participate in government and the factors that influence whether—and how—people vote.

In this chapter . . .

Political Participation

Because voting is the most common form of political participation in a democracy such as the United States, it is interesting to notice the difference between what Americans say about voting and their actions. According to the U.S. Bureau of the Census, 48.8 percent of all eligible voters in the **electorate** actually voted in the 1996 presidential election. But when Americans were asked by researchers from The National Election Studies at the University of Michigan, 72 percent said that they had voted. What explains the difference? Perhaps Americans are ashamed to admit that they didn't vote. If so, their answers reflect a belief in the fundamental value of political participation.

FORMS OF PARTICIPATION

Although voter turnout may be low, some studies suggest that many Americans do participate in a wide range of political activities besides voting, as shown below.

AMERICAN POLITICAL PARTICIPATION, 1996

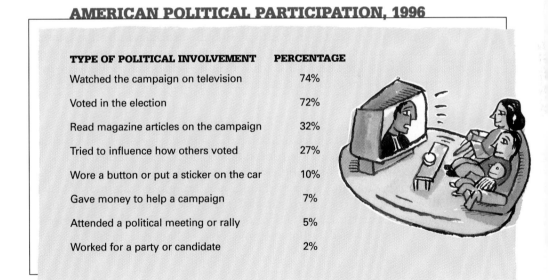

TYPE OF POLITICAL INVOLVEMENT	PERCENTAGE
Watched the campaign on television	74%
Voted in the election	72%
Read magazine articles on the campaign	32%
Tried to influence how others voted	27%
Wore a button or put a sticker on the car	10%
Gave money to help a campaign	7%
Attended a political meeting or rally	5%
Worked for a party or candidate	2%

Source: The National Election Studies, Center for Political Studies, University of Michigan

def·i·ni·tions

    electorate—the people who are qualified to vote in an election.

It is possible, of course, that people exaggerate the extent of such political participation, just as they seem to do with their voting habits. Still, research in **civics** suggests that many Americans do participate in a wide range of political activities at the national, state, or local level—from actively campaigning for a candidate to joining a community organization or contacting a local government official about a problem.

Clearly, many Americans are content for the most part to leave government up to the people who represent them. But a relatively small percentage of the entire population are **activists**, or people who regularly participate in many areas of political life—from involvement in national campaigns to participation in local protests or demonstrations. Activists often have a great deal of influence in the political process. For example, most delegates to national party conventions are political activists. Consider that only about half as many people vote in primaries as in the general election. Logically, a larger percentage of voters in primaries are activists than those that vote in the general election. Because primaries are crucial in determining the parties' candidates, activists have real input into the electoral process.

WHO PARTICIPATES AND WHY

Political scientists interested in **political socialization** have identified several social and economic characteristics that influence who participates and who does not. Most of the research focuses on voting—the most common form of participation—but many studies generalize to other types of participation.

★ Education

The single most important factor related to a high degree of political participation is an individual's level of education, because it is also related to a person's occupation, income, and economic status. Generally, people with more education are more interested in the political process and more likely to vote. For example, according to statistics from the U.S. Bureau of the Census, in 1996, citizens with bachelor's degrees were almost twice as likely (74 percent) to report that they voted as those without a high school diploma (39 percent).

def·i·ni·tions

activist—a person, often outside of government, actively and energetically engaged in political activities.

political socialization—the process by which people develop their political identity and their attitudes toward government, leaders, and issues.

civics—the branch of political science dealing with citizens and their activities.

★ Age

Participation is higher among people who are more than 35 years old than among those who are younger than age 35. More than 70 percent of those aged 55 to 74 voted in the 1996 election, but only a little more than 33 percent of those aged 18 to 24 did.

★ Racial and Ethnic Groups

If only race is considered, whites participate in politics at higher rates than do African Americans and Hispanics. For example, statistics from the U.S. Bureau of the Census for 1996 indicate that the voter turnout rate among citizens is higher for whites (61 percent) than for African Americans (53 percent) or Hispanics (44 percent). However, these statistics may be deceptive. Studies show that people of the same education and income levels, even if they are African American and Hispanic, participate at rates similar to those of whites. Recently, researchers have begun analyzing comparative voting statistics for even smaller populations, such as Asians and Native Americans.

Voting Rights and Eligibility

While voting is only one way for people to participate in politics, it is a critical one. The history of the United States can be characterized as the story of how the pool of eligible voters has expanded from the end of the eighteenth century to the end of the twentieth century.

EXPANSION OF VOTING RIGHTS

According to estimates from the U.S. Bureau of the Census, in November 1996, 179.9 million people 18 years and older were **citizens** eligible to vote. Included in that figure are members of groups that were granted the right to vote long after the first federal election in 1789.

def·i·ni·tions

citizen—a person who has certain rights and responsibilities as a member of a nation and who, by birth or naturalization, may vote.

REPORTED VOTING AND REGISTRATION: NOVEMBER 1996

	PERCENT OF CITIZEN VAP* REPORTED REGISTERED	PERCENT OF VAP* REPORTED VOTED
TOTAL, 18 YEARS AND OLDER	70.9	58.4
White	73.0	60.7
African American	66.5	53.0
Hispanic	59.0	44.3
Asian and Pacific Islander	57.2	45.0
EDUCATION		
Less than high school	54.2	38.8
High school graduate or GED equivalent	65.5	51.7
Some college or Associate's degree	76.1	63.1
Bachelor's degree	83.2	74.1
Advanced degree	89.8	83.3
AGE		
18 and 19 years	46.7	32.4
20 to 24 years	56.4	36.9
25 to 29 years	61.3	44.9
30 to 34 years	65.5	51.1
35 to 44 years	72.2	59.6
45 to 54 years	76.4	66.0
55 to 64 years	79.8	71.4
65 to 74 years	81.0	72.6
75 to 84 years	79.5	67.9
85 years and older	70.1	52.2

* VAP—voting age population

Source: U.S. Bureau of the Census

The Original Electorate

In 1789, only about 23 percent of the total population was eligible to vote. The Founders said little about the establishment of **suffrage** rights, leaving the question of voting requirements largely to the states. Article I of the Constitution states that members of the House of Representatives should be chosen by the "people of the several states." All states had property requirements at first, so that only white men who owned property could vote.

The End of Property Requirements

A very important part of President Andrew Jackson's (1829–1837) popularity was his appeal for "universal manhood suffrage," which meant that voting was reserved for all adult white men, regardless of property holdings. By 1852, all states had dropped property requirements for voting.

Voting and African Americans

After the Civil War (1861–1865), slaves were freed by the 13th Amendment, and voting rights were extended to African American men in 1870 by the 15th Amendment, although, as discussed in Chapter 16, the matter was not settled then. Because so many voting procedures were left up to the states, many former slave states chose to ignore the amendment. Such tactics as the **poll tax,** the **grandfather clause,** and **literacy tests** kept African Americans from voting for decades. Grandfather clauses were declared unconstitutional in 1915, but poll taxes went largely unchecked until 1964, and literacy tests were not banned until 1965.

Voting and Women

Starting in the late nineteenth century, states in the West were the first to extend voting rights to women. The 19th Amendment was not passed until 1920, when the right to vote was granted to all eligible women. Unlike African-American men, who had been kept from voting largely by intimidation and state and local laws, women almost immediately began to vote in large numbers.

def·i·ni·tions

suffrage—the right or privilege of voting.

poll tax—a fee, now unconstitutional, required of voters in many southern states; designed to discourage African-American voters.

grandfather clause—a now unconstitutional law that permitted persons to vote without meeting other requirements if they or one of their ancestors had been entitled to vote in 1866.

literacy test—an examination of reading and writing skills, now unconstitutional, that citizens had to pass before they were allowed to vote.

Then and Now

WOMEN IN WYOMING

Why did western states allow women to vote before those in the East? One explanation is that the nature of life in the Wild West did not allow women to be unequal. They faced the same dangers as men in crossing plains and mountains, and they shared work equally in clearing farms and building homes. Another possible explanation is that women were in short supply (what with so many men going first in response to gold and silver rushes), and, therefore, valued more.

In 1869 the territory of Wyoming was the first to give the right to vote to all its adult female citizens, making them the only women in the world who could legally cast ballots for officeholders at that time. Many easterners were alarmed by this radical move, and some members of Congress tried to force the territory to repeal the law before statehood would be granted. The Wyoming territorial legislature replied with this famous telegraph message: "We may stay out of the Union for 100 years, but we will come in with our women." And, in fact, they did. In 1890, Wyoming was admitted as a state.

Voting and 18- to 21-Year-Olds

A final major expansion of voting rights occured in 1971 when the 26th Amendment granted suffrage to 18- to 21-year-olds. Before that time, the general requirement was that individuals had to be at least 21 to vote. A few states—such as Georgia, Kentucky, Alaska, and Hawaii—had allowed people as young as age 18 to vote. The increased activism of young people, particularly on college campuses during the 1960s, almost certainly inspired this expansion of voting rights.

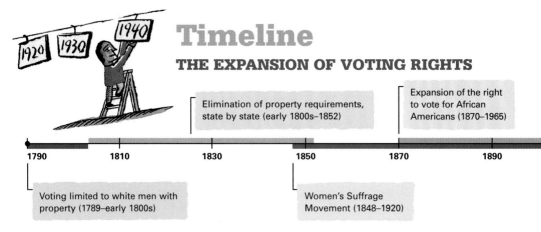

Timeline

THE EXPANSION OF VOTING RIGHTS

Elimination of property requirements, state by state (early 1800s–1852)

Expansion of the right to vote for African Americans (1870–1965)

| 1790 | 1810 | 1830 | 1850 | 1870 | 1890 |

Voting limited to white men with property (1789–early 1800s)

Women's Suffrage Movement (1848–1920)

VOTER ELIGIBILITY

Nearly all Americans age 18 and older today are eligible to vote. Some are still excluded from voting rights by the following limits:

★ Citizenship

Since 1926 most states have prohibited noncitizens from voting. Before that, some western states allowed aliens who had applied for citizenship to vote, probably in order to attract settlers. Only one state, Minnesota, requires a person to have been a citizen for at least three months before voting rights are granted. In a few states, noncitizens may vote in municipal elections only.

★ Residency

Most states require citizens to live within their borders for anywhere from 10 to 30 days before they can vote. Residency requirements were enacted largely to cut down on corruption and cheating in voting.

★ Registration

A controversial requirement for voting is **registration.** Voter identification is intended to prevent fraud in voting. It gives election officials a list of people qualified to vote, and if people's names are not on the list, they can't vote. Every state except North Dakota has some form of voter registration.

In some states, certain groups of citizens are not allowed to vote: people in mental institutions, others found to be mentally incompetent, people convicted of felonies, those dishonorably discharged from the armed forces, the homeless, and polygamists (those with more than one wife at a time). Each of these states differs in the groups that it excludes from voting, but the total number of people kept from voting is very low.

---

registration—the process of formally having one's name placed on a list of those eligible to vote.

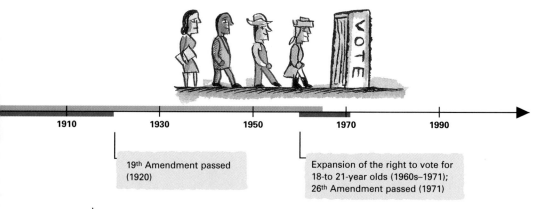

| 1910 | 1930 | 1950 | 1970 | 1990 |

19th Amendment passed (1920)

Expansion of the right to vote for 18-to 21-year olds (1960s–1971); 26th Amendment passed (1971)

Low Voter Turnout

Although the number of eligible voters in the United States has grown tremendously, the rate of voter turnout remains low. The 1996 turnout was the lowest rate of participation in a presidential election since 1924. Eighty million people who could have voted in the 1996 presidential election did not.

YEAR	VOTING AGE POPULATION	REGISTRATION	TURNOUT	% TURNOUT OF VAP*
1996	196,511,000	146,211,960	96,456,345	49.08%
1994	193,650,000	130,292,822	75,105,860	38.78%
1992	189,529,000	133,821,178	104,405,155	55.09%
1990	185,812,000	121,105,630	67,859,189	36.52%
1988	182,778,000	126,379,628	91,594,693	50.11%
1986	178,566,000	118,399,984	64,991,128	36.40%
1984	174,466,000	124,150,614	92,652,680	53.11%
1982	169,938,000	110,671,225	67,615,576	39.79%
1980	164,597,000	113,043,734	86,515,221	52.56%
1978	158,373,000	103,291,265	58,917,938	37.21%
1976	152,309,190	105,037,986	81,555,789	53.55%
1974	146,336,000	96,199,020**	55,943,834	38.23%
1972	140,776,000	97,328,541	77,718,554	55.21%
1970	124,498,000	82,496,747***	58,014,338	46.60%
1968	120,328,186	81,658,180	73,211,875	60.84%

* VAP—voting age population
** Registrations from Iowa not included
*** Registrations from Iowa and Missouri not included

Sources: Congressional Research Service reports, Election Data Services, Inc., and State Election Offices

Turnouts in nonpresidential elections are often worse. As the previous chart shows, congressional elections in off-presidential years have consistently lower rates than do those that take place when presidential candidates are on the ballot. Turnout rates for primary elections are about half those for general elections. In fact, some local officials are elected by less than 10 percent of the eligible voters.

How can we explain the low voter turnout rates? A common explanation for nonvoting is apathy—that people simply don't care. They simply don't pay enough attention to campaigns or make the effort to vote. But, the answer may not be that simple. For example, in a 1996 survey by The National Election Studies, 75 percent of adults responded that they were at least somewhat interested in the current campaign, and 78 percent reported that they cared a good deal about who would win the presidential election. Thus, factors other than apathy must help to explain the low voter turnout.

1. POLITICAL EFFICACY

Political efficacy is the sense that a person can actually make a difference by participating in government and politics. One explanation for nonvoting, then, is that most people don't believe that their one vote—out of millions— will make a difference in the outcome. The lack of political efficacy may be exaggerated by the election night practice in which television networks declare victors state by state in the East before polls in the West actually close. Why bother to vote if the election is already settled? Even though most networks now have agreed to delay making victory announcements until after all polls close, some people argue that just seeing results from the East Coast still discourages West Coast voters.

2. THE REGISTRATION PROCESS

Another possible reason for nonvoting is the voter registration requirement. Statistics show that the turnout of registered voters is significantly higher than the percentage of total voting age population. Indeed, in studies that compare low voter turnout in the United States to that in other countries, the United States turnout is often among the lowest. However, if the turnout is calculated by the percentage of registered voters who actually vote, America's rates compare more favorably with those in other democracies.

def·i·ni·tions

political efficacy—influence in political activities; the sense that one can make a difference through political participation.

States in this country do have strict voter registration requirements, in part because of abuses at the hands of political party machines in the late nineteenth and early twentieth centuries. In those days, political parties often recruited people to vote twice. Ballots were supposedly completed by people who were actually dead at election time, and ballot boxes were "stuffed" with fake votes. Most states now require people to register at least 10 to 30 days before an election. If voters are going to be out of town on election day, most states have complex absentee requirements. Although the procedures surely cut down on corruption, they may also have made it much harder for eligible voters to vote. One common complaint in the past came from college students who were only allowed to vote by **absentee ballot** in their home-towns, a time-consuming process that had to be completed several days before the election. Many states now allow students to register in their college town, avoiding the absentee balloting. In 1996, according to the U.S. Bureau of the Census, 8 percent of voters reported voting by absentee ballot.

★ The Motor-Voter Bill

In 1995 the National Voter Registration Act (NVRA), a law designed to make voter registration easier, went into effect. The motor-voter bill requires states to allow people to register to vote when applying for a driver's license and to permit registration through the mail and at some state offices. In 1996 more people reported registering when they renewed or obtained their licenses than by any other means. Somewhat suprisingly, the percentage of the voting age population who reported they were registered in 1996 did not increase. It is too soon to tell, however, whether the NVRA will eventually increase the percentage of eligible voters who register to vote.

OTHER BARRIERS TO VOTING

Three other factors might explain why many people did not vote in 1996.

★ Weekday Voting

Some critics of the American electoral system believe that holding elections on a weekday discourages people from voting. In most democracies, elections are held on weekends when many people are off work. More than one in five people who reported that they registered but did not vote in the 1996 election explained that they couldn't get time off work or school or were too busy.

def·i·ni·tions
_____

absentee ballot—a ballot marked and mailed in advance that allows a person to vote without being at the place where he or she is registered on election day.

★ **Weak Party Efforts**

In many other countries, parties put forth great efforts to get people to the polls. Party members call and often take people to the polls. In Mexico, the long-dominant PRI not only provides transportation to the polls but often provides food, drink, entertainment, and baby-sitting as well. Earlier in U.S. history, party machines actively recruited voters. Today American parties often contact voters before an election, but their efforts are not as intense as those in other countries.

★ **Voter Satisfaction**

Some people argue that low voter turnout is not bad. It indicates, they say, that people are actually satisfied with how things are going. People don't vote, in other words, because they don't feel the need for a change in the status quo.

Factors Influencing Voting

Socioeconomic characteristics influence whether or not people vote, but political scientists have also identified three factors that significantly influence the choices voters make.

1. CANDIDATE APPEAL

Voters frequently describe themselves as voting for a particular person, not a party. The personal appeal of candidates has affected voter behavior since the early days of American history. For example, military heroes have often won the presidency. George Washington, the leader of the Continental Army during the American Revolution, was the unanimous choice of the electoral college in 1789. His personal qualities and military experience helped establish his reputation as the "Father" of the country.

In recent years the growing role of electronic media has increased the importance of the candidates' personal appeal. Close-ups on television, interviews in magazines and newspapers, and even call-in talk shows put pressure on candidates to look good, speak clearly, and convey knowledge and warmth. Candidates who demonstrate experience, leadership qualities, good judgment, competence, strength, energy, and charisma almost certainly have advantages over their opponents at the polls.

2. PARTY IDENTIFICATION

As much as voters may assert their independence, research indicates that **party identification** is still the single most important predictor of who people will vote for. For example, voters may follow the presidential race carefully and assess the candidate's personal qualities in coming to a voting decision. But because they must make decisions in many other races—local, state, and national—voters often fall back on party labels when they don't have time to research each candidate.

Political scientists usually measure party identification by asking people if they generally consider themselves to be Republican, Democratic, independent, or something else. Those who indicate a party preference are asked a question that measures the strength of their identification. Independents are asked if they feel closer to one party or the other. For example, The National Election Studies at the University of Michigan received the following answers to their questions:

STRENGTH OF PARTISANSHIP—1952-1996

ELECTION YEAR												
PARTY IDENTIFICATION	'52	'56	'60	'64	'68	'72	'76	'80	'84	'88	'92	'96
Independent or Apolitical	9%	13%	12%	9%	12%	15%	15%	15%	13%	12%	13%	10%
Leaning Independent	17%	15%	13%	15%	19%	22%	22%	22%	23%	25%	27%	26%
Weak Partisan*	39%	37%	39%	38%	40%	39%	39%	37%	35%	32%	32%	34%
Strong Partisan*	35%	36%	36%	38%	30%	25%	24%	26%	29%	31%	29%	30%

* either Democrat or Republican

Source: The National Election Studies, Center for Political Studies, University of Michigan

Notice that the percentage of those that responded "Leaning Independent" did increase over the years. The percentage of those that either weakly or strongly identified with a party decreased. As of 1996, however, the percentages of those that identified with a party were still higher than those claiming to lean independent.

---

party identification—an individual's sense of loyalty to a political party.

3. ISSUES

A third factor that influences voters' choices—at least according to what they say in exit polls—is their sense of individual issues. For many voters economic conditions in the country largely determine which candidate they will support. Economic recession, or downturn, often hurts an incumbent's chances for re-election. In 1992, for example, discontent with the economy led many people to reject President George Bush in favor of Democratic challenger Bill Clinton. Exit polling suggested that jobs were the most important issue of the campaign to 43 percent of voters interviewed.

Exit polls and other studies show that the state of the economy is often the single most important issue in many election campaigns. But other issues—such as how the candidate would handle war issues, health care, family values, taxes, education, abortion, and the environment—also affect voters' choices.

Political participation is a vital part of a strong democracy. A country is not truly democratic if people are not interested in or allowed to participate in the political process. Partly because the United States is a representative, not a direct, democracy, voting for public officials has always been the most common form of political participation. While more and more people have become eligible to vote, the percent of those eligible who actually vote has not increased. However, low voter turnout does not necessarily indicate that people do not respect or care about their government or that their political opinions are poorly conceived.

Next, we will investigate how political opinions are formed, how the media influence the political process, and how the media shape popular attitudes toward government and politics.

8 | **Public Opinion and Mass Media**

W hat opinions do you have about government and politics? If your first reaction is, "I don't know," or "I don't have any," think again. What do you think about speed limit restrictions on your city streets? Do you approve of the rules that your school board sets for student behavior? How good a job is the President of the United States doing right now? Do you think government gun control laws are too strict? Do movies and television influence your attitudes? If so, is the influence bad or good? You probably do have opinions—some stronger than others—on these issues. The sum of these private—and widely differing—opinions held by the people is something that political scientists call public opinion.

Because the United States is a diverse country—with people of different ages, regions, racial and ethnic groups, religions, and occupations—public opinion is not simple to gauge. Politicians and media reports like to talk about what the American people want, but we must not assume that all citizens want the same thing. They most certainly do not. At the same time the United States government, as a representative democracy based on the consent of the governed, must be in touch with the opinions of the people even if its leaders choose at times not to follow, but lead, public opinion.

Mass media both reflect and influence public opinion. The media link public opinion and the government, and the influence of the mass media on politics is tremendous.

In this chapter . . .

Political Ideologies

Although all Americans have opinions on various political and social matters, some have more consistent, coherent sets of political beliefs, or political **ideologies.** Most Americans hold broadly shared values and beliefs that shape the direction of government. These core values—such as freedom, equality of opportunity, and individualism—were set in place by the Founders and are sometimes collectively called the American political culture. However, beyond these broad agreements, different ideologies abound.

In the United States, political ideologies are often described as falling into two broadly defined categories: **liberal** and **conservative,** with **moderate** falling in the area between. The terms mean different things to different people, but the fact that many Americans continue to use and relate to the terms indicates that they are important tools in trying to assess political opinion. In an ongoing study, Americans were asked where they would place themselves on a 7-point scale ranging from extremely liberal to extremely conservative. Their answers are reflected in the chart on the following page.

The extreme liberal position on the far left of the political spectrum is often called **radical.** The extreme conservative position on the far right is often called **reactionary.** Only about 4 percent of Americans identified themselves at the ends of the spectrum of ideologies. It's worth noting that most of those polled in 1996 seemed to understand the idea of conservative and liberal beliefs, since only one-fourth responded that they didn't know or didn't care.

Remember that political ideologies are consistent, coherent belief systems. In other words, if a person claims to have a conservative political ideology, we should be able to predict his or her opinion about many different issues.

def·i·ni·tions

ideology—a body of ideas or views of the world that reflect the social needs, values, and ideas of an individual or group.

liberal—a person expressing political views or policies that favor the use of governmental power to promote individual liberties and social progress.

conservative—a person expressing political views that generally favor traditional values, the status quo, and the idea that government should stay out of the affairs of private citizens.

moderate—a person opposed to extreme views; one whose political attitudes are between those of a conservative and a liberal.

radical—a person with extremely liberal political views who favors rapid and widespread change to the current political and social order.

reactionary—a person with extremely conservative political views who favors the widespread changes necesary to return to an earlier government or society.

LIBERAL-CONSERVATIVE SELF-IDENTIFICATION, 1972–1996

Year	'72	'74	'76	'78	'80	'82	'84	'86	'88	'90	'92	'94	'96
Extremely Liberal	1%	2%	1%	2%	2%	1%	2%	1%	2%	1%	2%	1%	1%
Liberal	7%	11%	7%	8%	6%	6%	7%	6%	6%	7%	8%	6%	7%
Slightly Liberal	10%	8%	8%	10%	9%	8%	9%	11%	9%	8%	10%	7%	10%
Moderate, Middle of the Road	27%	26%	25%	27%	20%	22%	23%	28%	22%	24%	23%	26%	24%
Slightly Conservative	15%	12%	12%	14%	13%	13%	14%	15%	15%	14%	15%	14%	15%
Conservative	10%	12%	11%	11%	13%	12%	13%	13%	14%	10%	13%	19%	15%
Extremely Conservative	1%	2%	2%	2%	2%	2%	2%	2%	3%	2%	3%	3%	3%
Don't Know, Haven't Thought	28%	27%	33%	27%	36%	36%	30%	25%	30%	33%	27%	24%	25%

Source: The National Election Studies, Center for Political Studies, University of Michigan

| radical | liberal | moderate | conservative | reactionary |

"left"   "right"

However, this consistency is not always, or even usually, found among either ordinary American citizens or among political leaders. Thus, we need to be cautious about using labels such as liberal or conservative. People's ideologies can and do also change over time. Even among conservative and liberal political leaders, attitudes vary significantly from one individual to the next. Despite these difficulties, researchers have put together some beliefs that are generally regarded as liberal and others as conservative.

LIBERALISM

The term *liberalism* first emerged in Europe in the seventeenth century. Up through the nineteenth century, liberals fought to keep governments small, allowing ordinary citizens freedom to run their own affairs. Liberals stressed the individual rights of the "little guy," and they saw the government as a threat to ordinary citizens. Liberalism in the United States has its roots in the political thinking of Thomas Jefferson and Andrew Jackson. For example, liberals during Andrew Jackson's presidency believed the government was controlled by big bankers and political elites. Opposed to the National Bank, they believed state banks would give ordinary people the breaks they needed to get ahead.

Today liberals still emphasize protecting individual rights. They embrace the image of representing ordinary folks, but their perceptions about the need for government have changed. The turnaround can best be seen during the Great Depression of the 1930s when many people were overcome by the economic crisis without much hope of surviving, much less getting ahead. Led by President Franklin Roosevelt and his "Brain Trust" of advisers, liberals began to believe that government could be a positive force for ordinary people and could ensure equality of opportunity and justice by giving a boost to the disadvantaged. During the 1930s, the New Deal programs gave jobs, loans, and government subsidies to all kinds of people, and, as a result, liberals began to support a larger role for government.

Today the support that liberals give to various issues—such as racial equality, foreign aid to countries in need, decreased military spending, and affirmative action programs—usually, but not always, emphasizes their long-held belief in the protection of individual rights and liberties.

CONSERVATISM

American conservatism has its roots in the political thinking of Alexander Hamilton, John Adams, and many of their contemporaries. Even though they believed in the consent of the governed, they emphasized that the United States was a representative democracy. Most decisions, they believed, should be left up to political leaders. Conservatives had less faith in the political judgments of ordinary citizens than did the liberals, and they tended to be more pessimistic about human nature in general. Originally they supported a stronger central government that had enough clout to bring order to the struggling new country. During the late nineteenth and early twentieth centuries, an era of great industrial development in the United States, conservatives asserted their strong belief in free enterprise and private property rights.

Like those of the liberals, conservatives' attitudes toward the size of government had been changed dramatically by the Great Depression. Conservatives generally opposed New Deal programs of the 1930s. In part, they believed government support to be ultimately damaging to character, making people dependent on government and unable to help themselves. Conservatives believed that big government, Roosevelt-style, was a mistake. Today, many conservatives adhere to these basic values, believing that human needs can and should be taken care of by families and charities, not by government.

PARTIES AND POLITICAL IDEOLOGIES

Recall that American political parties are primarily electoral, not ideological. They are broad umbrella organizations that emphasize winning elections, not being true to a particular set of political ideas. In order to win elections, both Democratic and Republican candidates tend to moderate their positions in their campaigns. Even so, research indicates that most people think of Democrats as being more liberal and Republicans as more conservative. Consider these research results:

IS ONE PARTY MORE CONSERVATIVE? 1970–1992

Year	'70	'72	'74	'76	'78	'80	'82	'84	'86	'88	'90	'92
Yes, Democrats	16%	15%	**	17%	**	**	**	15%	**	12%	18%	12%
Yes, Republicans	51%	57%	**	54%	**	**	**	53%	**	57%	44%	57%
No, Both Same, Don't Know	33%	28%	**	29%	**	**	**	32%	**	31%	38%	31%

** figures unavailable

Source: The National Election Studies, Center for Political Studies, University of Michigan

Forming and Measuring Public Opinion

Earlier discussion in Chapter 7 about what sorts of people participate in politics stressed how complicated the process of forming one's political identity is. Discussions with family and friends, relationships and experiences at home or school or work, images that the media bombard us with, and reports of **public opinion**—all combine to help us define ourselves politically.

INFLUENCES ON POLITICAL ATTITUDES

Each person experiences influences from many different, even contradictory, directions. Conflicting factors are known as crisscrossing influences. For example, a person raised in a liberal, Democratic family in a large eastern city may be exposed to contrasting political opinions from professors when he or she attends a religious liberal arts college in the South or marries a person of a different nationality. Sorting out the weight to give to different factors involved in the opinion-shaping process is almost impossible. Yet some interesting generalizations can be made about six key agents of political socialization.

1. Family

One of the most important determinants of political attitudes is an individual's family. Families are usually the first influence, and most research shows that the majority of young people identify with their parents' political party.

As people grow older, other influences crisscross, but many adults still share the party identification of their parents. The transfer of party identification from one generation to the next has been seriously undermined, however, by the decline in party affiliation in general and the corresponding increase in the percentage of people who identify themselves as independent. Although parents do influence political opinions significantly, their children are not as likely to agree with them on specific issues—such as equal rights for minorities, military spending, or school prayer—as they are to identify with their political party.

def·i·ni·tions

public opinion—the attitudes expressed by citizens of a country about government and politics.

2. Gender

Ever since women first won the right to vote in 1920, significant differences have existed between their political views and those of men. Gender-sensitive issues include war, gun control, pornography, and, earlier in American history, the prohibition of alcohol. Although the so-called gender gap has existed for a long time, the party receiving more female support has changed.

Women tended to support Republicans through the 1950s, but by the late 1960s, they were moving to the Democrats. Today women are more likely to be Democrats than men are. According to survey figures from The National Election Studies, 58 percent of women identified themselves as Democrats.

3. Religion

Religious beliefs and practices can also shape political attitudes, particularly in two categories: economic issues (such as taxes, welfare programs, and national spending) and social issues (such as equal rights, abortion, and school prayers). Many studies have found that Catholic families are somewhat more liberal on economic issues than are Protestants, and that Jewish families are much more liberal on both economic and social issues than are either Catholics or Protestants.

4. Education

Because schools teach young people the values of American political culture, introduce them to the study of government, and provide the opportunity to interact with peers, education is a significant agent of political socialization. For more than 50 years, studies have found evidence that political opinions of college-educated people are more liberal than those without a college educa- tion. Political scientists have noted that college students are more liberal than the general population, and the longer students have been in college, the more liberal they are. Former college students appear to maintain at least some of their liberalism for years after graduation.

5. Race and Ethnicity

Another factor that helps to shape an individual's political opinion is race or ethnicity. As a general rule, for the past half century African Americans have been consistently more liberal than whites on issues having to do with minority civil rights, such as school busing and affirmative action. The differences extend to other areas as well. African Americans are less supportive of the death penalty compared to whites and more supportive of national health care. However, on some issues, such as legalization of marijuana and abortion, there are few differences between African Americans and whites. African

Americans have voted overwhelmingly for the Democratic party and are widely perceived as the party's most loyal supporters. In a 1996 survey by The National Election Studies, 78 percent of African Americans (compared to 48 percent of whites) identified themselves as Democrats.

Fewer statistics are available for Latinos, but research does show that Mexicans and Puerto Ricans tend to vote Democratic as well, but not as strongly as African Americans. Among Asian Americans, the limited research available shows wide variations as well. Some studies have found Korean Americans to be the most liberal and Japanese Americans the most conservative of the Asian groups. Overall, Asian Americans appear to vote much more conservatively than African Americans and Latinos, and perhaps even more conservatively than whites.

Comparative voting in the 1992 and 1996 presidential elections provides evidence for the influence of race and ethnicity on political attitudes.

1992 AND 1996 PRESIDENTIAL ELECTION RESULTS

	1992			1996		
	CLINTON (D)	BUSH (R)	PEROT (IND.)	CLINTON (D)	DOLE (R)	PEROT (REFORM)
Total Vote	43%	38%	19%	49%	41%	8%
Whites	39%	40%	20%	43%	46%	9%
African Americans	83%	10%	7%	84%	12%	4%
Latinos	61%	25%	14%	72%	21%	6%
Asians	31%	55%	15%	43%	48%	8%

Source: Voter News Service exit polling, 1992 and 1996

6. Region

Although not usually as significant a factor as family, education, or race, one's place of residence can influence political attitudes. Northeasterners have long held the reputation of having more liberal political views than their southern and western counterparts, but this generalization masks some important variations. It is true that many western states are likely to support Republicans for public office, and southern members of Congress vote more conservatively than northern ones. At one time white southerners were much less liberal than citizens from other parts of the country on social issues, such as federal aid to minorities, legalizing marijuana, school busing, and police conduct. Their views on economic issues, however, were similar to those of residents from other regions.

Today, political opinions of Southerners are less distinct than before. One important trend among them is the gradual but clear erosion of their traditional support for the Democratic party, a tendency that earned the region the nickname Solid South from Reconstruction (1865–1877) until the 1950s. The Solid South held through the depression and New Deal legislation, but began to break up in the late 1950s when the Democratic party began to back civil rights legislation more vigorously. With the civil rights movements of the 1950s and '60s, conservative Democrats in the South began to affiliate with the Republicans. A number of southern Republican governors and members of Congress have been elected in recent years.

MEASURING PUBLIC OPINION

Through the years, politicians and government officials have used a variety of methods to determine what the American public is thinking. They read newspapers and magazines, meet with voters personally, consider letters and telephone calls they receive, and listen to the radio or watch television.

Informal Polling

Informal, unscientific polls—conducted by collecting information by phone, word of mouth, or mail—to measure public opinion have long been a part of the political scene. These **straw polls** are not reliable, however, even if a large number of responses are gathered. The problem lies with the quality, not the quantity, of the **sample.** In a straw poll, there is no guarantee that those who happen to respond accurately represent a cross section of the total population.

Scientific Polling

Political parties, interest groups, individual candidates, the media, and polling organizations now employ numerous experts to help make political decisions and more accurately determine public opinion.

Much of the scientific polling conducted today attempts to measure not only how many people hold a certain opinion, but how intensely people feel and how stable the opinion is, or how long it is likely to last. Scientific polling is conducted according to several basic rules. Proper sampling is based on random choice among members of a population, or the group whose attitudes

def·i·ni·tions

straw poll—an unofficial vote or poll indicating the trend of opinion about a candidate or issue.

sample—in polling, a small number of people drawn from and analyzed as representative of the total population to be surveyed.

114

the researchers are measuring. In a random sample, every individual has an equal chance of being selected. For example, a sample of 14 to 19-year-olds should not be taken solely from private schools, since most high school students do not attend private schools. The accuracy of poll results depends on questioning a representative sample, one that represents a microcosm of the entire population. If only 6 percent of the total high school population attends private schools, then only 6 percent of the sample should consist of private school students. To measure nationwide attitudes toward a particular issue, a sample should include students of different backgrounds and races who attend a variety of schools in different regions of the country.

e.g.

POLL QUESTIONS

How pollsters word a question can dramatically affect the answers they get. A 1993 article in the *New York Times* contrasted the results of a question devised by 1992 presidential candidate Ross Perot's organization with two similar ones constructed by professional polling firms using random samples. Perot's survey was criticized for wording the questions so as to shape the answers that were given.

PEROT'S QUESTION

Should laws be passed to eliminate all possibilities of special interests giving huge sums of money to candidates?

Yes	99%

QUESTIONS OF POLLING FIRMS

Should laws be passed to prohibit interest groups from contributing to campaigns, or do groups have a right to contribute to the candidate they support?

Prohibit contribution	40%
Groups have right	55%

Please tell me whether you favor or oppose the proposal: The passage of new laws that would eliminate all possibility of special interests giving large sums of money to candidates.

Favor	70%
Oppose	28%

Fair and clear questions are harder to construct than you might imagine. The wording of questions is extremely important to the reliability of the poll's findings. Good questions are unbiased and have been pretested. In an oral survey, it's important that those conducting the poll read the questions exactly as written, without inflections in their voices that suggest one response is preferable to another.

Thorough analysis and reporting of the results is also necessary if the poll is to have value. Reliable scientific polls should indicate a sufficient sample size, the margin of error for a standard question, and, because public opinion can change very quickly, when the poll was conducted. No poll can claim 100 percent accuracy. However, good scientific polls may come very close, indicating their margin of error, or the range in which the opinions of the population will fall. Experts have concluded that a properly drawn random sample of about 1,500 is able to reflect the nation's adult population to within a margin of plus or minus (+/-) 3 percent 95 percent of the time. For example, a 3 percent margin of error for a finding of 45 percent would reflect a range of 42 to 48 percent.

Politics and Mass Media

Because most of us watch television or listen to the radio, read newspapers or magazines, or spend time surfing the Internet, we are influenced to some degree by the **mass media.** Statistics abound regarding the use and influence of the media. One estimate is that by the time a person graduates from high school today, he or she has spent 15,000 hours watching television and only 11,000 hours in the classroom. So what? Although much that is written or programmed in mass media is primarily for entertainment, any medium that provides political information and reaches millions of people has tremendous power to shape political opinions and influence government decisions.

THE DEVELOPMENT AND TYPES OF MASS MEDIA

Today we may identify three kinds of media: the print media, which consist of newspapers and magazines; the broadcast media, which include television and radio; and the Internet. In the past 50 years, the broadcast media have gradually replaced the print media as the main source of political information for most Americans. Today, the Internet is the most rapidly growing type of mass media.

def·i·ni·tions

mass media—those sources of information and means of communication—such as radio, television, magazines, and the Internet—that reach large numbers of the public.

116

Quote

"... were it left to me to decide whether we should have a government with-out newspapers, or newspapers without a government, I should not hesitate a moment to prefer the latter."

Thomas Jefferson, 1787

1. Newspapers

The early newspapers in the United States were actually sponsored by political parties and blatantly supported a partisan point of view. For example, the Federalists, led by Alexander Hamilton, created the *Gazette of the United States* as an instrument for their point of view. Not to be outdone, Jefferson's Democratic-Republicans published the *National Intelligencer.* The first American daily newspaper, the *Pennsylvania Evening Post and Daily Advertiser*, was printed in Philadelphia in 1783.

Today, many of the 1,700 local newspapers published daily are part of massive media conglomerates—such as Gannett, Knight-Ridder, and Newhouse—which control most of the nation's daily circulation. Despite vigorous competition from the broadcast media, many Americans still read newspapers. Daily newspaper circulation has held fairly steady at about 60 million nationwide for the past 20 years.

2. Magazines

Magazines are the other major component of the print media, but those with the largest circulations—such as the *Reader's Digest, TV Guide*, and *Family Circle*—have little political content. Despite their limited circulation, news and political opinion magazines (such as *Time, Newsweek, Nation, The Weekly Standard,* or the *New Republic*) have had considerable influence on American government and politics. The first magazines to discuss issues of public policy—among them *Harper's Weekly* and the *Atlantic Monthly*—appeared in the mid-nineteenth century, and though their circulations were and are still relatively small, their influence among political activists is indisputable.

3. Radio

Invented in 1903, radio first broadcast election returns in 1920, and its popularity quickly grew. President Franklin Roosevelt took advantage of the new medium to communicate with the public in his famous fireside chats. Roosevelt understood that people needed a presidential father figure to comfort them during the stark depression years, and he talked to them reassuringly about the issues of the day.

Today almost everyone in the United States has access to a radio either at home, at work, in a car, or in a backpack. Although a great deal of radio broadcasting is strictly entertainment, in recent years talk shows that feature political issues have become very popular. Their hosts usually promote a definite point of view, and they feature call-ins—a straw poll of sorts—by ordinary citizens. The shows are sometimes criticized for screening callers in order to enhance their point of view, although few of the shows claim to be objective.

4. Television

Television's influence on the American public is enormous. Almost all Americans see television every day, and many homes have at least two sets, which are frequently turned on. Television technology is almost as old as radio, but televisions did not appear in the average American's living room until the early 1950s. While television is primarily a medium for entertainment, most Americans use it for news as well. By 1963, two major networks had doubled the length of their evening news broadcast from 15 to 30 minutes. By the mid-1960s, television had replaced newspapers as the American public's main source of political information. With the advent of cable television—for example, broadcasters such as Cable News Network (CNN) or MSNBC—viewers can watch news programs 24 hours a day. C-SPAN, the Cable-Satellite Public Affairs Network, presents both live and taped coverage of congressional floor debates, committee hearings, speeches, and press conferences. Americans not only get information from television, but they also get commentaries and analysis of the news.

"I'LL BELIEVE I'M A PRISONER WHEN I SEE IT ON TELEVISION."

5. The Internet

The newest type of mass media to become a source of political information and debate is the Internet, begun in the early 1970s primarily as a communications device for the military, government agencies, and scholars at major universities. The technology has developed rapidly, and by the late 1990s, the number of users as well as the amount of information available was growing dramatically. Total worldwide use in 1997 was estimated at between 50 to 60 million people. Many projected that the influence of the Internet would soon outpace that of any other medium, including television or newspapers. Thousands of Web sites—some sponsored by parties and candidates, government offices, and newspapers and magazines—provide a wealth of political information through which a person may search. (See Almanac page 461 for list of Web sites.) Interactive chat rooms allow people to communicate with others on many topics, including government and politics.

Critics of the Internet attack the lack of accurate information on the Web, claiming that print and broadcast media have professional guidelines and take more responsibility for the news that they give out. In contrast, people can create a Web site with almost any information they want, regardless of its accuracy. The Internet is also criticized for its loose organization and technical difficulties that make it difficult for many people to use.

GOVERNMENT REGULATION OF MEDIA

Government officials often depend on the media for news, but they give the media considerable freedom. However, the government does set some regulations.

Protection of Print Media

The print media receive a great deal of protection from the 1st Amendment to the Constitution: "Congress shall make no law . . . abridging the freedom . . . of the press." Since this guarantee is fundamental to democracy, many different types of protection are covered by these important words.

★ The power of the government to prevent publication of information it considers objectionable is called **prior restraint.** Today the Supreme Court has barred government from such practices except in extreme cases of national security and then mainly in time of war.

def·i·ni·tions

prior restraint—the governmental censorship of information before it is published or broadcast.

★ Journalists' rights not to reveal the sources of their information are protected by **shield laws.** Courts, police, and legislatures have at times tried to force the media to turn over the names of their sources under penalty of jail. In 1972, the Supreme Court ruled that the press does not have the right to conceal its sources. However, the Court also said that both Congress and individual state legislatures can enact shield laws. More than half of the states have now passed them.

★ Freedom of the press does not mean the freedom to print false statements. **Libel** is the publication of false statements that are damaging to a person's reputation. Public figures must be able to prove in court that untrue statements were knowingly published in order to intentionally harm their characters or reputations.

★ Right of access to courtrooms and other government outlets is a freedom the media have fought for over the years. The press has often argued that the 1st Amendment guarantees to the people the right to know and that the press is responsible for providing the information. The Supreme Court, to some degree, has limited the press in this area. As part of the *Branzburg v. Hayes* (1972) ruling, the Court stated that "the First Amendment does not guarantee the press a constitutional right of special access to information not available to the public generally."

Freedom in Broadcast Media

The broadcast media are more closely regulated by the government than the print media. One of the main reasons is that the airwaves through which radio and television stations send their signals are considered a public resource.

★ The government exercises its control over the broadcast media through the Federal Communications Commission (FCC). The FCC is responsible for licensing radio and television stations, as well as setting long-distance telephone rates and licensing cable television. Stations must comply with regulations that require them to devote a certain percentage of their broadcast time to such things as public service information, news, and political candidates in order to retain their license. In awarding the licenses, the FCC limits media ownership of multiple television and radio stations in the same area. These limits to ownership are designed to guarantee that the public hears different points of view.

def·i·ni·tions

shield law—a law that protects journalists from being compelled to reveal confidential sources of information against their will.

libel—written statements that defame a person's character, damage his or her reputation, or expose him or her to public ridicule.

120

★ One of the most important regulations imposed by the FCC on the broadcast media regards the allocation of time to political candidates. The **equal time doctrine,** in existence since 1934, requires that stations that either give or sell broadcast time to a political candidate must give or sell equal time to opponents of that candidate. Opposing candidates do not have to use that time, but it must be made available to them. In 1983, the FCC relaxed this rule regarding political debates at all levels, maintaining that stations could choose which candidates to invite to a debate. Notice that the FCC rules imply a two-party system and that third parties are often not included in the application of the fairness doctrine. Recent independent or minor party candidates, such as John Anderson in 1980 and Ross Perot in 1992 and 1996, have protested their exclusion and have managed to get more press attention as a result.

THE POLITICAL INFLUENCE OF THE MEDIA

By its very nature, a representative democratic government is meant to link policy making to the people it governs. Political parties and interest groups have long served as links between institutions. As the various mass media have developed, they have gradually become more important as links between institutions. Today most Americans count on mass media to connect them to government and politics on both local and national levels. Media influence is most prominent in two areas: its effect on campaigns and elections and on setting the public agenda.

1. Influencing Campaigns and Elections

As a vital link between the people and their government, the media hold a special power that operates in two ways: to influence the political opinions of the people and to shape the behavior of candidates and officials themselves. Both are illustrated by the media's growing influence in campaigns and elections and the corresponding loss of control by political parties. As increasing numbers of candidates are chosen by popular election in primaries, people receive most of their information and impressions of candidates through the media coverage.

The influence of media on popular political opinions is somewhat difficult to measure, but the changes in the behavior of the candidates and the nature of campaigns are clear. Candidates realize that their messages about policy are often ignored or given little attention by the media. The image they project is increasingly important. Candidates hire media professionals to help them

---

equal time doctrine—the Federal Communications Commission requirement that equal radio or television airtime must be made available to opposing candidates running for public office.

conduct polls, devise advertising, and get favorable media coverage. Campaigns center around carefully staged media events and photo opportunities. As a result, some worry that style is triumphing over substance, that a candidate's looks, gestures, and personality are becoming more important than his or her experiences, qualifications, or ideas. Of particular concern are the negative commercials that smear the opponent and almost certainly contribute to cynical attitudes toward government.

2. Setting the Public Agenda

The media serve as both observers and participants in the work of the government. As observers, they report about, reflect on, and react to what is going on in government and what leaders are doing. In so doing, the media themselves begin to shape public opinion; political leaders are influenced by media coverage and commentary.

Despite government regulations on the media, the media have an important power over government—agenda setting. As reporters choose to focus on certain stories, they help to set the government's priorities. Mass media not only reflect—but also create—public opinion. No matter what a President or congressional representatives really want to do, they often have to spend their time addressing topics the media call to their attention. As a result, the issues and events that garner the most media attention are likely the ones that people think are the most important. For example, amidst the scandals surrounding Bill Clinton's personal behavior, no matter how much he might want to focus on education or health care, the people's attention was drawn to the topic of possible misconduct.

Is agenda setting by the media a good or bad thing? Like so many other questions, the answer depends on your perceptions of the balance between liberty and order, government by the people or by representatives. The Founders intended that power should be spread among many different

Quotes

Media influence is a "beam of a search light that moves restlessly about, bringing one episode and then another out of the darkness and into vision."

Walter Lippmann, Public Opinion, *1922*

"The lowest form of popular culture—lack of information, misinformation, disinformation, and a contempt for the truth or reality of most people's lives—has overrun real journalism. Today, ordinary Americans are being stuffed with garbage."

Carl Bernstein, Guardian, *1992*

groups. They wanted the President's behavior to be "checked" and the power of Congress to be "balanced" by that of other branches. Perhaps it is appropriate for the media to provide that check and balance. On the other hand, do radio and television, newspapers and magazines, and the Internet have too much power? Critics complain that they should not be allowed to set agendas, especially since they are driven by their own desire for profits and their perceptions of what the American people want.

★ ★ ★

The relationship among American public opinion, mass media, and government and politics in the United States is complex. Many factors—family, education, gender, religion, racial and ethnic background, and even the media itself—shape public opinion, or more precisely the opinion of multiple publics. In recent decades, the mass media have developed an increasing importance as a link between the government and citizens, placing themselves at the heart of the democratic process. As a powerful link to the people, the media have in turn gained a great deal of influence over the opinions of American citizens and the behavior of government leaders. One of the most important issues of our time is the appropriateness of that influence of the media.

9 | Interest Groups

A
s we have seen, many ordinary citizens in a democracy take part in government and politics. Sometimes they participate directly, but more often their involvement occurs through such institutions as political parties, mass media, or interest groups. It's estimated that two-thirds of all adult Americans belong to at least one interest group. Interest groups organize around similar goals with the primary purpose of affecting public policy. Their activities often spark controversy. The United States has thousands of interest groups, and they almost always are criticized for having too much sway over government decisions. We must look closely at not only how much influence American interest groups have in the political process but also assess how positive or negative that influence in fact is.

In this chapter . . .

Formation of Interest Groups

The main purpose of most **interest groups** is to influence policy and gain political advantages for their members and their causes. The reasons people join interest groups and the amounts of time and money they commit vary widely. For some members of interest groups, the appeal is the contact with like-minded individuals. Other people are motivated by economic benefits, and still others by the opportunity to become active politically while advancing an issue they care about.

EARLY DEVELOPMENT

From the founding of our country to the present, people have argued about the influence of interest groups. For example, James Madison, the "Father of the Constitution," worried about their "mischief" in *The Federalist* No. 10 (1787). He warned that they, like political parties, would promote "instability, injustice, and confusion."

Believing that people are self-interested by nature, Madison saw interest groups and parties as power-hungry forces that must be checked before they took over government. He argued that their freedoms should be guaranteed but that their influence must be checked by the government structure provided for in the Constitution. While the power of political parties has weakened, both the number of interest groups and their political influence have grown.

def·i·ni·tions

interest group—a private organization of like-minded people whose goal is to influence and shape public policy.

Vs.

POLITICAL PARTIES vs. INTEREST GROUPS

James Madison did not distinguish between interest groups and political parties when he referred to both as "factions," but today they differ in several significant ways.

PARTIES

1. Political parties nominate candidates to run for elective office.

2. Political parties focus on a broad range of issues to appeal to a wide range of the electorate.

3. Political parties compete for control of the legislative branch by trying to win the majority of the seats in Congress.

INTEREST GROUPS

1. Interest groups may support certain candidates for office, but they do not nominate their own candidates.

2. Interest groups take a narrow focus on a specific issue, such as gun control, or a specific theme, such as the environment.

3. Interest groups compete for influence over elected officials so that they decide public policy issues in the interest group's favor.

At every stage of American history, interest groups reflecting the issues of the day have emerged. For example, a number of antislavery groups formed in the 1830s and 1840s as slavery became a major source of conflict in Congress. During the 1860s, trade unions began to represent the growing numbers of urban workers as the country industrialized, and dozens of business associations formed as the Industrial Revolution spread. The expansion of government programs in the 1930s led to the formation of even more interest groups. More recently, such issues as women's rights, environmental protection, and health care have led to an explosion of new interest groups.

126

CHARACTERISTICS OF INTEREST GROUPS

Groups vary widely in their membership, goals, methods, and effectiveness. It's useful, however, to compare them in terms of three key characteristics.

1. Size

Clearly the size of an interest group is important to its political power. An organization representing 5 million voters frequently has more influence than one speaking for 50,000 people. However, it does not follow that bigger groups are necessarily more powerful. Large groups may suffer from a free-rider problem, in which some members may do little or nothing to contribute to the group's efforts. The larger the group, the less motivated individual members may feel to work toward the group's goals. A big interest group faces the challenge of keeping an inactive and largely out-of-touch membership focused and involved.

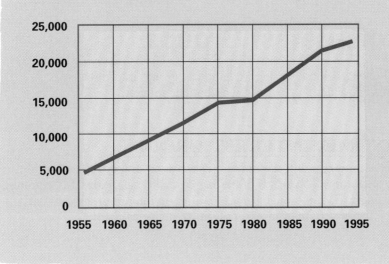

Headlines

THE GROWTH OF INTEREST GROUPS

One source that political scientists use to determine the number of interest groups is the *Encyclopedia of Associations*, a book that annually lists many of the associations operating in the United States. Note how quickly the number of groups has grown since 1956.

NUMBER OF ORGANIZATIONS

Sources: *Encyclopedia of Associations* and American Society of Association Executives

2. Resources

Groups also differ in the amount of money they have available to carry on their media campaigns, send out mass mailings, and attempt to influence government leaders. Most interest groups get some funding from membership fees, but they almost always need to find money from other sources as well. Some groups spend considerable effort writing proposals for grants from private foundations, such as the Ford Foundation or the Rockefeller Family Fund. Others benefit from federal grants, though many believe that the federal government should not support interest groups since they represent points of view or controversial causes with which many tax-paying citizens may not agree. One of the most important fund-raising techniques today is to go after prospective members by direct mail. By using computer lists, interest groups can target specially chosen people who are most likely to support their cause.

3. Intensity

Another characteristic important to some interest groups is intensity of feeling. By focusing on one issue about which people feel deeply, groups are able to rally members. Intensity is a psychological advantage that often makes politicians listen and support a cause. Through their strong emotions, single-issue groups can sway others to their point of view. For example, Mothers Against Drunk Driving (MADD) was started up by a woman whose child was killed in a drinking-related automobile accident. She mobilized others with similar experiences, and new members were attracted by the strong emotional appeal of the issue.

Types of Interest Groups

Political scientists loosely categorize interest groups into three types: economic, social action or equality, and public interest.

1. ECONOMIC INTEREST GROUPS

Much government policy has either a direct or an indirect effect on the country's economy. Thousands of businesses, trade associations, labor unions, and farming and professional groups have set up interest groups to try to influence the government to pass policies favorable to them.

A. Business Groups and Trade Associations

When people criticize interest groups for having too much political power in Washington, business groups and **trade associations** are often the targets of their concern. Part of their reputation for power rests on the fact that they represent about half of the total number of interest groups in Washington. Their general goal is to create a good economic climate in which the organizations they represent can prosper. Most large corporations, such as AT&T and Ford, now have organizations in Washington that monitor legislative activity. Two huge business organizations are the National Association of Manufacturers (NAM), which represents more than 12,000 manufacturers, and the Chamber of Commerce, which represents more than 180,000 businesses.

B. Labor Groups

Labor groups have more affiliated members than any other type of interest group. More than 13 million people belong to the powerful American Federation of Labor and the Congress of Industrial Organizations (AFL-CIO), itself a union of **labor unions.** Although the percentage of workers who belong to unions is considerably lower than it was at its peak (about 25 percent of all workers in 1970), labor organizations still have a great deal of political clout.

C. Agricultural Groups

Farmers make up only about 2 percent of the nation's population, but more than 150 interest groups represent various aspects of farming. Three of the best known agricultural interest groups are the American Farm Bureau Federation (AFBF), which has a membership of more than 4 million, and the National Grange (NG), whose members number about 300,000, and the National Farmers Union, which is particularly active in western states. Organizations such as the AFBF represent nearly every type of farming. Other organizations—such as the National Peanut Council, the American Mushroom Institute, and the National Potato Council—represent specific producers.

D. Professional Groups

People who work in professions requiring long and specialized training—such as medicine, law, and education—also have organized interest groups to advocate for them. Three professional organizations are among the strongest interest groups in the country: the American Medical Association (AMA), which has a membership of nearly 300,000 physicians; the American Bar Association (ABA), with about 375,000 attorneys; and the National Education Association (NEA), with about 2 million educators.

---

trade association—an interest group representing a specific part of the business community.

labor union—an organization of workers whose purpose is to serve the members' interests.

2. SOCIAL ACTION AND EQUALITY GROUPS

Instead of focusing on economic outcomes, other interest groups organize to bring about some kind of social change. Many of these focus on equality issues that promote civil liberties and civil rights. For example, the American Association of Retired Persons (AARP) looks out for the rights of elderly and retired people. The National Organization for Women (NOW) focuses on women's concerns and has lobbied for an end to sexual discrimination. The National Association for the Advancement of Colored People (NAACP), founded in 1909, has played an important role in the fight to ensure the civil rights of minorities. Numerous religious organizations, such as the Christian Coalition, have also advocated and influenced social action.

3. PUBLIC-INTEREST GROUPS

Public-interest groups rose from the political unrest of the 1960s. They profess to be different from other interest groups because they do not represent their own selfish interests but rather work for the best interests of the public. Perhaps the best known public-interest groups are those founded in the 1960s and 1970s by Ralph Nader. He first became a consumer advocate for automobile safety, later helping to create Public Interest Research Groups (PIRGs), which are concerned with organizing college student activists to work on local public-interest projects. An older public-interest group is the League of Women Voters, formed shortly after women got the right to vote in 1920. Their members' primary purpose is to educate both men and women about the candidates and issues in local, state, and national races and to promote citizen participation in elections. Causes of all kinds—from literacy to conservation to animal rights—have formed special interest groups to influence policies and lawmaking in Washington.

How Interest Groups Work

No matter how rich or powerful, no interest group has enough resources to achieve its policy goals on its own. Each group must choose carefully the best strategies for its own success. Generally speaking, the strategies of interest groups can be divided into four types: lobbying, electioneering, litigation, and influencing public opinion.

---

public-interest group—a group that works for the common good, not for the benefit of specific individuals or interests.

1. LOBBYING

The term **lobbying** is rooted in the early nineteenth century before members of Congress had private offices. During this time, people who wanted to speak with them would wait in the lobbies of Congress, state capitols, or hotels and boarding houses where legislators stayed during legislative sessions. While they waited, these individuals would descend on unsuspecting officials to get their attention on issues or policies. By the 1830s the term *lobbying* was coined to describe this practice. Today's lobbyists use more varied techniques. In direct lobbying, representatives of interest groups hold face-to-face meetings with public officials in an effort to convince them to support a certain position. Other times the groups try indirect lobbying, which includes arranging for a third party (businessperson or citizen) to meet with an official, writing letters or calling to pressure officials, publishing newsletters or voting records, and making campaign contributions to gain access to a politician.

Interest groups with large resources usually hire professional full-time lobbyists who are given titles such as "Director of Legislative Relations." They spend all of their time lobbying for that particular interest group. Other lobbyists work independently of a particular group. Instead, they contract with several interest groups with smaller budgets who will buy shares of their time. Thus, an independent lobbyist may spend 40 percent of his or her professional time lobbying for an agricultural interest, another 30 percent lobbying for a small chemical company, and another 30 percent lobbying for a group of radio stations.

e.g.

WHO ARE THE LOBBYISTS?

Whom do interest groups hire to represent them in government? There is no better lobbyist than someone who has actually served in a strategic government position. For example, if your group's main objective is to preserve the rights of landowners in western states, why not hire an important former official from the Department of the Interior? Such a person knows the people and the processes that directly affect your goals. This controversial practice is sometimes known as the "revolving door," and it is criticized for giving private interests an unfair inside track to influence government decisions.

def·i·ni·tions

lobbying—an organized process in which an individual or group tries to influence legislation or policy.

2. ELECTIONEERING

Because lobbying is generally more successful if elected officials already agree with the lobbyist, getting the right people into office or keeping them there is an important strategy of interest groups. **Electioneering** refers to the involvement of interest groups in political campaigns—to help elect those candidates who favor their positions or to help defeat those candidates who oppose their positions.

Interest groups closely monitor the voting records of elected officials to determine which ones agree with their views. They also send candidates running against incumbents lengthy questionnaires to try to determine their positions. This information is then analyzed along with other important factors—such as party affiliation—and a decision regarding endorsements is made. Electioneering is generally conducted by special political arms of interest groups called political action committees (PACs). (See page 88.)

PACs were created by interest groups to handle electioneering. Campaign finance reform laws passed in the early 1970s sharply restricted the amount of money that an interest group could give to a candidate for federal office, but the same laws made it legal for corporations and labor unions to form PACs. As a result, the number of PACs rose dramatically. Almost any kind of organization can form a PAC. More than half of all PACs are sponsored by corporations, about 10 percent by labor unions, and the rest by various other groups. About one-third of all money spent for elections to the House of Representatives comes from PACs. In 1995–1996, according to Federal Election Commission statistics, five congressional candidates each received more than $1 million in PAC contributions.

The Federal Election Commission oversees and regulates PACs and their contributions to candidates and campaigns. They must register with the government six months before an election and adhere to strict accounting and reporting procedures. No PAC may contribute more than $5,000 to a single candidate per primary or general election. However, there are no restrictions on the number of separate PACs an interest group can form, and individuals may contribute up to $5,000 to as many PACs as they wish. Such loopholes allow big interest groups and wealthy individuals to contribute large amounts to political campaigns.

PAC money is controversial for many reasons. Some critics see it as

def·i·ni·tions

electioneering—the process of actively and publicly supporting a candidate or political party.

little more than legalized bribery, in which money is used to buy access to members of Congress. Others point out that more PAC money goes to incumbents than to challengers, therefore discouraging real competitive elections. On the other hand, supporters claim that the dollar limitations on PAC contributions have encouraged many small donations from different sources, thus lessening the influence of "big money." Many members of Congress get money from PACs on both sides of an issue (for example, for and against gun control), and donations do not clearly favor one political party over the other.

Then and Now

THE NATIONAL RIFLE ASSOCIATION: FALTERING GIANT?

The National Rifle Association is one of the most controversial interest groups in the United States, drawing strong, emotional reactions from both its supporters and its critics. The NRA was founded in 1871 to provide shooting instruction, but by the 1960s it became widely known as a group dedicated to defending citizens' rights to own and use firearms for sporting and other legal purposes. During the 1980s, particularly after the attempted assassination of President Ronald Reagan, pro–gun control lobbies such as Handgun Control, Inc., and the Fraternal Order of Police gained many supporters. By the late 1990s, many observers believed that the NRA had lost much of its political support, even as it selected celebrity actor and longtime member Charlton Heston as its president.

Judging from the numbers alone, it's easy to see how the NRA won a reputation as a powerful interest group. Between January 1991 and mid-1998, it pumped $16.3 million into federal campaigns—more than the six largest defense contractors combined. In the 1992, 1994, and 1996 campaigns, the organization backed 714 general election winners in House and Senate contests; 315 of its candidates lost. The group has had its failures too, such as its large contributions to President George Bush's unsuccessful re-election campaign in 1992.

3. LITIGATION

If a group fails in Congress or with governmental agencies, it may turn to the courts to gain support for its causes. Much environmental legislation, such as the Clean Air Act, allows ordinary citizens to sue for enforcement. As a result, many federal agencies involved in environmental regulation now have hundreds of suits pending against them at any given time. Even if the suits are not successful, the constant threat of a lawsuit increases the likelihood that businesses will consider the environmental consequences of their actions. Perhaps the most famous interest group victories in court were by civil rights groups such as the NAACP in the 1950s. Getting no response from Congress, the civil rights groups turned to the courts to win major victories concerning school desegregation, equal housing, and employment opportunities.

One tactic that interest group lawyers employ is the filing of ***amicus curiae*** briefs, or written arguments submitted to the courts in support of one side of a case. In highly publicized and emotionally charged cases, numerous groups may file such briefs. Another tactic is the filing of **class–action lawsuits.** They allow a group of plaintiffs in similar situations to combine grievances into a single suit. The *Brown v. Board of Education of Topeka* (1954) case, for example, was a class–action lawsuit that established the principle that segregation in public places is unconstitutional.

4. SHAPING PUBLIC OPINION

Interest groups know that public opinion is a driving force in public policy decisions. Besides the practices of lobbying, electioneering, and litigation, interest groups invest their resources in trying to shape public opinion through three main techniques.

★ First, groups buy broadcast time on radio and television or ads in newspapers and magazines to promote their point of view. For example, in 1994, the Health Insurance Association of America ran a multimillion–dollar nationally televised advertising campaign criticizing President Clinton's health care reform plan. Their goal was accomplished; the reform did not pass Congress.

---

amicus curiae—literally, "a friend of the court"; legal arguments or advice in a case offered voluntarily.

class–action lawsuit—a lawsuit brought by a person or group both on their behalf and on behalf of many others in similar circumstances.

★ Second, interest groups often attempt to influence public opinion by publishing results of research studies that they sponsor. For example, environmental groups have published many studies that show how industrial pollution helps cause the greenhouse effect, or the gradual warming of the earth.

★ Finally, interest groups often work closely with media to stage events to draw public attention. Animal rights and environmental activists, such as Greenpeace, for example, regularly alert the media about their efforts to disrupt the whaling industry.

★ ★ ★

In recent years, as the number and power of interest groups have increased, public opinion about them has become increasingly negative. Many observers of American political culture focus not on their potentially useful functions—creating interest in public policy, promoting shared interests, serving as watchdogs for their causes, and providing valuable information to elected officials and the general public—but on the problems they can create. Critics argue that their money allows them to put undue pressure on policy makers and that their tactics need to be more closely regulated. Like it or not, interest groups play a role in almost every political decision made in the United States.

Unit III

Institutions of National Government

10 | Congress and the Legislative Branch

Suppose you were to ask a sampling of Americans the question, "Which one organization, person, or group holds the most policy-making power in our government?" Some people would name the President. But almost certainly, many people would just as readily name Congress as a major center of political power in the United States. These modern perceptions reflect the intent of the Founders, who wanted congressional powers checked by the other branches but nevertheless saw Congress as the cornerstone of the government.

Over the years the executive and judicial branches have gained powers that the Founders did not anticipate, and sometimes their efforts have overshadowed those of the legislature. However, Congress still remains central in setting the government's agenda for shaping policies that address important issues in American society.

In this chapter . . .

Structure and Powers of Congress

The legislative, or lawmaking, branch of government is the first to be described in the Constitution. The Founders intended Congress—with its bicameral structure and many powers—to lead the judicial and executive branches.

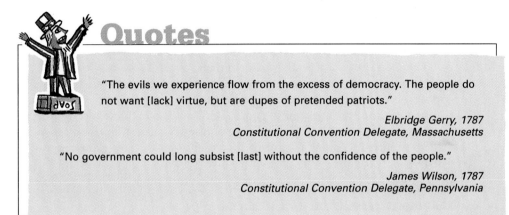

Quotes

"The evils we experience flow from the excess of democracy. The people do not want [lack] virtue, but are dupes of pretended patriots."

Elbridge Gerry, 1787
Constitutional Convention Delegate, Massachusetts

"No government could long subsist [last] without the confidence of the people."

James Wilson, 1787
Constitutional Convention Delegate, Pennsylvania

STRUCTURE OF CONGRESS

The two quotations above reflect the Founders' mixed feelings about popular government. They understood that the people should be represented, but they also believed that the legislature should provide order and stability. This balance between democracy and order resulted in the creation of a two-house legislature—the single most important characteristic of the United States Congress. In this structure, America imitated its parent. Britain's Parliament has two houses: the House of Lords (for the nobles) and the House of Commons (for everyone else). The United States had no lords and adapted the two houses—the House of Representatives and the Senate—to meet its needs.

The House of Representatives

The Constitution based the membership of the House of Representatives on population. The idea was that every voter in the country should be equally represented, so states with big populations had more representatives than states with small populations. For example, Virginia had ten representatives, and Massachusetts and Pennsylvania had eight. But little Rhode Island and Delaware had only one each. The original House of Representatives had 65 representatives, but it increased as the country's population grew. Finally, in the Reapportionment Act of 1929 the size was capped at 435, with every state being allowed at least one representative. (The District of Columbia, Puerto Rico, Guam, American Samoa, and the Virgin Islands each send one elected nonvoting delegate to the House.) With the population of the United States estimated at more than 271 million in 1999, each of the 435 members of the House represents an average of more than 624,000 people.

The Constitution provided that a **census,** an official survey of the population, be taken every ten years to count the people and that the **apportionment** of representatives be adjusted accordingly. As a result of this **reapportionment,** states whose populations increased rapidly received larger numbers of representatives. That practice continues today. After each census in the late twentieth century, California, Texas, and Florida have gained representatives at the expense of states with slower growth, such as New York and New Jersey.

REAPPORTIONMENT OF HOUSE SEATS

This map shows the changes in state representation as a result of the reapportionment of the House after the census of 1990.

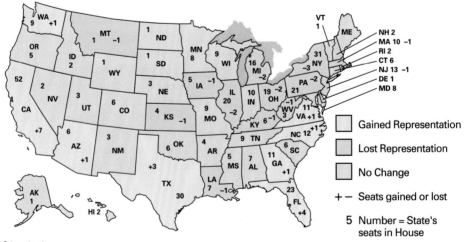

def·i·ni·tions

apportionment—the distribution of the number of members of the House of Representatives based on the population of each state.

reapportionment—the periodic redistribution of U.S. congressional seats according to changes in the census figures.

census—an official population count.

The Senate

The Constitution stated that members of the Senate would be chosen in a totally different way from those of the House. The states were to be equally represented with two senators each. Why? One very important reason is sovereignty, or the fierce sense that each state stands on its own. Within the federalist system, each state should be recognized as an equal to all other states regardless of population or geographic size. As states were added to the Union, the Senate grew until today 100 senators represent the 50 states.

Another major difference the Constitution made between senators and representatives was the way they were to be selected. While representatives were to be elected directly by the people, the senators were to be selected by their state legislatures. In 1913, the 17th Amendment changed the selection of senators, so that today all voters of a state elect their senators **at-large.** But for the first 133 years under the Constitution, senators were not directly elected by the people.

Qualifications and Terms

The Constitution also sets different qualifications and terms for the House and the Senate.

CONSTITUTIONAL PROVISIONS FOR LEGISLATORS

	HOUSE OF REPRESENTATIVES	SENATE
Age	25	30
Years of Citizenship	7	9
Length of Term	2 Years	6 Years
Number of Terms	No Limit	No Limit

Even though the Constitution did not say so, it is clear that the Founders intended the House of Representatives to be the lower house and the Senate the upper house. The House was directly elected, and the Senate was not. The terms of senators are three times longer than those of the representatives. Senators must be older and must be citizens longer before they can be elected. Representatives are intended to be closer to the people.

def·i·ni·tions

at-large—an election process in which the voters of a city, state, or country as a whole elect their government representatives.

As a result, the representatives were a less predictable but vital component of that new type of government—a democracy. The senators, although not lords, were thought of as elite. Their selection by the state legislatures meant they were not as vulnerable to being swept out of office by the masses. Besides making both the big and small states happy, the bicameral legislature provided the Framers with a balance between the experiment of a people's government and the stability of government with an elite group of experienced politicians.

Vs.

CHARACTERISTICS OF THE TWO HOUSES

When the first Congress was formed, the two houses had only the blueprint provided by the Constitution. Over the years, they have developed contrasting characteristics and procedures.

HOUSE OF REPRESENTATIVES

membership: 435

more formal and rigid rules

more hierarchically organized

acts more quickly

power concentrated

smaller constituencies

less prestige

limited debate

one major committee assignment

SENATE

membership: 100

less formal and rigid rules

less hierarchically organized

acts more slowly

power less concentrated

larger constituencies

more prestige

unlimited debate

two or more major committee assignments

POWERS OF CONGRESS

The Constitution gives Congress many specific powers. But its powers are limited, given the separation of powers and the checks and balances that are built into the government. The powers of Congress may be grouped into three major categories: delegated (or expressed) powers, implied powers, and nonlegislative powers.

1. Delegated Powers

Most of the lawmaking powers the Constitution grants to Congress are those that any sovereign nation would need. Article I, Section 8 lists the majority of them.

A. BORROWING POWER

Sometimes the government needs to borrow money in order to make ends meet—for example, to finance a war or pay for a new government program. The Constitution allows the government to borrow against its credit, the good faith of its people.

B. POWER TO TAX

The Constitution grants Congress financial powers to raise the money needed to pay for the government. Article I of the Constitution protects citizens from oppressive taxes. It specifies that the government must use the money it collects from "taxes, **duties, imposts,** and **excises**" to pay debts and provide for the well-being of its citizens.

C. COMMERCE POWER

The Commerce Clause allows Congress to regulate and promote trade. It keeps states from dealing individually with foreign countries and gives Congress many more powers than the states over trade within the country. Rivers, railroads, airspace, and most roads do not stop at state borders, so the national government needs a controlling influence over commerce.

---

duty—a governmental tax, especially on imports.

impost—a tax or duty.

excise—a tax on the production, sale, or consumption of products within the United States, such as tobacco, gas, or liquor.

D. CURRENCY POWER

Under the Articles of Confederation, the Second Continental Congress issued paper money, but since the national government had no money and no authority to raise money, the currency was almost worthless. To add to the problem, each of the states issued its own currency, so that a variety of different bills were used. The Constitution gave the right to coin money exclusively to Congress as a way to stabilize its value. It also allowed Congress to punish those who counterfeit the legal currency.

E. BANKRUPTCIES

Congress has the power to establish uniform bankruptcy laws. When a person is unable to pay his or her debts, declaring bankruptcy allows the individual's assets to be divided among the creditors.

F. WAR POWERS

The Constitution gives Congress a wide range of war powers, including the ability to declare war and "provide for the common defense and general welfare of the United States." Some of Congress's war powers are shared with the President, named as the commander in chief of the nation's armed forces. Clearly, the Founders were concerned that the new country be able to defend itself.

G. OTHER DELEGATED POWERS

The Constitution also gives Congress control over the naturalization process, the post office, the issuing of **copyrights** and **patents,** the establishment of standard weights and measures, the creation of federal courts below the Supreme Court, and the power to acquire territories and manage federal areas.

2. Implied Powers

The implied powers are those not stated specifically in the Constitution but considered as reasonable offshoots of delegated powers. The Elastic Clause (also known as the Necessary and Proper Clause) gives Congress authority to pass laws it deems "necessary and proper" to carry out its specified functions. Since the Supreme Court's decision in *McCulloch v. Maryland* (1819), Congress has exercised a wide range of implied powers. The Elastic Clause has been stretched a great deal through the years.

---

copyright—the legal right to publish, sell, perform, or distribute a literary or artistic work.

patent—the government's grant to inventors assuring them the rights to make, use, or sell their inventions for a specific period of time.

For example, Congress today often investigates suspected wrongdoing in the executive branch when it considers it "necessary and proper" to do so. When members of Congress accused President Clinton and Vice President Gore of illegal fund-raising during the 1996 campaign, congressional committees were formed to investigate the accusations. The implied powers are not unlimited, however; they must be based on one or more of the delegated powers.

3. Nonlegislative Powers

In addition to its lawmaking powers, Congress has nonlegislative duties and responsibilities. Some of them are outlined in the Constitution. These duties include such things as the power to propose constitutional amendments and to admit new states to the Union. Also included are the power to approve key presidential appointments and treaties and the House's selection of a President if no candidate receives a majority of the electoral vote. Certain duties, such as Congress's role as a watchdog over governmental activities, have developed through tradition. Two other important nonlegislative responsibilities are the power of impeachment and the powers of investigation and oversight.

A. IMPEACHMENT

The Constitution grants Congress the power to remove federal officials—such as the President, Vice President, and court justices—from office for "treason, bribery, or other high crimes and misdemeanors." The House may impeach an officer from his or her position by a two-thirds vote of its membership, but the Senate must try the **impeachment** and vote for conviction before the officer actually is removed. In the case of the President, the Chief Justice presides, and two-thirds of the Senate membership must vote for removal. If found guilty, the former official is disqualified from ever holding a government job again and may be tried in a regular court and punished like any other citizen. In the course of American history, seven federal judges have been removed from office by the Senate after being impeached by the House. Two Presidents have been impeached, and one President resigned as impeachment proceedings were beginning against him.

def·i·ni·tions

impeachment—the formal procedure by which a President or any federal official is removed for misconduct in office.

PRESIDENTS AND IMPEACHMENT

THE IMPEACHMENT AND TRIAL OF ANDREW JOHNSON

Andrew Johnson, an "accidental president" who gained the presidency after the assassination of Abraham Lincoln, was impeached in 1868. The leaders of the radical Republicans who controlled Congress strongly disliked Johnson and set a trap to remove him from the presidency. Congress passed a law over his veto, the Tenure of Office Act, which severely limited the power of the President. This act required a President to get permission from the Senate before removing any of his appointees. Congressional leaders knew that Johnson did not get along with some of his cabinet members, and they also knew that Johnson would consider the act unconstitutional (which it probably was). When Johnson dismissed his secretary of war, they used it as an excuse to impeach him. The vote in the Senate trial failed to support the House decision, however, and Johnson kept the presidency—by a margin of one vote.

THE IMPEACHMENT AND TRIAL OF BILL CLINTON

A second President, Bill Clinton, was impeached by the House of Representatives 130 years later. The impeachment came after several years of investigations by Independent Counsel Kenneth Starr of various aspects of Clinton's behavior, such as real estate dealings and personal conduct. In the fall of 1998, the *Starr Report* presented evidence to Congress suggesting that Clinton had attempted to cover up sexual encounters with a White House aide, Monica Lewinsky. After hearings conducted by the House Judiciary Committee, the House voted in December 1998 to impeach Clinton for perjury and obstruction of justice. The trial in the Senate began in January 1999 and lasted about a month. The Senate did not support the House decision, with many Senators agreeing that the behavior didn't represent "impeachable offenses."

THE RESIGNATION OF RICHARD NIXON

In 1974, Richard Nixon resigned rather than risk impeachment and possible removal from office. His resignation came more than two years after five men were arrested for breaking into the Democratic party's headquarters in the Watergate office-apartment complex in Washington. The investigation of these arrests revealed some questionable campaign tactics linked to the Republican Party, including "laundering" of funds through Mexican banks, electronic surveillance of competitors, shredding of government documents, and a cover-up of the break-in. Nixon claimed no knowledge of any of it, but in a televised congressional hearing a number of his associates were implicated. The hearing uncovered the existence of White House tape recordings that revealed Nixon knew about the cover-up shortly after the break-in. At that point, the House began to organize impeachment proceedings, and Nixon resigned.

B. OVERSIGHT AND INVESTIGATION

A second significant power of Congress is its **oversight function,** a process that often involves investigating the executive branch and its administration of policy. Through committee hearings, Congress has raised public awareness of issues such as the environment, crime, health care, consumer safety, and foreign trade. Ever since Congress first executed its investigative power in 1792, when it reviewed an army defeat of a Native American tribe, congressional investigations of the executive branch have occurred regularly. Congress may **subpoena** a person to an investigation. However, the Supreme Court has ruled that investigations should not be held only to expose personal affairs of private individuals and must not deprive citizens of their basic rights.

Another important oversight function deals with budgetary powers. When a law is passed setting up a government program, no money may be spent until Congress passes an **authorization** bill, stating the maximum amount of money available. Clearly, when the country's budget is set, there is only so much money to go around. Congress has to appropriate, or divide, the money among the programs and the agencies that run them. The money that has been authorized cannot be spent until an **appropriation** is made. Congress almost never appropriates as much as it has authorized. However, Congress can approve deficit spending, or the practice of spending more money than is brought in.

def·i·ni·tions

oversight function—the power of Congress to review the policies and programs of the executive branch.

authorization—a legislature's approval to implement or continue a governmental program or agency.

appropriation—a grant of money by Congress to be used for specific purposes.

subpoena—a legal order requiring a person to appear in court or turn over specified documents.

Organization and Membership of Congress

The two houses of Congress meet for terms of two years that begin on January 3rd of odd-numbered years. Each term is numbered. For example the 106th Congress begins in 1999 and ends in 2001. Each term is divided into two one-year sessions that include holidays and vacations. The President may also call special **sessions** of Congress in case of national emergencies. The Constitution gives each house the authority to determine the rules that its members must follow. The rules (there are far more in the House than the Senate) range from basic parliamentary procedure to restrictions on smoking, use of cell phones, and even the presence of flowers.

ORGANIZATION

Over the years, Congress has developed four important types of structures to organize its work: the party leadership, the committee system, caucuses, and the support agencies.

1. The Party Leadership

Even though most people think political parties are not as important as they used to be, the party is still very important to the organization of Congress. After each legislative election one party has the majority, and one is designated as the minority. Each house selects its own leaders by majority vote. Even though the whole house votes for its leaders—with the majority winning—the real selection is made by the majority party ahead of time and behind the scenes.

A. LEADERSHIP IN THE HOUSE OF REPRESENTATIVES

Because the membership in the House is so much larger than that in the Senate, power in the House tends to be centralized in the hands of its leaders—the **Speaker of the House,** the two **floor leaders,** and two assistant leaders.

def·i·ni·tions

Speaker of the House—the presiding officer of the House of Representatives, selected from the membership. The Speaker is always a leader of the majority party.

floor leader—a spokesperson for a party in Congress; one who directs party decisions and strategy.

session—the meeting of a legislative or judicial body for a specific period of time for the purpose of transacting business.

148

Then and Now

THE IMPORTANCE OF PERSONALITY

Even though the Speaker of the House has many powers, his influence depends largely on his personality and informal influence. Consider these Speakers from history:

HENRY CLAY entered the House in 1811 and almost immediately (at the age of 34) was elected Speaker. He was a brilliant and powerful orator, so admired by the other members that he and his "War Hawks" seized control of the chamber. Then they pressured President James Madison to declare war on Britain (the War of 1812). Clay is considered to have been the most powerful man in the nation from 1811 to 1825.

"CZAR" THOMAS REED, Speaker from 1889-1891 and from 1895-1899, exploited and manipulated the job to its full power. In 1890 he said, "The only way to do business inside the rules is to suspend the rules."

SAM RAYBURN, Speaker for 17 years between 1940 and 1961, invited a favored few to join him after House sessions at the "Board of Education," a hidden office under his formal office. They socialized and plotted strategy for House business, and an invitation meant that "Mister Sam" thought you were special. In 1945 Harry Truman was attending a "Board meeting" when he received a call telling him to come quickly to the White House, where he learned he was to become President after Roosevelt's sudden death.

NEWT GINGRICH gained the speakership in 1994 when Republicans and their "Contract with America" (a plan advocating a balanced budget, welfare reform, and a tax cut) swept so many Democrats out of office that Republicans gained majority status in the House for the first time in more than 40 years. He used his majority to centralize more power in the Speaker's position, but he offended so many members of his party that he nearly lost his job in 1996. Finally, after a disappointing Republican showing in the 1998 midterm elections, Gingrich resigned his position because he lost support from voters and colleagues.

The Speaker of the House is always a member of the majority party and is often the single most important member of Congress. The Speaker's influence depends partly on qualities of personality and the respect of colleagues, but also on several important powers. Usually a loyal party member who ranks high in seniority, the Speaker rules on questions of parliamentary procedure, influences committee assignments, channels bills to committee, appoints the party's other leaders, and presides over many House debates. If the Speaker or presiding officer doesn't call on a member, he or she can't say anything.

After the Speaker, the majority and minority leaders are the most important officers in the House. The **majority leader** is the Speaker's top assistant and helps plan the party's legislative program, making sure that the committees get important bills to the House floor and steering them through debate once they are on the floor. The **minority leader** heads and organizes the opposition to the majority party. Both leaders are assisted by party **whips.** They inform members when important bills will come up for a vote, count numbers of expected votes for the leadership, and pressure members to support the leadership in critical votes.

B. LEADERSHIP IN THE SENATE

Senate leadership is similar to that of the House. According to the Constitution, the president of the Senate is the Vice President of the United States. Partly because he is from another branch of government, the Vice President has little authority. One formal duty is to vote in case of a tie. Because the Vice President does not regularly attend Senate sessions, a **president *pro tempore,*** a leading—often senior—member of the majority party, is selected to preside. Unlike that of Speaker of the House, however, the role of the president *pro tempore* is largely ceremonial and lacks real power. The responsibility of presiding is purely an honor, and the president *pro tempore* usually gives it to a new member of the party in power.

The floor leaders hold the real leadership power in the Senate, although their power is much less centralized than it is in the House of Representatives. The majority leader is often the most influential person in the Senate and frequently represents, or speaks for, the Senate to outsiders. He has the privilege of speaking first on the floor, and he usually has a powerful say in making committee assignments. The majority leader usually consults with the minority leader in setting the agenda. In fact, the minority leader's power often depends on how well he gets along with the majority leader. The Senate also has party whips with responsibilities similar to those in the House, but the Senate whips have a particular challenge, because the senators are less tied to party and more independent in the way they vote.

def·i·ni·tions

majority leader—the legislative leader of the party holding the majority of seats in the House or Senate. In the House, the majority leader is second to the Speaker of the House.

minority leader—the legislative leader and spokesperson for the party holding the minority of seats in the House or Senate.

whip—a senator or representative who works with party leaders to communicate views, solicit support before votes are taken, and keep track of how voting is likely to go.

president *pro tempore*—the member of the U.S. Senate chosen as leader in the absence of the Vice President.

LEADERSHIP IN CONGRESS

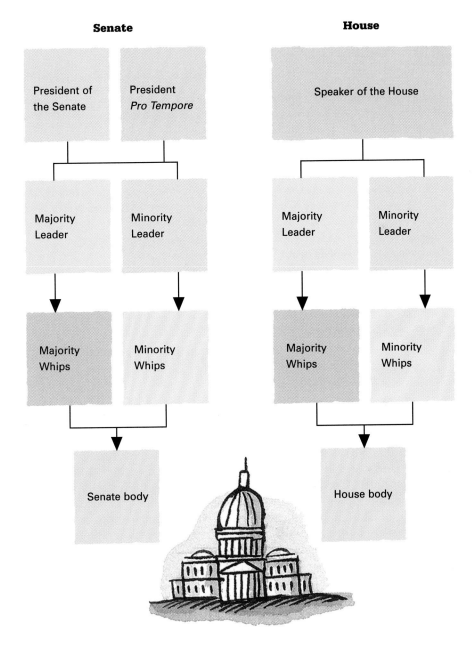

Senate

President of the Senate

President *Pro Tempore*

Majority Leader

Minority Leader

Majority Whips

Minority Whips

Senate body

House

Speaker of the House

Majority Leader

Minority Leader

Majority Whips

Minority Whips

House body

Quotes

2. The Committee System

Congress organizes its legislative work through a system of committees. More than 11,000 bills are presented by members to Congress during one two-year session, and it would be impossible to consider each of them on the floor of either house. Committees were created to divide the work of Congress, giving bills to groups of members who specialize in a field, such as national security or labor. Dozens of committees work simultaneously on different bills, and each committee divides the work further by sending bills to subcommittees. That's how they get the work done.

A. TYPES OF COMMITTEES

There are four types of powerful legislative committees.

★ **STANDING COMMITTEES** are the most important type because they stand from one Congress to the next. Standing committees can be combined or discontinued, but most of them have been around for a long time. The committees handle bills in different policy areas and shape legislation at a very

152

critical point. For example, after a bill about tax reform is introduced in the Senate, it would be referred to the Finance Committee. Each **standing committee** has several (some have more than others) subcommittees. The Senate currently has 17 standing committees. Even though the House has far more members, it currently has only 19 standing committees. The House allows representatives to serve on only one standing committee, while senators may serve on two or more. Many of the committees in the House have similar names to those in the Senate, but they function almost completely separately. It is just another way to check and balance and get a better bill as a result.

★ SELECT COMMITTEES are more temporary, set up to study specific issues. **Select committees** are appointed separately for each house. The Speaker of the House appoints the members to House committees, and the president of the Senate appoints those in the Senate. Of the four types of legislative committees, select committees usually have the least direct input into legislation, although their investigations may lead to the consideration of specific bills. Some longstanding select committees, such as the Select Committee on Indian Affairs and the Select Committee on Aging, produce legislation just as a standing committee does. Select committees look into all sorts of issues, such as hunger, minority group status or conditions, crime, narcotics abuse and control, and suspected wrongdoing by government officials.

★ JOINT COMMITTEES are similar to select committees, except that they are made up of members from both the House and the Senate. They meet together about a specific issue and report back their findings to each house. They often handle routine matters, such as printing government publications and supervising the Library of Congress. **Joint committees** tend to be more permanent than select committees.

★ CONFERENCE COMMITTEES are created when the House and the Senate have passed different versions of the same bill. They are similar to joint committees in that they have members from both the House of Representatives and the Senate. A **conference committee** is very temporary and lasts only as long as it takes to hammer out a compromise bill that can be sent back to each house before it goes on to the President.

def·i·ni·tions

standing committee—a permanent committee that evaluates bills and either kills them or passes them along for further debate.

select committee—a temporary congressional committee appointed for a limited purpose.

joint committee—a legislative committee made up of members of both houses of Congress.

conference committee—a temporary House-Senate committee whose goal is to find an acceptable compromise on conflicting versions of a bill.

Vs.

STANDING COMMITTEES OF CONGRESS

After a bill is introduced in either house, it's referred to the appropriate standing committee.

HOUSE COMMITTEES

Agriculture

Appropriations

Armed Services

Banking and Financial Service

Budget

Commerce

Education and the Workforce

Government Reform

House Administration

International Relations

Judiciary

Resources

Rules

Science

Small Business

Standards of Official Conduct

Transportation and Infrastructure

Veterans Affairs

Ways and Means

SENATE COMMITTEES

Agriculture, Nutrition, and Forestry

Appropriations

Armed Services

Banking, Housing, and Urban Affairs

Budget

Commerce, Science, and Transportation

Energy and Natural Resources

Environment and Public Works

Finance

Foreign Relations

Governmental Affairs

Health, Education, Labor, and Pensions

Indian Affairs

Judiciary

Rules and Administration

Small Business

Veterans Affairs

B. COMMITTEE ASSIGNMENTS

The ratio of party members on each committee mirrors the ratio of Democrats to Republicans in each house. Assignment to legislative committees is one of the most important decisions to a new member of Congress. Usually, the best committee is one that will allow the member to serve his or her district or state the most easily. However, a member from a "safe" (one likely to grant re-election) district who wants to make it big nationally may want to be named to a committee that receives much media attention, such as Foreign Relations or Judiciary, or one that holds lots of financial power. For the Republicans, the Committee on Committees (led by party leaders) makes committee assignments in the Senate and, along with the Policy Committee, makes assignments in the House. For the Democrats, the Democratic Steering Committee makes appointments in the Senate, and, in the House, the Democratic Steering and Policy Committee is responsible for committee assignments. The parties consider a member's wishes in making the appointments, but they also assess the appointee's region of the country, personality, and party connections.

e.g.

CONGRESS AND THE MOVIES

Consider how members of Congress, congressional staff, and congressional candidates have been portrayed in films.

MR. SMITH GOES TO WASHINGTON (1939)—Frank Capra classic starring James Stewart as a naïve senator who fights against political corruption.

THE FARMER'S DAUGHTER (1947)—Romantic comedy about a Swedish woman and her clash with the man she loves over a congressional election.

THE CANDIDATE (1972)—Story of a political hopeful, played by Robert Redford, facing the challenges of a California Senate race against a powerful incumbent.

THE SEDUCTION OF JOE TYNAN (1979)—Story of Senator Joe Tynan, played by Alan Alda, and the behind-the-scenes deal-making and romance in his life in Washington.

BOB ROBERTS (1992)—Satiric fake documentary about a millionaire's campaign for a seat in the Senate.

BULWORTH (1998)—Dark comedy about Jay Bulworth, a desperate and cynical Senator, played by Warren Beatty, who discovers the joy of speaking the truth after hiring a hit man to kill him.

3. Caucuses

Congress organizes formally through party leadership and the committee system, but a growing trend is for members to join informal groups called caucuses. Like the caucuses that select party candidates for public office, the congressional caucuses' purpose is to discuss an issue or advocate a political ideology. Their members, however, are all representatives and senators, and their goal is to plan legislative strategies, not select candidates. Today there are more than 70 of these caucuses. Many include both representatives and senators. Many members of Congress belong to more than one caucus. With the growing numbers of minority and female representatives, each has its own caucus: the Congressional Black Caucus, caucuses for women, and caucuses for Hispanics. Others form around special interests, such as the Steel Caucus and even a Mushroom Caucus.

4. The Support Agencies

In addition to their own internal organization and formal committees, support agencies serve members of the House and the Senate. Support agencies also provide services for other branches of government and sometimes for the public. Four of the most important support agencies are described below.

★ **THE LIBRARY OF CONGRESS** was created in 1800 so that members of Congress would have books available for reference as they deliberated the business of legislation. From that small start, it now contains almost 97 million items, and it also administers copyright law for most published works in the United States. The Library still addresses its original purpose, through the Congressional Research Service that conducts research for legislators and congressional staff.

★ **THE CONGRESSIONAL BUDGET OFFICE (CBO)** was established in 1974 to help Congress study and analyze the federal budget. The CBO studies the budget proposals from the President, and employees come up with their own statistics, predictions, and arguments—another instance of checks and balances.

★ **THE GENERAL ACCOUNTING OFFICE (GAO)**, created in 1921, provides another way for Congress to look over the shoulder of agencies in the executive branch. The staff of the GAO audits government programs to be sure the money appropriated by the committees is spent according to congressional guidelines. The GAO staff members also provide legal opinions on bills under consideration, testify before committees, do wide-ranging research, and develop questions for committee hearings.

★ **THE GOVERNMENT PRINTING OFFICE (GPO)** was created to print for members of Congress a daily record of bills introduced in both houses and the speeches supporting and disagreeing with them. For years that record has been known as the *Congressional Record*. The GPO now prints almost all the publications produced by all three branches of the federal government.

MEMBERS OF CONGRESS

Recall that the Constitution requires senators to meet stricter age and citizenship requirements and to hold longer terms than representatives. The Founders were concerned that the House elected by the people be balanced by the Senate, which provided stability. But today both houses are popularly elected, and our country has changed a great deal since 1787. What similar characteristics do members of Congress share, and in what ways are the members of the two houses different?

Personal and Political Characteristics

Although the 535 members of Congress represent the people of the United States, they do not reflect a true cross section of the American population. Senators and representatives tend to be older, wealthier, and better educated than those they represent. Nearly all members of the 106th Congress are married with children, while a few are divorced. Several claim no religious affiliation, but about 60 percent are Protestants, 25 percent are Roman Catholics, and about 8 percent are Jewish. Nearly half of them are lawyers. A large number come from business, banking, and education. Some are farmers,

RECENT HOUSES

HOUSE OF REPRESENTATIVES (435 MEMBERS)	105TH CONGRESS	106TH CONGRESS
Average age	53.4	52.6
Under 40	28	32
Advanced degrees	282	277
Military service	140	136
Held prior elected office	301	311
Women	54	58
African Americans	39	39
Hispanics	21	19
Asian/Pacific Islanders	5	4
Native Americans	0	0

Source: *Congressional Quarterly*

journalists, former teachers, or public servants. Some congressional members are millionaires. Nearly all went to college, and a number of them have advanced degrees as well.

The typical profile of congressional members has been changing in recent years. (See Almanac page 530.) Particularly in the House, an increasing number of women and minorities are being elected. Among the 40 House newcomers in 1999—23 Democrats and 17 Republicans—were a man born in Taiwan, a lesbian lawyer, and a 62-year-old grandmother.

Privileges, Benefits, and Penalties

As authorized by the Constitution, Congress sets its own salaries and benefits. Congressional salaries have increased substantially since 1789, when members received $6 per day. Salaries in 1999 for senators and representatives were set at $133,600 a year (except for the Speaker of the House, who makes $171,500 a year). Members also receive a wide array of fringe benefits—**perquisites,** or "perks." For example, each member of Congress has an office, large expense accounts for staff and supplies, generous travel allowances and pension plans, and low-cost health coverage. One benefit, the **franking** privilege, gives representatives and senators free postal service. Another important perk is that of privileged speech, the right to speak freely about political questions without fear of being sued or prosecuted for libel or slander.

Congress has a number of ways of dealing with the misconduct of its members, including **censure** or expulsion. Each house, for example, has an Ethics Committee to investigate accusations against its members. Between 1981 and 1990, 40 members were charged with misconduct, such as misuse of funds, failing to disclose personal income, and accepting illegal gifts. Despite the adoption in 1989 of a new code of ethics, members of Congress and their scandals still generate media attention and contribute to a cynical view of an American Congress unduly concerned with money and power.

In one well-publicized case in 1993, Representative Daniel Rostenkowski, the chairman of the powerful Ways and Means Committee, was forced to resign and went to prison after abusing the franking privilege, accepting gifts from lobbyists, and misusing campaign funds.

---

perquisite—a benefit received in addition to a regular salary or wage; a "perk."

franking—free postal service for letters sent by members of Congress to their constituents.

censure—an official expression of blame or disapproval.

Congressional Staff

Members of Congress are also entitled to hire staff members to assist them in their legislative duties. Even though the 535 members hold the lawmaking powers, the thousands of workers who help the members do their jobs should not be overlooked. Staff members often communicate with constituents, plan campaign strategies, do research for committees, attend committee meetings, and draft new bills for committee members. Their extensive responsibilities make them a largely unknown power in Congress that helps to shape the legislation process.

The numbers of congressional staff have increased dramatically from about 2,000 in 1947 to almost 12,000 today, and committee staff members have increased from nearly 400 to around 3,000. This growth is caused partly by the increasing numbers and growing complexity of proposed bills and partly by the increasing number of constituents.

Then and Now

A POWERFUL STAFF MEMBER

In the early 1930s, a young man arrived in Washington to become the staff secretary for Richard Kleberg, a nondescript representative from Texas. The young man knew almost no one, had no money, and stayed in a rickety boardinghouse for the few hours when he wasn't working. Representative Kleberg was a Democrat from a safe district where no one had voted for a Republican in years. He did not have to work too hard, so he was almost never in Washington, nor did he pay much attention to the needs of the folks back home. His new staff secretary did all his work for him. The secretary called other representatives to discuss legislation, got to know the party, and answered constituents' mail. Before long no one asked for Richard Kleberg when they called his office. Instead they asked for his staff secretary. The young man was Lyndon Johnson. He used his position as a staff secretary to become a representative himself, and later a senator, a powerful Senate majority leader, Vice President, and eventually President of the United States.

How a Bill Becomes a Law

One way to understand what representatives and senators really do is to look at the way they spend their days. While it is important for them to be in Washington when Congress is in session, it is also essential to keep in touch with the folks back home. Members travel back and forth between Washington and their districts or states numerous times during a year. When in Washington, members of Congress must split their time in many ways—meeting with staff, making telephone calls, answering mail, and preparing legislation and speeches. They must also be in the House or Senate chambers for debate and voting. Committee meetings and hearings also consume a good bit of time.

Of course, their major responsibility is to consider bills proposed for legislation. Fewer than 10 percent become law, but Congress manages to pass several hundred during each two-year period, each having gone through a complex process. A bill must pass through both houses before it can be sent for the President's signature. Usually, but not always, similar versions of the same bills (companion bills) pass through the House and Senate at the same time, although they do not have to. Some bills go through the process relatively quickly, but many take a full year or even more. Others fail to meet the end-of-the-year deadline and are either dropped completely or reintroduced in the next session to go through the entire process again.

A BILL'S PASSAGE THROUGH THE HOUSE AND SENATE

A bill may begin in either house, except that bills of revenue must begin in the House of Representatives.

HOUSE OF REPRESENTATIVES

A bill is introduced and assigned to a committee.

The bill is usually assigned to a subcommittee. Then it goes back to the full committee for approval.

The bill usually goes to the Rules Committee where rules are set for the debate of the bill on the floor.

The bill goes to the Committee of the Whole for further discussion and revision.

The bill goes to the House floor for highly restricted debate. Amendments may be offered. The entire membership votes on the bill.

SENATE

A bill is introduced and assigned to a committee.

The bill is usually assigned to a subcommittee. Then it goes back to the full committee for approval.

(No Rules Committee)

(No Committee of the Whole)

The bill goes to the Senate floor for an almost unrestricted debate. Amendments often are offered. The entire membership votes on the bill.

The bill may go to conference committee where members from both houses work out differences in House and Senate versions.

The bill goes back to the House for vote on the compromise bill.

The bill goes back to the Senate for vote on the compromise bill.

The bill goes to the President for his signature. If he vetoes it, it may be overridden by two-thirds vote of the membership of each house.

1. INTRODUCING A BILL

Although **bills** can be introduced on the House or Senate floor only by members of Congress, ideas for bills usually come from other people—private citizens, the President, other officials in the executive branch, or interest groups. There are two types of bills: public bills and private bills. Public bills apply to the entire nation, while private bills (about one-third of all bills proposed) apply only to certain persons or places. For example, a new tax law would be a public law; the awarding of a Congressional Medal of Honor to a war veteran would be a private law. Congress also considers resolutions. They differ from bills in that they deal with matters that affect only one house or the other, and they do not relate directly to the public will. Resolutions may change rules or procedures, or they may wish a member a happy birthday or a prosperous retirement. They do not go to the President for approval.

Concurrent resolutions affect both houses and are voted on by both memberships. They are used when Congress wants to make a statement without passing a law. For example, Congress may issue a concurrent resolution when it wants to make a policy statement on foreign affairs to other countries. The most serious of all are the **joint resolutions,** which require approval by the President. They have the force of law. They differ from bills in that they often address temporary matters or situations that need immediate attention.

When a bill or resolution is introduced in the House, a representative drops the bill into the hopper—a box near the clerk's desk. To introduce a bill in the Senate, the sponsor is recognized on the floor and then simply announces it or hands it to a clerk in the front of the Senate. In both houses the bill is assigned a title and a number—for example, H.R. 345 (the 345th bill presented in that term to the House of Representatives) or S. 237 (the 237th bill presented to the Senate). From there it is sent to a legislative committee.

2. BILLS IN COMMITTEE

New bills are sent to the legislative committee that deals with the same subject matter. The committee chair then may send it to subcommittee. Most bills (about 90 percent) die in committee or subcommittee. Ninety percent of those that die are **pigeonholed,** or simply forgotten and never discussed.

def·i·ni·tions

bill—a proposed law presented to a legislative body.

concurrent resolution—a statement of congressional opinion, without the force of law, that requires the approval of both the Senate and the House, but not the President.

joint resolution—a formal expression of opinion by both houses of Congress that has the force of law.

pigeonhole—to put aside or ignore a proposed piece of legislation.

The term comes from the old rolltop desks with little compartments called "pigeonholes" where papers were stuck and left forever.

On rare occasions and only in the House of Representatives, a bill may be forced from committee by a **discharge petition** that must be signed by a majority of the membership. In such a situation, members may force a bill to the floor after it has been in the committee for at least 30 days. This step keeps a committee chair from totally squelching a bill he or she does not like. But the discharge petition is almost never used because committees are considered to be experts in their fields, and other members generally do not question them.

Hearings

If a committee or subcommittee decides to act on a bill, the chair will set up hearings, in which people interested in the bill present their points of view to the committee members. Presenters may be experts, government officials, or interest group leaders. Hearings vary in length according to the bill's complexity, its controversial nature, or its seriousness.

After the hearings, committee members meet to "mark up" the bill, or go through it section by section, making changes as they go. Then the committee votes favorably to the full membership or reports to kill the bill. If the bill survives, it will be accompanied by a written report to all members, describing the bill and explaining why the committee thinks it should become law. Staff members usually write these reports, which are very important because many senators and representatives rely almost exclusively on them to determine their vote. A bill favorably reported out in the Senate is scheduled on one of the several calendars. However, in the House, a bill must go to the powerful House Rules Committee.

The House Rules Committee

Created originally to set the rules for debate when a bill came to the floor, the Rules Committee plays a crucial role in the legislative process. Not only does the committee limit floor debate, but it first must issue a "rule" before a bill can even reach the floor for consideration. Without grant of a rule, a bill is effectively dead. When the Rules Committee does grant a rule, time limits on debate and the process of offering amendments are also set forth. When time limits are very short and no amendments are allowed from the floor, the Rules Committee is said to have issued a "gag rule." If no rules were set in a body as large as the House of Representatives, debates could go on forever, and floor action could be chaotic.

---

discharge petition—a process designed to force a bill out of committee to the floor of the House of Representatives.

3. FLOOR ACTION AND DEBATE

A very odd thing often happens when the House of Representatives and the Senate debate bills on the floor. No one comes to the chamber. You can sit in the galleries and see people speaking formally in front of empty chairs. If others are present, they may be reading, talking to each other, or even sleeping. Certainly if the bill is particularly controversial or important, the numbers present increase, but senators and representatives frequently believe they can often use their time in better ways than listening to debate. Also, members and their staff follow the debates on television from their offices.

Quote

"So little is done on the Senate floor that a senator could run naked through the chamber and no one would notice."

Senator Ernest Hollings (D-SC)

The Constitution requires that for either house to do official business, a **quorum,** or majority of its members, must be present. But it is often difficult to get a quorum, especially in the House. To meet the requirement, the House calls a Committee of the Whole, in which the House becomes one large committee of itself. Only 100 representatives need be present to begin the work of the Committee of the Whole. Debate, proposal of amendments, and voting on each section of a bill proceed until the entire bill has been considered. At that point, with its work done, the Committee of the Whole dissolves itself, and the House goes into regular session to approve or reject the Committee of the Whole action.

A. Debate

Floor debate, a crucial part of the lawmaking process, occurs under strict rules in the House. No representative may speak for more than one hour without unanimous consent. The Speaker has the power to force a member to give up the floor at any time. Any member may "move the previous question," which means that, if a majority approves, a vote must be taken within 40 minutes of the motion. If amendments are allowed on a bill, opponents sometimes propose amendments to stall or kill it. One tactic is to attach so many objectionable

def·i·ni·tions

quorum—the minimum number of members of a group who must be present for the valid transaction of business.

amendments to a bill that other members decide not to support it. An amendment cannot be added unless a majority of the members present approves it.

Debates on the Senate floor are very different from those in the House. Because the Senate does not have a Committee of the Whole to work through bills before they go to the floor, a bill comes straight from committee to the full Senate for consideration. The majority and minority leaders are responsible for guiding the debate with few set rules. Senators may usually speak on any subject they wish, and they can have unlimited time, provided they are properly recognized and have the floor.

THE FILIBUSTER

A tactic called a **filibuster** allows a senator or small group of senators to talk a bill to death, extending debate to block a bill's passage. Senators may plan ahead, yielding the floor to one another to keep the discussion alive for days, even if it means simply asking for the roll call to be read repeatedly.

Then and Now

FAMOUS FILIBUSTERS

In 1808, Representative Barent Gardenier was shot and nearly killed by a Tennessee colleague who became irate as Gardenier droned on and on during floor debate. Eventually the House passed a rule forbidding the filibuster.

In 1953, Senator Wayne Morse pinned a rose on his lapel and promised to talk until the petals wilted. He talked for 22 hours and 26 minutes, and sure enough, the petals wilted.

Senator Strom Thurmond of South Carolina holds the record for the longest filibuster on record. In 1957, in an effort to stop the passage of a strong civil rights bill, Mr. Thurmond spoke on the Senate floor for more than 24 hours. He talked about civil rights for a while but also read and discussed several of his favorite food recipes and finally read names from a phone book.

def·i·ni·tions

filibuster—a tactic, often a lengthy speech or debate, designed to delay the Senate's vote on a bill.

Because senators value their freedom of expression so highly, they probably will never forbid the filibuster. Despite the senatorial desire for free debate, they agreed to one type of restriction in the early part of this century. In 1917, just before the United States entered World War I, "eleven willful men" (as President Woodrow Wilson named them) filibustered a measure that would arm U.S. merchant ships in the Atlantic Ocean. Most other senators were angry enough to bring about the passage of the almost revolutionary Senate Rule 22, known as **cloture.** Under this rule, still in effect today, a motion may be made to cut off debate. If 60 senators vote for the motion (originally, the number was 67), the filibuster can be stopped.

THE "CHRISTMAS TREE" BILL

Another consequence of freedom of expression in the Senate is called a **"Christmas tree" bill.** When amendments are added to a bill in the House of Representatives, they must be **germane,** or relevant to the topic of the bill. For example, if a bill deals with gun control, the amendments must also address gun control. In the Senate, no such rule exists; senators can tack any amendment they please on to a bill. For example, in 1966 the Foreign Investors Act had amendments that helped hearse owners, importers of scotch whisky, and candidates for the presidency. Nongermane amendments are called **riders,** and they exist only in the Senate. Sometimes so many riders are attached to a bill that it looks like a Christmas tree, with everything added to make it as elaborate as possible. The goal may be to attach a rider that senators know the President wants, in hopes that he will sign the bill. Or it may be done to achieve the opposite: attach a rider that the President is opposed to so that he will not sign the bill.

THE FOREIGN INVESTOR ACT—1966

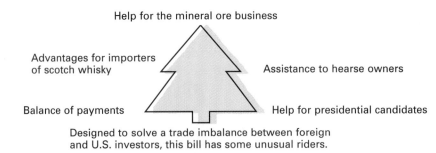

Help for the mineral ore business

Advantages for importers of scotch whisky

Assistance to hearse owners

Balance of payments

Help for presidential candidates

Designed to solve a trade imbalance between foreign and U.S. investors, this bill has some unusual riders.

def·i·ni·tions

cloture—the decision of three-fifths of the Senate to limit or end debate on an issue and call for a vote.

germane—having significant relevance to the point at hand.

rider—an addition or amendment to a bill that may have nothing to do with the bill's subject.

"Christmas tree" bill—a bill to which many irrelevant riders have been attached to increase the likelihood of its passage.

166

B. Voting

After the floor debate, a bill is printed in its final form and presented for a vote. Both houses require a quorum, or majority, to be present, and the members are signaled in their offices or committee meetings to come to the floor. Passage of a bill requires a majority vote by the members present, and members can't afford to miss too many important votes. The four options available to Congress members are:

★ to pass the bill as written and send it to the other house for consideration,

★ to table or kill the bill,

★ to send the bill back to committee, or

★ to offer amendments.

METHODS OF VOTING

Voting for a bill is different in the two houses. The House uses four different methods:

1. Voice votes are used for noncontroversial bills. The Speaker calls for "yeas" and "nays" and then announces the results.

2. In a standing vote, or a "division of the House," all in favor of a bill stand and are counted, followed by those who are opposed.

3. A teller vote may be called for by one-fifth of a quorum. Two tellers, one from each party, count representatives as they pass between the two tellers, first the supporters and then those opposed. Its use is rare.

4. In a roll-call vote, the names of the representatives are called, and they vote either "yea" or "nay."

   Since 1973, most teller and roll-call votes have been replaced by an electronic voting system. Roll-call votes took about 45 minutes, and the House was looking for a more efficient way to count votes. Members vote with a plastic card inserted in one of 48 boxes situated around the chamber. A master board shows how each member votes. They are given 15 minutes to vote, and then the Speaker locks the electronic system and announces the results.

   The Senate uses voice, standing, and roll-call votes, but it does not have an electronic voting process since a roll-call vote does not take very long.

CONFERENCE COMMITTEES

When a bill passes one house and is sent to the other, usually the members of the second house do not amend it. If they do, the changes are usually accepted by the first house, and the bill is sent to the President. But commonly the two houses are unable to agree on the exact terms of the bill. When this happens, a conference committee is formed to merge the two versions. The members are usually chosen from the standing committee that sponsored the bill and a comparable committee in the other house. For example, if a bill were sponsored by the House Agriculture Committee, some of its members would be joined on the conference committee by members from the Senate Agriculture, Nutrition, and Forestry Committee.

4. THE PRESIDENT'S ACTIONS

In keeping with the system of checks and balances established by the Constitution, a bill that passes both houses is sent to the President for action. The President signs the large majority of bills sent from Congress, and even if he does not act within ten days of receiving it, the bill becomes a law without a signature.

The President has the right to veto, or refuse to sign, but a veto represents a real stand-off between the executive and legislative branches of government. If vetoes happen too often, the tension can create **gridlock,** a situation in which nothing gets done because the two branches can't agree with one another. Often Presidents will meet with leaders of Congress before a bill is passed so that a veto can be avoided. After the meeting, congressional leaders may return to the committee to revise the bill. Or, in a more aggressive spirit, the President may announce to the public his intent to veto a bill, thereby warning Congress of measures he opposes. Members of Congress then have time to change the bill to avoid the veto, or they may send their own signals back to the President.

The President may also use a **pocket veto** within ten days of the end of a session of Congress. Congress tends to pass a large number of bills late in a session. To a certain extent, this makes sense because the bills need time to get to this point. If Congress gets a bill to the President within ten days of the end of a session, he does not have the full ten days to consider the bill. He can just "put it in his pocket" (ignore it), and the bill does not become law.

def·i·ni·tions

gridlock—conflict between the legislative and executive branches that commonly results in inaction.

pocket veto—a means by which a President kills a bill that Congress has sent by refusing to act on it until Congress has adjourned.

If a President vetoes a bill, it is returned to the house where it originated. The President also sends a veto message, or an explanation for his veto. Congress may then pass the bill over the veto by a two-thirds vote of the members present in both houses. If they are overridden, it is a serious indication of gridlock between the branches.

BILLS AND VETOES

Vetoes are seldom overridden; that has happened in history only in a relatively small number of the cases. For example, in the period between 1971 and 1988, 96.7 percent of bills passed. Of the 3.3 percent that were vetoed, only 12.7 percent of the vetoes were overridden.

INFLUENCES ON VOTING

You now know what procedures members follow to vote on bills presented for their consideration, but what factors shape their decisions to vote for or against a particular bill? As members of Congress, they represent the people. But is it the people of their home district or state—their **constituents**—or the country as a whole? And how much weight do they, or should they, give to the wishes of their party, interest groups, or even their own consciences? Political scientists have researched and argued these questions over and over, and no one has a clear answer. We can identify, however, several important considerations.

CONSTITUENTS' VIEWS—Citizens vote for people they want to represent them in Congress. Does that mean that those they elect usually vote according to these citizens' views? The answer is sometimes yes, and sometimes no. Some members of Congress are heavily influenced by their constituents' wishes and make it their primary goal to follow them.

PARTY MEMBERSHIP—The organization of Congress depends heavily on political parties, and party membership is an important influence on a member's voting record. Since leaders and committee members are chosen by party membership, it should not be surprising that members of one party generally vote similarly with other members of their party about three-fourths of the time.

---

constituent—a person represented by a government official and, as a result, to whom the official is accountable.

PERSONAL VIEWS—Do members ever vote according to their own personal views? Of course they do. As you might expect, Democratic representatives and senators tend to cast votes that reflect liberal views, and Republicans tend to cast more conservative votes. As a result, it is difficult to know whether the member is influenced by personal or party views. Nevertheless, some members of Congress feel that their own judgment—not the influences of party or constituents—is what should count most.

 e.g.

"PORK BARREL" AND "LOGROLLING"

One major criticism of members of Congress is that they too often vote for wasteful projects that are popular in their home districts. **Pork barrel** legislation happens when members—especially those who are in danger of losing the next election—"bring home the bacon" in bills that provide money for local roads, parks, mass-transit projects, or military bases that might benefit voters in specific areas but are not necessarily good for the country as a whole.

The custom of **logrolling** makes it easier for members of Congress to obtain such federal projects for their home state or district. In logrolling, lawmakers agree to support each other's bills. For example, one representative's district may be threatened with the closing of a key military base that will cost thousands of jobs, and another representative's district may be desperate for a new dam to prevent regular floods that ruin its farmland. So, the first representative will agree to vote for a bill that funds the dam in exchange for a vote to save the military base. Both districts get their pork barrel projects through logrolling, the agreement that "You scratch my back, and I'll scratch yours."

pork barrel—a government project that benefits a specific location or lawmaker's home district and constituents.

logrolling—the process of exchanging political favors for support.

Controversial Issues

Everybody has an opinion about Congress. To some, it is an effective legislative body in which ordinary Americans have their voices heard. To others, it is a slow-moving institution whose constantly bickering members are the pawns of special interest groups or rich capitalists. One window into Congress is through the controversial issues that preoccupy them. Three controversial issues that affect the public's perception of the work of Congress and its members include:

★ the seniority system,

★ incumbents and term limits, and

★ apportionment.

1. SENIORITY SYSTEM

One controversial congressional tradition is the **seniority system.** This refers to the practice of giving the key position of committee chair to the person from the majority party who has served on the committee the longest. It began as a reform to break the power of the Speaker, but the seniority system has itself become a problem. Critics argue that the seniority system ignores ability, discourages younger members, and can lead to a committee chair who is out of touch with current public opinion. Defenders of the system counter that the system is easy to apply, eliminates fighting within the party, ensures an experienced member is selected as chair, and protects the chair from party influence.

In the 1970s both houses decided to reform the seniority system by allowing committee chairs to be selected by secret ballots in some cases. Still, the seniority system is not dead. In most cases, when a chairmanship comes open, the senior member of the majority party on the committee becomes the chair. If the senior member is overlooked, it is usually for very serious reasons, and even if a junior member is better qualified, he or she just has to wait.

2. INCUMBENTS AND TERM LIMITS

Another controversial aspect of Congress has emerged from the tendency of voters to return incumbents to office. When the houses of Congress were first created, the Founders almost certainly believed that representatives and senators

def·i·ni·tions

seniority system—the congressional tradition in which members with the longest continuous service on a committee are automatically given the chairmanship position.

would serve for one or two terms and then go home to their regular lives as farmers, lawyers, or merchants. Representatives were expected to have particularly short tenures in office since they are elected every two years. Indeed, that pattern held for most members of Congress throughout the nineteenth century. But today incumbency is the rule rather than the exception. Indeed, the whole system of party leadership and seniority is based on the expectation that some members will stay in Congress for long periods.

Why should incumbents be re-elected so many times? One possible reason is that fund-raising and gaining the support of political action committees (PACs) are easier for incumbents. PACs provide a large percentage of the funds used in election campaigns. In recent elections, 88 percent of the donations from corporate and trade PACs went to incumbents in the House and more than 65 percent to incumbents in the Senate. According to Federal Election Commission records for 1995–1996, of the $159.8 million that PACs contributed to congressional campaigns, $117.2 million went to incumbents. For Senate races, $28.6 million of the total $55.4 million went to incumbents. PACs prefer to give their money to incumbents because they know how incumbents have voted in the past, and they keep a close watch over which members support them and which don't. A challenger is usually a mystery.

©1998 Wiley Miller/dist. By The Washington Post Writers Group

Another advantage for incumbents is their name recognition among voters. Members of Congress send newsletters from Washington, host families when they come to Washington, campaign with other well-known government officials, and get publicity in the local papers. All this publicity is virtually free; challengers often can't raise enough money to make themselves as well known. Incumbents can always "logroll" a little "pork" if their re-election is in trouble. If they get nice benefits for their districts, people remember them at election time. And incumbents can also remind constituents of their good works through mass mailings since they have the franking privilege.

In the early 1990s, a movement began that called for term limits—restricting the number of terms that a member of Congress can serve. After all, the President is currently limited to only one re-election or a maximum of ten years in office. In recent elections, the topic of term limits has caused heated debate.

TERM LIMITS

Term limits for Congress were proposed and heavily debated in 1995, but as yet, no limits have been imposed.

PRO

1. Incumbency keeps competent people from serving in Congress.

2. Democracy cannot be maintained if public offices are not rotated, allowing larger numbers of people to serve.

3. Congress would be reinvigorated by the new ideas that term limits would bring. Otherwise, Congress tends to be stale, and the same old ideas float around forever.

CON

1. Term limits would force experienced lawmakers to resign. Congress would lose the benefit of their experience.

2. Democracy is maintained as long as citizens vote. They have the ability to decide when people deserve re-election and when they do not.

3. The people can provide new ideas when they want them. Otherwise, citizens are kicking out experienced people who have much to contribute to Congress.

4. Term limits are actually unconstitutional since the Constitution does not provide for them.

3. APPORTIONMENT

Other controversial issues center around the problems in achieving a fair apportionment, or division, of representatives among the states. **Malapportionment** results from having districts of unequal size. Over the years, when the census indicated the need for redividing congressional districts, some states' legislatures created districts with greatly differing populations. The dominant political party, in an effort to maintain party control, was usually responsible for the establishment of districts of such unequal size.

Origins of Gerrymandering

Another problem with district boundaries is **gerrymandering,** a situation in which the population sizes of districts may be relatively even, but the boundary lines are drawn in odd shapes to favor a certain party or candidate or reduce the voting power of a racial or ethnic group. The term *gerrymandering* comes from a situation in 1812 when Governor Elbridge Gerry of Massachusetts redrew legislative districts to favor a prominent political party of the day, the Democratic-Republicans. Painter Gilbert Stuart made fun of Gerry's new district by adding a head, wings, and claws to make it look like the salamander below.

Governor Gerry was trying to create a district that would ensure the election of a Democratic-Republican. Many people did not think this redistricting was fair. By 1812, the practice of gerrymandering was well established, and it has continued to be a problem over the years.

Until 1964 the national government did nothing to interfere with each state's method of reapportionment. Then the Supreme Court acted on these controversial practices. In the landmark case of *Wesberry v. Sanders* (1964), also known as the "one man one vote" decision, the Court ruled that each district must represent approximately the same number of people as all others. Through its decision, the Court directly attacked malapportionment.

Gilbert Stuart's "Gerrymander"
The Granger Collection, New York

def·i·ni·tions

malapportionment—distribution of representatives among congressional districts in unequal proportion to the population.

gerrymandering—the process of dividing voting districts to give an unfair advantage to one candidate, party, or group.

Racial Gerrymandering

A new form of gerrymandering is much less clear-cut, and opinions around the country are widely split on it. Consider again the limited representation in Congress of minorities. Racial gerrymandering is intended to increase these numbers.

For example, the U.S. Justice Department rejected a redistricting plan submitted by the state of North Carolina after the census of 1990. North Carolina's plan included only one district with a majority of African-American voters, and the Justice Department decided that the state had a large enough African-American population that they should have at least two African-American districts. With only one majority African-American district, the number of African Americans elected might be unfairly limited. The state was ordered to go back to the drawing board in order to comply with the Federal Voting Rights Act, a law designed to protect the voting rights of African Americans and other minorities. The result was that in 1992 Democratic Representatives Melvin Watt and Eva Clayton became the first African Americans to represent North Carolina in Congress since 1901.

Other states followed the racial gerrymandering example, redesigning districts to allow for more minority representatives in the 1992 elections. For example, New York designed an X-shaped district that slithered through a dozen different school districts and several police precincts. At one point, it is only a block wide. However, a number of white voters began challenging the constitutionality of such districting, claiming that racial gerrymandering violated the white voters' right to equal protection of the laws.

The Supreme Court ruled against racial gerrymandering in *Shaw v. Reno* (1993), in a 5–4 decision. The Court reinstated a suit by five white citizens who maintained that North Carolina's redistricting violated their 14th Amendment right to "equal protection." Since then, the Supreme Court has ruled against other race-based districts in several cases, such as *Bush v. Vera* (1996). Still, many people continue to feel that given the number of districts in which whites remain the majority, racial gerrymandering is fair.

The Founders envisioned that the legislative branch, with its lawmaking power, would be the most important of the three branches of government. But they also wanted a system of checks and balances that would limit the power of Congress. It's time to look at the other two branches of government. Only then can we begin to understand how they interact and how the balance of power in the American political system shifts back and forth among them.

11 | **The Presidency**

hen the writers of the Constitution created the presidency in 1787, they could not have imagined the tremendous powers that a twentieth-century President of the United States would possess. George Washington became the first President in 1789 after winning an election with no primaries, no rival party candidate, no heated campaign, and only the 69 votes of the first electoral college. No one was sure of how he should spend his time or even how he should be addressed. Rejecting such titles as "His Excellency" or "Elective Majesty," Washington settled on the less formal "Mr. President."

The title remains the same today, but the process of winning the presidency and the strength of the President's powers and influence have changed dramatically since the time of George Washington. The President is America's most visible leader. He has the most explicit responsibility for guiding the course of the nation. The Founders probably would not be surprised to see that the presidency and the executive branch now serve as a strong check to legislative policy making. However, since they envisioned the legislature as dominant, they almost certainly could not have anticipated the gradual increase in presidential power. Today the President often sets the policy-making agenda, and Congress must sometimes respond, rather than lead.

In this chapter . . .

The Office of President

The modern presidency bears little resemblance to the office described by the Founders in 1787, but Article II of the Constitution provides a brief job description. It outlines the qualifications, terms, compensation, selection process, and several responsibilities of the presidency. Notice how Article II is much shorter than Article I, which details the duties and powers of Congress. Right away you get the point about which branch the Founders thought was most important. Remember, however, that the previous government, under the Articles of Confederation, provided for no President at all. Even though it's short, Article II represented a major shift.

★ QUALIFICATIONS

The Constitution includes only three formal requirements for becoming President. Previous experience in government is not one of them. First, the President must be a "natural-born citizen." Anyone born in a foreign country who later becomes a citizen is not eligible. The Founders no doubt were concerned that the leader of the newborn country be a loyal citizen who understood Americans and their needs. Second, the President must have lived in the United States for at least 14 years, although the years need not be consecutive. Third, the President must be at least 35 years old. The youngest man to take the office was Theodore Roosevelt at age 42 (succeeding William McKinley, who was assassinated in 1901), and the youngest ever elected was John F. Kennedy at age 43. So no President has been at all close to the minimum age of 35.

★ TERM

After seriously considering a single six-year or seven-year term, the Founders settled on a four-year term, with the President being eligible for re-election. The Constitution put no limit on the number of terms a President might serve. However, beginning with George Washington, no one had sought more than two terms, and so the unwritten tradition of "no third terms" continued. In 1940, Franklin Roosevelt broke that tradition, and in 1944, he was elected to a fourth term.

e.g.

PRESIDENTIAL FACTS

As of 1998, the United States has had 42 Presidents.

★ 41 belonged to political parties (George Washington did not).

★ 41 were Protestants (John Kennedy was a Catholic).

★ 37 had previous government experience before assuming office.

★ 34 were 50 years or older.

★ 31 went to college (all except one—Harry Truman—in the twentieth century).

★ 24 were lawyers.

★ 14 were former Vice Presidents.

★ None was a racial or ethnic minority.

★ None was a woman.

In 1951, the unwritten custom limiting presidential terms became the 22nd Amendment to the Constitution. A President can be elected to a maximum of two full terms, which generally means eight years in office. However, if a President succeeds to the office more than halfway into a term to which someone else was elected, the President could end up serving as many as ten years. For example, Lyndon Johnson filled the remainder of John Kennedy's term after Kennedy was assassinated in 1963. Because only a little more than one year of Kennedy's term remained, Johnson was eligible to run both in 1964 and 1968 (although he chose not to in 1968).

Although the intent of the 22nd Amendment was to reinforce the precedent set by Washington, the two-term limit has created the lame duck phenomenon. Because everyone knows that the President will be leaving office, his authority is somewhat undercut. Most Presidents are able to get things done despite the limitations, but almost none in the last 50 years has accomplished as much in the second term as in the first. However, a President sometimes finds the lame duck phenomenon working in his favor; the political motivation to be re-elected can't be seen in his actions.

★ PAY AND BENEFITS

Article II, Section 1 of the Constitution states that the President should be paid a "compensation" that cannot be increased or decreased during a term. First set at $25,000 a year in 1789, the President's salary since 1969 is $200,000. Besides the salary, Presidents receive a great many benefits—such as an expense account, residence in the White House, generous travel and entertainment funds, superb health care, a lifetime pension, and use of a yacht, a fleet of fancy automobiles, and *Air Force One*. So, is the President really well paid? The answer depends on your frame of reference. If you do the math, with a salary of $200,000, the President makes less than one penny for every thousand people he governs. Compare, for example, the pay and benefits of the President to those of chief executive officers (CEOs) of American businesses.

We need to recognize, of course, the important differences between being the President and being a CEO. The positions differ not just in pay and benefits but in power, fame, media praise and criticism, and public respect. CEOs head companies whose purpose is to make money, while Presidents are public servants whose salaries are paid by ordinary taxpayers. Presidents are in the glare of the public spotlight, with their appearance, conversation, leisure activities, and personal behavior the subject of often harsh scrutiny. Yet Presidents are traditionally given a degree of respect not generally given to successful CEOs. Libraries of collected documents, papers, and related articles are dedicated to former Presidents. Their birthplaces and boyhood homes are preserved and turned into museums. Impressive monuments are created for the great ones in Washington, such as the Jefferson, Lincoln, and Roosevelt memorials. Art and music centers and universities (such as Carnegie Hall and Stanford and Vanderbilt universities) are named for businessmen, but only if their money financed the buildings, the programs, or the grounds.

Quote

"I have had all the honor there is in this place [the White House], and have had responsibilities enough to kill any man."

William McKinley, President of the United States (1897–1901)

TOP CEO ANNUAL SALARIES AND BONUSES: 1996

Compare the President's annual salary ($200,000) and pension plan ($171,500) to the salaries and bonuses of these corporate leaders in 1996. These figures, from a study conducted by William M. Mercer Inc., don't include stock options or long-term incentive payouts.

EXECUTIVE	COMPANY	SALARY AND BONUS
Sanford I. Weill	Travelers Group, Inc.	$8,025,000
John F. Welch, Jr.	General Electric Co.	$6,300,000
Eckhard Pfeiffer	Compaq Computer Corp.	$4,250,000
Maurice R. Greenberg	American International Group Inc.	$4,150,000
John S. Reed	Citicorp	$3,466,667

Presidential Selection and Succession

Two other important topics addressed by the Founders were the selection of the President and the succession to the presidency. The guidelines they provided in the Constitution about the methods for electing a President and filling a vacancy in the presidency are complex. To some, they are even a bit controversial.

PRESIDENTIAL SELECTION

The Founders spent a great deal of time determining the methods of choosing the President. They sought a balance between the views of the people (a direct vote) and control by the political leaders (selection by Congress). When the Founders considered the selection of the President at the Constitutional Convention in 1787, they had already decided to allow the people to directly elect the House of Representatives and to leave selection of the Senate to the state legislatures. That compromise worked with a bicameral legislature, but how could they agree on the presidency? Some argued that citizens could not make a wise choice because they knew nothing of politics. Others believed that popular candidates would not make the best Presidents. Yet if Congress chose the President, then too much of the power of government would be in the hands of one branch.

The Electoral College

Alexander Hamilton suggested a compromise solution—the **electoral college.** It involved indirect popular participation, a solution the Founders finally accepted. The President would be selected by a special body of **electors,** none of whom could be members of Congress. They were to be chosen in each state as the state legislature directed. The number of electors allowed to each state would equal the total number of senators and representatives it had in Congress. The original plan provided that electors should meet together in each state separately and cast two votes each for presidential candidates. The **electoral vote** was to be counted before a joint session (both houses meeting together) of Congress. The one with the most votes would be President, and the one with the second most votes would be Vice President. In case of a tie,

def·i·ni·tions

electoral college—people selected in each state who gather to formally cast their ballots for the President and Vice President of the United States.

elector—a member of the electoral college.

electoral vote—the vote cast for President and Vice President by members of the electoral college.

CARTOGRAM OF 1996
ELECTORAL VOTE DISTRIBUTION

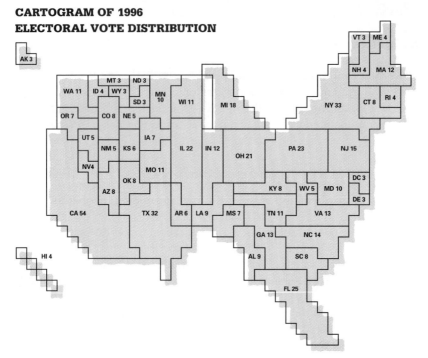

AK 3

VT 3   ME 4

NH 4   MA 12

MT 3   ND 3

WA 11   ID 4   WY 3

MN 10

WI 11

MI 18

NY 33

CT 8   RI 4

OR 7   CO 8   NE 5   SD 3

UT 5

IA 7

NM 5   KS 6

IL 22   IN 12

OH 21

PA 23

NJ 15

NV 4

MO 11

DC 3

OK 8

AZ 8

KY 8   WV 5   MD 10

DE 3

CA 54

TX 32

AR 6   LA 9   MS 7

TN 11

VA 13

GA 13   NC 14

HI 4

AL 9   SC 8

FL 25

Note: States are drawn proportionally to their number of electoral votes.

Source: Federal Election Commission

or if no one received a majority, the House of Representatives would choose the President. The Senate would choose the Vice President in case of a tie for that position. These were the original provisions laid out in Article II, Sections 2 and 4 of the Constitution.

The Election of 1800 and the 12th Amendment

The original electoral college worked as the Founders had hoped in 1789 and 1792 as George Washington was chosen unanimously by the electors. The system ran into trouble in 1800 because two political parties had formed— the Federalists and the Democratic-Republicans. Each party nominated its own candidates for President and also its own electors in each state. The Democratic-Republicans had the majority, so naturally their two candidates won: Thomas Jefferson and Aaron Burr. The problem was a tie for the presidency. Burr and Jefferson each got exactly the same number of votes because all the Democratic-Republicans had two votes each. The election then went to the House of Representatives. Even though the Democratic-Republican party clearly wanted Jefferson for President and Burr for Vice President, the House had to cast 36 ballots before the matter was settled. The debate caused many political tensions, especially between the newly selected President and Vice President, so the new administration got off to a hostile start.

As a result of the near-debacle of the election of 1800, the 12th Amendment was added in 1804 to the Constitution. It required that the electors cast separate ballots for President and Vice President. That system of separate presidential and vice-presidential elections continues today. So does the unwritten tradition of each party's selection of candidates for the two offices and the choice of electoral delegates who will be loyal to their party's choices.

THE ELECTORAL COLLEGE TODAY

Today political parties still nominate candidates for office, and citizens vote in presidential elections every four years on the Tuesday after the first Monday of November. What most people don't realize is that even though the candidates' names are on the ballot, they're voting for the electors, not for the candidates directly. The winning candidate is announced almost always on the same day as the popular election, but the electors do not formally meet in their respective state capitals until the Monday following the second Wednesday in December. While the Founders believed that each elector would use individual judgment in selecting a President, since political parties select the electors, the votes are predictable. Each party's electors are expected to vote automatically for their party's candidates. The electoral ballots are sealed and sent to the president of the Senate for a formal count. To become President or Vice President, a candidate must have at least 270 electoral votes (a majority of the 538 total). The formal announcement of the electoral college results comes in a joint session of Congress on January 6.

Criticisms of the Electoral College

The electoral college is criticized as having two main flaws.

1. First, some argue that the division of votes among states is not fair. Some small states have a greater percentage of the electoral college vote than their population should dictate. Other critics complain that the larger states carry too much importance because of their large number of electoral votes. A presidential candidate could, for instance, win the necessary 270 electoral votes by carrying only 11 big states. If the election had to be settled in the House of Representatives, additional problems could occur. According to the Constitution, each state has one vote. That means that a state with a small population, such as North Dakota, would have a vote equal to that of a state with a large population, such as California. The possibility of the House having to determine the winner increases if a popular minor party candidate runs.

1996 ELECTORAL VOTE DISTRIBUTION MAP

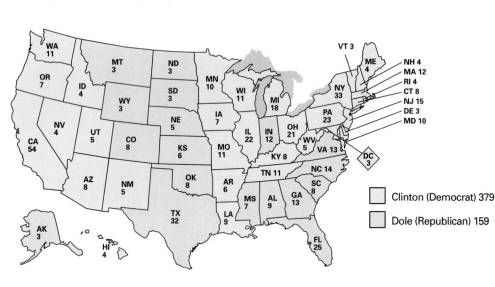

Clinton (Democrat) 379

Dole (Republican) 159

Source: Federal Election Commission

2. The main controversy surrounding the electoral college is the possibility that the person who wins the popular vote will not necessarily win the electoral college vote. Remember that the electoral college is a winner-take-all system. In other words, the electoral votes are counted state by state. Whoever wins a state's popular vote wins all of the state's electoral votes. It would be possible, in other words, to win the presidency without winning the majority of the popular votes. Three times this situation has actually happened. In the elections of John Quincy Adams in 1824, Rutherford B. Hayes in 1876, and Benjamin Harrison in 1888, those men actually received fewer popular votes than their opponents did. In several other presidential elections, a change of just a few thousand votes would have changed the result. For example, in 1960, the popular vote between Richard Nixon and John Kennedy was extremely close—Kennedy received just 114,673 more votes than Nixon out of the more than 68 million votes cast. Had Nixon received a few more votes in a few key states, he would have won the election.

Then and Now

POPULAR VOTE vs. ELECTORAL VOTE

In five elections in American history, the candidate who lost the popular vote won, or almost won, the presidential election.

DATE	CANDIDATES	PARTY	TOTAL POPULAR VOTE	TOTAL ELECTORAL VOTE
1824	John Quincy Adams*	Democratic-Republican	113,122	84
	Andrew Jackson	Democratic-Republican	151,271	99
	William H. Crawford	Democrat	40,876	41
	Henry Clay	Democrat	47,531	37
1876	Rutherford B. Hayes*	Republican	4,034,311	185
	Samuel Tilden	Democrat	4,288,546	184
1888	Benjamin Harrison*	Republican	5,443,892	233
	Grover Cleveland	Democrat	5,534,488	168
1960	John Kennedy*	Democrat	34,221,344	303
	Richard Nixon	Republican	34,106,671	219
1968	Richard Nixon*	Republican	31,785,148	301
	Hubert Humphrey	Democrat	31,274,503	191

* *winners of presidential elections*

Source: *The 1998 New York Times Almanac*

Ideas for Reform

A number of ideas for reforming the electoral college have been proposed over the years. Several plans would eliminate the problem of the winner-take-all system by awarding electoral votes on the basis of who won the popular vote in a particular congressional district or the share a candidate receives of a state's popular vote. Another possible solution is the elimination of the entire electoral college so that the people directly elect the President and the Vice President.

So why don't we throw the electoral college out? It's easier said than done. To change the system, an amendment supported by Congress and state legislatures would be necessary, and the constitutional amendment process is a difficult one. Probably the most compelling reason that we keep the electoral college system is that the country has had no significant problems with it in more than 100 years. As complex as it is, and as unfair as it might seem, it works fairly well. Since 1888, the person who has won the electoral vote has also won the popular vote.

e.g.

THE PRESIDENT'S INAUGURATION

At noon on January 20, following the November general election, the new—or re-elected—President takes office. Traditionally, an inaugural ceremony is held outside the Capitol. The President-elect takes the inaugural oath (as provided in Article II, Section 8), swearing to "faithfully execute the office of President of the United States," and "preserve, protect, and defend the Constitution of the United States."

After the oath, the President gives a speech, an Inaugural Address—sometimes short (the 135 words of George Washington in 1792), sometimes long (the 8,500 words of William Henry Harrison in 1841). Members of Congress, loyal supporters, other government leaders, and thousands of citizens attend the ceremony and festivities that follow, including a parade and elaborate evening parties. The inauguration brings to completion the long process of selecting a President, and it gives a new President a chance to express his hopes for his term in office.

PRESIDENTIAL SUCCESSION

The presidency may be vacated in any of four ways: death (either by assassination or natural causes), disability, resignation, or impeachment. Eight American Presidents have died in office, and one (Richard Nixon in 1974) has resigned. None has left office because of disability or after impeachment. The Constitution says little about the issue of **presidential succession,** stating

def·i·ni·tions

presidential succession—the specified procedure by which a vacancy in the presidency is filled.

186

only that "the powers and duties" of the office, not the office itself, would "devolve on the Vice President." The practice of the Vice President succeeding to the presidency began in 1841 (when John Tyler succeeded after William Henry Harrison's death) but was not officially added to the Constitution until the adoption of the 25ᵗʰ Amendment in 1967. The 1947 Presidential Succession Act established the line of succession after the Vice President: Speaker of the House, president *pro tempore* of the Senate, and then members of the President's **cabinet,** beginning with the secretary of state and according to the seniority of the department.

The 25ᵗʰ Amendment

Eight times in American history, the nation has had no Vice President, most recently when Lyndon Johnson became President after John Kennedy's assassination. Whatever the plan in place for presidential succession, some worried the nation was vulnerable without a Vice President. The 25ᵗʰ Amendment, ratified in 1967, addressed the problem of how to handle a vacancy in the vice presidency. Section 2 of the Amendment states that to fill a vacancy in the office of the Vice President, the President makes a nomination to Congress. After confirmation by a majority of both the House and the Senate, the nominated candidate shall take office.

The country didn't have to wait long for the 25ᵗʰ Amendment to be applied in a rather spectacular way. In 1973 Spiro Agnew resigned the office of Vice President after being charged with fraud during his previous position as Maryland's governor. (His case was later settled through plea bargain.) President Nixon appointed and Congress confirmed Gerald Ford as the new Vice President. The following year Nixon himself was forced to resign in the wake of the Watergate scandal, and Ford became President. Because the Vice President's position was again vacant, Ford appointed and Congress confirmed Nelson Rockefeller as Vice President. So for the only time in American history, both the President and Vice President were appointed figures, not elected to those offices.

What happens if the presidency and the vice presidency should be vacant at the same time? Only in that case does the 1947 Presidential Succession Act govern. The Speaker would become President, and the president *pro tempore* of the Senate would become Vice President. That's one reason the President and Vice President often travel in separate cars, and the Secret Service takes all kinds of precautions to keep them out of mutual danger.

def·i·ni·tions

cabinet—the group of persons, heading 14 executive departments, appointed by the President to act as official advisers and help establish policy.

Then and Now

VICE-PRESIDENTIAL VACANCIES

Eight times in American history, the United States has had no Vice President. When a vice president succeeded to the presidency, the country simply did without a Vice President until the next election.

1841–1845: John Tyler became President when William Henry Harrison died of pneumonia.

1850–1853: Millard Fillmore became President when Zachary Taylor died, probably from overeating or overheating at a July 4th picnic.

1865–1869: Andrew Johnson became President when Abraham Lincoln was assassinated by southern loyalist John Wilkes Booth.

1881–1885: Chester Arthur became President when James Garfield was assassinated in 1881 at a train station by a disgruntled campaign supporter.

1901–1905: Theodore Roosevelt became President when William McKinley was assassinated at the World's Fair in Buffalo, New York, by a man who hated capitalists.

1923–1925: Calvin Coolidge became President when Warren Harding died of a massive cerebral hemorrhage.

1945–1949: Harry Truman became President after Franklin Roosevelt died only weeks after his inauguration for a fourth term.

1963–1965: Lyndon Johnson became President when John Kennedy was assassinated in Dallas, Texas.

Presidential Disability

Besides the appointment of a Vice President, the 25th Amendment also addresses the problem of presidential disability. Up to then, neither the Constitution nor Congress specified what should happen if a President were to fall seriously ill and could not fulfill his duties. The situation has occurred on several occasions.

Two Presidents have been disabled for long periods of time. In 1881, James Garfield lay for 80 days before dying from an assassin's gunshot. He was seriously wounded, clearly unable to fulfill his duties, yet he was still the President. In 1919, Woodrow Wilson suffered a serious stroke that left him unable to speak or leave his bed for several months. His wife Edith took the responsibility of keeping him quiet and rested and began to make presidential decisions for him.

In the 1950s, Dwight Eisenhower suffered a massive heart attack that debilitated him for about 20 weeks. His assistants split his responsibilities among themselves, and his Vice President, Richard Nixon, filled in for him on ceremonial occasions. Eisenhower suffered two other shorter, less serious illnesses, but they were enough to frighten many people.

The 25th Amendment specifies a clear procedure to follow if a President can't perform his duties. The Vice President may serve as "acting President" under one of two conditions: if the President declares himself in writing to be unable to carry out his duties, or if the Vice President and a majority of the Congress decide that the President is incapacitated, even if the President disagrees. In such a case, a two-thirds majority of the Congress must confirm that the President is unable to serve. In either case, the President may resume his office by informing Congress that his illness is over. However, if the Vice President and a majority of the cabinet disagree, they can take the matter to Congress, which has 21 days in which to decide the issue. Unless Congress votes against the President by a two-thirds vote in each house, the President may reclaim his powers.

The issue of presidential disability arose twice during Ronald Reagan's presidency. In 1981, after Reagan was shot and wounded in an assassination attempt, he underwent emergency surgery before having time to sign over his powers to Vice President George Bush. He recovered quickly enough so that the Vice President and the cabinet did not have to ask for the transfer of powers. But for a short amount of time the President was unable to fulfill his duties. The disability provisions have officially come into effect only one time so far and then for only a few hours. On July 13, 1985, before President Reagan underwent surgery for a malignant tumor, he transferred the powers of the presidency to Vice President Bush for just under eight hours.

THE VICE PRESIDENCY

Did you ever hear of George Clinton, Daniel Tompkins, Richard M. Johnson, William R. King, William A. Wheeler, James S. Sherman, Thomas R. Marshall, or Henry A. Wallace? They were all Vice Presidents of the United States, yet their names are unfamiliar to most of us. On the other hand, you probably have heard of John Adams, Thomas Jefferson, Harry Truman, Richard Nixon, Lyndon Johnson, and George Bush. They also were Vice Presidents but then went on to become President. The two lists reflect something of the inconsistent expectations that go with the "second job" in the American national government.

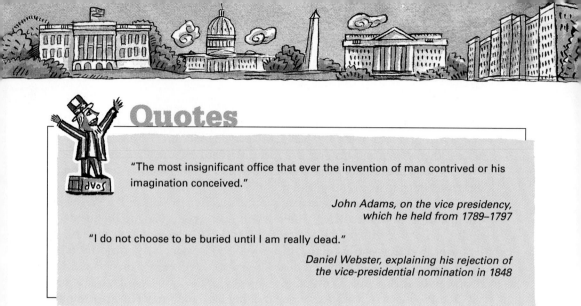

Quotes

"The most insignificant office that ever the invention of man contrived or his imagination conceived."

John Adams, on the vice presidency,
which he held from 1789–1797

"I do not choose to be buried until I am really dead."

Daniel Webster, explaining his rejection of
the vice-presidential nomination in 1848

The vice presidency has been viewed throughout American history with both disdain and respect because it is a rather peculiar position. The Vice President is always in the shadow of the President, with little real power in the **administration,** but merely one heartbeat away from the most powerful job on Earth.

1. Constitutional Duties

The writers of the Constitution paid little attention to the office of Vice President, assigning it only two formal duties.

★ The Vice President presides over the Senate (Article I, Section 3, Clause 4). Although the Vice President has this duty, he has no vote except to break a tie.

★ Under the 25th Amendment (Sections 3 and 4), the Vice President helps decide the question of presidential disability.

So far, since the Amendment was passed in 1967, the Vice President has never had to decide whether a President was unable to fulfill his duties. Nine times—because of death or resignation—a Vice President has had to take over the presidency. Despite the lack of specific powers given the Vice President by the Constitution, the position is clearly an important one.

2. The Role of the Vice President

What responsibilities and influence a Vice President has really depend upon the President. From the beginning, the President controls the Vice President by hand-picking him (or her—Geraldine Ferraro ran in 1984 as the only female vice-presidential candidate on a major party ticket in U.S. history).

def·i·ni·tions

administration—the people and organizations that make up the executive branch of a government.

The vice-presidential candidate traditionally has been chosen based on his or her ability to help the President win the election.

Beginning with Eisenhower, Presidents have given their Vice Presidents more responsibilities. Vice Presidents have headed commissions or organized major projects. For example, Al Gore, President Clinton's Vice President, led a national review of the federal bureaucracy and developed important suggestions for reorganizing the government. Often Vice Presidents go on goodwill missions abroad for the President or represent him at important international events. Today Vice Presidents are members of the National Security Council, a group of foreign policy and military advisers.

The real test of the role of a Vice President is whether or not the President regularly asks his advice and includes him in making decisions. That depends almost entirely upon the working relationship between the two people. President Carter often included Walter Mondale; President Reagan sometimes included George Bush; and President Clinton has generally included Al Gore as an important adviser. The 22nd and 25th Amendments have clarified and formalized the Vice President's power of succession, but the general duties of the Vice President are still subject to the goodwill and mood of the President.

Presidential Powers and Leadership

When the Founders created the presidency, they feared more than anything a monarchy, a government like that in England in which the king had all the power. That's why they created the two-house Congress, whose members are elected to represent the states and their citizens. But the Founders discovered that the country still needed a leader, someone who was responsible for the big picture, not just one state or district. So they provided for an executive branch with a President whose powers were much more restricted than those exercised by modern Presidents.

Quote

"No one who has not had the responsibility can really understand what it [the presidency] is like . . . not even his closest aides or members of his immediate family."

Harry Truman, President of the United States (1945–1953)

PRESIDENTS AND THE PRESIDENCY

PRESIDENTS OF THE UNITED STATES

PRESIDENT	IN OFFICE	AGE TAKING OFFICE	PARTY	PLACE OF BIRTH
George Washington (1732–1799)	1789–1797	57	None	Virginia
John Adams (1735–1826)	1797–1801	61	Federalist	Massachusetts
Thomas Jefferson (1743–1826)	1801–1809	58	Dem–Rep*	Virginia
James Madison (1751–1836)	1809–1817	58	Dem–Rep*	Virginia
James Monroe (1758–1831)	1817–1825	59	Dem–Rep*	Virginia
John Quincy Adams (1767–1848)	1825–1829	58	Dem–Rep*	Massachusetts
Andrew Jackson (1767–1848)	1829–1837	62	Democratic	South Carolina
Martin Van Buren (1782–1862)	1837–1841	55	Democratic	New York
William H. Harrison (1773–1841)	1841	68	Whig	Virginia
John Tyler (1790–1862)	1841–1845	51	Whig	Virginia
James K. Polk (1795–1849)	1845–1849	50	Democratic	North Carolina
Zachary Taylor (1784–1850)	1849–1850	65	Whig	Virginia
Millard Fillmore (1800–1874)	1850–1853	50	Whig	New York
Franklin Pierce (1804–1869)	1853–1857	48	Democratic	New Hampshire
James Buchanan (1791–1868)	1857–1861	65	Democratic	Pennsylvania
Abraham Lincoln (1809–1865)	1861–1865	52	Republican	Kentucky
Andrew Johnson (1808–1875)	1865–1869	57	Democratic	North Carolina
Ulysses S. Grant (1822–1885)	1869–1877	47	Republican	Ohio
Rutherford B. Hayes (1822–1893)	1877–1881	55	Republican	Ohio
James A. Garfield (1831–1881)	1881	50	Republican	Ohio
Chester A. Arthur (1830–1886)	1881–1885	51	Republican	Vermont
Grover Cleveland (1837–1908)	1885–1889	48	Democratic	New Jersey
Benjamin Harrison (1833–1901)	1889–1893	56	Republican	Ohio
Grover Cleveland (1837–1908)	1893–1897	56	Democratic	New Jersey
William McKinley (1843–1901)	1897–1901	54	Republican	Ohio
Theodore Roosevelt (1858–1919)	1901–1909	52	Republican	New York
William H. Taft (1857–1930)	1909–1913	52	Republican	Ohio
Woodrow Wilson (1856–1924)	1913–1921	56	Democratic	Virginia
Warren G. Harding (1865–1923)	1921–1923	56	Republican	Ohio
Calvin Coolidge (1872–1933)	1923–1929	51	Republican	Vermont
Herbert C. Hoover (1874–1964)	1929–1933	55	Republican	Iowa
Franklin D. Roosevelt (1882–1945)	1933–1945	50	Democratic	New York
Harry S Truman (1884–1972)	1945–1953	61	Democratic	Missouri
Dwight D. Eisenhower (1890–1969)	1953–1961	63	Republican	Texas
John F. Kennedy (1917–1963)	1961–1963	43	Democratic	Massachusetts
Lyndon B. Johnson (1908–1973)	1963–1969	55	Democratic	Texas
Richard M. Nixon (1913–1994)	1969–1974	56	Republican	California
Gerald R. Ford (1913–)	1974–1977	61	Republican	Nebraska
James E. Carter (1924–)	1977–1981	52	Democratic	Georgia
Ronald W. Reagan (1911–)	1981–1989	69	Republican	Illinois
George H. W. Bush (1924–)	1989–1993	64	Republican	Massachusetts
William J. Clinton (1946–)	1993–	46	Democratic	Arkansas

*Democratic–Republican

NATIONALITY	RELIGION	PREVIOUS OCCUPATION	VICE PRESIDENT
English	Episcopalian	Farmer, Soldier	John Adams
English	Unitarian	Lawyer, Diplomat	Thomas Jefferson
Welsh	—	Farmer, Lawyer	Aaron Burr, George Clinton
English	Episcopalian	Lawyer	George Clinton, Elbridge Gerry
Scotch	Episcopalian	Lawyer	Daniel D. Tompkins
English	Unitarian	Lawyer, Diplomat	John C. Calhoun
Scotch-Irish	Presbyterian	Lawyer, Soldier	John C. Calhoun, Martin Van Buren
Dutch	Dutch Reformed	Lawyer	Richard M. Johnson
English	Episcopalian	Soldier, Farmer	John Tyler
English	Episcopalian	Lawyer	None
Scotch-Irish	Presbyterian	Lawyer	George M. Dallas
English	Episcopalian	Soldier	Millard Fillmore
English	Unitarian	Lawyer, Teacher	None
English	Episcopalian	Lawyer	William R. King
Scotch-Irish	Presbyterian	Lawyer, Diplomat	John C. Breckenridge
English	—	Lawyer	Hannibal Hamlin, Andrew Johnson
English	Methodist	Tailor	None
English, Scotch	Methodist	Soldier	Schuyler Colfax, Henry Wilson
Scotch	Methodist	Lawyer	William A. Wheeler
English	Disciples of Christ	Teacher, Lawyer	Chester A. Arthur
Scotch-Irish	Episcopalian	Lawyer, Teacher	None
English-Irish	Presbyterian	Lawyer	Thomas A. Hendricks
English	Presbyterian	Lawyer, Soldier	Levi P. Morton
English-Irish	Presbyterian	Lawyer	Adlai E. Stevenson
Scotch-Irish	Methodist	Lawyer, Teacher	Garrett A. Hobart, Theodore Roosevelt
Dutch	Dutch Reformed	Rancher, Soldier, Writer	Charles W. Fairbanks
English	Unitarian	Lawyer	James S. Sherman
Scotch-Irish	Presbyterian	Teacher	Thomas R. Marshall
English	Baptist	Editor	Calvin Coolidge
English	Congregational	Lawyer	Charles G. Dawes
Swiss-German	Quaker	Engineer	Charles Curtis
Dutch	Episcopalian	Lawyer	John Nance Garner, Henry Wallace, Harry S Truman
English, Scotch	Baptist	Farmer, Haberdasher	Alben W. Barkley
Swiss-German	Presbyterian	Soldier	Richard M. Nixon
Irish	Roman Catholic	Writer	Lyndon B. Johnson
English	Disciples of Christ	Teacher	Hubert H. Humphrey
Eng., Scotch-Irish	Quaker	Lawyer	Spiro T. Agnew, Gerald R. Ford
English	Episcopalian	Lawyer	Nelson A. Rockefeller
English	Baptist	Farmer, Businessman	Walter F. Mondale
Eng., Scotch-Irish	Disciples of Christ	Actor, Union leader	George Bush
English	Episcopalian	Businessman	James Danforth Quayle
English	Baptist	Lawyer	Albert A. Gore

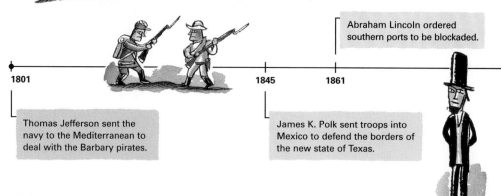

CONSTITUTIONAL POWERS

Article II of the Constitution contains the very important blueprint that has defined the presidency for more than 200 years. The powers it grants the President are, however, only vaguely described. While the beginning of Article II grants "executive power" to the President, the power itself is not defined. Like the Elastic Clause, the phrase in Section 3 stating that the President should "take care that all the laws be faithfully executed. . . ." has been stretched considerably as the justification for strengthening the power of the presidency.

1. Military Powers

The Constitution makes the President, a civilian, the commander in chief of the armed services. The Founders saw the importance of a centralized military to keep law and order and to defend the country from outside attack. However, they were cautious about the military becoming too powerful. The President, not a military general, was put in charge. To ensure that he did not have too much military power, Congress was given the power to authorize money for military forces.

Even though the Constitution splits control of the military between the President and Congress, during nearly every war in United States history the President has held more power than Congress. Presidents, such as Lincoln in the Civil War and Franklin Roosevelt in World War II, have made decisions about war policies and tactics, and Congress has usually funded the President's decisions.

Timeline

PRESIDENTS AND MILITARY ACTIONS

Notice that in each of the following cases a dangerous situation required a quick reaction from a chief executive, not from a deliberative body such as Congress.

Abraham Lincoln ordered southern ports to be blockaded.

1801

1845

1861

Thomas Jefferson sent the navy to the Mediterranean to deal with the Barbary pirates.

James K. Polk sent troops into Mexico to defend the borders of the new state of Texas.

THE WAR POWERS ACT

The President's role as commander in chief of the armed services seldom has been as controversial as during the Vietnam War. In response to a crisis, President Lyndon Johnson asked Congress for a resolution giving him power "to take all necessary measures to repel any armed attack against forces of the United States." Congress passed the Gulf of Tonkin Resolution, giving Johnson a "blank check." As a result, he dramatically stepped up the war. In 1973, after the United States finally ended its involvement in Vietnam, Congress overturned its 1964 action with the **War Powers Act.**

The War Powers Act, passed over President Nixon's veto, restricted the President's powers considerably. It requires him to report in writing to Congress within 48 hours after he places U.S. troops in trouble spots. Congress then must authorize the action within 60 days. If Congress does not authorize the action, the President must withdraw the troops. Congress may also pass a concurrent resolution (which the President may not veto) directing the removal of troops.

The power to pass a concurrent resolution nullifying a presidential action has been challenged. The Supreme Court's decision in *Immigration and Naturalization Service v. Chadha* (1983) declared unconstitutional a **legislative veto,** in which Congress writes laws that allow it to review and cancel actions of executive agencies. The Court ruled that the legislative veto violates the independent actions guaranteed the executive branch. Other parts of the War Powers Act have not yet been tested in court.

def·i·ni·tions

legislative veto—the powers of Congress to void an action of the executive branch.

War Powers Act—the law, passed in 1973, that restricts the President's use of U.S. combat troops abroad and authorizes Congress to order troops home.

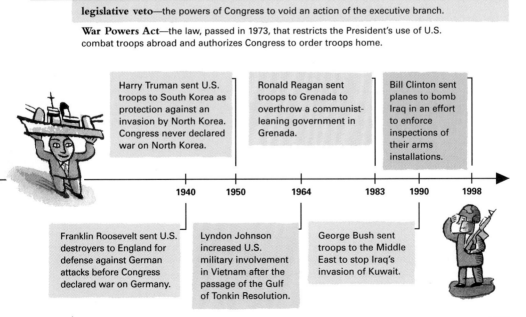

Harry Truman sent U.S. troops to South Korea as protection against an invasion by North Korea. Congress never declared war on North Korea.

Ronald Reagan sent troops to Grenada to overthrow a communist-leaning government in Grenada.

Bill Clinton sent planes to bomb Iraq in an effort to enforce inspections of their arms installations.

1940   1950   1964   1983   1990   1998

Franklin Roosevelt sent U.S. destroyers to England for defense against German attacks before Congress declared war on Germany.

Lyndon Johnson increased U.S. military involvement in Vietnam after the passage of the Gulf of Tonkin Resolution.

George Bush sent troops to the Middle East to stop Iraq's invasion of Kuwait.

2. Diplomatic Powers

The Constitution grants the President many diplomatic powers. The President is the chief negotiator with foreign nations, but the Senate must confirm all **treaties** by a two-thirds vote of approval. Treaties have the same legal standing as do acts passed by Congress. Because the Constitution includes treaties as part of the "supreme law of the land," logically, then, treaties—like laws—need congressional approval.

Executive agreements are pacts between heads of state, but they do not have the formal status of treaties. Most executive agreements involve routine matters and flow out of legislation passed by Congress or from treaties that the Senate has confirmed. Dozens of executive agreements are made each year. Some Presidents have kept executive agreements secret, even though Congress passed a law in 1950 that required them to be public. Presidents have tended to ignore the law, most notoriously during the Vietnam War. The "Pentagon Papers" scandal revealed several important executive agreements pledging American military support to South Vietnam and other countries of Southeast Asia.

Then and Now

THE DESTROYER DEAL

A very famous executive agreement between Franklin Roosevelt and Winston Churchill in 1940 had far-reaching consequences. The "Destroyer Deal" gave the British 50 older U.S. destroyers in return for 99-year leases to British island bases in the Atlantic Ocean. World War II was raging in Europe, but the United States had not yet joined the war. American destroyers helped the British protect themselves from German attack. The U.S. interest in island bases in the Atlantic to fortify U.S. defenses signaled to Germany that America was not truly neutral in the war. Since U.S. involvement in the war was still controversial, Roosevelt hardly would have wanted to subject the arrangement to Senate approval. Instead, he used an executive agreement.

def·i·ni·tions

treaty—a formal agreement between two or more sovereign nation-states.

executive agreement—a presidential agreement, not requiring the Senate's approval, with another head of state.

The Constitution also gives Congress the exclusive authority to set tariffs and enact other legislation governing international trade. The Founders did not want the President's power to go unchecked, as it was in European countries where kings had control of foreign policy. A short phrase in the Constitution, that the President "shall receive ambassadors and other public ministers" (Article II, Section 3), provides the basis for the President's role as head of state. As chief diplomat, the President recognizes new nations, represents the United States to other countries, and performs related ceremonial duties. The President is given the exclusive right to recognize foreign governments, but his negotiation powers are shared with other executives and Congress.

Headlines

"FAST TRACK"

Presidents have often tried to increase their control of trade agreements with other countries. In 1997, President Bill Clinton tried to speed up congressional consideration of trade agreements through "fast track," a procedure that earlier Presidents had had the authority to use. He believed that the Senate was hampering his ability to negotiate effective treaties because it often amended trade agreements. According to President Clinton, countries often were not willing to negotiate seriously with the United States because the Senate changed the rules after the agreement was made with the President. Under his proposed fast track, Congress would vote, within a fixed period of time, on an agreement without reopening any of its provisions. Fast track died, however, because the President could not get enough support, even from his own party members in Congress.

The President's negotiating powers have increased through the years, but the constitutional limitation on the President has had its price. At the Versailles Conference following World War I, President Woodrow Wilson was the only leader present who did not have the power to sign the treaty to end the war. He had to get consent from the Senate, who refused to confirm the peace treaty. As a result, the United States never joined the League of Nations, dooming the peace-keeping organization from the start. Controversial treaties, such as the Versailles Treaty, can cause gridlock, or a tug of war between the President and Congress, that can bring progress to a halt.

3. Executive Powers

As chief executive of the national government, the President executes, or administers, the decisions the houses make and enforces the laws they pass. He oversees how all federal law is carried out. To help him do this, the President has the power to issue **executive orders,** or rules and regulations that have the effect of law. The President also has the power to appoint other public officers and justices of the Supreme Court, but again, only with the approval of the Senate. Other powerful positions may be appointed by the President alone, but the positions themselves are created or removed by the Senate. The President may remove individuals at will from most appointed positions, but some major public officers, such as Supreme Court and other federal judges, can be removed only by impeachment.

PRESIDENTIAL APPOINTMENTS

One exception to the general trend of increasing presidential powers is the tendency in recent years for the Senate to question presidential appointments. Most presidential appointments still are approved by the Senate, but some appointees in recent well-publicized cases have been challenged. In 1987, the Senate refused to confirm Robert Bork's nomination to the Supreme Court, and in 1991 the Senate only narrowly confirmed Clarence Thomas. Several nominees to cabinet positions have been withdrawn from consideration when their personal lives were scrutinized. For example, President Clinton withdrew Zoe Baird's nomination for assistant attorney general when Congress questioned whether or not she reported to the Internal Revenue Service paying a salary to her children's nanny (the "Nanny-gate Scandal").

PRESIDENTIAL PARDONS

As chief executive, the President may grant **reprieves** and **pardons** for federal crimes. (Governors grant reprieves and pardons for people convicted in state courts.) The President's power is absolute in these matters, except in cases of impeachment. Presidents usually grant pardons to people after they have been convicted of a crime in federal court. A famous exception to this rule occurred in 1974 when President Gerald Ford granted former President Richard Nixon a pardon for any crimes connected to the Watergate scandal

def·i·ni·tions

executive order—a presidential directive to an agency that defines new policies or carries out existing laws.

reprieve—the postponement or setting aside of punishment.

pardon—the exemption of a convicted person from the penalties of a crime or offense.

198

before any court charged Nixon with a crime. Ford's action was so controversial that many observers believe that the pardon was the single most
important reason Ford lost the presidential election of 1976. Some critics
believe that Nixon's acceptance of the pardon was an admission of guilt,
and Ford was accused of allowing Nixon special privileges he did not
deserve. The President's pardoning powers also include the power to grant
amnesty, a general pardon offered to a group of citizens. For example, in
the 1970s Presidents Ford and Carter offered amnesty to Vietnam War draft
evaders, allowing a number of citizens to return from Canada and other
countries to the United States without danger of arrest.

4. Legislative Powers

The Constitution gives the President a limited number of legislative powers
that allow him to influence the actions of Congress. For instance, the President
may call Congress into special session to deal with an important, immediate
issue and may adjourn Congress if the two houses cannot agree on a date for
adjournment—a situation that has yet to happen. The Constitution requires
the President to deliver a State of the Union message "from time to time"
(Article II, Section 3). By tradition, soon after the beginning of each congressional session, the President calls together both houses, his cabinet, and the
Supreme Court to listen to his address, which calls on Congress to pass
legislation supporting his programs.

VETO POWER

If a President disapproves of a bill passed by Congress, he may veto the
bill by refusing to sign it. Along with the veto he may send a veto message
to Congress within ten days. If the bill is passed within ten days of the
adjournment of Congress, the President simply may ignore it through a
pocket veto, and the bill will die. A presidential veto may be overridden
by a two-thirds vote of both houses, but Congress rarely has the votes to
override, so the veto is a substantial presidential power.

In 1996, Congress passed the Line-Item Veto Act, which allows the President
to veto only sections of an appropriations bill ("items of new direct spending").
President Clinton exercised the new **line-item veto** on sections of the Balanced
Budget Act and the Taxpayer Relief Act. However, both the "actions of the
Congress that passed it and the President who signed it into law" were found to
be unconstitutional by the Supreme Court in *Clinton v. City of New York* (1998).
The Court argued that the line-item veto permits the President to construct
legislation, which is an abuse of the principle of separation of powers.

---

amnesty—the government's general pardon given to people who have broken the law.

line-item veto—an executive's power to reject part of a bill while approving the rest.

PRESIDENTIAL VETO POWER

PRESIDENT	REGULAR VETOES	POCKET VETOES	TOTAL	VETOES OVERRIDDEN
Washington (1789–1797)	2	—	2	—
Madison (1809–1817)	5	2	7	—
Monroe (1817–1825)	1	—	1	
Jackson (1829–1837)	5	7	12	—
Van Buren (1837–1841)	—	1	1	—
Tyler (1841–1845)	6	4	10	1
Polk (1845–1849)	2	1	3	—
Pierce (1853–1857)	9	—	9	5
Buchanan (1857–1861)	4	3	7	—
Lincoln (1861–1865)	2	5	7	—
Johnson (1865–1869)	21	8	29	15
Grant (1869–1877)	45	48	93	4
Hayes (1877–1881)	12	1	13	1
Arthur (1881–1885)	4	8	12	1
Cleveland (1885–1889)	304	110	414	2
Harrison (1889–1893)	19	25	44	1
Cleveland (1893–1897)	42	128	170	5
McKinley (1897–1901)	6	36	42	—
Roosevelt (1901–1909)	42	40	82	1
Taft (1909–1913)	30	9	39	1
Wilson (1913–1921)	33	11	44	6
Harding (1921–1923)	5	1	6	—
Coolidge (1923–1929)	20	30	50	4
Hoover (1929–1933)	21	16	37	3
Roosevelt (1933–1945)	372	263	635	9
Truman (1945–1953)	180	70	250	12
Eisenhower (1953–1961)	73	108	181	2
Kennedy (1961–1963)	12	9	21	—

CONTINUED

PRESIDENTIAL VETOES CONTINUED

PRESIDENT	REGULAR VETOES	POCKET VETOES	TOTAL	VETOES OVERRIDDEN
Johnson (1963–1969)	16	14	30	—
Nixon (1969–1974)	26	17	43	7
Ford (1974–1977)	48	18	66	12
Carter (1977–1981)	13	18	31	2
Reagan (1981–1989)	39	39	78	9
Bush (1989–1993)	29	15	46	1
Clinton (1993–1997)	17	0	17	2
	1,465	1,181	2,646	106

Presidents who are not listed
vetoed no measures.

Source: U.S. Senate Library

EVOLUTIONARY POWERS

According to nineteenth-century historian Henry Adams, "The American President resembles a commander of a ship at sea. He must have a helm to grasp, a course to steer, a port to seek." The Founders had no crystal ball to gaze into the future to see what history would demand of the President. To help the President have "a helm to grasp," leadership responsibilities that are not spelled out in the Constitution have evolved through history and are now accepted as rightful presidential powers. Even though his power is checked by the other branches, the President is still the nation's most visible leader. He has come to be not only the chief of his own political party but the chief citizen of the entire country, the representative of all the people. Among the many factors that have led to the strengthening of the presidency, four stand out: the power of economic planning, the power of executive privilege, the power of impoundment, and the power of persuasion.

1. The Power of Economic Planning

A very important evolutionary power of the President is that of chief economic planner. Franklin Roosevelt assumed that role during the Great Depression. Congress followed Roosevelt's lead in developing economic programs to help the country out of the economic crisis. The Employment Act of 1946 significantly strengthened this role by directing the President to submit an annual economic report to Congress. It created a Council of Economic Advisers to study and prepare reports on the economy for the President. It also declared for the first time that the federal government has the responsibility to promote employment of workers, encourage productivity of factories and businesses, and increase purchasing power for the consumer.

The President's powers were increased further during a serious recession in the early 1970s. Then Congress granted President Nixon power to control prices and wages. Even though the law had a time limit that expired and was not renewed, it allowed Nixon to freeze wages, rents, and prices for a 90-day period. Presidents have also increased their role as economic planners by taking a lead in preparing the federal budget every year.

The President also appoints the chairman and members of the Federal Reserve Board. Although the Board operates fairly independently, the President's appointments shape the country's monetary policy.

2. The Power of Executive Privilege

Executive privilege was not mentioned in the Constitution, but Presidents have claimed it for more than 200 years. This right of the President to confidentiality and to refuse to testify before or provide information to Congress or a court rests on the principle of separation of powers. Executive privilege has evolved from Presidents' claims that the advice they get and the private discussions they have in the Oval Office should not always be made public. Presidents believed that breaking confidentiality could lead to breaches of national security.

No one questioned executive privilege until 1974 when the Watergate scandal led to a major Supreme Court decision. Richard Nixon had secretly taped conversations with top aides about the Watergate cover-up. When a federal court ordered him to surrender the tapes, Nixon refused, claiming executive privilege. In *United States v. Nixon* (1974), the Court ruled that Nixon had to surrender the tapes, but it did not declare executive privilege unconstitutional. Instead, it held that since the privilege "relates to the effective discharge of a President's powers, it is constitutionally based." However, the Court further ruled that there is no

def·i·ni·tions

executive privilege—the President's right to withhold information from or refuse to testify before Congress or the courts.

"absolute unqualified Presidential privilege of immunity from judicial process under all circumstances." Presidents still may claim executive privilege, and advisers may continue to give private counsel. But neither the President nor his advisers may block a federal court from deciding criminal cases.

The decision in *United States v. Nixon* (1974) led to *Nixon v. Fitzgerald* (1982), in which the Supreme Court ruled that a President cannot be sued for damages related to official decisions he makes while in office. In 1997, President Clinton's lawyers used the 1982 decision to argue that a President is entitled to a reprieve from all civil suits while in office. The President was sued by Paula Jones, a former Arkansas state employee, for sexual harassment while Clinton was governor of Arkansas. Clinton's advisers argued that allowing civil suits against a chief executive would mean major distractions since he would have to spend time defending himself instead of performing his official duties. In *Clinton v. Jones* (1997), the Supreme Court unanimously rejected Clinton's argument.

In 1998, a U.S. Court of Appeals decided that Clinton did not have attorney-client privileges with government lawyers. The ruling stated that executive privilege does not apply in cases of criminal investigation, such as that conducted by independent prosecutor Kenneth Starr. The Supreme Court further ruled that the President could not claim executive privilege by barring from investigation the testimony of Secret Service agents. The rulings in these cases, which further restricted the President's use of executive privilege, allowed Starr to continue his investigation of President Clinton.

3. The Power of Impoundment

The Constitution did not address the issue of **impoundment.** Although the Founders didn't anticipate this practice, Presidents figured out almost from the beginning that they could assert their disapproval of a congressional action by refusing to execute it. Suppose that Congress passed a bill that provided for the building of new federal highways. What if the President didn't want to veto such a bill but was horrified by the amount of money Congress appropriated to it? When the appropriation got to the Department of Transportation, the President could simply refuse to approve execution of the project. Congress could then do nothing to force the President to spend the money.

The impoundment issue erupted during the presidency of Richard Nixon. The Democratic Congress appropriated money for programs that the Republican Nixon did not approve of, so he impounded the funds. Congress reacted with the Budget Reform Act of 1974. This act requires the President

def·i·ni·tions

impoundment—a President's refusal to spend money that Congress has appropriated.

to spend all appropriated funds, unless he gets approval from Congress to delay the spending. In other words, the President has to spend money that Congress has appropriated. Some critics complain that such a rule is unconstitutional because it keeps the President from exercising his power to check and balance Congress.

4. The Power of Persuasion

The Constitution clearly gives more explicit powers to the legislative branch than to the executive, but the President has one clear advantage. There is only one of him. Congress speaks with 535 voices, but the President with only one. This simple fact allows an articulate President to exercise his power of persuasion to set important agendas for the nation. He can meet with leaders of Congress regarding important legislation and convince them to go along with his point of view. He can also call members of Congress on the phone—members who are often flattered to be contacted personally by the President. The President also has the power to appeal to the real bosses—the American public—through public appearances, press conferences, and presidential addresses. Even though Presidents may have always understood the power of persuasion, its potential has been magnified in recent years by effective use of radio and television.

Savvy Presidents use many forms of mass media to communicate—to other officials in Washington, D.C., to party leaders and officials throughout the United States, and to the American public. Presidents have several ways to shape their images and communicate persuasively:

★ **NEWS RELEASES AND BRIEFINGS** A news release is prepared by the White House to call attention to a recent or pending presidential action or policy. A briefing allows the President or his press secretary to make announcements and gives reporters a chance to ask questions about news releases.

★ **PRESS CONFERENCES** The President announces ahead of time that he will meet with members of the press, who may ask questions regarding almost anything they like. The press conference is the perfect way for a President to get media attention to help build **bipartisan** public support for policies. On the other hand, a President may look foolish in a press conference if the questions stir up controversial issues or if his answers seem inadequate or evasive.

def·i·ni·tions
_____
bipartisan—made up of members of both political parties.

Then and Now

THE FIRST TELEVISED PRESIDENTIAL DEBATE

In the election of 1960, when John Kennedy, the Democratic candidate, faced Republican Richard Nixon in the first-ever televised presidential debate, the camera almost certainly made a difference in the public's perception of the two men. In the days preceding the debate, Kennedy spent his time reviewing and rehearsing as he relaxed by the swimming pool at the Kennedy compound in Florida. While preparing for the debate, he used a product called Man-Tan that reputedly enhanced a natural tan. Nixon, on the other hand, was maintaining a grueling campaign schedule, fulfilling his promise to visit all 48 contiguous states. On the day of the debate, Nixon looked thin and tired. The only enhancing product Nixon used was Burma Shave, an old-fashioned shaving cream. It failed to cover up a dark shadow that made him look as if he had not shaved at all. Kennedy's advisers knew that black-and-white television made white shirts look yellow; Nixon's did not. So, a rested, tanned Kennedy, dressed in a blue shirt, out-debated a tired, sick, Burma-Shaved Nixon who was dressed in a baggy white shirt. Kennedy won the election, and the age of television politics was off and running.

★ **PHOTO-OPS AND MEDIA EVENTS** Photographs certainly convey important messages both in print and television. The President is by far the most photographed person in the country, and a good photo can convey a message to the public more effectively than does a speech. Through carefully planned media events, Presidents can communicate their ideas as well as enhance or shape their images.

★ **SOUND BITES** A President must consider the importance of **sound bites,** or short video clips, any time he wants to get a message to the public through the media. Over the years, evening newscasts have shortened the average sound bite from about 42 seconds in 1968 to less than 10 seconds today. As a result, short, catchy phrases are just as important as well-constructed speeches, and a President must tailor his speeches and activities to suit the medium.

★ **BACKGROUNDERS AND LEAKS** The President may give reporters important information called backgrounders to test ideas or send unofficial messages to Congress or to foreign countries. For example, President Reagan once sent a not-too-subtle message to the Soviet Union when he called it an

---

sound bite—a short statement used on a radio or television news broadcast.

"evil empire." The message was given to the press, not officially or directly to the Soviet Union, but Brezhnev (the Soviet leader) got the point. Leaks can't always be traced to the President because they are given anonymously, but recent Presidents have been known to plant them.

e.g.

THE PRESIDENT IN THE MOVIES

Just as a skillful President can manipulate the media, sometimes the media can shape the public's image of the President. Consider the images of the President in these 1990s movies:

1993: *DAVE*

Actor Kevin Kline played an affable, gentle presidential look-alike who filled in when the real President was felled by a stroke.

1995: *THE AMERICAN PRESIDENT*

Michael Douglas depicted a widowed President as a handsome heartthrob who fell in love with a beautiful lobbyist.

1997: *ABSOLUTE POWER*

Gene Hackman portrayed a drunken President whose affair with a married woman caused a massive cover-up.

1997: *AIR FORCE ONE*

Harrison Ford played an action-hero President, an ex-Vietnam helicopter pilot, who knew how to fight and outsmart the enemy. When *Air Force One* was hijacked, Ford shot, kicked, and wrestled his way to a dramatic rescue of his family.

1997: *WAG THE DOG*

Dustin Hoffman and Robert Duvall advised an off-screen President who went to great lengths to cover up a romantic affair. The movie was an eery precursor to the Clinton-Lewinsky affair that came to light about the time the film was released.

1998: *PRIMARY COLORS*

John Travolta portrayed a complex presidential candidate (modeled after Bill Clinton), capable of great empathy and understanding but deeply flawed by political ambition.

PRESIDENTIAL LEADERSHIP AND STYLE

The Constitution outlines the qualifications, powers, selection and succession processes, and terms of the presidency. But it says nothing about the personal background, attitudes toward power, or personality traits that make up presidential style. Each person who has held the office has brought to it a style of his own. The frequency of his public appearances, his relationship with the media, the degree to which he isolates himself, the activities of the First Lady—all these contribute to the public's perception of the President's style as a national leader. During some administrations, the atmosphere of the White House has been restrained and quiet. At other times, life in the White House was more informal and lively. During the term of Theodore Roosevelt, for instance, the Roosevelt children often slid down stairways, bicycled and skated on polished floors, and once even took their pony upstairs on the President's private elevator.

e.g.

FIRST LADIES

Americans always have been fascinated with the First Lady, who is usually the wife of the President. Her influence most often has been informal, but her importance varies with the individual and appears to be changing along with general trends in American society.

1. **HOSTESS** Part of the President's job involves greeting, honoring, and entertaining foreign dignitaries, members of Congress, government officials in the executive and judicial branches, and other people from outside government. Traditionally, the First Lady has taken a major responsibility in organizing such events. For example, the relationships that the shy James Madison had with his work associates almost certainly were enhanced by his vivacious wife Dolley, who was renowned for the White House events she hostessed. Jacqueline Kennedy played a major role in defining the elegance and style associated with the presidency of John Kennedy in the early 1960s.

2. **ADVISER** Even though the First Lady has no official capacity as adviser to the President, perceptive staff members—and a little later, the American public—have recognized that the President's wife sometimes influences her husband's decisions and image. From Abigail Adams to Rosalyn Carter and Nancy Reagan, First Ladies often wield considerable power.

CONTINUED

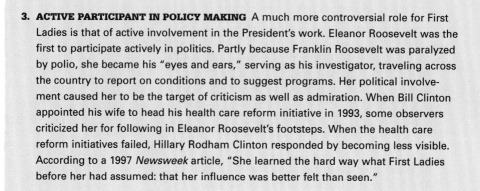

3. **ACTIVE PARTICIPANT IN POLICY MAKING** A much more controversial role for First Ladies is that of active involvement in the President's work. Eleanor Roosevelt was the first to participate actively in politics. Partly because Franklin Roosevelt was paralyzed by polio, she became his "eyes and ears," serving as his investigator, traveling across the country to report on conditions and to suggest programs. Her political involvement caused her to be the target of criticism as well as admiration. When Bill Clinton appointed his wife to head his health care reform initiative in 1993, some observers criticized her for following in Eleanor Roosevelt's footsteps. When the health care reform initiatives failed, Hillary Rodham Clinton responded by becoming less visible. According to a 1997 *Newsweek* article, "She learned the hard way what First Ladies before her had assumed: that her influence was better felt than seen."

Rating the Presidents

Recognizing differences in presidential styles can help explain why some Presidents are more popular with the public and why some seem to use their powers more effectively than others. History's judgment of presidential greatness is not necessarily reflected in presidential popularity polls.

Presidential greatness has long been a favorite topic of conversation. The game of rating the Presidents is played by ordinary Americans as well as scholars and media pundits. Harvard professor Arthur M. Schlesinger started the modern version of the game in 1948 when he invited 55 other historians to rate the Presidents up to that time. Lincoln, Washington, Franklin Roosevelt, Wilson, and Jefferson topped the list in that order. Since then, historians and political scientists have taken similar surveys. Although the results vary—and change somewhat through the years—some consistent patterns have emerged.

Abraham Lincoln, George Washington, and Franklin Roosevelt are always at the top. Thomas Jefferson, Andrew Jackson, James Polk, Theodore Roosevelt, Woodrow Wilson, and Harry Truman follow, but in varying order. Usually placed near the bottom are James Buchanan, Franklin Pierce, Millard Fillmore, Zachary Taylor, Calvin Coolidge, and Richard Nixon. Finally, Andrew Johnson, Ulysses S. Grant, and Warren Harding are usually rated as failures. It is worth noting that while a national crisis—such as a war or major economic depression—may provide an opportunity for greatness, it does not necessarily make the man.

Quote

"I do not believe that any man can lead who does not act . . . under the impulse of a profound sympathy with those whom he leads."

Woodrow Wilson, President of the United States (1913–1921)

Leadership Qualities

Great Presidents seem to have several leadership qualities in common.

★ Strong vision of an ideal America communicated clearly in both speeches and governmental actions

★ Good ability to see their own times in the context of what has happened in the past

★ Effective communication skills, and especially the ability to convince Congress and the electorate of the rightness of their course

★ Political courage to make decisions they know will be unpopular with voters

The modern President is a visible leader. The presidency has evolved into the most visible and powerful position in the world today. Even so, its development is firmly rooted in a fundamental constitutional principle that continues to guide our country: leadership within a system of checks and balances, always complex, not always efficient, and never easy.

The powers and responsibilities of the American presidency almost certainly would surprise the Founders. Today policy is made through the complex workings between Congress and the President. Added to that are a powerful judiciary, executive branch officials, and a bureaucracy not even mentioned in the Constitution. The presidency has become an immensely powerful, yet carefully watched and checked office.

The Executive Branch and the Bureaucracy

Many people think of the government as a remote, gigantic organization that never touches their own lives. If you agree, think again. In fact, just think about what you do almost every day. The radio station you like to listen to is licensed to operate by the Federal Communications Commission. The cereal you had for breakfast passed inspection by the Food and Drug Administration, and the processed meat in your sandwich at lunch was packed under the supervision of the Food Safety and Inspection Service of the U.S. Department of Agriculture. The cost of mailing your letters is determined by the U.S. Postal Service. You probably don't think about any of these federal bureaucracies, but they influence your daily life in many ways.

The bureaucracy, a complex web of people, procedures, departments, and agencies—not mentioned in the Constitution—has been created to make government decisions. As these people carry out broad policies, they have tremendous power. Their decisions can make or break programs supported by Congress and agendas set by the President.

In this chapter . . .

The Federal Bureaucracy

The combination of people, procedures, and agencies through which the federal government operates makes up the federal **bureaucracy.** About 100 years ago, Europeans first began to use the term *bureaucracy* to refer to a system of organization. Today we use the word to describe a complex system of organization, with power usually flowing from the top down. For many Americans the word *bureaucracy* brings up negative images of big government and its red tape, endless rules and regulations, waste, and inefficiency. However, bureaucracies are not found just in Washington, D.C. Bureaucracies are found in state and local governments, big corporations, schools, and even some families.

The Constitution only vaguely refers to a governmental bureaucracy. In describing the President's powers as chief executive, Article II, Section 2 says only that the President may need to consult with "the principal officer in each of the executive departments." The Constitution says little else about the organization of the executive branch or how **public policy** will be carried out.

Though the bureaucracy is administered by the executive branch, all of the agencies are regulated by the legislative branch, some of them directly supervised by Congress. The executive branch—besides the President and the Vice President—is made up of three basic parts: the Executive Office of the President, the cabinet departments, and independent agencies.

EXECUTIVE OFFICE OF THE PRESIDENT (EOP)

The Executive Office of the President is made up of agencies and individuals who directly help the President. It was created in 1939 by President Franklin Roosevelt to assist him as he coordinated all of the programs created by New Deal legislation. The government grew rapidly to execute the special programs that Congress approved. Today the EOP functions as the President's "right arm," helping him exercise his executive power. It has more than 1,500 full-time employees and consists of several important advisory bodies.

def•i•ni•tions

bureaucracy—a large and complex group of people and agencies whose purpose is to manage government and implement policy; often used to refer to the departments and agencies of the federal government.

public policy—all of a government's actions and programs that address issues and problems in a society or work toward a national goal.

EXECUTIVE OFFICE OF THE PRESIDENT

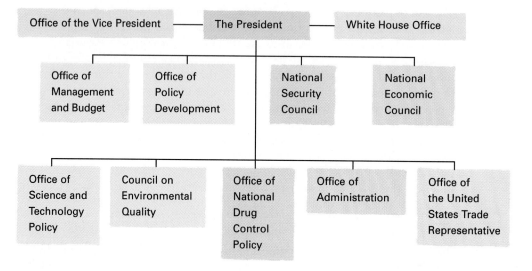

Office of the Vice President — The President — White House Office

Office of Management and Budget

Office of Policy Development

National Security Council

National Economic Council

Office of Science and Technology Policy

Council on Environmental Quality

Office of National Drug Control Policy

Office of Administration

Office of the United States Trade Representative

1. The White House Office

The early Presidents had little or no staff—family members served as secretaries and answered mail. Now some of the most influential people in government are in the President's White House Office. Appointed by the President, without the consent of Congress, they make up his closest personal and political staff. Their titles include special assistant, counsel, aide, and press secretary. They have offices in the White House, and they often compete for locations in the crowded West Wing, to be as close as possible to the President's Oval Office. The staff members attach great importance to whose office is closest to that of the President, who sees him regularly and for how long, and who has the right to see documents and memos before they go to the Oval Office.

Among the duties of White House staff members are gathering information and writing reports, giving advice, lobbying the lawmakers, and presenting the President's views to the media and the public. The chief of staff is usually particularly influential because he directs all of the operations of the White House Office. He often shapes the President's schedule and coordinates his work.

Over the years the White House Office has grown from about 50 people under Franklin Roosevelt to almost 600 under Nixon, and in the 1990s back to about 400 under Clinton. Many recent Presidents have given increasing authority to set policy to their top White House staff aides, so more and more policy decisions are made in the White House rather than in federal agencies.

Quote

"Forget the cabinet. This is where the loop begins. This is the loop. Right here, OMB. It's power central."

Richard Darman
Director of the Office of Management and Budget, 1992

2. The Office of Management and Budget (OMB)

George Bush's director of the Office of Management and Budget, Richard Darman, made the above comment to Robert Reich, Bill Clinton's incoming secretary of labor. Darman wanted to impress upon Reich the significance of this powerful executive office. The OMB is so important that many people believe its director should serve permanently on the President's cabinet. Until 1970 its director reported to the secretary of the treasury, and it was called the Bureau of the Budget. Today it is the largest office in the EOP, and it has the all-important job of preparing the national budget that the President proposes to Congress each year.

The **federal budget** gives a detailed estimate of the government's income and expenses for the coming **fiscal year.** The budget reflects priorities; bigger budgets may be allotted for programs the President supports, smaller ones for those he opposes. The budget is an important way for a President to influence what the government does and what policies it follows. The influence of the OMB has increased since the early 1980s when Ronald Reagan pledged to reduce federal spending. He ordered his budget director to prepare detailed plans to cut government spending. Even though the resulting budget proposals were controversial and Reagan's efforts to cut the budget failed, Congress supported many of them, and government priorities were greatly affected by the changes.

The influence of the OMB is increased by its right to monitor the spending of the funds approved by Congress. Departments and agencies are accountable for what they spend, and the OMB gives the President the ability to control more closely the activities of the executive branch by checking their budgets and recordkeeping. The OMB also makes studies of the organization, management, and work of all agencies. It helps prepare executive orders and veto messages and clears agency policies with the President.

def·i·ni·tions

federal budget—the document that details how much money the government collects and spends in a given year.

fiscal year—the 12-month period for which an organization plans its budget; for the government, from October 1 through September 30.

3. The National Security Council (NSC)

President Harry Truman created the National Security Council in 1947 to advise the President and help coordinate military and foreign policy. World War II had ended only two years before, and the country was deeply involved in the cold war with the Soviet Union. The nation's security was a top priority. The NSC continues today to be an important advisory body to the President. The President heads it, and the Vice President, secretary of state, and secretary of defense are members. Sometimes the President may ask the director of the Central Intelligence Agency (CIA) or the chairman of the Joint Chiefs of Staff to participate in NSC meetings.

The NSC staff of policy experts works under the direction of the President's assistant for national security affairs, who is usually called the national security adviser. Because the NSC is an advisory body, the degree to which a President relies on it has varied over the years. Presidents who have given the council a great deal of power include Dwight Eisenhower, Richard Nixon, and Ronald Reagan. For example, under Reagan the NSC staff actually conducted a number of secret operations, including a controversial sale of arms to Iran and the use of the revenues to aid the Contra rebels in Nicaragua. For the first time, many Americans realized how powerful the NSC had become. Many were shocked by the activities it conducted. This operation, sometimes known as the Iran-Contra scandal or "Iran-gate," was denounced because Congress had voted not to fund the Contras.

4. The National Economic Council (NEC)

The National Economic Council (formerly known as the Council of Economic Advisers) was created in 1946 to help the President in his role as chief economic planner. The council consists of three of the country's leading economists and about 60 other economists, attorneys, and political scientists. It is the President's major source of advice and information about the nation's economy. The NEC assesses the health of the economy, predicts future economic conditions, and sometimes advises other executive agencies involved in economic policy. The Council also helps to prepare the President's annual Economic Report to Congress, which is meant to influence legislation on economic matters.

5. Other Agencies

Although the relative influence of the Executive Office of the President agencies varies with each President, the OMB, the NSC, and the NEC usually are the most important advisory bodies to the chief executive. However, other agencies in the Executive Office also significantly affect policy decisions in the executive branch. The Office of National Drug Control Policy is a relatively new office established in 1988 to advise the President on programs to control the use and sale of illegal drugs. The Office of Policy Development advises the President on all matters of the nation's domestic (within the borders of the country) affairs. The Office of the United States Trade Representative advises the President on all matters of foreign trade. The President's main source for advice on all scientific and technological policies and programs, including the space program, is the Office of Science and Technology Policy. The Council on Environmental Quality provides assistance in environmental policy matters, and a seemingly endless list of general support services—such as data processing and clerical help—is provided by the Office of Administration.

THE CABINET

The cabinet is not mentioned by name in the Constitution, but this informal advisory body is probably the best known of all in the executive branch. As close advisers to the President, the members of the cabinet can wield considerable political power. They are appointees of the President (and confirmed by the Senate), and they serve at his pleasure. Abraham Lincoln captured the relationship of a President to his cabinet members when he announced the result of a vote on an issue: all seven cabinet members voted against it, he voted for it, and he won. The President can ignore advice from his cabinet and can even dismiss members without approval of Congress. Cabinet members often disagree with one another and at times disagree with the President himself.

At its first session in 1789, Congress established four executive positions: secretary of state, secretary of the treasury, secretary of war, and attorney general. Under George Washington, all members except the attorney general headed departments that executed policies in their areas. In time, the attorney general came to head the Department of Justice. Other secretaries and departments were added or reorganized or renamed through the years. Today the heads of 14 executive departments form the cabinet. Other top officials, such as the Vice President, the director of the OMB, the trade representative, the White House chief of staff, and the chief domestic policy adviser are often asked to join a President's cabinet.

GROWTH OF THE CABINET

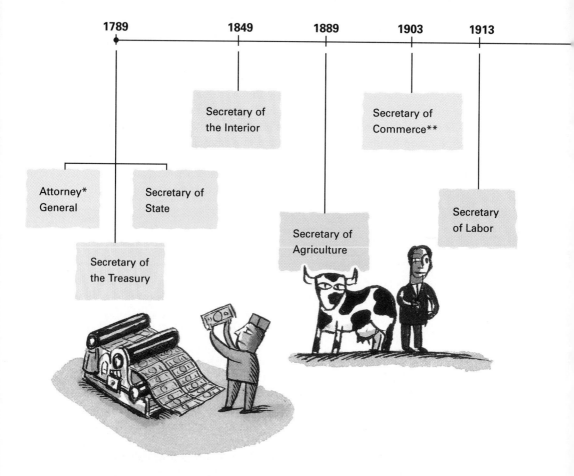

1789   1849   1889   1903   1913

Secretary of the Interior

Secretary of Commerce**

Attorney* General

Secretary of State

Secretary of the Treasury

Secretary of Agriculture

Secretary of Labor

    *   *Although the Attorney General (the department head) was an original cabinet post in 1789, the Department of Justice was not created until 1870.*

  **   *The Department of Commerce was originally the Department of Commerce and Labor. In 1913, a separate Department of Labor was created.*

 *** *The Department of War was created in 1789, but it was renamed the Department of Defense in 1947.*

**** *The Department of Health and Human Services was originally the Department of Health, Education, and Welfare. In 1979, a separate Department of Education was created.*

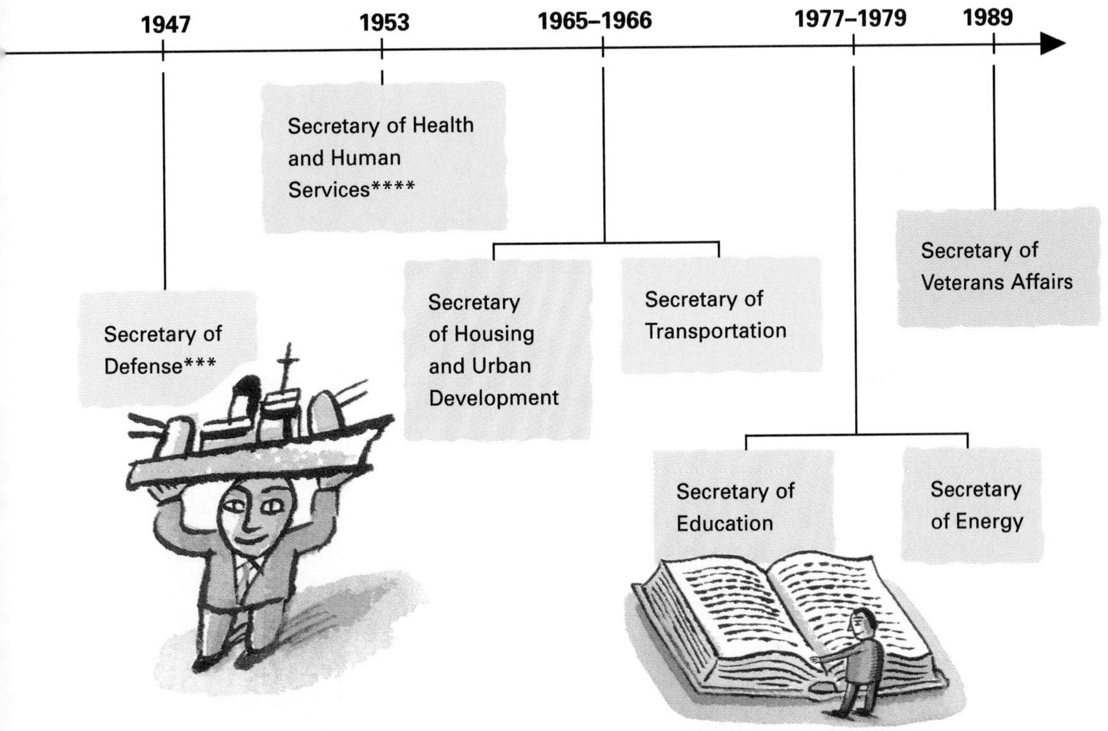

1947	1953	1965–1966	1977–1979	1989

Secretary of Health and Human Services****

Secretary of Defense***

Secretary of Housing and Urban Development

Secretary of Transportation

Secretary of Veterans Affairs

Secretary of Education

Secretary of Energy

The Organization of Cabinet Departments

Each of the 14 cabinet departments is headed by a secretary, or in the case of the Department of Justice, the attorney general. Beneath the secretary are undersecretaries, deputy undersecretaries, and assistant secretaries. Each department is made up of subunits—bureaus, services, offices, or administrations—that govern specific policy areas. For example, the Department of the Interior includes such subunits as Fish and Wildlife and Parks, Land and Mammals Management, Water and Science, the National Park Service, Minerals Management Service, and the U.S. Geological Survey. Only the top positions in each department are appointed by the President and subject to approval by the Senate.

Each department is organized a little differently according to its mission and traditions. Until the 1970s the largest department was the Department of Defense. Today the Department of Health and Human Services spends the most money (other than the Treasury Department) although the Department of Defense still has the most employees.

Cabinet Departments

★ **THE DEPARTMENT OF AGRICULTURE** helps farmers improve their incomes and expand their markets. The department provides financial credit, assists farmers in protecting water and soil, and develops conservation programs.

★ **THE DEPARTMENT OF COMMERCE** promotes the nation's international trade, economic development, and technological advancement. Its agencies include the Bureau of the Census, the Economic Development Administration, the United States Travel and Tourism Administration, and the Patent and Trademark Office.

★ **THE DEPARTMENT OF DEFENSE** supports and defends the national security and upholds the national interest through military action. It oversees the armed forces through the Joint Chiefs of Staff. The department supervises the Army, the Navy, the Marine Corps, and the Air Force.

★ **THE DEPARTMENT OF EDUCATION** coordinates federal assistance programs for public and private schools as well as programs to help students with limited English proficiency and physical impairments.

★ **THE DEPARTMENT OF ENERGY** sets national energy policies and researches and develops energy technology. The Federal Energy Regulatory Commission sets rates for interstate distribution of natural gas and electricity.

★ **THE DEPARTMENT OF HEALTH AND HUMAN SERVICES** supervises programs to protect public health and provide social services. Its agencies include the Public Health Service and the Food and Drug Administration. The Social Security Administration was a part of this department until 1994.

★ **THE DEPARTMENT OF HOUSING AND URBAN DEVELOPMENT** supports preservation of the nation's communities, protects equal housing opportunities, and conducts a number of insurance, rent subsidy, and grant programs. Examples of the agencies it oversees are the Government National Mortgage Association and the Office of Fair Housing and Equal Opportunity.

★ **THE DEPARTMENT OF THE INTERIOR** protects public lands and natural resources and oversees relations with Native Americans. Some of its agencies include the National Park Service, the Bureau of Mines, the Bureau of Indian Affairs, and the United States Fish and Wildlife Service.

★ **THE DEPARTMENT OF JUSTICE** represents the government in legal matters and provides the means for the enforcement of federal laws. Its agencies include the Federal Bureau of Investigation (FBI), the Immigration and Naturalization Service (INS), and the Drug Enforcement Administration (DEA).

★ **THE DEPARTMENT OF LABOR** promotes the welfare of workers by setting and enforcing a minimum wage, overseeing and ensuring safe working conditions, and protecting pensions. Agencies include the Bureau of Labor Statistics, the Employment and Training Administration, and the Office of Labor-Management Standards.

★ **THE DEPARTMENT OF STATE** is responsible for the foreign policy of the United States. It includes all U.S. embassies and consulates to countries throughout the world. The secretary of state, usually one of the President's most trusted advisers, is a high-profile negotiator in world affairs discussions.

★ **THE DEPARTMENT OF TRANSPORTATION** regulates policy development and planning for all forms of transportation, including air traffic, railroads, highways, and mass transit. It also supervises the United States Coast Guard and the Merchant Marine.

★ **THE DEPARTMENT OF THE TREASURY** formulates and sets finance and tax policy, manages the debt, collects taxes, manufactures coins and currency, and serves as financial agent for the United States. It also includes the Bureau of Alcohol, Tobacco, and Firearms and the United States Secret Service, which protects Presidents, Vice Presidents, candidates, visiting heads of state, and former Presidents.

★ **THE DEPARTMENT OF VETERANS AFFAIRS** administers laws that provide benefits for former members of the armed services and their dependents and beneficiaries.

The Selection of the Cabinet

Many factors influence a President's selection of cabinet members.

★ **BACKGROUND AND PROFESSIONAL EXPERIENCE** If a person is to head a huge bureaucracy, he or she should have some experience with and knowledge of what the department specializes in. Thus, the secretary of agriculture should know something about farming, and the secretary of housing and urban development should know about urban planning.

★ **POLITICAL PARTY** Republican Presidents almost never appoint Democrats, and vice versa. Presidents often choose their campaign managers or consultants as cabinet members.

★ **FRIENDS AND ACQUAINTANCES** Some cabinet members and White House advisers are people the President has known for many years. In some cases a trusted adviser will hold different positions during a President's time in office. For example, Donald Regan served as Ronald Reagan's chief of staff and also as his secretary of defense; Henry Kissinger served as national security adviser and as secretary of state for Richard Nixon.

★ **REGION** The cabinet is often regionally balanced so that most parts of the country are represented. Part of the balance is determined by the nature of the departments. For example, the secretary of interior is usually from the West, where most of the department's work is done.

★ **RACE AND GENDER** For the first 144 years of America's history, all cabinet members were white men. In 1933 Franklin Roosevelt appointed the first woman, but not for another 30 years was an African American appointed. Since the 1970s, women and minorities increasingly have been chosen for cabinet positions, and their appointments are fairly common today.

Senate rejection of the President's appointments of cabinet members is rare, although Congress has questioned them more often in recent years. Usually controversial presidential nominees are withdrawn from consideration before they are actually rejected.

The Cabinet's Roles

What do you think you would see and hear at a cabinet meeting—a weighty, philosophical discussion, much good advice and sympathetic listening to the woes of the President, a great deal of cooperative problem solving? You almost certainly would see some aggressive competition and hear some spirited arguments. Many Presidents have expressed disappointment and dismay over the lack of cooperation and objective advice they get from their cabinet members. Cabinet members have two important, but often contradictory, roles.

220

e.g.

CABINET FIRSTS

★ The first woman to serve on the cabinet was Frances Perkins, Franklin Roosevelt's secretary of labor from 1933 to 1945.

★ Robert Weaver, the first African-American cabinet member, was appointed by Lyndon Johnson in 1966 to be secretary of housing and urban development.

★ The first Hispanic cabinet member was Lauro F. Cavazos, appointed in 1988 as secretary of education by Ronald Reagan.

1. **ADVISORY ROLE** First, they are trusted advisers to the President. They have his needs and interests at heart. Their purpose is to ensure that his decisions are soundly based on their expertise. If the President knew any cabinet members before he took office, they were almost certainly appointed because the President anticipated that they would give good advice. An unusual example is John Kennedy's appointment of his brother, Robert Kennedy, as attorney general. Subsequent laws prohibited the appointment of members of the President's family to the cabinet.

2. **DEPARTMENTAL ROLE** In addition to being advisers, cabinet members head large departments that often compete with one another for funds and for the President's attention. Each of them is the primary link between the President and the cabinet member's department. They must promote the department to congressional committees, other government officials, and the public. They almost always "cross swords" with other cabinet members in defense of their departments' interests.

Presidents have tried to deal with these conflicting cabinet roles in different ways. Dwight Eisenhower, a former general, tried to relate to his cabinet members as a general to his staff officers. Some of Richard Nixon's cabinet members did not see him for months at a time because he seldom called them together. Jimmy Carter tried to revive cabinet meetings and give members more authority, but by the end of his term, he was relying much more heavily on the advice of the White House staff than on the cabinet. In the end, most Presidents have resigned themselves to the fact that their cabinets are generally not cooperative and supportive.

Then and Now

PRESIDENTS AND THEIR CABINETS

Through the years Presidents often have had high hopes for a good relationship with their cabinets. Although individual cabinet secretaries often have a great deal of power and authority over their departments, the cabinet has seldom operated as an effective advisory body to the President.

George Washington's cabinet meetings often were destroyed by the constant arguments that erupted between secretary of state Thomas Jefferson and secretary of the treasury Alexander Hamilton. The two had opposite points of view on almost everything, and they became the founders of the first two opposing political parties.

Andrew Jackson almost totally ignored his cabinet and rarely called cabinet meetings. Cabinet members had almost no influence on the President's decisions. He relied instead upon his "kitchen cabinet," an informal group of his close and most trusted friends.

Abraham Lincoln's cabinet met frequently, but they were hardly on good terms with one another. Often they argued about and criticized Lincoln's direction of the Civil War. His cabinet members almost unanimously agreed that Lincoln was incompetent, and they often treated him with disdain. Two of them, Edwin Stanton and William Seward, openly challenged Lincoln for the presidency in 1864. Lincoln only narrowly won the nomination of his party as the incumbent Republican presidential candidate.

Franklin Roosevelt almost never relied on his cabinet for advice but, like Andrew Jackson, turned to his own specially created group, the Brain Trust. Roosevelt assembled some of the most brilliant experts from many different fields to address the nation's problems.

INDEPENDENT AGENCIES

Although the majority of government employees work for one of the cabinet departments, many are employed by one of the nearly 150 independent agencies that Congress has created since the late nineteenth century. Most of these agencies are not free from presidential control and are independent only in the sense that they are not formally part of the 14 cabinet departments. A few, however, act almost independently from the executive branch.

Why aren't these agencies put within the cabinet bureaucracies? Many independent agencies perform tasks similar to those of cabinet agencies. Without question their existence complicates the organization of the executive branch, but there are three main reasons for their separation.

★ Some agencies were created for purposes that don't fit well within any department. For example, the Office of Personnel Management (OPM) was created as the hiring agency for nearly all other federal agencies.

★ Congress gave some agencies independent status to protect them from party politics. For example, Congress did not want the Federal Election Commission to be supervised by a department secretary and a President loyal to one political party.

★ Many regulatory commissions by their very nature need independence from a department and a branch of government. If an agency is created as a watchdog for other parts of government, it should operate independently.

Independent agencies can be classified into three types: independent regulatory commissions, government corporations, and independent executive agencies.

1. Independent Regulatory Commissions

Of all the independent agencies, the **independent regulatory commissions** operate the most independently. These ten agencies police different aspects of the nation's economy, making rules for large industries and businesses that affect the interests of the public. They gain their independence largely from the way they are structured. Each commission has from 5–11 commissioners. They are appointed to a long term of office by the President with the Senate's consent. But these commissioners do not report to the President, and the President cannot remove them. Examples of these commissions are the Securities and Exchange Commission, which regulates the stock market, brokers, and investment practices; the Federal Trade Commission, which enforces antitrust laws and prohibits unfair competition and false advertising; and the National Labor Relations Board, which prevents and remedies unfair labor practices.

def·i·ni·tions

independent regulatory commission—a federal agency whose purpose is to protect the public interest.

Sometimes when government tries to protect the welfare of the country, its regulations cause people to complain that government is robbing them of their freedom. These complaints led to a movement of **deregulation,** which started in the mid-1970s. Other complaints against the regulatory agencies were that they were heavily controlled by interest groups or that their restrictions were too complex to do any good. As a result, most regulatory agencies have been simplified. Two major commissions have been abolished altogether: the Civil Aeronautics Board, which governed commercial air traffic, and the Interstate Commerce Commission, which regulated the rates and routes of commercial transportation. Today, many of the nation's transportation industries—including airlines, bus companies, truckers, and railroads—have much greater freedom to operate than they did a few decades ago.

2. Government Corporations

About 60 independent agencies are **government corporations,** or businesses the federal government runs. Because they operate like private corporations, they charge customers for their services, and their profits are plowed back into the business. Like private companies, each government corporation has a board of directors and a general manager who are appointed by the President and approved by the Senate. Unlike private companies, Congress appropriates government funds to support the corporations. The largest government corporation is the U.S. Postal Service, which competes with private companies for mail service. One of the more controversial corporations is Amtrak, the passenger railway company. It has often operated at a huge loss, making some members of Congress argue that rail service should be turned over to private companies.

3. Independent Executive Agencies

Independent agencies that cannot be classified as regulatory agencies or as corporations are known as **independent executive agencies.** They vary in size. Some are almost as large as cabinet departments, and others have few employees and small budgets. Several are well known, such as NASA and the CIA. Some are not so well known, such as the Citizens' Stamp Advisory Committee and the Migratory Bird Conservation Commission.

def·i·ni·tions

government corporation—a business that the federal government runs. Government corporations perform functions that could be provided by private businesses.

independent executive agency—an executive branch agency outside of the cabinet departments that oversees a single area.

deregulation—the process of reducing, even removing, governmental control of industry.

Civil Service and the Power of the Bureaucracy

Federal civilian employment reached a peak of nearly 3.4 million people during World War II. In 1996, about 2.8 million civilians were employed by the federal government. Some facts about these **bureaucrats** may surprise you.

About 11 percent of the federal civilian employees work in or around Washington, D.C. The others work all around the country and even in other countries. For example, more than 350,000 federal employees work in California, more than all those employed in the District of Columbia. Many are employed by the Postal Service, the Social Security Administration, the FBI, and the Department of Agriculture.

Four executive departments—the Departments of Defense, Veterans Affairs, the Treasury, and Health and Human Services—account for almost 70 percent of the federal civilian workforce. Federal employees are more broadly representative of the nation than are legislators. About 43 percent are women, and 28 percent are minority (African Americans, Asians, Native Americans, Hispanics, and Pacific Islanders).

CHARACTERISTICS OF FEDERAL CIVILIAN EMPLOYEES

		1960	1994
Sex	Male	75%	57%
	Female	25%	43%
Race	White	n/a	72%
	Minority	n/a	28%
Employing	Defense Department	44%	30%
Agency	Postal Service	23%	38%
	All other	33%	32%
Location	Washington, D.C., area	11%	11%
	Elsewhere	89%	89%

n/a = not available

Source: *Statistical Abstract of the United States.*

def·i·ni·tions

bureaucrat—a person who works for a department or agency of the federal government.

1. CIVIL SERVICE

Only about 7,500 federal employees are appointed, usually to the top jobs. The others are **civil service** employees who apply for jobs through a competitive process. About 2,000 different job categories exist—from clerks, managers, and computer programmers to nurses, engineers, and lawyers.

A. The Historical Perspective

When Congress created the first cabinet departments, George Washington vowed to hire only people "as shall be the best qualified." Even so he found those to have "fitness of character" more often than not among members of the Federalist party. An important precedent was set when Thomas Jefferson, the first President from the opposing party, the Democratic-Republicans, came to office. Jefferson found that the Federalist workers opposed his policies, so he dismissed them and filled their jobs with Democratic-Republicans. With this action, he set a new standard for choosing government positions: patronage, or political acceptability.

Until the late nineteenth century, a person got a government job through the patronage system, or knowing the right people. Andrew Jackson is generally credited with beginning this practice, called the "spoils system," based on the old saying, "to the victor go the spoils." His election brought a whole new group of "Jacksonian Democrats" into office, and he rewarded those who helped him win the presidency with government jobs. The tradition was broken when a disappointed office seeker, Charles Guiteau, shot and killed President James Garfield in 1881 because he would not give Guiteau a job. In reaction, Congress passed the Pendleton Act (1883), which created the federal civil service. At first only about 10 percent of federal employees were members of the civil service; today about 85 percent are.

B. The Civil Service Today

The civil service replaced the patronage system with the merit principle, intended to base appointments to government jobs on talent and skill. To determine merit, a civil service entrance exam and promotion ratings were created. The Civil Service Commission administered examinations and supervised the operation of the new merit-based system. In 1979 the commission was replaced by two new agencies, the Office of Personnel Management (OPM) and the Merit Systems Protection Board.

def·i·ni·tions

civil service—name given to federal government employees who are hired and promoted based on merit.

Headlines

THE PENDLETON ACT: 1997

A relatively obscure part of the 1883 Pendleton Act is a ban on soliciting government employees for political support while they are on public property. The intent of the law was to keep patronage out of Washington. In 1996, Vice President Al Gore and President Bill Clinton were accused of violating the Pendleton Act when they made several phone calls to federal employees soliciting support for the Democratic party from their government offices. The charges were eventually dismissed by Attorney General Janet Reno.

GOVERNMENT JOBS

The OPM hires the vast majority of government employees. Its top positions are appointed by the President and confirmed by the Senate. The OPM sets strict rules about hiring and promotions. Candidates for jobs must first pass a test, either a general civil service test or special ones created by agencies for more specific needs. For example, the U.S. Postal Service has its own exam, as does the FBI. After candidates pass the test, they are sent to agencies when jobs open up. For each position open, the OPM sends three names (known as "the rule of three"), and the agency hires one of these three people. Once hired, a person is assigned a GS (General Service) rating ranging from GS 1 to GS 18. Salaries and responsibilities increase as the ratings get higher. At the top of the system are the members of the senior executive service, executives who earn high salaries and may be moved from one agency to another as leadership needs change. Government jobs are attractive to many because of their competitive pay, paid vacations, job security, and health insurance and pension plans.

The Merit Systems Protection Board is a three-member panel selected by the President and the Senate, and its job is to protect the merit principle in government jobs. If an individual believes that a job was filled through partisanship (favoring one political party over the other) rather than merit, that person may present the case to the Merit Systems Protection Board for review.

THE HATCH ACT

The merit system demands that the best qualified people get the jobs and that political party membership should have nothing to do with hiring. So in 1939 Congress passed the Hatch Act, which carried the merit principle one step further. Not only should party membership have nothing to do with the hiring process, but once employed, federal workers should have as little to

do with partisanship as possible. The Hatch Act forbids employees to be party activists. For example, they cannot run for public office, nor can they become an officer in a political organization or a delegate to a party convention. They also cannot raise funds for a political party or any of its candidates.

The Hatch Act was meant to prevent a party from using federal workers in election campaigns. Some bureaucrats have complained that the law violates their 1st Amendment rights, particularly their freedom of speech. The issue made its way to the Supreme Court in 1973, but the Court ruled that the Hatch Act did not place unreasonable restrictions on workers' rights. However, in 1993 Congress overhauled the old Hatch Act, making many forms of participation in politics permissible. Federal officials still cannot run as candidates in elections, but they may hold party positions and involve themselves in party fund-raising and campaigning.

2. BUREAUCRATIC DECISION-MAKING

After learning something about the bureaucracy, you might wonder about the role bureaucrats play in making decisions in government. Just how important are the bureaucrats compared to members of Congress or the President and Vice President?

A. Power

The power of the bureaucracy is not in the size of its staff or its budget. Bureaucracy's real power lies in the way it influences—even sets—public policy. Because they administer programs, federal bureaucrats have to issue rules and regulations that turn laws into action. As they administer policies, they also help shape what those policies are. Officials in the federal bureaucracy help Congress by providing members with information and generating ideas for new legislation, or writing drafts of new bills. Some agencies may need to settle disputes—with the authority of the courts—over how a law has been applied. For example, if a law grants money for persons who are handicapped, the bureaucrats help decide what exactly "handicapped" means. Many people believe that the bureaucracy is a kind of behind-the-scenes "subgovernment" and holds the real power in government.

B. Influences on the Bureaucracy

The bureaucrats don't make and carry out policy in isolation. From the beginning, the United States has rejected a single power source, believing instead that power should be checked and balanced. As a result, the American bureaucracy must report to and be controlled by more than one boss.

CONGRESS

The influence of Congress is particularly important when agencies are created, when major programs are put in place, and when congressional approval of appointments is necessary. Congress oversees the bureaucracy by overturning an agency's decisions with new legislation. Congress may hold hearings to investigate agency wrongdoing. The major power of Congress over the bureaucracy is the power of the purse; the legislature controls the agencies' budgets. Authorization for the maximum amount that an agency may spend comes from a legislative committee. Appropriations that determine the slice of the budget that agency programs get during a budget year are also set by congressional committees. Congress may refuse to appropriate money or may threaten to eliminate important agency programs.

THE PRESIDENT

Most Presidents try to impose their own political points of view on government agencies. As chief executive, the President may formally order an agency to take a particular action, and the agency must comply. More informally, a President may exert pressure by passing on his wishes through an aide. Even though Congress sets their budgets, agencies may feel the President's influence through the Office of Management and Budget.

The OMB sends recommendations for agency budgets in the President's initial budget to Congress, or it may threaten to cut or add to budgets within the guidelines set by Congress. Finally, a President may reorganize an agency, although only Congress may officially abolish one. If an agency head or a key assistant opposes the President, the President may replace the individual with someone more cooperative. Of course the agency then may find ways to ignore or reject the new boss, and Congress may refuse to approve budgets that reflect new priorities.

THE COURTS

Almost half the cases brought to federal court involve the United States government as either the prosecutor or the defendant. Agencies may be sued for policies or actions that adversely affect citizens. The Administrative Procedures Act of 1946 allows individuals directly affected by the actions of an agency to challenge the government in court. A federal court may then issue an **injunction** to the agency, either stopping an action or enforcing a regulation.

Other bureaucrats and the courts also influence the work of many agencies. Responsibilities of different agencies frequently overlap, either by design (for purposes of checks and balances) or by accident. For example, the Occupational Safety and Health Administration (OSHA) may set regulations about sanitation

---

injunction—a court order that demands or forbids a particular action.

standards in factories that contradict rules set by the Environmental Protection Agency. Agency heads or subheads may try to work out these differences. Sometimes interagency task forces or special committees must settle disputes.

IRON TRIANGLES

Agencies and departments are usually in close contact with interest groups that want to influence their actions. Lobbyists may provide valuable information to government agencies, and they are usually eager to impress their points of view on the bureaucrats. Of course, these interest groups also work with members of Congress, and so all three—interest groups, members of Congress, and agency bureaucrats—often work with one another. When agencies, interest groups, and congressional committees work closely together to make public policy, their cooperation is called a subgovernment, or **iron triangle.**

Think, for example, about how the government sets benefits for veterans or former members of the armed services, particularly people who have fought in the nation's wars. At one point of the triangle are the subcommittees of the House Veterans Affairs Committee and the Senate Armed Services Committee. They pass legislation that shapes veterans' benefits. At another point of the triangle are veterans' interest groups, such as the American

THE IRON TRIANGLE AND VETERANS' AFFAIRS

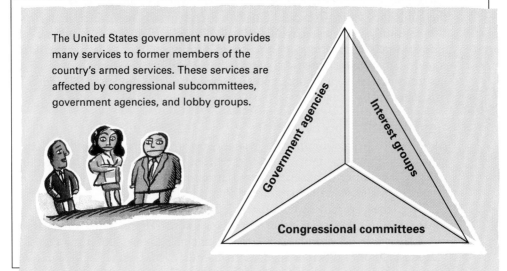

The United States government now provides many services to former members of the country's armed services. These services are affected by congressional subcommittees, government agencies, and lobby groups.

Government agencies

Interest groups

Congressional committees

def·i·ni·tions

iron triangle—a mutually advantageous relationship among congressional committees, interest groups, and governmental agencies in an effort to influence legislation and policy.

230

Legion, that push the legislation by giving campaign contributions and information to the subcommittees. At the third point of the triangle are the agencies of the Department of Veterans Affairs, which set rules on veterans' benefits and help with complaints. The people at each of the three points exchange political favors and information with one another. Multiply this example by all the policy areas with which the government is involved, and you have a powerful argument that supports the vital role played by bureaucrats in making important government decisions.

The bureaucracy in American politics and government is a favorite target of the public's complaints. Confusing regulations, endless forms, and wasted time and money fuel taxpayers' calls for reform. For instance, Vice President Al Gore undertook a national performance review at the request of President Clinton. His report, *From Red Tape to Results: Creating a Government That Works Better and Costs Less,* called for reinventing government, downsizing some agencies, and simplifying procedures. How successful such efforts are in reducing the size and improving the efficiency of the bureaucracy remain to be seen.

© Ed Stein. Reprinted courtesy of the *Rocky Mountain News*.

Beneath all the criticisms lies one simple truth: America divides the power in government in order to preserve its democracy, and ultimately a certain amount of inefficiency is a price the American people have to pay. Executive branch appointees, including the Executive Office of the President and the cabinet members, may not be mentioned in the Constitution, but they play a vital role in shaping policy and putting it into practice. The members of the vast bureaucracy in all branches and levels of government are less visible, but no less important, in the policy-making process. Collectively, they make many specific, concrete decisions that either support or challenge the powers of Congress and the President.

The Courts and the Judicial Branch

T he large courtroom sits behind huge double doors at the end of a waiting room lined with marble busts of stern-looking men. When the Court begins its session, those present stand as the judges, dressed in black robes, file in and take their seats at the bench in front of a red velvet curtain. When they are seated, everyone else sits down too. The attorneys are dressed formally, some in frock coats and striped trousers. Beside each justice is a spittoon for chewing tobacco, and on each attorney's desk is a goose quill pen. The lawyers on each side are allowed only 30 minutes to argue their points. When their time is up, a red light goes off on the desk, and the lawyer speaking must stop immediately, even if in mid-sentence. After both sides have been heard, the judges, who hold lifetime positions, meet in secret and eventually announce their decision, which is final.

Although it might sound like something from the late nineteenth or early twentieth century, that scene accurately describes a Supreme Court session in modern America. Why is it this way? The Court is operating much as the Founders intended. It serves as a stabilizing force for a democratic republican government. The U.S. judiciary plays an active role in policy making. It exerts a power unlike any other judicial system in the world. It equals the other two branches of government, checking and balancing them in ways that the Founders could not have foreseen.

In this chapter . . .

Foundations of the Judicial System

Like the presidency, the federal court system was first created by the Constitution. The national government had no judicial system under the Articles of Confederation. As powerful as the judicial branch is today, the Founders chose to give it only brief attention. Article III is devoted to the judiciary, and it consists of only three short sections compared to the much lengthier Articles I (about Congress) and II (about the presidency).

CONSTITUTIONAL ORIGINS

Article III specifically creates only the Supreme Court and gives Congress the power to create lower federal courts, or "inferior courts." Beginning with the Judiciary Act of 1789, Congress has established a variety of lower courts to handle the rising number of federal cases. The state court systems were already in place well before the Founders got together at the Constitutional Convention in 1787. Today the two levels—state and federal—exist side by side in a dual court system. While the federal courts base their authority on the Constitution and federal law, the powers of state courts come from state constitutions and laws. The principal job of the state courts is to decide disputes between private persons and between private persons and government.

Article III of the Constitution also provides guidelines of the terms of office and compensation of federal judges. To make the judiciary as powerful as the other two branches, the Founders tried to give federal judges considerable independence from the President or Congress. Federal judges may serve as long as they practice "good behavior," and their salary cannot be reduced while they are in office. (In 1998, Supreme Court justices made $167,900, the Chief Justice $175,400, and other federal judges between $125,700 and $145,000.) Once they are appointed by the President and confirmed by the Senate (as provided by Article II), they may be removed from office only by impeachment (outlined in Article I).

e.g.

THE JUDICIAL OATH

Even though the Constitution does not say anything about the duties of justices, the expectations were soon put into words in the form of the Judicial Oath all federal judges must take:

"I do solemnly swear that I will administer justice without respect to persons, do equal right to the poor and to the rich, and that I will impartially discharge and perform all the duties incumbent on me, according to the best of my abilities and understanding agreeably to the Constitution and the laws of the United States so help me God."

JURISDICTION OF THE COURTS

Every court—state or federal—has restrictions on the kinds of cases it may hear. This authority is called the **jurisdiction** of the court. Article III, Section 2 of the Constitution defines the jurisdiction of federal courts. They may try cases involving:

 ambassadors or other representatives of foreign governments,

 maritime law (the law of the sea),

 bankruptcy cases,

 two or more state governments,

 citizens of different states,

 a state and a citizen of a different state or foreign country,

 citizens of the same state claiming lands under grants of different states,

 U.S. laws and treaties, or the interpretation of the Constitution.

def·i·ni·tions

jurisdiction—the right to interpret and apply the law; a court's range of authority.

Federal question cases—cases "arising under the Constitution, the laws of the United States, and treaties"—are the **exclusive jurisdiction** of the federal courts. State courts may not hear them. For example, when a federal criminal law is broken, but not a state one, the case goes to federal court. A case involving a federal or foreign government official cannot be heard in a state court, nor can a case that arises out of an act of Congress. All cases involving interpretation of the Constitution must go to federal court, and disputes between two state governments must be heard only by the Supreme Court.

In some cases, federal and state courts share jurisdiction, a situation known as **concurrent jurisdiction.** Disputes involving citizens of different states may go to either state or federal court, although federal courts may take them only if they involve a claim of $50,000 or more. If a person commits a crime that violates both state and federal law, the case may go to either state or federal court. For example, if two people rob a state bank that is federally insured, they break both state and federal law. They may be tried in either or both types of courts. Under the dual sovereignty doctrine, state and federal authorities can prosecute an individual for the same crime.

Headlines

DUAL SOVEREIGNTY

The 5th Amendment of the Constitution prohibits double jeopardy, or a person being tried for a crime more than once. Dual sovereignty is not a violation of this amendment, since a person may break both a state law and a federal law with the same action or series of actions.

In cases such as *United States v. Lanza* (1922), the Supreme Court has upheld the dual sovereignty principle on two grounds: the right of each level of government to enact laws serving its own purposes and the need to prevent an accused person from avoiding prosecution by choosing a level more sympathetic to his case.

Sometimes the dual sovereignty doctrine can produce contradictory decisions. For example, in the 1992 Rodney King case, four Los Angeles police officers were acquitted of assault in a California state court for beating King during an attempt to arrest him. However, they were later prosecuted in federal court for violating King's civil rights. Two of the four police officers were found guilty.

---

exclusive jurisdiction—the authority of the federal courts alone to hear and rule in certain cases.

concurrent jurisdiction—the authority to hear cases shared by federal and state courts.

A trial court, the court in which a case is originally tried, has **original jurisdiction.** If a person who loses a case in a trial court wants to appeal a decision, he or she may take the case to a court with **appellate jurisdiction.** If the person loses in such a court of appeals, he or she may appeal the case to the Supreme Court, which has both original and appellate jurisdiction.

TYPES OF LAW

Both federal and state courts deal with civil law, criminal law, and constitutional law.

1. Civil Law

Most cases in federal courts involve **civil law**—the law that governs the relations between individuals and defines their legal rights. The **plaintiff** brings charges in a civil suit against a **defendant,** who must defend against the complaint. The plaintiff usually seeks damages in the form of money from the defendant. Whichever side wins, the other usually pays the court costs. Such cases are governed by equity law, which resolves the dispute on the grounds of fairness.

2. Criminal Law

Federal, state, and local governments are responsible for enforcing **criminal law**—law that defines crimes against the public order and provides for punishment. Most criminal cases are settled in state courts because they usually do not involve federal questions. But if a federal law is broken, a federal court may hear cases involving criminal law. Nevertheless, only about 2 percent of all the criminal cases in the United States are heard in federal courts; the rest are handled by state and local courts.

In all criminal cases, the government is always the prosecution and brings charges against the defendant. Examples of federal charges are kidnapping, tax fraud, selling narcotics, or driving a stolen vehicle across state lines. If someone is found guilty, that person may pay a fine or go to prison or may even receive the death penalty.

def·i·ni·tions

original jurisdiction—the court's authority to hear and decide a case for the first time.

appellate jurisdiction—the court's authority to hear cases on appeal.

civil law—the type of law dealing with the rights and relationships of private citizens.

plaintiff—a person who files suit in a civil case.

defendant—one against whom a legal charge has been made.

criminal law—the type of law dealing with crimes and providing for their punishment.

3. Constitutional Law

Federal courts, and occasionally state courts, consider cases based on interpretations of the U.S. Constitution, or **constitutional law.** Federal courts apply constitutional law when they decide whether a law or action conflicts with the Constitution. Most cases involving constitutional law decide the limits of the government's power and the rights of the individual.

JUDICIAL REVIEW

The power to decide the constitutionality of laws and other actions of government is the single most important responsibility of the judicial branch. The final decision is made by the Supreme Court, making it the ultimate authority on the meaning of the Constitution. This extraordinary power of **judicial review** is not specifically mentioned in the Constitution. It was claimed by the third chief justice of the Supreme Court, John Marshall, who served from 1801 to 1835. The debate between Thomas Jefferson and Alexander Hamilton concerning the interpretation of the Constitution set the stage. Jefferson, a **strict constructionist,** believed that the national government should exercise only the powers specifically mentioned in the Constitution. In contrast, Hamilton was a **loose constructionist,** believing that the government could claim broad powers only implied in the Constitution. In *Marbury v. Madison* (1803), Marshall sided with the loose constructionist point of view.

Marbury v. Madison

Marshall's landmark decision had its roots in the election of 1800. John Adams, seeking re-election as a Federalist, lost to Democratic-Republican Thomas Jefferson. Adams feared that Jefferson and his party would destroy all that the Federalists had worked to establish. So he did everything he could in his final days in office to see that the Federalist stamp not be removed from the presidency. He exercised his power of appointment to create and fill 59 federal judgeships (with lifelong terms) with loyal Federalists. William Marbury's appointment had been confirmed by the Senate, and Adams had

def·i·ni·tions

judicial review—the power of the courts to establish the constitutionality of national, state, or local acts of government.

strict constructionist—the view that judges ought to base their decisions on a narrow interpretation of the language of the Constitution.

loose constructionist—the view that judges have considerable freedom in interpreting the Constitution.

constitutional law—the type of law relating to the interpretation of the Constitution.

even signed the necessary paperwork. But it had not yet been delivered to Marbury when Jefferson became the President. At Jefferson's request, James Madison, the new secretary of state, refused to deliver the commission. Marbury asked the Supreme Court to force Madison to turn over the documents. Marbury argued that the Judiciary Act of 1789 compelled Madison to do so through the **writ of** *mandamus.*

Judicial Review

The Court's unanimous decision upheld the supremacy of the Constitution over Congress. Marshall ruled that the part of the Judiciary Act of 1789 that Marbury had cited was unconstitutional. Marshall wrote, "An act of the legislature repugnant [counter] to the Constitution is void," and "it is emphatically the province of the judicial department to say what the law is." With those words he established the power of judicial review, the ability of the courts to declare acts of Congress and the executive branch unconstitutional. As a result, a confrontation between Chief Justice Marshall and President Jefferson was avoided, and the power of the Supreme Court was clarified and expanded. This loose construction established the right of the Court to broadly interpret the Constitution, thus enlarging the power of the judiciary.

e.g.

READING COURT CASES

Court cases are identified by the names of the plaintiff and the defendant. The *v.* stands for the Latin word *versus,* meaning "against." The defendant's name always goes last. So, in *Marbury v. Madison,* Marbury is the plaintiff, who believes he has been wronged, and Madison is the defendant.

---

writ of *mandamus*—a court order that commands a government official to take a particular action.

Organization of the Federal Courts

Recall that the Constitution named only one specific court, the U.S. Supreme Court, and gave Congress the power to establish "such inferior courts" as deemed necessary.

In the Judiciary Act of 1789 Congress created **constitutional courts,** or the inferior courts referred to in Article III, Section 1. Although the basic structure of these courts remains intact today, over the years Congress also established **legislative courts** for specialized purposes. The large majority of all federal cases go to constitutional courts because they have general jurisdiction that covers most situations. The legislative courts are more specialized to correspond to the specific delegated powers of Congress.

THE FEDERAL COURT SYSTEM

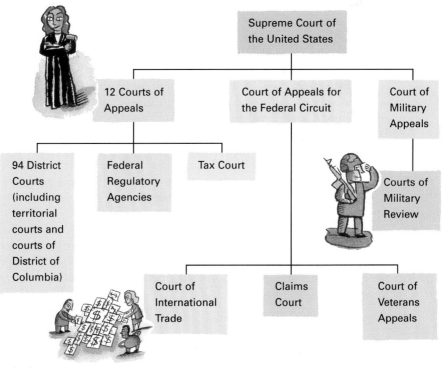

def·i·ni·tions

constitutional court—a federal court with constitutionally based powers and whose judges serve for life. The most important are the Supreme Court, the courts of appeals, and the district courts.

legislative court—a specialized court established to hear cases about and execute the legislative powers of Congress.

CONSTITUTIONAL COURTS

Constitutional courts include the federal district courts, the courts of appeals, and the United States Court of International Trade.

1. The District Courts

Congress created district courts in 1789 as the primary trial courts in the federal system. Originally each state was to have one district court, but as the population grew, some states were divided into more than one district. Today, the United States has 94 district courts, with the largest states having as many as four apiece. Washington, D.C., and Puerto Rico also have district courts assigned to them. The number of judges for each court varies with the population. It ranges from 28 judges who hear cases for the United States Judicial District for Southern New York, to only two judges assigned to several less populated areas.

The district courts are courts of original jurisdiction only; with just a few exceptions, they hear no appeals. District courts may receive appeals from state courts if constitutional questions are involved. They hear a wide range of both criminal cases and civil cases, and their jurisdiction extends to most cases that are heard in the federal courts.

The district courts are the only federal courts that regularly use grand juries to issue indictments and petit juries to try defendants. A **grand jury,** usually made up of 16 to 23 people, hears charges against a person suspected of having committed a crime. If the jury members believe there is sufficient evidence, the court orders the person to trial. A **petit jury,** usually made up of 6 to 12 people, weighs the evidence presented at a trial. If it is a civil case, the jury rules in favor of either the plaintiff or the defendant. In a criminal case, a petit jury reaches a verdict of guilty or not guilty.

District courts hear about 80 percent of all federal cases, and most federal cases end at this level. Very few verdicts are overturned by a higher court, although of those cases that district court judges actually decide (as opposed to those settled out of court), a fairly large percentage of the losers appeal their cases to a court of appeals.

---

grand jury—a group of people who evaluate whether there is enough evidence against a person to order him or her to stand trial.

petit jury—a jury that decides an individual's innocence or guilt; a trial jury.

e.g.

THE SUPPORTING CAST

A federal court needs more than just a judge. Much day-to-day administrative work goes into running the court. Some of the people who provide services include:

BAILIFFS They are the officers of the court who are responsible for prisoners during a trial and who guard the jurors in court.

CLERK This is the person appointed to have custody of the seal of the court and to keep a record of the court's proceedings. The clerk is assisted by deputy clerks, stenographers, and bailiffs.

FEDERAL MAGISTRATE This officer of the court is appointed for an eight-year term and issues warrants for arrest, determines whether or not to hold arrested persons for action by a grand jury, and sets bail (money the accused may be required to deposit with the court as a guarantee of his or her appearance at a future court date).

PROBATION OFFICERS These officers are appointed by the magistrate to watch and report on a person placed on probation, which is a conditional suspension of sentence.

ATTORNEY An attorney is appointed by the President and confirmed by the Senate to each federal judicial district. The U.S. attorneys and their staffs prosecute violations of federal law and represent the U.S. government in civil cases.

MARSHALL This officer is appointed to each district court to keep order in the court, carry out court orders, and perform functions similar to those of a sheriff, such as making arrests and keeping the accused in custody.

2. The Courts of Appeals

Congress created the U.S. courts of appeals in 1891 because so many people were appealing cases to the Supreme Court that the Court could not handle them. Today 13 courts of appeals handle about 41,000 cases a year, a figure that has almost doubled every ten years since 1970. The United States is divided into 12 judicial circuits, one of which is the District of Columbia. A justice of the Supreme Court is assigned to each circuit. The thirteenth is the Court of Appeals for the Federal Circuit, which hears cases from all across the nation from the legislative courts and from district courts in certain cases, such as those involving patents, trademarks, or copyrights.

The courts of appeals never have original jurisdiction. Usually a panel of three judges sits on each appeal, but for a very important case, all the judges in the circuit may hear it. Decisions are made by majority vote of the participating judges. The courts of appeals hold no trials and hear no testimony. These judges concentrate on determining if errors of procedure and law occurred in the original proceedings of the cases.

Most appeals come from the district courts within their circuits, but they also hear appeals arising from the decisions of federal regulatory agencies. Since many commissions decide disputes that arise over their regulations, their decisions may be appealed to the courts. For example, if the Securities and Exchange Commission, which governs the stock market, finds a stockbroker guilty of fraud in a dispute, the stockbroker may appeal the decision to a U.S. court of appeals. The decisions of the courts of appeals may be appealed to the Supreme Court, but the Court has almost full control over which cases it hears. Since thousands of cases are appealed and the Court can hear less than 150 cases each year, almost all the decisions of the courts of appeals are final.

3. The Court of International Trade

This court hears civil cases related to tariffs and trade. It was created in 1890 and was originally called the United States General Appraisers. The name was changed to the Court of Customs in 1926. In 1980, Congress changed its structure and gave it its present name. The Court of International Trade is based in New York City, but the judges also hear cases in other major port cities, such as New Orleans and San Francisco. The judges sit in panels of three, and their decisions may be appealed to the Court of Appeals for the Federal Circuit.

LEGISLATIVE COURTS

The legislative courts were created to help Congress exercise its powers as stated in Article I, Section 8. They are not governed by Article III as the constitutional courts are, and Congress narrowly defines their jurisdiction. These special courts handle a wide array of cases, but their narrow scope means that they hear many fewer cases than do the constitutional courts.

1. The Court of Military Appeals

Congress created the Court of Military Appeals in 1950 as the highest appeals court for the armed services. This court hears cases appealed to it from military courts by members of the armed forces convicted of breaking military law. Cases from the Court of Military Appeals may be appealed finally to the U.S. Supreme Court, although this rarely happens.

2. The United States Claims Court

Congress established this court in 1982 to handle claims against the United States for money damages. It is composed of 16 judges appointed by the President for 15-year terms. They hear claims throughout the country.

Then and Now

SUING THE GOVERNMENT

Amazingly, the United States government cannot be sued without its consent. The doctrine of sovereign immunity protects the government as a principle of old English public law, "The King can do no wrong." However, Congress long ago readily agreed to concede a long list of legitimate claims against the government. Still, even if the Claims Court upheld your lawsuit, you wouldn't receive your money until Congress appropriated it.

3. The Courts of the District of Columbia

Congress has developed a judicial system for the nation's capital. It includes a federal district court, a court of appeals for the District of Columbia, and local courts to hear civil and criminal cases.

4. The Territorial Courts

Because the Constitution gave Congress the power to make rules to govern U.S. territories, Congress created a court system for the Virgin Islands, Guam, the Northern Mariana Islands, and Puerto Rico. The courts function similarly to district courts, handling civil, criminal, and constitutional cases.

5. The Court of Veterans Appeals

Congress created this court in 1988. It hears appeals from the Board of Veterans Appeals in the Department of Veterans Affairs, a new cabinet department. The court was created to handle veterans' war claims for benefits and other veterans' problems.

6. The United States Tax Court

The power of Congress to tax affects most U.S. citizens. Inevitably, disputes arise over taxes. All civil (but not criminal) cases are heard in the Tax Court. Most cases are generated by the Internal Revenue Service and other Treasury Department agencies. Decisions may go to federal courts of appeals.

FEDERAL JUDGES

You know that the President appoints all federal justices, and, like all other major officials, the Senate must confirm the President's nominations. Consider, however, the numbers: 632 judges serve the district courts, and 179 circuit judges sit on the courts of appeals. Many more are appointed to the legislative courts. Of course, a President would not have to appoint all of them because they serve lifetime terms, but a number of positions always become vacant during a President's term in office. How can the President find time personally to interview candidates for all positions? Although the responsibility of selecting judges demands a great deal of time and effort from the chief executive, some important guidelines traditionally have served to streamline the process.

1. Selection Criteria

The Constitution provides no specific qualifications for federal judges. The criteria for selecting them have developed through history, with each President emphasizing some criteria more than others.

A. EXPERIENCE AND BACKGROUND

Almost all federal judges have law degrees, and most have been practicing lawyers. Many have held previous positions in law and government, as law school professors, members of Congress, or federal district attorneys. About one-third of district court judges have served as state court judges.

Supreme Court justices typically have held high administrative or judicial positions. Many are appointed from the courts of appeals, but surprisingly, some of the most distinguished justices have not had previous judicial experience. The work of the Court is so unique that previous experience is probably much less important than it is for service on the appeals courts. Many Supreme Court justices have worked as attorneys for the Department of Justice, and some have held elective office. For example, William Howard Taft was chief justice after he was President of the United States.

B. PARTY AFFILIATION

The President usually, but not always, appoints judges from his own political party. For example, 81 percent of Republican Gerald Ford's appointments were Republicans. Overall, about 90 percent of judicial appointments since the time of Franklin Roosevelt have gone to members of the President's party. Only 13 of 104 members of the Supreme Court have been nominated by Presidents of a different party, and even then, the exceptions were quite close to the President's political ideology.

The role of partisanship, the strong support of one party, in selecting judges may seem to contradict the idea that judges should be appointed because they are the best qualified for their positions. Remember Federalist John Adams's fear that his Democratic-Republican successor Thomas Jefferson would retract all that he had worked for as President. Even though the President may occasionally stand above politics, he almost certainly will consider a judicial candidate's political party in making his selections.

POLITICAL PARTIES AND JUDICIAL APPOINTMENT

PRESIDENT	PARTY	APPOINTEES FROM SAME PARTY
Franklin Roosevelt	Democrat	97%
Harry Truman	Democrat	92%
Dwight Eisenhower	Republican	95%
John Kennedy	Democrat	92%
Lyndon Johnson	Democrat	96%
Richard Nixon	Republican	93%
Gerald Ford	Republican	81%
Jimmy Carter	Democrat	90%
Ronald Reagan	Republican	94%
George Bush	Republican	89%
Bill Clinton	Democrat	90%*

*Clinton's figures for nominations during his first term (1992–1996)

C. POLITICAL IDEOLOGY

A person's political party can only suggest what one's political beliefs may be. For example, one survey of federal judges found that 75 percent of the Democrats, but only 28 percent of the Republicans, considered themselves to be liberals. A person's ideology, or set of beliefs, is also an important criterion for Presidents to consider as they select their nominations to the judiciary. A President quite understandably wants justices who will agree with his own political ideology. With a few exceptions, most justices appointed by conservative Presidents reflect conservatism in the decisions they make while on the court, and the same correlation exists for liberal Presidents and justices. However, Presidents have no real way of predicting how justices will rule on particular issues. Behavior doesn't always reflect ideology, and political views also change. For example, President Eisenhower was surprised—and dismayed—that two of his appointees, Earl Warren and William Brennan, were not the conservatives that he believed them to be. When asked if he'd ever made any mistakes, Eisenhower replied, "Yes, two, and they are both sitting on the Supreme Court."

e.g.

THE LITMUS TEST

A litmus test in chemistry determines whether a liquid is acid or alkaline. In politics, a type of "litmus test" is used to measure purity of beliefs, especially the political beliefs of Supreme Court justices. When potential nominees are questioned by a President's staff member, they may have to answer questions about school prayer, tax cuts, abortion, free speech, and many other "hot" issues that they might have to decide in court. Although Presidents usually deny the use of a litmus test in making their selections, the opposing political party often makes that accusation.

D. RACE AND GENDER

Until 1967, all Supreme Court justices were white males, as were most federal judges appointed to lower courts. The tradition was broken in 1967 with Lyndon Johnson's appointment of Thurgood Marshall, a distinguished African-American attorney who subsequently served on the Court for more than 20 years. In 1981, Ronald Reagan appointed the first woman justice, Sandra Day O'Connor. Since then, one other African American, Clarence

Thomas, and one more woman, Ruth Bader Ginsburg, have joined the Supreme Court. (See Almanac page 552.)

Although President Jimmy Carter did not have the opportunity to appoint a Supreme Court justice, he changed the composition of the lower federal courts dramatically. He appointed more African Americans, Hispanics, and women to the federal courts than all other Presidents combined—40 women, 38 African Americans, and 16 Hispanics. President Ronald Reagan did not appoint as many as did Carter, perhaps partly because fewer minority candidates could pass the Reagan administration's conservative ideology screening. Twenty percent of George Bush's appointments were women, 7 percent were African American, and 4 percent Hispanic.

E. SENATORIAL COURTESY

A President's judicial nominations must always be made with the "advice and consent" of the Senate. Quite naturally, a President wants to avoid the public embarrassment of having a nomination rejected, so a custom has emerged over the years that helps a President anticipate problems with nominations before they happen. The practice of **senatorial courtesy** governs the selection of judges to federal trial courts. Before officially nominating an individual to federal district court, a President usually submits the name of a candidate to the senators from the candidate's state before formally presenting it for full Senate approval. If either or both senators oppose the President's choice, the President usually withdraws the name and nominates a more acceptable candidate.

The practice of senatorial courtesy does not usually extend to appointments to the courts of appeals because the circuits of those courts cover more than one state. And, senatorial courtesy is not a factor in appointing Supreme Court justices because they are national, not state, appointments.

2. Selection Process

A President usually realizes that an appointment of a federal judge could leave an enduring mark on the American legal system. According to the Constitution, judges may serve "during good behavior," which gives them a lifetime position. They may be removed only through the impeachment process (impeachment by the House and conviction by the Senate). Of the thousands who have served as federal judges, only 13 have ever been impeached, and only 7 of them have been convicted. Only one Supreme Court justice, Samuel Chase in 1804, has been impeached by the House. The Senate failed to convict Chase, and so he remained in office.

def·i·ni·tions

senatorial courtesy—the practice in which a presidential nomination is submitted initially for approval to the senators from the nominee's state.

Headlines

IMPEACHED JUDGES

Seven judges have been removed from office through the impeachment process.

★ John Pickering of the district court in New Hampshire, for judicial misconduct and drunkenness, in 1804

★ West H. Humphreys of the district court in Tennessee, for disloyalty, in 1862

★ Robert W. Archbald of the old Commerce Court, for improper relations with litigants, in 1913

★ Halsted L. Ritter of the district court in Florida, for judicial misconduct, in 1936

★ Harry E. Claiborne of the district court of Nevada, for filing false income tax returns, in 1986

★ Alcee L. Hastings of the district court in Florida, on charges of bribery and false testimony, in 1989

★ Walter L. Nixon of the district court in Mississippi, for perjury, in 1989

A.   THE PRESIDENT'S CHOICE

On the surface it appears as if the President has the most control over judiciary appointments. But many others also have an important say in the process, especially in judgeships on federal district courts.

★ CONGRESS Typically when a vacancy appears on a district court, one or both of the senators of the President's party from the state where the judge will serve suggest candidates to the attorney general and the President. If the candidates pass FBI clearance, their appointment is automatic, with the White House playing only a formal role in their selection. So the custom of senatorial courtesy not only provides input from senators, but it gives the President's political party and the House of Representatives some power in the process too.

★ AGENCIES WITHIN THE EXECUTIVE DEPARTMENTS The Department of Justice and the FBI also get an opportunity to influence the selection. They conduct competency and background checks on the suggested candidates, and the President usually selects from those that they recommend. A President usually doesn't risk the political conflict that would result if he

248

turned down a senator's recommended candidate who survived this screening process. For example, President John Kennedy appointed Senator James O. Eastland's old college roommate to a district court even though Kennedy strongly disagreed with the candidate's racial and political views.

★ **SITTING JUDGES AND JUSTICES** Sometimes the Department of Justice asks sitting judges to evaluate prospective nominees. The judges often take it upon themselves to nominate candidates, and they usually feel free to try to block nominees that they don't support.

★ **PROSPECTIVE NOMINEES** Sometimes individuals who want judicial appointments campaign for themselves. They often work through their political party to gain support, or they contact members of Congress or judges to ask for their endorsements. Most people get judgeships by putting together a carefully orchestrated campaign to gain the necessary support to catch the President's attention.

★ **THE AMERICAN BAR ASSOCIATION (ABA)** This interest group for lawyers maintains a standing committee on the federal judiciary. It rates judicial nominees from a high category of "well qualified" to a low of "not qualified." Although its ratings do not bind a President or the Senate, Presidents usually don't nominate anyone rated "not qualified" by the ABA.

B. SENATE CONFIRMATION

Because most nominees for federal district courts are suggested by the senators in the appropriate states, the Senate confirmation required by the Constitution is only a formality for most. However, for appointments that Presidents control, such as appeals court judges and especially for Supreme Court justices, the confirmation process may be very important. Presidents usually rely on the attorney general, the Department of Justice, and the White House staff to identify and screen candidates for the Supreme Court. Although sitting justices may try to use their influence, the President's choice is usually made fairly independently.

The Senate Judiciary Committee interviews the nominee before he or she goes before the entire Senate. If the Judiciary Committee does not recommend the candidate, the Senate usually rejects the nomination. The committee hearing, then, is the most important step toward the nominee's success. Through 1998, 28 of the 146 individuals nominated to be Supreme Court justices have not been confirmed by the Senate.

Then and Now

CONFIRMATION CHALLENGES

In recent years the Senate has held heated confirmation hearings for Supreme Court nominees.

THE BORK REJECTION

In 1987, the Senate rejected President Reagan's nominee for the seat vacated when Lewis F. Powell stepped down from the Court. Reagan's nominee, Robert Bork, was portrayed by his supporters as a highly intelligent, learned man who would defer to Congress and state legislatures and adhere to the principles set by past court decisions. His critics saw him as a judicial activist who would overturn previous decisions and ignore Congress in order to achieve his extremely conservative political ends. After almost 4 months of politicized national debate, 12 days of hearings before the Judiciary Committee, and 23 grueling hours of debate on the Senate floor, the Senate voted 58 to 42 against Bork's confirmation.

THE THOMAS CONTROVERSY

Another Court nominee was only narrowly confirmed in a Senate vote of 52 to 48 in 1991. When the first African-American Supreme Court justice, Thurgood Marshall, retired in 1991, President Bush nominated as his replacement Clarence Thomas, a controversial member of the Court of Appeals for the District of Columbia. Thomas first ran into problems in the Judiciary Committee hearings when he refused to answer questions about his constitutional views. Critics believed that Clarence Thomas also would press his conservative views into active policy making. The committee narrowly recommended Thomas to the full Senate, where his trouble took a turn for the worse. The storm broke two days before the Senate was scheduled to vote on his confirmation. Information had been leaked to the press that a former associate of Judge Thomas, Anita Hill, had accused him of sexually harassing her when she worked for him in the Department of Education. Three days of emotionally charged hearings were telecast to the nation. Thomas denied the charges presented by Hill, and he narrowly escaped rejection by the closest Supreme Court confirmation vote in modern times.

C. SELECTION GRIDLOCK

Because the Senate must confirm the President's nominees, judicial appointments create opportunities for gridlock. When that happens, nothing gets done in government because the legislative and executive branches disagree. On the last day of 1997, Chief Justice William Rehnquist openly rebuked the Senate for failing to move more quickly on judicial appointments.

In an unusually strong statement, he claimed that the Senate's inaction left "too few judges and too much work" by allowing vacancies to remain unfilled. In 1997, the Senate confirmed only 36 judges, and only 17 in 1996, as compared to 101 judges in 1994. By early 1998, nearly 1 in 10 federal judgeships were vacant, with 26 of the 82 openings going unfilled for more than 18 months. The increasing workloads of the courts magnify the problem. Since 1990 the number of cases filed in courts of appeals has grown by 21 percent, and those brought to district courts have increased by 24 percent.

Quote

The President "should nominate candidates with reasonable promptness, and the Senate should act within a reasonable time to confirm or reject them."

Chief Justice William Rehnquist, 1997

The Supreme Court

Nine justices sit on the Supreme Court, although over the first 80 years of our nation's history the number varied from five to ten. The original number was set at six by the Judiciary Act of 1789 but has changed through the years. The number has been fixed at nine since 1869. Even Franklin Roosevelt could not change it, as he tried to do in 1937 when he asked Congress to increase it to 15. (See Almanac page 551.)

The Constitution does not list any specific responsibilities of the justices, but many duties have developed from laws and through tradition. Duties of the justices include deciding which cases to hear from among the thousands appealed to the Court each year, deciding the case itself, explaining the decision—called the Court's opinion—dealing with requests for special legal actions that come from their assigned circuits, and taking on occasional additional duties, such as serving on special commissions.

The chief justice has several additional duties, such as presiding over sessions and conferences. If he agrees with the majority decision, he usually writes the majority opinion. And, as the highest-ranking justice in the land, the chief justice supervises the general administration of the federal court system.

SUPREME COURT JUSTICES, 1999

JUSTICE	APPOINTING PRESIDENT	BIRTHPLACE	RACE/GENDER
William H. Rehnquist (Chief Justice of the United States)	Richard Nixon *	Wisconsin	White Male
John Paul Stevens	Gerald Ford	Illinois	White Male
Sandra Day O'Connor	Ronald Reagan	Texas	White Female
Antonin Scalia	Ronald Reagan	New Jersey	White Male
Anthony M. Kennedy	Ronald Reagan	California	White Male
David H. Souter	George Bush	Massachusetts	White Male
Clarence Thomas	George Bush	Georgia	African-American Male
Ruth Bader Ginsburg	Bill Clinton	New York	White Female
Stephen G. Breyer	Bill Clinton	California	White Male

* Appointed as chief justice in 1986 by President Reagan

PREVIOUS POSITION	YEAR APPOINTED
Assistant Attorney General Office of Legal Counsel, State of Arizona	1971
U.S. Seventh Circuit Court of Appeals	1975
Arizona Court of Appeals	1981
U.S. Court of Appeals, District of Columbia Judicial Circuit	1986
U.S. Ninth Circuit Court of Appeals, State of California	1987
New Hampshire Supreme Court	1990
U.S. Court of Appeals, District of Columbia Judicial Circuit	1991
U.S. Court of Appeals, District of Columbia Judicial Circuit	1993
U.S. First Circuit Court of Appeals, State of Massachusetts	1994

THE SUPREME COURT AT WORK

To many Americans, Supreme Court justices seem rather mysterious. We usually picture them in long, black robes holding court in a massive building nicknamed "The Marble Palace." We know little about them but consider them somehow "above politics."

Do the justices really have any important effect on the lives of citizens? A closer look at the Supreme Court shows the justices' important role in shaping government policy.

1. Choosing the Cases

The Court's term begins officially on the first Monday in October. The nine justices meet in a small conference room to decide which cases they will hear out of the 7,000 or so petitions they receive annually. The Supreme Court does not have to hear any appeals that they do not want to consider. About 90 percent of their cases are brought by **writ of *certiorari*,** an order to send up the case record because of a claim that the lower court mishandled the case. In the end the justices hand down about 80 to 120 signed rulings. The justices never explain the reason for their choices, a fact that reflects the nature of this least public of the three branches of government.

According to Chief Justice William Rehnquist in his 1987 book, *The Supreme Court: How It Was, How It Is*, three important factors determine whether or not a case is accepted. The first is whether the legal question has been decided differently by two lower courts. For example in *Koon v. United States* (1996), the California appeals court disagreed with the trial judge's sentence given to police officers accused of beating African-American motorist Rodney King. The Supreme Court took the case and sent it back to the California courts for reconsideration. A second reason a case may be heard is if a lower-court decision conflicts with an existing Supreme Court ruling. For example, the constitutionality of the all-male Virginia Military Institute's policy of not admitting women was the primary issue in the *United States v. Virginia* (1996). Finally, the Court may hear the case if the issue could have significance beyond the two parties in the case. For example, the Court struck down congressional districts in *Shaw v. Hunt* (1996), holding that race should not be the sole factor in drawing district boundaries.

The justices reject most of the appeals, but they discuss petitions flagged by one or more of them in earlier readings. Then they vote aloud, one at a time by seniority, starting with the chief justice. A petition will be heard if a minimum of four justices vote to accept the case, a practice known as the Rule of Four. The most junior justice takes notes that will be passed to a clerk for public announcement. Cases are refused for many reasons, not

---

writ of *certiorari*—literally, "made more certain"; an order from a higher court requiring a lower court to send the record of a case for review.

necessarily because the justices agree with the decision of the lower court. Some, for example, are rejected because they represent a controversy that the justices do not want to be involved in or because the person challenging a law has not actually been harmed.

2. Hearing the Cases

The hearings for the cases are public. On Mondays, Tuesdays, and Wednesdays, starting in October, the justices listen to lawyers present each side of two or three cases a day. (Some cases, however, are decided without oral arguments.) The public may attend on a first-come first-served basis. Since the Court's sessions end in June and cases do not carry over into the next session, as many as four cases a day may be heard.

Before a case is heard in open court, the justices receive briefs, in which lawyers from each side present legal arguments, historical materials, and related previous decisions. The justices often receive *amicus curiae* briefs from individuals, interest groups, or government agencies that have an interest in the case and claim to have information vital to the decision.

3. Deciding the Cases

After the public hearing, the justices again meet privately. Although the discussions in these meetings are secret, they may be described as spirited and substantial. The chief justice presides, usually opening the discussion by stating the facts of the case and making suggestions for deciding the case. Each member of the Court is then asked, in order of seniority, to give his or her views and conclusions. About one-third of the decisions are unanimous, and the rest are split. The Court is sometimes criticized for the large number of split decisions, but the cases that reach them are almost always the tough ones that have led to disagreement in the lower courts. The Court functions as the final say, and the decisions are rarely easy. After the vote, the most senior justice in the majority assigns the task of writing the **majority opinion.** This is the official opinion of the court. If the chief justice has agreed with the decision, he often will draft it in consultation with the others. The most senior justice on the losing side decides who will write the **dissenting opinion** of those justices who do not agree with the Court's majority decision. Sometimes one or more of the justices who agree with the Court's decision may write a **concurring opinion** to make or emphasize a point not made by the majority opinion.

def·i·ni·tions

majority opinion—the view of the Supreme Court justices who agree with a particular ruling.

dissenting opinion—a Supreme Court opinion by one or more justices in the minority who oppose the ruling.

concurring opinion—a Supreme Court opinion by one or more justices who agree with the majority's conclusion but wish to offer differing reasons.

Law clerks stay very busy at this point, writing draft opinions, researching past cases, and even making recommendations to the justices. The justices do not trade votes during this process, but they engage in a constant conversation by way of memos. Drafts may be circulated and discussed for weeks, or even months, but all decisions must be made by June when the Court generally finishes its session.

Beginning in mid-spring, the Court stops hearing oral arguments and focuses on public releases of decisions. Rulings traditionally are handed down on Mondays, although as June approaches, they are announced almost every day. The process again becomes public at this point, and the entire Court sits at the bench in the main courtroom. The justice who wrote the majority opinion announces the opinion and gives the facts of the case and details of the Court's decision. After the last case is announced, the session ends, and a new one begins the following October.

4. Implementing Decisions

Once a decision is made, sometimes the public responds quickly in implementing it. For example, in *United States v. Virginia* (1996) the Court ordered the all-male Virginia Military Institute to admit women. Later, the Citadel, a military college in Charleston, South Carolina, decided to admit female students for the first time. No court order was needed for the action. Other times action does not follow for many years. The famous *Brown v. Topeka* (1954) case declared "separate but equal" public facilities unconstitutional, but segregated school districts continued to exist for years thereafter. President Eisenhower refused to state clearly that Americans should comply with the decision. Southern governors—such as Orville Faubus of Arkansas and George Wallace of Alabama—blocked the decision from being implemented in their states. The Court needed more decisions and the cooperation of national and state executives and legislatures—as well as some media publicity—before the *Brown* decision was enforced across the country.

POLICY-MAKING POWER OF THE SUPREME COURT

The Supreme Court is the highest court in the most powerful judicial system in the world. As the Court interprets the meaning of laws, it also exerts great policy-making influence. Most people think of policy making as passing laws, but in truth all three branches of government shape policy. Congress certainly makes policies when it considers and passes new legislation. Although the executive branch theoretically carries out only the laws passed by Congress, its departments and agencies shape policy in the ways they execute the laws. The modern President now takes the initiative in developing a budget, influencing public opinion, and setting goals for the country in a way that his predecessors never did. Like it or not, the Supreme Court and other federal courts also determine policy through judicial review, setting precedents, and overturning decisions.

Precedents

An informal rule of judicial policy making has been *stare decisis,* a Latin term that means "let the decision stand." *Stare decisis* is based on using **precedents,** the custom of settling a court case in accordance with earlier decisions on similar cases. The personal values and beliefs of individual justices, the influence of one justice on another, changes in the American political climate and public opinion—these are just some of the factors that influence the decisions of the Court. Precedent gives continuity and stability to the meaning of law and sets the standard for the measurement of equal justice.

On the other hand, times and attitudes change, and the composition of the Court changes. The Supreme Court has overruled its own precedent dozens of times. One example is *West Virginia State Board of Education v. Barnette* (1943) in which the Court ruled that mandatory flag salute laws in public schools interfere with the free exercise of religion. In supporting a family that considered the flag a "graven image," and thus against their religious beliefs, that Court overturned the earlier *Minersville School District v. Gobitis* (1940) decision in which the Court had upheld the school policies.

Should the courts follow the lead of Congress and the President, waiting for the other branches to make laws and take actions that the courts may or may not judge to be constitutional? The argument that the courts go too far in policy making is an old one. The debate about policy-making power is evident in the conflicting points of view on judicial activism and judicial restraint.

def·i·ni·tions

precedent—a judicial decision that is used as a standard in later similar cases.

stare decisis—literally, "let the decision stand"; the practice of basing legal decisions on established Supreme Court precedents from similar cases.

U.S. SUPREME COURT JUSTICES

NAME	APPOINTED BY PRESIDENT	JUDICIAL OATH TAKEN	DATE SERVICE TERMINATED
CHIEF JUSTICES			
John Jay	Washington	1789	1795
John Rutledge	Washington	1795	1795
Oliver Ellsworth	Washington	1796	1800
John Marshall	John Adams	1801	1835
Roger Brooke Taney	Jackson	1836	1864
Salmon Portland Chase	Lincoln	1864	1873
Morrison Remick Waite	Grant	1874	1888
Melville Weston Fuller	Cleveland	1888	1910
Edward Douglass White	Taft	1910	1921
William Howard Taft	Harding	1921	1930
Charles Evans Hughes	Hoover	1930	1941
Harlan Fiske Stone	Franklin D. Roosevelt	1941	1946
Fred Moore Vinson	Truman	1946	1953
Earl Warren	Eisenhower	1953	1969
Warren Earl Burger	Nixon	1969	1986
William Hubbs Rehnquist	Reagan	1986	
ASSOCIATE JUSTICES			
James Wilson	Washington	1789	1798
William Cushing	Washington	1790	1810
John Blair	Washington	1790	1795
John Rutledge	Washington	1790	1791
James Iredell	Washington	1790	1799
Thomas Johnson	Washington	1792	1793
William Paterson	Washington	1793	1806
Samuel Chase	Washington	1796	1811
Bushrod Washington	John Adams	1799	1829
Alfred Moore	John Adams	1800	1804
William Johnson	Jefferson	1804	1834
Henry Brockholst Livingston	Jefferson	1807	1823
Thomas Todd	Jefferson	1807	1826
Gabriel Duvall	Madison	1811	1835
Joseph Story	Madison	1812	1845
Smith Thompson	Monroe	1823	1843
Robert Trimble	John Quincy Adams	1826	1828
John McLean	Jackson	1830	1861
Henry Baldwin	Jackson	1830	1844
James Moore Wayne	Jackson	1835	1867
Philip Pendleton Barbour	Jackson	1836	1841
John Catron	Van Buren	1837	1865

CONTINUED

U.S. SUPREME COURT JUSTICES   CONTINUED

NAME	APPOINTED BY PRESIDENT	JUDICIAL OATH TAKEN	DATE SERVICE TERMINATED
John McKinley	Van Buren	1838	1852
Peter Vivian Daniel	Van Buren	1842	1860
Samuel Nelson	Tyler	1845	1872
Levi Woodbury	Polk	1845	1851
Robert Cooper Grier	Polk	1846	1870
Benjamin Robbins Curtis	Fillmore	1851	1857
John Archibald Campbell	Pierce	1853	1861
Nathan Clifford	Buchanan	1858	1881
Noah Haynes Swayne	Lincoln	1862	1881
Samuel Freeman Miller	Lincoln	1862	1890
David Davis	Lincoln	1862	1877
Stephen Johnson Field	Lincoln	1863	1897
William Strong	Grant	1870	1880
Joseph P. Bradley	Grant	1870	1892
Ward Hunt	Grant	1873	1882
John Marshall Harlan	Hayes	1877	1911
William Burnham Woods	Hayes	1881	1887
Stanley Matthews	Garfield	1881	1889
Horace Gray	Arthur	1882	1902
Samuel Blatchford	Arthur	1882	1893
Lucius Quintus C. Lamar	Cleveland	1888	1893
David Josiah Brewer	Harrison	1890	1910
Henry Billings Brown	Harrison	1891	1906
George Shiras, Jr.	Harrison	1892	1903
Howell Edmunds Jackson	Harrison	1893	1895
Edward Douglass White	Cleveland	1894	1910*
Rufus Wheeler Peckham	Cleveland	1896	1909
Joseph McKenna	McKinley	1898	1925
Oliver Wendell Holmes	Theodore Roosevelt	1902	1932
William Rufus Day	Theodore Roosevelt	1903	1922
William Henry Moody	Theodore Roosevelt	1906	1910
Horace Harmon Lurton	Taft	1910	1914
Charles Evans Hughes	Taft	1910	1916
Willis Van Devanter	Taft	1911	1937
Joseph Rucker Lamar	Taft	1911	1916
Mahlon Pitney	Taft	1912	1922
James Clark McReynolds	Wilson	1914	1941
Louis Dembitz Brandeis	Wilson	1916	1939

Named Chief Justice

CONTINUED

U.S. SUPREME COURT JUSTICES

NAME	APPOINTED BY PRESIDENT	JUDICIAL OATH TAKEN	DATE SERVICE TERMINATED
John Hessin Clarke	Wilson	1916	1922
George Sutherland	Harding	1922	1938
Pierce Butler	Harding	1923	1939
Edward Terry Sanford	Harding	1923	1930
Harlan Fiske Stone	Coolidge	1925	1941*
Owen Josephus Roberts	Hoover	1930	1945
Benjamin Nathan Cardozo	Hoover	1932	1938
Hugo Lafayette Black	Franklin D. Roosevelt	1937	1971
Stanley Forman Reed	Franklin D. Roosevelt	1938	1957
Felix Frankfurter	Franklin D. Roosevelt	1939	1962
William Orville Douglas	Franklin D. Roosevelt	1939	1975
Frank Murphy	Franklin D. Roosevelt	1940	1949
James Francis Byrnes	Franklin D. Roosevelt	1941	1942
Robert Houghwout Jackson	Franklin D. Roosevelt	1941	1954
Wiley Blount Rutledge	Franklin D. Roosevelt	1943	1949
Harold Hitz Burton	Truman	1945	1958
Tom Campbell Clark	Truman	1949	1967
Sherman Minton	Truman	1949	1956
John Marshall Harlan	Eisenhower	1955	1971
William J. Brennan, Jr.	Eisenhower	1956	1990
Charles Evans Whittaker	Eisenhower	1957	1962
Potter Stewart	Eisenhower	1958	1981
Byron Raymond White	Kennedy	1962	1993
Arthur Joseph Goldberg	Kennedy	1962	1965
Abe Fortas	Lyndon Johnson	1965	1969
Thurgood Marshall	Lyndon Johnson	1967	1991
Harry A. Blackmun	Nixon	1970	1994
Lewis F. Powell, Jr.	Nixon	1972	1987
William H. Rehnquist	Nixon	1972	1986*
John Paul Stevens	Ford	1975	
Sandra Day O'Connor	Reagan	1981	
Antonin Scalia	Reagan	1986	
Anthony McLeod Kennedy	Reagan	1987	
David H. Souter	Bush	1990	
Clarence Thomas	Bush	1991	
Ruth Bader Ginsburg	Clinton	1993	
Stephen G. Breyer	Clinton	1994	

Named Chief Justice

Judicial Activism vs. Judicial Restraint

A number of prominent Supreme Court justices—from John Marshall in the early nineteenth century to Earl Warren in the 1950s and 1960s—have generally supported the view of **judicial activism,** the belief that it is appropriate for judges to make bold policy decisions and even chart new constitutional ground. Judicial activists believe that the other two branches represent the majority of Americans and that they usually make fair decisions for most people. However, sometimes an individual's rights may suffer because he or she is always outvoted by the majority. In this case, the courts are the best branch for defending the individual's rights and making policy to help those who are weak economically or politically. For example, most judicial activists would argue that the rights of African Americans were ignored for decades by Congress and Presidents. In *Brown v. Topeka Board of Education* (1954), for example, the Court led the other branches in policy making. The result was justice where it had previously been denied. (See page 317.)

Judicial activism is opposed by the policy of **judicial restraint,** the belief that the courts should leave policy decisions to the legislative and executive branches. Advocates of this view argue that the federal courts, composed of unelected judges, are the least democratic branch of government. They believe that judges should not get involved in political questions or conflicts between the President and Congress. Justices may be legal experts who specialize in defining rights and duties, but they have no special expertise in government.

Note that judicial activism or restraint differs from liberalism or conservatism. At any given time, the Supreme Court may be described as liberal, moderate, conservative, or divided. Since justices are appointed one by one, the Court tends to change gradually over a period of years. Although some might assume that liberals—who favor change—are activists, there is almost no correlation between activism and a liberal ideology. Nor do conservatives necessarily practice judicial restraint.

One reason that people tend to associate activism with liberalism is that the most activist Court in recent times, the Warren Court (1953–1969), was also known for its liberal political views. Led by Chief Justice Earl Warren, the Court rulings strengthened desegregation efforts and the civil liberties and rights of defendants. However, the actions of other Courts through the years illustrate that conservatism does not equal restraint, and liberalism does not equal activism.

def·i·ni·tions

judicial activism—the belief that Supreme Court justices should actively make policy and sometimes redefine the Constitution.

judicial restraint—the belief that Supreme Court justices should not actively try to shape social and political issues or redefine the Constitution.

Vs.

JUDICIAL ACTIVISM vs. JUDICIAL RESTRAINT

The debate between judicial activism and judicial restraint began in the early days of the United States and continues through the present.

JUDICIAL RESTRAINT

"The Constitution is not an empty bottle . . . it is like a statute, and the meaning doesn't change." A democratic system "is destroyed if the smug assurances of each age are removed from the democratic process and written into the Constitution."

Antonin Scalia
Associate Justice, 1996

(Referring to the Court of the 1970s): "For the most part, the Court was neither out in front of, or did it hold back, social change. Instead, what occurred was what engineers might call a positive feedback process, with the Court functioning as an amplifier sensitively responding to, and perhaps moderately accelerating, the pace of change."

Ruth Bader Ginsburg
Associate Justice, 1997

JUDICIAL ACTIVISM

"We are under a Constitution, but the Constitution is what the judges say it is."

Charles Evans Hughes
Associate Justice, 1910–1916
Chief Justice, 1930–1941

[The Supreme Court should be] "a leader in a vital national seminar that leads to the formulation of values for the American people."

Arthur S. Miller
legal scholar, 1982

"The genius of the Constitution rests not in any static meaning it might have had in a world that is dead and gone, but in the adaptability of its great principles to cope with current problems and current needs. What the constitutional fundamentals meant to the wisdom of other times cannot be the measure to the vision of our times."

William J. Brennan, Jr.
former Associate Justice, 1985

Then and Now

THE BURGER COURT (1969–1986)

The Burger Court demonstrates that liberalism does not necessarily mean activism. Richard Nixon chose Warren Burger, a conservative judge on the District of Columbia Court of Appeals, as chief justice. Although most of the justices were appointed by Republican Presidents, this moderate Court followed the activist tradition, knocking down 34 statutes compared to the Warren Court's 25. The Burger Court narrowed defendants' rights (a conservative view), but it also upheld a woman's right to have an abortion in *Roe v. Wade* (1973), required school busing in certain cases, and upheld affirmative action programs (all reflecting a liberal position).

Checks on Judicial Power

Despite the powerful policy-making role that courts play in the United States—especially those that practice judicial activism—they do not operate without restraint. There are a number of important checks on judicial power. For instance, the courts are limited in the types of cases and issues they may hear. Four other important constraints on judicial power are described below:

1. **LIMITED POWERS OF ENFORCEMENT** A judge has no police force or army. Although people who do not comply with a court order risk being charged with contempt of court, they can sometimes get away with ignoring the order for long periods of time. For example, long after the Supreme Court decided that prayers should not be allowed in public schools, schools all over the country were still allowing those prayers.

2. **CONGRESS** Congress may check the judiciary by its powers to:

★ confirm all presidential nominees to federal judgeships,

★ impeach judges and justices,

★ alter the organization of the federal court system (other than the Supreme Court), and

★ amend the Constitution.

Congress may also repass a slightly different version of a law the courts declare unconstitutional or restrict the kinds of remedies that courts may impose.

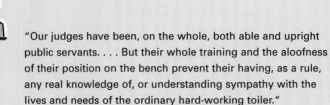

Quotes

"Our judges have been, on the whole, both able and upright public servants. . . . But their whole training and the aloofness of their position on the bench prevent their having, as a rule, any real knowledge of, or understanding sympathy with the lives and needs of the ordinary hard-working toiler."

Theodore Roosevelt,
President of the United States (1901–1909)

"Presidents come and go, but the Court goes on forever."

William Howard Taft, President of the United States (1909–1913)
Chief Justice of the United States (1921–1930)

"The law is at best an inexact science, and the cases our Court takes to decide are frequently ones upon which able judges in lower courts have disagreed. There simply is no demonstrably "right" answer to the question involved in any of our difficult cases."

Chief Justice William Rehnquist, 1987

"The Court should be the guardian of freedom that does not worry about elections and is not swayed by public opinion polls."

Senator Paul Simon (D-IL), 1992

264

3. **THE PRESIDENT** The President's ability to check the judiciary lies in his power to appoint justices and to enforce or ignore Court decisions. For example, President Dwight Eisenhower was initially reluctant to enforce the Court's 1954 ruling to integrate schools. He sent the National Guard to Little Rock, Arkansas, in 1957, after massive resistance by state and local officials convinced him to act.

4. **PUBLIC OPINION** In some ways it might seem federal judges are isolated from public opinion. After all, they are not elected and have no constituency to answer to. Some believe that society's views are irrelevant and that they should consider only the original intent of the Founders when interpreting the law. Yet, the courts are not entirely independent of popular opinion and changing political moods. For instance, if the Supreme Court strays too far from public opinion, the backlash can make the decision impossible to apply and weaken the Court's authority. In *Dred Scott v. Sandford* (1857), the Court declared that slaves cannot be citizens and that Congress had no power to forbid slavery in the U.S. territories. (See page 296.) The strong public outrage helped set off the Civil War. Decisions that go against popular opinion are sometimes overturned later as the views of the public—or the Court justices—change. For instance, the decision in *Plessy v. Ferguson* (1896) that "separate but equal" public facilities were constitutional was overturned by *Brown v. Board of Education* (1954). Court decisions often reflect the values of the American society during a particular historical era.

In 1788 Alexander Hamilton wrote in *The Federalist* No. 78 that the "judiciary is beyond comparison the weakest of the three [branches]...." Whether that assessment is still true today is debatable. The power of judicial review and the Supreme Court's increasing role as a shaper of public policy have established the U.S. judiciary as the most influential judicial system in the world. U.S. policies and laws are ultimately tested in the courts.

Unit IV

Civil Liberties and Civil Rights

1st Amendment Freedoms

T he great issue of America in the late eighteenth century was liberty. The American Revolution was fought to protest a mother country that restricted the freedoms of the colonists. Yet—perhaps surprisingly—the Constitution says little about the rights and freedoms guaranteed to the American people. As a result, people in many states were suspicious of the document. Anti-Federalists immediately protested that liberties would be unduly limited by the government proposed in the Constitution. They wanted a comprehensive list of liberties that the government could not violate. Since ratification was seriously threatened, the Founders agreed to add amendments that would guarantee liberties and rights. As a result, the Bill of Rights was introduced to the first Congress in 1789.

Americans often have been willing to fight for their liberties. No other topic has created more protest and argument through the years. Civil liberties disputes have taken many forms. They may be divided into two broad areas: freedoms guaranteed in the 1st Amendment (religion, speech and press, and assembly and petition) and liberties associated with crime and with due process. The overwhelming majority of court decisions that define American civil liberties are based on the Bill of Rights.

In this chapter . . .

Bill of Rights and Basic Freedoms

The Bill of Rights was a set of proposals based largely on the existing Virginia bill of rights. Twelve were approved by Congress, ten of which were ratified by the states and added in 1791 as amendments to the Constitution. (See Almanac page 507.)

THE BILL OF RIGHTS

★ 1ST AMENDMENT—RELIGIOUS AND POLITICAL FREEDOM
The 1st Amendment is the source of Americans' freedom of religion, speech, press, assembly, and the right to petition the government.

★ 2ND AMENDMENT—RIGHT TO BEAR ARMS The 2nd Amendment provides the right to bear arms. Individuals and groups on both sides of the gun control issue interpret the 2nd Amendment differently.

★ 3RD AMENDMENT—QUARTERING TROOPS This restriction on the quartering of soldiers (having them take over your house) was important to those with fresh and bitter memories of the American Revolution. While it may seem oddly out-of-date, this amendment has been used to support the right to privacy in court cases today.

★ 4TH AMENDMENT—SEARCH AND SEIZURE The 4th Amendment protects individuals against "unreasonable searches and seizures." It requires that authorities have warrants before they can search private property.

★ 5TH AMENDMENT—RIGHTS OF ACCUSED PERSONS
The 5th Amendment deals with the rights of the accused in criminal proceedings, such as the protection against self-incrimination or being tried twice for the same crime. It also provides the right not to be deprived of "life, liberty, or property without due process of law" and the right to be given "just compensation" when the government takes private land.

★ 6TH AMENDMENT—RIGHT TO A PUBLIC TRIAL Persons accused of a crime are guaranteed "a speedy and public trial, by an impartial jury" and must be informed of the crime that they are accused of. Witnesses against them must publicly confront them, defendants must be allowed to call witnesses in their defense, and defendants have the right to be represented by an attorney.

★ 7TH AMENDMENT—JURY TRIALS IN CIVIL CASES While the 6th Amendment addresses rights of individuals in a criminal trial, the 7th Amendment guarantees rights in civil cases. Individuals are guaranteed the right of trial by jury in situations where the value in question exceeds

$20. (Trial by jury for criminal cases had been guaranteed already in Article III.) The right to trial by jury may be, and often is, waived if both accused and accuser agree to a bench trial, in which only a judge hears the case.

⭐ **8TH AMENDMENT—PUNISHMENTS FOR CRIMES** The 8th Amendment is also concerned with protecting the rights of those accused of crimes. It guards against excessive bail, excessive fines, and "cruel and unusual punishment" for those found guilty of a crime. For example, a person found guilty of stealing $10 worth of groceries from the local deli cannot be sent to prison for life. Those opposed to the death penalty usually argue that the death penalty is "cruel and unusual punishment."

⭐ **9TH AMENDMENT—RIGHTS OF PEOPLE** This "elastic clause" for civil rights says that a right cannot be ignored just because it is not expressly mentioned in the Bill of Rights or in the body of the Constitution. Loose constructionists cite the 9th Amendment for support of such rights as the right to privacy.

⭐ **10TH AMENDMENT—POWERS OF STATES AND PEOPLE** This amendment was designed to ease the fears of the Anti-Federalists who worried that states' rights would be abused by the new national government. The amendment states that powers not specifically granted to the national government by the Constitution shall be reserved for the states.

The Bill of Rights clearly was intended to protect individuals from abuses by the national government. Those who insisted that amendments be added to the Constitution to check the power of the national government had no idea that these same restrictions would be applied to the state governments. For example, in *Barron v. Baltimore* (1833) the Marshall Court ruled that the Bill of Rights applied only to the national government, not to the states and cities. But now the Bill of Rights is routinely applied to states as well as to the national government.

INCORPORATION

No attempt was made to apply the Bill of Rights to the states for about 80 years, and then Congress added the 14th Amendment to the Constitution. Its Due Process Clause states that "no state shall . . . deprive any person of life, liberty, or property without the due process of law. . . ." It has been interpreted through the years—in cases such as *Gitlow v. New York* (1925), *Fiske v. Kansas* (1927), and *Near v. Minnesota* (1931)—to mean that the protections of the Bill of Rights must also apply to the states.

This case-by-case gradual extension of the Due Process Clause of the Bill of Rights to the states is known as **incorporation**. By the 1940s all provisions of the 1st Amendment—religion, speech, press, assembly, and petition—had been brought within the scope of the 14th Amendment. Through the 1960s, the Supreme Court selectively incorporated all of the Bill of Rights, except for the 2nd, 3rd, 7th, and 10th Amendments. The Court reasoned that rights not incorporated are those that could be replaced by other procedures without necessarily denying justice or freedom. For example, the 5th Amendment provision that requires a grand jury indictment before a person is brought to trial remains unincorporated because justice could be ensured through any number of other procedures.

CIVIL LIBERTIES AND CIVIL RIGHTS

Notice how often the word *right* appears in the Bill of Rights. Even the name of the first ten amendments, which are meant to preserve liberty, is the Bill of Rights. The Founders used the words *rights* and *liberties* often in the same sentence. For example, consider Thomas Jefferson's famous sentence from the Declaration of Independence:

"We hold these Truths to be self-evident, that all Men are created equal, that they are endowed by their Creator with certain unalienable Rights, that among these are Life, Liberty and the Pursuit of Happiness . . . to secure these Rights, Governments are instituted among Men."

According to Jefferson, liberty is a right fundamental enough to serve as a cornerstone for our government. Life and the pursuit of happiness are rights as well. But doesn't a guarantee of life and the pursuit of happiness imply liberty? As we will soon see, the distinction between rights and liberties was blurred from the very beginning, and today the two concepts are often used interchangeably.

def·i·ni·tions

incorporation—the gradual process of applying the Bill of Rights to the states.

Kinds of Protections

In general, **civil liberties** are protections against government. They are individual freedoms and rights guaranteed to every citizen. For example, the 1st Amendment says that Congress shall "make no law respecting an establishment of religion." This phrase is intended to safeguard the individual from a "government-sponsored" church with which people might disagree. So, the 1st Amendment gives the individual "liberty" from the actions of the government.

Civil rights, on the other hand, generally refer to positive acts of government protection against group discrimination. The Supreme Court has held that most, but not all, constitutional rights are guaranteed to all persons. Jefferson's famous phrase—"that all men are created equal"— sometimes doesn't work quite that way in real life. It requires government support and laws to achieve equality. As a result, the term *civil rights* is often associated with the protection of rights for minority groups. Positive actions by government counterbalance the natural tendencies of majority rule in a democracy, so that rights of minorities are protected.

Rights in Conflict

Over and over in American history, the tough civil liberties issues have to do with rights in conflict. The difficult questions are the ones most likely to end up in the Supreme Court. Consider, for example, the case of *Tinker v. Des Moines School District* (1969). In 1965, a group of adults and students in Des Moines, Iowa, decided to publicize their opposition to the Vietnam War by wearing black armbands during the winter holiday season. The principals of the Des Moines schools reacted by announcing the policy that any students wearing armbands to school would be asked to remove them and would be suspended if they refused. As a result, Mary Beth, John, and Christopher Tinker (and several other students) were suspended and sent home from school. Their parents took the case to court. Both sides believed that their rights had been violated.

There are many situations such as this in which different rights conflict—or are thought to conflict—with one another. The Court sided with the Tinkers, declaring that students' rights are not banned "at the schoolhouse gate."

def·i·ni·tions

civil liberties—constitutionally based freedoms guaranteed to individuals.

civil rights—rights belonging to a citizen or member of society, regardless of race, sex, or national origin, to receive equal treatment under the law.

Vs.

RIGHTS IN CONFLICT

In *Tinker v. Des Moines School District* (1969), the Supreme Court had to decide whether students could wear armbands as a form of symbolic protest. The case was not about speech—that is, what was said—as much as it was about "symbolic speech." The Court has often ruled that the 1st Amendment protects certain nonverbal behavior, such as hand movements, facial expressions, or wearing certain clothes. Do you agree with the Court's decision in favor of the students?

TINKER

★ The students had a 1st Amendment right to express their opinions, and they were as entitled to that expression in school as in any other place.

★ The armbands did not disrupt school discipline.

★ The school did not ban all political symbols. Selectively banning just black armbands is unconstitutional.

DES MOINES

★ Reasonable limits must be placed on freedom of expression. School is not the appropriate place for a political demonstration.

★ The ban was placed on armbands to avoid disruption of school discipline.

★ The orderly atmosphere of a classroom is entitled to constitutional protection.

Freedom of Religion

The 1st Amendment guarantees freedom of religion in two clauses. The first, known as the **Establishment Clause,** states that "Congress shall make no law respecting an establishment of religion." The second, called the **Free Exercise Clause,** requires that Congress not prohibit the free exercise of religion.

THE ESTABLISHMENT CLAUSE

Notice that the phrase "separation of church and state" does not appear in the 1st Amendment, nor is it found anywhere else in the Constitution. Instead, Thomas Jefferson coined it in his writings during the American Revolution. He opposed having the Church of England as the established church of his native Virginia. As President, Jefferson wrote that the 1st Amendment's freedom of religion clause was designed to build "a wall of separation between Church and State." Jefferson's interpretation has surely influenced the Supreme Court through the years. The Court has consistently ruled that a separation between church and state is required by the Constitution. The Court has declared that the 1st Amendment not only means that no national religion may be established but that government can have no involvement with religion at all.

Quote

"Be it enacted . . . that no man shall be compelled to frequent or support any religious worship . . . nor shall otherwise suffer on account of his religious opinions or belief. . . ."

The Virginia Statute of Religious Liberty, *1786*

def·i·ni·tions

Establishment Clause—the part of the 1st Amendment that prohibits the establishment of a national religion.

Free Exercise Clause—the part of the 1st Amendment that states that Congress may not make laws restricting or prohibiting a person's religious practices.

Everson v. Board of Education

The first case that the Court heard based on the Establishment Clause was *Everson v. Board of Education* (1947). The case involved a New Jersey town that reimbursed parents for the costs of transporting their children to school, including parochial schools operated by the Catholic Church. Some parents in the town challenged the New Jersey law that allowed the reimbursement, claiming that the state was supporting religion in violation of the Establishment Clause. The Court decided that the law was constitutional and that transportation is a "religiously neutral" activity. However, it made it clear that the Establishment Clause applied to the states. The ruling specified that the government cannot aid one or more religions and that it can't spend any tax money in support of religious activities or institutions. The *Everson* case still guides the Court, but it leaves open the question of just how high the wall of separation is and what issues are "religiously neutral."

School Prayer

Other Supreme Court cases involving the Establishment Clause have centered on student religious groups, the teaching of evolution, tax exemptions for religious organizations, state aid to parochial schools, and "released time" programs, in which public schools provide students time in school to attend religious classes. School prayer has been the most controversial of the separation of church and state issues. In five major cases, the Supreme Court has ruled about the constitutionality of saying prayers and reading the Bible in public schools.

1. *ENGLE v. VITALE* (1962) The Court banned the use of a prayer written by the New York State Board of Regents. It read, "Almighty God, we acknowledge our dependence upon Thee, and we beg Thy blessings upon us, our parents, our teachers, and our country."

2. *ABINGTON SCHOOL DISTRICT v. SCHEMPP* (1963) The Court overturned a Pennsylvania law requiring the saying of the Lord's Prayer and a Bible reading.

3. *STONE v. GRAHAM* (1980) The Court ruled that a Kentucky law requiring copies of the Ten Commandments be posted in all public school classrooms was unconstitutional.

4. *WALLACE v. JAFFREE* (1985) Alabama's "moment of silence" law that provided for a one-minute period of silence for "meditation or voluntary prayer" was found to be unconstitutional.

5. *LEE v. WEISMAN* (1992) The Court decided that prayer could not be offered as part of a graduation ceremony of a Rhode Island public school.

© Glenn McCoy *Belleville News-Democrat*

While the Supreme Court has held that public schools can't sponsor religious activities, it has ruled that the practice of prayers at daily sessions of Congress are constitutional. Not only are prayers permissible, but a chaplain—paid with public funds—offers the opening prayer. How could this be? The Court makes three distinctions between school and legislative prayers. First is tradition. Prayers have been offered in the nation's legislative bodies since colonial times. Second, the legislators are adults who are not so easily swayed to religious indoctrination or peer pressure as are children. Third, attendance at the beginning of the daily sessions is voluntary.

THE FREE EXERCISE CLAUSE

A second clause in the 1st Amendment that addresses freedom of religion is the Free Exercise Clause. It disallows any laws "prohibiting the free exercise of religion." The courts have interpreted the 14th Amendment to extend this freedom to protection from state governments as well. How could anyone disagree? It is a basic, straightforward guarantee that few people would challenge, right? Wrong! As with other civil liberties and rights, the issues almost never have clear-cut answers.

Headlines

ORDER IN THE COURT

The issue of separation of church and state in schools and in government offices was raised again in 1997. A circuit court judge in Alabama ruled that Judge Roy Moore's display of the Ten Commandments in his courtroom was unconstitutional. Nonetheless, Moore pledged that he would not remove his display. Alabama's Governor Fob James declared that he would use the "force of arms" to prevent a court order removing the Ten Commandments from being carried out.

Circuit Court Judge Charles Price maintained the unconstitutionality of the display with these words:

"The Ten Commandments are not in peril. They are neither stained, tarnished nor thrashed. They may be displayed in every church, synagogue, temple, mosque, home, and storefront. They may be displayed in cars, on lawns and in corporate boardrooms. Where this precious gift cannot and should not be displayed as an obvious religious text or to promote religion is on government property (particularly in a courtroom)."

Difficult Questions

Think about whether you would guarantee the right to practice one's religion in these cases.

★ Should a Mormon who practices polygamy (the marriage of one man to more than one woman) be allowed to live next door to you with five wives and assorted children?

★ Should people be permitted to use poisonous snakes in their religious rites?

★ Should a man be denied unemployment benefits because he violated state drug laws when he took a hallucinogenic drug (peyote) as part of a religious ceremony?

★ Should a sick child whose parents' religion prohibits medical treatment be allowed to die?

★ What if a religious group sincerely believes that its gods require human sacrifice? Should that practice be allowed?

Freedom of Religion Cases

Each year the courts face tough questions regarding free exercise of religion. Religions sometimes require actions that violate the rights of others or forbid actions that society thinks are necessary. The Supreme Court has never allowed religious freedom to be an excuse for any behavior. But it has consistently ruled that people have the absolute right to believe what they want, but not necessarily the right to religious practices that may harm society. In six important cases, the Court has set guidelines on people's rights to practice their religion freely.

1. *REYNOLDS v. UNITED STATES* (1879) In this precedent-setting case for free exercise of religion, George Reynolds, a Mormon who had two wives, appealed his conviction on a charge that he'd violated U.S. laws prohibiting polygamy. The Court ruled against his claim that he should be able to practice his religion freely. A precedent was set. The right to free exercise of religion may be restricted if the practice violates a law that protects the health, safety, or morals of the community.

2. *CANTWELL v. CONNECTICUT* (1940) The Court has ruled that a number of other government restrictions on religious practices are unconstitutional. In this landmark case, for instance, the Court overturned a law requiring a license before an individual could raise money for a religious cause.

3. *MINERSVILLE SCHOOL DISTRICT v. GOBITIS* (1940) The issue in this case was whether schoolchildren could be required to salute the American flag. In this case the Jehovah's Witnesses, a religious group, believed that saluting the flag violated the Christian commandment of not bowing to a "graven image" or idol. The Court upheld the school regulation, reasoning that the salute didn't infringe on religious freedom. But three years later in another case, the Court reversed itself. In *West Virginia Board of Education v. Barnette* (1943), it determined that a compulsory flag salute was unconstitutional.

4. *BUNN v. NORTH CAROLINA* (1949) In this case the Supreme Court ruled against the use of poisonous snakes in religious rituals. In this and subsequent cases, the Court followed the precedent in the *Reynolds* case to restrict the ways people may worship. In *Oregon v. Smith* (1990), for example, the Court ruled that workers may be denied unemployment benefits for using drugs as part of a religious ceremony.

5. *WELSH v. UNITED STATES* (1970) Free exercise of religion may be restricted if it conflicts with military service. The ruling in this case permitted the federal government to draft those who hold religious objections to military service. The decision in a later case, *Goldman v. Weinberger* (1986), followed this precedent, declaring that an Orthodox Jew does not have the right to wear a yarmulke (skullcap) while on active duty in the Air Force.

6. *WISCONSIN v. YODER* (1972) In this case, the Court again ruled that some restrictions violate the Free Exercise Clause. According to the justices, the state can't require Amish parents to send their children to school after eighth grade. To do so would violate long-held and important religious beliefs of the Amish community.

Headlines

THE RELIGIOUS RIGHT

The longstanding practice of separation of church and state has been reconsidered in recent years through the visible political activism of conservative religious groups, sometimes known as the "religious right." Their political activism began in the 1970s with an organization called the Moral Majority, formed by the Reverend Jerry Falwell. The Moral Majority sought to legalize school prayer and balance the teaching of Darwinian evolutionary theory with creation science. Weakened by sexual and financial scandals, the Moral Majority was disbanded in 1989. The visible political activism of the religious right was renewed by Ralph Reed in the movement known as the Christian Coalition. Reed broadened the issues that concern the religious right to include welfare, abortion, unemployment, and crime rates. Their members' active campaigning for and financial support of particular candidates—as well as the efforts of other religious groups—have caused heated debates about the role religious groups play in the political process.

Freedom of Speech and Press

Ask most any Americans whether they believe in free speech, and you will almost certainly hear a resounding "yes." After all, a democracy depends on free expression of ideas. Americans often take pride in the belief that their government, unlike many others, does not muffle the voices and opinions of its people. But again, free speech often conflicts with other rights and liberties, and the courts have been confronted with the challenge of deciding the limits of free speech.

THREE TYPES OF SPEECH

Everyone knows what speech is. Or do they? Actually, there has been much argument about the definition of speech. The courts have spent considerable time and energy trying to clarify its meaning. The results are three categories of public speech protected by the 1st Amendment:

1. PURE SPEECH is the verbal expression (with the vocal cords) of thoughts and opinions before a voluntary audience. The Supreme Court has generally provided strong protection of **pure speech** from government regulation.

2. SPEECH PLUS is a category that involves actions—such as marching or demonstrating—as well as words. **Speech plus** is not generally protected as strictly as pure speech because actions may endanger safety or conflict with the rights of others. The courts have ruled that speech plus must not obstruct street or sidewalk traffic, nor may it illegally trespass or endanger public safety.

3. SYMBOLIC SPEECH is the most controversial protected form of speech, partly because it may involve technically no speech at all. **Symbolic speech** is expression by conduct. The courts have interpreted that actions and symbols are forms of free expression too and thus may be protected by the 1st Amendment. Symbolic speech first became an issue during the 1960s, when many cases revolved around Vietnam War protests. The courts' decisions during this era with regard to symbolic speech were varied. For example, the Supreme Court upheld the arrest and conviction of three men who burned their draft cards to protest the war in *United States v. O'Brien* (1968). But it protected the right of students to wear black armbands to public high schools to protest the war in *Tinker v. Des Moines School District* (1969).

---

pure speech—verbal communication of ideas and opinions.

speech plus—speech combining words with some sort of action, such as picketing, marching, or chanting.

symbolic speech—nonverbal action that expresses a political message, such as wearing an armband or burning a draft card.

Then and Now

THE MEANING OF FREE SPEECH

Even the Supreme Court justices don't agree on the meaning of free speech. Justice Oliver Wendell Holmes believed that speech must be controlled in some instances. He offered a classic example in 1919: "The most stringent protection of free speech would not protect a man in falsely shouting 'fire' in a theater and causing a panic."

In contrast, Justice Hugo Black believed that freedom of expression is absolute. Referring to the guarantee in the 1st Amendment, he said: "I read no law abridging [free speech] to mean no law abridging."

Flag Desecration

The controversial nature of symbolic speech is reflected in the flag desecration issue—that is, violating the sacredness of the flag as an important symbol. It has polarized American points of view on free speech for more than a decade. Members of Congress have made several recent unsuccessful attempts to pass a constitutional amendment prohibiting flag desecration, including flag burning and displaying the flag in disrespectful ways, such as letting it touch the ground. Most flag burnings represent protests to actions by the U.S. government.

All three branches of the federal government became involved in the issue in 1989. Gregory Johnson had set a flag on fire during the 1984 Republican National Convention in Dallas, Texas, to protest the buildup of nuclear arms. When his case reached the Supreme Court, the justices reversed an earlier decision by categorizing flag burning as symbolic speech that is protected by the 1st Amendment. *Texas v. Johnson* (1989) declared that the Texas law prohibiting flag desecration was unconstitutional.

The *Texas v. Johnson* decision was challenged by President George Bush, who announced his support for a constitutional amendment to prohibit flag desecration. Bush was spurred on not only by the Johnson case but by a highly criticized art exhibition that opened in February of 1989 at the Art Institute of Chicago. The exhibit, entitled "What Is the Proper Way to Display the United States Flag?" included a large flag placed on the floor that people could walk across. Critics objected to that and many other parts of the exhibit, claiming that it desecrated the flag and that artists had no license to treat the flag in such a disrespectful manner.

Flag Protection Act

Congress reacted with a debate about the best method of making flag burning a crime: by statute or by constitutional amendment. Although Bush and the House of Representatives supported an amendment, the Senate did not agree. The final result was the Flag Protection Act of 1989, which was passed into law by both houses of Congress. President Bush allowed the act to become law without his signature, showing his continued preference for a constitutional amendment.

What followed was a rash of protests. People burned flags and danced and walked on flags to protest the law. The issue went to the courts when protesters were arrested. Two district courts, one in Seattle and one in the District of Columbia, dismissed desecration charges on the grounds that the new law was unconstitutional according to *Texas v. Johnson*. The Supreme Court heard appeals in 1990 and upheld the decisions of the lower courts. In other words, they confirmed the unconstitutionality of the Flag Protection Act. Congress reacted by renewing an effort to pass a Flag Protection Amendment, which failed to pass either house in June 1990. The debate was renewed again in the fall of 1995. Many Democrats who had opposed the amendment in 1990 were no longer in office, and the House passed the amendment. But it was narrowly rejected by the Senate. Since two-thirds of the membership is required to pass an amendment, the 63–36 vote in favor was just shy of the necessary support.

Headlines

DISPLAYING THE AMERICAN FLAG

The controversy continued in 1996 when the Phoenix Art Museum exhibited "What Is the Proper Way to Display the United States Flag?" Protesters from the American Legion, a patriotic organization, removed the flag from the floor and folded it so that it could not be stepped on. Then Speaker of the House Newt Gingrich announced his opposition to the exhibit. He even declined an invitation by the museum's director to see the artwork before passing judgment. He responded with the words, "I don't have to look at a United States flag in the toilet to know that it's wrong"—the point of view shared by many supporters of the proposed Flag Protection Amendment.

REGULATING SPEECH

The question of how far government can go in limiting free speech is a tough one. For example, speech that damages a person's good name, character, or reputation—known as **slander**—is not permitted. Freedom of expression must be balanced with the need for the government to protect the nation's security. Not surprisingly, freedom of speech has been questioned most seriously during times of war or threatened war, when national security is a top priority.

The government clearly has the right to prohibit espionage, sabotage, and **treason** to protect the nation's security. **Sedition** is more controversial because it does not necessarily involve an act against the government. The government's right to control sedition—and its very definition— has changed dramatically through U.S. history.

Speech has almost always been more closely controlled during time of war or threat of war. The first sedition act was passed in 1798 when a war with France seemed near at hand (it never happened), but the act was allowed to expire when the threat subsided. More than 60 years later, President Abraham Lincoln was criticized for restricting freedom of speech during the Civil War. The next sedition acts were passed during World War I, making it a crime to encourage disloyalty, interfere with recruitment of soldiers, incite insubordination, or write or publish disloyal or abusive remarks about the government. More than 2,000 people were convicted of violating the Espionage Act of 1917 and the Sedition Act of 1918.

def·i·ni·tions

sedition—actions or language inciting rebellion against a lawful authority, especially advocating the overthrow of a government.

slander—spoken statements intended to injure the well-being or reputation of a person.

treason—the betrayal of one's own country by acting to aid its enemies.

During the twentieth century, rulings in four landmark cases have helped to define the limits on free speech.

1. *SCHENCK v. UNITED STATES* (1919) Charles Schenck, an official of the Socialist party who disapproved of U.S. participation in World War I, had been arrested and convicted for sending 15,000 young men leaflets that encouraged them to ignore their draft notices. Schenck argued that the 1st Amendment protected his actions. The Supreme Court upheld his conviction. In writing the majority opinion, Justice Oliver Wendell Holmes created a precedent that has been used throughout the twentieth century for deciding the limits of free speech in relation to national security. In times of war, Holmes claimed, speech that will create "a clear and present danger" will not be protected by the 1st Amendment.

2. *DENNIS v. UNITED STATES* (1951) In the 1940s, Congress passed a new sedition law called the Smith Act. It extended restrictions to peace time. Under the Smith Act, it was unlawful for any person to advocate the violent overthrow of government or to belong to an organization with such goals. In *Dennis v. United States,* the Court upheld the conviction of 11 Communist party leaders under this act. The men argued that the Smith Act violated the freedom of speech guaranteed under the 1st Amendment and that they were not a "clear and present danger" to the national security of the United States. The Court disagreed.

3. *YATES v. UNITED STATES* (1957) In this case, the Court overturned the Smith Act conviction of several Communist party leaders. In narrowing the definition of seditious speech, the Court ruled that merely urging people to believe something is different from inciting them to take action.

4. *BRANDENBURG v. OHIO* (1969) Here the Court further narrowed its definition of sedition. Clarence Brandenburg, a Ku Klux Klan leader, was arrested for not clearing the streets after a police order. As he left, he cried, "We'll take the . . . streets later." He was convicted of inciting lawless mob activities. But the Supreme Court overturned the conviction because the activities he called for were not "imminent," and there was no reason to believe that the listeners would take violent action.

LIMITING THE PRESS

Closely related to the freedom of speech is the freedom of the press. Freedom of the press had a very different meaning in 1791 than it does today. The Founders were concerned that opinions would be written and circulated in newspapers. Today that freedom includes writing in magazines, radio, television, and on the Internet. Many of the same principles that apply to freedom of speech apply to the press. However, decisions involving government censorship, the public's right to know, the confidentiality of news sources, and the issue of obscenity have proved controversial over the years. In four significant rulings, the Supreme Court has established guidelines that clarify the freedoms of the press.

1. *NEAR v. MINNESOTA* (1931) In this precedent-setting case, the Supreme Court defined its position on censorship. A weekly newspaper, *The Saturday Press,* was shut down by Minneapolis officials under a Minnesota state law that prohibited the publication of "malicious, scandalous, or defamatory" periodicals. Even though the editor had called local officials "grafters" and "Jewish gangsters," the Supreme Court ruled the Minnesota law unconstitutional because it involved prior restraint, or censorship of information before it is written and published. Except in cases involving national security, such censorship is not allowed.

2. *NEW YORK TIMES COMPANY v. UNITED STATES* (1971) The Court's position about prior restraint was reaffirmed in the fight over the "Pentagon Papers." A Pentagon employee leaked to the *New York Times* classified documents that revealed damaging secret government involvement in the Vietnam War. After the *New York Times* printed a few reports that showed that government officials had lied to the public, the government tried to stop further publication of the papers. The Court rejected the government's argument that the reports endangered national security and upheld the newspaper's right to publish.

3. *BRANZBURG v. HAYES* (1972) In this case, the Supreme Court ruled that the 1st Amendment does not protect reporters from having to reveal confidential sources of information. In order to get a good story, reporters sometimes promise an individual confidentiality—that is, that the person's identity will not be revealed publicly as the source of information. The problem comes when the source has evidence that might be valuable in court. The Supreme Court has generally agreed that reporters who refuse to divulge their sources are obstructing justice. Since the ruling in *Branzburg v. Hayes* (1972), some 30 states have passed shield laws that give reporters some protection against disclosure of sources.

4. *MILLER v. CALIFORNIA* (1973) Material considered obscene or pornographic has never been protected by the 1st Amendment. However, there has been great difficulty in defining precisely what obscenity is. In *Miller v. California,* the Supreme Court attempted to define standards for judging a work to be obscene: what an average person would find appealing to only sick or prurient interests, whether a local law or courts objected to the depiction of sexual conduct, and whether the work as a whole lacked "serious literary, artistic, political, or scientific value." Still, the definition of obscenity remains controversial, and court decisions on obscenity issues have varied widely.

RECENT ISSUES

The writers of the Constitution could not have predicted the growth of technology and the evolution of electronic media in the last 100 years. New issues regarding free speech and free press have emerged with the development of radio, motion pictures, television, and the Internet. For instance, radio and television are censored much more strictly than newspapers. This may seem unfair at first glance. Why should they be treated differently? The main reason is that broadcasters use public airwaves that require licenses to operate. The Federal Communication Commission (FCC) regulates radio and television today. It is expressly forbidden to censor content. However, the FCC may require that a certain amount of broadcast time be devoted to public service, news, and children's programs and that equal time be allotted to political candidates and their opponents. The Court has upheld these requirements, reasoning that only a limited number of broadcast frequencies are available, so companies must provide fair and equal public services.

The growth of cable television and satellite dish technology has also presented new questions about the interpretations of the 1st Amendment's application to broadcasting. For example, the Supreme Court ruled that decency standards for cable can't be as strictly regulated as those for traditional television.

Censorship and the Internet

A whole new set of problems about free speech has emerged with the Internet. This medium is neither print nor broadcast. The Court clearly cannot apply the same reasoning for strict supervision that it has used for broadcast media. Many people are concerned about the consequences of the lack of laws governing the Internet. One potential problem is that individuals may publish anything directly on the World Wide Web. People with the technical knowledge to do so may post anything they like with little fear of censorship. Second, since the World Wide Web does not respect national boundaries, many question the right and ability of a single country or state to place regulations on Web publications. There is no central authority in charge of the Internet.

Most debates for and against censoring the Internet focus on obscenity or pornography. The controversy heightened in 1996 when Congress created some Internet laws with the passage of the Communications Decency Act (CDA). The following year Vice President Al Gore was criticized by free speech supporters when he headed a White House summit on Internet censorship.

One result of the summit was the creation of a Web site that provided direct links to a variety of blocking programs. But the use of blocking software also raises questions about who should decide what views and values should be blocked. The American Civil Liberties Union demanded that the summit attendees provide full disclosure of their lists of blocked sites and the criteria for blocking.

Vs.

THE WEB AND CENSORSHIP

The rapid growth of the Internet has left the public and the courts with difficult questions about when cyberspeech does—and doesn't—deserve 1st Amendment protection.

FOR CENSORSHIP

★ Uncensored Web sites give children access to pornographic and erotic materials that they do not have access to in print.

★ People hide behind the anonymity of the Web and say outrageous things that would not be allowed in any other public medium.

★ Even if the government does not get involved, the industry should self-censor, just as the movie industry does. Some people have suggested a rating system that identifies questionable materials.

★ Uncensored Web sites are physically dangerous, as proved by several criminal cases in which acquaintances made through chat room conversations on the Web have led to real-life encounters in which individuals have been harmed or killed.

★ Filtering devices should be readily available for parents, schools, and other organizations that do not wish to provide access to violent or sexually explicit materials.

AGAINST CENSORSHIP

★ Internet censorship is a violation of the 1st Amendment.

★ Censoring the Web is equivalent to the practice of burning books, which is associated with repressive societies, such as Nazi Germany.

★ A self-rating system for the Internet is equivalent to requiring publishers of books and magazines to rate each article and story, to require everyone engaged in a street corner conversation to rate his or her comments, or to require people to rate their telephone conversations.

★ Censorship violates another precious value of American culture: unrestricted thought and creative expression.

★ Software programmers and their blocking programs should not be in the business of promoting social agendas.

Internet Court Decisions

In 1996, Jake Baker, the first person to be criminally charged for objectionable Internet content, was found not guilty when a federal court ruled that his communications were constitutionally protected free speech. Although he wrote about torturing and murdering women, the court ruled that he did not threaten them, so the charges against him were dismissed. In 1997, the legislatures of Georgia and New York attempted to pass and enforce state laws that would regulate Internet communications, but both laws were declared unconstitutional.

The Supreme Court became involved in 1997 with *Reno v. ACLU.* The justices ruled that the Communications Decency Act was unconstitutional. The Court decision seems to support the point of view that the Internet is comparable to books, not broadcast, and deserves the highest 1st Amendment protection.

Headlines

HUCKLEBERRY FINN AND CENSORSHIP

A court ruling in October 1998 addressed a complaint against Mark Twain's *Huckleberry Finn*, published more than a hundred years ago. The case was brought by an African-American parent in Arizona who challenged the mandatory assignment of the novel to high school students. She claimed that Twain's frequent use of a racial epithet reflected racial discrimination and caused students to taunt her daughter and other African-American students.

The U.S. Court of Appeals for the 9th Circuit ruled against the parent because removing controversial books from the curriculum would be a violation of students' 1st Amendment rights to receive information. Though the court acknowledged that school districts have a duty under federal law to correct racially hostile environments, they concluded that "permitting lawsuits against school districts on the basis of the content of literary works . . . could have a significant chilling effect on a school district's willingness to assign books with themes, characters, snippets of dialogue, or words that might offend. . . ."

Freedom of Assembly and Petition

Freedom of assembly and petition—the freedom to meet, protest, march, or picket—are 1st Amendment liberties closely related to freedom of speech. After all, when people gather, they almost always have something to say or a message to communicate, and a petition is a written form of expression. Assemblies take many forms today, both public and private. Sometimes their purpose is to get attention for a cause, like street demonstrations, strikes, and picketers with banners. Other times people may quietly gather in someone's house to share a common interest, which could be an interest in political change. Without the freedom of assembly and petition, political parties and groups could not function.

One of the first freedom of assembly cases to go to the Supreme Court was *DeJonge v. Oregon* (1937). When the Great Depression threatened to end American capitalism, concern about the number of Communist party members in the country increased. Before the Smith Act of 1940, Oregon had passed a law that prohibited "any unlawful acts" intended to bring about "industrial or political change or revolution." The law was clearly intended to limit the spread of communism. Dirk DeJonge was arrested and convicted by a state court for helping to organize and for speaking at a public meeting of the Communist party. The Supreme Court overturned the lower court's decision, ruling Oregon's law unconstitutional according to the 1st as well as the 14th Amendments, which protect against violation of freedoms and rights by state governments.

LIMITS ON ASSEMBLIES

The Supreme Court has ruled that the right of peaceful assembly—including parades and demonstrations—in public places should be guaranteed. People cannot be stopped from assembling just because their views are unpopular. Whatever a group's cause, its members have the right to assemble. But people cannot simply hold a demonstration anytime or anyplace they choose. If the assembly is public, it may conflict with other people's rights if it disrupts public order, traffic flow, freedom to go about normal business, or peace and quiet. Usually a group must apply to a local city government for a permit and post a bond of a few hundred dollars as a kind of security deposit. The government body must grant a permit as long as the group holds its demonstration at a time and place that allow officials to prevent major disruptions. There are almost no restrictions on the content of the messages expressed, but the government can make and enforce reasonable rules covering the time, place, and manner of assemblies.

e.g.

THE NAZIS IN SKOKIE, ILLINOIS

One of the most controversial cases regarding freedom of assembly happened in Skokie, Illinois, in 1977. Skokie is a suburb of Chicago with a large Jewish population. At the time, many survivors of German concentration camps lived in Skokie. The American Nazi party, a modern descendant of the Nazi party that executed millions of Jews during World War II, wanted to march in Skokie. Skokie's city government required that they post a $300,000 bond to get a parade permit. The city took the position that the march could easily lead to violence. The Nazis claimed that the high bond was meant to prevent their march and that it violated their freedoms of speech and assembly. The American Civil Liberties Union (ACLU), despite its disapproval of the Nazis, defended the Nazis' right to march. As a result, the ACLU lost half its Illinois membership. A federal district court protected the Nazis' rights, ruling that no community could use parade permits to interfere with free speech and assembly.

After all the trouble, the march never happened because the Nazis changed their minds and canceled it.

A review of four cases from the past shows the difficulties in establishing limits and guidelines for the freedom of assembly.

1. *ADDERLEY v. FLORIDA* (1966) In this case, the Court's ruling helped to clarify the limits on public demonstrations in such public facilities as libraries, schools, parks, and jails. The justices held that demonstrators could not enter the grounds of a county jail without permission.

2. *GRAYNED v. CITY OF ROCKFORD* (1972) Determining what kind of assembly violates other people's rights has been a major concern of the Supreme Court. In this case, the Court upheld a city ordinance that prohibits making noise that could disrupt the activities at a nearby school.

3. *LLOYD CORPORATION v. TANNER* (1972) The right of assembly does not give demonstrators the right to trespass on private property, even if they wish to make a political statement. In this case, the Court ruled that a group protesting the Vietnam War did not have the right to gather in a privately owned shopping mall. Later, the Court narrowed this principle. It allowed state supreme courts to require owners of shopping centers to allow the "reasonable exercise" of the right of petition on their private properties.

4. *SCHENCK v. PRO-CHOICE NETWORK OF WESTERN NEW YORK* (1997)
In recent years, various groups have sought to restrict the right to assemble and demonstrate outside private abortion clinics. In this case, the Court upheld the creation of "fixed buffer zones," which prohibited demonstrations and blockades within 15 feet of entrances to abortion clinics, parking lots, or driveways. According to the Court, such "buffer zones" protect the government's interest in public safety and free traffic flow, while still allowing the demonstrators to be heard.

FREEDOM OF ASSOCIATION

The Court has also ruled that the freedom of assembly and petition includes a guarantee of association. People who wish to promote political, economic, and other social causes—even if those causes are unpopular—have the right to associate with one another. In a famous case in 1958, Alabama tried to force the state chapter of the National Association for the Advancement of Colored People to turn over its membership list. When the organization refused, the issue went to the Supreme Court. It found no good reason why the state should have the membership list. The justices in *NAACP v. Alabama* found the demand to be an unconstitutional restriction on freedom of association. In *Rotary International v. Rotary Club of Duarte* (1987), the Supreme Court rejected the efforts of an all-male organization to exclude women. The men had tried to use the principle of freedom of association to deny women's membership.

Most Americans cherish their 1st Amendment freedoms of religion, speech, assembly and petition and feel deeply wronged if they are violated. These freedoms strike at the very heart of American political values. Yet they are not always easy to protect. More often than not, conflicts involving 1st Amendment freedoms pit one individual's or group's rights against another, and the issues they raise call for frequent interpretation by the courts. As you will see in the next chapter, some of the most difficult civil liberties cases involve due process for those accused of crimes and for those being punished after having been convicted of crimes.

15 | **Rights of Due Process**

To many people, the Bill of Rights is the guarantee of freedoms to American citizens. The 1st Amendment—with its provisions for freedom of religion, speech, press, assembly, and petition—is perhaps the most controversial of the first ten amendments. Yet another important part of the Bill of Rights protects Americans from certain injustices. These constitutional guarantees of fairness and equality under the law are based on the concept of due process.

Due process protects individuals from government power that would threaten those natural rights identified by English philosopher John Locke: life, liberty, and property. These rights are important to all Americans, not just those accused of crimes, and they are claimed by the right of citizenship.

In this chapter . . .

The Principle of Due Process

The concept of **due process** was brought from England to the American colonies and was well established by the time the U.S. government was formed. The constitutional basis for due process is most clearly stated in the 5th and 14th Amendments. Both declare that the government shall not deprive any person of "life, liberty, or property, without due process of law. . . ." The 5th Amendment protects people from actions of the federal government, while the 14th Amendment protects against civil liberties violations by state and local governments.

The Supreme Court originally interpreted due process, as England had, to mean that laws must be applied fairly and equally to all people, especially to a citizen accused of a crime. This type of due process, which refers to the methods by which laws are carried out, is called **procedural due process.** Toward the end of the nineteenth century, the Court began to focus on unfair laws, not only procedures. This kind of due process, which refers to the reasonableness of the laws themselves, is called **substantive due process.** Most of the amendments in the Bill of Rights are intended to ensure that all citizens' rights of procedural due process are safeguarded.

Quote

"The history of liberty has largely been the history of observance of procedural safeguards."

Felix Frankfurter, Associate Justice of the U.S. Supreme Court (1939–1962)

def·i·ni·tions

due process—the principle, guaranteed by the Constitution, that federal and state government must not deprive an individual of life, liberty, or property by unfair or unreasonable actions.

procedural due process—the rules that police officers, courts, and lawyers must follow to protect persons who are suspected, accused, or convicted of a crime.

substantive due process—the principle that ensures that laws must be fair to all citizens.

Citizenship in the United States

The Constitution guarantees the civil liberties of all citizens. The 14th Amendment contains the Due Process Clause through which many rights protected by the federal government are extended to protection by state and local governments. But Section 1 of the 14th Amendment is important for another reason. It defines citizenship. In a democracy, citizenship carries with it both rights and responsibilities.

e.g.

SEARCHES AT SCHOOL: PROCEDURAL DUE PROCESS?

In the case of *New Jersey v. T.L.O.* (1985) the Supreme Court ruled that school officials do not need warrants or probable cause to search students or their property. They simply need reasonable grounds to believe that a search will prove that a student has broken school rules.

The New Jersey case began when an assistant principal searched a student's purse for cigarettes and found marijuana as well. The student (whose initials were T.L.O.) was suspended from school and prosecuted by juvenile authorities. Had a police officer searched the girl's purse, the justices almost certainly would have ruled in favor of the student. School officials are bound by different standards because school is a "special place" where rules must be enforced to keep order.

What do you think? Was procedural due process upheld in this case?

THE BASIS OF CITIZENSHIP

There are three ways to become a U.S. citizen.

1. Almost everyone born in the United States or in American territories is automatically granted citizenship. The 14th Amendment, written to clarify the rights of former slaves freed by the 13th Amendment, serves as a basic guarantee of U.S. citizenship. But not everyone born in the United States is a U.S. citizen. For instance, children of foreign diplomats working in the United States are not American citizens even if they were born in the country.

2. A child born to U.S. citizens living or traveling abroad is also granted automatic citizenship. The rules covering particular cases—for instance, how long a parent lived in the United States and whether the child must live in the United States at some point to keep his or her citizenship—can be quite complicated and have changed frequently.

3. Citizenship may also be acquired through the process of **naturalization.** To start the process, an applicant who is at least 18 years old, who can read, write, and speak English, and who has lived in the United States for 5 continuous years (3 years if he or she is married to a citizen) may file a petition requesting citizenship. Then, at a hearing conducted by the Immigration and Naturalization Service (INS), applicants are asked about their background and character and are asked questions about American government and history. If they pass, they attend a final hearing where they swear an oath of allegiance to the laws and Constitution of the United States. About 97 percent of **aliens** who seek citizenship meet these requirements and become naturalized citizens.

Americans may lose their citizenship in three ways: through expatriation (the giving up of one's citizenship by leaving the United States to live in a foreign country), as punishment for a federal crime (such as treason), or as a result of fraud during the naturalization process. It is possible for a citizen born in the United States also to be a citizen of another country. A person can become a dual citizen through birth, marriage, or naturalization. However, a person who becomes a naturalized citizen of another nation loses his or her American citizenship.

def·i·ni·tions

naturalization—the process by which a person becomes a citizen.

alien—a person who is not a citizen of the country in which he or she lives.

Then and Now

DRED SCOTT v. SANDFORD (1857)

The passage of the 14th Amendment in 1868 took the control of determining citizenship from the states and put it in the hands of the federal government. The problems that had risen from allowing individual states to determine citizenship are clearly illustrated in a case 11 years before, *Dred Scott v. Sandford* (1857). Scott was a slave in Missouri, a state that allowed slavery. His master, Dr. John Emerson, took him to Illinois and the territory of Wisconsin, both free soil areas. Scott sued for his freedom in a Missouri court after his master died. His argument was based on the grounds that he had lived on free soil and had voluntarily returned to Missouri. Scott won, but the decision was appealed to the Supreme Court. The Court held that because the Constitution contains no definition of federal citizenship, Scott could not be considered a U.S. citizen. Legally, he remained property—not a citizen—in Missouri.

IMMIGRANTS AND IMMIGRATION

More than 250,000 aliens become naturalized citizens each year. America is a nation of immigrants. Everyone living in the United States—except for Native Americans—either immigrated here by themselves or are descended from immigrants. The INS estimated that in 1996 approximately 10.5 million legal immigrants were living in the United States. About 5.8 million of them were eligible to apply for naturalization.

Congress has the power to regulate immigration by setting restrictions on who may be admitted to live in the United States. Until the late nineteenth century, no limitations were placed on immigration. Starting with the passage of the Chinese Exclusion Act in 1882, Congress set quotas for immigration from various countries. The 1990 Immigration Act governs the admission of aliens today. While it sets no quotas on the number of immigrants from different nations, the 1990 act sets a ceiling—675,000—on the number who are allowed to enter the United States each year.

THE RIGHTS OF ALIENS

Because most of the rights mentioned in the Constitution are guaranteed to "persons"—not "citizens"—aliens are entitled to many constitutional rights. Aliens who are in the country legally can own property, run a business, and attend public schools. They are guaranteed 1st Amendment freedoms and due process rights, and they must pay taxes. However, they can't vote, and they

Headlines

IMMIGRATION TRENDS

The number of immigrants—both legal and illegal—has increased steadily since 1960, affecting both the size and ethnic make-up of the American population. The upsurge in the numbers of Asian and Hispanic immigrants has been especially dramatic. More than half of the legal immigrants each year are from those two ethnic backgrounds.

According to figures from the Immigration and Naturalization Service, the top countries of birth for U.S. immigrants in 1995 were as follows:

COUNTRY OF BIRTH	PERCENT OF TOTAL IMMIGRANTS
1. Mexico	12.5%
2. Philippines	7.1%
3. Vietnam	5.8%
4. Dominican Republic	5.3%
5. China	4.9%
6. India	4.8%
7. Cuba	2.5%
8. Ukraine	2.4%
9. Jamaica	2.3%
10. Korea	2.2%

can't hold public office. Aliens, unlike citizens, may be deported or legally required to leave the United States. The most common reason for deportation today is illegal entry into the country.

For instance, the long, easily crossed border that separates Mexico from the southwestern states makes it difficult to control the illegal flow of people into the United States. In recent years, thousands who have been caught by the Border Patrol, the police arm of the INS, are deported. Thousands of others are not caught. The INS estimates that in 1996 about 5 million illegal aliens were living in the United States. The passage of the 1986 Immigration Reform and Control Act created an amnesty program so that many illegal, or undocumented, aliens could become U.S. residents. More than 2 million aliens used the program to establish their legal residence in the United States.

The same 1986 law also made it a crime for anyone to hire a person who is in this country illegally. (Until then, it was not illegal to hire undocumented

aliens.) In 1996, Congress toughened its stance further with the Illegal Restrictions Act. The act increased the size of the Border Patrol, simplified deportation procedures, and increased penalties for smuggling aliens into the United States. A highly criticized provision of this act prevents illegal aliens from qualifying for Social Security benefits or public housing and allows checks on the legal status of any alien who has applied for welfare benefits.

e.g.

IMMIGRANTS, ALIENS, AND REFUGEES

People often use the terms *immigrant, alien,* and *refugee* to mean the same thing— someone who came here from another country. The U.S. government, however, uses five different legal classifications of groups of people who enter this country.

1. **RESIDENT ALIENS** This is the legal term for those whom most people call immigrants. This status is given to people who enter the United States with the intention of permanently living here. Once granted this status, they may stay as long as they wish. Most eventually apply for citizenship and become naturalized citizens. Some, however, choose to remain resident aliens who have taken up permanent residence in the United States.

2. **NON-RESIDENT ALIENS** This term is applied to people from foreign countries who visit the United States for a short period of time. This might include people who travel for business or students who come to study at an American university.

3. **ENEMY ALIENS** This is the status given to citizens from foreign nations who are at war with the United States. Enemy aliens living here are entitled to protection under the law. However, public fear and mistrust of these citizens has, at times, resulted in restrictions being placed on them or even discriminatory practices. In World War I, for example, German citizens living in America had to register with the government and were restricted in terms of their travel.

4. **ILLEGAL ALIENS** This status is given to people who enter this country illegally without a passport, visa, or entry permit. Most of these people evade guards and illegally cross U.S. borders. Others stay in this country after their permit expires.

5. **REFUGEES** Refugees have fled their own nation to avoid persecution or hardship. Under the provisions of the Refugee Act of 1980, Congress limited refugee admission to 50,000 per year. However, the President has been able to raise these numbers in emergency situations. Thus, between 1990 and 1995, U.S. Bureau of the Census data indicate that more than 700,000 refugees were admitted to the United States.

Rights of Persons Accused of Crimes

How do we protect people accused of crimes from being punished for deeds they didn't commit? How do we ensure that individuals under suspicion of criminal behavior are not abused by their captors while awaiting trial? A significant part of the Bill of Rights protects those accused of crimes under the principle of "innocent until proved guilty."

The law and the courts deal with the rights of persons accused of crimes in the original Constitution and the 4th, 5th, 6th, and 8th Amendments.

PROVISIONS IN THE CONSTITUTION

Recall that the Framers of the Constitution were criticized by the Anti-Federalists for creating a strong central government that would suppress individual freedom. To answer the concerns of the Anti-Federalists, the Bill of Rights was added. However, three important provisions in the original Constitution provide important civil liberties safeguards. They are the right of a writ of *habeas corpus,* the protection against *ex post facto* laws, and a ban of bills of attainder.

1. **THE WRIT OF *HABEAS CORPUS*** This writ is a court order directing an official to bring a prisoner to court and explain to the judge why the prisoner is being held. Persons who believe they are being held in custody wrongfully may apply to a judge, usually through an attorney, for release. The jailer must show cause for holding the prisoner. If the judge finds the detention unlawful, he or she may order the person's immediate release. Critics claim that the **writ of *habeas corpus*** is often abused by prisoners. They can delay an execution for years by raising objection after objection. Because of this alleged abuse, the Supreme Court has recently severely restricted the use of *habeas corpus* by judges. Article I, Section 9 provides that Congress can suspend *habeas corpus* only during times of rebellion or invasion.

2. ***EX POST FACTO* LAWS** These laws are passed after an act has been committed. Imagine that you record your neighbor's loud arguments with his wife in his backyard. Then you play the tapes for all to hear in the neighborhood grocery store. Your intention is to embarrass him because he is obnoxious. Then imagine that your neighbor goes to the city council and persuades its

def·i·ni·tions

writ of *habeas corpus*—literally, meaning "you shall have the body"; a court order that requires a judge to evaluate whether there is sufficient cause for keeping a person in jail.

members to pass a local law forbidding your action (playing taped arguments in a public place). If the police arrest you for your previous action, they are doing something unconstitutional. They have arrested you under an *ex post facto* law—that is, a law that did not exist when you committed the act. You cannot be arrested unless you play your tapes again after the law is passed.

3. **A BILL OF ATTAINDER** This law declares a person or group guilty of a crime without a court trial. Under the Constitution, **bills of attainder** are forbidden. It is the job of the courts, not Congress, to decide that a person is guilty of a crime and then impose a punishment. A bill of attainder is not only an abuse of the individual's civil liberties but a violation of the principle of separation of powers.

Then and Now

EX PARTE MILLIGAN (1866)

During the Civil War, President Abraham Lincoln temporarily suspended the writ of *habeas corpus*. However, after the war, in the case of *Ex parte Milligan*, the Supreme court ruled that Lincoln had lacked the authority to do so.

Lambden P. Milligan had been imprisoned and sentenced to death by a military commission in Indiana for engaging in acts of disloyalty. Milligan claimed his rights to a fair trial had been interfered with, questioned the authority of the military court, and sought release through the writ of *habeas corpus.*

The Court held that the presidential powers to suspend the writ in time of war didn't apply. Trials of civilians by presidentially created military commissions are unconstitutional. No President since Lincoln has attempted to suspend *habeas corpus.*

def·i·ni·tions

ex post facto—literally, "after the fact"; a law, prohibited by the Constitution, that makes criminal an action that was legal when it was committed.

bill of attainder—a law, prohibited by the Constitution, that pronounces a person guilty of a crime without trial.

THE 4ᵀᴴ AMENDMENT AND LIMITS ON INVESTIGATIONS

The 4th Amendment extends the Constitution's protections of the privacy of the individual. Its words have formed the foundation of how searches and seizures should be conducted, how evidence can be obtained and used, and what surveillance techniques (such as wiretapping) are permissible.

Searches and Seizures

According to the 4th Amendment, people have the right "to be secure in their persons, houses, papers, and effects, against unreasonable searches and seizures . . . and no warrants shall issue, but upon probable cause . . . describing the place to be searched, and the persons or things to be seized." The vagueness of the word *unreasonable* has created many arguments about the 4th Amendment and when police searches can be justified. The rules covering searches and seizures apply not only to searching people or their homes, offices, and cars; the Supreme Court considers wiretapping, eavesdropping, and other kinds of electronic surveillance to fall under search and seizure. The 1978 Foreign Intelligence Surveillance Act, for instance, requires a court order for wiretapping and bugging, even in national security cases.

Searches are generally considered to be reasonable under two circumstances:

1. THE POLICE HAVE A SEARCH WARRANT. A **search warrant** is an order from a judge allowing the search. As required by the 4th Amendment, the warrant must describe what is to be searched for and seized. A judge can issue it only if there is good reason—called **probable cause**—to believe that searching a place may provide evidence in a criminal case. Of course, the police may search a place if the occupant gives them permission.

2. THE INDIVIDUAL HAS BEEN LAWFULLY ARRESTED. Lawful arrests include those in which a judge has issued an arrest warrant, a crime has been committed in the presence of a police officer, or if an officer has probable cause to believe that an individual has committed a serious crime.

The rules can be complicated. They also change often, but the general principle is that searches are valid methods of enforcing law and order, but unreasonable searches are prohibited by the 4th Amendment. However, some exceptions are made to the requirement for a warrant.

---

search warrant—a judge's order authorizing the search of a place or person and specifying what evidence can be seized.

probable cause—the reasonable belief that a search of property will provide evidence in a criminal case.

EXCEPTIONS TO THE WARRANT REQUIREMENT

1. **THE AUTOMOBILE EXCEPTION** Police don't need a warrant to search automobiles, partly because they move. By the time police got a warrant to search a car, only a very foolish suspect would have kept the car in the same place. Also, the courts just don't see autos as places quite as private as homes.

2. **THE TERRY EXCEPTION** The decision in *Terry v. Ohio* (1968) allows brief investigatory stops and searches when the police have good reason to believe that a person has committed or is about to commit a crime. A Terry search is limited to a quick pat-down to check for weapons or contraband, to determine identity, or to allow time to question the suspect. If evidence is found, then the officer may conduct a full search.

3. **SEARCHES FOLLOWING A LAWFUL ARREST** Police may make a full search of all persons involved with the arrest, the areas around the arrest, and all the possessions that the suspects have at the time of their arrest. These searches may not, however, become an excuse for a general rummaging in order to discover incriminating evidence.

4. **SEARCHES FOR EVIDENCE** When probable cause allows an arrest, even if it hasn't yet been made, the police may conduct limited searches if necessary to preserve evidence, such as scrapings under fingernails.

5. **BORDER SEARCHES** People—and their possessions—may be searched when they cross a border into the United States. Officials may also open mail entering the country if they have probable cause to suspect that illegal activities or substances, such as drugs, are involved.

6. **PLAIN-VIEW EXCEPTION** Evidence in plain view of the officer may be seized without a warrant. In such cases, the officer must be in a legal position to see an object that is obviously evidence of a crime. However, a police officer who forces his way into an apartment without a warrant and sees illegal drugs on the coffee table cannot seize the evidence because he has illegally entered the residence.

7. **EXIGENT CIRCUMSTANCES** In urgent or critical situations, exceptions may be made to the requirement to have a warrant. For example, if evidence is about to be destroyed because a house is burning, or if a criminal is about to escape capture, an officer does not have adequate time to get a warrant.

302

THE EXCLUSIONARY RULE

The **exclusionary rule** upholds the principle that evidence gathered illegally cannot be used in a trial. Although this rule was established in a landmark 1914 case (*Weeks v. United States*), the courts did not apply the exclusionary rule to the states until 1961 in *Mapp v. Ohio*. The justices ruled that the Cleveland police conducted an unreasonable search and seizure of Dollree Mapp's home and property. The police hadn't obtained a search warrant before they searched her home for evidence related to bomb-making. They found obscene pictures, and Mapp was tried and convicted for possessing obscene materials. In *Mapp v. Ohio*, the Supreme Court overturned her conviction. The Court further ruled that such illegally gathered evidence could not be used in Mapp's trial.

Critics of the exclusionary rule, including Chief Justice William Rehnquist, express doubts that criminals should go free just because of mistakes or sloppiness on the part of police. Since the 1970s, the Supreme Court has made some exceptions, such as cases in which police have relied in good faith on a search warrant that was later proved to be granted improperly. But the Court has refused to abandon the exclusionary rule.

e.g.

LIMITING THE EXCLUSIONARY RULE

In recent years, the Supreme Court has ruled that evidence obtained in illegal searches and seizures can sometimes be used. Two 1984 cases clearly demonstrate how the exclusionary rule has been relaxed.

In *Nix v. Williams* the Court approved an "inevitable discovery" exception. Even if evidence is obtained in violation of a suspect's rights, it can still be used if prosecutors can show that the evidence would have eventually been discovered by legal means.

In *United States v. Leon*, the Court ruled that there is a "good faith" exception to the exclusionary rule. Evidence seized on the basis of a mistakenly issued warrant can be used in court as long as police acted in good faith when they requested the warrant.

def·i·ni·tions

exclusionary rule—the rule that evidence gathered in violation of the Constitution cannot be presented in trial.

THE 5TH AMENDMENT AND PROTECTION OF THE ACCUSED

The 5th Amendment adds more protection for citizens accused of crimes. It states that a person can't be charged with a serious crime unless a grand jury investigation takes place. If this group of people believes the evidence is persuasive, a formal charge, or **indictment,** is made. If the grand jury feels the evidence is weak, the case is dropped. Two other important elements of the 5th Amendment concern double jeopardy and the right to remain silent.

Double Jeopardy

The 5th Amendment prohibits **double jeopardy,** or being tried for the same crime twice. This law seems simple enough, but it isn't. For example, when a single crime is committed, a person can violate both federal and state law. That person can be tried in both federal and state courts. This situation often happens when an individual is caught selling illegal drugs. A single act can also result in charges for several crimes. If someone breaks into a house, steals jewelry and money, and kills the owner, three crimes (at least) have been committed. The person can stand separate trials for each. Other limitations on double jeopardy are that it applies only to criminal cases, and it is not prohibited when a case is appealed to a higher court.

RIGHTS OF THE ACCUSED: THE MIRANDA RIGHTS

1. You have the right to remain silent.
2. Anything you say can and will be used against you in a court of law.
3. You have the right to talk to a lawyer and have one present while you are being questioned.
4. If you cannot afford to hire a lawyer, one will be appointed to represent you before any questioning, if you wish.
5. You can decide at any time to exercise these rights and not answer any questions or make any statements.

---

indictment—a legal statement charging a person with a crime or other offense.

double jeopardy—the act of bringing a person to trial a second time for the same crime.

304

The Right to Remain Silent

Probably the most famous phrase from the 5th Amendment states that a person shall not "be compelled in any criminal case to be a witness against himself" (often called "pleading the Fifth," or refusing to answer on the grounds of self-incrimination). This clause was originally intended to prevent the use of torture or high-pressure police tactics to force a suspect to confess to a crime. Although the Supreme Court had long held that involuntary confessions could not be used in federal courts, the ban was not applied to the states until the *Malloy v. Hogan* (1964) decision. The landmark case of *Miranda v. Arizona* (1966) clarified when suspects should be told they have the right to remain silent.

Ernesto Miranda was convicted in Arizona of raping and kidnapping a young woman. Miranda's conviction was based on a written confession that he signed after two hours of police questioning. The Court decided that a confession should be presumed to be involuntary unless the suspect had been fully informed of his or her rights, including the right to remain silent and to have an attorney present. Since Miranda did not have an attorney present, the evidence fell under the exclusionary rule; it was judged to be illegally gathered, and the conviction was overturned.

The Court interpreted the Due Process Clause to require that local police departments issue warnings—known as "Miranda Rights"—to people they are arresting. (See page 304.) To some, the *Miranda* decision guarantees important rights to those accused of a crime. To others, it is an obstacle to efficient law enforcement.

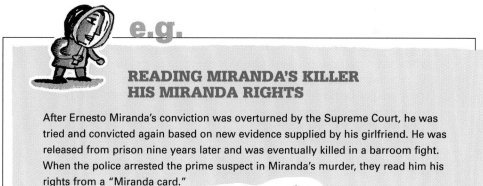

e.g.

READING MIRANDA'S KILLER HIS MIRANDA RIGHTS

After Ernesto Miranda's conviction was overturned by the Supreme Court, he was tried and convicted again based on new evidence supplied by his girlfriend. He was released from prison nine years later and was eventually killed in a barroom fight. When the police arrested the prime suspect in Miranda's murder, they read him his rights from a "Miranda card."

THE 6TH AMENDMENT AND TRIALS

The 6th Amendment guarantees several additional rights to a person accused of a crime. Two important ones are the right to counsel and the right to a fair trial.

The Right to Counsel

The 6th Amendment guarantees that an individual accused of a crime has the right "to have the assistance of counsel for his defense." However, this right was not applied to states until the *Gideon v. Wainwright* (1963) case. Clarence Earl Gideon was arrested and sentenced to prison for breaking into a poolroom in Bay Harbor, Florida, in 1961. Gideon pleaded not guilty, but he was poor and had no money to contribute to his defense. The judge denied Gideon's request for the state of Florida to provide him with an attorney. He defended himself and lost the case.

Since Gideon felt strongly that he had been wronged, he used the prison library to research his rights. After futile attempts to convince Florida appeals courts to reconsider his case, Gideon sent a handwritten petition to the U.S. Supreme Court. Fortunately for Gideon, the Court saw his issue as important. The Court used it as a way to re-examine one of its earlier decisions, *Betts v. Brady* (1942). In the earlier case, the Court had held that the 14th Amendment's Due Process Clause did not cover the right to counsel except in cases in which "a denial of fundamental fairness" would exist. In Gideon's case, the Court extended the interpretation of fundamental fairness to include all poor persons facing a felony charge.

The Right to a Fair Trial

The Founders were reacting to perceived abuses by the British government when they guaranteed the right to a speedy and public trial in the 6th Amendment. Ironically, the backlog of cases in federal and state courts today makes the "speedy" part of this amendment a problem. To try to address this problem, Congress passed the Speedy Trial Act of 1974. It says that in a federal criminal trial, the time between a person's arrest and the beginning of the trial cannot be more than 100 days.

The guarantee of a public trial, with the accused having the right to call and confront witnesses, was meant to keep government from quickly and secretly holding a trial designed to find an accused person guilty of a crime. Today the idea of a public trial has become something of a nightmare, particularly for celebrities. When famous people are involved in a trial, the media are a major issue. Should TV cameras be allowed in court? How many newspaper reporters should be permitted to sit in the audience? What about the curious public? Too many people in a courtroom can disrupt proceedings. Judges have the right to limit both the number and the kinds of spectators. The Court has struggled to balance the rights of spectators with those of the accused.

THE 8TH AMENDMENT AND PUNISHMENT

The 8th Amendment offers guidelines to ensure that the rights of the accused are protected not just before and during a trial but also after persons have been convicted of a crime. One important part of the 8th Amendment is the requirement that citizens in jail have a reasonable opportunity to be released on **bail.** While the amendment states that "excessive bail shall not be required," precisely how much is considered "excessive" varies from case to case. The seriousness of the crime and factors such as the person's age, employment record, residence, and ability to pay are all considered when the court sets bail.

Cruel and Unusual Punishment

The most controversial part of the 8th Amendment is the phrase that forbids "cruel and unusual punishment" in criminal cases. Just what is "cruel and unusual punishment"? The courts have interpreted and reinterpreted its meaning for more than 100 years. The first Supreme Court case involving cruel and unusual punishment was *Wilkerson v. Utah* (1879). In this case, a court had sentenced a man to die by firing squad, a death penalty that the Court judged not to be protected by the 8th Amendment. The majority opinion was that only barbaric tortures—such as burning at the stake or beheading—were forbidden. Since then the Court has heard only a few cases that address cruel methods of execution. For example, in *Louisiana v. Rosweber* (1947), the Supreme Court ruled that it was not unconstitutional to electrocute a convicted murderer a second time if the chair doesn't work the first time.

Lower courts still consider a few cruel and unusual punishment cases every year. For example, in February of 1997, a federal magistrate ruled against the practice of using a "hitching post" in the Alabama prison system. The "hitching post" consisted of a series of outdoor, chest-high horizontal bars that prisoners were shackled to for as long as seven hours in the heat of the summer, as well as in damp, cold winters. Prisoners claimed that while they were chained, they had no opportunity to eat or drink, nor were they allowed to use the toilet.

Capital Punishment

By far the most controversial punishment for criminals is the death penalty, often referred to as "capital punishment." Does the government have the right to take a person's life, even if he or she has committed a serious crime? The question has been passionately debated.

---

bail—an amount of money exchanged for the release of an arrested person as a guarantee of his or her appearance for trial at a specified time.

e.g.

LAW AND ORDER IN THE LONE STAR STATE

After the execution of Larry Wayne White in May of 1997, the state of Texas had executed a record 122 men since the reinstatement of capital punishment in 1976. No other state even came close to that number. Virginia and Florida tied for second place with 39 executions each.

Although opponents of the death penalty have wanted the Supreme Court to abolish it for years, the Court did not challenge the death penalty until 1972 in *Furman v. Georgia*. Even then, the Court did not judge capital punishment to be cruel and unusual punishment. It did warn the states that the death penalty was to be carried out in a fair and consistent way. The Court charged that judges and juries imposed capital punishment in arbitrary ways for a wide variety of crimes. Statistics indicated that the death penalty was imposed in ways that discriminated against racial minorities and the poor.

For four years executions were halted as states revised their death penalty laws in several ways. Some states made the death penalty mandatory for certain crimes, such as the murder of a police officer or murder that takes place while another felony is being committed. Other states provided a two-stage process for serious crimes: first a trial to determine guilt or innocence; then a second hearing to decide whether the person deserves the death penalty. In 1976, the Court defined its position in *Woodson v. North Carolina* when it judged the mandatory death sentence unconstitutional according to the 8th Amendment. However, in that same year the Court allowed the two-stage process to stand (*Gregg v. Georgia*). It stated that the "punishment of death does not invariably violate the Constitution." According to the justices, the effectively written two-stage laws could almost eliminate "the risk that [the death penalty] will be inflicted in an arbitrary or capricious manner."

A recent issue surrounding the death penalty concerns the large numbers of juveniles arrested and convicted for committing felonies. Some believe that young people should not be held to the same standards of guilt or innocence as adults are. In *Thompson v. Oklahoma* (1988), the Court ruled that the 8th and 14th Amendments prohibited the execution of a man for a murder he had committed when he was only 15 years old. The next year, however, in *Wilkens v. Missouri* (1989), the Court allowed the execution of a man for a murder he committed when he was 16.

308

Property and Privacy Rights

The rights of due process protect more than just the rights of the accused. They extend to basic rights of property and privacy. The Founders generally believed that the most essential rights were life, liberty, and property. Even though in the Declaration of Independence Thomas Jefferson changed "property" to "pursuit of happiness," the importance of property rights was clear. The original phrase appears several times in the Constitution. For example, the Due Process Clauses in the 5th and 14th Amendments refer to "life, liberty, and property." Today the rights of an individual to own, use, rent, invest in, buy, and sell property are rarely questioned.

PRIVATE PROPERTY

A major restriction on private property rights is **eminent domain,** the power of government to take private property for public use. The 5th Amendment states that private property shall not be "taken for public use, without just compensation." Of course, the government's idea of "just compensation" may be very different from what the property owner believes is fair market value. In case of a dispute, it's up to the courts to decide. Usually the courts have held that the owner is entitled to receive what a private buyer would pay to a willing seller at the time the property was taken. Compensation would then be determined by assessments of comparable properties in the neighborhood.

Headlines

IS BIG BROTHER WATCHING?

In April of 1997, the Oakland, California, police department felt the need to modernize their efforts to reduce crime. They introduced to the city council a set of powerful video cameras that swiveled in every direction and could zoom in to read the fine print on a flyer or read a license plate from more than a mile away. After criticism from horrified community members and groups, the police department reconsidered and recommended that the cameras not be used. The Oakland Public Safety Committee voted in September 1997 to cancel the proposed high-tech video surveillance pilot project.

---

eminent domain—the government's right to take control of private property for public use.

PRIVACY RIGHTS

The right to privacy is not specifically mentioned in the Constitution. But the Supreme Court has in several cases implied recognition of some rights to privacy. The rights to private property also extend to personal behavior. Justice William Douglas identified privacy rights in the majority opinion in *Griswold v. Connecticut* (1965). He reasoned that a right to privacy can be inferred from other provisions of the Bill of Rights—for example, the 1st Amendment's guarantee of free association and the 4th Amendment's protection from "unreasonable searches and seizures."

Since 1965, the courts have protected several aspects of the right to privacy: the right to be free from governmental surveillance and intrusion, the right not to have private affairs made public by the government, and the right to be free in thought and belief from governmental compulsion. For instance, the 1974 Family Educational Rights and Privacy Act allowed people to review and challenge information about themselves in the files of federal agencies. Parents and students 18 or over can check the school files, including test scores and advisers' comments.

Privacy rights have presented many new and troubling civil liberties issues.

★ Who should have access to databases of e-mail communications, medical histories, or purchase records?

★ Can schools require drug testing of students?

★ Can questions about sexual orientation be asked on a job application?

Abortion Rights

A controversial application of the right to privacy has centered on abortion rights. Until 1973, it was up to the states to decide whether and under what circumstances women could have abortions. States had very different regulations. For example, New York allowed almost any abortion during the first 24 weeks of pregnancy, while Texas completely banned any abortions unless the mother's life was in danger.

In the landmark *Roe v. Wade* (1973) case, the Supreme Court declared the Texas law unconstitutional. The Court asserted that the 14th Amendment implies a right to privacy that protects a woman's right to choose during the first three months (the first trimester) of pregnancy whether or not to have an abortion. The Court further ruled that during the second trimester the states could regulate abortion procedures to protect the mother's health, and they could ban abortions during the final trimester. The majority opinion made it clear that the Court was trying to balance the mother's right to privacy with the unborn child's right to life—a classic example of rights in conflict.

Recent Decisions

The Court's decision immediately stirred a heated debate. The Court almost certainly did not intend to determine at what point a fetus becomes a baby, but that question of viability became the center of the issue. Those who believe that a baby's life begins at conception came to describe their position as "pro-life," or the "right to life." Those who supported the mother's right to decide whether or not to continue the pregnancy called themselves "pro-choice," or supporting the "right to choose." The labels are still in use today, and abortion remains one of the most divisive issues in America.

So far, Congress has refused to pass any national laws or constitutional amendments that would take the issue out of the hands of the states. The guidelines set by *Roe v. Wade* are still in place. For 16 years the Court reaffirmed and broadened its decision, declaring any laws unconstitutional that required a woman to have the consent of her husband or to be counseled by her doctor about the facts of abortion. Then, in *Webster v. Reproductive Health Services* (1989), the Court began to uphold some state restrictions on abortions. This action led many to believe that *Roe v. Wade* would eventually be overturned, especially if more conservative justices came to the bench. The big challenge came in *Planned Parenthood v. Casey* (1992). In a close 5-4 vote, the Court upheld the decision in *Roe,* agreeing that a right to abortion does exist. On the other hand, it has upheld a number of state restrictions, such as a mandatory 24-hour waiting period, the requirement that teenagers have the consent of at least one parent, and a requirement that women be given pamphlets explaining alternatives to abortion.

The rights of due process are guaranteed in the Bill of Rights. Even though the first ten amendments were written more than 200 years ago, the meaning of their protections continues to evolve. Today due process protects many rights—including citizenship, property, privacy, and those of the accused. Because due process is part of the Constitution, courts must define its meaning by interpreting the words of the Framers. We can't know how the courts may decide to interpret and apply these words in the future. But we can be confident that the rights of due process will continue to protect the civil liberties that Americans cherish.

Civil Rights

EQUAL RIGHTS

"I have a dream that one day this nation will rise up and live out the true meaning of its creed: 'we hold these truths to be self-evident; that all men are created equal.'

I have a dream that one day on the red hills of Georgia the sons of former slaves and the sons of former slave owners will be able to sit down together at the table of brotherhood. . . ."

Martin Luther King, Jr., spoke these words in his famous "I Have a Dream" speech, given at a momentous gathering of civil rights supporters in Washington, D.C., in 1963. He stated the all-American dream begun almost 200 years before. By quoting Jefferson's words in the Declaration of Independence, King masterfully linked the struggle for racial equality to the most fundamental philosophical beliefs of the United States. The enormous effect of his rhetoric on that late summer day in Washington is rooted in two of the most deep-seated values in democratic societies: equality and freedom.

The struggle for equal rights has been one of the most bitter and long-lasting in the history of the United States. Today civil rights issues center on three types of inequality: inequality based on racial and ethnic group membership, on gender, and on age, disability, and sexual orientation. These issues represent the desire to attain goals set in place by the Declaration of Independence, the Constitution, and the Bill of Rights. Modern-day civil rights conflicts are real, intense, and far from over.

In this chapter . . .

Civil Rights for Racial and Ethnic Minorities

Saying, as Thomas Jefferson did in the Declaration of Independence, that "all men are created equal" sounds good, but what does it really mean? Certainly people are not all exactly the same. Obviously, some are shorter, older, richer, and smarter than others. And should people always be expected to be treated exactly the same or to have the same qualities and possessions? Even though civil liberties and civil rights are included in the original Constitution and are emphasized in the Bill of Rights, the word *equality* does not appear in either place.

The only place that equality is really addressed is in the 14th Amendment, which was not added until after the Civil War—about 80 years after the original Constitution was written. The amendment forbids states to deny anyone "equal protection of the laws." The full force of the 14th Amendment was not felt for another 100 years. Even today, the equal treatment of all people before the law is an elusive value that does not always exist hand-in-hand with liberty.

The United States has always been home to many different racial and ethnic groups. When Europeans first arrived in the Americas, their cultures clashed with those of the Native Americans. African Americans first arrived on the eastern shores in the early seventeenth century, and they have long been the largest racial minority group in the country. American history is also one of immigration, a process that has continually brought in people with diverse racial and ethnic backgrounds. New groups have always had to establish their equality in the face of those already here, and patterns of prejudice and **discrimination** are found through the centuries. The modern civil rights movement was begun by African Americans. Today Hispanics, Asians, and Native Americans have joined the struggle to attain equality for all.

def·i·ni·tions

discrimination—the unfair treatment of an individual based on group membership (such as race) alone.

16 | Civil Rights

313

EQUALITY FOR AFRICAN AMERICANS

The unique history of African Americans includes 250 years of bondage followed by more than a century of widespread discrimination. Their efforts to secure equal rights and eliminate **segregation** have led the way in establishing principles that protect equal rights.

1. Slavery and the Post–Civil War Amendments

The first African immigrants to America came as slaves. Most of these African Americans lived in bondage until 1865 when the 13th Amendment abolished slavery. Up until that time, slaves were property and could be bought and sold as their masters pleased. They could neither vote nor own property. Most lived in the southern states, whose plantations required large numbers of agricultural laborers.

Slavery was a major source of disagreement between North and South, and it eventually contributed to the hostilities that led to the Civil War in 1861. Shortly after the Civil War ended in 1865, Congress passed three landmark constitutional amendments that appeared to guarantee equality for African Americans:

★ **13TH AMENDMENT—SLAVERY ABOLISHED** Slavery and involuntary servitude were abolished, except as punishment for a crime. In other words, people tried and convicted of crimes can still be put in prison and be forced to work, but no one else can be held as a slave or servant against his or her own will.

★ **14TH AMENDMENT—CIVIL RIGHTS** Citizenship and due process rights were protected. For the first time "equal protection of the law" was guaranteed.

★ **15TH AMENDMENT—RIGHT TO VOTE** The right to vote was protected. It stated that the vote could not be denied or abridged by state or federal governments "on account of race, color, or previous condition of servitude."

def·i·ni·tions

segregation—the policy or practice of separating racial or ethnic groups in schools, housing, and industry.

2. A Century of Discrimination

The Civil War ended slavery, and the post-war amendments were intended to protect the new citizens' rights. But the quest for equality was far from over. In an effort to reclaim power lost as a result of their defeat in the war and to preserve something of their destroyed society, southern states passed **Jim Crow laws.** These laws supported the separation of African Americans from whites. For example, hundreds of state laws and local ordinances created separate public facilities, such as restaurants, hotels, rest rooms, and water fountains, as well as separate school systems. These laws created *de jure* **segregation,** or separation by law. Although no such laws were passed in states outside the South, real or *de facto* **segregation** commonly existed in the North as well.

e.g.

WHO WAS JIM CROW?

No one knows whether a person named Jim Crow actually existed. The term "Jim Crow" comes from a song staged in vaudeville (a type of variety show) in the late 1820s by a white entertainer, Thomas D. Rice. Rice blackened his face and sang a song entitled "Wheel About and Turn About and Jump, Jim Crow." The term "Jim Crow" eventually came to refer to African Americans. Later it was used to describe the state and local laws and practices that segregated African Americans from whites.

3. The Separate-But-Equal Doctrine

The Supreme Court's decision in the landmark case of *Plessy v. Ferguson* (1896) supported the segregation laws. Homer Plessy was arrested for violating a Louisiana state law that required the races to ride in "equal but separate" coaches on trains. Plessy, who was seven-eighths white, refused to leave a railway car reserved for whites and appealed his case to the Supreme Court. He claimed that the law violated the equal protection clause of the 14th Amendment. The Court upheld the law, saying that segregation was not unconstitutional as long as the facilities were substantially equal. Only one justice, John Marshall Harlan, disagreed, arguing that "Our Constitution is

---

Jim Crow laws—state and local laws that discriminated against African Americans and supported segregation.

de jure **segregation**—segregation that is authorized by the government and the law.

de facto **segregation**—literally, segregation "in fact"; racial or ethnic separation that occurs without the backing of laws or political action.

color-blind, and neither knows nor tolerates classes among citizens. In respect of civil rights, all citizens are equal before the law."

Harlan did not speak for most white Americans, however. In later decisions, the Court paid more attention to the "separate" than to the "equal" part of *Plessy v. Ferguson*. For example, southern states were allowed to maintain high schools and professional schools for whites, even when there were no such schools for African Americans. Even major league baseball was segregated, and African-American players played in Negro leagues. The **separate–but–equal** doctrine created by *Plessy v. Ferguson* and upheld by later court decisions set in place the legal precedent that segregation was constitutional. As a result, Jim Crow laws—and *de jure* segregation—stayed in place until the mid-1950s, when they were finally declared unconstitutional.

Then and Now

THE NAACP FIGHTS BACK

In 1909 African-American activists led by W.E.B. Du Bois formed the National Association for the Advancement of Colored People (NAACP). The organization attempted to promote the goals of full political rights for African Americans, an end to all racial distinctions, and the creation of a new spirit of brotherhood. The NAACP's legal team began to challenge discriminatory practices in the courts. It won an important victory in the case of *Guinn v. United States* (1915), which threw out the grandfather clauses of the Maryland and Oklahoma constitutions. These legal provisions permitted individuals to vote without passing a literacy test if they or one of their ancestors had been entitled to vote in 1866.

The NAACP followed this victory with a strategy of changing segregation and discrimination by influencing court decisions. Because they believed that they had little hope of persuading white state legislators to overturn the Jim Crow laws, they pursued their fight through the courts. This strategy proved slow and difficult. The NAACP sponsored a series of cases in which the court decisions chipped away at the separate-but-equal doctrine. Those rulings inspired civil rights proposals in Congress during the late 1940s and culminated in the *Brown v. Board of Education of Topeka* decision in 1954.

def·i·ni·tions

separate-but-equal—the doctrine that segregation of the African-American and white races was legal as long as separate facilities were comparable in quality.

4. The Modern Civil Rights Movement

In the era following World War II, federal judges started to use the 14th Amendment to reverse earlier decisions that supported the separate-but-equal doctrine. For example, in *Sweatt v. Painter* (1950) judges ruled that an African-American student at the University of Texas Law School was given unequal educational opportunities when he was not allowed to attend classes and study in the same building with whites. But the breakthrough came in 1954, in a landmark case argued by the NAACP.

A. BROWN v. BOARD OF EDUCATION OF TOPEKA

In the 1950s, schools in Topeka, Kansas—like schools in many places across the country—were racially segregated. The NAACP took the case of Linda Brown, an eight-year-old African-American student excluded from enrolling in her all-white Topeka neighborhood school. A federal district judge ruled that the African-American school that Brown could attend was equal in quality to the white school her family wanted her to attend. The NAACP appealed to the Supreme Court on the grounds that racially separate schools were unconstitutional, even if they were equal. The NAACP successfully argued that segregated schools inflicted a sense of inferiority on African-American children that affected their motivation to learn. The Supreme Court ruled that segregated schools were not, and could never be, equal. Thus they were unconstitutional.

Brown v. Board of Education of Topeka (1954) was a class-action suit, one that applied not only to Linda Brown but to other similar cases. That meant the Court's unanimous decision applied to separate policies in other states. The Court's decision changed the interpretation of the 14th Amendment, overturning the separate-but-equal doctrine put in place almost 60 years before by *Plessy v. Ferguson*. Enforcing the *Brown* decision was difficult. More than 20 years later, many segregated school systems still existed. In the 1970s, for example, the controversial practice of court-ordered busing began in an attempt to break up racially segregated districts.

Quote

"Segregation of white and colored children in public schools has a detrimental effect upon the colored children. . . . for the policy of separating the races is usually interpreted as denoting the inferiority of the Negro group. . . . We conclude that in the field of public education the doctrine of 'separate but equal' has no place. Separate educational facilities are inherently unequal. . . . "

Chief Justice Earl Warren
Brown v. Board of Education of Topeka *decision (1954)*

B. INCREASED ACTIVISM

The *Brown* decision established a precedent for Supreme Court decisions to strike down segregation not only in public schools but in other public facilities. The Court's support was complemented by the appearance of a leader, Martin Luther King, Jr. The Baptist minister led nonviolent protest marches and demonstrations against segregation. King's leadership inspired African Americans to break laws deliberately and peacefully in an effort to end racial segregation. Such massive resistance was intended to bring about change through the cooperative efforts of large numbers of protesters. In 1955 in Montgomery, Alabama, an African American named Rosa Parks refused to give up her seat in the front of a bus, despite a regulation that African Americans had to sit in the back. She was forced to leave the bus, and the incident inspired a bus boycott. King organized Montgomery's African-American residents to conduct a year-long bus boycott. King insisted on nonviolent resistance to discriminatory laws, using such tactics as demonstrations, marches, and sit-ins at segregated places. Nevertheless, violence often erupted.

The actions of the protesters soon gathered media attention and drew sympathy from many Americans. Crucial support came from the other two branches of government, the President and Congress. The success of the civil rights movement is due to the ability of leaders such as Dr. King to push for changes in attitudes in the federal government. The movement pressured state and local governments to comply with its demands to end racial discrimination.

C. CIVIL RIGHTS LAWS

Civil rights bills were first proposed in Congress during the 1950s and 1960s, but the early laws were weakened by compromise with a number of Dixiecrats, or Southern Democrats, as exemplified by Strom Thurmond's famous filibuster of 1957. The most important changes took place during the administration of President Lyndon Johnson (1963–1969). Johnson pressured Congress successfully for passage of two landmark civil rights acts—the Civil Rights Act of 1964 and the Voting Rights Act of 1965—that paved the way for others.

★ **THE CIVIL RIGHTS ACT OF 1964** is the most comprehensive anti-bias legislation in American history. By making discrimination based on race, color, religion, or national origin illegal in hotels, motels, restaurants, and other public places, the law forced public establishments all over the United States to open their doors to all customers. It also forbade employers with more than 15 employees to deny persons employment on the basis of race, color, religion, or national origin. Once hired, employees were to be treated equally in terms of pay, working conditions, and privileges. To enforce employment restrictions and listen to complaints, Congress created the Equal Employment Opportunity Commission (EEOC). This commission consists of five members appointed by the President and confirmed by the Senate.

★ **THE VOTING RIGHTS ACT** followed in 1965. This legislation made it possible for African Americans to register and vote in every district in the United States. Even though the 15th Amendment supposedly had done the same thing almost a century before, Jim Crow laws had made the amendment almost meaningless. The Voting Rights Act of 1965 authorized the appointment of federal examiners to register voters in areas where local authorities had discriminated in the past. The act also abolished literacy tests for any person who had gone to school beyond the sixth grade. Another type of Jim Crow law, the poll tax, was abolished by the 24th Amendment, passed in 1964. The results came quickly and dramatically. In the following few years, hundreds of thousands of African Americans registered to vote in southern states and counties for the first time in their lives. In 1965, only 70 African Americans held public office in the 11 southern states; by the early 1980s more than 2,500 held elected offices in those states.

Then and Now

THE LITTLE ROCK NINE

Sometimes ordinary but courageous people can make as much difference in history as judges or elected leaders. In the fall of 1957, nine African-American Arkansas teenagers made history when they tried to enroll in Little Rock's all-white Central High School. On the first day of school, when Elizabeth Eckford got off the bus near the high school, she was followed by a mob of white people. Guards refused to allow her in school. She was rescued by a local woman who accompanied her to a bus that carried her safely home.

Elizabeth and the others persisted in their efforts to go to school, but Arkansas Governor Orville Faubus posted Arkansas National Guardsmen around the school to prevent the African-American students from entering. Finally, President Eisenhower sent more than 1,000 troops of the 101st Airborne Division of the National Guard to defend the nine African-American students. The students finally entered the school accompanied by federal troops. All year the students had to put up with being taunted, kicked, and tripped.

The Little Rock Nine played a pivotal role in the success of the civil rights movement, courageously pioneering equal access to education for all students in the United States.

D. RIGHT TO OWN PROPERTY

Another important civil right addressed by Congress in 1968—following the assassination of Martin Luther King, Jr.—was the right to own property. The Civil Rights Act of 1968 remedied a well-established type of discrimination: the refusal to sell or rent property to a person because of race, color, religion, national origin, sex, or disability or to a family with children. For 20 years, enforcement of the law depended mostly on lawsuits from people who experienced the discrimination. In 1988, Congress strengthened the law by allowing the Justice Department to bring criminal charges against those in violation of its terms. The struggle for African-American civil rights continues today. *De jure* segregation (that is, segregation according to law) has been abolished, and African Americans have an increasing amount of political power.

PRESIDENTS DURING THE CIVIL RIGHTS MOVEMENT

HARRY TRUMAN One of the first supporters of the modern civil rights movement, Harry Truman desegregated the armed services just after World War II ended. Truman also unsuccessfully pushed Congress to pass a strong civil rights act during the late 1940s.

DWIGHT EISENHOWER For most of his two terms in office (1953–1961), Eisenhower generally ignored issues of civil rights. He believed these matters were best settled by the states, but the refusal of Arkansas Governor Orville Faubus to uphold a federal court order in the 1957 incident in Little Rock forced Eisenhower to send in the National Guard to restore order. He took a stand, sending the message that the federal government supported African-American civil rights.

JOHN KENNEDY Kennedy and his brother, Attorney General Robert F. Kennedy, often took decisive action against southern resistance to desegregation. One famous example occurred in 1961 when a young African American, James Meredith, was granted admission to the University of Mississippi. When those who opposed integration refused to allow him to enroll, the two Kennedys backed their directives to integrate with national troops.

LYNDON JOHNSON When Lyndon Johnson became President in 1963 after Kennedy was assassinated, he used his unusual clout with Congress (he was the former majority leader in the Senate) to push both houses to pass landmark legislation: the Civil Rights Act of 1964, the Voting Rights Act of 1965, and the 24th Amendment. Johnson was also responsible for appointing the first African American, Thurgood Marshall, to the Supreme Court. In Johnson's term of office, the civil rights movement finally received what it had been denied for almost 100 years, the support of all three branches of the federal government.

EQUALITY FOR OTHER RACIAL AND ETHNIC MINORITIES

By the mid-1960s other minority groups were beginning to pay attention to what was happening in the African-American civil rights movement and to the civil rights legislation that protected all groups from discrimination. Prejudice and discrimination against people of different religions or nationalities had existed for years. Other ethnic and racial groups started to organize their own efforts for fair and equal treatment.

Since the 1960s, congressional support for civil rights legislation has grown so that other supportive measures have easily been passed into law. For example, a 1972 law prohibited gender discrimination in education programs receiving federal aid. A 1988 law ruled that if any part of an organization receives federal aid, no part of that organization may discriminate on the basis of race, sex, age, or physical handicap. The Civil Rights Act of 1991 made it easier to sue over job discrimination and collect damages. The 1991 act reflects the fact that the courts and the judicial branch no longer consistently led civil rights reform. Just as the Founders intended, each of the three branches was offering checks and balances on the work of the other two.

The Rights of Hispanic Americans

More than 23 million Americans have Hispanic origins, sharing Spanish as a common language. They currently make up approximately 10 percent of the population, and their numbers have increased by 60 percent since 1980. As one of the most rapidly growing minority groups, Hispanics are making their voices heard in many civil rights issues, such as representation in government, voting rights, and education. Organization of their efforts for equal rights has been made harder because the Hispanic American population is widely separated geographically and by the diversity of their subgroups.

Hispanic influence in government is increasing. President Clinton has appointed three Hispanic cabinet members, and, as of 1999, 19 members of the House of Representatives are of Hispanic origins. However, in the United States overall, less than 1 percent of elected local officials are Hispanic. Hispanics have traditionally been slow to register to vote, and their voting rates are lower than those for African Americans and Asians.

e.g.

HISPANIC SUBGROUPS

★ **MEXICAN AMERICANS** form the largest subgroup of Hispanics, with almost 14 million people concentrated in the area closest to the Mexican border. Although Mexican Americans have settled all over the country, the majority live in the Southwest: Texas, New Mexico, Arizona, and California. Traditionally, Mexican Americans are strong supporters of the Democratic party.

★ **PUERTO RICANS** make up the second largest group, and 2.7 million live primarily in northern cities, such as New York and Chicago. Partly because of Puerto Rico's commonwealth status with the United States and partly because of strong family ties, many move back and forth between island and homeland.

★ **CUBAN AMERICANS** have sometimes come to Florida to escape the government of Fidel Castro's Cuba. When Castro gained control of the country and formed a communist government in 1959, many Cubans who did not support him asked for and received asylum in the United States. The immigration has continued over the years. In many areas of southern Florida, Cuban Americans have now become the majority group.

★ About 5 million Hispanics are refugees from political and social upheavals in Central and South American countries, such as Nicaragua, El Salvador, and Chile. Their numbers are growing rapidly. As political unrest in those areas continues, people are joining relatives already in the United States.

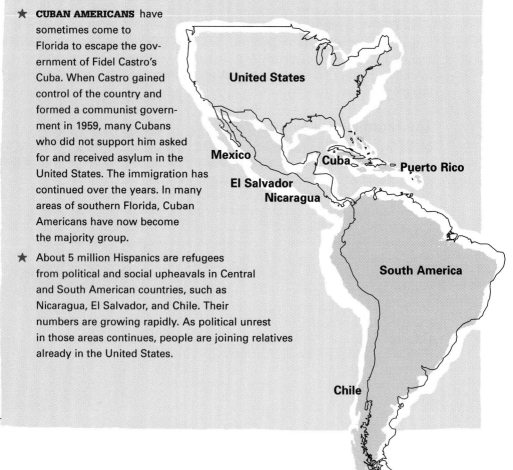

United States

Mexico   Cuba   Puerto Rico

El Salvador
Nicaragua

South America

Chile

Vs.

BILINGUAL EDUCATION

Should public schools teach students only in English? Or should they offer students who don't speak English instruction in their native language? Because Hispanics are such a large ethnic group in many areas, arguments over bilingual education have centered on the use of Spanish in the classroom. However, the debate over bilingual education applies to any student who does not speak English.

PRO

1. Spanish is a part of the Hispanic cultural tradition and should be preserved.

2. Hispanic students can learn more quickly in Spanish; thus they won't fall behind.

3. Students can learn English better if they are introduced to it gradually.

4. Teaching in English only is a denial of the world as it is today: a multilingual planet.

5. Being placed in English-only classes is a guarantee of failure or slow progress for children of immigrants.

CON

1. English is the primary language of the United States. Anyone who wants to be a citizen should learn it.

2. Immersion in English is the only way to learn it; otherwise, students remain too dependent on Spanish.

3. Teaching students in Spanish separates them from other students and limits their chances for success.

4. Teaching students in Spanish keeps them from learning English and hurts them in the long run.

5. Time spent educating students bilingually is time taken away from working on subjects such as mathematics and history.

The Rights of Asian-Pacific Americans

About 7.5 million Americans are of Asian origin. Like Hispanics, they come from many different countries with various cultural traditions, mostly from the Philippines, China, Taiwan, Korea, Vietnam, Cambodia, Pakistan, and India. But unlike Hispanics, they speak different languages. The Chinese were the first major group of Asians to come to the United States, attracted by expansion in California and the opportunities to work in mines and railroads and on farms.

As their numbers grew, so did resentment and prejudice. Californians began to pressure Congress to restrict immigration. In 1882, the Chinese Exclusion Act was passed. This and other American immigration laws strictly limited the number of Asian immigrants until the 1960s. The Asian-American population is growing rapidly and is expected to exceed 12 million by the year 2000. Besides the Chinese and the Japanese, other sizable subgroups include those from Korea, the Philippines, and the Indo-China region of Vietnam, Laos, and Cambodia. Most live on the West Coast and the Northeast, particularly in and around New York City, and growing numbers are settling in Texas. Today Asian-Pacific Americans represent about 3 percent of the total American population. Some estimates suggest that by 2050 that number will climb to as high as 10 percent.

Then and Now

JAPANESE AMERICANS AND DISCRIMINATION

The most radical discriminatory practice toward Asians occurred during World War II, after Pearl Harbor was bombed in 1941. The U.S. government, fearful of a Japanese invasion of the Pacific Coast, placed Japanese Americans in internment camps. About 110,000 Americans of Japanese descent were rounded up from their homes and sent to government camps located in the West, mostly in barren, unpopulated areas. They were guilty of no crimes, and their property was often sold quickly at very low prices. Critics likened these "internment camps" to Hitler's concentration camps, but in 1944 the Supreme Court upheld the internment as constitutional in *Korematsu v. United States*. After the war, Japanese Americans sought restitution for the property they had lost. Finally, in 1988, Congress made a formal apology to former internees. President Ronald Reagan signed a law providing $20,000 each to the approximately 60,000 surviving World War II internees.

The Rights of Native Americans

Almost two million people in America identify themselves as Native American. They hold the unique characteristic of not immigrating from any other country. As the original inhabitants of the land, they were treated as separate "nations" until the late nineteenth century. As settlers moved west after the establishment of the government on the East Coast, they often came into conflict with the native groups, and almost from the beginning, tensions and stereotypes dominated the relationship.

By the 1870s, the number of Native Americans had fallen to less than 250,000 as the result of European diseases and a succession of military campaigns as America expanded westward. The government began moving Native Americans to reservations (public lands set aside by the government for their use), out of the way of advancing settlers. After the Indian wars of the 1880s, the remaining groups were regulated by the Bureau of Indian Affairs, a part of the Department of the Interior that still exists today. As a result, vast tracts of land, including the best farmland, passed out of Native American control. Between 1887 and 1937, Native American land holdings in the United States decreased from 138 million acres to 48 million acres. The Indian Reorganization Act of 1934 prohibited further allotment of Native American lands, and the role of the government was redefined to help Native Americans become economically independent.

CIVIL RIGHTS AND SOVEREIGNTY

Government policies varied through the first half of the twentieth century. Without question, Native Americans have had to struggle against discrimination. The issue of the sovereignty of Native-American nations—not just the rights of individual Native Americans—adds to the complexity of their civil rights struggle.

RESERVATIONS

After World War II, a series of budget-cutting measures, known as the policy of termination, cut down on government-provided services to reservations. The policy created hardships just at a time when some tribes were becoming self-supporting. The federal government eventually abandoned termination, and in 1970, at the recommendation of President Nixon, Native American tribes were brought under federal funding once again.

Today almost one million Native Americans live on or near a reservation and are registered as members of one of 308 tribes within the continental United States or one of about 200 Native Alaskan communities. As tribes, they are a separate people with power to regulate their own affairs, but they are supervised by Congress. State control of tribal affairs is strictly limited. By an act of Congress, they have the right to vote. Native Americans living off reservations and working in the general community pay the same taxes as other citizens.

Most Native Americans on reservations live in poverty, have shorter life spans, and are in worse health than other Americans. Many reservations lack adequate sanitation and housing facilities, health care, schools, and job opportunities. However, the civil rights movement of the 1950s and 1960s created more concern for Native Americans. As a result, Congress has approved some compensation for past injustices, and courts are more protective of Native American rights.

LEGAL CASES

The Native American Rights Fund, a legal defense firm, has brought more Native American law cases to court in the last 25 years than at any time in the history of the country. For example, in 1980 the U.S. Supreme Court upheld a decision to award the Sioux $122.5 million for illegal seizure of their land in the Black Hills of South Dakota in 1877. In recent years, in an attempt to bring income to their impoverished reservations, some groups have opened gambling casinos on their lands and have come into conflict with state gaming laws. Even though Native Americans' defense of the practice has not always been successful, their efforts have brought attention to current inequalities that many Americans considered to be past history.

Currently, Native Americans are still not well represented in Congress. Ben Nighthorse Campbell of Colorado is the first Native American to ever serve as a U.S. senator. Campbell joined the 100th Congress in 1986.

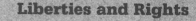

Headlines

"YOU'VE TAKEN OUR LAND— NOW TAKE OUR IDEAS"

Some Native Americans believe that their rights have not received as much atten- tion as have those of African Americans. Many Native-American activists currently are working hard to see that the government does not ignore their problems. For example, in early 1998, activists denounced President Bill Clinton's "One America in the 21st Century" race initiative as a sham because his race advisory commission did not include a Native American on its seven-member board. They marched outside a meeting of the commission in Denver, Colorado, with signs that read, "You've Taken Our Land, Now Take Our Ideas," in reference to the board's omis- sion. The board, headed by an African American, had included Native Americans in its discussions and had heard their ideas, but from the activists' point of view, the commissioners were using their ideas to further the causes of other groups, not Native Americans.

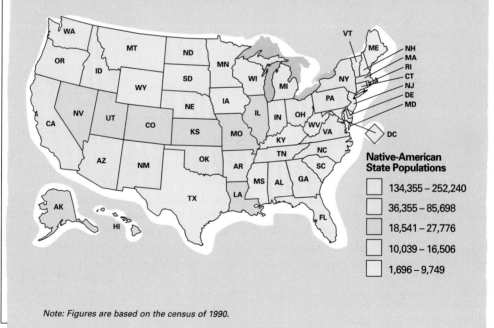

Native-American State Populations

- 134,355 – 252,240
- 36,355 – 85,698
- 18,541 – 27,776
- 10,039 – 16,506
- 1,696 – 9,749

Note: Figures are based on the census of 1990.

Civil Rights for Women

Who would claim that throughout all history men have so abused women that they deserve to be referred to as tyrants? The quote below is the introduction to the *Declaration of Sentiments,* a document modeled after the Declaration of Independence and signed by 100 women and men at the first Woman's Rights Convention. The meeting in Seneca Falls, New York, in the summer of 1848 marks the beginning of the women's rights movement in this country. The 19th Amendment, which gave women the vote, was ratified 72 years later. Only one signer of the declaration, Charlotte Woodward, was still alive to cast a vote in the presidential election of 1920.

Quote

"The history of mankind is a history of repeated injuries and usurpations on the part of man toward woman, having in direct object the establishment of an absolute tyranny over her."

Declaration of Sentiments
July 19, 1848

The story of women's rights has at least four stages:

1. EARLY ATTITUDES AND THE SUFFRAGE MOVEMENT

In the late eighteenth century, not only were women denied the vote, but they were denied legal rights, education, and choices regarding work. The legal doctrine known as coverture deprived married women of any identity separate from that of their husbands. Wives could not sign contracts or dispose of property. Both men and women found it almost impossible to end marriages. But circumstances began to change in the nineteenth century.

The first women's rights activists were products of the abolitionist movement (the attempt to abolish slavery). Two of these women, Lucretia Mott and Elizabeth Cady Stanton, attended an international meeting of abolitionists in London in 1840. There the ladies had to sit in a separate section of the hall and were not allowed to participate equally with the men at the convention. The women vowed to organize a convention to promote women's rights when they returned home. As a result of their hard work, a meeting was held in 1848 in Seneca Falls, New York.

After the 1848 declaration, leaders of the movement decided to concentrate on gaining suffrage for women. They successfully brought about changes in a number of states, especially in the Northwest, and several states allowed women to vote before the 19th Amendment passed in 1920. The suffrage movement was closely linked to a campaign for temperance (a ban on alcohol). The Women's Christian Temperance Union (WCTU) campaigned against saloons and bars, which they believed were responsible for keeping men from spending time with their families. Not accidentally, the two movements accomplished their goals at almost the same time: the 18th Amendment established the prohibition of alcohol in 1919, and the 19th Amendment gave women the vote in 1920.

2. DISCRIMINATION AND GROWING CONCERNS

Once women received the right to vote, they joined the labor movements of the 1920s and 1930s to ensure that demands for better working conditions and salaries included women workers. Still, many people did not question basic, established roles for men and women, seeing the right to vote as an extension of women's home and family responsibilities. Public officials were not so concerned with equality for women as they were about protection for women. Laws protecting workers from long hours and grueling conditions protected women from hardships that might take them away from their families. Men were legally required to support their families, even after a divorce, and to pay child support (although they sometimes did not).

The African-American civil rights movement of the 1950s and 1960s attracted the support of many who understood that equality was a valid issue for women as well as for African Americans. In 1963, Betty Friedan, a suburban housewife with a college degree in psychology, wrote a best-selling book, *The Feminine Mystique,* that inspired the women's liberation movement and motivated **feminists** to become politically active. Women's interest groups, such as the National Organization for Women (NOW) and the National Women's Political Caucus formed. The Civil Rights Act of 1964 addressed women's concerns when it banned gender discrimination in employment. Eight years later, **Title IX** of the Education Act of 1972 forbade gender discrimination in federally subsidized education programs, including athletics. The nature of court decisions, too, changed during the 1970s.

def·i·ni·tions

feminist—a person who advocates the political, social, and economic rights of women.

Title IX—the requirement that all schools receiving federal funds offer male and female students equal classroom and extracurricular activities.

3. COURT DECISIONS

By the early 1970s, the Supreme Court had altered its policies toward women to reflect more equal protection of the laws. The issue the Court faced was how much gender discrimination the Constitution allows, if any at all. The Court applied two general standards when considering gender equality:

★ **REASONABLENESS STANDARD** Different treatments are justified as long as they are "reasonable." Governments do have the right to make reasonable discriminations among people and groups.

★ **STRICT SCRUTINY STANDARD** Some instances of discrimination are "inherently suspect." In other words, they have been based historically on prejudices, such as treating certain races differently. Therefore, the Court would look more carefully at these treatments than at others.

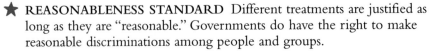

OCCUPATION: HOUSEWIFE

Betty Friedan believed that in 1963 men ran American life. Even though women were a numerical majority, they were treated like a minority, with unequal access to good jobs, property rights, and good educations. In *The Feminine Mystique* she argued that the "glorification" of the menial tasks of housekeeping was blocking women from reaching their true potential as human beings.

According to Friedan, women were trapped by a "feminine mystique." They so completely occupied their time they didn't realize they were second-class citizens. Many of her critics believe that Friedan undermined family life by creating a false discontent among women. Critics also said Friedan made women believe they only had worth if they worked outside the home.

At first the Court applied only the reasonableness standard to sexual discrimination. For example, the *Reed v. Reed* (1971) decision invalidated a state law preferring men to women in court selection of an estate's administrator. Such a discrimination was ruled to be "unreasonable." In later cases, the Court has tended to apply a standard somewhere between "reasonableness" and "strict scrutiny." For example, in 1976 it ruled against an Oklahoma law that set different legal drinking ages for men and women. Other rulings established that employers cannot require women to take mandatory pregnancy leaves, nor can girls be barred from Little League baseball teams.

4. RECENT ISSUES

The American public—even the courts—often have conflicting views about whether gender-based laws should be allowed. Issues involving women in the military, equal opportunities in school athletics, child custody, pregnancy leaves, abortion, and credit practices continue to generate discussion.

The Equal Rights Amendment

Many felt that only a constitutional amendment would truly guarantee the equal rights of women. The Equal Rights Amendment (ERA), passed by Congress in 1972, declared: "Equality of rights under the law shall not be denied or abridged by the United States or by any state on account of sex."

These words, drawn from the wording of the 14th and 15th Amendments, might seem to say nothing that anyone today would disagree with. Yet there was heated debate about the meaning of those words. A major issue developed regarding the military draft. If women are equal to men, should they be drafted to military service, just as men are? The ERA was still three states short of ratification when its extended time limit ran out in 1982. Although introduced in every congressional session, the ERA has never been resubmitted to the states. (See Almanac page 536.)

Women at Work

One of the most important recent issues regarding women's rights is "equal work for equal pay." Critics point out that even though the gap is closing, women still earn about 80 cents for every dollar men do. Traditional "female jobs" (secretaries and child care workers) pay less than traditional "male jobs" (construction workers and police officers). In 1983, the Washington Supreme Court ruled that its state government had for years discriminated against women by denying them equal pay for jobs of "comparable worth." Out of this decision was born the doctrine of **comparable worth**, which requires that a worker be paid by the "worth" of his or her work, not by what employers are willing to pay. The issue is equitable pay within an organization, and comparisons apply "job factors" that determine pay in order to detect gender bias. Sophisticated job evaluation systems are used by almost 80 percent of large companies to determine pay scales for jobs within their structures.

def·i·ni·tions

comparable worth—the principle that women should be paid salaries equal to those of men for equivalent job responsibilities and skills.

Civil Rights for All Americans

The gains by women, African Americans, and other racial and ethnic groups who have suffered discrimination have motivated other groups to organize efforts to work for equal rights. Three of the most visible are older Americans, the disabled, and homosexuals. All three groups are represented politically by powerful interest groups, and all have made progress toward making other Americans aware of their situations.

EQUALITY FOR OLDER AMERICANS

The name "baby boomers" is given to the large number of Americans born shortly after World War II. As they grow older, the number of Americans over the age of 50 is rapidly increasing. This demographic change in our population is sometimes referred to as "the graying of America." As of 1998, about 45 percent of the nation's population was age 50 or older. Some political issues that interest older Americans are mandatory retirement ages and discrimination in hiring and firing practices in business.

When the Social Security program began in the 1930s, the retirement age was set arbitrarily at 65. In many companies, retirement at 65 was mandatory, and employers routinely refused to hire people over a certain age. During the downsizing of companies in the early 1990s, the older—more expensive—employees were often let go. Many of these people had worked for the same company for years. Older Americans suspected discriminatory behavior against them, based primarily on their age. Congress has enacted several age discrimination laws, starting in 1967. In 1975, a civil rights law denied federal funds to any institution discriminating against people over 40 years old. The Age Discrimination in Employment Act was amended in 1978 to raise the general compulsory retirement age to 70. Since then, retirement age has become much more flexible, and people retire at widely different ages. In many areas, compulsory retirement has been phased out entirely.

One of the most influential interest groups in Washington is the American Association of Retired Persons (AARP). This group has more than 30 million members, an annual operating budget of more than $200 million, and a cash flow estimated at an incredible $10 billion. They successfully pressure Congress to consider the rights of older Americans on a variety of topics. They provide members with an assortment of services, such as low-cost life insurance, mail-order discount drugs, tax advice, and group travel plans. About one out of every four registered voters belongs to the AARP. Older Americans also influence public policy in such areas as health, housing, taxes, and transportation.

EQUALITY FOR DISABLED AMERICANS

The slogan below reflects another group that has often felt ignored by the civil rights movement. Disabled Americans, who make up about 17 percent of the population, recently asked Congress to pass civil rights legislation to protect them from discrimination. They have often been denied rehabilitation services, education, and jobs.

The first rehabilitation laws were passed in the late 1920s. These laws were mostly to help veterans of World War I. Laws that addressed the lack of access to offices, stores, restaurants, and other public buildings were not passed until the 1970s. The Rehabilitation Act of 1973 added disabled people to the list of groups protected from discrimination. The Education for All Handicapped Children Act of 1975 gave all children the right to a free public education. The most comprehensive law of all, the Americans with Disabilities Act (ADA), was passed in 1990. It extended many of the protections established for racial minorities and women to disabled persons. The ADA defines a disabled person as anyone who has a physical or mental impairment that substantially limits one or more major activities of his or her life, such as employment; anyone who has a record of such impairment; or anyone who is regarded as having such an impairment.

Civil rights laws for disabled persons have met with stiff opposition. Some critics believe that we have over-accommodated and that the laws require expensive programs and alterations to existing buildings. Others criticize the laws as not being consistently enforced in comparison to laws that apply to racial and ethnic groups and women. The most important reason for the lack of enforcement appears to be the high cost of providing equal access. Activists for the disabled claim that equal access for the disabled is enforced only when it does not put "undue hardship" on the owners of public buildings, including the government.

Quote

"Once, blacks had to ride at the back of the bus. We can't even get on the bus."

a pro-disabled Americans' slogan

THE AMERICANS WITH DISABILITIES ACT

The ADA guarantees disabled people the following rights:

★ **EMPLOYMENT** Disabled people may not be denied employment or promotion solely because of their disability. If they can perform the duties without putting "undue hardship" on the employer, they cannot be denied the right to work or be promoted.

★ **GOVERNMENT PROGRAMS** Disabled persons may not be denied the right to government programs or benefits.

★ **PUBLIC ACCOMMODATIONS** The disabled must have full and equal access to hotels, restaurants, stores, schools, parks, museums, auditoriums, and other public buildings. Owners of existing buildings must alter them, and new buildings must include access to the disabled in their plans.

★ **PUBLIC TRANSPORTATION** All new buses, taxis, and trains have to be accessible to disabled persons, including those in wheelchairs.

★ **TELEPHONES** Telecommunications devices for hearing- and speech-impaired people must be available to the extent possible and in the most efficient manner.

EQUALITY BASED ON SEXUAL ORIENTATION

Homosexuals make up an estimated 10 percent of the adult population in the United States. In the last decade, this large group has become much more active in its fight against prejudice and discrimination in hiring, education, access to public accommodations, and housing. The Supreme Court first addressed sexual orientation in 1986 when it ruled in *Hardwick v. Georgia* that Georgia's law forbidding homosexual relations was constitutional. The Court relied on the concept of original intent, noting that all 13 colonies had laws against such behavior, as did all 50 states until 1961. This ruling still holds today, and government responsibility for upholding rights of homosexuals remains more problematic than for those of various ethnic and racial groups and women.

As the gay rights movement has grown, several well-organized, active interest groups have worked to promote the rights of homosexuals and lobby for issues such as AIDS research funding and federal hiring procedures. More than 100 cities have banned discrimination, and many colleges and universities have gay rights organizations on campus. Despite these changes, Americans have not readily endorsed sexual orientation as a basis for "equal protection of the law." In recent years cities in Colorado passed ordinances to ban discrimination against people because of their sexual orientation. But opponents lobbied the state to adopt a constitutional amendment that made it illegal to pass any law to protect persons based on their "homosexual, lesbian, or bisexual orientation." The Supreme Court struck down the state amendment in *Romer v. Evans* (1996), stating that it violated the equal protection clause of the Constitution by singling out as unworthy of protection one specific group of people. As Associate Justice Anthony Kennedy wrote in the majority opinion, "If the constitutional conception of 'equal protection of the laws' means anything, it must at the very least mean that a bare desire to harm a politically unpopular group cannot constitute a legitimate governmental interest."

The controversial nature of civil rights for homosexuals came to national attention in 1993 when the Clinton administration advocated protection of gay rights in the military. The resulting "don't ask, don't tell" policy has not resolved the unclear status of gays in the military, and the Supreme Court has not yet ruled on its constitutionality.

Affirmative Action

The groups that have organized for equality have used different methods in attaining their goals, but they usually think alike concerning **affirmative action.** Once the government said that it would not tolerate *de jure* segregation, many people began to argue that it was not enough to stop there. Elimination of discriminatory laws does not erase the scars remaining from generations of discrimination. *De facto* segregation still puts minority groups at a disadvantage. They reason that if nothing else changes, people who suffered from discrimination in the past still cannot participate equally in American life.

FIRST EFFORTS

Supporters of affirmative action believe that the government should go one step further than simply removing discriminatory laws and should actively promote equality. That is, the government should see that minorities are admitted to public colleges and universities and are employed in good jobs in proportional numbers to whites. Starting in 1965, the government has put in place various affirmative action programs. Some are simply plans that require jobs to be widely advertised, but many programs establish guidelines and timetables to overcome past discriminations. Affirmative action applies to the federal government, all state and local governments, and to all private employers who sell goods or services to the federal government. To comply with the policy, many employers have had to hire or promote more women and minorities than they previously did. Colleges and universities had to revise admission policies to create a more diverse student body. Affirmative action thus set into motion the practice of setting **quotas,** or minimum numbers of various minority groups that must be hired, promoted, or admitted.

Almost from the beginning, affirmative action was controversial. Some argue that preferential treatment is itself discriminatory. Critics of affirmative action claim that it promotes **reverse discrimination,** or discriminatory actions toward the racial majority. Not surprisingly, the first significant clash between affirmative action and its critics took place in the Supreme Court.

def·i·ni·tions

affirmative action—government and private policies designed to provide equal opportunity for minority groups that have suffered from discrimination in the past.

quota—a minimum number of people from a minority group that may be admitted to an institution or hired by a company or organization.

reverse discrimination—a situation in which affirmative action policies violate the rights of the majority group.

THE BAKKE CASE

The Court's first major case, *Regents of the University of California v. Bakke,* was decided in 1978. A white male, Allan Bakke had been rejected for admission to the university's medical school at Davis. He sued the university because the admissions office had set up a quota of 16 nonwhite students out of the 100 spaces in the entering class. Bakke claimed reverse discrimination because the university admitted these 16 students, whose qualifications were inferior to his.

The intensity of the disagreement over affirmative action programs was reflected in the Court's 5 to 4 split decision. Justice Powell wrote the majority opinion, and the Court ordered that Bakke be admitted to the medical school. But the Court stopped short of declaring affirmative action programs and quotas unconstitutional. A university could adopt an "admissions program where race or ethnic background is simply one element—to be weighed fairly against other elements—in the selection process." It could not set aside a quota of spots for particular groups, thus making minority group member-ship the only factor in making the affirmative action decisions.

The *Bakke* case set a precedent for later affirmative action decisions. The Supreme Court has upheld a number of policies, but it has tended to put more and more restrictions on them. In general, there are no legal requirements for affirmative action, but, short of quotas, practices are allowed that are temporary in nature and aim at remedying the effects of past discrimination.

IMPORTANT COURT DECISIONS

A number of important cases reveal the evolution of court opinion on affirmative action.

★ *UNITED STEELWORKERS v. WEBER* (1979) Inspired perhaps by Allan Bakke's success, Brian Weber, a white worker in Louisiana, sued the Kaiser Aluminum Company after it rejected him for a special training program set up jointly by the company and the union. One goal of the program was to make up for years of past employment discrimination. Preference for admission was given to African Americans. The Court found that the training program, although built on quotas, was designed to "overcome manifest racial imbalances," and therefore was not in violation of the Civil Rights Act of 1964. Significantly, Justice Brennan's majority opinion strongly emphasized the "narrowness of our inquiry." Clearly, the Court did not intend the decision to be a blanket endorsement of affirmative action programs.

★ *FULLILOVE v. KLUTZNICK* (1980) The Court again upheld quotas in this case, which centered on a federal law that provided $4 billion in grants to state and local governments for public works projects. A "minority set-aside" provision of the law required that at least 10 percent of each grant had to be set aside for minority-owned businesses. A white contractor sued, claiming reverse discrimination since the set-asides did not give white contractors an equal chance to obtain federal funds. The Court held the law to be a constitutional attempt to overcome extreme and long-standing bias in the construction industry.

★ *JOHNSON v. TRANSPORTATION AGENCY OF SANTA CLARA COUNTY* (1987) This case dealt with sexual, not racial discrimination. It began when a white man challenged the promotion of a woman to a job that until then had always been held by a man. Johnson claimed reverse discrimination because he had scored higher on a qualifying interview than did the woman who was eventually hired. The Court upheld affirmative action in its 6 to 3 decision that neither the 14th Amendment nor Title VII of the 1964 law forbids the promotion of a woman over a man. As an employment practice, the promotion was seen as a temporary practice designed to remedy past discrimination.

Headlines

AFFIRMATIVE ACTION BAN IN CALIFORNIA

In November 1996, voters in California passed Proposition 209. It banned considering race, ethnicity, and sex in the public sector, including all state universities. Its supporters believe that allowing admissions offices to favor students from lower socio-economic classes would take care of imbalances in admission rates for minority groups. The first results of the new law came in the spring of 1998. The new policy has had a major negative effect on enrollments of African Americans, Native Americans, and Hispanics.

As of April 1, 1998, the most selective universities showed dramatic declines in admission of minority students for the fall of 1998. At the University of California at Berkeley African Americans, Hispanics, and Native Americans together made up 10.4 percent of the total pool of admitted freshmen for 1998; in 1997, they made up 23.1 percent. At the University of California at Los Angeles, minority representation fell to 12.7 percent, from 19.8 percent in 1997.

⭐ *ADARAND CONSTRUCTORS v. PENA* (1995) This case about contracting, not employment, began when a white-owned Colorado company challenged an affirmative action policy of the Federal Highway Administration. Until *Adarand,* the Court had generally accepted affirmative action laws, regulations, and programs as necessary instances of race-conscious policy making. In *Adarand,* however, the Court made it much more difficult for the federal government to use affirmative action programs. The Court held that whenever government provides preferential treatment based on race, that action is almost certainly unconstitutional. Justice Sandra Day O'Connor wrote in the majority opinion: "The Constitution protects persons, not groups. . . , Whenever the government treats any person unequally because of his or her race, that person has suffered an injury [established by] . . . the Constitution's guarantee of equal treatment."

Affirmative action remains a major civil rights issue today. The Court has upheld affirmative action on numerous occasions, but it gradually has placed more and more limits on such programs. Any government-created quota system will be subject to "strict scrutiny." All levels of government must show that affirmative action policies are needed to correct an actual past or present pattern of discrimination. And those who claim to be victims of discrimination must identify the actual practices that have negatively affected them. Meanwhile, various state court decisions and laws are continuing to define affirmative action programs, and the issues surrounding them still make headlines.

Are we closer to Martin Luther King's dream of equality than we were when he made his famous speech in 1963? Probably. Courageous people and groups are responsible for real accomplishments that make civil rights goals more realizable today than in almost any other era in American history. But the struggle is still difficult. Equality must be balanced with liberty, effects of past discrimination must be balanced with current needs, and one person's or group's equal rights must be balanced with those of another.

Struggles for civil rights in the United States continue. In the future, more groups undoubtedly will assert the need for equal rights and seek protection from discrimination. Even the use of the term "minority" will need to change, as the membership of the the so-called "minorities" is growing faster than those of "majority" whites. But amidst the changes, the pursuit of the basic American value of equality remains constant, from the signing of the Declaration of Independence to the beginning of the twenty-first century.

Unit V

Public Policy and Comparative Government

Public Policy

I n a 1790 letter to a French count, George Washington described his view of government's role in the making of public policy. According to Washington, "The aggregate happiness of society, which is best promoted by the practice of a virtuous policy, is, or ought to be, the end of all government."

Many people would readily agree with Washington. One of government's primary roles is to make policy that will solve society's problems. But there is less agreement about what "virtuous policy" is and who should have the power to design and enact it. All three branches of government help to make policy. The bureaucracy, special interest groups, research institutes, corporations, state and local governments, and even the public itself try to influence government decisions and programs.

Who makes policy and how they make it are the subjects of this chapter. As you read, ask yourself, "Who is making the real decisions here?" Your answers will identify the people and groups that hold real political power in the United States.

In this chapter . . .

Policy-Making Process

Every day the media call attention to the policy-making process. The Senate passes a law allowing private use of government land. The Supreme Court announces a decision regarding the President's right to privacy. A corporation is fined for polluting an ocean. Groups clash over the right for women to have abortions. Most Americans see such headlines as isolated incidents, but they are actually glimpses of the policy-making process.

Quotes

"Government includes the art of formulating a policy and using the political technique to attain so much of that policy as will receive general support. . . ."

Franklin Roosevelt, 1932
President of the United States (1933-1945)

"The really basic thing in government is policy. Bad administration, to be sure, can destroy good policy, but good administration can never save bad policy."

Adlai Stevenson, Jr., 1952
Democratic presidential nominee

Every policy has a unique history, but each one generally goes through five basic stages:

1. **RECOGNIZING THE PROBLEM** Almost no policy is made unless a need is recognized. Nearly anyone can bring a problem or issue to government's attention—interest groups, court cases, the President, members of Congress, bureaucrats, other countries, even individual citizens. Often pressure to place an issue on the national agenda comes from many different sources and sometimes for many years. Someone will almost always disagree with the need for government action. One group may call for new government regulations for air pollution, but others may believe that current regulations are adequate.

2. **FORMULATING THE POLICY** If enough people agree that government needs to act, then a plan of action must be formulated. At this stage, usually several conflicting plans from various political interests are formed. For example, a public-interest group may suggest tough regulations for air pollution and heavy fines for violators, but a corporation accused of being a polluter may argue for looser regulations in order to control costs.

3. **ADOPTING THE POLICY** In this third stage, the policy becomes an official action by the government. It may take the form of legislation, a bureaucratic order, a presidential action, or a court decision. Policy is often built in a series of small steps passed over time, until finally a complex policy emerges.

4. **IMPLEMENTING THE POLICY** For an adopted policy to be effective, government must see that it's applied to real situations. For example, if air pollution regulations are set up, government officials must make sure that the general public knows about them. They must also monitor pollution and see that violators are punished appropriately.

5. **EVALUATING THE POLICY** Evaluation of the good or the harm created by a policy usually takes place over an extended period of time. Seemingly excellent policies may have unforeseen negative consequences or excessive costs. Inevitably, some will call for changes and corrections, and others will disagree. The whole process occurs again, starting with recognition—or re-recognition—of the problem. As a result, policy making is a continuous process, and government at any given time is at various stages with countless issues.

THE POLICY-MAKING STAGES

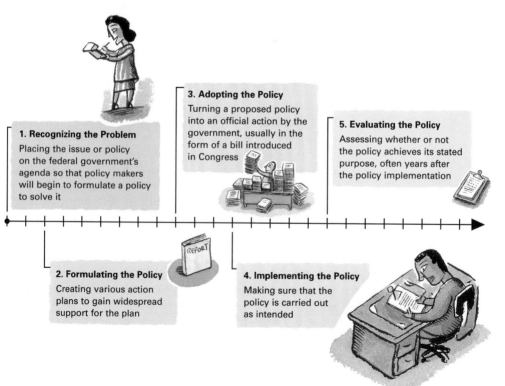

1. Recognizing the Problem
Placing the issue or policy on the federal government's agenda so that policy makers will begin to formulate a policy to solve it

2. Formulating the Policy
Creating various action plans to gain widespread support for the plan

3. Adopting the Policy
Turning a proposed policy into an official action by the government, usually in the form of a bill introduced in Congress

4. Implementing the Policy
Making sure that the policy is carried out as intended

5. Evaluating the Policy
Assessing whether or not the policy achieves its stated purpose, often years after the policy implementation

Economic Policy

When we speak of the economy of the United States, we are referring to the whole system of producing, distributing, and consuming wealth. America's economic system is based on **free enterprise,** or the practice of allowing businesses, industry, property, and money to operate on their own without government interference. Logically, under a true free enterprise, government would have no economic policy. However, since the government itself must have a budget supported by taxes from its citizens, some economic guidelines are necessary.

GOVERNMENT'S ROLE IN THE ECONOMY

Since the late nineteenth century, the United States has gradually moved away from a purely "hands off" free enterprise economic policy. Today the central issue is not whether the government should set economic policy, but how much, when, and in what ways.

1. Historical Background

The free enterprise theory was explained by the Scottish economist Adam Smith in his book *The Wealth of Nations.* Smith believed that the force behind the economy should be the "invisible hand" of competition, not the forceful hand of government. Under Smith's system, the laws of supply and demand should govern the marketplace. If demand increases, prices will rise, and producers will scramble to meet the demand. Once demand is met, supplies will naturally dwindle, since people won't be willing to pay for the product. To Smith, any government control is "interference" with supply and demand.

Smith's theory always assumed that part of a free market is a cycle in which some times are more prosperous than others. Recessions, small market downturns, or even depressions—big downturns—will happen. And, in those times of economic downturn, the government should play a role to protect people until the forces of the marketplace eventually restore economic health.

But free enterprise hit a major roadblock during the 1930s with the Great Depression. When the stock market crashed in 1929, President Herbert Hoover waited for market forces to turn around naturally. When they didn't and the depression worsened, he was voted out of office in 1932. The new President, Franklin Roosevelt, searched for a new philosophy. He found it in the writings of English economist John Maynard Keynes, who warned that if

def·i·ni·tions
_____

free enterprise—the freedom of private businesses to compete for profit with little government regulation.

people do not consume enough or invest enough, the national income will fall. Keynes argued that the best way to increase national income is for the government to do the spending and investing if private enterprise can't or won't. Roosevelt reasoned that people and businesses in the United States had been so burned by terrifying experiences during the early days of the Great Depression that they were too afraid to consume or invest. Roosevelt began a great number of New Deal programs, which involved massive government spending.

The U.S. government borrowed heavily during the 1930s and 1940s, first to get the country out of the depression and then to fight World War II. When the federal government spends more than it takes in, a **deficit** is created. As the government continued its deficit spending, the **national debt,** or public debt, increased. The annual deficit runs in the billions of dollars, the national debt in trillions. The money government spends may stimulate the economy, but it has tended to produce inflation—an increase in the price of goods— and high taxes. Furthermore, the government now has to pay about 15 percent of all the money it takes in just to pay interest on the debt. That's money that could have been used to provide services to the public.

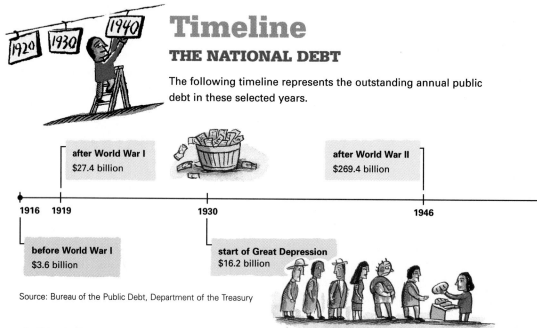

Timeline

THE NATIONAL DEBT

The following timeline represents the outstanding annual public debt in these selected years.

after World War I
$27.4 billion

after World War II
$269.4 billion

1916   1919   1930   1946

before World War I
$3.6 billion

start of Great Depression
$16.2 billion

Source: Bureau of the Public Debt, Department of the Treasury

def·i·ni·tions

deficit—an economic condition in which a government's spending exceeds its revenues.

national debt—the sum of money borrowed by the federal government but not yet repaid. The figure for the national debt also includes any interest owed.

346

Concerns about deficit spending and the increasing national debt have continued through the years. After decades of discussion, in 1997 Congress passed a law that would eliminate the annual budget deficit by the year 2002. A combination of a booming economy and budget cuts made the goal seem possible. Then, in April 1998, to almost everyone's surprise, Congress passed the first balanced budget (with no deficit spending) in 30 years. However, even though the government had a surplus (more money coming in than going out), the years of accumulated national debt did not disappear. The question is how best to manage the changed economy using two types of policy control: monetary policy (control of the money supply) and fiscal policy (control of taxing and spending).

2. Monetary Policy

Did you ever think about how much money is circulating in this country at any one time? The amount is so vast that it is hard to think that any one person or group could control it. But such a group does exist. Its members largely determine how much interest you pay when you buy a car or a house. They also have the power to slow down or speed up the economy and can make the difference between whether you are or are not able to find a job. This powerful group is called the Federal Reserve Board. It is responsible for **monetary policy,** or the control of the money supply.

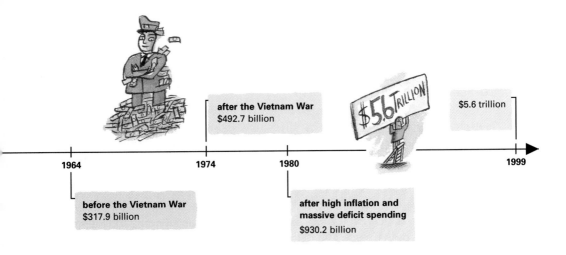

after the Vietnam War
$492.7 billion

$5.6 trillion

1964   1974   1980   1999

before the Vietnam War
$317.9 billion

after high inflation and massive deficit spending
$930.2 billion

def·i·ni·tions

monetary policy—economic policy that controls the money supply, mainly through the Federal Reserve System.

THE FEDERAL RESERVE SYSTEM

The Federal Reserve Board's seven members are appointed by the President, with the consent of the Senate, for 14-year, nonrenewable terms. The chair serves for four years and is one of the most powerful people in the United States. The Board heads the Federal Reserve System, often called "the Fed." It was created by Congress in 1913 to regulate the lending practices of banks. The Fed consists of 12 regional banks, each heading its own district. About 5,000 of the approximately 12,000 banks in the United States are members of the Federal Reserve System, including most of the large, important ones. The banks affiliated with the Federal Reserve control the largest share of total bank deposits in the United States.

3. Fiscal Policy

Just as individual families can control their budgets by regulating their incomes and spending habits, so the government can control its **fiscal policy,** or its methods of raising money and spending it. Two different theories have influenced the U.S. economy recently, and both have had important effects on problems with the national debt and inflation.

KEYNESIAN ECONOMICS

According to this theory, named after John Maynard Keynes, government must manage the consumers' demand for goods and services. In times of depression, the government should increase spending, even if it has to borrow money. In contrast, in times of inflation, government should raise taxes to reduce the amount of money in circulation. Franklin Roosevelt based his economic policy on Keynesian theory.

SUPPLY-SIDE ECONOMICS

In contrast to Keynesian theory, supply-siders believe that government should concentrate its effort on increasing the supply—not the demand—of services. Supply-side economics holds that large cuts in taxes will give people and companies more money to spend. That new money will cause the economy to grow because companies will grow, fewer people will be unemployed, and the initial loss of tax money will be offset by less government spending. During the 1980s, Ronald Reagan supported supply-side economics, pledging to eliminate the deficit by cutting taxes and government spending. But supply-side economics didn't work, and deficits soared during the Reagan years.

def·i·ni·tions

fiscal policy—policy that affects the economy by making changes in government spending and borrowing and tax rates.

e.g.

THE FEDERAL RESERVE BOARD

The Federal Reserve Board controls monetary policy in four ways:

1. **SETTING DISCOUNT RATES** **Discount rates** represent the interest that the Fed charges banks for the money it loans them. If the rates are high, banks pass their increased costs along to their customers. Fewer customers, in turn, will want to take out loans if the rates are high, and less money will be in circulation.

2. **SETTING RESERVE REQUIREMENTS** When you deposit money in a bank, the bank uses your money to make loans or to invest. Of course, it must keep a certain amount of money for customers who want to make withdrawals. The Fed determines the amount of money that banks must keep in reserve at all times. When they increase requirements, less money is available, and vice versa.

3. **SETTING MARGIN REQUIREMENTS** The Fed can influence the money supply by setting the margin rate—the percentage of money people can borrow to buy stocks on credit. Lowering the margin rate makes stock purchases easier and increases the supply of money.

4. **CREATING MORE MONEY** The Fed can't just print more money because of the fear of inflation. But it can exercise control over the money supply by creating more money to sell to the banks through buying securities (bonds and treasury notes). When the Fed sells securities, it takes more money out of circulation. During times of inflation, the Fed practices a "tight money" policy to reduce the money supply. In recessions, the Fed tries to increase the money supply, practicing "loose money" policies.

---

discount rate—the interest rate member banks pay when they borrow from the Federal Reserve.

RAISING MONEY

Most governments, including the United States, raise the largest share of their money through taxes. Some revenue comes from nontax sources, such as the Federal Reserve System, the sale or lease of public lands, fines, and fees for patents, copyrights, and passports. In fiscal year 1997, the U.S. government collected about $1.5 trillion in taxes. Taxes may take many shapes and forms, with some being far larger sources of revenue than others.

1. Federal Income Taxes

The income tax is the largest source of federal revenue today, accounting for about 39 percent of the government's total tax collections. Income was first taxed in 1861 to help finance the Civil War. The income tax is **progressive**— people with higher incomes generally pay larger percentages of their incomes than people with lower incomes. Over the years the income tax has become increasingly complex, and the current tax code runs about 7 million words. Nevertheless, the almost $673 billion dollars collected in 1997 paid for a lot of government expenses. Note that corporations must pay income taxes too. They provide about 10 percent of the total revenue.

2. Other Tax Revenues

The second largest source of federal money—about 32 percent of all collected revenues—is social insurance taxes. These include Social Security, Medicare, and unemployment compensation. They totaled about $536 billion in 1997. Many people actually pay more in Social Security tax than in federal income tax. These taxes are **regressive;** low-income people generally pay larger percentages of their income than high-income people.

Headlines

THE TAX LOAD

The Tax Foundation has estimated that in 1997 average taxpayers had to work **36 days** to pay their federal income tax. Think about it this way: of every 8 hour day, the average American worked **1 hour and 53 minutes** just to pay federal taxes. However, this tax burden is lower than that of citizens in most countries in Western Europe and Japan.

---

progressive tax—a tax that requires higher-income citizens to pay more than lower-income citizens.

regressive tax—a tax that is more burdensome for low-income people than for those with high incomes.

350

e.g.

PROGRESSIVE AND REGRESSIVE TAXES

Amidst complaints about loopholes, tax cheating, complicated forms, and high rates, there are frequent calls for tax reform. How fair is the U.S. tax system? Should rich people pay more than poor people, or should we all be treated equally? Think about two different philosophies of fair taxation.

PROGRESSIVE TAXES vary with a person's ability to pay. For example, the income tax is progressive because the wealthier you are, the higher your tax bracket or rate. Everyone pays the same percentage (currently 15%) on the first $25,000 or so, and then with each bracket above, the rate progresses up to a maximum of 39.6 percent. These rates are much less progressive than they were before President Reagan's tax reforms of the early 1980s. Before that, the highest bracket was actually 94 percent!

REGRESSIVE TAXES are not based on the ability to pay. They tend to hit the poor harder than the rich. For example, a simple sales tax is regressive. Everyone pays the same tax for an item, but a poor person misses the money more. In the 1996 presidential race, Republican contender Steve Forbes made the **flat tax** the corner-stone of his campaign. Forbes proposed an income tax set at a flat rate of 17 percent for all Americans, regardless of income.

★ EXCISE TAXES These taxes on the manufacture, transportation, sale, or consumption of goods and the performance of services accounted for about $57 billion in revenue in 1997. For example, excise taxes are levied on liquor, tobacco, gasoline, telephones, air travel, and other luxury items.

★ ESTATE AND GIFT TAXES These taxes bring in about 1 percent of federal money. An estate tax is a tax on the money belonging to the estate of a person who has died. These taxes are progressive: the more the estate is worth, the higher the tax rate. Gifts of money or property of more than $10,000 each year from one individual to another are also taxed.

★ CUSTOMS, DUTIES, AND TARIFFS Taxes levied on goods imported into the United States account for a little more than 1 percent of federal revenue, or about $17 billion. The main purpose of these customs, duties, and tariffs is to protect goods made in America from lower-priced foreign-made goods.

---

flat tax—a tax figured at a fixed rate.

3. Borrowing

Taxes are not the government's only source of revenue. Recall that the Constitution (Article I, Section 8) gives Congress the power "to borrow money on the credit of the United States." Since the Great Depression, the government has regularly borrowed money to finance its budget. Deficit spending has in recent years accounted for an increasingly small share of total revenue. For example, in 1995, borrowing accounted for about 17 percent of all sources of federal revenue. In 1998, it was estimated to be about 12 percent.

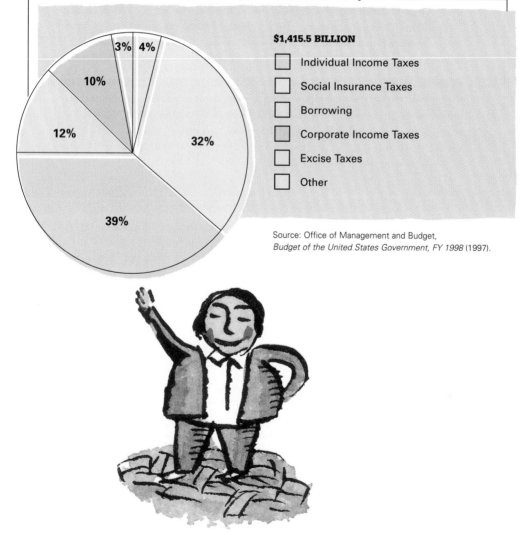

FEDERAL GOVERNMENT REVENUES, FY 1998

$1,415.5 BILLION

- Individual Income Taxes
- Social Insurance Taxes
- Borrowing
- Corporate Income Taxes
- Excise Taxes
- Other

3% 4% 10% 12% 32% 39%

Source: Office of Management and Budget, *Budget of the United States Government, FY 1998* (1997).

SPENDING MONEY

How does the government spend the money it raises—more than $1.5 trillion a year? Each year the President submits a federal budget to be approved by Congress. Federal spending patterns reflect trends in national policies. Analyses of the President's budget focus on several major categories. Three categories that account for the largest amounts of spending are entitlements, national defense, and the national debt.

★ **ENTITLEMENTS** The largest chunk of money goes to **entitlement** programs, or required government payments. Examples are Social Security (benefits for older Americans), Medicare (medical benefits), unemployment insurance, veterans' benefits, and federal retirement pensions. The government has to pay these expenses because, according to the guidelines of the programs, the recipients are "entitled" to them. In 1997, entitlements accounted for about 48 percent of federal spending.

★ **NATIONAL DEFENSE** The second largest amount of money goes for national defense. In 1997, the federal government spent approximately 16 percent of its budget for military defense, a figure that has dropped considerably in recent years. Just ten years earlier, in 1987, more than 28 percent of the budget went to defense. Even when defense spending was much higher, however, the figure was still much lower than that for entitlement programs.

★ **NATIONAL DEBT** About 16 percent of the budget must be set aside to pay interest for the huge national debt. Even though deficit spending was curbed in 1998, the accumulated national debt still costs a bundle in interest.

Much of the remaining money goes for such non-defense items as highway construction, housing, education, foreign aid, and space exploration. A significant portion of this money takes the form of grants to states and localities.

def·i·ni·tions

entitlement—a payment required by law, given to people meeting particular eligibility requirements, such as Social Security payments.

The Budget Process

The budget process is a kind of policy making. The budget requires coming up with solutions to government problems and social issues. It involves a complex series of interactions between the executive and legislative branches. Although the President's various government departments and agencies and Congress all play specified policy-making roles in the budget process, other voices are also heard—especially those of political parties and interest groups. There are four main phases in the budget process, as shown on the following page. Note that work on the budget begins about a year and a half before the budget goes into effect.

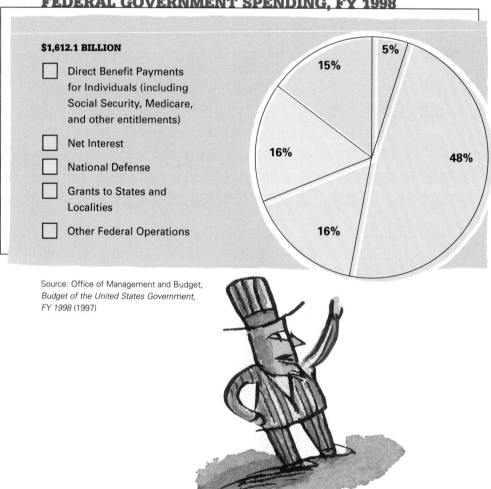

FEDERAL GOVERNMENT SPENDING, FY 1998

$1,612.1 BILLION

- ☐ Direct Benefit Payments for Individuals (including Social Security, Medicare, and other entitlements)
- ☐ Net Interest
- ☐ National Defense
- ☐ Grants to States and Localities
- ☐ Other Federal Operations

15%
5%
16%
48%
16%

Source: Office of Management and Budget, *Budget of the United States Government, FY 1998* (1997)

THE FEDERAL BUDGET PROCESS

May	Federal agencies and departments submit detailed budget requests to Office of Management and Budget (OMB).	**PHASE 1**—Estimating Needs and Making Requests
June	OMB reviews requests.	**PHASE 2**—Reviewing, Revising, and Submitting Budget
July	OMB analyzes budget requests and submits recommendations to White House.	
August	The President and his advisers adjust budget to reflect their economic goals.	
September	Budget is returned to agencies and departments for revision and final preparation.	
October	OMB submits a revised budget to White House for final presidential review.	**PHASE 3**—Developing and Approving a Congressional Budget Resolution
November December January	Budget is delivered to Congress along with a message from the President.	
February	House and Senate Budget Committees and Congressional Budget Office (CBO) analyze budget.	
March April	House and Senate Budget Committees issue the first concurrent budget resolution.	
May	Full House and Senate approve first budget resolution.	
June	Congressional committees and subcommittees work on appropriation bills and any changes in revenue bills to be consistent with first budget resolution.	**PHASE 4**—Creating Final Budget
August September	Congress passes appropriation bills and then a binding second budget resolution. Both are sent to the President to sign or veto.	
October	Budget goes into effect.	

Checking Expenses

Deadlines call for the budget process to be completed by October 1, the beginning of the fiscal year. In reality Congress does not always meet this deadline. Sometimes Congress must pass emergency spending legislation to keep agencies and programs running. An annual audit, or official review of the budget, takes place between the end of the fiscal year on September 30 and November 15. The audit is conducted by the Government Accounting Office (GAO), an independent agency under the supervision of Congress.

e.g.

BUDGET UNCONTROLLABLES

The President does not have total control over making up the budget. About 70 percent of the items in it are called uncontrollables. These are items required by law or resulting from earlier budgetary allotments. Two large uncontrollables are entitlements—such as Social Security, Medicare, Medicaid, and veterans' benefits—and the interest on the national debt.

Domestic Policy

Besides economic policy, there are two other broad categories of public policy: domestic policy and foreign policy. Although the two areas often overlap, **domestic policy** generally focuses on concerns within the United States, and **foreign policy** deals with U.S. interactions with other countries. Here we will consider two types of domestic policy: regulatory and social.

1. REGULATORY POLICY

Most Americans take government regulations for granted because almost every activity in the United States is somehow regulated by the federal government. Through regulatory policies, the federal government oversees the activities of individuals, businesses, and governmental institutions. Regulatory policies cover a wide range of activities and services—from regulations on advertising and transportation to those on food and drugs and public utilities. This section will focus on government restrictions of business, labor, the environment, and energy as examples of regulatory policy making.

A. Regulating Business

Free enterprise has always been the foundation of the American economic system. But starting in the late nineteenth century, protests about abuses of big businesses led to government intervention. Cutthroat competition and big companies were running small companies out of business. The very future of free competition seemed in doubt. Influenced by the strong leadership of President Theodore Roosevelt, Congress passed three key restrictions on businesses to eliminate **monopolies.**

★ **THE INTERSTATE COMMERCE ACT** was passed in 1887 to curtail certain unfair practices by the powerful railroad industry. The big companies would temporarily lower their rates to force the little guys out of business. Once a big company gained a monopoly, it raised the rates even higher than before. The farmers, who relied on railroads to ship their produce, were the losers. The Interstate Commerce Act set up the Interstate Commerce Commission, a government agency designed to oversee industry. Companies also had to post their rates publicly.

def·i·ni·tions

domestic policy—the decisions, actions, and principles that guide the government's approach to issues and problems within the United States.

foreign policy—the actions, decisions, and principles that guide the U.S. government's relationships with other nations.

monopoly—a business or group having exclusive control and lacking competition.

★ **THE SHERMAN ANTITRUST ACT** of 1890 made trusts, or monopolistic companies, illegal. But the provisions of this bill, as well as those of the Interstate Commerce Act, were vague. They had little immediate effect on big business but were used against labor unions instead.

★ **THE CLAYTON ACT** of 1914 also tried to crack down on monopolies. It gave the federal government new powers to prosecute big corporations and outlawed many common techniques used to gain control of an industry. In that same year, Congress established the Federal Trade Commission (FTC) to enforce the Clayton Act.

Today monopolies have largely disappeared but in their place are two newer threats to competition: the **oligopoly,** a situation in which a few firms dominate a market, and the **conglomerate,** a firm that owns businesses in many industries.

Headlines

MICROSOFT: A MODERN TRUST?

The members of Congress in 1890 would not have believed that the Sherman Antitrust Act would eventually regulate the massive computer industry of the late twentieth century.

In 1991, the Federal Trade Commission began to look into complaints that the computer software giant Microsoft was abusing its monopoly in PC operating systems. In 1997, Microsoft launched Internet Explorer 4.0 as a challenge to a rival called Netscape, whose share of the browser market consequently slipped from 90 percent to around 60 percent. In October of 1997, the Justice Department sued Microsoft, alleging that the company was forcing computer makers to use Internet Explorer as a condition of licensing Windows 95, a Microsoft operating system.

According to the Justice Department, Microsoft violated the Sherman Antitrust Act, by using a monopoly in one field to wedge into other lines of the business. Microsoft threatened PC company Compaq with revoking its Windows license if Compaq chose Netscape's Web browser Navigator over Microsoft's Internet Explorer.

Bill Gates, CEO of Microsoft, insisted that his company was just trying to give the American consumer more and more "functionality" at lower and lower prices. Gates did eventually agree to modify his licensing agreements with computer manufacturers, but the Justice Department pressed Microsoft for concessions to break its monopolistic control. As of mid-1999, the case was still not settled.

---

oligopoly—the domination of a kind of business by only a few companies.

conglomerate—a corporation that controls a variety of businesses.

B. Regulating Labor

Many labor policies have provided safeguards for the American worker, attempted to guarantee equal employment opportunities, and improved workplace safety standards. Many labor laws are designed to regulate workers' relations with their employers. Congress passed four important federal regulations regarding labor.

★ **THE WAGNER ACT** of 1935 guaranteed the right for workers to organize into unions and use **collective bargaining** strategies. The law prohibited employers from punishing or terminating an employee for union activities. The National Labor Relations Board (NLRB) was created to enforce the provisions of the law.

★ **THE FAIR LABOR STANDARDS ACT** of 1938 prohibited child labor (under 16 years of age, or under 18 in hazardous occupations) in industries that engaged in, or that produced goods for, interstate commerce. This famous law also set a maximum work week of 40 hours for all employees engaged in interstate commerce, and it set a minimum wage for all workers. The minimum wage was first set at 25 cents an hour. The Bureau of Labor Statistics (BLS) compiles the cost-of-living index or the consumer price index. It is used in negotiations to make salaries and benefits match increases in the cost of living. The amount and frequency of increases in the minimum wage have been a source of great controversy among policy makers.

★ **THE TAFT-HARTLEY ACT** of 1947 was sponsored by pro-business interests who believed that labor had gained too much power through the Wagner Act. Taft-Hartley outlawed closed shops—that is, the requirement that only union members can be hired by a business or factory. It also forbade federal employee unions to strike. The law placed restrictions on strikes in vital services, and today it serves as the legal basis for the government's right to order strikers back to work.

★ **THE LANDRUM-GRIFFIN ACT** of 1959 was designed to clean up corruption in labor unions. It set standards to make union elections fairer, required unions to file annual reports, and guaranteed workers the right to sue their unions for unfair practices.

---

collective bargaining—the negotiation between the representatives of organized workers and their employers, often to determine pay, hours, and working conditions.

C. Regulating the Environment and Energy

The preservation of the nation's natural resources—its land and waterways—
has long been a goal of federal environmental policy. Throughout American
history the national government has been responsible for huge amounts of
public land. For years it focused on encouraging people to claim and settle it.
However, starting in the late nineteenth century, as industry boomed, farmland
lost its fertility from overuse, and forests disappeared. The federal government began to think about conservation, not development, of public land.
One of the first conservation efforts was the founding of the first national park
in 1872. This vast area of forests, dramatic waterfalls, hot springs, and geysers
was named Yellowstone National Park.

From this beginning, the conservation effort broadened. The National
Park Service was established in 1916 to manage Yellowstone. Over the
years, many other parks have been added to the system. The U.S. Forest
Service was created to manage vast acreage of national forests. More
recently, the federal government has become more involved in preserving
other natural resources, such as water and air. Today environmental policy
is the responsibility of many government departments and agencies. Of
particular importance is the Environmental Protection Agency (EPA),
which enforces policies on pesticides, waste disposal, radiation, and water
and air pollution.

Policies regulating energy use are also tremendously important. Consider
that in 1995 the United States consumed 25 percent of the world's energy.
That includes nonrenewable energy sources (fossil fuels, such as coal, oil, and
natural gas), nuclear energy, and renewable energy sources (such as hydroelec-
tric, geothermal, solar, and wind).

The dwindling supply of cheap energy in the last several decades has
placed energy policies near the top of the national agenda. The federal
government began to design a long-term energy policy after the energy
crisis in 1973–74. Because the United States supported Israel during an
Arab-Israeli war, leaders of Arab countries pressured OPEC (Organization
of Petroleum Exporting Countries) to cut off shipments of their oil to
America and other "unfriendly" countries. Many gas stations had to close,
gas purchases were restricted, some businesses closed, and some states
lowered speed limits.

Conflicting interests, from energy companies to conservation groups,
wanted their concerns heard. Energy policies have varied widely from
one administration to the next. For example, both the Reagan and the
Bush administrations encouraged the use of nuclear energy, but the
Clinton administration opposed its further development.

MAJOR ANTI-POLLUTION POLICIES

1. **AIR POLLUTION ACT OF 1955.** This act was the first recognition of modern air pollution by the federal government.

2. **CLEAN AIR ACT OF 1963.** It provided funds to state and local governments that wished to hold conferences to deal with air pollution problems in their area.

3. **MOTOR VEHICLE AIR POLLUTION CONTROL ACT OF 1965.** This act is considered the first significant law affecting air pollution. It authorized the federal government to set emission standards for automobiles.

4. **AIR QUALITY CONTROL ACT OF 1967.** This act required states to set standards for clean air as well as to construct a plan to achieve these standards.

5. **CLEAN AIR ACT OF 1970.** This act established air quality standards for particulate matter, carbon monoxide, and four other pollutants. Companies not meeting these standards could not build new industrial plants without EPA approval. In addition, the law set tighter automobile emissions standards and regulated the amount of lead in gasoline.

6. **FEDERAL WATER POLLUTION CONTROL ACT OF 1972.** Enforced by the EPA, this law established two goals: 1) to make U.S. waters clean enough for swimming and to support fish and wildlife; 2) to end all discharges of pollutants into the nation's waterways. Since 1972, this act has dramatically improved the quality of the nation's water.

7. **SAFE DRINKING WATER ACT OF 1974.** Enforced by the EPA, this law set standards that limit the amount of certain pollutants in drinking water.

8. **RESOURCE CONSERVATION AND RECOVERY ACT OF 1976.** This act empowered the EPA to determine which chemicals are hazardous and to decide on the best methods for disposal of them. Disposal of the chemicals by anyone requires a permit from the EPA. The law also required states to close all open dump sites that were used to dispose of solid wastes such as garbage and trash.

9. **COMPREHENSIVE ENVIRONMENTAL RESPONSE, COMPENSATION, AND LIABILITY ACT OF 1980.** This act established the "Superfund," a $1.6 billion budget for locating and cleaning up toxic waste sites. It also allowed the government to locate those responsible for creating these hazardous sites and sue them for the cost of the cleanup.

10. **CLEAN WATER ACT OF 1986.** Passed by Congress over President Reagan's veto, this law provided funds for sewer construction, cleanup of lakes and rivers, and reduction of run-off pollution.

11. **CLEAN AIR ACT OF 1990.** This act reimposed air quality standards on urban areas and established new emission standards for automobiles.

2. SOCIAL POLICY

A second type of domestic policy, besides regulatory, is social policy. What, if any, responsibility should the U.S. government take for the safety of its citizens? What about transportation systems, urban renewal, housing, job security, or helping farmers, the disabled, or the homeless? The government's role in social issues is extremely controversial. Some people believe that these concerns are best left to private organizations, families, and individuals. Others believe that the government should take full responsibility for them. We will focus on three key social policy issues: health care, welfare, and education.

A. Health Care

The controversy regarding government's role in social policy making is clearly illustrated by the issue of health care. The government has become involved in health care policy in three ways.

★ RESEARCH AND SUPERVISION

The government has developed numerous programs to promote research, target diseases, regulate drugs, gather information, and monitor health care providers. States receive federal grants to build hospitals and research facilities and maintain medical programs, such as maternal and child welfare services. The Public Health Service, headed by the surgeon general, carries out research through the National Institutes of Health. The Food and Drug Administration polices the labeling and processing of most foods, drugs, and cosmetics; the Department of Agriculture inspects sanitary conditions in factories and monitors the processing, packaging, and labeling of food products.

★ COST CONTROL

Government pays for more than 40 percent of health care costs through veterans' hospitals and programs for the poor, the elderly, and the disabled. One of the largest and costliest programs is Medicare, a national health insurance program created in 1966 mainly for people 65 years of age and older. Costs have skyrocketed. In 1966, Medicare cost the federal government $3.2 billion. In 1997, the cost was nearly $190 billion.

★ ACCESS

Good medical care is vital to everyone's health, but it is also expensive. What does government do for people who need care but can't afford it? Many argue that the matter should be left up to private organizations, such as churches and charity groups, or perhaps to local government. However, since the 1960s the national government has taken an active role in improving access to health care. Besides Medicare, Congress created Medicaid, which provides medical benefits for low-income people, the disabled, and the unemployed.

The health care issue—its rising costs and the increasing numbers of Americans without health insurance—was a major part of Bill Clinton's 1992 campaign. Not long after his inauguration, he selected his wife, Hillary Rodham Clinton, to lead a health care task force. After extensive research and analysis, President Clinton submitted a national health insurance proposal to Congress in 1993. The plan would have provided all citizens with basic insurance coverage for doctor fees, hospitalization, and prescription drugs.

Early public reaction to the program was favorable. However, opposition grew quickly. Powerful groups—such as the American Medical Association (AMA), the Pharmaceutical Manufacturers Association (PMA), and the National Federation of Independent Businesses (NFIB)—lobbied heavily against it. Anticipating a decisive defeat, the Clinton administration withdrew the proposal before a vote was taken.

President Clinton's proposed health care policy got stuck in the policy formulation stage. He placed it on the national agenda but was unable to forge a sufficient base of support. Perhaps his proposal was too abrupt a change. Perhaps Clinton should have worked out compromises with the influential interest groups that opposed him. The fate of Clinton's proposal illustrates the complicated interaction—and conflict—among different policy makers. Still, the issue appears to be not whether the government is responsible for health care, but how much and in what ways.

© Jimmy Margulies

Headlines

E. COLI OUTBREAK

In June of 1998, a number of people in Alpine, Wyoming, became seriously ill with stomach pains, diarrhea, and paralyzing stomach cramps. When two victims went to the local doctor, they started a process that illustrates the policy implementation phase of policy making.

A doctor strongly suspected that the illness was caused by *e. coli,* a bacterium with an unusual ability to change and multiply. He contacted other doctors in the area and confirmed several other similar cases. Then he notified Alpine Mayor Donn Wooden and the county infectious disease nurses. They in turn reported it to Gayle Miller, the state of Wyoming's chief epidemiologist, a specialist in infectious diseases. Within a week, the state office had located 26 confirmed *e. coli* cases. Since the problem went beyond the state's capabilities, Miller e-mailed the Centers for Disease Control (CDC), a federal agency headquartered in Atlanta, Georgia. Groups of their scientists were dispatched to Wyoming. They set up shop in the Alpine city hall and traced the outbreak to the city's water supply. How did the water become contaminated? After a winter storm had toppled some fences, farm animals had wandered into springs that fed the city water source. The bacteria from the farm animals had contaminated the entire city's water supply.

In this case, private citizens, doctors and nurses, city and state officials, and finally federal authorities were involved. Such incidents have inspired new pressure in Washington for a more concerted federal effort to research and control infectious diseases. If these demands are heard, their input undoubtedly will feed the policy-making process for health care issues.

364

B. Welfare

Another highly controversial area of social policy is that of **public assistance and social insurance programs**, more commonly known as **welfare.** Entitlements, or the costs associated with social welfare policies, make up almost a half of the federal budget. Federal social welfare programs got started during the 1930s when Franklin Roosevelt's New Deal programs gave aid to those in need. Employees and employers contribute to a trust fund through payroll taxes. The worker receives benefits at retirement age. The best-known New Deal program is Social Security, a social insurance plan for the elderly. During the 1960s and 1970s, public assistance programs expanded greatly, to include Medicare, Medicaid, Aid to Families with Dependent Children (AFDC), Supplemental Securities Income (SSI), and food stamps. Today these and other social service programs are targeted at the more than 37 million people living under the official poverty line, or roughly 15 percent of the population.

Reform of social insurance programs has been debated for years. Rising medical costs, increasing numbers of people receiving benefits, and longer life expectancies have jeopardized the financial stability of the Social Security system. Experts estimate that by 2019 more money will be paid out than is brought in.

Some of the controversy surrounding welfare reflects the split between conservative and liberal political ideologies. Conservatives tend to oppose welfare programs on the grounds that they can corrupt recipients' character, destroy their desire to work, and reward plain laziness. In contrast, liberals tend to believe that government should help those who can't seem to help themselves. They see welfare benefits as government's responsibility to provide a decent standard of living for all. A 1997 program, Welfare to Work, was proposed by President Clinton as a compromise between the two points of view. The program, jointly sponsored by the federal government and various large corporations and companies, serves as a pipeline for welfare recipients to get and keep steady jobs with the participating companies. The federal government is responsible for weaning people from welfare and putting them in touch with the companies.

def·i·ni·tions

public assistance—aid programs funded by state and federal tax money. They are available to those who meet eligibility requirements based on need.

social insurance programs—programs created to help elderly, ill, and unemployed citizens. They are funded by personal contributions and available to those who have paid into them.

welfare—aid given by the government or private agencies to the needy or disabled.

C. Education

Americans have always believed that local communities should be primarily responsible for educating their children. The federal government first became involved in education policy when Congress passed the Morrill Land Grant Act in 1862, which provided money to state colleges. More than 80 years later, after World War II, the government paid college tuition for war veterans under the G.I. Bill. Today the majority of federal funds for education goes to higher education, primarily as student loans and grants. During the late 1950s and the 1960s, the federal government initiated programs to upgrade science, language, and mathematics courses. As part of his Great Society program, President Lyndon Johnson sponsored such education programs as Head Start (for pre-schoolers and kindergartners) and signed the Elementary and Secondary Education Act, which focused on helping underprivileged public school students. Still, the federal government today funds less than 10 percent of the more than $60 billion spent on education in the United States. Most education policy is set by local school boards and state governments.

EDUCATIONAL REFORMS

The heated debate over several policy issues reveals disagreement about the extent of the government's involvement in education. For example, Congress didn't approve President Bush's educational reform package, America 2000, in part because it called for merit pay for good teachers, national standards, and a school-choice plan. Another controversial issue surrounds the funding of public schools by property taxes. Schools in wealthy districts receive a lot more property tax money than schools in poorer neighborhoods. State and federal governments have recently stepped in to help eliminate the inequality.

VOUCHERS AND CREDITS

A related and still quite controversial issue involves school vouchers. All property owners in a school district pay taxes to fund the schools. If children from outside the district want to attend their schools, school boards generally charge their parents tuition. Partly as an incentive to encourage poor school districts to improve, school vouchers have been introduced in some communities. They allow students "credits" toward attending the school of their parents' choice, including out-of-district schools and private schools. Supporters of the system claim that vouchers give underprivileged students an opportunity to escape the weak school systems. Opponents claim that the voucher system breaks down the separation of church and state (since many private schools are religious) at the expense of the taxpayer. The voucher issue is at various stages in the policy-making process around the country. Some areas are already implementing a policy, but many others are still trying to identify problems and formulate policy.

Foreign Policy and National Defense

The early 1990s marked a critical juncture for U.S. foreign policy. After the end of World War II in 1945, Americans had grown accustomed to the strong tensions of the **cold war,** a struggle between the United States and the Soviet Union for world power. In 1991, the Soviet Union collapsed. In its place were the individual republics, so diminished and preoccupied by internal problems that competition for world power was out of the question. Within a matter of a few months in 1991, the United States came to realize that the cold war was over. What would happen next?

Today the United States is a major player in a whole new age of world affairs. For the first time in centuries, no superpower rivalries immediately threaten world peace. Yet the world is still full of volatile, dangerous situations. Among major foreign policy concerns today are the increasing number of nations with nuclear weapons, biological and chemical warfare, and the threat of terrorism. It is up to the nation's foreign and defense policy makers to decide how to react to and even avoid these situations.

© Signe Wilkinson/Cartoonists & Writers Syndicate

---

cold war—the period of hostility and tensions between the United States and the Soviet Union, lasting from the end of World War II until the early 1990s.

FOREIGN POLICY PRIORITIES

According to the State Department, American foreign policy goals include the following:

★ Preserving the national security of the United States and promoting a safe, secure global environment, an essential element of the success of the other goals

★ Promoting world peace, maintaining a balance of powers, and working with allies to solve international problems

★ Promoting democratic values and human rights, particularly encouraging countries with political choice and the rule of law

★ Furthering foreign trade and global economic and cooperative involvement in international organizations, such as the International Monetary Fund and the World Bank

Quote

American policy "is directed not against any country or doctrine but against hunger, poverty, desperation, and chaos. Its purpose should be the revival of political and social conditions in which free institutions can exist."

Secretary of State George Marshall
commencement address at Harvard University, 1947

FOREIGN AND DEFENSE POLICY MAKERS

Foreign and defense policy makers may be divided into two groups. The first group consists of those whose job it is to use diplomacy to solve problems. Diplomats are specialists in foreign policy, and they negotiate to solve problems peacefully. They try to keep problems from escalating to the second level, which is the responsibility of defense policy specialists. The second are those who must defend the country against outside threats, including military strikes or war. In practice, the two levels overlap and require cooperation and interaction among foreign policy specialists and defense policy specialists.

According to the Constitution, Presidents share with Congress the responsibility for making foreign policy and defense policy decisions. For example, the Constitution names the President as commander in chief of the armed forces. Implied in that position are policy-making responsibilities. However, only Congress may declare war on another country. Obviously, each branch must cooperate with the other. In reality, the President almost always has had the primary responsibility to shape foreign and defense policies. Presidents, or their executive branch representatives, bargain, negotiate, apply pressure, persuade, and threaten.

Within the executive branch, the President relies on many people to advise him on foreign policy. Each President reorganizes or emphasizes the importance of different positions or departments, so that identifying the key policy makers is a constant challenge. Competition to get the ear of the President is usually intense. Below are four areas with responsibility for foreign policy decisions:

1. THE STATE DEPARTMENT The primary duty of the State Department has always been the security of the nation. It serves as a first line of defense against the serious situation in which the armed services might be called on to take care of an international conflict. Its priorities include negotiating with other nations, protecting American citizens and interests abroad, providing humanitarian relief funds, and promoting American commercial interests and enterprises.

Usually the President's principal foreign policy adviser is the secretary of state. He or she administers the State Department and is the chief coordinator of all governmental actions that affect relations with other countries. Many day-to-day responsibilities of running the department usually fall to under-secretaries, and the secretary of state spends a great deal of time negotiating with the leaders of other countries.

The **Foreign Service** is part of the State Department, but it represents the entire government and works directly with many other agencies. Foreign Service diplomats are a select, specially trained group expected to take assignments anyplace in the world on short notice. The United States sends **ambassadors,** or official representatives, to more than 160 countries in the world today. In each country, the ambassador, along with a staff, establishes an embassy, which represents an American presence abroad. The embassy carries out policy under the direction of the secretary of state, protects Americans within the country, and cultivates friendly relationships with other countries.

2. **THE NATIONAL SECURITY COUNCIL (NSC)** The NSC serves directly under the President. It was created by Congress in 1947 to help the President integrate foreign, military, and economic policies that affect national security. By law, it consists of the President, the Vice President, the secretary of state, and the secretary of defense. Sometimes Presidents have included the director of the CIA, the White House chief of staff, the attorney general, and the national security adviser. The national security adviser, appointed by the President, sometimes rivals the influence of the secretary of state. Over the years, the NSC has claimed a major role in making and implementing foreign policy.

3. **THE CENTRAL INTELLIGENCE AGENCY (CIA)** The CIA, one of the best known arms of foreign policy, was created in 1947 to coordinate the gathering and analysis of information that flows into the U.S. government

Then and Now

DIPLOMACY IN HISTORY

The right of legation, or the right for countries to send and receive diplomatic representatives, is a time-honored practice. Its roots can be traced back 6,000 years to the ancient Egyptians, who used diplomacy as well as military campaigns to protect and expand their kingdom. A few thousand years later, around 550 B.C., the Greek city-state of Sparta established through diplomacy, the Peloponnesian League, a union of city-states intended to promote cooperation and avoid war. Almost 2,300 years later, the Second Continental Congress of the United States sent its first foreign service officer to France—Benjamin Franklin.

def·i·ni·tions

Foreign Service—the diplomatic staff that represents the U.S. government in other nations.

ambassador—an official appointed to represent a nation in diplomatic or foreign policy matters.

Headlines

CHANGES IN DEFENSE SPENDING

Defense spending during the 1950s and early 1960s amounted to more than half the entire federal budget. America was paying off debts from World War II, fighting new wars (Korea and Vietnam), and defending itself from cold war threats all at the same time. Starting in the mid-1960s and continuing until the early 1980s, defense spending crept downward. In the early 1980s, President Reagan bolstered defense, but the downward trend has continued since 1990. At 16 percent of the total budget, defense spending is close to $250 billion a year. About half the people employed by the national government work in the Defense Department. The defense cutbacks, though probably inevitable, have been controversial nonetheless. The questions of how much to cut, when, and in what areas have not been easily answered. One major issue in the defense cutbacks has been the closing of military bases.

from around the world. Although most information that the CIA gathers is made public, the term *intelligence* stirs visions of papers marked "Top Secret" and undercover agents. The CIA does supply critical information, but most of its work is routine. Under a director appointed by the President and approved by the Senate, the CIA reports on developments around the world, analyzes data, and transmits the right information to the right people at the right time.

4. **THE DEPARTMENT OF DEFENSE (DOD)** Although the Department of Defense advises the President on foreign policy, it specializes in defense policy. Its headquarters is the Pentagon, which houses about 25,000 military and civilian personnel. All three military departments—Army, Navy, and Air Force—are under the general supervision of the secretary of defense.

The Joint Chiefs of Staff is a five-member body that serves as the main military advisory body to the President, the National Security Council, and the secretary of defense. It includes the chiefs of staff of the three military departments, the commandant of the Marines, and a chair. All the service chiefs are appointed by the President, with the consent of the Senate. The President selects the chair, a top-ranking military officer.

DIPLOMATIC POLICIES

A major responsibility of the foreign and defense policy makers is the decision as to what strategy to follow in solving international problems. According to conventional diplomacy, much foreign policy is conducted by the foreign service and ambassadors in face-to-face discussions with representatives from other countries. Foreign policy is also enacted around the world in regional or international organizations.

American diplomatic policies encourage other countries to act favorably toward the United States. Providing foreign aid, using economic sanctions, and forming alliances are three key types of diplomatic policy.

e.g.

DIPLOMACY IN THE UNITED NATIONS

The United Nations (UN) is probably the best-known international peace-keeping organization. It was created in 1945 at the end of World War II, when its members renounced war and vowed to respect human and economic freedoms. Most countries today belong to the UN, and they are represented equally in the General Assembly. The real seat of power, however, is the Security Council, whose five permanent members (United States, Britain, France, China, and Russia), and six rotating members make binding decisions. In addition, the UN sponsors international programs focused on economic development, health, education, and welfare concerns. Although the United Nations has fallen short of the goal of eliminating warfare, it still plays an important part in the policy-making process for the United States and most other nations.

1. FOREIGN AID By providing countries with **foreign aid**—assistance including military weapons, medical care, loans, and food—the United States can achieve better relationships with other countries. Foreign aid began in the early 1940s when the United States gave nearly $50 billion in weapons, food, and other supplies to U.S. allies in World War II. In 1997, the United States gave about $12 billion in foreign aid, less than 1 percent of the total U.S. budget.

def·i·ni·tions

foreign aid—a government's financial or military assistance to other countries.

2. ECONOMIC SANCTIONS **Sanctions** show disapproval of the actions or policies of another country. The United States has frequently put economic pressure on countries perceived to be a threat or whose behavior presents a problem. For example, during the 1980s many nations placed economic sanctions on South Africa to protest that nation's practice of apartheid, or separation and inequality of racial groups. Those sanctions almost certainly were a factor in bringing apartheid to an end in South Africa. In contrast, although economic sanctions during the 1990s against Iraq negatively affected the Iraqi economy, they were unsuccessful in removing Saddam Hussein as president.

3. ALLIANCES The United States is a member of several regional alliances. In these collective security pacts, nations agree to view an attack on one country as an attack on all. Besides encouraging friendly relations among countries, the alliances can be an effective means of **deterrence** to nations considering military action against a member. One powerful alliance is the North Atlantic Treaty Organization (NATO). It consists of 18 nations in Western Europe and the United States.

e.g.

WHERE DOES OUR MONEY GO?

America gave $12 billion in foreign aid in 1997.

★ The money went to 156 countries.

★ The largest recipients of U.S. economic and military aid in 1996 were Israel, which got some $3 billion, and Egypt, which received some $2 billion. These two countries alone made up about 40 percent of the entire foreign aid budget. Next in line was Bosnia, which received $298 million.

★ Military and security assistance accounted for about 25 percent of all aid.

★ Humanitarian and disaster relief assistance made up about 15 percent.

★ Economic and development assistance was about 60 percent.

def·i·ni·tions

sanction—a penalty against a nation that has violated international law.

deterrence—the U.S. defense policy that uses the threat of military attack to discourage enemy attack or hostile action.

DEFENSE POLICIES

If diplomacy breaks down, the United States must be able to defend itself. There are several common defense strategies.

1. **COVERT OPERATIONS** Covert, or secret, operations are generally meant to avoid full-scale military involvement. During the cold war several Presidents endorsed covert operations in Southeast Asia, which were controversial when they were revealed. For example, President John Kennedy almost certainly allowed the American military to be involved in a 1963 plot to assassinate Ngo Dinh Diem, the president of North Vietnam. Covert operations that involved a complex ploy to divert money for weapons to Central America from Iran were at the heart of the Iran-Contra scandal of the Reagan presidency.

2. **POLITICAL COERCION** This is the last resort before military intervention in dealing with a country that the United States perceives as a threat. Techniques include breaking diplomatic ties, boycotts, and restricting tourist and business travel between the countries. For example, diplomatic relations were broken with Iran in 1979 when the shah, who favored a strong relationship between Iran and the United States, was overthrown by Islamic fundamentalists. Diplomatic relations were also broken with Iraq after Saddam Hussein invaded Kuwait.

3. **MILITARY INTERVENTION** Military action is usually the last resort in dealing with an international crisis. It represents a total collapse of diplomacy. Most interventions are brief, such as the invasion of Panama ordered by George Bush in 1989 or the Persian Gulf War and the invasion of Kuwait in 1990. Since Vietnam, the United States has avoided extensive, sustained military operations. The success of military intervention varies. The United States achieved its objectives in Panama and Kuwait. However, the success of its participation in the UN peacekeeping forces in Bosnia and Kosovo is unclear.

Headlines

STRIKING AT TERRORISM

In August of 1998, bombs exploded in the U.S. embassies in Kenya and Tanzania. They killed hundreds of people, both natives and Americans, who were apparently the victims of a coordinated terrorist attack. A few days later, the United States launched military strikes at a terrorist training center in Afghanistan and a factory in the Sudan.

These events were hardly the first blow in the struggle between terrorist organizations and the U.S. government. For example, a terrorist organization was linked to the 1993 World Trade Center bombing in New York. In 1986, the United States bombed Libya after terrorists killed an American soldier at a Berlin discotheque. In 1988, a Pan Am jet blew up over Scotland, an attack the Justice Department blamed on two Libyan intelligence agents.

The 1998 attacks, however, were described by President Bill Clinton and Secretary of State Madeline Albright not as retaliatory but as "pre-emptive." That is, they were designed to stop later terrorist attacks that U.S. intelligence claimed were being planned for other U.S. embassies.

Policies are plans of action that take us from where we are to where we want to be. Political parties, interest groups, the media, Congress, the executive branch, the courts, and the President—they have a say in setting domestic and foreign policy. It is important to understand that no one group operates alone. Getting an issue on the government's agenda and then deciding what to do about it is a complicated process. The economic, domestic, and foreign policies that are implemented affect us all. One of the main duties of citizens is to judge the quality of the current policies and let their representatives know how they feel about those policies. If the public's views are not heard and reflected in government policies, then important problems in American society won't be solved.

18 | Comparative Economic and Political Systems

conomics and politics . . . you may think of them as very different. One has to do with your wallet and the other with your government. But often economic issues are also political issues, and vice versa. To separate the two is hard. For example, most adults in the United States have jobs, make money, buy clothes, and pay bills in a capitalistic economic system. Likewise, people follow a democratic system when they vote, pay taxes, and follow traffic rules. Most U.S. citizens never think about carrying on these day-to-day activities in any other way.

In fact, people in other countries accept an array of economic and political rules that are different from those in America. Each country arranges its economic and political system in its own way. But the systems of some countries have some general similarities to others. These similarities, or patterns, allow us to identify basic types of political and economic systems. And that, in turn, allows us to understand similarities in the ways citizens of different countries conduct their affairs.

In this chapter . . .

Comparative Economic Systems

Economic systems define the basic rules for producing, distributing, and consuming goods that people need or want. Three different modern economic systems are capitalism, communism, and socialism.

CAPITALISM

Capitalism, also known as the free enterprise system, has five basic rules for production, distribution, and consumption:

1. **PRIVATE OWNERSHIP** Most of the means of production—such as factories, stores, or businesses—are owned privately rather than publicly. Individuals or groups of individuals hold them freely with few or limited controls by government. Decisions about how much and when to produce and how to price products are made by private owners, not by the government.

2. **FACTORS OF PRODUCTION** In order to produce goods and services that people need, four types of resources are necessary. First, producers need land for agriculture, mining, forestry, or simply the space for building a factory. Second, human resources are needed—people to work in the factories, offices, or farms. A third factor is **capital**—the money, machinery, or buildings that are necessary to make the products. Fourth, management is needed to organize the other factors and make them run efficiently.

3. **FREE COMPETITION** Who controls production, distribution, and consumption? The basic rule of capitalism is that people should compete ethically and freely. The assumption is that, in most cases, the most deserving person is the one who succeeds. In theory, competition keeps prices down and quality high because consumers will seek the best product for the least amount of money.

4. **LAWS OF SUPPLY AND DEMAND** Prices in the free market are determined by how many products there are to go around and how much people want them. When supplies become plentiful, prices tend to drop; and if prices drop, demand usually increases until supplies are used up. Then prices will go up once more, but only until demand goes down. These laws work in a cycle to control prices, keeping them from getting too low or too high.

def·i·ni·tions

capitalism—an economic system characterized by open competition in a free market and based on private ownership.

capital—money or property invested in businesses by one or more individuals.

5. FREEDOM OF CHOICE Capitalism assumes that all people involved in the economic cycle may freely choose when and how to participate. People may produce and consume goods when and how they choose. **Entrepreneurs**—that is, people who start businesses or invent new means of production—may switch businesses. People who are hired as workers choose where, when, and how much they will work. And consumers have choices among a variety of products and services.

CAPITALISM AND SHOES

Let's look at how a capitalist system would handle the production, distribution, and consumption of a particular product: shoes. Under capitalism, some individuals in the society will decide to start producing shoes. They will get the land, workers, capital, and management they need. People who need shoes can freely decide where to go for their shoes. Although it may not be convenient to go to the factory where they are produced, other people will figure out how to distribute the shoes, getting them to those who need them. Others will open stores to sell shoes. The price of the shoes will vary according to the demand for them. If too many people are producing shoes, the supply goes up. The producers will have to compete for customers by lowering their prices. Once shoes are priced so low that people decide to buy them again, the supply goes down, causing more competition for shoes. Then the price goes up again, starting the whole cycle over again.

Adam Smith's influential theory of the free enterprise system was based on enlightened self-interest and *laissez-faire* theory. Smith believed that in the pursuit of personal wealth, people will see how their interest is tied to the interests of others. By providing goods, services, jobs, and opportunities for new enterprises, individuals enrich the entire community. In Smith's view, government should not interfere with business, except to protect and promote free competition and the process of supply and demand. However, American capitalism has not operated on pure *laissez-faire* principles. The government has been involved in many aspects of American economic life—from prohibiting monopolies and protecting the environment to operating toll highways and setting consumer safety standards.

---

entrepreneur—a person who organizes and develops new ideas for a business.

laissez-faire—an economic theory that opposes governmental interference in big business; literally, "leave it alone."

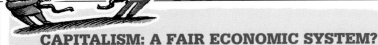

Vs.

CAPITALISM: A FAIR ECONOMIC SYSTEM?

Capitalism is an accepted or preferred economic system in many countries today—for example, the United States, Japan, and Germany. In nearly all countries, restrictions have been placed on capitalistic economies because of some important criticisms of its effects. Look at both sides:

PRO

1. Capitalism rewards those who deserve it: the most intelligent, the hardest working, and the most ambitious.

2. Competition brings out good qualities in people; they try harder than they would without it.

3. Capitalism allows people to compete; therefore, almost everyone has a chance to do well.

CON

1. Capitalism rewards people who are the most ruthless, and others less able to compete (such as the sick) are hurt by the system.

2. Competition brings out the bad side of human nature. It encourages people to be selfish and greedy.

3. Capitalism eventually results in monopoly, or only one company controlling an industry, because everyone else will be driven out of business.

COMMUNISM

The two quotes below begin and end *The Communist Manifesto,* one of the most influential political documents in modern history. The authors, strong critics of the capitalist system, suggested a powerful new economic system called **communism.** Communism has very different answers to the question of who should control production, distribution, and consumption. In communist systems, such as those in Cuba or China, the government controls economic life.

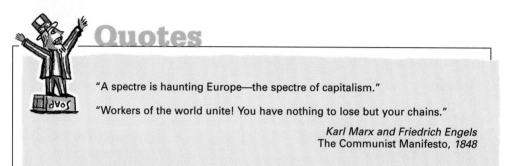

Quotes

"A spectre is haunting Europe—the spectre of capitalism."

"Workers of the world unite! You have nothing to lose but your chains."

Karl Marx and Friedrich Engels
The Communist Manifesto, *1848*

The Theory of Karl Marx

In 1867, Karl Marx carefully explained the development of capitalism in his major work, *Das Kapital.* For him, capitalism was an outmoded economic system that exploited workers. Capitalism was the past; communism was the future. Marx's economic and political views are known as **Marxism,** and they provide an important foundation for communism. *Das Kapital* explained both Marx's interpretation of history and his vision for the future in six basic principles:

1. ORIGINAL COMMUNAL SOCIETIES Marx believed that originally people lived in communal societies, or groups, in which everyone was basically equal. People didn't own property individually. They shared their resources as a community. Even though they had different responsibilities, their survival depended on sharing and cooperating. People did what they were able to do and took what they needed.

2. CLASS STRUGGLE According to Marx, as soon as the idea of private property came to be accepted, problems began. People for centuries were split into two social classes—the controlled and the controllers, the oppressed and the oppressors. For example, many ancient civilizations waged wars with others, seizing their land and taking the defeated people as slaves, creating two classes: slave owners and slaves. During the Middle Ages, defenseless people turned to more powerful

def·i·ni·tions

communism—a system of government in which the state controls the means of production.

Marxism—the political and economic ideas, developed by Karl Marx, that emphasize class struggle.

ones for protection. The two classes in feudalism were nobles and serfs. During the capitalist era in which Marx lived, the two classes were called the **bourgeoisie** (the owners of the factories and other means of production) and the **proletariat** (the workers or laborers).

3. LABOR THEORY OF VALUE According to the communist view, a product has no value unless a worker transforms it into something useful. For example, wood and bricks are useless unless a laborer uses them to build something. Because laborers give the product its value, they deserve to be paid for it. But, in the capitalist system, workers are paid as little as possible. In the fierce competitive battle between producers trying to gain control of the marketplace, workers' salaries are a major expense. The entrepreneurs' ability to cut salaries may be the factor that causes them to win the competition. As a result, workers are paid only enough to survive. According to Marx, the capitalists stole their profits from the workers. The root of all this evil is the desire for private property, which creates greed and selfishness.

4. ECONOMIC CONTROL OF SOCIETY AND GOVERNMENT Marx believed that whoever controls the economy controls everything else, including the government. Under a system in which one class economically oppresses the other, the government is just a tool of those in control. Capitalists then will do whatever is necessary to keep the system going.

5. REVOLUTION OF THE PROLETARIAT Marx believed that capitalism exaggerated the class-based oppression to the point that the proletariat would finally revolt. Workers would become so enraged that they would overthrow the bourgeoisie in a massive, violent revolution. The main point of the revolution would be to do away with the evil—private ownership of property that had divided people into classes for centuries. The two social classes would disappear. According to Marx, a new world of equality and cooperation would emerge under the system of communism. Marx's view of philosophy was, "To each according to his need, from each according to his ability." This, he felt, would bring human society back to its purer state.

6. DICTATORSHIP OF THE PROLETARIAT Marx understood that the revolution would not automatically bring about an organized society. He saw the need for a transitional phase during which the state would represent and enforce the interests of the masses. Marx called this phase "the dictatorship of the proletariat," a period of authoritarian rule that would supervise the change to a property-less society without classes. After a time, the dictatorship would "wither away." Without private property and its social class distinctions, centralized government would be unnecessary.

---

bourgeoisie—in Marxism, the social class that profits from the work of the proletariat.
proletariat—in Marxism, the social class that is taken advantage of by the bourgeoisie.

Marxism and Communism

Marx's revolution of the proletariat did not occur in the most industrialized countries of the nineteenth century, as he thought it would. Instead, communism took hold first in Russia in 1917 and in China in 1949. Capitalism in both countries had been nonexistent. In Russia and China, communist control of the economy extended into other areas, such as controlling elections and requiring persons to pool their livestock and tools to work together on large farms. In those two countries the property-less society without classes that Marx envisioned has not yet occurred.

In fact, since the late 1980s, many countries—particularly those in Eastern Europe—have drifted away from communism. In 1990, for example, East Germany, a former communist state, united with West Germany under a capitalist economic system. The former Soviet Union has also now moved away from communism. By the late 1980s, dissatisfaction with the scarcity and quality of consumer goods and slow economic growth led to calls for reform. *Perestroika,* or restructuring, began in 1985 under Soviet President Mikhail Gorbachev, but it failed to stimulate the economy. Prices rose, inflation soared, and discontent increased. In 1991, when several of the republics declared independence, the Union of Soviet Social Republics was officially dissolved. A loose association, called the Commonwealth of Independent States, emerged in its place. Real questions remain about how much genuine democratic reform can be achieved.

SARGENT © 1992 *Austin American-Statesman.* Reprinted with permission of UNIVERSAL PRESS SYNDICATE. All rights reserved.

SOCIALISM

Socialism, as it has emerged in the twentieth century, is an economic system that rejects most of the basic tenets of capitalism. But it does not accept the extreme communist beliefs regarding the inevitability of the proletariat revolution. The term *socialism* can be confusing because its meaning has evolved over the course of a century. In fact, Marx himself sometimes used the term *socialism* for *communism*. He often referred to the "dictatorship of the protelariat"—the transition time after the overthrow of the bourgeoisie—as socialistic.

Theory of Socialism

Socialism does not support the Marxist idea that a more equal society must come about through the violent overthrow of the ruling class. Instead socialists believe that changes may be brought about peacefully, through the democratic process. Socialists do not value the concepts of private ownership and competition that characterize capitalism. They believe that wealth should be distributed more equally than in capitalist societies and that the extremes of wealth and poverty should be eliminated. Under socialism, the most important means of production and distribution should be held by the public, usually under government control.

Then and Now

SOCIALISM IN THE UNITED STATES

Even though the United States is usually considered a capitalist nation, some socialist principles have influenced our twentieth-century government. The socialist influence was most obvious during times of economic problems, such as the post-World War I recession and the Great Depression of the 1930s. The New Deal programs were often criticized for being socialist because they gave the government a great deal of control over free enterprise. When questioned, President Roosevelt declared that his programs were neither "fish nor fowl, but they taste mighty good" when they worked. In other words, he refused to label them capitalist or socialist.

Others of this era carried the idea of redistribution of wealth further. For example, Governor Huey Long of Louisiana proposed a "share the wealth" plan that included provisos to limit the fortunes of multi-millionaires, restrict the amount a person can earn or inherit in 1 year to $1 million, and guarantee education for every child through college.

def·i·ni·tions

socialism—the economic system that advocates government ownership of the means of production.

Basic Elements of Socialism

Although a purely socialist economic system doesn't exist today, many countries have a blend of capitalism and socialism. Good examples are Austria, Sweden, the Netherlands, Israel, and Italy. Influential socialist political parties exist in many other nations, including France and Great Britain. Socialist economic systems usually share many of the following four characteristics:

1. NATIONALIZATION Under nationalization, some major industries formerly owned by private companies or citizens are taken over by the government. For example, in Mexico during the 1930s, President Lazaro Cardenas nationalized many privately owned companies, including some owned by American oil companies. He created "Pe-Mex," a government-run company that took over almost all the oil industry. In this case, as in most others, companies were nationalized without receiving any compensation.

2. PUBLIC ASSISTANCE Socialists want to limit wealth, but they also want to limit poverty. Usually, socialists ask the government to ensure that everyone has housing and food. Public services are considered to be the government's responsibility. Today the governments of many countries, including the United States, provide some social assistance in the form of pensions, health insurance, and unemployment insurance. Countries in which socialism is more influential provide many more services, such as free medical and dental care.

3. TAXATION Since social welfare services are expensive, taxes in socialist countries tend to be high. It is not uncommon for taxes to take 50 or 60 percent of an individual's total income. Tax rates for the wealthy may amount to 80 or 90 percent of their income.

4. COMMAND ECONOMY Under capitalism, key economic decisions are made by thousands of private individuals and companies, a situation called a **market economy.** Under socialism, and also under communism, the government can plan how an economy will develop over a period of years. It may set targets for production and guide investments into specific industries. As a result, the system is called a **command economy.**

---

market economy—an economic system in which government plays a limited role.

command economy—an economic system in which the government has great control of the economy.

Vs.

SOCIALISM: A FAIR ECONOMIC SYSTEM?

In socialist economic systems, the governments own basic industries, but citizens have some economic freedom. How fair do you think socialism is?

PRO

1. Socialism levels the inequalities between the rich and the poor.

2. Socialism is morally superior to capitalism. It emphasizes social responsibility and cooperation.

3. Socialism makes political democracy work more smoothly by comple-menting it with economic democracy.

CON

1. Socialism removes people's right to earn as much money as they are capable of earning.

2. Socialism deprives people of freedom and the incentive to be as good as they can be.

3. Socialism turns government into a bureaucratic nightmare. Economies are too complex to be directed by central planners.

MIXED ECONOMIES

Today, many economies are not wholly capitalistic or socialistic, but are mixed, with some characteristics of each. Often, political parties within a country will advocate one system or the other, so that governments may lean socialist for a time and capitalist at another time. For example, during the early 1980s in France, the Socialist party gained control of the government. Under the leadership of François Mitterrand, the government nationalized many industries and strengthened public assistance programs. The socialist influence diminished by the early 1990s. Expensive welfare programs that were creating large government debts were abandoned, and government control of business lessened.

In many developing parts of the world, a socialist party may challenge high-control governments (often run by the military) that do not support redistribution of the wealth. At times, the Socialist party may prevail, but many countries teeter back and forth between the two economic systems.

TYPES OF ECONOMIC SYSTEMS

DIRECTED BY THE FREE MARKET		DIRECTED BY COMMAND
Capitalism	**Socialism**	**Communism**
Right to own private property is unlimited	Right to own private property is unlimited	Right to own private property is greatly restricted
Most industry is owned by private individuals	Basic industry is owned by the government	All industry is owned by the government
Competition and profit are not regulated by the government	Competition and profit are regulated by the government	Competition and profit are prohibited

Comparative Political Systems

While economic systems concentrate on meeting needs of production, distribution, and consumption, political systems address collective needs of a society. These needs are coordinated by the government, which forms the heart of the political system. It maintains order, allocates power and resources, and promotes common values. In reality, so much overlap exists between economic and political systems that it is often impossible to separate them. In many modern countries, the government takes a major responsibility for a stable economy. The responsibility varies, and capitalist systems generally allow less government control than do socialist and communist regimes. But almost all countries expect some government involvement in economics.

Nevertheless, political systems do emphasize different needs from those emphasized by economic systems. Political systems may be divided into two categories—democratic and authoritarian. The two may be distinguished by the degree of citizen involvement in policy making.

DEMOCRATIC POLITICAL SYSTEMS

The more citizens are involved and the more meaningful their choices, the more democratic the system. The people have supreme political authority in a democracy. There are six key measures of democracy.

Measures of Democracy

1. POLITICAL PARTICIPATION BY CITIZENS Participation that is dictated by the government or a dominating political party is not democratic. If participation comes from individuals and groups—apart from the government—the degree of democracy is higher. Interest groups formed freely and on their own initiative are good examples.

2. FREEDOM OF COMMUNICATIONS AND SPEECH If the government owns and censors the newspapers, freedom of expression is limited. However, government ownership of major sources of information does not necessarily indicate a lack of democracy. For example, the British Broadcasting Corporation (BBC) is government owned but is generally an objective source of news with little actual censorship. However, *Pravda,* the official newspaper of the Soviet Union, was little more than a propaganda mouthpiece for the government.

3. RECRUITMENT OF POLITICAL LEADERS Do leaders come from the same few families, the same schools and colleges, or the same part of the country? If so, the country is probably a lot less democratic than you might think.

4. EFFECT OF CITIZEN PARTICIPATION In democracies, citizens have a high degree of political efficacy, or the feeling that their opinions do count. Their political participation actually influences the decisions of the leaders.

5. RULE OF LAW, NOT INDIVIDUALS Democracies have championed the value of agreed-upon laws. Those laws will govern everyone, including the leaders, whose rule will be subject to the law.

6. COMPETITIVE POPULAR ELECTIONS A political system is not democratic just because the government sponsors elections for public officials. In a democratic political system, the elections are fair and give the people a real choice between candidates who wish to stand for election.

No political system is 100 percent democratic. Think back to our study of the beginnings of American government and recall how many checks the Founders placed on democracy. Although the United States has become more democratic over the years, few people would claim that it fully meets all six of the measures of democracy listed above.

Headlines

ELECTIONS WITH NO CHOICES

Some elections appear to be democratic when in fact they are not. For example, elections were held regularly in the authoritarian Soviet Union, but until the late 1980s, people were given no choices except the communist candidates. Until recently, elections in Mexico were not truly democratic. Even though it allowed competition from other political parties whose candidates' names appeared on the ballot, the government-sponsored party, the PRI, usually rigged elections so that other parties never won.

Case Study: Great Britain

By most measures, the political system of Great Britain is democratic. It was, after all, the primary model for democracy in the United States. Despite their similarities, the governments of Great Britain and the United States differ in at least two important ways: British government is unitary (rather than federal), and it is parliamentary (rather than presidential).

UNITARY GOVERNMENT

Political power in Great Britain is centered in London in Whitehall. The most powerful figure in the central government is the prime minister, who lives nearby on Downing Street. The Houses of Parliament are located in the area as well, as are many of the executive branch bureaucracies, such as the Exchequer (the treasury) and the Home Office (for domestic affairs).

e.g.

GREAT BRITAIN'S FOUR PARTS

Great Britain's official name is "the United Kingdom of Great Britain and Northern Ireland." Its population of 58 million lives in four parts: England, which is the largest part; Wales, a small area that was conquered by England in the 1200s; Scotland, which joined with England in 1707; and Northern Ireland, which was added by treaty in 1800.

Great Britain has numerous local governments, but they generally just carry out the decisions made in London. In the United States, local and state governments have their own bases of authority, making its system federalist.

Great Britain is one of the few democracies in the world that still has a monarch, or hereditary ruler. This fact, however, does not weaken Britain's status as a democracy because the monarch has no real political power. For many years that power has been held by Parliament. Today the prime minister and his or her cabinet have that control. British democracy is unique, too, in its lack of a written constitution. Certainly, Britain has many important volumes of written laws and documents, such as the Magna Carta, that provide guidelines for the government. However, the British political system relies heavily on unwritten customs and traditions that are widely accepted by government and citizens.

PARLIAMENTARY GOVERNMENT

In Britain's parliamentary government, legislative and executive branches are fused together. The prime minister and the cabinet are members of Parliament, and they share executive authority. Together they make up the government. The prime minister is the leader of the majority party in Parliament, and he or she chooses the cabinet members from among the members of the legislature. The opposition party selects a so-called shadow cabinet that would immediately take over the government should it win the parliamentary election.

The House of Lords and the House of Commons are the two houses of Parliament. The House of Lords is one of the only hereditary legislative bodies in the world today. Most of its 1,100 members inherited their positions. The real power lies with the 650 members in the House of Commons, partly because the prime minister and his cabinet always come from the House of Commons. Recent proposals have called for changes to the legislative branch, including elimination of the hereditary lords in the House of Lords.

PARTIES AND ELECTIONS

Political parties are very powerful in Britain, particularly since the majority party's leader automatically becomes prime minister and other party members form the cabinet. Parliament runs on the assumption that there will be a majority party and an opposition party. The two major parties, the Conservative and Labor parties, usually control more than 90 percent of seats in Parliament. In reality, Britain has a fairly large minor party, the Liberal Democrats, and several other smaller ones, including nationalist parties that represent Scotland, Northern Ireland, and Wales. The members of Britain's political parties almost always vote the way their leaders advise them to. As a result, most of the legislation that the prime minister and the cabinet want usually passes.

e.g.

PARLIAMENT AND TRADITION

The British Parliament is not the bunch of stuffy old men droning away about boring topics that you might imagine. Members of Parliament love to argue, partly because they have a lot to gain from their oratory. After all, the top leaders of the country come only from Parliament, so all MPs (members of Parliament) with political ambitions do a lot of strutting. Particularly rowdy is an event known as "question time," when the opposition party grills the prime minister and his cabinet about controversial decisions. MPs sit crammed into a small room on long, plain benches with an aisle down the center. The members of the majority party sit on one side. The opposition sits on the other side, facing them. The prime minister and his cabinet sit in the first row, with the shadow cabinet just across the aisle. They insult one another loudly, yell and scream, stalk out, and often throw objects (like fruit) at the other side. Down the middle of the center aisle is a table, the prime minister on one side and his would-be successor on the other, face-to-face. The ancient table was specially designed to sit exactly where it is, keeping the two leaders two sword-lengths apart.

Elections are called by the prime minister, and they must be held at least every five years. In national elections, people elect only the representative to the House of Commons; they do not vote directly for the prime minister. Elections are occasionally triggered by a vote of no confidence, in which MPs vote against an important measure proposed by the cabinet. If that happens, the government falls, and immediate elections are held. If the opposition wins the elections (that is, if enough of their members are elected as MPs so that they become the majority), the shadow cabinet takes over.

AUTHORITARIAN POLITICAL SYSTEMS

Authoritarian political systems do not value democracy and individual expression. They depend on the authority of one central figure. It is important not to confuse unitary governments with authoritarian ones. Unitary governments, like that of Great Britain, can be democratic. They can have competitive elections, recruitment of leaders from many different levels, and a great deal of political participation from citizens. Authoritarian governments, unlike democratic ones, do not give citizens free choice; instead, they determine what the people can or cannot have.

Authoritarianism also differs from communism. One is a political system, the other an economic system. Authoritarian governments may be ruled by a king, a small group of leaders, the military, or a dictator. Political leaders in an authoritarian political system may preside over a regime that is capitalist, socialist, or communist. There are five important measures of an authoritarian system.

Measures of Authoritarian Systems

1. CITIZENS AS SUBJECTS In an authoritarian system, citizens have little influence on the policies made by the government. Citizens may come into frequent contact with government officials, but they act only as subjects, or people who must obey. Democracies allow input, even criticism or ridicule of the government. An authoritarian government does not.

2. RESTRICTIONS OF COMMUNICATIONS AND SPEECH Authoritarian governments do not allow open criticism of the political system. They usually censor print and broadcast materials heavily. Since they often assert their authority through force, reactions to violators can be brutal.

3. NARROW RECRUITMENT OF POLITICAL LEADERS Political leaders are selected through a narrow process that eliminates most citizens from consideration. For example, in a communist regime such as the former Soviet Union or China, leaders are carefully selected from the Communist party. In a hereditary monarchy, leaders inherit the throne.

4. RULE OF INDIVIDUALS, NOT LAW Authoritarian rulers make their own decisions about policies in their countries. Their decisions are not bound by law; people are subject to the good (or bad) judgment of the rulers.

5. NO COMPETITIVE ELECTIONS Authoritarian governments may have no election process at all. Leaders may be chosen by a monarch or a dictator or a small group of leaders. Sometimes authoritarian governments have elections, but they do not offer citizens any real choices. The government merely looks for confirmation of its policies.

Case Study: Communist China

China has always been something of an enigma to most Westerners, partly because for centuries its leaders cared little about sharing the country's well-developed and self-sufficient culture with outsiders. China is one of the oldest political systems in existence today. Its independence dates back to 221 B.C. China's political and economic powers are growing, and many observers believe that China already is, or soon will be, one of the most influential countries in the world.

AUTHORITARIAN TRADITION

Historically China's government has consistently had authoritarian character-istics, even though its economy has changed dramatically. For centuries, China was ruled by emperors in a succession of dynasties, or eras dominated by one family in which authority was transferred from father to son. Political authority rested with the emperor, whose dictates were executed and interpreted by an efficient, highly educated bureaucracy. The scholarly members of this bureaucratic elite were chosen by a sophisticated merit-based examination system. Theoretically, as youngsters, anyone could study for the tests, which required extensive cultural and philosophical knowledge. Their test results determined whether or not they were admitted to the elite. Most citizens were poor farmers, subjects who almost never participated in government decisions. Their children didn't have time to study for the exams.

The Qin (221 B.C.) and Han (206 B.C.) dynasties expanded the empire's territory and established the basic tradition of authoritarian government. Later major dynasties include the Song (960-1279), Ming (1368-1644), and Qing (1644–1911).

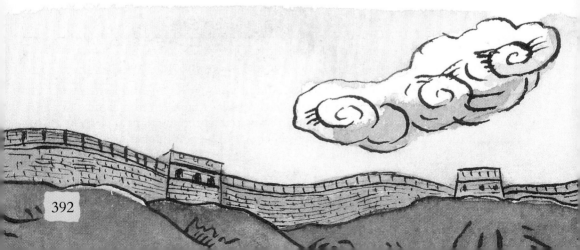

IMPERIALISM AND REVOLUTION

The power of the dynasties ebbed and flowed with the centuries. Sometimes leaders had a great deal of control, but at other times leaders were weak, inefficient, and vulnerable. During the nineteenth century, the dynasty was particularly weak and became a target of strong European countries that saw the rich trade potential with China. These imperialist countries, bent on empire building, made agreements with the emperors and literally carved China into economic pieces, or spheres of influence. By 1900, Britain, France, Germany, Russia, and Japan had almost full control of China's economy.

Chinese nationalists (people who wished to preserve China for the Chinese) rebelled against their new masters many times, and in 1911 a leader who wished to establish democracy led a successful rebellion. That leader, American-educated Dr. Sun Yat-sen, became the first president of a new nationalist China. His hopes for democracy were frustrated by the centuries-old tradition of authoritarianism. The country went through a period of intense upheaval—including regional infighting and an invasion by Japan that lasted until 1949.

COMMUNISM IN CHINA

During the 1920s, a time of great disorder in China, the communist leader Mao Zedong emerged. With the support of the Soviet Union, he posed a threat to the nationalist government for two decades. In 1949 his forces ran the Nationalist leader Chiang Kai-shek off the Chinese mainland to the island of Taiwan. A new political system named the People's Republic of China (PRC) was put in place, and the Chinese Communist party (CCP) controlled the government. Party members hold all important government positions, and the National People's Congress (NPC) has little real independent power.

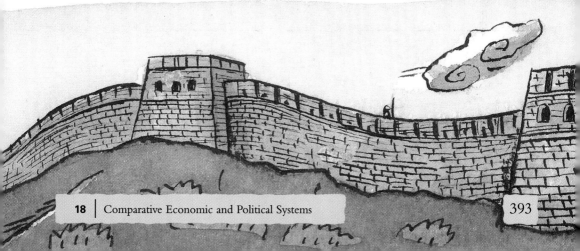

Headlines

TIANANMEN SQUARE—1989

Supporters of democracy around the world are still haunted by a single image captured by a TV camera in Tiananmen Square: a lone Chinese student standing his ground as a military tank rolled slowly but surely toward him. Although his identity is still unknown, his bravery earned him the designation by *Time* magazine as one of the "100 most influential people of the 20th century."

In Tiananmen Square in Beijing, students led a protest demonstration against the government. It caught the attention of media around the world. The Chinese government reacted by sending armed troops to clear the square. They opened fire, killing hundreds of demonstrators. Thousands more were arrested. Nations around the world—including the United States—implemented temporary sanctions against China, and tourism declined. Concerns about Chinese human rights policies have continued in the late 1990s. In June of 1997, Congress voted to renew China's most-favored trade status despite concerns about China's human rights record. But the debate in Congress revealed serious divisions about the issue in both political parties.

Remember that the ultimate goal of Marxism is a property-less society where people contribute what they can and receive what they need. How can this economically based dream take place in a country with a strong tradition of authoritarianism, such as China? Conflicts were obvious from the beginning. The modern history of the Chinese and Soviet governments may be viewed as a struggle to resolve the clash between a political system (authoritarianism) and an economic system (communism).

CAPITALISM IN CHINA

Today China's emerging global power is based partly on its developing economic strength. To achieve those ends the government has gradually steered away from a communist economic system and toward capitalism. Beginning in the late 1970s, modernization plans emphasized developing agriculture, industry, national defense, science, and technology. Individuals and families were encouraged to enrich themselves, and they did, through capitalist principles such as ownership of property and free trade. Chinese modernization has embraced an "open door" trade policy with countries with capitalist economic systems that Karl Marx would have seen as the root of all evil. Small-scale free enterprise has been encouraged, and despite high inflation, China's economic growth has led to higher wages and increased consumer spending. In 1979, the United States formally recognized the PRC government.

Through the centuries, the economic system of China has changed dramatically—from peasant-based agriculture to communism to capitalism. The changes have caused much turmoil. Although the political system is no longer headed by an emperor, it has consistently remained authoritarian—oppressive and rigid. China continues to pursue economic reform goals while repressing political dissent. Demands for democracy in China are met with resistance from a centuries-old tradition of authoritarian governments.

The array of economic and political rules that countries follow varies widely, and each country arranges them in its own unique ways. However, three broad types of economic systems—capitalism, socialism, and communism—and two broad types of political systems—democratic and authoritarian—allow us to make comparisons among countries.

The practice of classifying economic and political systems may be traced back 2,000 years to Aristotle, a philosopher who contrasted the economies and social structures of the many Greek city-states. His work set the standards for our goal: to recognize how political institutions and policies are shaped by a country's unique environments. Comparing economic and political systems helps us understand how governments and politics operate in the modern world and how practices and customs in the United States fit in the larger global picture.

Unit VI

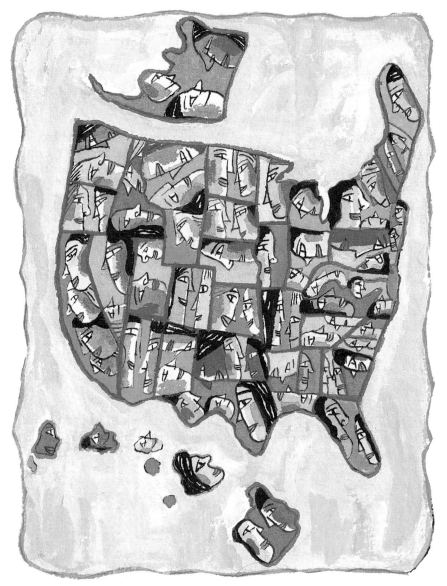

State and Local Government

Structure of State and Local Government

W hen was the last time you had direct contact with a government office or government employee? It probably was not a conversation with the President of the United States or even a senator or a representative. Most of our day-to-day political dealings have to do with the clerk in the motor vehicles office, a local police officer, or even the voice mail that explains the process for getting a passport. Think about the last 24 hours of your life. Did you talk to a teacher, the school principal, a coach, a nurse, or a custodian? If you attend a public high school, all of those people are probably state or local government employees. In fact, many more Americans hold jobs at state and local levels than at the national level, and they carry a tremendous amount of behind-the-scenes responsibility for the day-to-day work of government.

Federalism, or the division of political power between national and state governments, is one of the cornerstone principles of the American political system. But the workings of the federal government get a lot more media attention. How much real policy-making power do state and local governments have? Do they have important responsibilities, or has their power diminished since earlier days? What are their financial responsibilities? Are state and local governments more democratic than the national government? These are the questions that the next two chapters will address.

In this chapter . . .

Levels of Government

The United States has thousands of units of government—one national, 50 for states, and almost 87,000 local ones. The state and local governments vary tremendously. State and local governments are not carbon copies of national government. While they share some common characteristics, they also have key differences.

SIMILARITIES

Seven main similarities exist between the national government and governments at the state and local levels.

1. At all levels, government is to some degree democratic.
2. Popular, competitive elections are held to select public officials on all levels.
3. All levels are staffed by both elected and appointed officials.
4. The federal and state governments all have three branches of government and written constitutions.
5. The federal and all state legislatures (except Nebraska) are bicameral, with a lower and an upper house.
6. All levels of government get revenue through taxes.
7. Court systems operate at all levels.

DIFFERENCES

Four main differences separate the national government from governments at the state and local levels.

1. At the state and local level, people often vote not just for officials but also on important decisions that officials make, such as budgets or zoning.
2. Many executive branch officials at the state and local level are elected. At the national level, the only elected executive branch officials are the President and Vice President.
3. Party leaders in state legislatures have much more influence over who gets and retains committee chairmanships than do party leaders in the House or Senate.
4. Federal judges are appointed by the President and confirmed by the Senate. Many state judges are directly elected by the voters.

DISPERSED vs. CONCENTRATED POWER

Recall that the concentration of political power was one of the first major political issues after the founding of the U.S. government. Under the leadership of Alexander Hamilton, the Federalists supported a strong national government at the expense of state power, and the Anti-Federalists believed that state governments should have a great deal of control over their own affairs. Even though national supremacy eventually won the struggle, the Anti-Federalist voices were heard in many state and local governments. The tradition of dispersed (spread-out) power rather than concentrated power was evident in state governments from the beginning.

Power Divided

In the early nineteenth century, voters tended to be suspicious of government. As a result, new restrictions were placed on the power of state governments, particularly the executive branch. To keep the governor weak, state constitutions were amended to divide power among numerous elected officials, such as lieutenant governors, treasurers, auditors, secretaries of state, and attorneys general. At the local level, power was divided between mayors and elected city councils. Thus, radical decentralization of power occurred at both the state and local levels.

As often happens when power is spread among many people, policy became much more difficult to organize and execute. For example, if the decision to fix city streets is left to a city council, all the members must somehow agree on the same projects, the schedules, and their costs. Political parties helped solve this problem, coordinating efforts and getting voters out to the polls to support them. By the late nineteenth century, many states and cities were controlled by political parties, and the most powerful came to be known as political machines.

Power Concentrated

With party government came corruption and inefficiency. Many elected positions were filled by incompetent or dishonest people controlled by political parties that operated through bribes and kickbacks. This situation sparked the progressive movement, which called for major government reforms. Since parties were controlling elections, the progressives called for fewer elected officials, less power for legislatures, and more power placed in the hands of appointed officials in the executive branch. In other words, progressives supported a concentration of power in the hands of fewer government positions.

This historic tension between those who favor dispersed power and those who want concentrated power is still a central issue in many states and cities today. We will see evidence of the conflict as we examine the structures and functions of both state and local governments.

Organization of State Government

Of course, the structures of state governments vary widely, but we can categorize them into types based on the degree to which power is dispersed or concentrated among officials and branches. Some states disperse power by having many elected officials, weak executives, and part-time legislatures. Examples of this type are Indiana and Texas. On the other hand, California and Wisconsin concentrate power in the hands of a strong governor and have relatively few elected officials and a full-time, professional legislature. The states that concentrate power tend to be more active policy makers, often experimenting with new models that other states imitate. Every state's concentration of power is different, and no state is 100 percent one type or the other.

STATE CONSTITUTIONS

Even before the American colonies declared their independence from Great Britain in 1776, states had written constitutions, most based on their old charters granted from the king. States have written a total of about 150 constitutions, and several states throw out old constitutions and write new ones rather regularly. For example, Louisiana has had 11 constitutions, and Georgia has had 10. State constitutions determine the structure, role, and financing of state and local levels of government. The constitutions also define the process for proposing constitutional amendments.

State constitutions are much longer than the U. S. Constitution, which explains why they tend not to last as long. The average length of a state constitution is around 28,000 words, approximately four times as long as the U.S. Constitution, including the amendments. The longest state constitution is Alabama's, which weighs in at 174,000 words. By and large, the more detailed the constitution, the less freedom public officials have in policy making.

e.g.

STATE CONSTITUTIONAL TRIVIA

Some state constitutions get very specific, creating the likelihood of frequent amendments. Consider some examples:

★ California's much-amended constitution sets rules governing the length of wrestling matches.

★ Georgia's constitution offers a $250,000 reward to the first person who strikes oil in the state.

★ Oklahoma's constitution proclaims: "Until changed by the Legislature, the flash test for all kerosene oil for illuminating purposes shall be 115 degrees Fahrenheit; and the specific gravity test for all such oil shall be 40 degrees."

★ South Dakota's constitution authorizes a twine and cordage plant at the state penitentiary.

States have a variety of ways to allow citizens to participate in the law-making process. In 18 state constitutions, there are provisions for legislation by **initiative,** a measure that allows voters to propose legislation. If a group gets enough signatures (usually between 5 and 15 percent of the total number who voted in the last election), their proposed legislation goes right onto the voting ballot. Forty-nine states allow the **referendum,** which permits voters to reject a measure adopted by the state legislature. In 15 states, voters can remove an elected official from office through a procedure known as the **recall.**

These procedures illustrate how different state constitutions are from the federal constitution. The Founders would probably have found the initiative, the referendum, and the recall to be far too democratic—much too likely to lead to the tyranny of the majority. Is it good, then, that state constitutions allow so much popular input? Opinions are split. Some argue that the result of so much popular input is chaos. Others believe that the differences between state and national constitutions reinforce the basic principle of federalism and the division of power among groups.

def·i·ni·tions

initiative—the process by which citizens can propose a law or state constitutional amendment to be voted upon in an election.

referendum—the process by which a proposed public measure is voted upon.

recall—the process by which voters can vote to remove a public official from office.

402

GOVERNORS

Do you know what your governor looks like? How often do you see photos of your governor in newspapers or magazines? When have you seen him or her on television—perhaps surveying a disaster area, giving a speech, dedicating a new building, or meeting with law enforcement officials? The image that you have is shaped by your governor's personality or programs, and less conspicuously (but just as importantly) by the structure of your state government.

Most governors never enter national politics and are not well-known outside their states. But a number of U.S. Presidents have first been governors. The New York governorship, in particular, gained the reputation as a stepping-stone to the presidency, after both Roosevelts—Theodore (1901–1909) and Franklin (1933–1945)—served first as New York governors. More recently, Ronald Reagan (1981–1989) was governor of California. Two recent Presidents have come from the governor's office of Georgia and Arkansas, Jimmy Carter (1977–1981) and Bill Clinton (1993–), respectively.

e.g.

GOVERNORS AS CELEBRITIES

Electronic media have made it easier for governors to be known outside their states, especially if they are from big states that get more attention. Even if a governorship does not lead to the presidency, consolation prizes are available. For example, when two well-known governors, Ann Richards of Texas and Mario Cuomo of New York, left their positions in the mid-1990s, they took to the airwaves. The two politicians flaunted their talents by advertising tortilla chips on prime-time TV. According to the ratings, they were quite successful.

In 1998, the newly elected governor of Minnesota became an instant media celebrity. Jesse "The Body" Ventura, a former professional wrestler and radio personality, won a stunning political upset—the first candidate of Ross Perot's Reform party to win a statewide office. Ventura, former mayor of a Minneapolis suburb, claimed that grass-roots resentment of elite politicians and entrenched bureaucracy led to his victory.

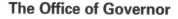

The Office of Governor

In almost all states, governors must meet specific age, citizenship, and residency requirements. Today, the median age for governors is the mid-50s. Nearly all governors have been white, and only a handful have been female. Most governors live in a residence provided to them by the state or a state foundation.

In every state, the governor is chosen by popular vote. In all but five states—Arizona, Georgia, Louisiana, Mississippi, and Vermont—only a plurality is needed for election. The candidate does not need to get 50 percent or more of the vote. One recent trend is to provide for the joint election of the governor and lieutenant governor in much the same way that the President and Vice President run as a team on the national ticket.

Almost all the states elect governors to four-year terms, and more than half now restrict the number of times a governor may be elected to office. The usual term limit is two, just as it is at the national level. Governors' salaries average a little more than $90,000 a year. In most states, the governor's administration consists of several other elected officials, including a lieutenant governor, an attorney general, and a secretary of state.

GOVERNORS' SALARIES

FIVE LOWEST	
Montana	$59,310
Arkansas	60,000
Nebraska	65,000
North Dakota	69,648
Rhode Island	69,900
FIVE HIGHEST	
New York	$130,000
Michigan	121,166
Washington	121,000*
California	120,000
Maryland	120,000

Official salary; governor accepts less and returns a portion of salary. Figures are from 1997.

Source: Council of State Governments, *The Book of the States,* 1996–1997

Powers

Most governors run large and complex organizations and serve as chief policy makers in their states. In addition, they have seven more specific powers:

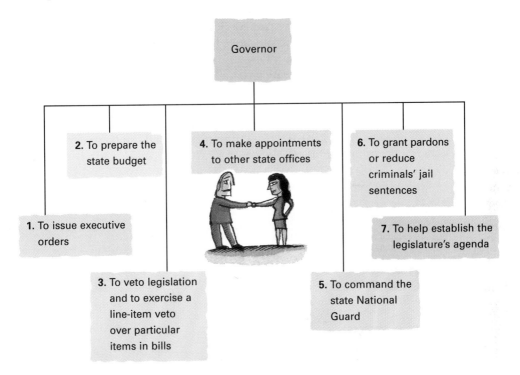

Governor

2. To prepare the state budget

4. To make appointments to other state offices

6. To grant pardons or reduce criminals' jail sentences

1. To issue executive orders

7. To help establish the legislature's agenda

3. To veto legislation and to exercise a line-item veto over particular items in bills

5. To command the state National Guard

States whose constitutions concentrate power in the executive branch generally allow their governors broader authority for making appointments, setting the budget, prescribing programs to the legislature, and vetoing legislative bills. In some states—such as Arkansas, Massachusetts, Illinois, Hawaii, and New York—the governor's powers go far beyond these basic powers. For example, the power of the governor to appoint other executive officers varies greatly from state to state. The more officials who are directly elected, generally the less is the appointment power of the governor. In about 30 states, six or more executive officials, in addition to the governor and lieutenant governor, are directly elected; about 20 states elect five or fewer officials. States in the South and the Midwest tend to have more elected officials than those in the East or West. Likewise, some states, such as California, have strong civil service laws that make appointments merit-based and that restrict the governor's discretion in hiring.

STATE LEGISLATURES

State legislatures are the oldest part of U.S. government. They existed before the U.S. Constitution was written and were the most powerful governing bodies in the country during the American Revolution. Even though the Constitution diminished their power, today state legislatures still play a vital role in state politics and policy making. As on the national level, most state legislatures counterbalance the executive branch, some more successfully than others.

State legislatures vary in size, from 20 members in Alaska's upper house to 400 in New Hampshire's lower house. The size of the legislature does not necessarily reflect the state's population. Most state legislatures are similar to Congress in organization. (Recall that Nebraska has a one-house legislature.) The same basic steps are involved in passing a bill, and a system of party leaders and committees is established.

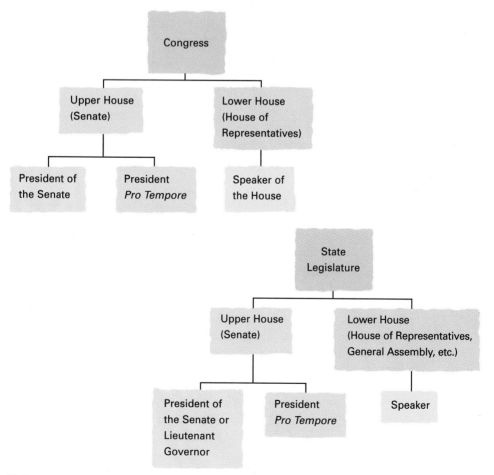

Qualifications, Elections, and Terms

Guidelines for age, residency, and compensation vary from state to state. Most states, for example, require representatives to be at least 21 and senators to be at least 25. Annual salaries for state legislators range from $200 in New Hampshire to $72,000 in California. Legislators are selected in every state by popular election. Nearly all candidates for the legislature are nominated at party primaries, and opposing candidates face one another in the general election. In most states legislative elections are held in even-numbered years. Four states (Louisiana, Mississippi, New Jersey, and Virginia) hold legislative elections in odd-numbered years in an effort to keep local and state issues separate from national politics. Legislators serve either two-year or four-year terms, and the rate of turnover is fairly high.

Sessions

Forty-two state legislatures now meet in annual sessions, and the California legislature meets in a continuous two-year session. Until the last decade or so, many more state legislatures met only every other year. But the workload is now so heavy that most state legislators find themselves not only meeting every year but spending more and more hours at work during the sessions. The governor (and in some states the state legislature) can also call special sessions.

State Legislators

The characteristics of state legislators have not historically been much different from those of national legislators—middle-aged, white males, most usually with backgrounds in the legal profession.

Largely as a result of court rulings, state legislative districts are fairly uniform in the numbers of people they represent within a state. However, the numbers vary greatly across the states. For example, a California legislator typically represents about 300,000 people, but in New Hampshire, a district may have only about 2,000 people. Generally, the more people a legislator represents, the more time he or she must devote to the job. Of course, as the population of the country grows, the districts tend to grow as well. Pressure is increasing for more and more legislatures to become professional rather than remain amateurs. In other words, being a state representative or senator is likely to be a full-time job. Professional legislatures—such as those in Wisconsin, Pennsylvania, California, Illinois, Massachusetts, and New York—meet most of the year. Their members are relatively well paid, and they have sizable, year-round staffs.

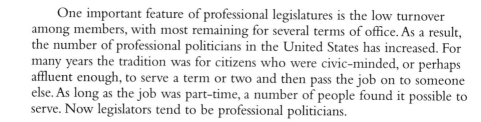

One important feature of professional legislatures is the low turnover among members, with most remaining for several terms of office. As a result, the number of professional politicians in the United States has increased. For many years the tradition was for citizens who were civic-minded, or perhaps affluent enough, to serve a term or two and then pass the job on to someone else. As long as the job was part-time, a number of people found it possible to serve. Now legislators tend to be professional politicians.

MINORITY REPRESENTATION RISING

More and more women and minorities are winning seats in state legislatures. Out of 7,424 state legislators,

★ more than 500 are African Americans,

★ more than 190 are Hispanic Americans,

★ approximately 55 are Asian Americans,

★ more than 40 are Native Americans, and

★ more than 1,600 are now women. According to figures from the Center for the American Woman and Politics at Rutgers University in 1999, 22 percent of the state legislators in the United States are women. The number of female state legislators has increased more than five-fold since 1969 when 301 women served in state legislatures. The five states with the highest percentages of women state legislators are Washington (41 percent), Nevada (37 percent), Arizona (36 percent), Colorado (33 percent), and Kansas (33 percent).

STATE COURTS

The most powerful judges in the country sit on the U.S. Supreme Court. They make the ultimate decisions on the most controversial issues, and their power to interpret the Constitution is unmatched. However, in most cases, state judges have the final say. State courts deal with millions of cases each year, while the caseload in federal courts is less than half a million a year. Through writs of *habeas corpus*, those accused of crimes may get federal district judges to review the actions of the state courts. If a constitutional question is involved, the case may even make its way to the Supreme Court. Of the hundreds of thousands of decisions made by state judges each year, only a handful reach the Supreme Court.

The structure of state courts is very similar to that of the federal system. There are two main kinds of courts: trial courts and appeals courts.

1. TRIAL COURTS—These are roughly comparable to the federal district courts, but they are much more diverse and specialized. In most states, a basic distinction exists between courts that handle minor cases and those that deal with serious crimes. In urban areas, municipal courts handle traffic tickets, small claims, truancy, adoptions, divorce settlements, and minor criminal offenses. In rural areas, minor cases go to justices of the peace. Trial courts with broad jurisdiction over all criminal and civil matters are called by various names, such as superior courts, county courts, circuit courts, or district courts. These courts handle major criminal cases and lawsuits.

Then and Now

LAW WEST OF THE PECOS

In 1885, a sparsely settled area of west Texas was organized into Val Verde County, consisting of 3,242 square miles (which is three times the size of Rhode Island). That same year the new county elected as its first justice of the peace, Roy Bean, a citizen of the tiny town of Langtry, which is west of the Pecos River. He served until his death in 1904. Judge Bean's home, place of business, courthouse, and jail was his saloon.

People came to regard Judge Roy Bean as the "Law West of the Pecos" because he dispensed his own unique brand of justice from the Jersey Lily Saloon. His antics formed the basis for many legends. Judge Bean would often recess trials to sell liquor to the courtroom. Among his unorthodox exploits were fining a dead man and staging a heavyweight boxing match in the middle of the Rio Grande River. The match had been outlawed by both Texas and Mexico, so Judge Bean reasoned that a sandbar in the middle of the river was neither government's jurisdiction.

2. **APPEALS COURTS**—All states have a court of appeals that is similar to the U.S. Supreme Court. In most states it is called the state supreme court. Two states have separate supreme courts for civil or criminal matters. Some, but not all, states have intermediate appeals courts between the highest court and the trial courts. State supreme courts may declare state and federal laws unconstitutional, but both are subject to review by the U.S. Supreme Court.

State judges are chosen by popular vote, appointment by the state legislature, appointment by the governor, or a combination of the three. Popular election is the most widely used method of selecting judges, and selection by the legislature is the least commonly used. Governors appoint about one-fourth of all state judges. In general, those states that disperse power tend to elect their judges, just as they do other officials, and states with concentrated powers tend to allow the governor or the legislature to appoint judges. Many states use the Missouri Plan, a method that combines the election and appointment processes. In the Missouri Plan, the governor makes each appointment from a list of names recommended by a nominating commission. After a judge has served an initial term, his or her name appears on the ballot without opposition. Voters are asked whether or not that judge should be kept in office. If the vote is favorable, the judge serves a regular term; if the vote is unfavorable, the judge leaves office, and a new appointment is made.

Qualifications for state judges vary from state to state. More than half of the states have no minimum residency requirement or minimum age limits for judges. Terms also range from state to state. Generally, the higher courts have longer terms. Salaries for state judges are set by state law.

Quote

"In no country in the world does the law hold so absolute a language as in America; and in no country is the right of applying it vested in so many hands."

Alexis de Tocqueville
Democracy in America *(1835)*

Organization of Local Government

In his classic observations of American society, Frenchman Alexis de Tocqueville described political power in the United States as being spread out among a great number of people. His travels in America persuaded him that much of the strength of American democracy lay in the citizens' attachments to their local governments, especially as they existed in New England townships.

A century later, two sociologists from Columbia University, Robert and Helen Lynd, reached a different conclusion. They lived in and investigated community relationships in Muncie, Indiana, hoping to understand better the social, political, and economic influences in middle-sized, typical American towns. They asked questions and observed how people made their living, related to their families, and got involved in civic and social associations. In their 1929 book, *Middletown*, the Lynds concluded that despite the appearance of democratic rule, a social and economic elite actually ran the town.

Who was right—de Tocqueville or the Lynds? One stressed the spirit of democracy, and the others saw elitism and control in the hands of a few. Their conflicting views represent the struggle that still characterizes American government on all levels today. Local government organization and functions are, in effect, answers to that question: Is it best to concentrate political power in a few hands or disperse power in the hands of many?

CHARACTERISTICS OF LOCAL ELECTED OFFICIALS

Sex, Race, and Hispanic Origin	Total	GENERAL PURPOSE			SPECIAL PURPOSE	
		County	Municipal	Town, Township	School District	Special District
Total	493,830	58,818	135,531	126,958	88,434	84,089
Male	324,255	43,563	94,808	76,213	54,443	55,228
Female	100,531	12,525	26,825	27,702	24,730	8,749
Sex (not reported)	69,044	2,730	13,898	23,043	9,261	20,112
White	405,905	52,705	114,880	102,676	73,894	61,750
African American	11,542	1,715	4,566	369	4,222	670
Native American, Eskimo, Aleut	1,800	147	776	86	564	227
Asian, Pacific Islander	514	80	97	16	184	137
Hispanic	5,859	906	1,701	216	2,466	570
Non-Hispanic	413,902	53,741	118,618	102,931	76,398	62,214
Race, Hispanic origin not reported	74,069	4,171	15,212	23,811	9,570	21,305

Note: Numbers refer to office holders in 1992.
Source: U.S. Bureau of the Census, *Statistical Abstract of the United States,* 1998

TYPES OF LOCAL GOVERNMENTS

The United States organizes local governments into four basic types: the county, the township, the special district, and the municipality. Because local governments have no separate power base guaranteed by the U.S. Constitution, they often spend a great deal of time and energy carrying out state business. Many state governments now grant larger cities the power of **home rule.** Through home rule, cities have some independence from the state.

1. COUNTY—The **county** is usually the largest political subdivision of the state. As creations of the state, counties administer state laws and such county laws as are allowed by the state constitution. Historically, counties were formed to organize the vast, largely unpopulated areas of the state. Their present functions reflect their history: to keep the peace, maintain jails, assess property, collect taxes, build and repair roads and bridges, record deeds and marriages, register voters, supervise elections, and administer wills. The number of counties in each state varies widely. For instance, Texas has 254 counties, but Delaware has just three. The largest county in the country is Los Angeles County, California, with a 1996 population of more than 9 million. County governments usually are led by an elected group, called supervisors or commissioners.

2. TOWNSHIP—The **township** exists as a unit of local government in fewer than half the states, and its meaning varies from region to region. In New England, township is another name for a town, a small community with a population less than about 5,000. In some mid-Atlantic states—such as New Jersey and Pennsylvania—and throughout the Midwest, a township is a large subdivision of the county. In no state do townships blanket the state, but, like counties, they generally were formed to provide services to people in rural areas. Township governments are usually run by elected supervisors or trustees.

3. SPECIAL DISTRICT—The **special district** is a unit of local government that has a special function—for example, education, transportation, or water supply. The local school district is the most common example of a special district. Most special districts make their own policies, levy taxes, and borrow money. Special districts are the newest and fastest-growing type of government in the United States. In 1992, there were 31,355 special district governments, compared to about 3,000 county governments, 19,000 municipalities, and 16,500 township governments. Special districts are particularly useful in handling problems that are not handled by other local governments.

---

home rule—a city or local government's power to govern itself.

county—a subdivision of a state; the largest unit of local government.

township—a unit of local government; a subdivision of a county.

special district—a unit of local government that provides certain services that the local government does not provide.

e.g.

THE NEW ENGLAND TOWN

Thomas Jefferson once described politics in the typical New England town as "the perfect exercise of self-government." In colonial days and during the early republic, town meetings were open to all voters. There people could express their opinions, participate in the lawmaking process, decide tax rates, and appropriate money for public projects. They elected town officials, selectmen, who were responsible for administering the local government between meetings.

Today larger populations make the town meeting impractical, but in some very small towns, the town meeting still operates as it always has. In larger towns, voters elect representatives to attend the meetings, and in many places, the selectmen, or hired town managers, make many decisions formerly made by the town meeting.

4. MUNICIPALITY—The **municipality** is a unit of government— a town, city, borough, or urban district whose legal rights are granted by the state through a written agreement. In 1790, only about 5 percent of the nation's population lived in municipalities. Early charters were unique, each with different powers and relationships to the state. After about 1850, they tended to be much more uniform and general. Today, about four out of every five people in the United States live in municipalities, and municipal governments affect the lives of many people. More than half of the American population now lives in a large city or its metropolitan area (that is, the suburbs and towns that surround it).

CITY GOVERNMENT

City governments also illustrate the tension between dispersing and concentrating power that has characterized American government on all levels since the founding days. Many scholars classify American cities as "reformed" or "unreformed." Those terms don't describe how good or bad a city is. Rather, they describe the degree of concentration of governmental power.

---

municipality—a political unit, such as a town or city, that is self-governing.

Concentration of Power

Unreformed cities have many elected officials who run under a party banner. Executive power lies in the hands of an elected mayor who shares decision-making with a city council. The city council is elected from small districts, a system that allows the members to be more closely tied to their constituents. Power is shared among elected leaders, and appointed civil servants have little decision-making authority. Cities with an unreformed structure include New York, Philadelphia, and St. Louis.

In contrast, in reformed cities, city council candidates run as individuals, not as party nominees. The city councils are elected at-large, or from the whole city. Executive power lies in the hands of an appointed city manager, not an elected mayor. Much responsibility is delegated to a strong civil service, whose members are appointed, paid professionals. Power is concentrated in the city manager, who consults with the city council and directs the work of the civil service. Cities with a reformed structure include Cincinnati, Dallas, and San Diego.

BIG CITY MAYORS: 1999

CITY	POPULATION	MAYOR	SALARY
1. New York City, NY	7,380,906	Rudolph Guiliani	$165,000
2. Los Angeles, CA	3,553,638	Richard Riordan	$117,876
3. Chicago, IL	2,731,743	Richard M. Daley	$170,000
4. Houston, TX	1,744,058	Lee Brown	$133,000
5. Philadelphia, PA	1,524,249	Edward G. Rendell	$110,000
6. San Diego, CA	1,197,000	Susan Golding	$68,239
7. Phoenix, AZ	1,159,014	Skip Rimsza	$37,500
8. San Antonio, TX	1,067,816	Howard W. Peak	$50*
9. Dallas, TX	1,053,292	Ronald Kirk	$50*
10. Detroit, MI	1,000,272	Dennis Archer	$143,000

Note: Salary figures are from 1997.
* per each council meeting

Sources: U.S. Bureau of the Census, *Current Population Reports*, 1997; U.S. Conference of Mayors

VOTING AT-LARGE OR BY DISTRICT?

In district-by-district voting, each city council member represents a particular neigh-borhood within a city. In the early twentieth century, progressives wanted to replace the old system with voting at-large, in which all members were voted in by citizens throughout the city. The progressives believed that district voting encouraged council members to think only of their neighborhoods and not about what would be good for the city as a whole. Also, they thought that council members could more easily be controlled by powerful people within their neighborhoods. As a result, many cities changed to at-large voting procedures.

The changes sparked controversy over racial consequences of voting at-large. Many city councils found themselves without representatives of minority groups. Theoretically, minorities may be elected at-large, but few of them actually were. In a large city, for example, it is much easier for a member of a minority group to get elected to the city council from a neighborhood district than in an at-large election. Federal courts have interpreted voting rights laws to require that minorities have a reasonable chance of winning elections. As a result, they have ordered many cities and counties (especially in the South) to switch from at-large to district elections.

Types of City Government

The tendencies toward dispersal or concentration of power can be seen in three forms of city government: the mayor-council, the council-manager, and the commission.

1. MAYOR-COUNCIL PLAN The most common form of city government is one in which authority is given to a popularly elected mayor and council. Mayor-council systems come in two sorts: strong-mayor and weak-mayor. Under the strong-mayor form, mayors have the power to propose the city's budget and to veto ordinances passed by the council. The mayor also has the authority to appoint and remove the various heads of city departments. This form is typical of very large cities (over 250,000 population). Examples are New York City and Boston. The weak-mayor form allows mayors to preside over council meetings but gives them few budgetary, veto, or appointment powers. A mayor often must share executive authority with various boards and commissions and does not have a lot of influence in the city council. Often the mayor is not popularly elected but is chosen from among the council members. The weak-mayor form is usually found in very small cities (under 10,000 population).

2. COUNCIL-MANAGER PLAN Under the council-manager system, people vote only for city council members, who then appoint a professional city manager to control most or all of the city's administration. Usually elections are nonpartisan and at-large, and the civil service is strong. The council-manager plan appears most commonly in mid-sized cities with a population in the 10,000 to 200,000 range.

3. COMMISSION PLAN The commission form of municipal government began in Galveston, Texas, after a hurricane devastated the city in 1900, killing 6,000 people. The city's mayor-council form of government could not cope with the disaster, so the city was granted permission by the Texas legislature to form a special commission to rebuild the community. In this form, power is held by an elected commission that does not have a single head. Instead each commissioner takes responsibility for some part of city administration. One commissioner may be in charge of utilities, another may supervise roads and highways, and yet another may direct the fire and police departments. This plan is now the least popular, but it exists in some big cities, including St. Paul, Minnesota, and Tulsa, Oklahoma.

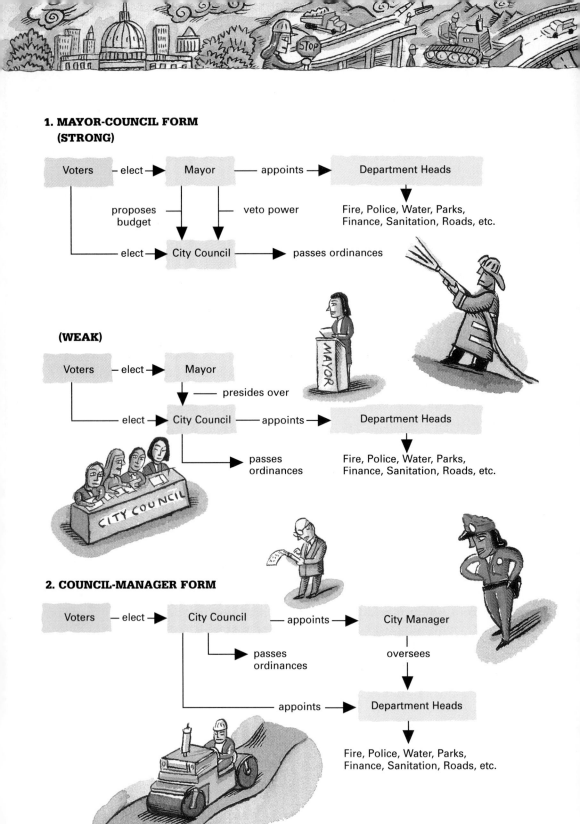

1. MAYOR-COUNCIL FORM
(STRONG)

Voters — elect → Mayor — appoints → Department Heads

Mayor: proposes budget | veto power

Department Heads: Fire, Police, Water, Parks, Finance, Sanitation, Roads, etc.

Voters — elect → City Council → passes ordinances

(WEAK)

Voters — elect → Mayor

Mayor — presides over

Voters — elect → City Council — appoints → Department Heads

City Council → passes ordinances

Department Heads: Fire, Police, Water, Parks, Finance, Sanitation, Roads, etc.

2. COUNCIL-MANAGER FORM

Voters — elect → City Council — appoints → City Manager

City Council → passes ordinances

City Manager — oversees →

City Council — appoints → Department Heads

City Manager — oversees → Department Heads

Department Heads: Fire, Police, Water, Parks, Finance, Sanitation, Roads, etc.

418

3. COMMISSION FORM

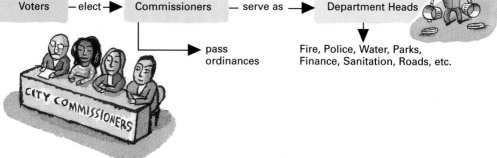

| Voters | — elect ➔ | Commissioners | — serve as ➔ | Department Heads |

➔ pass ordinances

Fire, Police, Water, Parks, Finance, Sanitation, Roads, etc.

Although there is, of course, great variety in how city governments operate, these three basic forms are the most common. According to 1992 figures from the U.S. Bureau of the Census, only 531 of approximately 19,100 cities did not have a mayor-council, council-manager, or commission form of government.

There is a healthy tension among local, state, and federal governments and between state and local governments and the federal government. Americans are citizens of the same nation but also citizens of 50 states and thousands of local governments. Most of the services people use every day and the government officials they routinely see are associated with the local and state governments. While the federal government—the President, the Congress, the bureaucracy, and the Supreme Court—may get most of the headlines, local and state governments remain the foundation of American democracy.

Recall that the 10th Amendment says that all powers not specifically granted to the national government "are reserved to the States, respectively, or to the people." In the operation of state and local government, the people have opportunities to practice their citizenship responsibilities both in small and large ways.

20 | Policies and Finances of State and Local Government

Although the Constitution gives broad policy-making power to the federal government, it leaves much policy-making authority to the states. The kind of textbooks used in your school, the speed limits on the roads, and what shots kids need before they can go to kindergarten are decided by state and local governments. Other examples include how much property tax your family pays, what lands are set aside for parks and playgrounds, the choices you have for cable TV service, and where and if a new fire station is built. Each state creates policies that affect the daily lives of all of us in important ways.

A number of factors influence the policy-making process in each state, county, township, or municipality. Among the most important are geography, population, and economics. For instance, a city in a dry area of the Southwest may need to adopt strict policies on water use. Densely populated urban counties may restrict construction more than rural areas. And states with high unemployment may decide to expand health care services in public clinics to serve the needs of residents.

Whatever policies state and local governments adopt, they must figure out how to pay for them.

In this chapter . . .

Policy Responsibilities

State and local governments provide a wide range of vital services. Many of their policies overlap with those of the federal government—such as regulating business and encouraging economic growth, providing social services, and protecting the environment. The Constitution gives some guidelines that distinguish between national and state powers, but it does not even mention local governments. Over the years, many decisions regarding who is responsible for what have been made. Some responsibilities are clearly recognized as belonging to one level or the other, and others are shared, or vaguely defined. Let's investigate three areas that state and local governments control.

EDUCATION

In the 1997–98 school year, a record 52.2 million U.S. students attended elementary and secondary schools. Most people today take for granted that free public school education is provided in almost every part of the United States. It was not always so. Only during the past century has the idea become generally accepted that government should provide tax-supported schools. Opponents of free education believed that it would give the government control over the minds of the young and that it was unfair to tax people who themselves did not have children in school.

Today about 37 percent of all state and local government costs are for education—a higher percentage than for any other function. Typically, state and local governments provide most of the money. The national government provides some funding, but in smaller amounts. In 1995–96, New Jersey led the nation in expenditures per pupil, at $9,318.

The city, county, and township may have some say in local schools, but the school district is chiefly responsible for providing public elementary and secondary education. In almost all of the 15,000 school districts in the country, voters elect a board of education that sets the school tax rate, appoints a superintendent of schools and other personnel, and runs the schools from kindergarten or first grade through high school.

Although local officials take most of the responsibility for the schools, states have important supervisory and financial responsibilities. States often set curriculum requirements and building codes, monitor the quality of local schools, and almost always distribute financial assistance to the communities. State money is passed out according to many formulas, but the trend is toward giving more money to poorer communities.

In recent years many states have become concerned about the unequal amounts that school districts have to spend on public education. Because most schools are funded by property taxes, many well-to-do communities are able to collect more taxes because property is worth more than it is in poor communities. Critics believe that this situation creates inequities in the quality of schools, resulting in inadequate education for children in poor communities. States have responded with a variety of programs, but many have redistributed state funding by giving more financial assistance to poor districts than to wealthy ones. Some of these plans have been quite controversial.

REVENUES FOR PUBLIC ELEMENTARY AND SECONDARY SCHOOLS

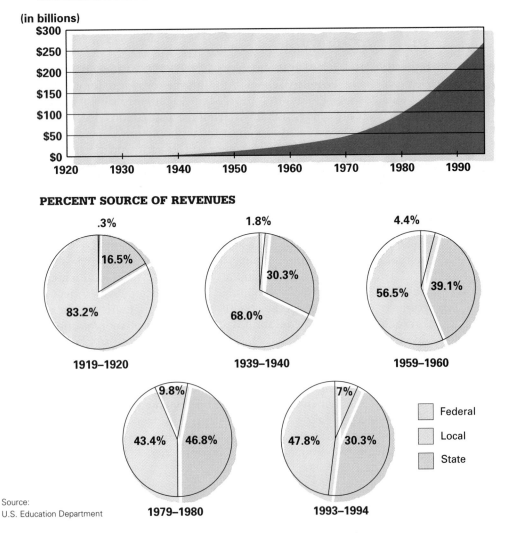

PERCENT SOURCE OF REVENUES

.3%
16.5%
83.2%
1919–1920

1.8%
30.3%
68.0%
1939–1940

4.4%
56.5%
39.1%
1959–1960

9.8%
43.4%
46.8%
1979–1980

7%
47.8%
30.3%
1993–1994

☐ Federal
☐ Local
☐ State

Source:
U.S. Education Department

422

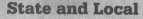

Headlines

REVOLT OF THE GENTRY

In 1998, Vermont passed a controversial law called Act 60, which aimed to correct the disparities in school spending between wealthy and poor towns. Act 60 required that property taxes not be collected locally. Instead, they should be sent to the state capital, Montpelier, and sent back to the towns in the form of block grants of $5,000 per student. This way all students in Vermont would have the same amount of money spent on their education, regardless of the affluence of their town. The rich school districts have to share the property-tax revenue they formerly spent on their own schools. Initially, 41 "gold" towns were told they must send part of their revenue to 211 receiver towns, giving away as much as 60 or 70 cents on the dollar.

Some of the towns rebelled, claiming that they could not possibly maintain the quality of their schools with their budgets so severely slashed. Rather than cut programs and fire teachers, three districts refused to send their taxes to Montpelier, and others considered joining the revolt. The issue split people in the state. Some believe Act 60 to be a fair solution to the problem. Others express outrage at robbing one community to pay another. And still others worry that children of prosperous citizens will leave the public schools to attend private ones, leaving only the poor to attend public schools.

WELFARE AND PUBLIC HEALTH

Americans don't agree on what responsibility government has for providing basic housing, health, and food. Welfare policy forms an intricate web of federal, state, and local programs that often involves shared or matching financial responsibilities. The national government pays for aid to the aged, the blind, and the disabled. It also supports the Medicare and food stamp programs. Joint federal and state funds go to Aid to Families with Dependent Children, public housing, and Medicaid. (See page 365.)

e.g.

HMOs AND PATIENT RIGHTS

Health maintenance organizations (HMOs) have sparked heated debate, particularly about what they will and will not pay for. They have been criticized for valuing cost reductions more than care of patients. As a result, in 1998 President Clinton asked Congress for a "Bill of Rights" for patients. The Democrats proposed such things as guaranteeing emergency-room access without prior approval from an HMO, allowing patients to sue health plans for improperly denying coverage, and assuring patients that they will be treated even if their doctor is dropped from a health plan. Before the debate over Clinton's plan had begun, however, many states already had in place their own regulations for managed care:

★ Oregon's comprehensive Patient Protection Act forces health plans to disclose financial incentives offered to physicians to control costs, gives consumers the right to a full appeals process if denied treatment, and allows access to emergency-room care.

★ Texas has its own patients' bill of rights and recently decided to make all HMO complaint records public. Texas is the only state that allows consumers the right to sue insurance companies if they do not use "ordinary care" in denying or delaying payment for treatment.

★ New Jersey published its first HMO report cards in 1997, showing that New Jersey HMOs fell short of national averages in preventive care—such as immunizations for children and screenings for breast cancer.

★ Maryland requires state-based health plans to guarantee adequate hospital stays for new mothers and to cover mental health and substance-abuse care.

Every state has a department of human services or welfare that either directly administers welfare programs or supervises local programs. Federal guidelines for welfare assistance are detailed, but each state makes important decisions about the size and nature of its own welfare programs. States generally pay for and administer **unemployment compensation** programs, special hospitals and institutions for the ill, and certain assistance programs that supplement federal aid to the aged, the disabled, and the poor. More and more states also provide **workfare** programs designed to help welfare recipients get and keep jobs. These programs have been promoted by the federal government, especially during the administration of Bill Clinton, but the states generally administer and budget for them.

When disease epidemics hit communities and countries, people often look to government for help. In America, the state governments take the lead in establishing boards of health to deal with the protection of public health. State officials inspect food, set and enforce cleanliness standards, oversee waste disposal systems, and license physicians, nurses, pharmacists, and other health care professionals. Today thousands of local governments, as well as all the states, have some kind of public health programs. Doctors are required to report cases of communicable disease. Health department officials also investigate to discover the source of infections, isolate the sick, and take whatever action is necessary. Some major illnesses, such as tuberculosis and AIDS, have special programs devoted to their prevention and control.

LAW ENFORCEMENT AND PUBLIC SAFETY

Traditionally crime control has been a responsibility of state and local governments, not of the federal government. Part of the reason derives from the Constitution. Police power—that is, the power of states to use physical force to protect the safety of citizens—is among the reserved powers not expressly given to the federal government. Not until the 1920s did the United States have the FBI, and even then people worried about giving power to a "national police force." Until the 1960s, most citizens believed that local law enforcement matters ought to be handled by local authorities.

---

unemployment compensation—government money given to unemployed workers.
workfare—social programs designed to help welfare recipients find and keep jobs.

Then and Now

THE STATE POLICE

The famous Texas Rangers were the first state police unit, organized in 1835 as a small border patrol. The first real state police system, organized in 1905, was the Pennsylvania State Constabulary, whose force was a mounted and uniformed body with a military organization. A superintendent, who reported directly to the governor, supervised this police force. Many states followed the Pennsylvania model, and today every state maintains a police force to preserve law and order.

Some state police systems evolved from highway patrols established in the 1930s. As road systems grew and automobiles made travel faster, highway safety became important, and states established highway patrols to enforce traffic rules. Since criminals could now make a fast getaway in cars, the highway patrol's authority was extended to include the usual powers of the police.

The role of the federal government in law enforcement increased as the power to regulate interstate commerce increased. A growing number of criminal activities were viewed as interstate activities. For instance, in response to the sensational 1932 kidnapping of aviator Charles Lindbergh's child, Congress made it a federal offense to transport a kidnapped person across state lines. Similarly, in 1968, loan sharking (loaning money at very high interest rates) was made a federal crime. As crimes rates rose significantly, presidential candidates began to talk more and more about federal responsibility for crime, especially as it connected to international drug trade. In 1994, Congress passed the Violent Crime Control and Law Enforcement Act, which authorized $8.8 billion over six years for grants to local police to add 100,000 officers. Still, crime control and law enforcement remain primarily the responsibility of state and local authorities.

Police and fire protection usually makes up a large part of a local community's budget. Police protection is often the second largest expense in communities, after public education. Counties still have sheriffs and deputies, and some townships have their own police officers. Altogether, more than 40,000 separate law enforcement agencies in the United States employ more than 600,000 people. Local governments pay for more than 70 percent of all law enforcement costs.

States also spend large amounts of money on building public highways and keeping them safe. The design of bridges and roads and their building and maintenance are a major responsibility of state governments. Maintaining safe and efficient transportation systems—such as buses, subways, and rail lines—is another challenge that local governments face.

Taxing and Spending

Just like the federal government, state and local governments must make decisions about how to collect revenue and how to budget and spend their tax money. Each state government has a budget, and most are prepared under the direct supervision of the governor. Most states have yearly budgets; 18 prepare budgets that run two years. While specific steps in preparing the budget differ from state to state, the general process in state and local governments is similar to the way the federal budget is prepared. Because the U.S. Constitution reserves for the states the power to tax, most citizens pay many different types of taxes to all levels of government.

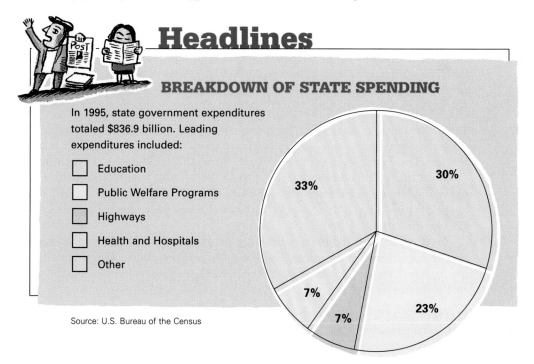

Headlines

BREAKDOWN OF STATE SPENDING

In 1995, state government expenditures totaled $836.9 billion. Leading expenditures included:

☐ Education

☐ Public Welfare Programs

☐ Highways

☐ Health and Hospitals

☐ Other

33% 30% 23% 7% 7%

Source: U.S. Bureau of the Census

TYPES OF STATE AND LOCAL TAXES

Spending by state and local governments has risen dramatically in recent years because of inflation, increases in population, and the public's growing demands that the state and local governments provide more—and better— services. Counties, townships, cities, and states collect some of their money from licenses and fees, federal aid, gambling and lotteries, and state-operated businesses. State and local governments may also borrow money by selling bonds. But about half of state revenues come from taxes.

State and local governments may levy taxes in any way they please, as long as they stay within constitutional guidelines. However, most rely on a combination of four types of taxes:

1. THE SALES TAX—The **sales tax** is placed on the sale of various products and is paid by the customer. It may be a general tax on most products, or it may apply only to select items, such as cigarettes, liquor, or gasoline. Today 45 states have a general sales tax, which accounts for about one-third of all tax monies these states collect each year. Some cities apply a local sales tax as well. A sales tax is regressive—it is the same for everyone, rich or poor. Sometimes states try to make it fairer by levying an extra "luxury tax," which applies to expensive items, such as fur coats, fancy cars, or jewelry.

2. THE INCOME TAX—In 43 of the 50 states, and a number of municipalities, citizens must pay **income tax** not only to the federal government but also to the state or city. This progressive tax assesses higher incomes at a higher rate. The rates vary from 1 percent on lower incomes to 10 percent or more on the highest incomes in some states. Corporate income taxes are used in 45 states as well.

3. THE PROPERTY TAX—The **property tax** is the chief source of income for local governments today, accounting for about 80 percent of all their tax receipts. Taxes are levied on real property—land and buildings—and personal property. Intangible property (such as stocks, bonds, and bank accounts) is easily hidden, so many states do not bother to tax it. Property must be assessed for its value, and most cities have tax assessors for that job. The property tax is criticized today because it often does not measure an individual's ability to pay as closely as it did in the past. Until the twentieth century, real property was probably the clearest indication of wealth in this country. Today, when intangibles account for a large portion of a well-to-do person's net worth, that is no longer true.

4. OTHER TAXES—Other taxes imposed by states include inheritance, estate, and certain business taxes. Inheritance taxes are applied to each heir, and an estate tax is assessed on the deceased person's entire estate. Business taxes include such things as severance taxes for removing natural resources (such as oil, gas, coal, or fish) from state land or water. States also require corporations to be licensed to do business. Most states require licensing, for example, of doctors, lawyers, dentists, plumbers, and teachers.

def·i·ni·tions

sales tax—a tax on purchased items.

income tax—a tax on annual income.

property tax—a tax on land and buildings, usually levied by local government.

STATE AND LOCAL GOVERNMENT SPENDING: 1980–1995

TOTAL (MIL. DOL.)

EDUCATION

1980	$133,211
1990	$288,148
1995	$378,273

HIGHWAYS

1980	$33,311
1990	$61,057
1995	$77,109

PUBLIC WELFARE

1980	$45,552
1990	$110,518
1995	$193,110

HEALTH AND HOSPITALS

1980	$32,174
1990	$74,635
1995	$105,946

RETIREMENT AND UNEMPLOYMENT COMPENSATION

1980	$26,078
1990	$54,854
1995	$96,631

UTILITY*

1980	$33,600
1990	$74,875
1995	$91,215

* Includes water supply, gas supply, and electric power systems.

Source: U.S. Bureau of the Census

TAX REVOLTS

When citizens pay federal income tax, they seldom have the opportunity to see what their money pays for. An individual's payment to the Internal Revenue Service (IRS) seems to disappear among the vast numbers of others' payments. State and local taxes pay for things that people can see more easily—local schools, hospitals, public buildings, police, and firefighters. Perhaps partly because they feel more ownership, people are more likely to complain about how their state and local tax money is spent. In fact, from the late 1970s on into the 1990s, citizens across the country staged "tax revolts," or active movements to reduce state and local taxes.

Proposition 13

A major reason for the revolts was that taxes, particularly those on property, were increasing more rapidly than people's incomes. For example, throughout the 1970s, California property taxes rose dramatically. Taxpayers put pressure on the legislature to do something, and the result was Proposition 13, a measure adopted by the voters in 1978. Proposition 13 limited property taxes to 1 percent of the property's market value and stipulated that property assessments could not go up more than 2 percent a year. It required a two-thirds vote of the legislature before new state taxes could be levied. Several other states, including Massachusetts, Missouri, and Texas, have adopted similar tax-limitation measures.

Lotteries

State and local governments tried to cope with tax revolts and declining revenue by cutting budgets, reducing services, and inventing new fees for various services. Others turned to state-run lotteries, designating a portion of the profits for an expense, such as education, the arts, building projects, or subsidies to municipal governments. During the 1980s, lotteries became more and more popular; gross receipts totaled $18.7 billion by 1990 and $31.9 billion in 1995. States retained about one-third of the money as proceeds. Despite their growing popularity, lotteries are a controversial source of revenue. Critics complain that lotteries hurt lower-income people, who buy most of the tickets. Supporters of lotteries counter that buying a ticket is a matter of choice and that the money goes to worthwhile causes.

Federalism, like the separation of powers between branches of government, is a basic principle of American government. The Founders' intentions to spread power among levels of government are alive and well today as the thousands of government units that now exist throughout the United States today. State and local governments have real policy-making power in crucial areas, such as education, welfare, public health, and law enforcement. The services they provide—such as public education, fire and police protection, water and sanitation, transportation, road maintenance, and upkeep of parks and forest preserves—affect our lives as U.S. citizens every day in ways we take for granted.

Even though state and local governments generally get less attention than the national government, they are much closer to the people and more likely to be contact points of citizens with their government. The very fact that citizens organize initiatives and stage tax revolts indicates that they feel empowered to participate in state and municipal governments.

Do state and local governments encourage democracy in a way that supports and improves the political process? Or are they ineffective because they listen to too many voices? Each state, city, and town balances the democratic wish to disperse power with the need to centralize responsibilities in order to rule effectively. Every day, in thousands of ways all over the country, state and local governments continually reinforce the delicate balance between liberty and order that has kept the U.S. government running for more than 200 years.

Unit VII

Skills Handbook

Skills Handbook

1 | Studying and Writing Effectively

"Writing and rewriting are a constant search for what it is one is saying."

—John Updike

No matter how good a student you are, you could probably stand some work on your reading, thinking, writing, and study skills. After all, who wouldn't want to take better notes, get higher test scores, or turn out better papers?

Taking Notes

You may resist taking notes because you consider it a waste of time or because you don't really know what you should be doing. But it's a skill worth learning and doing. Taking notes—as you listen and as you read—helps you learn.

Checklist

TAKING NOTES AS YOU LISTEN

Listen with a pen in hand. Be ready to write the moment something grabs your attention.

✔ If your teacher acts like something is important, it probably is.

✔ Stay focused. Make an effort to ignore any distractions.

✔ Keep your notes organized. Write the date and topic at the top of each page.

✔ Be brief. Write in short phrases and use a shorthand method of abbreviations.

✔ Create pictures, lists, charts, or anything else that will help you visualize—and remember—the information.

✔ Don't let your notebooks sit until it's time for a test. Look over your notes every so often to refresh your memory.

TAKING NOTES AS YOU READ

Taking notes as you read is as important as taking notes during a lecture. Try one of the strategies below to help you organize the information you read.

 K-W-L

To use a K-W-L note-taking strategy (What I **K**now—What I **W**ant to Know—What I **L**earned), set up a chart similar to the one below.

WHAT I KNOW ABOUT TERMS OF OFFICE:	**WHAT I WANT TO KNOW:**	**WHAT I LEARNED:**
President = 4-yr. term	Why are terms of different officials different lengths?	Representatives have short terms to keep them closer to the people.
Senators = 6-yr. term		
Reps. = 2-yr. term	Is there a limit to the number of terms a President or members of Congress can have?	Presidents' terms are limited; terms of others aren't.
State and local officials have various length terms.		

2. Graphic Organizers

Another useful strategy is to create graphic organizers that clarify the information you are reading. Below are two kinds:

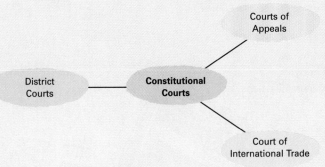

District Courts — Constitutional Courts

Courts of Appeals

Court of International Trade

DESCRIBING Write the main subject of the section or article in the center. List important details on the spokes or in new circles as you read. (This covers material on pages 240–242.)

FINDING CAUSE AND EFFECT Begin with an event, and then identify possible effects. (This covers material on page 198.)

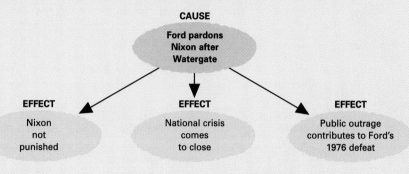

CAUSE

Ford pardons
Nixon after
Watergate

EFFECT

Nixon
not
punished

EFFECT

National crisis
comes
to close

EFFECT

Public outrage
contributes to Ford's
1976 defeat

3. Outlining

When you outline, you divide ideas and information from your reading into a few large groups. Then subdivide each group into smaller groups. For example, you might give each section of your reading a different Roman numeral. Each subsection within a section could begin with a different uppercase letter, and so on. (The outline below is based on material on pages 77–80.)

I. THE ELECTORAL PROCESS

    A. Scheduling Elections

    B. Polling Places and Ballots

II. TYPES OF ELECTIONS

    A. Primaries

    B. Caucuses

    C. General Elections

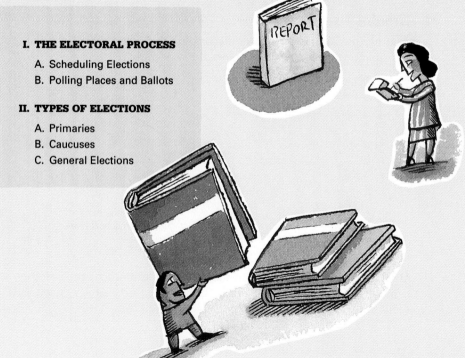

Annotating a Selection

Whenever possible, annotate what you're reading by underlining, highlighting, and circling words, phrases, and sentences. Mark anything that seems interesting, important, or puzzling. If you can, use the margin of the text to record questions, comments, and reactions.

Checklist

ANNOTATING

Annotating will prove useful when you're reviewing for a test or trying to answer a question in class.

✔ Watch for main ideas and key definitions. Mark them carefully.

✔ Keep an eye out for the topic sentence of each paragraph. They're often important clues to the meaning of the paragraph.

✔ Use special symbols—stars, asterisks, check marks, and so forth—to emphasize important information.

✔ Avoid highlighting too much. The point of highlighting is to allow you to quickly see a few things that are very important. If everything is highlighted, nothing will stand out.

Below is a sample of how one reader might annotate a passage from Ronald Reagan's First Inaugural Address in 1981:

So as we begin, let us take inventory. We are a nation that has a government—not the other way around. And this makes us special among the nations of the Earth. Our Government has no power except that granted by the people. It is time to check and reverse the growth of government which shows signs of having grown beyond the consent of the governed. It is my intention to curb the size and influence of the Federal establishment. . . . All of us need to be reminded that the Federal Government did not create the States; the States created the Federal Government. . . . Government can and must provide opportunity, not smother it; foster productivity, not stifle it.

Annotations: Are we so special? — what signs? when was growth? — main idea* — a conservative view! — How? — What does this mean?

Taking Tests

If you're like most students, one of your biggest worries is taking tests. No matter what you do, and no matter how hard you study, you just can't seem to overcome "test anxiety." What should you do? There are two basic ways to treat test anxiety: learn test-taking strategies for different kinds of exams and be well prepared.

OBJECTIVE TESTS

The great thing about objective tests is that the answer to every test question is always right there in front of you. So, think positively.

Checklist

MULTIPLE-CHOICE TESTS

On this kind of test, you'll need to decide which answer or answers best suit the question.

✔ Be sure to read the directions carefully. Be sure you know whether you are to find the correct answer or the best answer. Check to see whether you can list more than one choice for each question.

✔ Read each question twice. Try to answer it in your head before looking at the choices.

✔ Read through all the choices before deciding which answer is correct.

✔ If one of your choices is "all of the above," "none of the above," or "more than one of the above," proceed with caution. These options usually signal a tricky question.

Some tests are quick measures of your understanding. They tend to be fast, efficient checks of what you know. But many true-false tests, for example, also often require close and careful reading.

Checklist

TRUE-FALSE TESTS

These exams have a reputation for being easy. Easy or not, tests still require advance preparation and careful reading.

✔ Read the entire question before answering.

✔ Pay attention to names, dates, numerals, and questions with negative words like *not* and *never*. They can be confusing.

✔ Don't mark a statement true unless the whole statement is true. If half is true and half is false, mark the entire statement false.

✔ Think carefully about questions that use an absolute: *always, never, all,* and *every.* Most absolute statements end up being false.

Relationships and connections are emphasized by matching tests. Quite often matching tests are vocabulary tests.

Checklist

MATCHING TESTS

Matching tests require patience. Sometimes it can be tempting to jump at an answer without considering all the possibilities.

✔ Quickly read through both lists or columns before you begin.

✔ Be sure you know whether an answer can be used more than once. If not, then cross out each answer when you use it.

✔ Make your letters or answers legible. You don't want to confuse yourself—or the person correcting the test.

✔ If you get stuck, skip the question and come back to it later. By then, you might have eliminated some of the possible answers.

To assess overall understanding, essay tests are often used. An essay exam tests whether you can put the information you learned "in your own words."

Checklist

ESSAY TESTS

For an essay test, you'll have to read, think, plan, and write—all under time pressure. Don't make the common mistake of trying to write down everything you know about the subject. It's best to follow a plan.

✔ Read the essay question carefully several times. Be sure you understand what you are being asked to do: that is, explain, evaluate, compare, classify, and so forth.

✔ Come up with a one-sentence answer—a thesis statement—to use as your main idea. (Often it helps to reverse the test question: How has the President's power increased? The President's power has increased. . . .)

✔ Make a brief outline of what points you'll want to cover and in what order.

✔ Begin with your thesis statement. If you're planning on more than one paragraph, start new paragraphs for each new point.

✔ Be sure to include at least one or more supporting detail for each paragraph.

✔ Avoid abbreviations, slang, and nonstandard language (like *awesome* or *idiot*).

✔ Proofread what you've written. Leave at least three minutes at the end to read over your answer. Make corrections neatly. A brilliant answer won't mean much if a teacher can't read it.

WATCH YOUR WORDING

Often the language of an essay question can give you important clues about how to answer the question. Here is a list of key terms commonly used. Some questions may use more than one term, so read carefully.

COMPARE to use examples to show how things are similar and different, mainly similar

CONTRAST to use examples to show how things are different

TRACE to explain in a step-by-step sequence how facts or events are related

JUSTIFY to tell why a position or viewpoint is good or right

EXPLAIN to make clear or to break something up into its parts to show how it works

DISCUSS to talk about all sides of something

SUMMARIZE to express only the main points of an idea, event, issue, or reading, not the specific details

ILLUSTRATE to show examples of something, often a law, idea, or principle

REVIEW to reexamine or summarize the major elements or characteristics of something

PROVE to offer a persuasive argument about the truth of something by providing convincing evidence

CLASSIFY to categorize or group things or people according to similarities and differences

ESSAY TEST

According to President Woodrow Wilson, "Congress in session is Congress on display. Congress in committee is Congress at work." Discuss how committees help to organize the work of Congress. Compare and contrast the functions of several different kinds of committees as you trace how a bill would progress from introduction in the House through passage in the Senate.

STUDYING FOR TESTS

No matter what kind of test you're going to take, it pays to be well prepared and confident. Chances are good that you probably know more than you think you do. Studying helps you be sure of your own abilities. One way to help you feel more confident is to develop a study plan.

★ Find out what type of test questions you should expect and what exactly the test will cover.

★ Then look at your schedule. Set aside 1 or 2 specific days and times for your reviewing.

★ Spend extra time on topics the teacher stressed or that you've found difficult.

★ Make outlines or diagrams to help you see how information fits together.

★ Try to predict what the questions will be and then practice answering them.

★ And, don't put everything off until the night before. Get a good night's rest, wear a watch, and make sure you bring everything you need to the exam.

The Writing Process

An important part of being a successful athlete is having a routine—a set of steps that you can follow each time you step into the batter's box, shoot a free throw, or serve a match point in tennis. Like athletes, writers need a routine, too. That's what the writing process is—a routine you can use when it comes time to write a short essay, a letter, or a longer research project.

Those who know a lot about writing break the writing process down into four steps: planning (or prewriting), drafting, revising, and proofreading.

STEP 1: PLANNING

The planning stage involves understanding the assignment and settling on a topic and preliminary plan of organization.

★ Begin by looking over the assignment. Ask questions about anything you don't understand.

★ Make sure you know who your audience is, if there are length guidelines, and when the writing is due.

★ If you can choose your own topic, try a prewriting activity to help you select a promising subject.

QUICKWRITING Choose a related topic that interests you. Write, without stopping, for five or six minutes on the subject. Put down anything that comes to mind. Sometimes just moving your pencil across the paper is enough to get your brain working.

CLUSTERING Create a cluster that explores a subject. Begin with a word or phrase and then surround it with related words and phrases that come to mind.

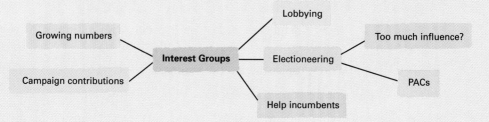

LISTING Listing is sort of like quickwriting. Begin with an idea or key word (for example, gun control), and then list words and phrases that relate to it. Write quickly. Full sentences will just slow you down.

> Gun Control:
>
> the NRA   freedom to bear arms
> rising crime rates   handguns vs. semi-automatic weapons
> gun-related deaths   the Brady Bill? changes?

 If your topic is assigned, it may help to get a quick overview by skimming through your book, notes, encyclopedias, articles, Web sites, or other resources.

 Write a thesis statement—the main point you want to make about the topic.

> topic   +   your thoughts about topic   =   thesis statement
>
> gun control   +   a good thing   =   Gun control laws will effectively keep
>   guns out of the hands of minors.

 Create a brief outline, jot down some ideas, or make a flow chart of the ideas you'll want to explore.

 Begin writing once you've thought through the plan. You wouldn't start building a house without some sort of blueprint, would you?

STEP 2: DRAFTING

Once you've finished planning, you are ready to start on your first draft. Keep your writing plan and your thesis statement in front of you as you write.

 Gather all your materials before you begin drafting. Stopping to find a book or a pencil can ruin your concentration.

 Write quickly to get your ideas down. If you get stuck on one idea or sentence, just put an X and move on.

 Remember that rough drafts are messy. They are full of question marks, arrows to show passages that should be moved around, and crossed-out words, lines, and paragraphs.

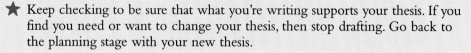

★ Keep checking to be sure that what you're writing supports your thesis. If you find you need or want to change your thesis, then stop drafting. Go back to the planning stage with your new thesis.

★ Try for an introduction that grabs the reader's attention and introduces your thesis. Just because it's the first thing a reader reads doesn't mean it's the first thing you have to write. If starting with the introduction causes writer's block, move on. Start somewhere else.

★ As you write the body paragraphs, use a separate paragraph for each new point.

★ Don't just let your writing trail off. Even if it's short, write a conclusion to give the reader a sense of closing and to re-emphasize your main point.

★ Think about what story your paper tells about your subject.

STEP 3: REVISING

Some writers often make the mistake of treating their first draft as their final draft. Often they skip revising because they haven't left themselves enough time or because they don't really know what changes to make to improve their writing. However, the revising stage is crucial. It's your chance to go back and look at the things you skipped over as you drafted. It's your chance to be sure that your writing says just what you want it to.

★ Let your draft sit for a while—overnight or at least for an hour—before beginning to revise. This way you can look at your words with the fresh eye of an editor.

★ Start by considering the "big picture" things—the content and the organization. Make sure the thesis is clear and that your body paragraphs follow in a clear order.

★ Sometimes it helps to try to outline your own draft. If you have trouble, so will a reader.

★ Adding transitional words—such as *in contrast, but, next,* or *therefore*—may help make connections among paragraphs clearer.

★ Look next for places where details should be added or passages should be removed. Add support to weak paragraphs, and cut any wordy expressions and unnecessary details.

★ Move from paragraphs to sentences. Read your writing out loud, listening to how it sounds. Mix up the structure and the length of sentences. Try to make some short, some long.

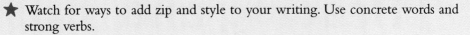
★ Watch for ways to add zip and style to your writing. Use concrete words and strong verbs.

★ Check that your tone is consistent. You don't want to use formal language throughout only to jolt the readers with slang, contractions, or sentence fragments at the end.

★ Add a title. Think of it as one more way to get your point across to your readers.

★ Cut out the deadwood. Get rid of any words that don't add much.

★ When you think you're finished revising, reread the assignment again. Check one more time that you've met the requirements in content, length, and format.

STEP 4: PROOFREADING

At the final stage of the writing process, proofread your writing for grammatical and spelling errors. These problems distract readers from the points you want to make. Errors can undermine your credibility.

★ Proofreading is not skimming, so go slowly. Read through your paper out loud. Make your eyes see each word—what's actually on the paper, not what you think is there.

★ If you haven't typed up your paper yet, now's the time. It's harder to find errors in your own handwriting.

★ Check for errors in spelling, wrong or missing punctuation, grammar mistakes, problems with mechanics, and careless typos.

★ Proofreading means focusing on errors, not content or style. Try what some professional proofreaders do—start from the last paragraph of the last page and work backward. That way you can't be distracted by the ideas you're expressing.

★ You will probably want to read through your paper more than once. Proofread especially for errors you know you tend to make—punctuation, grammar, or spelling problems you've had before.

★ Use a spell check or grammar check program if you're working on a computer. Just be aware that software programs can't catch all errors. They're not a substitute for your brain.

★ Make any last-minute corrections neatly in ink.

★ When you think you've finished proofreading, proofread again!

Reading and Thinking Critically

"The public buys its opinions as it buys its meat, or takes in its milk, on the principle that it is cheaper to do this than to keep a cow. So it is, but the milk is more likely to be watered."

—*Samuel Butler*

How much you read or think is not as important as how well you read or think. That is, it's important how efficiently and effectively you pull meaning from a book, solve a problem, analyze an issue, or evaluate an idea.

Reading Effectively

Critical readers are thoughtful and active readers. Each time they pick up an article, book, or newspaper, they know that they'll need to work with the text a bit before they can thoroughly understand what they're reading.

Checklist

IMPROVING READING SKILLS

Know what your purpose is—whether you're reading to find background information, evaluate an idea, prepare for a test, or locate a specific fact.

✔ Preview what you're reading. Get a general sense of what's there. Pay attention to headings, subheadings, graphic organizers, words in boldface, and illustrations.

✔ Get in the habit of reading with a pen or pencil in hand. Take notes, jot down ideas, highlight terms, make lists, or note your reactions. (See page 439 on annotating.)

✔ Ask yourself questions as you read. Who is involved? What is being described? When and where does this occur? How does the process occur? Why is something happening?

✔ Reread anything that is difficult or confusing. Try reading more slowly.

✔ Summarize (to yourself, out loud to someone else, or in writing) the main points.

✔ Reflect on what you've read after you've finished.

Thinking Clearly

When you think clearly, everything gets easier—listening, taking notes, speaking in front of groups. So, consider these fundamentals of thinking:

DEFINING Defining is a higher-level thinking skill that you use constantly. It's a way of being specific. Defining pinpoints exactly what you are talking about. For example, you might say, "His argument is full of red herrings, or distractions from the main point."

Of course, you'll need to offer longer definitions for words that are more complex or abstract—for example, *freedom*, *equality*, or *policy*. If a definition is one paragraph or longer, it is called an extended definition. You can develop an extended definition by using a combination of synonyms, giving examples, giving characteristics, even explaining what the word is not.

CLASSIFYING When you classify, you "lump" and "split." You sort similar things together into a single category and then break the category into smaller subgroupings. When you classify, present the categories in the order that makes the most sense. Be sure that the categories don't overlap and that there is one—and only one—category for each thing to fit in.

TYPES OF SPEECH

pure speech	symbolic speech	speech plus

COMPARING AND CONTRASTING When you compare, you mainly point out similarities; when you contrast, you point out differences. Although it's possible to compare or contrast any two subjects, make sure there is a good reason behind the comparison. Why, for example, would someone want to point out obvious differences between two things that everyone already knows are different? What's more worthwhile is to point out differences between two things that people think are similar.

A Venn diagram can help you organize the key similarities and differences.

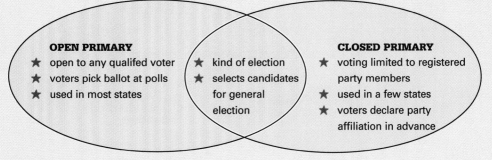

OPEN PRIMARY
★ open to any qualifed voter
★ voters pick ballot at polls
★ used in most states

★ kind of election
★ selects candidates for general election

CLOSED PRIMARY
★ voting limited to registered party members
★ used in a few states
★ voters declare party affiliation in advance

DETERMINING CAUSE-AND-EFFECT In a cause-and-effect relationship, a cause triggers an event that can then become the cause of another event. Ask why something (the effect) happened. The answer tells the cause, or the reason. Because effects are sometimes obvious, it's usually more important to spend time discussing the causes and how they really caused the events. Be clear about immediate or long-term causes and effects, too.

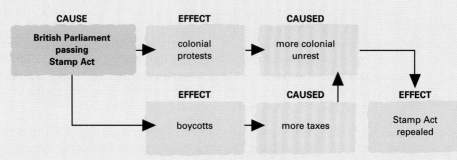

PERSUADING To think, speak, and write effectively, you must be able to argue effectively. You need to be able to take a clear stand on an issue and then convince others to share your viewpoint. The challenge in being persuasive is to find solid evidence that supports your position, to keep a calm and moderate tone, and to take into consideration any opposing arguments.

EVALUATING When you evaluate, you make a value judgment about how good or bad something is. Book and movie reviews or consumer product reports are common forms of informal evaluation. Remember that an opinion or judgment is of little use unless it can be supported with evidence.

As you begin to evaluate something, try to identify 3 to 4 specific standards or criteria on which your judgment is based. For example, to evaluate whether a particular plan for educational reform in your city is good, you'd need to settle on several characteristics that, in your opinion, all good educational reform plans need to have. The next step would be to decide—perhaps based on some research—whether the specific plan in your city has these characteristics.

STANDARDS FOR EVALUATING ANY EDUCATIONAL REFORM

most important *

1. Increases students' learning in measurable ways
2. Has support of all stakeholders—administration, staff, parents, community, and students
3. Is based on solid research
4. Is not excessively expensive

450

Avoiding Fallacies

A fallacy of thinking—or logical fallacy—is a false or flawed argument that can't stand up to close scrutiny. If one isn't thinking critically, however, fallacies can be very convincing. Look through the list of several common fallacies below. Think about the number of times you've seen these techniques used in advertising, editorials, or political campaigns and speeches. Sometimes fallacies are the result of fuzzy or sloppy thinking. Other times they are used intentionally to appeal to emotion, not logic. Try to recognize fallacies in what you read and hear, and then work to avoid them in your own writing.

★ **EITHER/OR** This fallacy occurs when you analyze a complex situation as if it has only two sides when more alternatives exist. You fail to take into account possibilities that are neither black nor white, but gray.

Example: Either we ban all guns for private citizens or we have no gun control. Those are the only two choices facing the United States today.

★ **STRAW MAN** This fallacy involves an unfair representation of an opposing view. You exaggerate or oversimplify the other side so that it can be dismissed as ridiculous. You try to turn the opposition into a "straw man" who is easily knocked down.

Example: Those who want to expand welfare programs don't believe in the value of hard work and personal responsibility. Expansion of welfare means the celebration of laziness.

★ **CIRCULAR THINKING** Most arguments move from one point to another to another. But in circular thinking, you don't really get anywhere. You just go around in a circle. Instead of providing a reason for your conclusion, you begin with the very point you're trying to prove.

Example: The Supreme Court decision restricting prayer in schools is bad because I think prayer in schools is a good thing.

★ *AD HOMINEM* You commit this fallacy (in Latin, "to the man") when you attack the person making the argument rather than the validity of the argument itself. Many of the negative personal attacks on political candidates in heated campaigns are attempts to divert attention from an issue to a person.

Example: Why are you supporting the bill for tougher air pollution regulation? The representative who proposed it just got caught cheating on his income tax.

★ BANDWAGON This fallacy confuses what is popular—what everyone else does or says—with what is right or good. You use the bandwagon appeal when you claim something or someone should be accepted because a large number of people favor it. This technique appeals to a person's desire to belong or be in the majority.

Example: Most polls show Representative Katherine Benjamin is quite popular. You should vote for her, too.

Distinguishing Facts from Opinions

Facts are those things that are known to be true and that can be checked for accuracy. They are likely to be found in many sources. Opinions, on the other hand, are expressions of people's beliefs or attitudes. Although many opinions are based on facts, the opinions themselves can't be proved true or false, right or wrong. Opinions often contain adjectives that imply approval or disapproval (such as *good, bad, wonderful, disappointing*) or that are introduced by such signals as "in my view" or "it's his feeling that."

Critical thinkers can make sound judgments partly because they're able to pick out the facts from the opinions in what they're reading or listening to. Look at the way facts and opinions are mixed in the passage below:

opinion | Medicare is in <u>deep trouble.</u> Current estimates suggest that the Medicare trust fund will be out of money by 2008. Increasing numbers of older Americans and rising costs of medicine are pushing Medicare toward bankruptcy. The National Bipartisan Commission on the Future of Medicare has
opinion | <u>an almost impossible task</u> ahead of it. It's <u>a challenge that should worry</u> the | opinion
77 million baby boomers who haven't yet retired. As it is, the program covers only 53 percent of the health care costs for beneficiaries, and <u>that</u>
opinion | <u>figure is likely to go down.</u>

Some paragraphs, such as the one below, seem at first glance to contain only facts.

Francis Bellamy, a writer for *Youth's Companion* magazine, is acknowledged as the author of the Pledge of Allegiance. The original version first appeared in the September 8, 1892, issue. Congress has since approved two minor unfortunate wording changes. In 1923, "my flag" was changed to "the Flag of the United States of America," and in 1954, the phrase "under God" was added. The Pledge of Allegiance is recited daily at a number of schools throughout the United States.

Unless you read carefully and critically, you might not recognize that the word *unfortunate* is an opinion, not a fact.

Recognizing Assumptions

Critical thinkers not only know how to tell the difference between fact and opinion, but they know how to identify the assumptions. Assumptions are the things that people expect to be true. Even though they're often left unsaid, they form the foundation on which many opinions are built. As you read or listen to discussions and arguments about political issues, get in the habit of asking yourself what the speaker or writer is taking for granted. Look for words that express underlying judgments or values.

Recognizing assumptions helps you make sound evaluations of different issues. Paying attention to assumptions makes you aware of when people are trying to subtly influence your opinions. For example, suppose someone conducting a poll asked you to respond to this question:

"Do you think congressional campaign financing laws go far enough in restricting the harmful effects that result from big money contributions by interest groups?"

The question asks for an opinion on congressional campaign financing laws. But it also contains an assumption about another topic. Notice how the pollster has used the word *harmful* to describe the effects of interest group contributions. He or she has made two assumptions: first, that the money given to congressional campaigns has noticeable effects; second, that those effects are negative. Did you recognize both of those assumptions? The wording of the question slants the response.

Making Generalizations and Drawing Conclusions

Generalizations are broad statements based on facts. By making generalizations you can synthesize—or pull together—lots of different information.

★ Make a generalization only if you have evidence to support it. Avoid making general statements based on hunches or guesses—at least not without admitting it's only a feeling.

★ Collect enough data. Suppose you know that both Bill Clinton and Jimmy Carter became President after serving as governor of a southern state. Are you ready to conclude that being a governor in the South is a good stepping stone to the presidency? Probably not. That's a broad conclusion to draw from just two cases. You'd need to find out how many of the Presidents were southern governors.

★ Avoid using absolute words such as *all*, *every*, or *no*. Their use will make your generalization too broad. If someone finds one exception, the validity of your conclusion is damaged. For instance, suppose you survey two-thirds of the teachers at your school, and no one you talk to supports a school voucher program. Be careful to say that "most" or "the majority" do not favor the plan, not that "all" do not. Just one teacher who supports school vouchers would make your generalization false.

★ Examine the data collected below. What conclusions can you draw based on the information?

NUMBER OF WOMEN IN THE HOUSE

CONGRESS	YEARS	TOTAL
101ST	1989–1991	25
102ND	1991–1993	28
103RD	1993–1995	47
104TH	1995–1997	47
105TH	1997–1999	53
106TH	1999–	58

Source: *Congressional Quarterly*

Faulty Conclusions

Why would a critical thinker have to reject these conclusions based on the data?

1. The number of women has increased each year since 1989. (There was no increase in the 104th Congress.)

2. Women's political power is growing. (The chart tells us nothing about judgments of the political power of women.)

3. In the last two decades of the twentieth century, the number of women in the Senate has more than doubled. (The chart gives figures about the number of women in the House, not the Senate.)

3 | **Doing Research**

Searching and researching go together. When you search, you look for something. When you research, your search again or start anew. Sometimes what you're looking for is very specific—the date of someone's birth for a homework assignment, a book to review in a speech, a summary of a Supreme Court decision for a debate, or the latest developments in a current events issue for the school newspaper. Sometimes your search is less focused. You might want to read about an issue to satisfy your own curiosity. You might follow up on something your teacher said in class or browse a topic to see whether it would make a good subject for a paper assignment.

To do research effectively—and efficiently—you need to sharpen your ability to use the library and the Internet, know how to evaluate and keep track of sources, and properly use and document the information you find.

Interviews and Questionnaires

When you think of doing research, you probably think about finding out what other people have said or written about a topic, right? Well, published sources (such as books, newspapers, journal articles, and speeches) are excellent resources. But sometimes you may want to do what is often called field research, gathering your own information firsthand through interviews and questionnaires.

You might need a face-to-face meeting or a phone call to ask questions of an expert in a particular policy area. The opinions of a city official about next year's budget might be useful. A description of a political event by someone who was there could be persuasive. Perhaps you need a survey of the seniors in your school about an upcoming election. All of this information would be collected through field research. Conducting successful interviews and using questionnaires take considerable planning. You'll need to clearly define your purpose, ask carefully worded questions, and be ready to document your sources.

Using the Library

The library is a great place to begin your research. But even a small library can seem overwhelming. You need to have a basic idea of what's available. And don't be afraid to ask a librarian for help.

ENCYCLOPEDIAS Most student researchers begin their search with encyclopedias, either in book or CD form. They can provide you with a general overview of a subject and clue you in to what's known (and unknown) about a topic. In addition, the subdivisions in an encyclopedia's treatment of a large subject can help you narrow down your topic. Finally, the bibliography list that appears at the end of many encyclopedia articles can point you to other valuable sources of information.

You'll probably want to begin with a general encyclopedia such as *Encyclopedia Britannica* or *Encarta*. For some topics in government and political science, you may want to consult specialized encyclopedias, such as the *Encyclopedia of Black America* or the *Worldmark Encyclopedia of Nations*.

GENERAL REFERENCE WORKS Especially when you're searching for a specific bit of information—for example, a name, a date, or a brief explanation or description—your best bet will be a work in the reference section of the library. Among the most useful reference works on government and politics are:

1. *Statistical Abstract of the United States* Published annually, with hundreds of charts, tables, and graphs on the population, the budget, crime, and so on.

2. *Congressional Quarterly Almanac* Annual summary of legislation, debate, and votes.

3. *The Weekly Compilation of Presidential Documents* Documents, memos, speeches, and articles from the Oval Office.

4. *Current Biography* A useful source for biographical information.

5. *Washington Information Directory* A good source of government postal addresses.

6. *Budget of the United States Government* A comprehensive and current listing of taxing and spending.

7. *The World Almanac and Book of Facts* One of several almanacs published annually; extensive information on the United States, last year's news, and so on.

8. *Facts on File* A weekly news digest arranged by subject headings such as world, national, and foreign affairs; maps and tables are included.

BOOKS Besides locating general reference books, the card catalog can help you locate fiction, nonfiction, and some periodicals. Every book in the library is listed in the card catalog in three different ways: by title, by author's name, and by subject. Many good-sized libraries are connected together into networks. If your local library does not have a book, a librarian usually can order it for you or borrow it from another library. Ask the librarian for help using various search options that may be available on on-line card catalogs.

In the Dewey decimal system, numbers in the 300s are given to books about government, law, politics, education, and economics. Sometimes you can find treasures by just browsing the shelves.

INDEXES A library's periodical section is an extremely useful place for research about current issues. To find what you're looking for more easily, use one of the library's many indexes. Some are devoted exclusively to newspapers or magazines. Others are for professional or academic journals, and still others include both books and periodicals. All periodical indexes give you the title of the article published, the author, and the date and place of publication. In addition, most periodical indexes can be searched by topic.

Among the most useful library indexes are the following:

1. *Readers' Guide to Periodical Literature* An easy-to-use index of more than 200 popular magazines and journals; often also available on-line or in CD-ROM versions.

2. *Social Sciences Index* Indexes periodical articles in political science and economics.

3. *Social Issues in Research Index* Useful for contemporary social issues.

4. *New York Times Index/Wall Street Journal Index* Good place to start looking for newspaper articles.

5. *Biography Index* Excellent source for finding small parts of books or articles about famous people.

6. *InfoTrac, Public Affairs Information Service (PAIS), Educational Resources Information Center (ERIC)* Among the most common and comprehensive on-line or CD-ROM systems that can save you from having to consult several different indexes.

PERIODICALS Many students go straight to books and forget how much valuable information can be found in magazines, newspapers, and journals. Of course, not all libraries have all titles, and some collections may not go back in time as far as you may need. But you can learn the current thinking about a subject very quickly by tracking down several recent articles about it.

1. *American Political Science Review* One of the premier journals about government.

2. *Atlantic Monthly* In-depth articles on politics, society, arts, and culture.

3. *Congressional Quarterly Weekly Report* News and analysis of what's happening in Congress; follows the federal government and current political events.

4. *Congressional Digest* One of the oldest publications on congressional activity; provides background, testimony, and debate from the House and the Senate.

5. *George* A blend of serious features about politics and government and pop culture; published by John F. Kennedy, Jr.

6. *Mother Jones* An irreverent look at today's politics.

7. *Nation Weekly* News magazine with a special emphasis on current affairs.

8. *The New Republic* Weekly journal of opinion, emphasizing politics.

9. *Time, Newsweek, U.S. News & World Report* The "big three" weekly news magazines; extensive coverage of national news and politics; some international news.

10. *Business Week* Information about politics and foreign affairs as it relates to the economy.

Using the Internet

Think of the Internet as a library, meeting room, and classroom all in one. You can use it to do research about current issues and topics. You can also use the Internet to make your views known and to communicate with others—around the world, the United States, your state, or even your school. Its value for researchers is tremendous. But its lack of organization can prove frustrating. That's why you need to know how to search on the Internet.

SEARCH ENGINES

Almost any research you do on the Internet will probably begin at the Web site of one of the major search engines. Using a search engine is similar to using an online card catalog, although a search engine is much more powerful. Most searches are conducted with query words, or keywords. Because the Internet is so huge, the more specific you can be in your search, the better. Often it helps to try different combinations of words; for example, you could try "affirmative action," "law and affirmative action," and "courts and affirmative action." Read the instructions each search engine provides about the ways to limit and define searches.

COMMON INTERNET SEARCH ENGINES

Yahoo!: www.yahoo.com	**Infoseek:** www.infoseek.com
Lycos: www.lycos.com	**AltaVista:** www.altavista.com
Excite: www.excite.com	**LookSmart:** www.looksmart.com

WEB SITES

A few moments after you submit your search request, the results are displayed. For each file, article, or picture that is found, a World Wide Web address, or Web site, will be listed. The sites that are university- or college-affiliated will have addresses that end in *.edu.* The official government sites have addresses that end in *.gov.* The educational and government sites would be likely to provide reliable information. Sites that end in *.org* may promote a certain viewpoint. One potential problem with doing research on the Web is the possibility that a site that you access one day is no longer there—having closed down or moved—the next.

USEFUL GOVERNMENT WEB SITES

The White House www.whitehouse.gov
The House of Representatives www.house.gov
The Senate www.senate.gov
The Bureau of the Census www.census.gov
The Federal Election Commission www.fec.gov
The Department of Agriculture www.usda.gov
The Department of Commerce www.doc.gov
The Department of Defense www.defenselink.mil
The Department of Education www.ed.gov
The Department of Health and Human Services www.dhhs.gov
The Department of Housing and Urban Development www.hud.gov
The Department of the Interior www.doi.gov
The Department of Transportation www.dot.gov
The Department of the Treasury www.ustreas.gov
Centers for Disease Control and Prevention www.cdc.gov
Central Intelligence Agency www.odci.gov/cia
Federal Bureau of Investigation www.fbi.gov
FedWorld Information Network www.fedworld.gov
Food and Drug Administration www.fda.gov
Library of Congress www.loc.gov
Consumer Information Center www.pueblo.gsa.gov
National Archives and Records Administration/Presidential Libraries
    (Hoover through Bush) www.nara.gov

OTHER USEFUL GOVERNMENT AND POLITICS SITES

Democratic party www.democrats.org
FindLaw, Inc. (law resources) www.findlaw.com
Gallup Organization (polls) www.gallup.com
National Conference of State Legislatures www.ncsl.org
Republican party www.rnc.org
Supreme Court www.cornell.edu/supct or oyez.nwu.edu
United Nations www.un.org
National Election Studies www.umich.edu/~nes
See also the Web site for *American Government* at www.greatsource.com/amgov/

Organizing Sources

Finding information is definitely an important step in the research process. But it's not the only one. One challenge is keeping track of what you've found. You don't want to lose anything, waste time checking the same source twice, or forget where a piece of information came from. If you're simply searching for one fact or locating one or two sources, keeping track of your sources isn't a big deal. But with longer research projects and a dozen sources, it can be tricky.

Two basic systems—with many varieties and combinations—are often used. Each has its own advantages and disadvantages. If you don't already have a system that works well for you, ask your teacher to recommend one. Some students find that the note-taking system helps them avoid procrastination because they read and take notes on a source as they go. Others prefer the convenience of making copies of sources at the library and reading and highlighting them later. Many students use a combination of the two systems.

1. **TAKING NOTES** One of the oldest methods, still used by many students today, is to take research notes on 3 × 5 or 4 × 6 index cards. The basic idea is to take notes from or copy quotes from one source on a card. This system works best when you know—or have a good idea about— what you are looking for. You give each card a heading, include the name of the source and the page number, and keep the stack of cards together.

2. **MAKING PHOTOCOPIES** Many students prefer to photocopy material from books and magazines and print out information they find on the computer. Instead of a stack of note cards, they have a folder full of copies of their source materials. As they read through the sources, they underline, highlight, and jot notes in the margins. This system—collect now, sift later—works best for general searches when you're not sure exactly what you're looking for.

Evaluating Sources

What's the next step after locating and organizing your sources? You evaluate them. Not all sources are created equal. Some are more credible and reliable than others. Just because you found what seems like a good quote in a newspaper article or an interesting theory on a Web site doesn't mean those sources are accurate. So, how do you know whether a source is a good one?

The issue is a complicated one, with no simple answers. With the rapid—and unsupervised—growth of the Internet and the increasing numbers of Web sites, the issue of evaluating sources has become especially important. Although the Internet is often called the "information superhighway," there's a mind-boggling amount of misinformation floating around cyberspace. Use some of the questions below as a guide to know what sources you should have confidence in.

1. Source Questions

What, if anything, do you know about whoever is responsible for publishing the source? Is it a well-respected university, government department, major television network, or long-established book publisher? If so, the information is likely to be reliable. If you don't know much about the organization or Web site, do a little homework. Is it mentioned in other sites or publications? How long has it been around? How objective does the information seem? Remember that almost anyone who can access a computer and has a little programming knowledge can create a Web site and put almost anything on it—fact or fiction.

2. Author Questions

If the author is a "big name," or you know that he or she's an expert in the area you're investigating, your confidence in the information should go up. Just because you don't know anything about the author doesn't mean he or she isn't credible either. What can you find out about the author's work experience, education, or other publications? Have any other works you've seen mentioned the author's name? A work can be both reliable and anonymous, of course. But if you've never heard of an author and can't seem to find out any information about him or her, be a little cautious.

3. Information Questions

It's a good idea to check out the specific information you're interested in, even if the author and the publisher seem reliable. Are all necessary sources cited? Are facts up-to-date and authoritative? If the material is more than five years old, you may want to try to find something published more recently. Is the information—all or part—confirmed in other sources? If you find obvious bias, dubious facts, sloppy writing, or quotations attributed to "unnamed sources," warning bells should go off.

EVALUATING INFORMATION FROM SOURCES

Some sources are more reliable than others. To help you determine which sources to
have confidence in, ask teachers, librarians, and others whose opinions you respect.

✔ Who collected the information?

✔ What do you know about the author of the information?

✔ What is the point of view of the source?

✔ How "expert" or recognized are the authors cited?

✔ What sources are provided to allow you to check the information?

✔ How current and up-to-date is the information?

Using Sources Responsibly

When you include source information—whether in an informal speech, a
take-home essay test, or a formal research paper—it's important that you
don't confuse your own ideas with the ideas you've picked up from your
research. If you allow others to think—intentionally or by accident—that
ideas and information you got from sources are yours, you may be guilty of
plagiarism, the act of representing someone else's ideas as your own.

THREE WAYS OF USING SOURCES

1. SUMMARIES When you summarize all or part of a
source, you present only the main idea or ideas. The
details, descriptions, and specific examples are left
out as you concentrate on only the essential
meaning. A summary is, then, much shorter
than the original. It should sound like you,
with your vocabulary and your style, but
it will express the ideas of the source.
Summaries, except for common knowledge, need documentation. When you
summarize, you'll need to give credit to
your source in the body of your paper.

464

2. PARAPHRASES A paraphrase is similar to a summary. When you paraphrase, you restate the ideas in the source in your own words, just as you do in a summary. However, a paraphrase is about the same length as the original. Try to change both the vocabulary and the sentence structure of the original so that your paraphrase sounds quite different from the source. Because you're presenting someone else's ideas, citing the source in the body of your paper is necessary. But because you've used your own words, you don't use quotation marks around a paraphrase.

3. QUOTATIONS Use a direct quotation when you feel that an author's exact words are particularly powerful. Don't quote too much, and keep the quotes you do use short. If you do use a direct quotation, be sure you copy the author's words precisely. Use the same punctuation marks, spelling, and capitalization. Check a grammar handbook such as *Writer's Inc.* for rules about when to use brackets and ellipses and how to set off a long quotation. Like summaries and paraphrases, direct quotations need to be cited in the body of your paper.

Documentation

All uses of source material—whether summaries, paraphrases, or quotations—need to be documented, or credited. The only exception is information that is considered common knowledge, factual information about which there is no disagreement (such as where George Washington was born or who the current chief justice is).

Different fields of study use different forms of documentation. Two of the most widely used are those recommended by the Modern Language Association (MLA) and the American Psychological Association (APA). Instructors in the humanities usually prefer MLA style, while instructors in education and the social sciences often prefer APA style. Both combine some kind of in-text citations with a separate list of all the sources you used. Unless your teacher tells you otherwise, use MLA style for your writing. Below are brief summaries of each format.

For complete information about MLA and APA documentation, check out the most recent edition of *The MLA Handbook for Writers of Research Papers, The Chicago Manual of Style,* or the *Publication Manual of the American Psychological Association.*

PARENTHETICAL CITATIONS

The MLA author-page system requires that you give credit to your sources in the body of your writing, not in footnotes or endnotes. To do this, insert the author's last name and page number(s) in parentheses after the words or ideas that you borrowed. The APA author-year system calls for the last name of the author and the publication year. If the cited material is a quotation, APA also requires the page number. In both styles, the final period comes after the parentheses.

MLA   According to the author, George Washington didn't want to run for a second term because he was "tired of the squabbling" (Shields-West 7).

APA   According to the author, George Washington didn't want to run for a second term because he was "tired of the squabbling" (Shields-West, 1992, p. 7).

  If you mention the author's name in your sentence, the format changes slightly.

MLA   Eileen Shields-West described Lyndon Johnson as acting "like a circus ringmaster" at the 1964 Democratic Convention (208).

APA   Eileen Shields-West (1992) described Lyndon Johnson as acting "like a circus ringmaster" at the 1964 Democratic Convention (p. 208).

Check *The MLA Handbook* for details about how to handle works with more than one author, anonymous works, and sources without page numbers, such as Web sites, interviews, and CD-ROMs.

LIST OF WORKS CITED OR REFERENCES

Every source cited in the text must refer to an entry in a full list of references, which you should include at the end of your paper. Each entry in the list must correspond to at least one parenthetical citation; in other words, don't list items that you may have looked at but didn't use.

The MLA system uses the title "Works Cited" while the APA uses the term "References." Both arrange entries alphabetically according to the author's last name. If no author is identified, alphabetize by the first key word of the title. The basic difference between MLA and APA styles of listing sources is the order in which information is given. Notice the differences in capitalization and punctuation in the sample entries below.

FOR A BOOK:

MLA Shields-West, Eileen. *Presidential Campaigns.* New York: World Almanac, 1992.

APA Shields-West, E. (1992). *Presidential campaigns.* New York: World Almanac.

FOR A PERIODICAL:

MLA Hirsh, Michael. "It Only Gets Worse: Election Eve Pledges." *Newsweek* 22 Dec. 1994: 130.

APA Hirsh, M. (1994, Dec. 22). It only gets worse: election eve pledges. *Newsweek*, p. 130.

FOR A GOVERNMENT PUBLICATION:

MLA United States. Department of Health and Human Services. *Why Vaccinate?* Washington: GPO, 1998.

APA U.S. Department of Health and Human Services. (1998). *Why vaccinate?* Washington, D.C.: U.S. Government Printing Office.

For details about setting up Works Cited and References pages and specific information about other kinds of entries—such as reference books, letters, interviews, network sources, and CD-ROMs—see www. thewritesource.com or the latest edition of *The MLA Handbook.*

4 | Interpreting Special Sources

"Few things in life are harder to put up with than the annoyance of a good example."

—*Mark Twain*

Students studying government and political science today need to know how to read and interpret a variety of special sources. Original documents, cartoons, maps, and the like enrich and expand our appreciation of America's political history and culture. Interpreting them requires time, patience, curiosity, an eye for detail, and the willingness to look beyond the obvious.

Original Documents

Reading documents—such as diaries, laws, Supreme Court opinions, speeches, treaties, and letters— written by people in other eras can sometimes be intimidating. For example, try to make sense out of these words from Article III, Section 3 of one version of the Constitution:

"The Congress shall have Power to declare the Punishment of Treason, but no Attainder of Treason shall work Corruption of Blood, or Forfeiture except during the Life of the Person attainted."

Not only is the sentence full of unfamiliar words and strange capitalizations, but its structure seems awkward and confusing to most modern readers. It is easier, then, for most of us to rely on a paraphrase: Congress may punish citizens for disloyal actions against the United States, but the case can't extend beyond the

468

person's lifetime, nor can his or her children or relatives be punished for the acts committed. That's better. So why even bother to try to interpret the original?

Once learned, the skill of reading original documents immensely enriches your understanding of principles of government and the eras that produced them. If you must rely exclusively on a textbook interpretation, you are in effect putting a filter between you and the document, allowing someone else to take charge of and translate the meaning. Besides, it's interesting—and sometimes amusing—to see how different words may be used in different eras to convey the same messages.

Consider this line from a 1776 letter John Adams wrote to his wife Abigail while he was away from home:

"... you are so saucy. ... you know that [our Masculine systems] are little more than Theory ... in Practice you know We are the subjects."

Think about what Adams is trying to say. Put into your own words, the distinction he's making between what happens in theory and what happens in reality, or practice. Who is the "We" that he refers to? Soon you will see that Adams is teasing his wife with the age-old accusation that men are suckers for women and that it's women who truly control the world. Doesn't knowing this is how Adams related to his wife make him seem a bit more human? His voice speaks to us across the centuries.

So dig in. Don't just skim excerpts from original documents. With practice, you'll be able to interpret them on your own. Understanding original documents can make you appreciate government and politics a great deal more.

Political Cartoons

Political cartoons have played an important role in American politics since the first American newspaper was published in 1783. Cartoonists use satire, sarcasm, exaggeration, and irony to poke fun at government officials, political issues, the media, and sometimes the public itself.

Although they can be very entertaining, political cartoons also serve a serious purpose. They are meant to be subtle—or not-so-subtle—comments on government, politicians, and current events. A political cartoon can be as influential as a front-page newspaper article or the top story on the evening news.

In the cartoon below, political "handlers" (not shown) are working to create a presidential candidate who will appeal to the American public. You probably recognized Lincoln and noted his unhappy expression right away. So what's the message? Who's being criticized? Probably two groups are: the handlers who focus on a candidate's appearance rather than important issues and the public who will be impressed by a certain image.

© The 5th Wave by Rich Tennant

In the cartoon below, published in 1998, the caption and art work together to show a cowardly President Clinton hiding behind his wife, Hillary Rodham Clinton, as she protects him during his scandal-ridden second term.

1/27/98

STATE OF
THE UNION~

Checklist

INTERPRETING POLITICAL CARTOONS

Interpreting political cartoons requires an eye for detail.

✔ Read the caption first, then any other dialogue or text.

✔ Next look at the art. Ask yourself who or what is pictured. Then study the cartoon again, looking for details you missed the first time.

✔ Look for caricatures of famous leaders, well-known settings (such as the White House or the Capitol), or traditional political symbols (such as an elephant to represent the Republican party or Uncle Sam to represent the United States).

✔ Put it all together. Think about how the art and the text connect. Read between the lines and draw inferences about what we are to think of what's pictured.

✔ State the message the cartoonist is trying to get across in one sentence.

Maps

Reading maps is another crucial skill. Maps are everywhere—in textbooks, magazines, newspapers, and cars and on television. They generally contain an outline of a geographical region. On most maps, north is at the top, although you should always check the directional finder. Other important information is in the map legend, or key, which is usually located at a bottom corner of the map. In the legend, you can find information about distances, symbols, abbreviations, or coloring that's used.

Take a look at this map showing percentages of citizens who reported voting in the 1996 presidential election.

**REPORTED VOTING, BY STATE: NOVEMBER 1996
(AS A PERCENT OF THE CITIZEN POPULATION)**

Source: U.S. Bureau of the Census

First look at the legend in the bottom right. Are you clear about what each color represents? Then think about the "big picture." What conclusions can you draw? Do the states in which under 50 percent of the population voted have any characteristics in common? Did one geographical region seem to have a larger percentage of people voting than another? And, if so, why?

A cartogram, such as the one on page 182 representing the electoral vote, is a special kind of map that tries to present complex statistical information in a simple way. For instance, Montana's small size represents the small proportion of the country's total electoral votes that state has, not its actual land mass.

472

Graphs, Charts, and Tables

A graph, chart, or table can make even the most complex information easy to understand by creating a visual image. The ability to interpret graphs, charts, and tables—as well as to create them yourself—can make you a more critical reader and thinker. You'll be able to understand and communicate complicated amounts of information more effectively and efficiently.

LINE GRAPH

A line graph is used to show changes over a period of time. Line graphs—such as the one below about the minimum wage—have L-shaped grids. The horizontal line stands for passing time, from 1961 to 1997. The vertical line shows the subject of the graph, the dollar amount of the minimum wage.

It's easy to see the general upward trend in the bottom line. Over the years, the minimum wage has steadily risen, faster in some decades than in others. But what do you make of the top line? Do the two graphs contradict each other? Are people who earned the minimum wage in 1997 ($5.15) better off than they were in 1968 when the minimum wage was $1.60? The answer is no. While the minimum wage has increased numerous times, it has not kept pace with the rate of inflation. Think about how you might look at each graph differently if it stood by itself.

MINIMUM-WAGE HISTORY

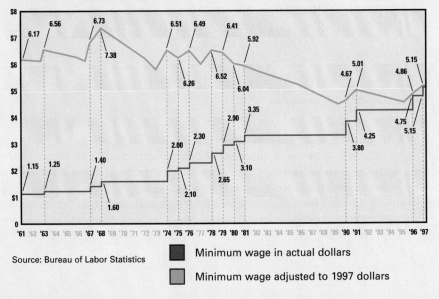

Source: Bureau of Labor Statistics

■ Minimum wage in actual dollars

■ Minimum wage adjusted to 1997 dollars

BAR GRAPH

A bar graph uses columns (bars) to represent the subjects (persons, places, or things) of the graph. A bar graph is especially helpful in comparing quantities. It shows the relationship between different subjects at one point in time. The bar graph below shows the reasons registered voters gave when asked why they didn't vote. Putting information from the two years together allows us to see changes over time. The most common specific reason given in 1980 was illness/emergency. But it was having no time off or being too busy in 1996. What do you think accounts for the change?

REASONS GIVEN FOR NOT VOTING
AMONG THOSE REGISTERED: 1980 AND 1996

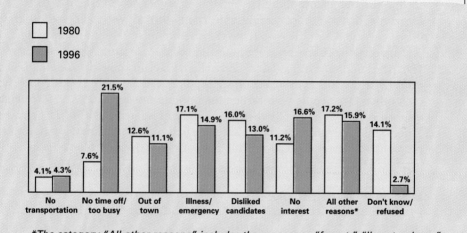

*The category "All other reasons" includes the responses "forgot," "lines too long," and "other reasons" for 1996.

Source: U.S. Bureau of the Census

You will improve your ability to interpret bar graphs if you get in the habit of asking yourself questions about the information presented. For instance, in the graph above, why did the number of people who said they had no interest in voting increase so much between 1980 and 1996? What might account for the decline in those who said they didn't vote because they disliked candidates?

PIE CHART

A pie chart (or pie graph or circle chart) is used to show percentages or proportions. A well-done pie chart will clearly show how each proportion or part relates to the other parts as well as to the whole. The pie chart below gives us information about how many Americans belong to various religious groups according to a poll in 1996.

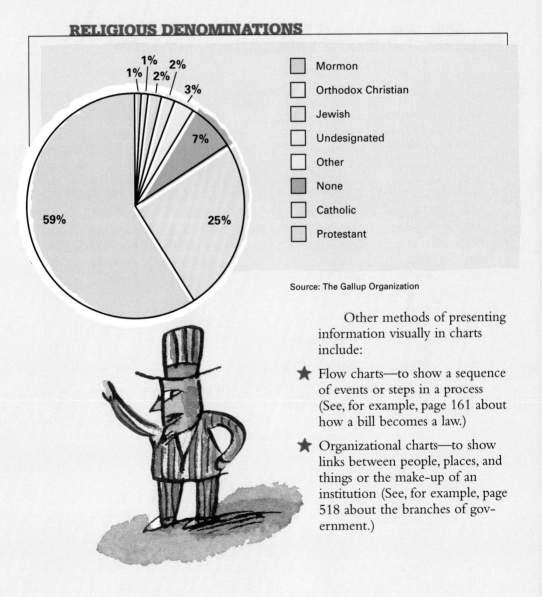

RELIGIOUS DENOMINATIONS

- Mormon
- Orthodox Christian
- Jewish
- Undesignated
- Other
- None
- Catholic
- Protestant

1% 1% 2% 2% 3% 7% 25% 59%

Source: The Gallup Organization

Other methods of presenting information visually in charts include:

★ Flow charts—to show a sequence of events or steps in a process (See, for example, page 161 about how a bill becomes a law.)

★ Organizational charts—to show links between people, places, and things or the make-up of an institution (See, for example, page 518 about the branches of government.)

TABLE

A table organizes words and numbers so that you can see how they relate to one another. Tables have columns and rows and can be read from left to right and top to bottom. The table below lists the two most successful minor party or independent candidates who ran for President from 1936 to 1996, their party, and the number of votes each received.

LEADING MINORITY PARTY OR INDEPENDENT CANDIDATES FOR PRESIDENT: 1936 TO 1996

YEAR	CANDIDATE	PARTY	POPULAR VOTE (1,000)	CANDIDATE	PARTY	POPULAR VOTE (1,000)
1956	T. Coleman Andrews	States' Rights	111	Eric Hass	Socialist Labor	44
1960	Eric Hass	Socialist Labor	48	Rutherford Decker	Prohibition	46
1964	Eric Hass	Socialist Labor	45	Clifton DeBerry	Socialist Workers	33
1968	George Wallace	American Independent	9,906	Henning Blomen	Socialist Labor	53
1972	John Schmitz	American	1,099	Benjamin Spock	People's	79
1976	Eugene McCarthy	Independent	757	Roger McBride	Libertarian	173
1980	John Anderson	Independent	5,720	Ed Clark	Libertarian	921
1984	David Bergland	Libertarian	228	Lyndon H. La Rouche	Independent	79
1988	Ron Paul	Libertarian	432	Lenora B. Fulani	New Alliance	217
1992	H. Ross Perot	Independent	19,742	Andre Marrou	Libertarian	292
1996	H. Ross Perot	Reform	8,085	Ralph Nader	Green	685

Source: *Statistical Abstract of the United States,* 1998

Can you identify which candidate received the most votes? (H. Ross Perot did in 1992.) Other information is harder to pick out. For instance, in what year was there the smallest difference between the two candidates' popular vote total? (Only 2,000 votes separated them in 1960.) Many tables, like this one, require—and reward—careful study.

476

Public Opinion Polls

A public opinion poll can be enormously important to voters and politicians alike. Polls give voters a chance to express their opinions and provide politicians with valuable information about the public's attitudes on issues. Many polls are conducted by polling firms, media organizations, political parties, interest groups, or candidates themselves. Of course, some polls are more reliable than others. So critical thinkers need to analyze a poll carefully before they take the results too seriously. (See pages 114–116.)

Checklist

ANALYZING A PUBLIC OPINION POLL

Look first at the heading. It should tell you the poll's purpose, when and where it was conducted, and the size of the sample (the number of people polled).

✔ Determine whether the size of the sample is adequate. For a poll to represent the views of the American population, for instance, a randomly selected sample of between 1,200 and 1,500 people is most often used. Sample sizes of 100 to 200 are often too small to be reliable.

✔ Determine whether the sample is random. Do you know how the people were chosen? If one person were as likely as any other to be asked to participate, the sample is random. Random samples are likely to give more accurate and reliable results than polls on radio call-in shows, for example, when people ask to be included and volunteer to answer the questions.

✔ Evaluate, as best you can, whether the sample was representative—that is, how well those polled accurately reflect the total population. For instance, the results of a poll asking whether your high school's music budget should be increased would likely differ significantly depending on who was asked. Imagine the results if only band, orchestra, and chorus students were polled or if only varsity athletes were surveyed.

✔ Check the questions themselves. Are they easy to understand? Are they unbiased? Many times opinion poll questions have a built-in bias. Poorly worded questions can also lead to misunderstandings or inaccurate results.

✔ Finally, see if the margin of error is indicated. This is the statisticians' way of saying how much the sample results may differ from those of the entire population. Large margins of error should make you question the validity of the poll's results.

Let's look closely at a sample poll:

THE PUBLIC'S PERCEPTIONS OF
THE ACCURACY OF NEWS ORGANIZATIONS

This poll was conducted by the Gallup Organization in July of 1998. Those surveyed were asked to respond to the question: "In general, do you think news organizations get the facts straight, or do you think that their stories and reports are often inaccurate?"

Facts Straight	49%
Often Inaccurate	47%
No Opinion	4%

Source: The Gallup Organization

How reliable is this poll? Before you can judge its reliability, you need more information.

★ What was the sample size—10 people or 10,000?

★ How were people selected to participate?

★ Was polling done in person or by phone?

★ What sorts of people responded? Were they a mix of men and women, liberals and conservatives, old and young?

★ Were people from all over the United States surveyed?

You need specific answers to questions like these in order to interpret poll results. These Gallup Poll results were based on evening telephone interviews with a randomly selected national sample of 619 adults, 18 years and older. The margin of error is calculated at $+/-4$. The Gallup Organization claims the results are likely to be reliable within 4 percent. Still, can you think of other factors that might have affected the results of this poll one way or the other? What other information about the sample or the polling process do you wish you had?

5 | # Completing Special Assignments

"Next to the originator of a good sentence is the first quoter of it."

—*Ralph Waldo Emerson*

Assignments in government classes naturally vary from teacher to teacher, year to year, and state to state. Yet most teachers probably have a common goal. They want their students to think. Their assignments challenge you to interpret what you read, explore and connect ideas, consider new information, make judgments, form opinions, back up opinions with support, and communicate your thoughts effectively.

This section contains background information about several of the most common kinds of assignments you may be given: speeches, letters, position papers, and research projects.

Giving a Speech

In high school, in college, and in business, people will often judge you by the way you speak. The most successful students, teachers, politicians, business leaders, and so on are those who speak well, argue persuasively, and rarely lose hold of their audience.

Checklist

GIVING A SPEECH

PLANNING

✔ Be sure you understand who your audience is and what your main purpose is (usually to persuade, to inform, or to entertain).

✔ Find out how much time you have and narrow your topic accordingly.

✔ After gathering the necessary information, organize the facts and details into an introduction, a body, and a conclusion.

✔ Grab your audience's attention right away as you introduce your topic. Try beginning with a startling fact, a strong statement, a series of questions, or a personal anecdote.

✔ Keep the organization clear and simple. Try, for example, to arrange information in order of importance, in chronological order, or by describing a problem and then presenting a solution.

✔ Use your conclusion to emphasize your main point and explain why it's important or what you want your audience to do next.

REHEARSING AND DELIVERING

✔ Rehearse the speech in front of a mirror or ask a friend or family member to listen. Practice saying it out loud.

✔ Go through it several times, until you feel comfortable.

✔ Practice a few gestures and changes in the tone of your voice or your facial expression. If they don't feel natural, don't include them.

✔ Mark up your notes or copy to remind yourself where to pause, where to speed up, what words to emphasize, and so forth.

✔ Face the audience, make eye contact as you begin, and try not to fidget.

✔ Speak slowly in a loud, clear voice. Most people tend to rush when they're nervous.

THREE TYPES OF SPEECHES

★ **IMPROMPTU SPEECH** You have little or no time to prepare this speech so you're speaking "off the cuff." You may not even know in advance that you'll be asked to speak or what the topic is. Talk slowly, giving yourself time to think as you speak. Watch the audience's faces and body language to help you shape your speech as you go. These talks are often brief, so try to stick to one main point.

★ **OUTLINE SPEECH** You can and should carefully plan this speech. Prepare an outline of main ideas that you want to cover, perhaps on note cards. Don't write out each word. You'll want to glance only occasionally at your outline. Try to sound conversational.

★ **MANUSCRIPT SPEECH** For this formal type of speech you write out— word for word—what you will say. Decide whether you will memorize the speech, read it to your audience, or look at the manuscript only from time to time. Be sure to keep the audience engaged by establishing good eye contact and varying your tone of voice.

Writing a Letter

Writing letters is a good way to get involved in government. Two common letter assignments are writing to a local, state, or federal official and writing a letter to the editor. Writing those types of letters is a great way to let people know what's on your mind. The chief advantage of writing a letter instead of making a phone call is that there are no busy signals for letters. Most government officials and editors—or their staffs—devote at least part of each day to their mail. Politicians also tend to think letters are important because the writer has taken the time to express his or her feelings in writing.

Checklist

CHECKLIST FOR WRITING LETTERS

You'll have a better chance of having your letter read carefully—and answered or published—by making it clear, well written, and to the point.

✔ Decide on a clear purpose. Make the topic timely. No one wants to read old news.

✔ Use a clear organization, with each paragraph expressing a new point.

✔ Keep sentences and paragraphs fairly short. Aim generally for no more than one page total. Make it short, but powerful.

✔ Use a moderate and respectful tone. Don't rant and rave. No matter how strongly you feel about an issue, stay calm and polite.

✔ Make sure your letter is neatly typed, in proper business letter format, and free from distracting errors in grammar, spelling, and punctuation. Type it or write it neatly in ink.

✔ Sign your letter and provide your home address and phone number. Most editors won't print letters without that information, though you can request that your name be withheld.

✔ Double-check the name and title of the person you're writing. Be sure you have the current and complete address. The Blue Pages of the phone book list addresses of many state and local offices. Newspapers and magazines often specify where letters to the editor should be sent right on the page where letters are printed.

✔ The fastest way to send your letter is to fax it. Call first to find out the number. If you don't want to fax, e-mail is another quick alternative to regular mail.

Read this student's letter to her state's governor. Notice her purpose, structure, and tone.

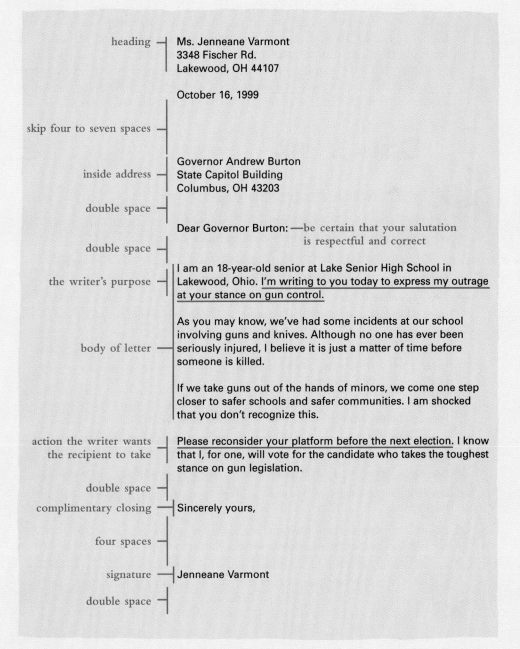

heading — Ms. Jenneane Varmont
3348 Fischer Rd.
Lakewood, OH 44107

October 16, 1999

skip four to seven spaces —

inside address — Governor Andrew Burton
State Capitol Building
Columbus, OH 43203

double space —

Dear Governor Burton: —be certain that your salutation
double space —   is respectful and correct

the writer's purpose — I am an 18-year-old senior at Lake Senior High School in
Lakewood, Ohio. I'm writing to you today to express my outrage
at your stance on gun control.

body of letter — As you may know, we've had some incidents at our school
involving guns and knives. Although no one has ever been
seriously injured, I believe it is just a matter of time before
someone is killed.

If we take guns out of the hands of minors, we come one step
closer to safer schools and safer communities. I am shocked
that you don't recognize this.

action the writer wants — Please reconsider your platform before the next election. I know
the recipient to take — that I, for one, will vote for the candidate who takes the toughest
stance on gun legislation.

double space —
complimentary closing — Sincerely yours,

four spaces —

signature — Jenneane Varmont

double space —

Writing a Position Paper

Writing a position paper requires you to look critically at your own thinking and understand other people's points of view. The goal of a position paper is to persuade readers to adopt your position. When that's not possible, you try to make the best possible case for your view and strongly refute the opposing side's position. The most convincing arguments appeal to logic—by gathering persuasive evidence—and to emotion—by making readers share your concern about the issue. As citizens in a democracy, it's both a privilege and a responsibility to participate in the public debate over controversial issues.

Checklist

WRITING A POSITION PAPER

As for any writing assignment, you'll want to budget time for moving through the planning, drafting, revising, and proofreading stages. (See pages 444–447.)

✔ If your topic isn't assigned, brainstorm a list of controversial topics—ones that reasonable people can disagree about. Be sure it's narrow enough.

✔ Form your opening statement. It should be an assertion—an opinion you want your readers to adopt or an action you want them to take. Make it brief and clear. Don't be wishy-washy.

✔ Sometimes you may already have a clear opinion on the topic. Other times you won't know at first what you think. And sometimes you'll find yourself changing your mind as you write. That's all right.

✔ As supporting evidence, consider using your own experiences, those of people you know, or authoritative research. Evidence should be reliable and relevant.

✔ Keep a calm, but determined, tone. If you sound hysterical or rant like a maniac, people won't take you seriously.

✔ Open with something catchy. Use a surprising fact, a snappy quote, or an anecdote.

✔ Work through your evidence, one piece at a time. Most writers like to save the best for last.

✔ Devote some time to opposing views. Anticipate and acknowledge what the opposition will say and then do your best to explain the weaknesses in their position.

✔ Restate your position in the conclusion. Try not to introduce any new ideas or evidence at the end. And don't apologize for not giving a longer or stronger argument.

484

Study the following draft of a brief position paper that uses personal experience to make an argument about a problem in local government. What are its strengths? What revisions should the author make?

Time for a Change

engaging opening anecdote — The next time you open your bedroom window or step outside your backdoor, listen carefully. Do you hear the sweet chirping of the birds or the low grumble of a bulldozer? Do you hear the buzz of the bumblebee or the whine of the chain saw? What has happened to our "garden of Eden," our scenic, wooded, and beautiful Bucks County?

What has happened is this: almost everywhere you look in Bucks County, construction companies are tearing down landscapes, back filling rivers and streams, and planting houses where farmers used to plant summer wheat. Our farms, forests, and open spaces are being snatched up by builders who *specific detail* — are putting up house after house, development after development. In the last year alone, 153 new houses were begun. These developers will keep on building so long as our local government allows this unrestricted construc*clear position* — tion to continue. Local officials need to start saying "no" to developers and "yes" to those who are trying to preserve the land for the entire community.

As the county's population increases, so does our need for parks, playgrounds, athletic fields, and campgrounds. For every acre the local government sells or deeds to a developer, two acres should be put *specific action suggested* aside as open space for the community. As part of this proposal, every developer would be required to "give back" to the community by building a playground, park, or other site that would benefit the community as a whole. Residents, zoning officials, and developers could all work together.

Of course, few builders will be happy about a one-two acre policy. A policy like this would make building in Bucks County a much more expensive process. As a result, we might end up with fewer houses than currently *acknowledgment of opposing views* anticipated. Less development would mean a slower rate of population growth and possibly a loss of economic revenue to the county. Still, the trade-offs would be worth it. Our open lands would be preserved, our roads would be less congested, and our community would have a variety of public places to enjoy.

It's time for us to take the future of Bucks County out of the hands of developers and put it back where it belongs: in the capable hands of the *restatement of position* people who live here. Beginning now, let's tell our local government that we are ready, willing, and able to take charge of Bucks again.

Writing a Research Paper

Most students moan and groan when asked to write a research paper. However, a research project is not a horrible undertaking. The key is starting early, having a plan, and sticking to it. Writing a research paper requires moving through the usual stages of the writing process—planning, drafting, revising, and proofreading. (See pages 444–447.) But it also adds two additional challenges: finding source material and using and documenting those sources in your writing. Doing Research (pages 456–467) presents the basics of how to find and work with sources.

CHOOSING A RESEARCH TOPIC

Sometimes you may be assigned a particular topic. But if you're not, think carefully about possible topics. Because you'll be working on the paper for more than just a few days, you want to choose something you'll really be interested in. Ask other people, look in your book's table of contents, skim through some magazines, check out some Web sites, and so forth.

What if you have a basic topic but don't know how to break it down further? Suppose you chose (or were assigned) the Supreme Court. Try looking at the topic from a variety of angles. Use the approaches described on pages 449–450.

 DEFINE Define the concept of judicial review and show how several justices have used the power.

 CLASSIFY Research several Courts of the past and divide them into categories based on how activist they are.

 COMPARE/CONTRAST Contrast the lives and values of two current justices.

 DETERMINE CAUSE AND EFFECT Consider how the Court has recently dealt with a particular issue, such as sexual harassment or censorship, and show what the effects of those decisions have been on ordinary Americans.

 PERSUADE Argue for/against the idea that justices should not be able to serve past the age of 70.

 EVALUATE Select one particular controversial case and make a judgment about the ruling.

Checklist

WRITING A RESEARCH PAPER

It's important to consider your audience. Know who you are writing for and how much you can assume they already know about your subject.

✔ Find out what kinds of sources—the number and the type—you are supposed to use.

✔ Don't think that just because you're doing research, you don't have to have a thesis. You can't just string together a bunch of quotes or facts that other people have collected. You need a main point for the research to support.

✔ Whatever time you budgeted for researching, drafting, and revising—double it.

✔ Develop—and use—some system for taking notes and keeping track of sources. The longer the paper and the more sources you use, the more you need a system.

✔ It can be tempting to keep researching—looking for that "one perfect source"—instead of sifting through what you have and starting to write. Don't fall into this trap.

✔ Make a detailed first outline or "blueprint." When you find information on a certain point, make a note on the outline. That way you'll have a visual picture of where the gaps in your research are and what information you still need to find.

✔ Summarize or paraphrase most of your sources. Save the quotations for the really striking language.

✔ Be tough on yourself when you're revising. If something's not clear to you—and you wrote it—imagine what a reader will think.

✔ Check your documentation format before you proofread so you can concentrate on finding and correcting other errors.

Unit VIII

Almanac

Almanac

Beginnings of American Government and the Constitution

Declaration of Independence

In Congress, July 4, 1776

W HEN in the Course of human Events, it becomes necessary for one People to dissolve the Political Bands which have connected them with another, and to assume among the Powers of the Earth, the separate and equal Station to which the Laws of Nature and of Nature's God entitle them, a decent Respect to the Opinions of Mankind requires that they should declare the causes which impel them to the Separation.

WE hold these Truths to be self-evident, that all Men are created equal, that they are endowed by their Creator with certain unalienable Rights, that among these are Life, Liberty, and the Pursuit of Happiness — That to secure these Rights, Governments are instituted among Men, deriving their just Powers from the Consent of the Governed, that whenever any Form of Government becomes destructive of these Ends, it is the Right of the People to alter or to abolish it, and to institute new Government, laying its Foundation on such Principles, and organizing its Powers in such Form, as to them shall seem most likely to effect their Safety and Happiness. Prudence, indeed, will dictate that Governments long established should not be changed for light and transient Causes; and accordingly all Experience hath shown, that Mankind are more disposed to suffer, while Evils are sufferable, than to right themselves by abolishing the Forms to which they are accustomed. But when a long Train of Abuses and Usurpations, pursuing invariably the same Object, evinces a Design to reduce them under absolute Despotism, it is their Right, it is their Duty, to throw off such Government, and to provide new Guards for their future Security. Such has been the patient Sufferance of these Colonies; and such is now the Necessity which constrains them to alter their former Systems of Government. The History of the present King of Great Britain is a History of repeated Injuries and Usurpations, all having in direct Object the Establishment of an absolute Tyranny over these States. To prove this, let Facts be submitted to a candid World.

HE has refused his Assent to Laws, the most wholesome and necessary for the public Good.

HE has forbidden his Governors to pass Laws of immediate and pressing Importance, unless suspended in their Operation till his Assent should be obtained; and when so suspended, he has utterly neglected to attend to them.

HE has refused to pass other Laws for the Accommodation of large Districts of People, unless those People would relinquish the Right of Representation in the Legislature, a Right inestimable to them, and formidable to Tyrants only.

HE has called together Legislative Bodies at Places unusual, uncomfortable, and distant from the Depository of their public Records, for the sole Purpose of fatiguing them into Compliance with his Measures.

HE has dissolved Representative Houses repeatedly, for opposing, with manly Firmness, his Invasions on the Rights of the People.

HE has refused for a long Time, after such Dissolutions, to cause others to be elected; whereby the Legislative Powers, incapable of the Annihilation, have returned to the People at large for their exercise; the State remaining in the mean time exposed to all the Dangers of Invasion from without, and Convulsions within.

HE has endeavoured to prevent the Population of these States; for that Purpose obstructing the Laws for Naturalization of Foreigners; refusing to pass others to encourage their Migration hither, and raising the Conditions of new Appropriations of Lands.

HE has obstructed the Administration of Justice, by refusing his Assent to Laws for establishing Judiciary Powers.

HE has made Judges dependent on his Will alone, for the Tenure of their Offices, and the Amount and Payment of their Salaries.

HE has erected a Multitude of new Offices, and sent hither Swarms of Officers to harrass our People, and eat out their Substance.

HE has kept among us, in Times of Peace, Standing Armies, without the consent of our Legislatures.

HE has affected to render the Military independent of and superior to the Civil Power.

HE has combined with others to subject us to a Jurisdiction foreign to our Constitution, and unacknowledged by our Laws; giving his Assent to their Acts of pretended Legislation:

FOR quartering large Bodies of Armed Troops among us;

FOR protecting them, by a mock Trial, from Punishment for any Murders which they should commit on the Inhabitants of these States:

FOR cutting off our Trade with all Parts of the World:

FOR imposing Taxes on us without our Consent:

FOR depriving us, in many Cases, of the Benefits of Trial by Jury:

FOR transporting us beyond Seas to be tried for pretended Offenses:

FOR abolishing the free System of English Laws in a neighboring Province, establishing therein an arbitrary Government, and enlarging its Boundaries, so as to render it at once an Example and fit Instrument for introducing the same absolute Rules into these Colonies:

FOR taking away our Charters, abolishing our most valuable Laws, and altering fundamentally the Forms of our Governments:

FOR suspending our own Legislatures, and declaring themselves invested with Power to legislate for us in all Cases whatsoever.

HE has abdicated Government here, by declaring us out of his Protection and waging War against us.

HE has plundered our Seas, ravaged our Coasts, burnt our Towns, and destroyed the Lives of our People.

HE is, at this Time, transporting large Armies of foreign Mercenaries to compleat the Works of Death, Desolation, and Tyranny, already begun with circumstances of Cruelty and Perfidy, scarcely paralleled in the most barbarous Ages, and totally unworthy of the Head of a civilized Nation.

HE has constrained our fellow Citizens taken Captive on the high Seas to bear Arms against their Country, to become the Executioners of their Friends and Brethren, or to fall themselves by their Hands.

HE has excited domestic Insurrections among us, and has endeavoured to bring on the Inhabitants of our Frontiers, the merciless Indian Savages, whose known Rule of Warfare, is an undistinguished Destruction, of all Ages, Sexes, and Conditions.

IN every stage of these Oppressions we have Petitioned for Redress in the most humble Terms: Our repeated Petitions have been answered only by repeated Injury. A Prince, whose Character is thus marked by every act which may define a Tyrant, is unfit to be the Ruler of a free People.

NOR have we been wanting in Attentions to our British Brethren. We have warned them from Time to Time of Attempts by their Legislature to extend an unwarrantable Jurisdiction over us. We have reminded them of the Circumstances of our Emigration and Settlement here. We have appealed to their native Justice and

Magnanimity, and we have conjured them by the Ties of our common Kindred to disavow these Usurpations, which would inevitably interrupt our Connections and Correspondence. They too have been deaf to the Voice of Justice and of Consanguinity. We must, therefore, acquiesce in the Necessity, which denounces our Separation, and hold them, as we hold the rest of Mankind, Enemies in War, in Peace Friends.

WE, therefore, the Representatives of the UNITED STATES OF AMERICA, in GENERAL CONGRESS assembled, appealing to the Supreme Judge of the World for the Rectitude of our Intentions, do, in the Name and by Authority of the good People of these Colonies, solemnly Publish and Declare, That these United Colonies are, and of Right ought to be, FREE AND INDEPENDENT STATES; that they are absolved from all Allegiance to the British Crown, and that all political Connection between them and the State of Great Britain is, and ought to be, totally dissolved; and that as FREE AND INDEPENDENT STATES, they have full Power to levy War, conclude Peace, contract Alliances, establish Commerce, and to do all other Acts and Things which INDEPENDENT STATES may of right do. And for the support of this Declaration, with a firm Reliance on the Protection of divine Providence, we mutually pledge to each other our Lives, our Fortunes, and our sacred Honor.

John Hancock.

Georgia, Button Gwinnett, Lyman Hall, Geo. Walton.

North Carolina, Wm. Hooper, Joseph Hewes, John Penn.

South Carolina, Edward Rutledge, Thos Heyward, Jr., Thomas Lynch, Jr., Arthur Middleton.

Maryland, Samuel Chase, Wm. Paca, Thos. Stone, Charles Carroll, of Carrollton.

Virginia, George Wythe, Richard Henry Lee, Ths. Jefferson, Benja. Harrison, Thos. Nelson, Jr., Francis Lightfoot Lee, Carter Braxton.

Pennsylvania, Robt. Morris, Benjamin Rush, Benja. Franklin, John Morton, Geo. Clymer, Jas. Smith, Geo. Taylor, James Wilson, Geo. Ross.

Delaware, Caesar Rodney, Geo. Read.

New York, Wm. Floyd, Phil. Livingston, Frank Lewis, Lewis Morris.

New Jersey, Richd. Stockton, Jno. Witherspoon, Fras. Hopkinson, John Hart, Abra. Clark.

New Hampshire, Josiah Bartlett, Wm. Whipple, Matthew Thornton.

Massachusetts Bay, Saml. Adams, John Adams, Robt. Treat Paine, Elbridge Gerry.

Rhode Island and Providence, C. Step. Hopkins, William Ellery.

Connecticut, Roger Sherman, Saml. Huntington, Wm. Williams, Oliver Wolcott.

NOTE: Some spellings and punctuation have been modernized for easier reading.

Constitution

The 55 delegates of the Constitutional Convention that met in May 1787 wrote the document that established the government for the United States. Government under the Constitution began operating in 1789—in a nation of 13 states and fewer than 4 million people. (See pages 37–38.)

AN OUTLINE OF THE CONSTITUTION OF THE UNITED STATES

Article I	Legislative Branch
Article II	Executive Branch
Article III	Judicial Branch
Article IV	Relations Among the States
Article V	Amending the Constitution
Article VI	Supremacy of National Government
Article VII	Ratification

BILL OF RIGHTS

1st Amendment	Religious and Political Freedom (1791)
2nd Amendment	Right to Bear Arms (1791)
3rd Amendment	Quartering Troops (1791)
4th Amendment	Search and Seizure (1791)
5th Amendment	Rights of Accused Persons (1791)
6th Amendment	Right to a Public Trial (1791)
7th Amendment	Jury Trials in Civil Cases (1791)
8th Amendment	Criminal Punishment (1791)
9th Amendment	Rights of People (1791)
10th Amendment	Powers of States and People (1791)

OTHER AMENDMENTS

11th Amendment	Lawsuits Against States (1798)
12th Amendment	Election of the President and Vice President (1804)
13th Amendment	Abolition of Slavery (1865)
14th Amendment	Citizenship and Civil Rights (1868)
15th Amendment	Right to Vote (1870)
16th Amendment	Income Tax (1913)
17th Amendment	Direct Election of Senators (1913)
18th Amendment	Prohibition (1919)
19th Amendment	Woman's Suffrage (1920)
20th Amendment	Terms, Congressional Sessions, and Presidential Succession (1933)
21st Amendment	Repeal of Prohibition (1933)
22nd Amendment	Limits on Presidential Terms (1951)
23rd Amendment	Voting in District of Columbia (1961)
24th Amendment	Abolition of Poll Taxes (1964)
25th Amendment	Presidential Succession, Disability, and the Vice President (1967)
26th Amendment	18-Year-Old Right to Vote (1971)
27th Amendment	Congressional Pay (1992)

THE CONSTITUTION OF THE UNITED STATES OF AMERICA

We the people of the United States, in order to form a more perfect union, establish justice, insure domestic tranquility, provide for the common defense, promote the general welfare, and secure the blessings of liberty to ourselves and our posterity, do ordain and establish this Constitution for the United States of America.

Article I Legislative Branch

SECTION 1. CONGRESS

All legislative powers herein granted shall be vested in a Congress of the United States, which shall consist of a Senate and House of Representatives.

SECTION 2. THE HOUSE OF REPRESENTATIVES

1. Elections The House of Representatives shall be composed of members chosen every second year by the people of the several states, and the electors in each state shall have the qualifications requisite for electors of the most numerous branch of the state legislature.

2. Qualifications No person shall be a Representative who shall not have attained to the age of twenty-five years, and been seven years a citizen of the United States, and who shall not, when elected, be an inhabitant of that state in which he shall be chosen.

3. Number of Representatives Representatives and direct taxes shall be apportioned among the several states which may be included within this union, according to their respective numbers, ~~which~~ ~~shall be determined by adding to the whole number of free persons, including those bound to service for a term of years, and excluding Indians not taxed, three fifths of all other Persons.~~ The actual Enumeration shall be made within three years after the first meeting of the Congress of the United States, and within every subsequent term of ten years, in such manner as they shall by law direct. The number of Representatives shall not exceed one for every thirty thousand, but each state shall have at least one Representative; ~~and until such enumeration shall be made, the state of New Hampshire shall be entitled to choose three, Massachusetts eight, Rhode Island and Providence Plantations one, Connecticut five, New York six, New Jersey four, Pennsylvania eight, Delaware one, Maryland six, Virginia ten, North Carolina five, South Carolina five, and Georgia three.~~

4. Vacancies When vacancies happen in the Representation from any state, the executive authority thereof shall issue writs of election to fill such vacancies.

5. Officers and Impeachment The House of Representatives shall choose their speaker and other officers; and shall have the sole power of impeachment.

NOTE: Parts of the Constitution no longer in use have been crossed out. Headings have been added and the spelling and punctuation modernized for easier reading.

SECTION 3. THE SENATE

1. Number of Senators The Senate of the United States shall be composed of two Senators from each state, ~~chosen by the legislature thereof,~~ for six years; and each Senator shall have one vote.

2. Terms of Office Immediately after they shall be assembled in consequence of the first election, they shall be divided as equally as may be into three classes. The seats of the Senators of the first class shall be vacated at the expiration of the second year, of the second class at the expiration of the fourth year, and the third class at the expiration of the sixth year, so that one third may be chosen every second year; ~~and if vacancies happen by resignation, or otherwise, during the recess of the legislature of any state, the executive thereof may make temporary appointments until the next meeting of the legislature, which shall then fill such vacancies.~~

3. Qualifications No person shall be a Senator who shall not have attained to the age of thirty years, and been nine years a citizen of the United States and who shall not, when elected, be an inhabitant of that state for which he shall be chosen.

4. Role of Vice President The Vice President of the United States shall be President of the Senate, but shall have no vote, unless they be equally divided.

5. Senate Officers The Senate shall choose their other officers, and also a President pro tempore, in the absence of the Vice President, or when he shall exercise the office of President of the United States.

6. Impeachment Trials The Senate shall have the sole power to try all impeachments. When sitting for that purpose, they shall be on oath or affirmation. When the President of the United States is tried, the Chief Justice shall preside: And no person shall be convicted without the concurrence of two thirds of the members present.

7. Punishment for Impeachment Judgment in cases of impeachment shall not extend further than to removal from office, and disqualification to hold and enjoy any office of honor, trust or profit under the United States: but the party convicted shall nevertheless be liable and subject to indictment, trial, judgment and punishment, according to law.

SECTION 4. CONGRESSIONAL ELECTIONS

1. Regulations The times, places and manner of holding elections for Senators and Representatives shall be prescribed in each state by the legislature thereof; but the Congress may at any time by law make or alter such regulations, except as to the places of choosing Senators.

2. Sessions The Congress shall assemble at least once in every year, ~~and such meeting shall be on the first Monday in December, unless they shall by law appoint a different day.~~

SECTION 5. RULES AND PROCEDURES

1. Quorum Each House shall be the judge of the elections, returns and qualifications of its own members, and a majority of each shall constitute a quorum to do business; but a smaller number may adjourn from day to day, and may be authorized to compel the attendance of absent members, in such manner, and under such penalties as each House may provide.

2. Rules Each House may determine the rules of its proceedings, punish its members for disorderly behavior, and, with the concurrence of two thirds, expel a member.

3. Records Each House shall keep a journal of its proceedings, and from time to time publish the same, excepting such parts as may in their judgment require secrecy; and the yeas and nays of the members of either House on any question shall, at the desire of one fifth of those present, be entered on the journal.

4. Adjournment Neither House, during the session of Congress, shall, without the consent of the other, adjourn for more than three days, nor to any other place than that in which the two Houses shall be sitting.

SECTION 6. PAYMENT AND PRIVILEGES

1. Salaries The Senators and Representatives shall receive a compensation for their services, to be ascertained by law, and paid out of the treasury of the United States. They shall in all cases, except treason, felony and breach of the peace, be privileged from arrest during their attendance at the session of their respective Houses, and in going to and returning from the same; and for any speech or debate in either House, they shall not be questioned in any other place.

2. Restrictions No Senator or Representative shall, during the time for which he was elected, be appointed to any civil office under the authority of the United States, which shall have been created, or the emoluments whereof shall

have been increased during such time: and no person holding any office under the United States shall be a member of either House during his continuance in office.

SECTION 7. HOW A BILL BECOMES LAW

1. Tax Bills All bills for raising revenue shall originate in the House of Representatives; but the Senate may propose or concur with Amendments as on other Bills.

2. Law Making Process Every bill which shall have passed the House of Representatives and the Senate shall, before it become a law, be presented to the President of the United States; if he approve he shall sign it, but if not he shall return it, with his objections to that House in which it shall have originated, who shall enter the objections at large on their journal, and proceed to reconsider it. If after such reconsideration two thirds of that House shall agree to pass the bill, it shall be sent, together with the objections, to the other House, by which it shall likewise be reconsidered, and if approved by two thirds of that House, it shall become a law. But in all such cases the votes of both Houses shall be determined by yeas and nays, and the names of the persons voting for and against the bill shall be entered on the journal of each House respectively. If any bill shall not be returned by the President within ten days (Sundays excepted) after it shall have been presented to him, the same shall be a law, in like manner as if he had signed it, unless the Congress by their adjournment prevent its return, in which case it shall not be a law.

3. President's Role Every order, resolution, or vote to which the concurrence of the Senate and House of Representatives may be necessary (except on a question of adjournment) shall be presented to the President of the United States; and before the same shall take effect, shall be approved by him, or being disapproved by him, shall be repassed by two thirds of the Senate and House of Representatives, according to the rules and limitations prescribed in the case of a bill.

SECTION 8. POWERS GRANTED TO CONGRESS

1. Taxation The Congress shall have power to lay and collect taxes, duties, imposts and excises, to pay the debts and provide for the common defense and general welfare of the United States; but all duties, imposts and excises shall be uniform throughout the United States;

2. Credit To borrow money on the credit of the United States;

3. Commerce with Foreign Nations To regulate commerce with foreign nations, and among the several states, and with the Indian tribes;

4. Naturalization and Bankruptcies To establish a uniform rule of naturalization, and uniform laws on the subject of bankruptcies throughout the United States;

5. Power to Coin Money To coin money, regulate the value thereof, and of foreign coin, and fix the standard of weights and measures;

6. Counterfeiting To provide for the punishment of counterfeiting the securities and current coin of the United States;

7. Post Office To establish post offices and post roads;

8. Patents and Copyrights To promote the progress of science and useful arts, by securing for limited times to authors and inventors the exclusive right to their respective writings and discoveries;

9. Federal Courts To constitute tribunals inferior to the Supreme Court;

10. International Law To define and punish piracies and felonies committed on the high seas, and offenses against the law of nations;

11. War Powers To declare war, grant letters of marque and reprisal, and make rules concerning captures on land and water;

12. Armed Forces To raise and support armies, but no appropriation of money to that use shall be for a longer term than two years;

13. Navy To provide and maintain a navy;

14. Armed Forces To make rules for the government and regulation of the land and naval forces;

15. Militia To provide for calling forth the militia to execute the laws of the union, suppress insurrections and repel invasions;

16. Organizing the Militia To provide for organizing, arming, and disciplining the militia, and for governing such part of them as may be employed in the service of the United States, reserving to the states respectively, the appointment of the officers, and the authority of training the militia according to the discipline prescribed by Congress;

500

17. District of Columbia To exercise exclusive legislation in all cases whatsoever, over such District (not exceeding ten miles square) as may, by cession of particular states, and the acceptance of Congress, become the seat of the government of the United States, and to exercise like authority over all places purchased by the consent of the legislature of the state in which the same shall be, for the erection of forts, magazines, arsenals, dockyards, and other needful buildings;—And

18. Elastic Clause To make all laws which shall be necessary and proper for carrying into execution the foregoing powers, and all other powers vested by this Constitution in the government of the United States, or in any department or officer thereof.

SECTION 9. POWERS DENIED CONGRESS

1. Slave Trade ~~The migration or importation of such persons as any of the states now existing shall think proper to admit, shall not be prohibited by the Congress prior to the year one thousand eight hundred and eight, but a tax or duty may be imposed on such importation, not exceeding ten dollars for each person.~~

2. Habeas Corpus The privilege of the writ of habeas corpus shall not be suspended, unless when in cases of rebellion or invasion the public safety may require it.

3. Illegal Punishment No bill of attainder or ex post facto Law shall be passed.

4. Taxes No capitation, ~~or other direct,~~ tax shall be laid, unless in proportion to the census or enumeration herein before directed to be taken.

5. Export Tax No tax or duty shall be laid on articles exported from any state.

6. Preference of States No preference shall be given by any regulation of commerce or revenue to the ports of one state over those of another: nor shall vessels bound to, or from, one state be obliged to enter, clear or pay duties in another.

7. Public Money No money shall be drawn from the treasury, but in consequence of appropriations made by law; and a regular statement and account of receipts and expenditures of all public money shall be published from time to time.

8. Titles of Nobility No title of nobility shall be granted by the United States: and no person holding any office of profit or trust under them, shall, without the consent of the Congress, accept of any present, emolument, office, or title, of any kind whatever, from any king, prince, or foreign state.

SECTION 10. POWERS DENIED THE STATES

1. Restrictions on States No state shall enter into any treaty, alliance, or confederation; grant letters of marque and reprisal; coin money; emit bills of credit; make anything but gold and silver coin a tender in payment of debts; pass any bill of attainder, ex post facto law, or law impairing the obligation of contracts, or grant any title of nobility.

2. Import and Export Taxes No state shall, without the consent of the Congress, lay any imposts or duties on imports or exports, except what may be absolutely necessary for executing its inspection laws: and the net produce of all duties and imposts, laid by any state on imports or exports, shall be for the use of the treasury of the United States; and all such laws shall be subject to the revision and control of the Congress.

3. Peacetime and War Restraints No state shall, without the consent of Congress, lay any duty of tonnage, keep troops, or ships of war in time of peace, enter into any agreement or compact with another state, or with a foreign power, or engage in war, unless actually invaded, or in such imminent danger as will not admit of delay.

Article II Executive Branch

SECTION 1. THE PRESIDENCY

1. Term of Office The executive power shall be vested in a President of the United States of America. He shall hold his office during the term of four years, and, together with the Vice President, chosen for the same term, be elected, as follows:

2. Electoral College Each state shall appoint, in such manner as the Legislature thereof may direct, a number of electors, equal to the whole number of Senators and Representatives to which the State may be entitled in the Congress: but no Senator or Representative, or person holding an office of trust or profit under the United States, shall be appointed an elector.

3. Former Method of Electing the President The electors shall meet in their respective states, and vote by ballot for two persons, of whom one at least shall not be an inhabitant of the same state with themselves. And they shall make a list of all the persons voted for, and of the number of votes for each; which list they shall sign and certify, and transmit sealed to the seat of the government of the United States, directed to the President of the Senate. The President of the Senate shall, in the presence of the Senate and House of Representatives, open all the certificates, and the votes shall then be counted. The person having the greatest number of votes shall be the President, if such number be a majority of the whole number of electors appointed; and if there be more than one who have such majority, and have an equal number of votes, then the House of Representatives shall immediately choose by ballot one of them for President; and if no person have a majority, then from the five highest on the list the said House shall in like manner choose the President. But in choosing the President, the votes shall be taken by States, the representation from each state having one vote; A quorum for this purpose shall consist of a member or members from two thirds of the states, and a majority of all the states shall be necessary to a choice. In every case, after the choice of the President, the person having the greatest number of votes of the electors shall be the Vice President. But if there should remain two or more who have equal votes, the Senate shall choose from them by ballot the Vice President.

4. Election Day The Congress may determine the time of choosing the electors, and the day on which they shall give their votes; which day shall be the same throughout the United States.

5. Qualifications No person except a natural born citizen, or a citizen of the United States, at the time of the adoption of this Constitution, shall be eligible to the office of President; neither shall any person be eligible to that office who shall not have attained to the age of thirty-five years, and been fourteen Years a resident within the United States.

6. Succession In case of the removal of the President from office, or of his death, resignation, or inability to discharge the powers and duties of the said office, the same shall devolve on the Vice President, and the Congress may by law provide for the case of removal, death, resignation or inability, both of the President and Vice President, declaring what officer shall then act as President, and such officer shall act accordingly, until the disability be removed, or a President shall be elected.

7. Salary The President shall, at stated times, receive for his services a compensation, which shall neither be increased nor diminished during the period for which he shall have been elected, and he shall not receive within that period any other emolument from the United States, or any of them.

8. Oath of Office Before he enter on the execution of his office, he shall take the following oath or affirmation:—"I do solemnly swear (or affirm) that I will faithfully execute the office of President of the United States, and will to the best of my ability, preserve, protect and defend the Constitution of the United States."

SECTION 2. POWERS OF THE PRESIDENT

1. Military Powers The President shall be commander in chief of the Army and Navy of the United States, and of the militia of the several states, when called into the actual service of the United States; he may require the opinion, in writing, of the principal officer in each of the executive departments, upon any subject relating to the duties of their respective offices, and he shall have power to grant reprieves and pardons for offenses against the United States, except in cases of impeachment.

2. Treaties and Appointments He shall have power, by and with the advice and consent of the Senate, to make treaties, provided two thirds of the Senators present concur; and he shall nominate, and by and with the advice and consent of the Senate, shall appoint ambassadors, other public ministers and consuls, judges of the Supreme Court, and all other officers of the United States, whose appointments are not herein otherwise provided for, and which shall be established by law: but the Congress may by law vest the appointment of such inferior officers, as they think proper, in the President alone, in the courts of law, or in the heads of departments.

3. Vacancies The President shall have power to fill up all vacancies that may happen during the recess of the Senate, by granting commissions which shall expire at the end of their next session.

SECTION 3. PRESIDENTIAL DUTIES

He shall from time to time give to the Congress information of the state of the union, and recommend to their consideration such measures as he shall judge necessary and expedient; he may, on extraordinary occasions, convene both Houses, or either of them, and in case of disagreement between them, with respect to the time of adjournment, he may adjourn them to such time as he shall think proper; he shall receive ambassadors and other public ministers; he shall take care that the laws be faithfully executed, and shall commission all the officers of the United States.

SECTION 4. IMPEACHMENT

The President, Vice President and all civil officers of the United States shall be removed from office on impeachment for, and conviction of, treason, bribery, or other high crimes and misdemeanors.

Article III Judicial Branch

SECTION 1. FEDERAL COURTS AND JUDGES

The judicial power of the United States shall be vested in one Supreme Court, and in such inferior courts as the Congress may from time to time ordain and establish. The judges, both of the supreme and inferior courts, shall hold their offices during good behaviour, and shall, at stated times, receive for their services a compensation, which shall not be diminished during their continuance in office.

SECTION 2. THE COURT'S AUTHORITY

1. **Judicial Power** The judicial power shall extend to all cases, in law and equity, arising under this Constitution, the laws of the United States, and treaties made, or which shall be made, under their authority;—to all cases affecting ambassadors, other public ministers and consuls;—to all cases of admiralty and maritime jurisdiction;—to controversies to which the United States

shall be a party;—to controversies between two or more states;—between a state and citizens of another state;—between citizens of different states;—between citizens of the same state claiming lands under grants of different states, and between a state, or the citizens thereof, and foreign states, citizens or subjects.

2. **Authority** In all cases affecting ambassadors, other public ministers and consuls, and those in which a state shall be party, the Supreme Court shall have original jurisdiction. In all the other cases before mentioned, the Supreme Court shall have appellate jurisdiction, both as to law and fact, with such exceptions, and under such regulations as the Congress shall make.

3. **Jury Trial** The trial of all crimes, except in cases of impeachment, shall be by jury; and such trial shall be held in the state where the said crimes shall have been committed; but when not committed within any state, the trial shall be at such place or places as the Congress may by law have directed.

SECTION 3. TREASON

1. **Definition of Treason** Treason against the United States shall consist only in levying war against them, or in adhering to their enemies, giving them aid and comfort. No person shall be convicted of treason unless on the testimony of two witnesses to the same overt act, or on confession in open court.

2. **Punishment of Treason** The Congress shall have power to declare the punishment of treason, but no attainder of treason shall work corruption of blood, or forfeiture except during the life of the person attainted.

Article IV Relations Among the States

SECTION 1. ACTS AND RECORDS

Full faith and credit shall be given in each state to the public acts, records, and judicial proceedings of every other state. And the Congress may by general laws prescribe the manner in which such acts, records, and proceedings shall be proved, and the effect thereof.

SECTION 2. RIGHTS OF CITIZENS

1. **Privileges of Citizens** The citizens of each state shall be entitled to all privileges and immunities of citizens in the several states.

2. **Extradition** A person charged in any state with treason, felony, or other crime, who shall flee from justice, and be found in another state, shall on demand of the executive authority of the state from which he fled, be delivered up, to be removed to the state having jurisdiction of the crime.

3. **Fugitive Slaves** No person held to service or labor in one state, under the laws thereof, escaping into another, shall, in consequence of any law or regulation therein, be discharged from such service or labor, but shall be delivered up on claim of the party to whom such service or labor may be due.

SECTION 3. NEW STATES

1. **Admission of States** New states may be admitted by the Congress into this union; but no new states shall be formed or erected within the jurisdiction of any other state; nor any state be formed by the junction of two or more states, or parts of states, without the consent of the legislatures of the states concerned as well as of the Congress.

2. **Congressional Authority** The Congress shall have power to dispose of and make all needful rules and regulations respecting the territory or other property belonging to the United States; and nothing in this Constitution shall be so construed as to prejudice any claims of the United States, or of any particular state.

SECTION 4. GUARANTEES TO STATES

The United States shall guarantee to every state in this union a republican form of government, and shall protect each of them against invasion; and on application of the legislature, or of the executive (when the legislature cannot be convened) against domestic violence.

Article V Amending the Constitution

The Congress, whenever two thirds of both houses shall deem it necessary, shall propose amendments to this Constitution, or, on the application of the legislatures of two thirds of the several states, shall call a convention for proposing amendments, which, in either case, shall be valid to all intents and purposes, as part of this Constitution, when ratified by the legislatures of three fourths of the several states, or by conventions in three fourths thereof, as the one or the other mode of ratification may be proposed by the Congress; provided that no amendment which may be made prior to the year one thousand eight hundred and eight shall in any manner affect the first and fourth clauses in the ninth section of the first article; and that no state, without its consent, shall be deprived of its equal suffrage in the Senate.

Article VI Supremacy of National Government

SECTION 1. VALID DEBTS

All debts contracted and engagements entered into, before the adoption of this Constitution, shall be as valid against the United States under this Constitution, as under the Confederation.

SECTION 2. SUPREME LAW

This Constitution, and the laws of the United States which shall be made in pursuance thereof; and all treaties made, or which shall be made, under the authority of the United States, shall be the supreme law of the land; and the judges in every state shall be bound thereby, anything in the Constitution or laws of any State to the contrary notwithstanding.

SECTION 3. LOYALTY TO THE CONSITUTION

The Senators and Representatives before mentioned, and the members of the several state legislatures, and all executive and judicial officers, both of the United States and of the several states, shall be bound by oath or affirmation, to support this Constitution; but no religious test shall ever be required as a qualification to any office or public trust under the United States.

Article VII Ratification

The ratification of the conventions of nine states shall be sufficient for the establishment of this Constitution between the states so ratifying the same.

Done in convention by the unanimous consent of the states present the seventeenth day of September in the year of our Lord one thousand seven hundred and eighty-seven and of the independence of the United States of America the twelfth. In witness whereof We have hereunto subscribed our Names,

G. Washington—Presidt. and deputy from Virginia

New Hampshire: John Langdon, Nicholas Gilman

Massachusetts: Nathaniel Gorham, Rufus King

Connecticut: Wm: Saml. Johnson, Roger Sherman

New York: Alexander Hamilton

New Jersey: Wil: Livingston, David Brearly, Wm. Paterson, Jona: Dayton

Pennsylvania: B. Franklin, Thomas Mifflin, Robt. Morris, Geo. Clymer, Thos. FitzSimons, Jared Ingersoll, James Wilson, Gouv Morris

Delaware: Geo: Read, Gunning Bedford jun, John Dickinson, Richard Bassett, Jaco: Broom

Maryland: James McHenry, Dan of St Thos. Jenifer, Danl Carroll

Virginia: John Blair—, James Madison, Jr.

North Carolina: Wm. Blount, Richd. Dobbs Spaight, Hu Williamson

South Carolina: J. Rutledge, Charles Cotesworth Pinckney, Charles Pinckney, Pierce Butler

Georgia: William Few, Abr Baldwin

THE BILL OF RIGHTS: AMENDMENTS 1–10

[These Amendments were ratified by Congress on December 15, 1791.]

The Conventions of a number of the States having, at the time of adopting the Constitution, expressed a desire, in order to prevent misconstruction or abuse of its powers, that further declaratory and restrictive clauses should be added, and as extending the ground of public confidence in the Government will best insure the beneficent ends of its institution;

Resolved, by the Senate and House of Representatives of the United States of America, in Congress assembled, two-thirds of both Houses concurring, that the following articles be proposed to the Legislatures of the several States, as amendments to the Constitution of the United States; all or any of which articles, when ratified by three-fourths of the said Legislatures, to be valid to all intents and purposes as part of the said Constitution, namely:

Amendment I. Religious and Political Freedom (1791)

Congress shall make no law respecting an establishment of religion, or prohibiting the free exercise thereof; or abridging the freedom of speech, or of the press; or the right of the people peaceably to assemble, and to petition the government for a redress of grievances.

Amendment II. Right to Bear Arms (1791)

A well regulated militia, being necessary to the security of a free state, the right of the people to keep and bear arms shall not be infringed.

Amendment III. Quartering Troops (1791)

No soldier shall, in time of peace, be quartered in any house, without the consent of the owner, nor in time of war, but in a manner to be prescribed by law.

Amendment IV. Search and Seizure (1791)

The right of the people to be secure in their persons, houses, papers, and effects, against unreasonable searches and seizures, shall not be violated, and no warrants shall issue, but upon probable cause, supported by oath or affirmation, and particularly describing the place to be searched, and the persons or things to be seized.

Amendment V. Rights of Accused Persons (1791)

No person shall be held to answer for a capital, or otherwise infamous crime, unless on a presentment or indictment of a grand jury, except in cases arising in the land or naval forces, or in the militia, when in actual service in time of war or public danger; nor shall any person be subject for the same offense to be twice put in jeopardy of life or limb; nor shall be compelled in any criminal case to be a witness against himself, nor be deprived of life, liberty, or property, without due process of law; nor shall private property be taken for public use, without just compensation.

Amendment VI Right to a Public Trial (1791)

In all criminal prosecutions, the accused shall enjoy the right to a speedy and public trial, by an impartial jury of the state and district wherein the crime shall have been committed, which district shall have been previously ascertained by law, and to be informed of the nature and cause of the accusation; to be confronted with the witnesses against him; to have compulsory process for obtaining witnesses in his favor, and to have the assistance of counsel for his defense.

Amendment VII Jury Trials in Civil Cases (1791)

In suits at common law, where the value in controversy shall exceed twenty dollars, the right of trial by jury shall be preserved, and no fact tried by a jury shall be otherwise reexamined in any court of the United States, than according to the rules of the common law.

Amendment VIII Criminal Punishment (1791)

Excessive bail shall not be required, nor excessive fines imposed, nor cruel and unusual punishments inflicted.

Amendment IX Rights of People (1791)

The enumeration in the Constitution, of certain rights, shall not be construed to deny or disparage others retained by the people.

Amendment X Powers of States and People (1791)

The powers not delegated to the United States by the Constitution, nor prohibited by it to the states, are reserved to the states respectively, or to the people.

THE OTHER AMENDMENTS 11–27

Amendment XI Lawsuits Against States (1798)

The judicial power of the United States shall not be construed to extend to any suit in law or equity, commenced or prosecuted against one of the United States by citizens of another state, or by citizens or subjects of any foreign state.

Amendment XII Election of the President and Vice President (1804)

The electors shall meet in their respective states and vote by ballot for President and Vice President, one of whom, at least, shall not be an inhabitant of the same state with themselves; they shall name in their ballots the person voted for as President, and in distinct ballots the person voted for as Vice President, and they shall make distinct lists of all persons voted for as President, and of all persons voted for as Vice President, and of the number of votes for each, which lists they shall sign and certify, and transmit sealed to the seat of the government of the United States, directed to the President of the Senate;—The President of the Senate shall, in the presence of the Senate and House of Representatives, open all the certificates and the votes shall then be counted;— the person having the greatest number of votes for President, shall be the President, if such number be a majority of the whole number of electors appointed; and if no person have such majority, then from the persons having the highest numbers not exceeding three on the list of those voted for as President, the House of Representatives shall choose immediately, by ballot, the President. But in choosing the President, the votes shall be taken by states, the representation from each state having one vote; a quorum for this purpose shall consist of a member or members from two-thirds of the states, and a majority of all the states shall be necessary to a choice. And if the House of Representatives shall not choose a President whenever the right of choice shall devolve upon them, before the fourth day of March next following, then the Vice President shall act as President, as in the case of the death or other constitutional disability of the President. The person having the greatest number of votes as Vice President, shall be the Vice President, if such number be a majority of the whole number of electors appointed, and if no person have a majority, then from the two highest numbers on the list, the Senate shall choose the Vice President; a quorum for the purpose shall consist of two-thirds of the whole number of Senators, and a majority of the whole number shall be necessary to a choice. But no person constitutionally ineligible to the office of President shall be eligible to that of Vice President of the United States.

Amendment XIII Abolition of Slavery (1865)

Section 1. Neither slavery nor involuntary servitude, except as a punishment for crime whereof the party shall have been duly convicted, shall exist within the United States, or any place subject to their jurisdiction.

Section 2. Congress shall have power to enforce this article by appropriate legislation.

Amendment XIV Citizenship and Civil Rights (1868)

Section 1. All persons born or naturalized in the United States, and subject to the jurisdiction thereof, are citizens of the United States and of the state wherein they reside. No state shall make or enforce any law which shall abridge the privileges or immunities of citizens of the United States; nor shall any state deprive any person of life, liberty, or property, without due process of law; nor deny to any person within its jurisdiction the equal protection of the laws.

Section 2. Representatives shall be apportioned among the several states according to their respective numbers, counting the whole number of persons in each state, excluding Indians not taxed. But when the right to vote at any election for the choice of electors for President and Vice President of the United States, Representatives in Congress, the executive and judicial officers of a state, or the members of the legislature thereof, is denied to any of the male inhabitants of such state, being twenty-one years of age, and citizens of the United States, or in any way abridged, except for participation in rebellion, or other crime, the basis of representation therein shall be reduced in the proportion which the number of

such male citizens shall bear to the
whole number of male citizens twenty-
one years of age in such state.

Section 3. No person shall be a Senator
or Representative in Congress, or elector
of President and Vice President, or hold
any office, civil or military, under the
United States, or under any state, who,
having previously taken an oath, as a
member of Congress, or as an officer of
the United States, or as a member of any
state legislature, or as an executive or
judicial officer of any state, to support
the Constitution of the United States,
shall have engaged in insurrection or
rebellion against the same, or given aid
or comfort to the enemies thereof. But
Congress may by a vote of two-thirds of
each House, remove such disability.

Section 4. The validity of the public
debt of the United States, authorized by
law, including debts incurred for payment of pensions and bounties for services in suppressing insurrection or
rebellion, shall not be questioned. But
neither the United States nor any state
shall assume or pay any debt or obligation incurred in aid of insurrection or
rebellion against the United States, or
any claim for the loss or emancipation of
any slave; but all such debts, obligations
and claims shall be held illegal and void.

Section 5. The Congress shall have
power to enforce, by appropriate legislation, the provisions of this article.

Amendment XV Right to Vote (1870)

Section 1. The right of citizens of the
United States to vote shall not be denied
or abridged by the United States or by
any state on account of race, color, or
previous condition of servitude.

Section 2. The Congress shall have
power to enforce this article by appropriate legislation.

Amendment XVI Income Tax (1913)

The Congress shall have power to lay
and collect taxes on incomes, from whatever source derived, without apportionment among the several states, and without regard to any census or enumeration.

**Amendment XVII Direct Election of
Senators (1913)**

1. The Senate of the United States shall
be composed of two Senators from each
state, elected by the people thereof, for
six years; and each Senator shall have one
vote. The electors in each state shall have
the qualifications requisite for electors of
the most numerous branch of the state
legislatures.

2. When vacancies happen in the representation of any state in the Senate, the
executive authority of such state shall
issue writs of election to fill such vacancies: Provided, that the legislature of any
state may empower the executive thereof
to make temporary appointments until
the people fill the vacancies by election
as the legislature may direct.

3. This amendment shall not be so construed as to affect the election or term of
any Senator chosen before it becomes
valid as part of the Constitution.

Amendment XVIII Prohibition (1919)

Section 1. ~~After one year from the ratification of this article the manufacture, sale, or transportation of intoxicating liquors within, the importation thereof into, or the exportation thereof from the United States and all territory subject to the jurisdiction thereof for beverage purposes is hereby prohibited.~~

Section 2. ~~The Congress and the several states shall have concurrent power to enforce this article by appropriate legislation.~~

Section 3. ~~This article shall be inoperative unless it shall have been ratified as an amendment to the Constitution by the legislatures of the several states, as provided in the Constitution, within seven years from the date of the submission hereof to the states by the Congress.~~

Amendment XIX Woman's Suffrage (1920)

The right of citizens of the United States to vote shall not be denied or abridged by the United States or by any state on account of sex.

Congress shall have power to enforce this article by appropriate legislation.

Amendment XX Terms, Congressional Sessions, and Presidential Succession (1933)

Section 1. The terms of the President and Vice President shall end at noon on the 20th day of January, and the terms of Senators and Representatives at noon on the 3d day of January, of the years in which such terms would have ended if this article had not been ratified; and the terms of their successors shall then begin.

Section 2. The Congress shall assemble at least once in every year, and such meeting shall begin at noon on the 3d day of January, unless they shall by law appoint a different day.

Section 3. If, at the time fixed for the beginning of the term of the President, the President elect shall have died, the Vice President elect shall become President. If a President shall not have been chosen before the time fixed for the beginning of his term, or if the President elect shall have failed to qualify, then the Vice President elect shall act as President until a President shall have qualified; and the Congress may by law provide for the case wherein neither a President elect nor a Vice President elect shall have qualified, declaring who shall then act as President, or the manner in which one who is to act shall be selected, and such person shall act accordingly until a President or Vice President shall have qualified.

Section 4. The Congress may by law provide for the case of the death of any of the persons from whom the House of Representatives may choose a President whenever the right of choice shall have devolved upon them, and for the case of the death of any of the persons from whom the Senate may choose a Vice President whenever the right of choice shall have devolved upon them.

Section 5. Sections 1 and 2 shall take effect on the 15th day of October following the ratification of this article.

Section 6. This article shall be inoperative unless it shall have been ratified as an amendment to the Constitution by the legislatures of three-fourths of the several states within seven years from the date of its submission.

Amendment XXI Repeal of Prohibition (1933)

Section 1. The eighteenth article of amendment to the Constitution of the United States is hereby repealed.

Section 2. The transportation or importation into any state, territory, or possession of the United States for delivery or use therein of intoxicating liquors, in violation of the laws thereof, is hereby prohibited.

Section 3. This article shall be inoperative unless it shall have been ratified as an amendment to the Constitution by conventions in the several states, as provided in the Constitution, within seven years from the date of the submission hereof to the states by the Congress.

Amendment XXII Limits on Presidential Terms (1951)

Section 1. No person shall be elected to the office of the President more than twice, and no person who has held the office of President, or acted as President, for more than two years of a term to which some other person was elected President shall be elected to the office of the President more than once. But this article shall not apply to any person holding the office of President when this article was proposed by the Congress, and shall not prevent any person who may be holding the office of President, or acting as President, during the term within which this article becomes operative from holding the office of President or acting as President during the remainder of such term.

Section 2. This article shall be inoperative unless it shall have been ratified as an amendment to the Constitution by the legislatures of three-fourths of the several states within seven years from the date of its submission to the states by the Congress.

Amendment XXIII Voting in District of Columbia (1961)

Section 1. The District constituting the seat of government of the United States shall appoint in such manner as the Congress may direct:

A number of electors of President and Vice President equal to the whole number of Senators and Representatives in Congress to which the District would be entitled if it were a state, but in no event more than the least populous state; they shall be in addition to those appointed by the states, but they shall be considered, for the purposes of the election of President and Vice President, to be electors appointed by a state; and they shall meet in the District and perform such duties as provided by the twelfth article of amendment.

Section 2. The Congress shall have power to enforce this article by appropriate legislation.

Amendment XXIV Abolition of Poll Taxes (1964)

Section 1. The right of citizens of the United States to vote in any primary or other election for President or Vice President, for electors for President or Vice President, or for Senator or Representative in Congress, shall not be denied or abridged by the United States or any state by reason of failure to pay any poll tax or other tax.

Section 2. The Congress shall have power to enforce this article by appropriate legislation.

Amendment XXV Presidential Succession, Disability, and the Vice Presidency (1967)

Section 1. In case of the removal of the President from office or of his death or resignation, the Vice President shall become President.

Section 2. Whenever there is a vacancy in the office of the Vice President, the President shall nominate a Vice President who shall take office upon confirmation by a majority vote of both Houses of Congress.

Section 3. Whenever the President transmits to the President pro tempore of the Senate and the Speaker of the House of Representatives his written declaration that he is unable to discharge the powers and duties of his office, and until he transmits to them a written declaration to the contrary, such powers and duties shall be discharged by the Vice President as Acting President.

Section 4. Whenever the Vice President and a majority of either the principal officers of the executive departments or of such other body as Congress may by law provide, transmit to the President pro tempore of the Senate and the Speaker of the House of Representatives their written declaration that the President is unable to discharge the powers and duties of his office, the Vice President shall immediately assume the powers and duties of the office as Acting President.

Thereafter, when the President transmits to the President pro tempore of the Senate and the Speaker of the House of Representatives his written declaration that no inability exists, he shall resume the powers and duties of his office unless the Vice President and a majority of either the principal officers of the executive department or of such other body as Congress may by law provide, transmit within four days to the President pro tempore of the Senate and the Speaker of the House of Representatives their written declaration that the President is unable to discharge the powers and duties of his office. Thereupon Congress shall decide the issue, assembling within forty-eight hours for that purpose if not in session. If the Congress, within twenty-one days after receipt of the latter written declaration, or, if Congress is not in session, within twenty-one days after Congress is required to assemble, determines by two-thirds vote of both Houses that the President is unable to discharge the powers and duties of his office, the Vice President shall continue to discharge the same as Acting President; otherwise, the President shall resume the powers and duties of his office.

Amendment XXVI 18-Year-Old Right to Vote (1971)

Section 1. The right of citizens of the United States, who are 18 years of age or older, to vote, shall not be denied or abridged by the United States or any state on account of age.

Section 2. The Congress shall have the power to enforce this article by appropriate legislation.

Amendment XXVII Congressional Pay (1992)

No law varying the compensation for the services of the Senators and Representatives shall take effect until an election of Representatives shall have intervened.

Constitutional Trivia

★ Seventy-four delegates to the Constitutional Convention were selected by 12 states, but only 55 of them attended.

★ No more than 30 delegates were usually present at any one time.

★ Rhode Island decided not to send a delegate.

★ The average age of the delegates was 44.

★ The oldest was Benjamin Franklin (PA), at 81; the youngest was Jonathan Dayton (NJ), at 26.

★ Of the 55 delegates, 34 were lawyers.

★ Eight of the men had signed the Declaration of Independence.

★ The delegates kept their deliberations secret. Two days after the convention adjourned, a Philadelphia newspaper published the entire Constitution.

★ Three delegates—Edmund Randolph, Elbridge Gerry, and George Mason— chose not to sign the document. Mason opposed the Constitution the rest of his life, but Randolph later supported ratification, and Gerry became Vice President under Madison.

★ It took fewer than 100 working days for the Constitution to be drafted.

★ Delaware was the first state to ratify the Constitution, in a unanimous vote on December 7, 1787. Rhode Island was the last state to ratify, after a 34–32 vote on May 29, 1790.

Federalists and Anti-Federalists

The Federalist (or the *Federalist* papers) is a group of 85 essays originally written as newspaper articles in 1787–1788. In them, John Jay, Alexander Hamilton, and James Madison analyzed the document and tried to move public opinion toward ratification. The Anti-Federalists, who opposed the Constitution, raised their objections in letters, articles, and speeches.

THE FEDERALIST NO. 1

THE
FEDERALIST:
A COLLECTION
OF
E S S A Y S,
WRITTEN IN FAVOUR OF THE
NEW CONSTITUTION,
AS AGREED UPON BY THE FEDERAL CONVENTION,
SEPTEMBER 17, 1787.

IN TWO VOLUMES.

VOL. I.

NEW-YORK:
PRINTED AND SOLD BY J. AND A. M'LEAN,
No. 41, HANOVER-SQUARE.
M,DCC,LXXXVIII.

"It has been frequently remarked that it seems to have reserved to the people of this country, by their conduct and example, to decide the important question, whether societies of men are really capable or not of establishing good government from reflection and choice, or whether they are forever destined to depend for their political constitutions on accident and force."

—*James Madison (1787)*

Corbis–Bettman

James Madison was born in 1751 to a prosperous Virginia family. He helped draft Virginia's state constitution, served in the Continental Congress from 1780 to 1783, and became the nation's fourth President. Because of his leadership, he is called the Father of the Constitution. Before Madison died in 1836, he was the last remaining Framer of the Constitution.

THE FEDERALIST NO. 45

"The powers delegated by the proposed Constitution to the federal government are few and defined. Those which are to remain in the state governments are numerous and indefinite."

—*James Madison (1787)*

THE FEDERALIST NO. 51

"In the extended republic of the United States, and among the great variety of interests, parties, and sects which it embraces, a coalition of a majority of the whole
society could seldom take place on any other principles than those of justice and the
general good."

James Madison (1788)

ANTI-FEDERALIST RESPONSE

"Every man of reflection must see that the change now proposed is a transfer of
power from the many to the few, and the probability is the artful and ever active
aristocracy will prevent peaceful measures for changes, unless when they shall
discover some favorable moment to increase their own influence."

Richard Henry Lee,
"Letters from the Federal Farmer to the Republican" (1787)

"We dissent . . . because the powers vested in Congress by this Constitution must
necessarily annihilate and absorb the legislative, executive, and judicial powers of the
several states, and produce from their ruins one consolidated government, which
from the nature of things will be an iron-handed despotism. . . ."

"The first consideration that this review suggests is the omission of a Bill of Rights
ascertaining and fundamentally establishing those unalienable and personal rights of
men, without the full, free, and secure enjoyment of which there can be no liberty. . . ."

William Findley, Robert Whitehill, and John Smilie,
"The Address and Reasons of Dissent of the Minority of the Convention of the State of
Pennsylvania to their Constitutents" (1787)

"In a word, the new constitution will prove finally to dissolve all the power of the
several state legislatures, and destroy the rights and liberties of the people; for
the power of the first will be all in all, and of the latter a mere shadow and form
without substance."

Robert Yates,
in the New York Daily Patriotic Register *(1788)*

Thoughts on the Constitution

"I first saw the Constitution of the United States in a foreign country. Irritated by no literary altercation, animated by no public debate, heated by no party animosity, I read it with great satisfaction, as the result of good heads prompted by good hearts, as an experiment better adapted to the genius, character, situation, and relations of this nation and country than any which had ever been proposed or suggested."

President John Adams, First Inaugural Address (1787)

"We must never forget that it is . . . a Constitution intended to endure for ages to come, and, consequently, to be adapted to the various crises of human affairs."

Chief Justice John Marshall, McCulloch v. Maryland (1819)

"When they [the Founders] found, after a short trial, that the confederacy of States was too weak to meet the necessities of a vigorous and expanding republic, they boldly set it aside, and in its stead established a National Union, founded directly upon the will of the people, endowed with full power of self-preservation and ample authority for the accomplishment of its great object."

President James A. Garfield, First Inaugural Address (1881)

"Our Constitution of 1787 was not a perfect instrument; it is not perfect yet. But it provided a firm base upon which all manner of men, of all races and colors and creeds, could build our solid structure of democracy."

President Franklin D. Roosevelt, Fourth Inaugural Address (1945)

"And the American Founders were themselves mixes of worldliness and intellect, self-interest and nobility. If they had been only brilliant and noble, they might not have won the Revolution. If they had been only worldly and self-interested, there would have been little to win."

Eugene McCarthy, former Senator and 1968 presidential candidate
No-Fault Politics: Modern Presidents, the Press, and Reformers (1998)

Government of the United States

THE CONSTITUTION

LEGISLATIVE BRANCH

Congress

Senate   House

Architect of the Capitol

United States Botanic Garden

General Accounting Office

Government Printing Office

Library of Congress

Congressional Budget Office

EXECUTIVE BRANCH

President

Vice President

Executive Office of the President

White House Office

Office of the Vice President

Council of Economic Advisers

Council on Environmental Quality

National Security Council

Office of Administration

Office of Management and Budget

Office of National Drug Control Policy

Office of Policy Development

Office of Science and Technology Policy

Office of the U.S. Trade Representative

JUDICIAL BRANCH

Supreme Court of the United States

United States Courts of Appeals

United States District Courts

Territorial Courts

United States Court of International Trade

United States Court of Federal Claims

United States Court of Appeals for the Armed Forces

United States Tax Court

United States Court of Veterans Appeals

Administrative Office of the United States Courts

Federal Judicial Center

United States Sentencing Commission

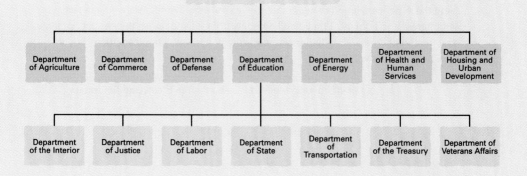

Department of Agriculture	Department of Commerce	Department of Defense	Department of Education	Department of Energy	Department of Health and Human Services	Department of Housing and Urban Development

Department of the Interior	Department of Justice	Department of Labor	Department of State	Department of Transportation	Department of the Treasury	Department of Veterans Affairs

2 | Voting, Elections, and Public Opinion

Election 1998

★ Voter turnout was estimated at 38 percent. Since 1970, the voter turnout in midterm elections has been between 37 percent and 40 percent.

★ Less than 20 percent of eligible voters aged 18 to 24 went to the polls.

BALANCE OF POWER

	OLD	NEW	+/−
Senate			
Republicans	55	55	0
Democrats	45	45	0
House			
Republicans	228	221	−7
Democrats	206	211	+5
Independents	1	1	0
Governorships			
Republicans	32	31	−1
Democrats	17	17	0
Independents	1	2	+1

* Numbers cited from the beginning of first session, excluding vacancies.

Source: CNN

- In picking up 5 seats in the House, the Democrats bucked historical tradition. Not since 1934 has the party in control of the White House gained seats in an off-year election. Since World War II, losses in the House have averaged 27 seats.

- Democrats gained about 45 state legislature seats nationwide and made a net gain of 3 legislative chambers.

CONTROVERSIAL ISSUES—1998

- California voters approved slot machines and unrestricted expansion of gambling on Native American land.

- Voters in Hawaii approved a constitutional amendment giving their state legislature the power to ban same-sex marriage.

- Michigan voters rejected a proposal that would have legalized physician-assisted suicide.

- In Alaska, Arizona, Nevada, and Washington state, voters supported a variety of ballot measures allowing the medical use of marijuana and protecting doctors who recommend its use to ease pain and nausea for some patients.

- Voters in the state of Washington approved an initiative to abolish most of their government affirmative action programs.

1996 Presidential Election

- Bill Clinton received 49 percent of the popular vote (379 electoral votes).

- Bob Dole received 41 percent of the popular vote (159 electoral votes).

- Ross Perot received 8 percent of the popular vote (0 electoral votes).

- In 1996, 2.4 million fewer voters aged 18 to 24 went to the polls than four years earlier.

520

1996 PRESIDENTIAL ELECTION EXIT POLL RESULTS

	CLINTON	DOLE	PEROT
Men	43%	44%	10%
Women	54%	38%	7%
White	43%	46%	9%
African Americans	84%	12%	4%
Hispanics	72%	21%	6%
Asians	43%	48%	8%
Other	64%	21%	9%
18–29 years	53%	34%	10%
30–44 years	48%	41%	9%
45–59 years	48%	41%	9%
Over 60 years	48%	44%	7%
18–64 years	49%	40%	9%
65 years and older	50%	43%	6%
Less than $15,000	59%	28%	11%
$15–30,000	53%	36%	9%
$30–50,000	48%	40%	10%
$50–75,000	47%	45%	7%
$75–100,000	44%	48%	7%
Over $100,000	38%	54%	6%
Democrat	84%	10%	5%
Republican	13%	80%	6%
Independent	43%	35%	17%
No High School	59%	28%	11%
High School Graduate	51%	35%	13%
Some College	48%	40%	10%
College Graduate	44%	46%	8%
Post Graduate	52%	40%	5%
No College Degree	51%	37%	11%

Source: CNN; sample size 16,359

STATE	CLINTON	DOLE	PEROT	ELECTORAL VOTE CLINTON	ELECTORAL VOTE DOLE
Alabama	662,165	769,044	92,149	—	9
Alaska	80,380	122,746	26,333	—	3
Arizona	653,288	622,073	112,072	8	—
Arkansas	475,171	325,416	69,884	6	—
California	5,119,835	3,828,380	697,847	54	—
Colorado	671,152	691,848	99,629	—	8
Connecticut	735,740	483,109	139,523	8	—
Delaware	140,355	99,062	28,719	3	—
District of Columbia	158,220`	17,339	3,611	3	—
Florida	2,546,870	2,244,536	483,870	25	—
Georgia	1,053,849	1,080,843	146,337	—	13
Hawaii	205,012	113,943	27,358	4	—
Idaho	165,443	256,595	62,518	—	4
Illinois	2,341,744	1,587,021	346,408	22	—
Indiana	887,424	1,006,693	224,299	—	12
Iowa	620,258	492,644	105,159	7	—
Kansas	387,659	583,245	92,639	—	6
Kentucky	636,614	623,283	120,396	8	—
Louisiana	927,837	712,586	123,293	9	—
Maine	312,788	186,378	85,970	4	—
Maryland	966,207	681,530	115,812	10	—
Massachusetts	1,571,763	718,107	227,217	12	—
Michigan	1,989,653	1,481,212	336,670	18	—
Minnesota	1,120,438	766,476	257,704	10	—
Mississippi	394,022	439,838	52,222	—	7
Missouri	1,025,935	890,016	217,188	11	—
Montana	167,922	179,652	55,229	—	3
Nebraska	236,761	363,467	71,278	—	5
Nevada	203,974	199,244	43,986	4	—

CONTINUED

1996 PRESIDENTIAL ELECTION RESULTS CONTINUED

STATE	CLINTON	DOLE	PEROT	ELECTORAL VOTE CLINTON	ELECTORAL VOTE DOLE
New Hampshire	246,214	196,532	48,390	4	—
New Jersey	1,652,329	1,103,078	262,134	15	—
New Mexico	273,495	232,751	32,257	5	—
New York	3,756,177	1,933,492	503,458	33	—
North Carolina	1,107,849	1,225,938	168,059	—	14
North Dakota	106,905	125,050	32,515	—	3
Ohio	2,148,222	1,859,883	483,207	21	—
Oklahoma	488,105	582,315	130,788	—	8
Oregon	649,641	538,152	121,221	7	—
Pennsylvania	2,215,819	1,801,169	430,984	23	—
Rhode Island	233,050	104,683	43,723	4	—
South Carolina	506,283	573,458	64,386	—	8
South Dakota	139,333	150,543	31,250	—	3
Tennessee	909,146	863,530	105,918	11	—
Texas	2,459,683	2,276,167	378,537	—	32
Utah	221,663	361,911	66,461	—	5
Vermont	137,894	80,352	31,024	3	—
Virginia	1,091,060	1,138,350	159,861	—	13
Washington	1,123,323	840,712	201,003	11	—
West Virginia	327,812	233,946	71,639	5	—
Wisconsin	1,071,971	845,029	227,339	11	—
Wyoming	77,934	105,388	25,928	—	3
Total	**47,402,357**	**39,198,755**	**8,085,402**	**379**	**159**
	49.24%	**40.71%**	**8.40%**	Total electoral vote = 538 Total electoral vote needed to win = 270	

Source: *The Wall Street Journal Almanac,* 1998

Recent Presidential Elections

Richard Nixon's election in 1968 began a period of divided government. For the most part, the party that has captured the presidency has not also controlled Congress.

POPULAR VOTE FOR PRESIDENT BY MAJOR POLITICAL PARTY

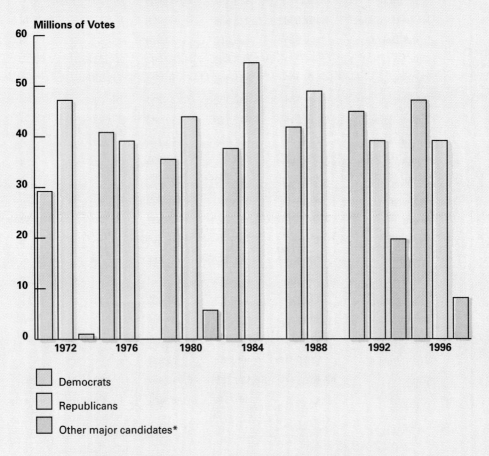

Democrats

Republicans

Other major candidates*

* 1972—American, John Schmitz; 1980—Independent, John Anderson;
1992—Independent, Ross Perot; 1996—Reform, Ross Perot

Source: U.S. Bureau of the Census

Campaign Financing: Facts and Trends

THE RUSH FOR MONEY

★ Political fund-raisers estimate that a viable presidential candidate in campaign 2000 must raise between $22 million and $25 million by the end of 1999. That amounts to more than $60,000 a day.

★ The candidate with the most cash at the end of the year before the election has become the party's nominee in the past five elections.

★ The cost of presidential campaigns has steadily increased. In 1992, presidential candidates spent about $296 million. According to Federal Election Commission (FEC) records, in 1996 presidential candidates spent more than $393 million.

★ The amount the government is contributing to presidential campaigns is rising fast. In 1996, Clinton and Dole received $61.8 million from the FEC. In 1976, the amount of federal campaign money awarded to candidates was $21.8 million.

★ In 1998 congressional races, the fund-raising total was $665.1 million for Senate and House candidates. That's a slight increase over the $659.6 million raised in 1996.

POLITICAL PARTIES AND FUND-RAISING

★ Fund-raising by both major political parties increased substantially during the 1995–1996 election cycle. Republican party committees at the national, state, and local levels reported a 62 percent increase, and Democratic committees reported a 36 percent increase over their spending in the 1991–92 election cycle.

★ Democratic and Republican parties raised $628 million for the 1998 midterm election, an increase of 41 percent compared to the same period from the 1994 midterm election.

★ Both parties raised much more soft money than in previous years. Republicans' soft money accounts in the 1998 election showed a 112 percent increase compared to the 1994 midterm election, and Democrats' accounts an 82 percent increase.

Sources: Sheila Kaplan. "Campaign 2000, by the numbers." *U.S. News & World Report,* January 18, 1999, 20-21; Federal Election Commission

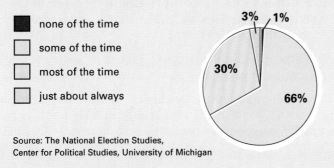

Snapshot of Public Opinion

The National Election Studies has asked people to characterize the trust they have not in Democrats or Republicans, but in government in general. The question they ask is "How much of the time do you think you can trust the government in Washington to do what is right—just about always, most of the time or only some of the time?" Consider these results from 1996:

■ none of the time
□ some of the time
□ most of the time
□ just about always

3% 1%
30%
66%

Source: The National Election Studies,
Center for Political Studies, University of Michigan

POLL RESULTS: *What do you think is the most important problem facing this country today?*

The top five answers, based on telephone interviews with a randomly selected national sample of adults, were as follows:

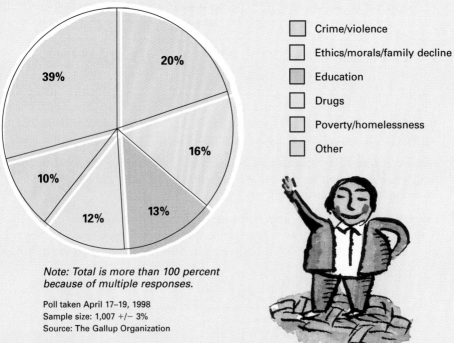

39%
20%
16%
10%
12%
13%

□ Crime/violence
□ Ethics/morals/family decline
□ Education
□ Drugs
□ Poverty/homelessness
□ Other

Note: Total is more than 100 percent because of multiple responses.

Poll taken April 17–19, 1998
Sample size: 1,007 +/− 3%
Source: The Gallup Organization

Political Campaigns, Advertising, and the Media

The Committee for the Study of the American Electorate reports that spending on political advertising, primarily on television, is the driving force behind increasing campaign costs. Between 1976 and 1992, for instance, political advertising costs in House races climbed by more than 196 percent.

"Campaign media is not only the principal cause of increased campaign cost, it is also a principal cause of voter disaffection and the decivilizing of the American dialogue."

Curtis Gans, Director, Committee for the Study of the American Electorate (1998)

More than half of all voters said they got most of their information about the 1996 presidential race from television, 17 percent from newspapers, 11 percent from radio, 2 percent from magazines, and less than 1 percent from the Internet. In the same report from the Research Group of the Media Studies Center, 83 percent of a random sample of 2,000 voters worried that media coverage leads candidates to perform for cameras rather than focus on issues.

Negative political television advertising was born in 1964 in the presidential race between Democrat Lyndon Johnson and Republican Barry Goldwater. In hopes of presenting Goldwater as a radical who wouldn't hesitate to use nuclear warfare, a Johnson ad featured a little girl picking daisy petals. She looks startled, as the video cuts to the mushroom cloud from an atomic bomb explosion. A male voice states, "We must either love each other, or we must die," and the phrase "Vote for President Johnson on Nov. 5" fills the screen.

Source: *Advertising Age*

Corbis

Courtesy of Lyndon Baines Johnson Library

3 | Congress

Profile of the 106th Congress

U.S. HOUSE

221 Republicans

211 Democrats

1 Independent

Speaker of the House	Dennis Hastert (R–IL)
Majority Leader	Dick Armey (R–TX)
Majority Whip	Tom DeLay (R–TX)
Minority Leader	Dick Gephardt (D–MO)
Minority Whip	David Bonior (D–MI)

U.S. SENATE

55 Republicans

45 Democrats

President of the Senate	Vice President Al Gore
President *Pro Tempore*	Strom Thurmond (R–SC)
Majority Leader	Trent Lott (R–MS)
Majority Whip	Don Nickles (R–OK)
Minority Leader	Thomas Daschle (D–SD)
Minority Whip	Harry Reid (D–NV)

Note: Figures and leadership as of January of 1999.

★ The current annual salary for members of Congress is $136,673.

★ Two senators and 13 representatives are physicians.

★ The one Independent serving in Congress is Representative Bernard Sanders from Vermont.

★ Only 7 of the 401 House incumbents and 3 of the 34 Senate incumbents were defeated in the 1998 elections.

★ In the Senate, 8 members are freshmen, and in the House, the newcomers total 40.

★ The Republican party's only African-American lawmaker is J. C. Watts of Oklahoma, the chair of the House Republican Conference.

★ In the House, the most common occupation of representatives of the 106th Congress is law (162), followed by business (160). The average age of House members is 52.6 years, with 32 members under the age of 40.

Courtesy of the Office of the Speaker

Dennis Hastert, an Illinois Congressman with a solid conservative voting record, took his place as Speaker of the House at the opening of the 106th Congress in January of 1999. In a short opening speech, Hastert called for a spirit of bipartisanship and admitted that "Hastert is not exactly a household name across America." The former high school teacher, wrestling coach, and state legislator was the consensus choice of the House Republicans after a series of dramatic events following the midterm elections in 1998.

First, **Newt Gingrich** gave up the Speaker's job under pressure after a poor Republican showing in the November 1998 elections. For only the second time since the Civil War, the party not in control of the White House lost seats in a midterm election. **Rep. Bob Livingston,** of Louisiana, was chosen to succeed Gingrich, but he never assumed the position. In December 1998, the day the House voted to impeach President Clinton, Livingston acknowledged having an extramarital affair and stepped aside.

Born in 1942 in Aurora, Illinois, Hastert is a graduate of Wheaton College and Northern Illinois University. First elected to the House of Representatives in 1986, Hastert served as the House Republicans' Chief deputy whip from 1995 to 1999 and earned a reputation for his plain talk and low-key persuasive talents. Explaining in 1998 what his political priorities as Speaker would be, Hastert promised "to make a particular effort to build bridges across the aisle, not just to pass legislation, but to ensure that common-sense ideas and principles become law."

Recent Congresses

	HOUSE OF REPRESENTATIVES						SENATE					
	101st	102nd	103rd	104th	105th	106th	101st	102nd	103rd	104th	105th	106th
Democrats	259	267	258	204	206	211	55	56	57	48	45	45
Republicans	174	167	176	230	228	221	45	44	43	52	55	55
Independents/ Other	—	1	1	1	1	1	—	—	—	—	—	—
Women	25	28	47	47	53	58	2	2	7	8	9	9
Men	408	407	388	388	382	375	98	98	93	92	91	91
African Americans	24	25	38	40	39	39	—	—	1	1	1	—
Hispanic Americans	10	11	17	17	21	19	—	—	—	—	—	—
Asian/Pacific Islanders	5	3	4	4	5	4	2	2	2	2	2	2
Native Americans	—	—	—	—	—	—	1	1	1	1	1	1

Note: Numbers cited from the beginning of first session, excluding vacancies

Sources: *Congressional Quarterly;* U.S. Bureau of the Census

CONGRESSIONAL TRIVIA

★ Carl T. Hayden of Arizona has the all-time record for length of service. Hayden served a total of 56 years, 10 months, and 28 days (in the House from 1912 to 1927 and then in the Senate between 1927 and 1969).

★ Strom Thurmond (SC) is the longest-serving member of the Senate. He began serving on November 7, 1956, in the second session of the 84th Congress.

★ John Dingell (MI) is the longest-serving member of the House. He began his service on December 13, 1955, in the first session of the 84th Congress.

1998—THE YEAR OF PARTISAN VOTING

The December 1998 vote in the House to impeach President Clinton followed party lines. Indeed 1998 was marked by a rise in partisan voting in Congress. The Republicans and Democrats voiced strong differences on such emotional issues as abortion, school vouchers, affirmative action, gay rights, and the minimum wage.

An analysis of 1998 roll-call votes done by *Congressional Quarterly* found that 56 percent of the votes in both the House and Senate pitted a majority of one party against a majority of the other. That figure represents an increase of about 5 percentage points over 1997 votes. The spirit of bipartisanship marked the first year of the 105th Congress, symbolized by the balanced-budget agreement of 1997 in which Democrats and Republicans agreed on a plan to eliminate the deficit in five years.

In 1998, parties battled over the sampling in the 2000 census, "partial birth" abortion, managed health care, tobacco-related lawsuits, and campaign finance. Despite the party-line votes, Congress did reach bipartisan agreement on some significant legislation in 1998: Internal Revenue Service reforms, an overhaul of housing programs, and reauthorization of Head Start.

"Partisan feelings have been rubbed raw."

—*Representative David E. Price (D-NC), 1999*

PARTY STRENGTH

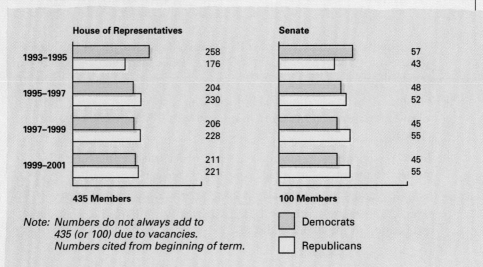

	House of Representatives		Senate	
1993–1995		258		57
		176		43
1995–1997		204		48
		230		52
1997–1999		206		45
		228		55
1999–2001		211		45
		221		55

435 Members   100 Members

Note: Numbers do not always add to
435 (or 100) due to vacancies.
Numbers cited from beginning of term.

☐ Democrats

☐ Republicans

Lobbying

According to statistics from the Center for Responsive Politics, lobbying in 1997 was a $1.26 billion business, with more than 11,500 lobbyists reporting their efforts to sway Congress and the executive branch. That's more than 21 active lobbyists and some $2.4 million in lobbying expenses for each member of Congress. The stricter reporting requirements in the Lobbying Disclosure Act of 1995 make it easier to tally how much money really does change hands.

TOP 10 SPENDERS, 1997

1.	American Medical Association	$17.28 million
2.	Philip Morris	$15.80 million
3.	Bell Atlantic	$15.67 million
4.	U.S. Chamber of Commerce	$14.24 million
5.	General Motors	$10.60 million
6.	Boeing Co.	$10.02 million
7.	Edison Electric Institute	$10.02 million
8.	Pfizer Inc.	$10.00 million
9.	American Automobile Manufacturers Association	$9.92 million
10.	Business Roundtable	$9.48 million

According to the Center for Responsive Politics, many of the biggest spenders on Capitol lobbying in 1997 were—not surprisingly—effective in getting their way.

★ The American Medical Association has been successful in getting efforts to ease restrictions on managed health care plans high on the congressional agenda.

★ Tobacco company Philip Morris has so far succeeded in avoiding new regulations meant to discourage smoking by teenagers.

★ Bell Atlantic won federal approval of its 1997 merger with NYNEX, despite the 1996 telecommunications act that was intended to spur more competition in the phone industry.

Source: Center for Responsive Politics

Congressional Milestones

1794—THE END OF SECRECY

For the first five years the Senate conducted its business in secret, meeting in New York and Philadelphia behind closed doors. The House had immediately opened its doors to the public, however. By 1795 public pressure had encouraged the Senate to allow a public gallery for visitors.

1830s–1860s—POWERFUL ORATORS

Many of the nation's most talented speakers and leading political figures had joined the Senate: Daniel Webster, John C. Calhoun, and Henry Clay. Divisive debate over states' rights, slavery, and secession marked this time period. Southern members resigned from the Senate as their states seceded, and the new Republican party became the majority. Members began to sit together according to party membership, and committee assignments began to be made based on political party caucuses.

Corbis

Henry Clay (1777–1852)

Born in Virginia, Clay served as both a senator and a representative from Kentucky. He was a powerful Speaker of the House in several Congresses, a secretary of state under John Quincy Adams, and three-time unsuccessful candidate for President—each time running under a different party: the Democratic-Republicans in 1824, the National Republican party in 1832, and the Whig party in 1844. Known as the "Great Compromiser" for his efforts to resolve disputes about slavery, Clay also advocated America's westward expansion.

Daniel Webster (1782–1852)

A champion of a strong national government, Daniel Webster represented New Hampshire in both the House and the Senate. Webster was a graduate of Dartmouth College, a successful lawyer, and one of the best-known orators of his time. Active in the Whig party, he ran unsuccessfully for President in 1836. Webster served as secretary of state under Presidents William Henry Harrison, John Tyler, and Millard Fillmore.

1917—FIRST WOMAN REPRESENTATIVE

Corbis

In 1917, **Jeannette Rankin** (1880–1973) became the first woman to be elected to Congress, three years before the 19th Amendment giving women the right to vote was passed. Born in 1880 near Missoula, Montana, Rankin was a college graduate, a social worker, and an active supporter of woman's suffrage efforts. Elected as a Republican to the 65th Congress, Rankin did not seek re-election. She ran unsuccessfully for the Senate and resumed her social work before being elected to the 77th Congress in 1941. Rankin remained a leader and lobbyist for peace and women's rights until her death.

1919—DEFEAT OF THE LEAGUE OF NATIONS

A series of weak Presidents after Abraham Lincoln helped the Senate to become the strongest part of the legislative branch of the government. But by the beginning of the twentieth century, Presidents **Theodore Roosevelt** and **Woodrow Wilson** had begun to challenge the Senate's authority and bring back power to the White House. Still, the Senate delivered a major defeat to Wilson by rejecting the Treaty of Versailles, which ended World War I and created the League of Nations. A group of senators, led by Republican **Henry Cabot Lodge,** refused to vote for the treaty without attaching reservations that Wilson opposed. After rejecting the treaty, Wilson declared that the 1920 presidential contest between **Warren G. Harding**—who opposed the treaty— and **James G. Cox**—who supported it—should be considered a public forum on the treaty. Harding won in an overwhelming victory. Wilson's fight for the League of Nations was over once and for all.

1946—LEGISLATIVE ACTION AND REORGANIZATION

President **Franklin D. Roosevelt's** New Deal programs of the 1930s prompted a flurry of legislative activity designed to lift the country out of the Great Depression. The 1946 Legislative Reorganization Act was a major turning point in Senate history. It reorganized the committee system and provided the first professional staff for senators and committees. As a result, the size of the federal bureaucracy greatly increased.

1954—McCARTHYISM

An atmosphere of fear and intimidation swept through America during the 1950s as Senator **Joseph McCarthy** claimed that numerous communists held government positions. As chairman of a subcommittee of the Senate Government Operations Committee, McCarthy launched investigations into possible communist influence. His targets ranged from the State Department and the armed services to the media and Hollywood. His baseless accusations harmed many innocent people. When McCarthy's investigation of the U.S. Army was televised in 1954, public sentiment turned against McCarthy. A special bipartisan committee began hearings on a censure resolution, with the quiet support of President **Dwight Eisenhower**. The Senate formally censured McCarthy in November 1954. He lost his subcommittee chairmanship the next year but continued to serve in the Senate until his death in 1957. Today the term *McCarthyism* has come to mean unfounded character attacks.

1964—CIVIL RIGHTS LEGISLATION

Heated congressional debates and lengthy filibusters over civil rights policies characterized much of the 1950s and 1960s. In 1964, for instance, the Senate took 57 working days to consider the Civil Rights Act of 1964. Finally, on the morning of June 14, after Senator **Robert Byrd** completed a 14-hour speech, the Senate invoked cloture to end the debate. Nine days later, the Senate approved the act, which stated that no person may be denied access to or refused service in various public places because of race, color, religion, or national origin. It is considered the most far-reaching of the civil rights statutes of the late 1950s and 1960s.

Corbis

1973–1978—WATERGATE AND THE INDEPENDENT COUNSEL STATUTE

In the mid-1970s Congress struggled to assert itself and its authority against that of the President and the executive branch. The efforts of President **Richard Nixon** and his aides to block an investigation of a 1972 break-in at the offices of the Democratic National Committee led to a political crisis known as Watergate. Nationally televised Senate hearings severely damaged the public's faith in the President—and government in general. In July of 1974, the House Judiciary Committee recommended that Nixon be impeached for obstruction of justice, abuse of presidential power, and contempt of Congress. To avoid impeachment and the likelihood of conviction in the Senate, Nixon resigned.

The Independent Counsel Statute, signed by President **Jimmy Carter** in 1978, was a direct result of the Watergate scandal. Presidents had long had the power to appoint special prosecutors to investigate corruption. But after Nixon ordered his attorney general to fire the prosecutor investigating him, government officials felt there should be someone with authority outside of the executive branch. Supporters felt that the appointment of an independent counsel—upon the recommendation of the attorney general and selected by three federal judges—would effectively check the conduct of high officials in the executive branch. However, **Kenneth Starr's** exhaustive and expensive investigation of President **Bill Clinton's** land deals and personal behavior in the 1990s jeopardized the future of the independent counsel. Critics complained about the lack of accountability. Once appointed, independent counsels have no limits on their spending, may expand their jurisdictions fairly easily, are difficult to fire, and don't fall clearly under the supervision of the Justice Department.

1983—THE EQUAL RIGHTS AMENDMENT, AGAIN

In 1983, the Equal Rights Amendment (ERA) was reintroduced to Congress. In essence it stated that "Equality of rights under the law shall not be denied or abridged by the United States or by any State on account of sex." This was not the first time members of Congress had been asked to consider such a bill. From 1923 to 1971 some form of an Equal Rights Amendment had been introduced in Congress annually. In 1972, the time seemed right for its passage. The Senate and House approved it quickly and by big margins. Public opinion was favorable, and both political parties supported its passage. It was approved quickly in 22 of the 38 states needed for ratification.

However, opposition soon grew, and a multi-year struggle began—with heated debates, protests, rallies, and economic boycotts of states that didn't ratify it. The Republican party withdrew its endorsement, and several states voted to withdraw their approval. Even with an extension of the original ratification deadline, the ERA fell three states short of passage in 1982. After it was reintroduced, the House defeated the proposal to resubmit it to the states the next year. Since 1984, the ERA has been reintroduced in every session of Congress, but it has never been approved with the necessary two-thirds majority.

4 | Presidents and the Presidency

Presidential Milestones

Corbis

1829—THE INAUGURATION OF ANDREW JACKSON

The election of Andrew Jackson is often seen as a turning point in ideas about the presidency. Jackson made an effort to establish a direct relationship between himself and the people. In fact, his presidency got off to a wild start. The first President born in a log cabin and born west of the Allegheny Mountains, he was also the first President not descended from an aristocratic family. At his inauguration in 1829, a huge crowd of people—city workers, farmers, old soldiers, western pioneers—descended on Washington, D.C. The White House reception turned into chaos, with a crowd of 20,000 people pouring into the White House through windows, spilling whiskey, breaking china, and spitting tobacco juice.

1861—LINCOLN'S WAR POWERS

In February 1961, seven southern states seceded from the United States to form the Confederate States of America. President **James Buchanan** had told Congress that he had no constitutional power to stop them. However, the next President, **Abraham Lincoln,** disagreed. He used his March 1861 inaugural address to warn the states that he would not let them leave. Lincoln again acted on his own authority to delay the meeting of Congress, mobilize militia, increase the size of the army and navy, blockade southern ports, and suspend the writ of *habeas corpus.* Lincoln established important precedents that demonstrated the President's ability to expand his powers in a national emergency.

1901-1909—THEODORE ROOSEVELT'S POWERS

Theodore Roosevelt dominated the U.S. political scene in the first decade of the twentieth century. He believed that the President should be an energetic leader in both foreign and domestic affairs. Roosevelt's actions—particularly measures to curb big business—extended executive authority as far as the Constitution would permit. He saw himself as a leader of public opinion and began the tradition of using public speeches as a means of accomplishing his agenda. He acquired land for the Panama Canal, championed health and consumer regulations, and supported conservationist causes. The beginnings of the White House press corps occurred during Roosevelt's administration. He also gave reporters unprecedented access to the White House.

Library of Congress

1933—FRANKLIN ROOSEVELT'S "ONE HUNDRED DAYS"

Franklin Roosevelt's proposed legislation to respond to the crisis of the Great Depression marked a turning point in political history. Up until then, Congress had dominated government, and the President had made few proposals. But the flood of programs Roosevelt outlined at the beginning of his first term, known as the "One Hundred Days," dominated the congressional agenda and marked a change in the relationship between the legislative and executive branches. One day after he was sworn in, Roosevelt issued the Bank Holiday Proclamation, and four days later, in a special session, Congress passed the Emergency Banking Bill. Among the major pieces of legislation enacted in Roosevelt's first three months were bills to legalize the sale of alcoholic beverages and to create public works and relief programs.

1973—THE WAR POWERS ACT

Congressional concern over the President's increasing powers in foreign affairs led to the Senate's passage of the War Powers Act of 1973. President **Richard Nixon** had opposed it, but his veto was overridden. The War Powers Act required the notification and approval of Congress whenever American troops are sent into combat. Within 60 days, the forces must be withdrawn unless Congress votes to authorize their continued involvement. Every President since Nixon has, however, questioned the constitutionality of the War Powers Act.

538

1998–1999—THE IMPEACHMENT AND TRIAL OF BILL CLINTON

The long-term effects of the impeachment and trial of President Bill Clinton have yet to be determined. Only time will tell what, if any, damage the Clinton scandal has done to the presidency. When will deep divisions between the parties heal? Has the standard for future impeachments been lowered? Will the public become even more disillusioned by and distrustful of government? Will investigations into officials' private lives and what has been called "the politics of personal destruction" continue? These questions—along with many others—remain unanswered.

The Beginnings

Independent Counsel **Kenneth Starr** began his investigation of Bill Clinton in 1994. Its focus then was Whitewater, a Clinton real-estate deal from the 1970s. But the inquiry into the affair that led to Clinton's impeachment did not begin until January of 1997. At that point **Linda Tripp**, a confidant of former White House intern **Monica Lewinsky**, turned over taped telephone conversations about Lewinsky's relationship with Clinton. Just days before, Lewinsky had signed an affidavit—denying a sexual relationship with Clinton—in a sexual harassment lawsuit filed by **Paula Jones** against Clinton in 1994 when he was governor of Arkansas. Several days later Clinton denied a sexual relationship with Lewinsky in his testimony in the Jones lawsuit. That's when the first media reports of the affair surfaced, and Starr opened a grand jury inquiry into Clinton's relationship with Lewinsky.

Grand Jury Testimony

Facing a subpoena from Starr, in July of 1998, Clinton agreed to testify before the grand jury. A few days later, Lewinsky received immunity from prosecution and testified for the first time. On August 17, 1998, Clinton underwent more than four hours of closed-circuit television questioning

"Even presidents have private lives. It is time to stop the pursuit of personal destruction and the prying into private lives and get on with our national life. Our country has been distracted by this matter [investigations into his sexual behavior] for too long, and I take my responsibility for my part in all of this. That is all I can do."

—*Bill Clinton's televised address*
August 17, 1998

from the Oval Office before the grand jury. In a televised address to the nation later that night, the President admitted that he did have a "relationship with Ms. Lewinsky that was not appropriate."

Accusation

In September of 1998, Starr released his report to the Senate—delivering 36 boxes containing evidence for his conclusion that there were 11 possible grounds for impeachment. Soon after, the *Starr Report* was released to the public, and Clinton's videotaped grand jury testimony was released and broadcast on television.

"Pursuant to Section 595 (c) of Title 28, the Office of Independent Counsel (OIC) hereby submits substantial and credible information that President Clinton obstructed justice during the *Jones v. Clinton* sexual harassment lawsuit by lying under oath and concealing evidence of his relationship with a young White House intern and federal employee, Monica Lewinsky. After a federal criminal investigation of the President's actions began in January 1998, the President lied under oath to the grand jury and obstructed justice during the grand jury investigation. There is also substantial and credible information that the President's actions with respect to Monica Lewinsky constitute an abuse of authority inconsistent with the President's constitutional duty to faithfully execute the law."

—*Excerpt from the* Starr Report

House Judiciary Committee Hearings

On October 5, 1999, the House Judiciary Committee, chaired by **Henry Hyde (R–IL)**, voted to conduct a full impeachment inquiry. Pressure was put on Republicans to conclude the impeachment inquiry by year's end. In the nationally televised committee hearings, Starr defended his investigation's conclusions, witnesses testified on both sides, and members of the Judiciary Committee debated. On December 11, 1999, the committee voted—along party lines—to impeach Clinton on two counts of perjury and one each of obstruction of justice and abuse of power. Clinton's job approval ratings remained high.

The Impeachment of a President

On December 19, 1998, in H-Res 611, Clinton was impeached on two articles. The first, which passed by a vote of 228–206, accused Clinton of committing perjury in his grand jury testimony about his relationship with Monica Lewinsky. His deposition in the sexual harassment case of Paula Jones, the statements he allowed his lawyer to make, and his efforts to influence the testimony of witnesses were other parts of the accusations. The obstruction of justice article, which passed in a vote of 221–212, focused on Clinton's attempts to find Lewinsky a job, his suggestion that Lewinsky file a false affidavit in the Jones case, and misleading statements made to his secretary, **Betty Currie**.

"The charges in the two Articles of Impeachment do not permit the conviction and removal from office of a duly elected President. The President has acknowledged conduct with Ms. Lewinsky that was improper. But Article II, Section 4 of the Constitution provides that the President shall be removed from office only upon 'Impeachment for, and Conviction of, Treason, Bribery or other high Crimes and Misdemeanors.' The charges in the articles do not rise to the level of 'high Crimes and Misdemeanors' as contemplated by the Founding Fathers, and they do not satisfy the rigorous constitutional standard applied throughout our Nation's history. Accordingly, the Articles of Impeachment should be dismissed."

Preamble to the "Answer of President William Jefferson Clinton
to the Articles of Impeachment"
Office of the White House Counsel
January 11, 1999

The Senate Trial

The trial against Clinton began on January 7, 1999. With **Chief Justice Rehnquist** presiding, the attorneys for the White House sat on one side of the Senate floor, the 13 managers appointed by the House on the other side. On January 27, in a partisan vote, senators decided not to dismiss the charges against Clinton. House prosecutors won the right to videotape depositions from Lewinsky, Clinton friend and adviser **Vernon Jordan,** and aide **Sidney Blumenthal**. Excerpts from Lewinsky's deposition were televised. After both sides offered their closing remarks, senators met for three days in secret sessions to deliberate the case, although there was little doubt about the verdict. In a roll-call vote on February 12, 1999, President Clinton was acquitted by a vote of 55 to 45 on the first article (10 Republicans voted with all the Democrats) and by a vote of 50 to 50 on the second article (5 Republicans voted with all the Democrats). A move to censure Clinton was tabled.

"Now that the Senate has fulfilled its constitutional responsibility, bringing this process to a conclusion, I want to say again to the American people how profoundly sorry I am for what I said and did to trigger these events and the great burden they have imposed on the Congress and the American people."

Bill Clinton's response to his acquittal in the Senate
February 12, 1999

REFLECTIONS AND REACTIONS: 1999

"We don't have a good balance between Congress and the president. We still have the rivalry, the war. The president won this time, but it revealed a political system that is very much in disorder."

James MacGregor Burns, Pulitzer Prize–winning historian

"With their verdict . . . the Senate has set the president above all other Americans and left him unaccountable for illegal actions."

Randy Tate, Christian Coalition executive director

"Presidents are not ordinary citizens. They are extraordinary, in that they are vested with so much more authority and power than the rest of us. We have a right; indeed, we have an obligation, to hold them strictly accountable to the rule of law."

Senator John McCain (R–AZ)

"All of the institutions of government—the presidency, the House of Representatives, the Senate, the system of justice and law, yes, even the media—all have been damaged by this unhappy and sorry chapter in our nation's history."

Senator Robert Byrd (D-WV)

"Now that the Cold War is over, we regard the president as less the person with his finger on the button than another figure in the culture of celebrity, scandal, and sensation. . . . His presidency and reputation were tarnished and diminished by the very trends that he rode to office, namely the culture of confession and personal disclosure, the soap opera-ification of American life."

Michael Sandel, Harvard University philosopher

CLINTON IMPEACHMENT—
WINNERS AND LOSERS

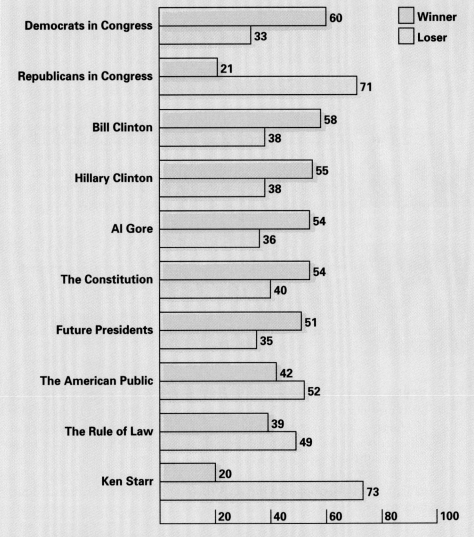

In a survey taken in February of 1999, the Gallup Organization asked the public this question: "Do you consider each of the following to be a winner or loser as a result of the entire impeachment matter?"

☐ Winner
☐ Loser

Democrats in Congress — 60 / 33
Republicans in Congress — 21 / 71
Bill Clinton — 58 / 38
Hillary Clinton — 55 / 38
Al Gore — 54 / 36
The Constitution — 54 / 40
Future Presidents — 51 / 35
The American Public — 42 / 52
The Rule of Law — 39 / 49
Ken Starr — 20 / 73

Note: Poll conducted Feb 12–13, 1999; sample size of 1,034; +/− 3 margin of error

Source: CNN/*USA Today*/Gallup Poll

Vice Presidents

Fourteen Vice Presidents have gone on to become President. The first was John Adams in 1797, and the most recent was George Bush in 1988. Eight Vice Presidents since 1900 have run unsuccessfully for President: Thomas Marshall in 1920, Charles Dawes in 1928 and 1932, John Nance Garner in 1940, Henry Wallace in 1948, Alben Barkley in 1952, Richard Nixon in 1960, Hubert H. Humphrey in 1968, and Walter Mondale in 1984. Only 45 individuals have held the office of Vice President.

Corbis

Aaron Burr (1756–1836) was a colorful and complex political figure, the first Vice President (under Thomas Jefferson) who was not eventually elected President. His ambition to be President and refusal to concede forced the House to elect Jefferson after 36 ballots—a situation that led to the 12th Amendment's change in the electoral college. In 1804, Burr killed Alexander Hamilton in a duel. Burr had objected to negative remarks Hamilton had made about him in a previous campaign. A few days after the shooting, Burr returned to his duties in the Senate as if nothing had happened.

Corbis

John C. Calhoun (1782–1850) was the first Vice President to resign. A powerful member of the House of Representatives and passionate supporter of states' rights, Calhoun and President Andrew Jackson grew apart. A frustrated Calhoun resigned the vice presidency nine weeks before his term was to expire so that he could be appointed to a vacant Senate seat from South Carolina.

William Almon Wheeler (1819–1887), a five-term member of the House of Representatives, became Vice President under Rutherford B. Hayes in 1877. Hayes had not even met Wheeler before 1876, and many believed Wheeler was added to the ticket because he was from the electorally important state of New York and had a reputation for integrity and honesty. In fact, in 1873, when Congress voted itself a 50 percent pay raise and back pay of $5,000, Wheeler opposed the act. When it passed, Wheeler returned the back pay.

John Nance Garner (1869–1967), who served as Vice President in Franklin Roosevelt's first two terms, probably got the job in a political deal. Garner had run for the 1932 presidential nomination but ran a distant third behind Roosevelt and Alfred E. Smith. He released his 90 delegates to avoid a destructive deadlock in the party. Roosevelt got the nomination and offered Garner the second spot. Garner was the first Vice President to make an official trip abroad. He also suggested what has now become a tradition—a weekly meeting between the President and congressional leaders. During their second term, Garner began to break from Roosevelt, opposing his court-packing plan and Roosevelt's expansion of executive powers. Garner ran—unsuccessfully—against Roosevelt for the presidential nomination in 1940.

Corbis

Alben Barkley (1877–1956) was 71—the oldest Vice President ever to take office—when he was sworn in in 1949. Frustrated that Franklin Roosevelt's four-term grip on the Democratic nomination had kept him from running for President, Barkley decided that he was too old to run against Harry Truman but would like the vice presidency. A native of Kentucky, Barkley served longer in Congress than any other Vice President or President—for 36 years, first in the House and then in the Senate. His grandson called him the "Veep," a name that continues to be used to refer to Vice Presidents today.

Nelson Rockefeller (1908–1979) was born into one of the country's wealthiest families. He advised several Presidents and served as governor of New York before becoming Vice President under Gerald R. Ford. He served from December 1974 to January 1977. Neither Ford nor Rockefeller had been elected to their office. Ford had succeeded to the presidency after the resignation of Richard Nixon and then had appointed Rockefeller. It took senators four months to approve Ford's nomination of Rockefeller and assure themselves that he had not used his wealth improperly and would have no conflicts of interest.

Memorable First Ladies

The use of the term "first lady" to refer to the wife of the President is believed to have been used for the first time in 1877 in an article describing the inauguration of Rutherford B. Hayes. Of the 41 Presidents, only James Buchanan did not marry.

Corbis

DOLLEY MADISON (1768–1849)

Dolley Madison was well known for her social graces and her responsibilities as the nation's hostess. She presided at the first inaugural ball in 1809 and began the longest-lasting White House tradition: children rolling eggs on the White House lawn the Monday after Easter. During the War of 1812, as the British approached Washington, D.C., Mrs. Madison refused to leave the White House until she had saved as many government documents and valuable pieces of art as she could. When she finally slipped out the back door, her carriage was full of historical treasures—including an original copy of the Declaration of Independence and Gilbert Stuart's portrait of George Washington.

SARAH POLK (1803–1891)

Her wealthy family sent young Sarah from her home in Tennessee to a "female academy" in Salem, North Carolina, one of just a few institutions of higher learning available to women in the early nineteenth century. Her education prepared her for—and sparked her interest in—helping her husband in his political life. With no children of her own, Mrs. Polk spent much time serving as her husband's unofficial secretary—helping him with speeches, keeping his schedule, and copying his correspondence. A devout Presbyterian, Mrs. Polk believed in keeping Sundays holy. She made it known that no visitors were to come to the White House on Sunday, but if some did come over, she took them to church with her.

LUCY HAYES (1831–1889)

Lucy Hayes was the first college graduate to be a First Lady. A graduate of Cincinnati's Wesleyan Female College, Mrs. Hayes was a strong advocate of women's suffrage, but she focused on her home and children, involving herself little in politics. She began the first significant art collection at the White House. A strong supporter of social reform, she was given the nickname "Lemonade Lucy" because she stopped the tradition of serving alcohol at White House social events.

EDITH WILSON (1872–1961)

The second wife of Woodrow Wilson, Edith Bolling Wilson kept busy volunteering for the Red Cross in addition to helping her husband and managing the White House. After President Wilson's stroke in 1919 (which left him partially paralyzed), Vice President Thomas Marshall refused to assume the presidency because he believed it would divide the nation and set a bad precedent. Doctors advised Mrs. Wilson that she must protect her husband from stress. For the next six months she kept the President isolated. She read his correspondence, reviewed reports, dictated notes, and screened his visitors. Critics felt she was too involved in making government decisions, calling her "Presidentress" or "First Man" and complaining about "Petticoat Government." However, she insisted in her memoirs that "The only decision that was mine was what was important and what was not, and the very important decision of when to present matters to my husband."

Corbis

ELEANOR ROOSEVELT (1884–1962)

When Anna Eleanor Roosevelt married her distant cousin Franklin Delano Roosevelt in 1905, her uncle, President Theodore Roosevelt, gave the bride away. When Franklin was stricken with polio in 1921, Mrs. Roosevelt became his eyes and ears, traveling, making speeches, and reporting on meetings. As such a visible figure, Mrs. Roosevelt redefined the roles and images of the First Lady. She broke precedent by holding her own press conferences, hosting a radio program, and even writing a daily syndicated newspaper column, "My Day." After her husband's death, Mrs. Roosevelt continued to work for the rights of the underprivileged. A champion of human rights, she became the U.S. delegate to the United Nations General Assembly.

Corbis/David Valdez

BARBARA BUSH (1925–   )

Barbara Bush projected a homey, grandmotherly style when she came to the White House in 1989. Although she didn't actively involve herself in politics and tried to steer clear of political controversy, Mrs. Bush campaigned effectively for her husband. She had a chief focus—volunteerism and literacy programs—just as Lady Bird Johnson had focused on conservation and beautification efforts and Nancy Reagan had chosen drug abuse prevention. Mrs. Bush was one of the most popular First Ladies in recent history.

Presidential Trivia

PRESIDENTS WHO DID NOT . . .

MARRY
James Buchanan

ATTEND COLLEGE
George Washington, Andrew Jackson, Martin Van Buren, Zachary Taylor, Millard Fillmore, Abraham Lincoln, Andrew Johnson, Grover Cleveland, Harry Truman

SERVE IN THE MILITARY
John Adams, Thomas Jefferson, John Quincy Adams, Martin Van Buren, Grover Cleveland, William Howard Taft, Woodrow Wilson, Warren Harding, Calvin Coolidge, Herbert Hoover, Franklin D. Roosevelt, Bill Clinton

WIN THEIR BIDS FOR A SECOND TERM
John Adams, John Quincy Adams, Martin Van Buren, Millard Fillmore, Grover Cleveland, Benjamin Harrison, Theodore Roosevelt, William Howard Taft, Herbert Hoover, Gerald Ford, Jimmy Carter, George Bush

© Robert Ariail. The State

5 | **Supreme Court**

Supreme Court Milestones

1790–1795—THE EARLY DAYS

Only three of the six justices (John Jay, James Wilson, and William Cushing) were even present for the Court's opening session in 1790. The next day a fourth justice showed up—John Blair—but there were no cases to hear. After organizing matters and appointing a clerk, they adjourned. The first formal opinion was not handed down until the third year of the Court's existence. It may seem surprising that the first chief justice, John Jay, resigned in 1795 to become the governor of New York. That Jay thought being the chief executive of New York a more important job than chief justice shows the diminished role the early Court had.

Corbis

1801–1835—THE MARSHALL COURT

John Marshall, who became chief justice in 1801, is generally acknowledged as one of the finest leaders of the Court. He was the first cabinet member to become a justice. In fact, he had little legal training and no experience as a judge before his appointment. For three decades he led the Court, establishing its power to review and nullify acts of Congress and establishing national supremacy over the individual states. Perhaps his greatest achievement was to increase the public respect for the Supreme Court. Marshall started the practice of issuing just one dominant opinion. Until then, the Supreme Court followed the English system of having each justice read his individual opinion. Marshall gave the Supreme Court an authoritative voice.

1836–1864—THE TANEY COURT

President Jackson nominated Roger B. Taney to the Supreme Court twice. The Senate indefinitely postponed his selection in 1835 by a close vote. Later that same year, Jackson nominated Taney again, this time as chief justice after the death of John Marshall. Despite vigorous opposition, led by Henry Clay and Daniel Webster, Taney was confirmed. He served for 28 years.

The Taney Court, in contrast to the Marshall Court, usually backed states' rights issues. Born to a slaveholding family, Taney himself personally accepted the idea of slavery. The Court's decision in *Dred Scott v. Sandford* (1857) that African Americans could not become citizens and that Congress lacked the authority to ban slavery in the territories caused an uproar. Taney's opinion was strongly criticized in the North on both legal and political grounds. It fueled conflict between the North and the South and contributed to the election of Abraham Lincoln in 1860. Newspapers ridiculed the elderly Taney as being "out of touch," and anti-slavery forces felt the decision weakened the reputation and authority of the Supreme Court for several decades.

1916—THE CONFIRMATION OF LOUIS BRANDEIS

Louis D. Brandeis, the son of Jewish immigrants, was born and raised in Louisville, Kentucky. A graduate of Harvard Law School, Brandeis brought extraordinary credentials as a lawyer to the Supreme Court. However, intense opposition arose when President Wilson nominated him in 1916. Brandeis's work against corporate monopolies had given him the label of the "people's attorney" but had created many enemies among the leaders of business and industry. Further, an undercurrent of anti-Semitism emerged in the bitter confirmation hearings, which lasted four months. Justice James Clark McReynolds openly shunned Brandeis, refusing to speak with him for several years or even have their picture taken together. The generally liberal Brandeis was an advocate of judicial restraint.

Corbis

1916–1941—THE TWO TERMS OF CHARLES EVANS HUGHES

Charles Evans Hughes has the distinction of being the only justice to have served two separate terms on the Court. First appointed by President Taft in 1916, Hughes served for six years before resigning to run for the presidency in 1916. Some believe Hughes had expected to be promoted to chief justice when a vacancy occurred. His disappointment that Taft chose someone else may have contributed to his decision to leave the Court. Hughes lost his presidential bid to Woodrow Wilson by just 23 electoral votes. But, in 1930, President Hoover named Hughes chief justice after he had served as secretary of state. A champion of 1st Amendment rights, Hughes placed a high value on harmony among justices and moderation in points of view.

550

1937—FRANKLIN ROOSEVELT'S COURT-PACKING PLAN

"By bringing into the judicial system a steady and continuing stream of new and younger blood, I hope, first, to make the administration of all Federal justice speedier and, therefore, less costly; secondly, to bring to the decision of social and economic problems younger men who have had personal experience and contact with modern facts and circumstances under which average men have to live and work. This plan will save our national Constitution from hardening of the judicial arteries."

With those words in a March 1937 radio address, Franklin Delano Roosevelt explained his plan to increase the size of the Supreme Court, from 9 justices to 15. His judicial "reorganization" plan met with intense criticism, however, and eventually failed. Most members of Congress—as well as the American public—realized that Roosevelt's expressed concern for the efficiency of the Court's operation masked his frustration over the conservative Court's rulings against his early New Deal programs. The average age of the justices in 1937 was 72, and Roosevelt wanted to be able to appoint younger men who would look more favorably on his legislative agenda. Establishing a mandatory retirement age would have called for a constitutional amendment, however, and Roosevelt wanted more immediate results. Under the terms of his proposal, the President could appoint an additional new justice if a sitting justice did not retire by the age of 70.5. If the proposal had passed, Roosevelt could have immediately added six new justices to the Court. However, the court-packing scheme became one of Roosevelt's most significant political defeats.

Evansville Courier

1967—THE FIRST AFRICAN-AMERICAN JUSTICE

Corbis

Thurgood Marshall became the first African-American member of the Supreme Court in 1967. Born in Baltimore and a graduate of Howard University, his confirmation was slowed by the intense questioning and opposition of mostly southern congressmen. He was not a stranger to the Supreme Court. He had been counsel for the NAACP and in that position had successfully argued the *Brown v. Topeka Board of Education* case and 31 others. After nominating Marshall, Lyndon Johnson said, "He has already earned his place in history." Marshall remained one of the most consistently liberal justices in Supreme Court history. As the Court became increasingly conservative under Warren Burger and William Rehnquist, Marshall found himself dissenting from the majority opinion. Frustrated by his role, and citing his advanced age, Marshall retired in 1991.

1981—WOMEN ON THE COURT

Dane Penland/Smithsonian Institution

Sandra Day O'Connor made history in 1981 when Ronald Reagan made her the first woman to be nominated to the Court. Born in El Paso, Texas, and a graduate of Stanford University Law School, O'Connor was a judge on the Arizona Court of Appeals at the time she was nominated by Ronald Reagan. It had not been easy for O'Connor, an outstanding student, to find a job when she graduated in 1952 because there were few female lawyers. One law firm offered her a job—but as a secretary, not an attorney.

In 1993, Ruth Bader Ginsburg joined O'Connor as the second woman on the Court. The first tenured female professor at Columbia University Law School, she brought a long record as a champion of women's rights to the Court. Between 1973 and 1976, Ginsburg had argued six women's rights cases before the Court and won five of them. As director of the Women's Rights Project of the American Civil Liberties Union, Ginsburg's strategy had been to convince the justices that laws that discriminated between men and women were based on unfair and harmful stereotypes.

©AP/Wide World Photos

552

Supreme Court Trivia

FIRST CATHOLIC JUSTICE
Roger Taney, appointed in 1836

FIRST JEWISH JUSTICE
Louis Brandeis, appointed in 1916

YOUNGEST CHIEF JUSTICE
John Jay, appointed in 1789 at age 44

OLDEST CHIEF JUSTICE
Harlan Stone, appointed in 1941 at age 69

FIRST WOMAN TO BE ADMITTED TO PRACTICE BEFORE THE SUPREME COURT
Belva Lockwood in 1879

OLDEST APPOINTED JUSTICE
Horace Lurton, joined the Court in 1910 at age 65

YOUNGEST JUSTICES
William Johnson, appointed in 1804, and Joseph Story, appointed in 1811, both at age 32

LONGEST-SERVING JUSTICE
William O. Douglas, sitting on the bench for 36 years (1939–1975)

SHORTEST-SERVING JUSTICE
Edwin Stanton, who died after serving only 4 days

NUMBER OF TIMES COURT HAS REVERSED ITSELF
about 200

NUMBER OF JUSTICES WHO HAVE NOT BEEN LAWYERS
0

JUSTICES BORN OUTSIDE THE UNITED STATES.
James Wilson (Scotland)—1789; James Iredell (England)—1790;
William Paterson (Ireland)—1793; David J. Brewer (Turkey)—1890;
George Sutherland (England)—1922; Felix Frankfurter (Austria)—1939

Important Supreme Court Cases

Marbury v. Madison (1803)
Established the power of the Supreme Court to declare an act of Congress or of the executive branch unconstitutional

McCulloch v. Maryland (1819)
Expanded Congress's ability to use its implied powers

Trustees of Dartmouth College v. Woodward (1819)
Held that the Constitution protects private charters

Cohens v. Virginia (1821)
Ruled that a state court's decision is subject to review by the U.S. Supreme Court

Gibbons v. Ogden (1824)
Broadened the definition of commerce and established that a state cannot interfere with Congress's right to regulate interstate commerce

Commonwealth v. Hunt (1842)
Ruled that workers have the right to organize

Dred Scott v. Sandford (1857)
Ruled that African Americans cannot be U.S. citizens and that Congress has no power to forbid slavery in U.S. territories

Ex parte Milligan (1866)
Limited the President's power to suspend the writ of *habeas corpus*

Munn v. Illinois (1877)
Established that states may regulate privately owned businesses in the public's interest

Plessy v. Ferguson (1896)
Ruled that separate but equal facilities for African Americans are constitutional

Schenck v. United States (1919)
Held that the clear-and-present danger principle should be used as the test of whether a government may limit free speech

Gitlow v. New York (1925)
Held that 1st Amendment rights to freedom of speech applied to states as well as the federal government

Patton v. United States (1930)
Upheld the 6th Amendment's requirements for a jury trial in federal courts

Near v. Minnesota (1931)
Held that the guarantee of a free press does not allow a prior restraint on publication, except in extreme cases, such as during wartime

Chaplinsky v. New Hampshire (1942)
Ruled that insults and fighting words—like profanity and libel—are not protected by the 1st Amendment

West Virginia State Board of Education v. Barnette (1943)
Held that a school's required flag salute violated the 1st Amendment's guarantees of freedom of religion

Everson v. Board of Education (1947)
Maintained that although public funds could be used to bus children to parochial schools, the wall separating church and state must be kept high and strong

Brown v. Board of Education of Topeka (1954)
Ruled that separation of the races in public schools is unconstitutional; reversed the *Plessy v. Ferguson* decision

Engle v. Vitale (1962)
Held that public schools cannot require students to say prayers

Edwards v. South Carolina (1963)
Ruled that the 14th Amendment doesn't permit a state to prohibit the peaceful expression of unpopular views

Gideon v. Wainwright (1963)
Held that defendants have the right to be represented by counsel in state trials and that lawyers must be provided to defendants who cannot afford to pay for them

Wesberry v. Sanders (1964)
Ruled that congressional districts within states should be as nearly equal as possible

Reynolds v. Sims (1964)
Held that "one person, one vote" must apply to apportionment of both houses of a state legislature

Griswold v. Connecticut (1965)
Ruled that the Constitution did guarantee certain zones of privacy

Miranda v. Arizona (1966)
Declared that if accused persons have not been informed of their right to remain silent, then any statements they make may not be used as evidence against them

Sheppard v. Maxwell (1966)
Overturned a murder conviction based on unfair pretrial publicity and ordered a new trial

Katz v. United States (1967)
Expanded the 4th Amendment protection against illegal searches to cover electronic surveillance

Terry v. Ohio (1968)
Upheld the police practice of "stop and frisk" when an officer suspects a crime is about to be committed

Tinker v. Des Moines School District (1969)
Ruled that schools would need to show evidence of the possibility of substantial disruption before students' free speech at school could be limited

Lemon v. Kurtzman (1971)
Established a three-part test to determine whether state aid to parochial schools was constitutional

New York Times Co. v. United States (1971)
Affirmed the 1st Amendment guarantee of a free press and limited "prior restraint" of the press

Miller v. California (1973)
Attempted to clarify 1st Amendment rights by defining obscenity

Roe v. Wade (1973)
Established a woman's legal right to an abortion under certain circumstances

United States v. Nixon (1974)
Limited the scope of a President's use of executive privilege

Gregg v. Georgia (1976)
Established that the death penalty does not necessarily violate the Constitution

Regents of the University of California v. Bakke (1978)
Held that colleges and universities may consider a person's race as one factor in admission policies

Rostker v. Goldberg (1981)
Upheld the decision of Congress to exclude women from the military draft

Island Trees School District v. Pico (1982)
Limited a school board's powers to remove books from its school library

Immigration and Naturalization Service v. Chadha (1983)
Disallowed the legislative veto

New Jersey v. T.L.O. (1985)
Established a "reasonable suspicion" rule for school searches

South Dakota v. Dole (1986)
Upheld the federal government's right to attach strings to highway funds to states

Hazelwood School District v. Kuhlmeier (1988)
Affirmed that school administrators could censor official school publications

Texas v. Johnson (1989)
Ruled that a state law against flag burning was an unconstitutional limit on freedom of expression

Cruzan v. Director, Missouri Dept. of Health (1990)
Clarified the need to have "clear and convincing" evidence that an individual would have wanted to die before intravenous feeding could be terminated

Westside Community Schools v. Mergens (1990)
Ordered a school to permit students to meet on campus and discuss religion because it does not amount to a "state sponsorship of a religion"

Clinton v. City of New York (1998)
Overturned the Line-Item Veto Act

United States: Political

Map © by Rand McNally R.L #99-544

World: Political

ARCTIC OCEAN

GREENLAND
(Den.)

Baffin
Bay

ICELAND

ALASKA
(U.S.)

Reykjavik

UNITED
KINGDOM

Dawson

Anchorage

NORTH

Hudson
Bay

ALEUTIAN IS.

C A N A D A

Edmonton

IRELAND

Vancouver

Winnipeg

Seattle

Montréal

St. John's

NEWFOUNDLAND

AMERICA

Detroit

Ottawa

AZORES
(Port.)

PORTUGAL

Chicago

New York

San Francisco

UNITED STATES

Washington

GIBRALTAR
(U.K.)

Atlanta

MIDWAY IS.
(U.S.)

Los Angeles

CANARY ISLANDS
(Sp.)

Tropic of Cancer

Houston

New Orleans

HAWAIIAN ISLANDS
(U.S.)

MEXICO

Gulf of Mexico

BAHAMAS

ATLANTIC

MAURITANIA

PACIFIC

Mexico City

Veracruz

Havana

CUBA

DOM. REP.

PUERTO RICO (U.S.)

CAPE VERDE

SENEGAL

BELIZE

HAITI

JAMAICA

GUADELOUPE (Fr.)

Dakar

THE GAMBIA

GUAL.

HOND.

MARTINIQUE (Fr.)

BARBADOS

GUINEA-BISSAU

EL SAL.

NIC.

COSTA
RICA

TRINIDAD AND TOBAGO

SIERRA LEONE

LIBERIA

PALMYRA
(U.S.)

PANAMA

VENEZUELA

Caracas

Georgetown

GUYANA

SURINAME

FRENCH GUIANA

Equator

COLOMBIA

Bogotá

KIRIBATI

GALAPAGOS ISLANDS
(Ecua.)

Quito

ECUADOR

Belém

MARQUESAS IS.
(Fr.)

Manaus

Fortaleza

OCEAN

SOUTH

BRAZIL

Recife

SAMOA

PERU

Lima

AMERICA

Salvador

OCEAN

AMERICAN
SAMOA

TAHITI

BOLIVIA

Brasília

TONGA

COOK
ISLANDS
(N.Z.)

FRENCH POLYNESIA

La Paz

Sucre

Tropic of Capricorn

EASTER ISLAND
(Chile)

Antofagasta

PARAGUAY

Rio de Janeiro

São Paulo

ARGENTINA

CHATHAM IS.
(N.Z.)

Valparaíso

ARCH. DE JUAN
FERNÁNDEZ
(Chile)

Santiago

URUGUAY

Buenos
Aires

Montevideo

FALKLAND IS.

SOUTH GEORGIA
(U.K.)

Punta Arenas

TIERRA DEL FUEGO

SOUTH SANDWICH IS.
(U.K.)

SOUTH ORKNEY IS.
(U.K.)

Antarctic Circle

SOUTH SHETLAND IS.
(U.K.)

Weddell
Sea

Scale 1:100,000,000; one inch to 1578 miles
Robinson Projection

0   400   800   1200   1600   2000 Miles
0   500   1200   1800   2400   3000 Kilometers

Map © by Rand McNally R.L #99-544

ARCTIC OCEAN

BERING SEA

R U S S I A
Okhotsk
Sea of Okhotsk
SAKHALIN

FINLAND
SWEDEN
St. Petersburg
Moscow
Novosibirsk
Irkutsk
Ulan Bator
Vladivostok
HOKKAIDŌ
HONSHŪ

BELARUS
Warsaw
Kiev
UKRAINE
MOLD.
KAZAKHSTAN
MONGOLIA
NORTH KOREA
Sea of Japan
JAPAN
Tōkyō

POLAND
ROM.
BUL.
Istanbul
Black Sea
UZBEKISTAN
KYRG.
Beijing
SOUTH KOREA
Seoul
KYŪSHŪ

Rome
Athens
TURKEY
Ankara
ARM. AZER.
TURKMENISTAN
TAJIK.
C H I N A
Shanghai
PACIFIC

MEDITERRANEAN SEA
CYPRUS LEB.
SYRIA
IRAQ
Baghdad
IRAN
Tehrān
AFGHANISTAN
Kābol
NEPAL
Tropic of Cancer

Tripoli
ISRAEL JORDAN
KUWAIT
PAKISTAN
New Delhi
Guangzhou
TAIWAN
WAKE (U.S.)

LIBYA
EGYPT
SAUDI ARABIA
Riyadh
QATAR
U.A.E.
Karachi
Calcutta
MYANMAR (BURMA)
Ha Noi
MACAU (Port.)
Hong Kong
NORTHERN MARIANA ISLANDS (U.S.)

NIGER
CHAD
SUDAN
Mecca
YEMEN
OMAN
Mumbai
I N D I A
LAOS
HAINAN
South China Sea
GUAM (U.S.)

AFRICA
ERIA
Addis Ababa
SOCOTRA (Yem.)
Aden
DJIBOUTI
ARABIAN SEA
Chennai
LAKSHADWEEP (INDIA)
Yangon
Bangkok
THAILAND
CAMBODIA
VIETNAM
Manila
PHILIPPINES

CAMEROON
ETHIOPIA
SOMALIA
Colombo
SRI LANKA
Thanh Pho Ho Chi Minh
PALAU
FED. STATES OF MICRONESIA
MARSHALL ISLANDS

GABON
RWANDA
KENYA
Nairobi
MALDIVES
MALAYSIA
BRUNEI

razzaville
DEM. REP. OF THE CONGO
Kinshasa
BURUNDI
TANZANIA
Dar es Salaam
SEYCHELLES
SINGAPORE
BORNEO
OCEAN
Equator

ANGOLA
ZAMBIA
COMOROS
INDIAN
SUMATRA
Jakarta
I N D O N E S I A
JAVA
NEW GUINEA
PAPUA NEW GUINEA
SOLOMON ISLANDS

ZIMBABWE
MADAGASCAR
COCOS ISLANDS (Aust.)
Darwin
CORAL SEA
VANUATU
FIJI

NAMIBIA
BOTSWANA
Antananarivo
MAURITIUS
REUNION (Fr.)
OCEAN
NEW CALEDONIA (Fr.)
Tropic of Capricorn

Pretoria
Maputo
SWAZILAND
Durban
Brisbane

SOUTH AFRICA
LESOTHO
Perth
Sydney
Auckland
NORTH I.

Cape Town
Melbourne
Canberra
NEW ZEALAND
Wellington

ÎLES KERGUÉLEN (Fr.)
TASMANIA
Hobart
SOUTH I.

Antarctic Circle

A N T A R C T I C A
Copyright by Rand McNally & Co.
Made in U.S.A.

6 | Maps

561

Glossary

absentee ballot—a ballot marked and mailed in advance that allows a person to vote without being at the place where he or she is registered on election day (p. 102)

activist—a person, often outside of government, actively and energetically engaged in political activities (p. 94)

administration—the people and organizations that make up the executive branch of a government. (p. 190)

affirmative action—government and private policies designed to provide equal opportunity for minority groups that have suffered from discrimination in the past (p. 336)

alien—a person who is not a citizen of the country in which he or she lives (p. 295)

ambassador—an official appointed to represent a nation in diplomatic or foreign policy matters (p. 370)

amendment—a formal statement of change to a law or constitution (p. 38)

amicus curiae—literally, "a friend of the court"; legal arguments or advice in a case offered voluntarily (p. 134)

amnesty—the government's general pardon given to people who have broken the law (p. 199)

Anti-Federalists—those who opposed the adoption of the Constitution (p. 30)

appellate jurisdiction—the court's authority to hear cases on appeal (p. 236)

apportionment—the distribution of the number of members of the House of Representatives based on the population of each state (p. 140)

appropriation—a grant of money by Congress to be used for specific purposes (p. 147)

Articles of Confederation—the first constitution of the United States, adopted by the original 13 states in 1781 and lasting until 1788 when the present Constitution was ratified (p. 24)

at-large—an election process in which the voters of a city, state, or country as a whole elect their government representatives (p. 141)

Australian ballot—a uniform ballot printed by the government distributed at the polls and able to be marked in secret (p. 78)

authorization—a legislature's approval to implement or continue a governmental program or agency (p. 147)

bail—an amount of money exchanged for the release of an arrested person as a guarantee of his or her appearance for trial at a specified time (p. 307)

bicameral—having or consisting of two legislative chambers or houses (p. 19)

bill—a proposed law presented to a legislative body (p. 162)

bill of attainder—a law, prohibited by the Constitution, that pronounces a person guilty of a crime without trial (p. 300)

Bill of Rights—the first ten amendments to the Constitution of the United States (p. 38)

bipartisan—made up of members of both political parties (p. 204)

blanket primary—a type of open primary in which voters may vote for candidates of more than one party on an office-to-office basis (p. 79)

block grants—a type of grant-in-aid given by the federal government to a state for general purposes, such as fighting crime or improving education (p. 55)

bourgeoisie—In Marxism, the social class that profits from the work of the proletariat (p. 381)

boycott—a method of expressing protest in which people are urged not to use or buy goods and services or deal with certain people or companies (p. 20)

bureaucracy—a large and complex group of people and agencies whose purpose is to manage government and implement policy; often used to refer to the departments and agencies of the federal government (p. 211)

bureaucrat—a person who works for a department or agency of the federal government (p. 225)

cabinet—the group of persons, heading 14 executive departments, appointed by the President to act as official advisers and help establish policy (p. 187)

capital—money or property invested in businesses by one or more individuals (p. 377)

capitalism—an economic system characterized by open competition in a free market and based on private ownership (p. 377)

categorical grants—a type of grant-in-aid given by the federal government to a state for specific purposes (p. 55)

caucus—a meeting of leaders of a political party to select candidates. In a congressional caucus, legislators meet to decide party strategies and conduct party business (p. 79)

censure—an official expression of blame or disapproval (p. 158)

census—an official population count (p. 140)

certiorari, **writ of**—literally, "made more certain"; an order from a higher court requiring a lower court to send the record of a case for review (p. 254)

charter—a legal document issued by a monarch or other authoritative power conferring certain rights and powers upon a person, people, or corporation (p. 18)

checks and balances—a system in which political power is divided among the three branches of government, with each having some control over the others (p. 34)

"Christmas tree" bill—a bill to which many irrelevant riders have been attached to increase the likelihood of its passage (p. 166)

citizen—a person who has certain rights and responsibilities as a member of a nation and who, by birth or naturalization, may vote (p. 95)

civics—the branch of political science dealing with citizens and their activities (p. 94)

civil law—the type of law dealing with the rights and relationships of private citizens (p. 236)

civil liberties—constitutionally based freedoms guaranteed to individuals (p. 272)

civil rights—rights belonging to a citizen or member of society, regardless of race, sex, or national origin, to receive equal treatment under the law (p. 272)

civil service—name given to federal government employees who are hired and promoted based on merit (p. 226)

class-action suit—a lawsuit brought by a person or group both on their behalf and on behalf of many others in similar circumstances (p. 134)

closed primary—a type of direct primary in which only registered party members may vote (p. 78)

cloture—the decision of three-fifths of the Senate to limit or end debate on an issue and call for a vote (p. 166)

coalition—an alliance, often temporary, of people, parties, or nations to achieve a common goal (p. 63)

coattail effect—the favorable influence that a popular candidate has on the voters' selection of other candidates in his or her party (p. 87)

cold war—the period of hostility and tensions between the United States and the Soviet Union, lasting from the end of World War II until the early 1990s (p. 367)

collective bargaining—the negotiation between the representatives of organized workers and their employers, often to determine pay, hours, and working conditions (p. 359)

command economy—an economic system in which the government has great control of the economy (p. 384)

communism—a system of government in which the state controls the means of production (p. 380)

comparable worth—the principle that women should be paid salaries equal to those of men for equivalent job responsibilities and skills (p. 331)

concurrent jurisdiction—the authority to hear cases shared by federal and state courts (p. 235)

concurrent powers—the powers that both national and state governments have (p. 47)

concurrent resolution—a statement of congressional opinion, without the force of law, that requires the approval of both the Senate and the House, but not the President (p. 162)

concurring opinion—a Supreme Court opinion by one or more justices who agree with the majority's conclusion but wish to offer differing reasons (p. 255)

confederation—a political system in which a weak central government has limited authority, and the states have ultimate power (p. 10)

conference committee—a temporary House-Senate committee whose goal is to find an acceptable compromise on conflicting versions of a bill (p. 153)

conglomerate—a corporation that controls a variety of businesses (p. 358)

consensus—collective opinion, general agreement (p. 67)

conservative—a person expressing political views that generally favor traditional values, the status quo, and the idea that government should stay out of the affairs of private citizens (p. 107)

constituent—a person represented by a government official and, as a result, to whom the official is accountable (p. 169)

constitution—a plan, often written, that details the rules, functions, and principles of a government (p. 24)

constitutional court—a federal court with constitutionally based powers and whose judges serve for life. The most important are the Supreme Court, the courts of appeals, and the district courts (p. 239)

constitutional law—the type of law relating to the interpretation of the Constitution (p. 237)

copyright—the legal right to publish, sell, perform, or distribute a literary or artistic work (p. 144)

county—a subdivision of a state; the largest unit of local government (p. 413)

criminal law—the type of law dealing with crimes and providing for their punishment (p. 236)

cross-over vote—a vote in which a member of one party votes in the other party's primary (p. 78)

dark horse candidate—one who receives unexpected support as a candidate for the nomination of a political convention (p. 83)

de facto **segregation**—literally, segregation "in fact"; racial or ethnic separation that occurs without the backing of laws or political action (p. 315)

defendant—one against whom a legal charge has been made (p. 236)

deficit—an economic condition in which a government's spending exceeds its revenues (p. 346)

de jure **segregation**—segregation that is authorized by the government and the law (p. 315)

delegated powers—the powers, also called enumerated or expressed powers, that are specifically granted to the federal government by the Constitution (p. 46)

democracy—a system of government by the people, exercised either directly or through elected representatives (p. 13)

deregulation—the process of reducing, even removing, governmental control of industry (p. 224)

deterrence—the U.S. defense policy that uses the threat of military attack to discourage enemy attack or hostile action (p. 373)

dictatorship—a form of government in which an absolute ruler controls the power, often through fear or force, and ignores the will of the people (p. 12)

direct democracy—a democratic system of government in which all citizens participate in politics and decision-making, such as New England town meetings (p. 13)

direct primary—a nominating election in which all party members may vote to choose the party's candidate for the general election (p. 78)

discharge petition—a process designed to force a bill out of committee to the floor of the House of Representatives (p. 163)

discount rate—the interest rate member banks pay when they borrow from the Federal Reserve (p. 349)

discrimination—the unfair treatment of an individual based on group membership (such as race) alone (p. 313)

dissenting opinion—a Supreme Court opinion by one or more justices in the minority who oppose the majority ruling (p. 255)

divine right—the belief that rulers derive their authority directly from God and are accountable only to Him (p. 6)

domestic policy—the decisions, actions, and principles that guide the government's approach to issues and problems within the United States (p. 357)

double jeopardy—the act of bringing a person to trial a second time for the same crime (p. 304)

due process—the principle, guaranteed by the Constitution, that federal and state government must not deprive an individual of life, liberty, or property by unfair or unreasonable actions (p. 293)

duty—a governmental tax, especially on imports (p. 143)

economic protest party—a political party dominated by feelings of economic discontent (p. 72)

Elastic Clause—the clause in the Constitution that allows Congress to pass laws as necessary to carry out its authorized powers; also known as the Necessary and Proper Clause (p. 46)

electioneering—the process of actively and publicly supporting a candidate or political party (p. 132)

elector—a member of the electoral college (p. 181)

electoral college—people selected in each state who gather to formally cast their ballots for the President and Vice President of the United States (p. 181)

electoral vote—the vote cast for President and Vice President by members of the electoral college (p. 181)

electorate—the people who are qualified to vote in an election (p. 93)

elite—a small and privileged group who have a disproportionate share of money or political influence (p. 7)

eminent domain—the government's right to take control of private property for public use (p. 309)

entitlement—a payment required by law given to people meeting particular eligibility requirements, such as Social Security payments (p. 353)

entrepreneur—a person who organizes and develops new ideas for a business (p. 378)

equal time doctrine—the Federal Communications Commission requirement that equal radio or television airtime must be made available to opposing candidates running for public office (p. 121)

Establishment Clause—the part of the 1st Amendment that prohibits the establishment of a national religion (p. 274)

excise—a tax on the production, sale, or consumption of products within the United States, such as tobacco, gas, or liquor (p. 143)

exclusionary rule—the rule that evidence gathered in violation of the Constitution cannot be presented in trial (p. 303)

exclusive jurisdiction—the authority of the federal courts alone to hear and rule in certain cases (p. 235)

executive agreement—a presidential agreement, not requiring the Senate's approval, with another head of state (p. 196)

executive order—a presidential directive to an agency that defines new policies or carries out existing laws (p. 198)

executive privilege—the President's right to withhold information from or refuse to testify before Congress or the courts (p. 202)

ex post facto—literally, "after the fact"; a law, prohibited by the Constitution, that makes criminal an action that was legal when it was committed (p. 300)

extradition—the legal process in which an alleged criminal is returned to the state or country where the crime was committed (p. 49)

federal budget—the document that details how much money the government collects and spends in a given year (p. 213)

federal government—a form of government in which governmental powers are divided between a central authority and a number of regional political subdivisions (p. 9)

federalism—the division of governmental power, as expressed in the United States Constitution, between the national government and the fifty states (p. 35)

Federalists—supporters of a strong federal government, as described in the Constitution (p. 30)

feminist—a person who advocates the political, social, and economic rights of women (p. 329)

filibuster—a tactic, often a lengthy speech or debate, designed to delay the Senate's vote on a bill (p. 165)

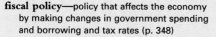

fiscal policy—policy that affects the economy by making changes in government spending and borrowing and tax rates (p. 348)

fiscal year—the 12-month period for which an organization plans its budget; for the government, from October 1 through September 30 (p. 213)

flat tax—a tax figured at a fixed rate (p. 351)

floor leader—a spokesperson for a party in Congress; one who directs party decisions and strategy (p. 148)

foreign aid—a government's financial or military assistance to other countries (p. 372)

foreign policy—the actions, decisions, and principles that guide the U.S. government's relationships with other nations (p. 357)

Foreign Service—the diplomatic staff that represents the U.S. government in other nations (p. 370)

franking—free postal service for letters sent by members of Congress to their constituents (p. 158)

free enterprise—the freedom of private businesses to compete for profit with little government regulation (p. 345)

Free Exercise Clause—the part of the 1st Amendment that states that Congress may not make laws restricting or prohibiting a person's religious practices (p. 274)

Full Faith and Credit Clause—the clause in the Constitution stating that acts or documents considered legal in one state must be accepted as valid by all other states (p. 49)

general election—a regularly scheduled election in which all voters select the winners for each office (p. 78)

germane—having significant relevance to the point at hand (p. 166)

gerrymandering—the process of dividing voting districts to give an unfair advantage to one candidate, party, or group (p. 174)

government corporation—a business that the federal government runs. Government corporations perform functions that could be provided by private businesses (p. 224)

government—the institutions, people, and processes by which a nation-state or political unit is ruled and its public policy created and administered (p. 3)

grandfather clause—a now unconstitutional law that permitted persons to vote without meeting other requirements if they or one of their ancestors had been entitled to vote in 1866 (p. 97)

grand jury—a group of people who evaluate whether there is enough evidence against a person to order him or her to stand trial (p. 240)

grants-in-aid—federal funds given to a state or local government for a particular project or program (p. 54)

grassroots—people at the local level; average voters, not professional politicians (p. 65)

gridlock—conflict between the legislative and executive branches that commonly results in inaction (p. 168)

habeas corpus, **writ of**—literally, meaning "you shall have the body"; a court order that requires a judge to evaluate whether there is sufficient cause for keeping a person in jail (p. 299)

home rule—a city or local government's power to govern itself (p. 413)

ideological party—a political party based on a particular set of beliefs or ideology (p. 72)

ideology—a body of ideas or views of the world that reflect the social needs, values, and ideas of an individual or group (p. 107)

impeachment—the formal procedure by which a President or any federal official is removed for misconduct in office (p. 145)

implied powers—those delegated powers of the national government that are not specifically stated in the Constitution, but that are implied by the interpretation of the Elastic Clause (p. 46)

impost—a tax or duty (p. 143)

impoundment—a President's refusal to spend money that Congress has appropriated (p. 203)

income tax—a tax on annual income (p. 428)

incorporation—the gradual process of applying the Bill of Rights to the states (p. 271)

incumbent—a person currently holding a political office or position (p. 87)

independent—a voter who does not belong to or consistently support one of the main political parties (p. 65)

independent executive agency—an executive branch agency outside of the cabinet departments that oversees a single area (p. 224)

independent regulatory commission—a federal agency whose purpose is to protect the public interest (p. 223)

indictment—a legal statement charging a person with a crime or other offense (p. 304)

inherent powers—powers, usually in foreign affairs, that grow out of the very existence of the national government (p. 46)

initiative—the process by which citizens can propose a law or state constitutional amendment to be voted upon in an election (p. 402)

injunction—a court order that demands or forbids a particular action (p. 229)

interest group—a private organization of like-minded people whose goal is to influence and shape public policy (p. 125)

iron triangle—a mutually advantageous relationship among congressional committees, interest groups, and governmental agencies in an effort to influence legislation and policy (p. 230)

Jim Crow laws—state and local laws that discriminated against African Americans and supported segregation (p. 315)

joint committee—a legislative committee made up of members of both houses of Congress (p. 153)

joint resolution—a formal expression of opinion by both houses of Congress that has the force of law (p. 162)

judicial activism—the belief that Supreme Court justices should actively make policy and sometimes redefine the Constitution (p. 261)

judicial restraint—the belief that Supreme Court justices should not actively try to shape social and political issues nor redefine the Constitution (p. 261)

judicial review—the power of the courts to establish the constitutionality of national, state, or local acts of government (p. 237)

jurisdiction—the right to interpret and apply the law; a court's range of authority (p. 234)

keynote address—an opening speech of a national nominating convention that sets the tone of the upcoming campaign (p. 84)

labor union—an organization of workers whose purpose is to serve the members' interests (p. 129)

laissez-faire—an economic theory that opposes governmental interference in big business; literally "leave it alone" (p. 378)

lame duck—an elected official during the period between failure to win reelection and the inauguration of a successor (p. 38)

legislative court—a specialized court established to hear cases about and execute the legislative powers of Congress (p. 239)

legislative veto—the power of Congress to void an action of the executive branch (p. 195)

libel—written statements that defame a person's character, damage his or her reputation, or expose him or her to public ridicule (p. 120)

liberal—a person expressing political views or policies that favor the use of governmental power to promote individual liberties and social progress (p. 107)

limited government—a system in which government's powers are restricted and individuals' rights are protected (p. 17)

line-item veto—an executive's power to reject part of a bill while approving the rest (p. 199)

literacy test—an examination of reading and writing skills, now unconstitutional, that citizens had to pass before they were allowed to vote (p. 97)

lobbying—an organized process in which an individual or group tries to influence legislation or policy (p. 131)

logrolling—the process of exchanging political favors for support (p. 170)

loose constructionist—the view that judges have considerable freedom in interpreting the Constitution (p. 237)

majority leader—the legislative leader of the party holding the majority of seats in the House or the Senate. In the House, the majority leader is second to the Speaker of the House (p. 150)

majority opinion—the view of the Supreme Court justices who agree with a particular ruling (p. 255)

malapportionment—distribution of representatives among congressional districts in unequal proportion to the population (p. 174)

mandamus, writ of—a court order that commands a government official to take a particular action (p. 238)

mandate—a rule issued by the federal government to the states (p. 57)

market economy—an economic system in which government plays a limited role (p. 384)

Marxism—the political and economic ideas, developed by Karl Marx, that emphasize class struggle (p. 380)

mass media—those sources of information and means of communication—such as radio, television, magazines, and the Internet—that reach large numbers of the public (p. 116)

minority leader—the legislative leader and spokesperson for the party holding the minority of seats in the House or Senate (p. 150)

moderate—a person opposed to extreme views; one whose political attitudes are between those of a conservative and a liberal (p. 107)

monarchy—government in which the ruler's power is hereditary (p. 12)

monetary policy—economic policy that controls the money supply, mainly through the Federal Reserve System (p. 347)

monopoly—a business or group having exclusive control and lacking competition (p. 357)

multiparty system—a political system in which many parties exist and compete for control of the government (p. 63)

municipality—a political unit, such as a town or city, that is self-governing (p. 414)

national debt—the sum of money borrowed by the federal government but not yet repaid. The figure for the national debt also includes any interest owed (p. 346)

nation-state—a political unit, with a defined territory, organized under a government and having the authority to make and enforce law (p. 3)

naturalization—the process by which a person becomes a citizen (p. 295)

nomination—the process of selecting and naming candidates for office (p. 78)

oligopoly—the domination of a kind of business by only a few companies (p. 358)

one-party system—a political system in which only one party exists or routinely controls the government (p. 61)

open primary—a type of direct primary in which voters may choose on election day the party primary they want to vote in (p. 79)

original jurisdiction—the court's authority to hear and decide a case for the first time (p. 236)

oversight function—the power of Congress to review the policies and programs of the executive branch (p. 147)

pardon—the exemption of a convicted person from the penalties of a crime or offense (p. 198)

parliamentary government—a form of government in which the executive leaders are chosen by and responsible to the legislature (p. 11)

party identification—an individual's sense of loyalty to a political party (p. 104)

patent—the government's grant to inventors assuring them the rights to make, use, or sell their inventions for a specific period of time (p. 144)

patronage—the practice of rewarding political allies and supporters with jobs (p. 66)

perquisite—a benefit received in addition to a regular salary or wage; a "perk" (p. 158)

petit jury—a jury that decides an individual's innocence or guilt; a trial jury (p. 240)

pigeonhole—to put aside or ignore a proposed piece of legislation (p. 162)

plaintiff—a person who files suit in a civil case (p. 236)

platform—the formal written statement of the principles and beliefs of a political party (p. 83)

pocket veto—a means by which a President kills a bill that Congress has sent by refusing to act on it until Congress has adjourned (p. 168)

political action committee (PAC)—a political arm of an interest group set up to contribute to political campaigns (p. 88)

political efficacy—influence in political activities; the sense that one can make a difference through political participation (p. 101)

political party—a group of people organized to influence government through winning elections and setting public policy (p. 61)

political socialization—the process by which people develop their political identity and their attitudes toward government, leaders, and issues (p. 94)

politics—the methods or tactics involved in managing government and gaining power (p. 4)

poll tax—a fee, now unconstitutional, required of voters in many southern states; designed to discourage African-American voters (p. 97)

popular sovereignty—the fundamental principle that the power to govern belongs to the people and that government must be based on the consent of the governed (p. 33)

pork barrel—a government project that benefits a specific location or lawmaker's home district and constituents (p. 170)

precedent—a judicial decision that is used as a standard in later similar cases (p. 257)

precinct—an election district of a city or town, often the smallest voting district (p. 77)

presidential government—a form of government in which the legislative and executive branches are separate and function independently (p. 11)

presidential succession—the specified procedure by which a vacancy in the presidency is filled (p. 186)

president *pro tempore*—the member of the U.S. Senate chosen as leader in the absence of the Vice President (p. 150).

prior restraint—the governmental censorship of information before it is published or broadcast (p. 119)

probable cause—the reasonable belief that a search of property will provide evidence in a criminal case (p. 301)

procedural due process—the rules that police officers, courts, and lawyers must follow to protect persons who are suspected, accused, or convicted of a crime (p. 293)

progressive tax—a tax that requires higher-income citizens to pay more than lower-income citizens (p. 350)

prohibited powers—the powers that are denied to the federal government, the state government, or both; also called restricted powers (p. 47)

proletariat—in Marxism, the social class that is taken advantage of by the bourgeoisie (p. 381)

property tax—a tax on land and buildings, usually levied by local government (p. 428)

proportional representation—a system in which candidates are elected in proportion to the popular vote they received (p. 63)

public assistance—aid programs funded by state and federal tax money. They are available to those who meet eligibility requirements based on need (p. 365)

public-interest group—a group that works for the common good, not for the benefit of specific individuals or interests (p. 130)

public opinion—the attitudes expressed by citizens of a country about government and politics (p. 111)

public policy—all of a government's actions and programs that address issues and problems in society or work toward a national goal (p. 211)

pure speech—verbal communication of ideas and opinions (p. 280)

quorum—the minimum number of members of a group who must be present for the valid transaction of business (p. 164)

quota—a minimum number of people from a minority group that may be admitted to an institution or hired by a company or organization (p. 336)

radical—a person with extremely liberal political views who favors rapid and widespread change to the current political and social order (p. 107)

ratification—the formal approval, or act of validating, a constitution, a constitutional amendment, or a treaty (p. 30)

reactionary—a person with extremely conservative political views who favors the widespread changes necessary to return to an earlier government or society (p. 107)

reapportionment—the periodic redistribution of U.S. congressional seats according to changes in the census figures (p. 140)

recall—the process by which voters can vote to remove a public official from office (p. 402)

referendum—the process by which a proposed public measure is voted upon (p. 402)

registration—the process of formally having one's name placed on a list of those eligible to vote (p. 99)

regressive tax—a tax that is more burden-some for low-income people than for those with high incomes (p. 350)

representative democracy—a democratic system of government in which policies are made by officials accountable to the people who elected them (p. 14)

representative government—a system in which policies are made by officials accountable to the people who elected them (p. 17)

reprieve—the postponement of or setting aside of punishment (p. 198)

republic—a democracy in which the supreme power lies with the citizens who vote for officials and representatives responsible to them (p. 25)

reserved powers—the powers that the Constitution sets aside for the state govern-ments (p. 47)

revenue sharing—government financing in which money collected in federal income tax is distributed to state and local govern-ments (p. 56)

reverse discrimination—a situation in which affirmative action policies violate the rights of the majority group (p. 336)

rider—an addition or amendment to a bill that has nothing to do with the bill's subject (p. 166)

runoff primary—a second primary between the two candidates who received the most votes in the first primary (p. 79)

sales tax—a tax on purchased items (p. 428)

sample—in polling, a small number of people drawn from and analyzed as repre-sentative of the total population to be surveyed (p. 114)

sanction—a penalty against a nation that has violated international law (p. 373)

search warrant—a judge's order authorizing the search of a place or person and specify-ing what evidence can be seized (p. 301)

sedition—actions or language inciting rebellion against a lawful authority, especially advocat-ing the overthrow of a government (p. 283)

segregation—the policy or practice of separat-ing racial or ethnic groups in schools, housing, and industry (p. 314)

select committee—a temporary congres-sional committee appointed for a limited purpose (p. 153)

senatorial courtesy—the practice in which a presidential nomination is submitted initially for approval to the senators from the nominee's state (p. 247)

seniority system—the congressional tradition in which members with the longest continuous service on a committee are automatically given the chairmanship position (p. 171)

separate-but-equal—the doctrine that segre-gation of the African-American and white races was legal as long as separate facilities were comparable in quality (p. 316)

separation of powers—the division of a government's executive, legislative, and judicial powers into three separate branches (p. 34)

session—the meeting of a legislative or judi-cial body for a specific period of time for the purpose of transacting business (p. 148)

shield law—a law that protects journalists from being compelled to reveal confidential sources of information against their will (p. 120)

single-issue party—a political party focused on one issue (p. 72)

single-member district—an electoral district in which only the one candidate with the most votes is elected to office (p. 68)

slander—spoken statements intended to injure the well-being or reputation of a person (p. 283)

social contract—the concept that the gov-erned and those governing have obligations to each other, that the people being gov-erned will support the government, and that the government will protect the basic rights of the people (p. 6)

social insurance programs—programs created to help elderly, ill, and unemployed citizens. They are funded by personal contri-butions and available to those who have paid into them (p. 365)

socialism—the economic system that advo-cates government ownership of the means of production (p. 383)

soft money—money, not regulated by federal law, used by political parties for general expenses (p. 90)

sound bite—a short statement used on a radio or television news broadcast (p. 205)

sovereignty—the authority of a nation-state's right to rule itself (p. 4)

Speaker of the House—the presiding officer of the House of Representatives, selected from the membership. The Speaker is always a leader of the majority party (p. 148)

special district—a unit of local government that provides certain services that the local government does not provide (p. 413)

speech plus—speech combining words with some sort of action, such as picketing, marching, or chanting (p. 280)

splinter party—a political party that has split off from a major party because of a serious disagreement (p. 72)

split ticket—a vote for candidates of more than one party in the same election (p. 71)

standing committee—a permanent committee that evaluates bills and either kills them or passes them along for further debate (p. 153)

stare decisis—literally, "let the decision stand"; the practice of basing legal decisions on established Supreme Court precedents from similar cases (p. 257)

straw poll—an unofficial vote or poll indicating the trend of opinion about a candidate or issue (p. 114)

strict constructionist—the view that judges ought to base their decisions on a narrow interpretation of the language of the Constitution (p. 237)

subpoena—a legal order requiring a person to appear in court or turn over specified documents (p. 147)

substantive due process—the principle that ensures that laws must be fair to all citizens (p. 293)

suffrage—the right or privilege of voting (p. 97)

symbolic speech—nonverbal action that expresses a political message, such as wearing an armband or burning a draft card (p. 280)

tariff—a duty or tax imposed on imported or exported goods (p. 26)

Title IX—the requirement that all schools receiving federal funds offer male and female students equal classroom and extracurricular activities (p. 329)

township—a unit of local government, a subdivision of a county (p. 413)

trade association—an interest group representing a specific part of the business community (p. 129)

treason—the betrayal of one's own country by acting to aid its enemies (p. 283)

treaty—a formal agreement between two or more sovereign nation-states (p. 196)

two-party system—a political system in which only two major parties compete for control of the government (p. 62)

unemployment compensation—government money given to unemployed workers (p. 425)

unicameral—having or consisting of one legislative chamber or house (p. 19)

unitary government—a form of government in which all of the powers of the government are held by a single unit or agency (p. 9)

War Powers Act—a law, passed in 1973, that restricts the President's use of United States combat troops abroad and authorizes Congress to order the troops home (p. 195)

welfare—aid given by the government or private agencies to the needy or disabled (p. 365)

whip—a senator or representative who works with party leaders to communicate views, solicit support before votes are taken, and keep track of how voting is likely to go (p. 150)

winner-take-all—an electoral system in which the person with the most votes wins; no majority is needed (p. 67)

workfare—social programs designed to help welfare recipients find and keep jobs (p. 425)

Index

D

Dark horse candidate, 83

Darman, Richard, 213

Dartmouth College, Trustees of, v. Woodward, 554

Das Kapital, 380

Declaration of Independence (1776), 10, 22, 24, 27, 309, 312, 492–95

Declaration of Rights, 21

Declaration of Sentiments, 328

De facto segregation, 315

Defense, U.S. Department of (DOD), 216, 218, 225

    role of, in foreign and defense policy, 370

Defense spending, changes in, 371

Deficit, 346

Deficit spending, 347, 352

DeJonge, Dirk, 289

DeJonge v. Oregon, 289

De jure segregation, 315, 320

Delaware, 19, 30

    local government in, 413

Delegated powers, 46, 143

Democracy, 142, 387–88

    direct, 13

    minority rights in, 15

    participatory, 13

    representative, 14

Democratic centralism, 14

Democratic National Committee, 87

Democratic party, 65, 69–70, 73, 110, 543

Democratic political systems, 387–90

Democratic-Republicans, 69, 182, 533

    Thomas Jefferson as, 117

Dennis v. United States, 284

Deportation, 297

Depressions, 345

Deregulation, 224

Deterrence, 373

de Tocqueville, Alexis, 411

Dictatorship, 12, 381

Dingell, John, 530

Diplomacy

    in history, 371

    in United Nations, 372

Diplomatic policies, 372

    alliances, 373

    covert operations, 374

    defense, 374

    economic sanctions, 373

    foreign aid, 372, 373

    military intervention, 374

    political coercion, 374

Diplomatic powers, 196–97

Direct democracy, 13

Direct primaries, 78

Disabled Americans, equality for, 333

Discharge petition, 163

Discount rates, 349

Discrimination, 313, 349

    reverse, 336

Dispersed power, 400, 411

Dissenting opinion, 255

District-by-district voting, 416

District courts, 240

District of Columbia, 140, 225

Divided government, 71

Divine right, definition of, 6

Divine Right Theory, 6

Dixiecrats, 72, 73

Documentation, 466–67

Dole, Bob, 87, 89, 90, 525

Domestic policy, 357

    education, 366

    health care, 362–64

    regulatory, 357–61

    welfare, 365

Double jeopardy, 304

Douglas, William O., 553

Dred Scott v. Sandford, 265, 296, 550, 554

Dual federalism, 45

Dual sovereignty, 235

Du Bois, W. E. B., 316

Due process

    procedural, 293, 294

    substantive, 293

Due Process Clause, 53, 271, 305, 306

Duties, 143, 351

E

Early colonial governments, 18–19

Early native governments, 7

Eavesdropping, 301

Economic control of society and government in communism, 381

Economic interest groups, 128–29

Economic planning, power of, 202

Economic policy, 345

    government's role in economy, 345–49

    raising money, 350–52

    spending money, 353–56

Economic protest parties, 72

Economics

    Keynesian, 348

    supply-side, 348

Economic sanctions, 373

Economic systems

    capitalism, 377–79

    communism, 380–82

    mixed economies, 385

    socialism, 383–85

Economy, government's role in, 345–49

Education, 366, 421

    bilingual, 323

    influence on political attitudes, 112

    and political participation, 94

    reforms, 366

    state and local government responsibility for, 421–23

Education, U.S. Department of, 216, 218

Education Act (1972), Title IX of, 329

Education of All Handicapped Children Act (1975), 333

Edwards v. South Carolina, 555

18–21 year olds, voting rights for, 98

Eighteenth Amendment, 41, 511

Eighth Amendment, 270, 307–8, 508

Eisenhower, Dwight D., 221, 246, 535

    and civil rights, 48, 257, 265, 319–320

    in elections of 1952 and 1956, 72

    and judicial appointments, 245

    and National Security Council (NSC), 214

    and presidential succession, 189

    and vice presidency, 191

Elastic Clause, 46, 50, 144–45

Electioneering, 132

Election(s). See also Campaigns

    of 1800, 182–83

    of 1824, 184, 185

    of 1876, 184, 185

    of 1888, 184, 185

    of 1912, 74

    of 1952, 71

    of 1956, 71

    of 1960, 184, 185

    of 1968, 185

    of 1972, 524

    of 1976, 524

    of 1980, 524

    of 1984, 524

    of 1988, 524

    of 1992, 105, 524

    of 1996, 520–23, 524

    of 1998, 519–20

    conducting, 49